NINETY DEGREES NORTH

NINETY
DEGREES
NORTH

The Quest for the North Pole

Fergus Fleming

GROVE PRESS
New York

Copyright © 2001 by Fergus Fleming

First published in Great Britain in 2001 by
Granta Books, London, England

Published simultaneously in Canada
Printed in the United States of America

FIRST GROVE PRESS PAPERBACK EDITION

Library of Congress Cataloging-in-Publication Data

Fleming, Fergus, 1959–
 Ninety degrees North : the quest for the North Pole / Fergus Fleming.
  p. cm.
 "First published in Great Britain by Granta Books 2001"—T.p. verso
 Includes bibliographical references (p.)
 ISBN 0-8021-4036-X (pbk.)
 1. North Pole—Discovery and exploration. 2. Arctic regions—
Discovery and exploration. I. Title: 90 degrees North. II. Title.

G620 .F58 2002
919.804—dc21   2002021469

Grove Press
841 Broadway
New York, NY 10003

03 04 05 06 07   10 9 8 7 6 5 4 3 2 1

'God gave man "dominion over *all* the earth" and made no exception of the North Pole.'

Sir John Barrow, 1846

'But what is the Pole? A point without magnitude, one extremity of the axis on which the terrestrial sphere revolves, without length, breadth or thickness.'

Blackwood's Magazine, 1875

'Is it the struggle towards the goals which makes mankind happy? What is the value of having goals for their own sake? . . . they all vanish . . . It is merely a question of time.'

Fridtjof Nansen, c. 1900

'The Pole at last!!! The prize of 3 centuries, my dream and ambition for 23 years. *Mine* at last.'

Robert Edwin Peary, 1909

CONTENTS

Preface and Acknowledgements		ix
Chronology of Major Expeditions		xv
Maps		xxiii
1	THE GATEWAY	1
2	THE BOAT JOURNEY	24
3	THE BLOWING PLACE	38
4	'AMERICANS CAN DO IT'	50
5	THE OPEN POLAR SEA	61
6	POLAR CRUSADER	80
7	THE SAGE OF GOTHA	92
8	A LAND UNKNOWN BEFORE	111
9	THE VOYAGE OF THE *POLARIS*	132
10	OSBORN'S LEGACY	158
11	HIS WORD IS LAW	191
12	IN THE LENA DELTA	211
13	*FRAM*	230
14	MIRACLE AT CAPE FLORA	252
15	THE FLIGHT OF THE *EAGLE*	269

16   'I MUST HAVE FAME'   283
17   'A FEW TOES AREN'T MUCH . . .'   304
18   THE POLAR DUKE   314
19   FARTHEST NORTH   333
20   1909   348
21   PRINCE OF IMPOSTORS   369
22   THE LAST HEROES   390

     EPILOGUE   419
     APPENDIX
     PAPER ON SCURVY BY DR DONNET AND DR FRASER   424

     Sources and References   427
     Bibliography   454
     Index   459

PREFACE AND
ACKNOWLEDGEMENTS

Seven years ago, I decided to write a two-volume history of the Arctic. Like many grand plans, mine fell apart almost immediately. The first volume became *Barrow's Boys*, a history of British exploration in the first half of the nineteenth century which encompassed not only the Arctic but the Antarctic, Australia and West Africa. The second became the book you are now holding. Both books stand on their own, but they can still be read sequentially, for the exploits described in the first lead directly to those in the second. It was Sir John Barrow who promoted nineteenth-century interest in the Arctic; and it was the search for one of his 'boys', Sir John Franklin, who disappeared in the North-West Passage, that set later explorers on their quest for the North Pole. Indeed, so long was the shadow of Barrow's programme that in 1927 Roald Amundsen, conqueror of both Poles, still cited Franklin as his inspiration.

As a narrative of North Pole exploration this is aimed at those who are new to the subject. Of necessity it includes episodes that will be recognisable to Arctic buffs. Tomes have been written about American explorers such as Kane, Hall, De Long, Greely and Peary; and books similar to this have been published in the past, the best and most comprehensive being Pierre Berton's *The Arctic Grail* of 1988. Alongside the familiar, however, there is much that I hope will be new. The Austro-Hungarian and Italian expeditions, for example, have been ignored by most historians; the story of Germany's expedition has hardly been told since its return in 1870; the Russian attempt of 1913–14 is all but unknown; and a book could be written about Britain's 1875–6 expedition, the heroic failure of which was to be replicated in Antarctica by Captain Scott – the *éminence grise* in both cases being Sir Clements Markham (who, as it happens, was an admirer of Sir John Barrow). In addition, the story of the Pole ends habitually with its 'conquest' in 1909 by Robert Peary – or by his competitor Frederick Cook, if the fancy takes you – but as most authorities now accept that both men falsified their findings, I have included Sedov's 1914 attempt, the Amundsen–Ellsworth flight of 1925, the Byrd flight of 1926 and the Amundsen– Ellsworth–Nobile expedition by airship of the same year, the last of which was indisputably the first to reach the spot.

The question of priority is a thorny one. Did Peary reach the Pole? There are scientists who have spent years on floating ice stations and who have seen conditions so smooth that Peary's exaggerated mileage may have been possible. Some Polar explorers, too, have been reluctant to dismiss his claim. In 1988 the National Geographic Society studied his photographs and produced 'evidence' that he had reached the Pole. Other, less partisan, bodies in the US studied his readings and concluded that he had not. Did Cook do it? There are die-hards who insist that he did, despite overwhelming evidence that he was a fraud. Did Byrd do it? Once again the camps are split – some saying he did, others saying he was a publicity-seeker who lied throughout and a third, more generous faction saying that although he did not do it he genuinely thought that he had. All one can say for certain is that Amundsen, Ellsworth and Nobile were the first to see the Pole; that the first to set foot on it were a twenty-four-strong team of Cold War scientists under Alexander Kuznetsov, who flew there in 1948 on the orders of Joseph Stalin; and that an expedition led by British explorer Wally Herbert became, in 1969, not only the first to reach the Pole by sledge but the first to traverse the Arctic pack – an astonishing feat. By rights, Kuznetsov and Herbert should feature prominently in this book. That they do not is due solely to narrative constraints. As the Arctic historian Christopher Pala has pointed out, it was the dream of centuries to stand at the North Pole; but those who did the standing were not those who did the dreaming. This story is about a dream, and it stops in 1926.

Hitherto, the North Pole has been treated pictorially as a poor cousin of its southern counterpart. This is a shame, because every Arctic expedition had something unique to record, albeit in different ways: early explorers, like Kane and Hayes, took sketches and gave them to the best available painter with instructions to get on with it; later expeditions brought along at least one illustrator, sometimes also a photographer, and in later cases, simply a camera; some explorers, such as Julius Payer, were artists in their own right. Here, therefore, reproduced at Great Personal Expense (Joanna: I know you would be disappointed if I didn't say that) are a selection of their works, some of which have not been aired in more than a century.

In writing this narrative I have used, wherever possible, the original journals of those involved. Nevertheless I owe a debt to the groundwork of previous authors who have written extensively on individuals and/or expeditions which are here covered in mere chapters. I urge anybody who is interested in Arctic history to read them. To name but a few: Wally Herbert's *The Noose of Laurels* provides a definitive analysis of Peary and his controversy with Cook; Roland Huntford's *Nansen* is a work of unimpeachable scholarship that should be read by anyone wanting to know about this great and enigmatic man; Beau Riffenburgh's *The Myth of the Explorer* is a goldmine of carefully annotated material; Leonard Guttridge's *Icebound* tells the full story of De Long, and his *Ghosts of Cape Sabine* does the same for Greely; Chauncey Loomis's *Weird and Tragic Shores* reveals all about Hall; George Corner and Oscar Villarejo have separately plumbed the journals relating to Kane's expedition; and Pierre Berton's *Arctic Grail*, as mentioned above, is required reading for all enthusiasts.

*

I would like to thank: my agent Gillon Aitken; my editor and publisher Neil Belton, whose attention to the manuscript was masterful;
Eugene Rae, Caroline Hoyle and Janet Turner of the Royal
Geographical Society library, for their tireless assistance; Joanna
Scaddon who went out of her way to provide access to the RGS picture collection; Andrew Tatham who gave me access to the RGS
archives; everybody from the Scott Polar Research Institute, in particular Lucy Martin who provided photographs and Robert
Headland who pointed me in the right directions and scoured the
manuscript for its many errors; Dr Peter Broucek of the Österre-
ichisches Staatsarchiv, Vienna; Mick Conefrey of the BBC who
generously provided material from his *Icemen* documentary; also the
staff of the British Library; the Kensington and Chelsea Library;
the London Library; the National Maritime Museum; the National
Portrait Gallery; the National Register of Archives; the Library of
Congress, Washington, DC; also Sajidah Ahmad, Clare Alexander,
Charlie Fletcher; Tora Fost; Sally Riley, Jane Robertson, Angela
Rose, Leslie Shaw; plus Claudia Broadhead, Sam Lebus and Milly
Simpson.

A note on the text

Measurements. In their journals, explorers usually described distance in
nautical miles. One degree of latitude = 60 minutes = 60 nautical
miles – each mile being about 2,026 yards or 1.85 kilometres. They
also used statute miles (which are smaller, at 1,760 yards or 1.609
kilometres), German miles (which are approximately three times the
length of a nautical mile), kilometres and occasionally Russian versts
(1,167 yards or 1.067 kilometres). For temperature they used
Fahrenheit, Celsius and Reamur (convertible to Celsius by a
multiplication of 1.25). Ideally, all these measurements should be
translated to metric. Perversely, I have stuck with imperial. All temperatures are therefore in Fahrenheit, and all mileages are nautical
unless they relate to minor forays, in which case they are statute.

The rule is: if it's north-south progress, it's nautical; if it's so many miles around a headland, or similar, it's statute.

Names. Eskimos are now known by their own appellation – Inuit. However, as most explorers of the time called them Eskimos, I have kept the term. Place names have been treated similarly – Spitsbergen instead of Svalbard, Prince Rudolf Island instead of Ostrov Rudolfa, and so on.

Scurvy. This disease crops up in all polar histories and without much explanation is generally accepted as being a Bad Thing. The Appendix explains just how bad it was. Reproduced from the *Scurvy Report* on Nares's 1875–6 expedition, it describes the symptoms, pathology and (as far as was known at the time) the causes.

CHRONOLOGY OF
MAJOR EXPEDITIONS

1845   Sir John Franklin RN steers the *Erebus* and *Terror* into
            the North-West Passage. Neither he, his ships, nor his
            crew are ever seen again. Subsequent rescue missions
            resurrect the centuries-old quest for the North Pole.

1852   While searching for Franklin, Commander Edward
            Inglefield RN discovers Smith Sound to be navigable.
            His 'Peep into the Polar Basin' suggests that ships
            might be able to sail through Smith Sound to a theo-
            retical Open Polar Sea and from there to the Pole itself.

1853–5   Elisha Kent Kane commands a US expedition aboard
            the *Advance* up Smith Sound, purportedly in search of
            Franklin but also to find the North Pole. He survives
            mutiny, the loss of his ship, and a perilous boat journey
            home to announce that he has found the Open Polar
            Sea. In reality he has found only a stretch of water that
            happens temporarily to be ice-free.

1860–61 One of Kane's officers, Isaac Israel Hayes, takes another expedition up Smith Sound aboard the *United States*. He too sees the Open Polar Sea. He, too, is mistaken.

1860–69 Cincinnati printer, Charles Francis Hall, makes two journeys into the Arctic in search of Franklin. Returning with Eskimo testimony as to the fate of the survivors, he turns his attentions to the North Pole.

1869–70 Germany launches a polar expedition under the command of Captain Karl Koldewey. The *Germania* and *Hansa* reach the east coast of Greenland whereupon they become separated. Sledgers from the *Germania* explore the coast, reaching 77°01′N. The *Hansa* is crushed and its crew drift south on a floe for 600 miles before reaching safety.

1871–3 Hall reaches a farthest north of 82°11′ via Smith Sound aboard the *Polaris*. After his death – or possibly his murder – the expedition disintegrates. The *Polaris* is subsequently wrecked. Half the crew drift south on an ice floe, to be rescued six months later.

1872–4 Captain Karl Weyprecht and Lieutenant Julius von Payer of Austria-Hungary explore the possibility of the Gulf Stream creating a 'thermometric gateway' to the Pole. Their ship, the *Tegetthoff*, becomes trapped in the ice. They drift north to discover a group of islands which they name Franz Josef Land. Threatened by scurvy, they abandon ship and drag their boats south until they meet open water.

1875–6 Captain George Nares RN leads the *Alert* and *Discovery* through Smith Sound. His man-hauled sledge teams

chart the north-west coast of Greenland, and much
of the north coast of Ellesmere Island. Travelling
over the pack one group reaches 83°20′N. Crippled
by scurvy, the expedition returns a year before
schedule.

1878–9   In command of the *Vega*, Baron Nils Adolf Erik
Nordenskiöld of Sweden successfully traverses the
North-East Passage.

1879–82   Sponsored by the US press magnate James Gordon
Bennett, Lt. George Washington De Long takes the
Jeannette through Bering Strait in search of a second
'thermometric gateway' to the Pole. The ship sinks.
Twelve men, including De Long, perish in the Lena
Delta.

1881–4   On Weyprecht's instigation, Europe and America
adopt 1882 as the First Year of International Polar
Cooperation. Adolphus Greely of the US Army sets up
post at Fort Conger on Ellesmere Island. One of his lieutenants reaches a new farthest north of 83°23.8′. When
supplies fail to arrive, Greely evacuates his men overland. By the time they are rescued only six of the
twenty-four-strong team are alive, some of them having
resorted to cannibalism.

1883   Nordenskiöld tries and fails to cross Greenland.

1886   Robert Edwin Peary, a US civil engineer, makes an
unsuccessful attempt to cross Greenland.

1888   Fridtjof Nansen, a Norwegian neuro-scientist, makes
the first crossing of Greenland. In doing so he intro-
duces skis as a tool of Arctic exploration.

1891–2   Peary attacks Greenland again, sledging with two men to Independence Bay which he believes – erroneously – to be Greenland's northernmost point.

1893–6   Nansen puts the *Fram* – a ship designed to resist ice pressure – into the polar pack, hoping that it will drift from Siberia to the Atlantic. During the voyage, Nansen and a crew member, Hjalmar Johanssen, leave ship to ski to the North Pole. They reach a new farthest north of 86°10′ before retreating to Franz Josef Land where they are rescued by Frederick Jackson. The *Fram* completes its journey under Otto Sverdrup.

1893–5   Peary repeats his sledge voyage over Greenland. He achieves little new.

1894–7   Frederick Jackson leads the Harmsworth–Jackson Expedition to Franz Josef Land. Three years' meticulous surveying is interrupted by the arrival of Nansen and Johanssen. Inspired by their example, Jackson makes his own attempt on the Pole. He sledges no further than the northern limits of the archipelago.

1897   Salamon Andrée flies from Spitsbergen for the Pole, aboard the balloon *Eagle*. At 82°93′N the *Eagle* is driven down by bad weather, forcing Andrée and his two companions to walk to safety. They nearly make it. Their remains are discovered in 1930 on a small island to the east of Spitsbergen.

1898–1902 Otto Sverdrup takes the *Fram* up Smith Sound and successfully explores the area west of Ellesmere Island.

1898–1902 Peary loses all but two of his toes to frostbite in an effort to outstrip Sverdrup, whom he believes, mistakenly, is trying to steal his glory. From Ellesmere Island he travels over the pack to reach 84°17′N.

1899   Walter Wellman, a US journalist, tries to sledge to the Pole from Franz Josef Land. He is brought home a near-cripple, never having left the archipelago.

1899–1900   The Duke of Abruzzi leads an Italian expedition to the Pole via Franz Josef Land. Captain Umberto Cagni and three others sledge to a new farthest of 86°33′N before making a hazardous return journey. Three of their support team vanish in the ice.

1901–2   On the direction of US industrialist William Ziegler, Evelyn Baldwin tries to reach the Pole from Franz Josef Land using dogs and ponies. He fails ignominiously.

1903–5   The second Ziegler expedition, under Anthony Fiala, lands on Franz Josef Land. It fares little better than the first.

1905–6   Peary sledges across the Arctic pack from Ellesmere Island, reaching 87°06′N. His readings are open to doubt.

1906   Wellman tries again, this time by airship from Spitsbergen. He is unable to take off due to engine failure.

1907   Wellman brings a more reliable airship to Spitsbergen. It crashes on a glacier.

1907–9   Frederick Cook, Peary's erstwhile companion, travels

through the Arctic west of Ellesmere Island and states
that he has, in addition, reached the Pole. Greeted initially as a conqueror he is soon shown to be a fraud.

1908–9   Peary sledges to the Pole over the Arctic pack from
              Ellesmere Island. Unlike Cook, his claim is believed.
              His readings are later proved to be false.

1909   Wellman arrives in Spitsbergen with a new and
              improved airship. It flies a few miles north before
              being forced back. Then it blows up.

1913–14   Gregoriy Sedov, a Russian surveyor, steams towards
              the Pole aboard the *Foka*. Underfunded and under-
              provisioned, his expedition manages to survey parts of
              Novaya Zemlya and Franz Josef Land. Sedov dies on a
              sledge journey over Franz Josef Land leaving the *Foka*
              to limp home.

1925   Roald Amundsen and Lincoln Ellsworth leave
              Spitsbergen on two Dornier flying boats. They reach
              88°N before engine failure forces them down. They
              leave one flying boat on the ice and, after two weeks'
              repairs, escape (narrowly) on the other.

1926   Robert Evelyn Byrd flies for the Pole from Spitsbergen.
              Later research suggests that he did not achieve his
              goal.

1926   Roald Amundsen, Lincoln Ellsworth and Umberto
              Nobile fly from Spitsbergen to Alaska on the airship
              Norge. They are the first people to see the North Pole.

1948   On the instructions of Joseph Stalin, a team of scien-
              tists fly north for scientific and strategic purposes. Led

by Alexander Kuznetsov, they are the first to set foot on the Pole.

1968–9   British explorer Wally Herbert becomes the first man not only to reach the Pole on foot but to traverse the polar pack.

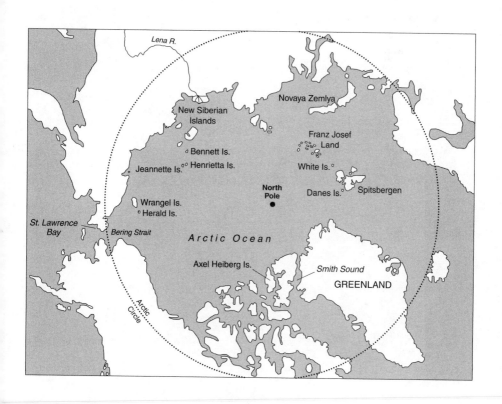

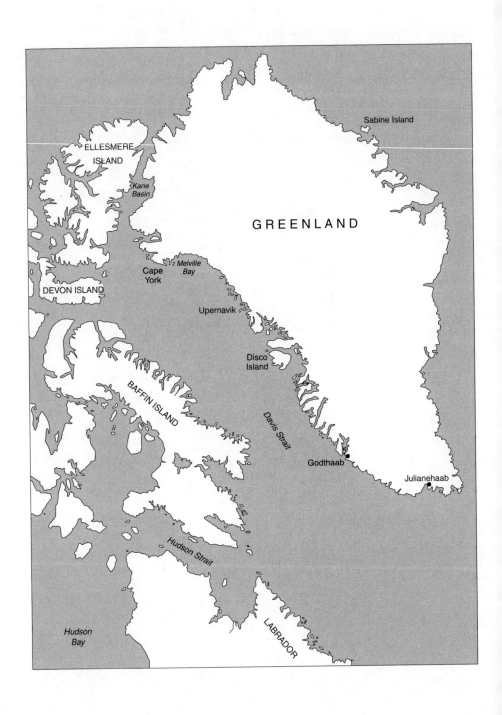

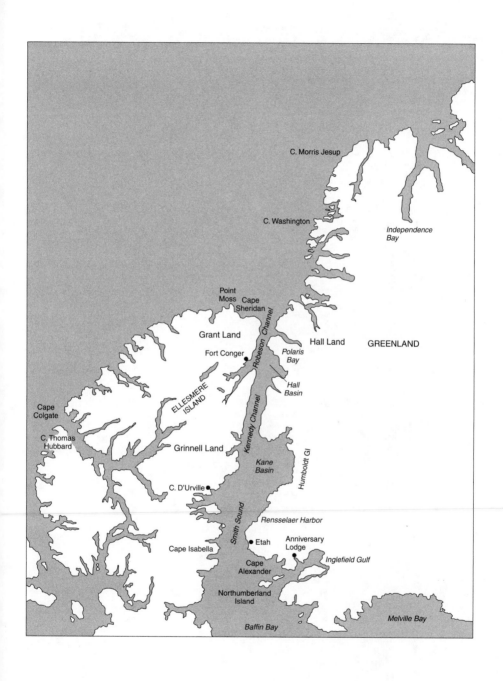

C. Morris Jesup

C. Washington

Independence
Bay

Point
Moss   Cape
        Sheridan

Grant Land   Hall Land   GREENLAND

Fort Conger   Polaris
                    Bay

ELLESMERE   Hall
ISLAND   Basin

Cape
Colgate

C. Thomas
Hubbard

Grinnell Land

Kane
Basin

C. D'Urville

Rensselaer Harbor

Smith Sound

Cape Isabella   Etah   Anniversary
                          Lodge

Cape   Inglefield Gulf
Alexander

Northumberland
Island

Baffin Bay   Melville Bay

Robeson Channel

Kennedy Channel

Humboldt Gl

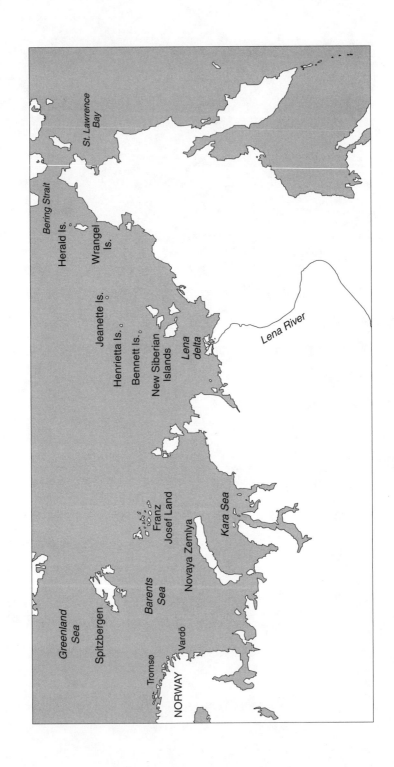

St. Lawrence Bay

Bering Strait

Herald Is.

Wrangel Is.

Jeanette Is.

Henrietta Is.

Bennett Is.

New Siberian Islands

Lena delta

Lena River

Franz Josef Land

Kara Sea

Novaya Zemlya

Barents Sea

Greenland Sea

Spitzbergen

Tromsø

Vardö

NORWAY

1

THE GATEWAY

There are five North Poles: the North Geographical Pole, the absolute, fixed cap of the globe; the North Magnetic Pole, to which our compasses point, and which is not stationary but rambles at present through the Canadian Arctic; the North Geomagnetic Pole, which centres the earth's magnetic field and sits today over north-west Greenland; the Northern Pole of Inaccessibility, a magnificently named spot in the Arctic Ocean north of Alaska, which represents the point farthest in all directions from land (currently, 684 statute miles from the nearest coast); and there is even a Pole in the sky, the North Celestial Pole, the astronomical extension of a line drawn through the earth's axis which nearly – but not quite – hits Polaris.

John Cleve Symmes did not know this. Had he done so, he would probably have dismissed it as miserably unadventurous. For Symmes, an ex-officer in the United States army, had a vision of the North Pole that has yet to be equalled for ingenuity. During the early decades of the nineteenth century he lectured to packed halls using a specially constructed wooden globe to demonstrate his theory of polar geography. His globe had two rings representing the ice fields at either end of the earth's axis. So far so good. It was common knowledge that the polar regions were cold and icy places. Where Symmes's globe departed from the norm, however, was in its countersunk holes which represented the Poles themselves. These, according to Symmes, were gateways to a series of seven worlds that nestled within each other like the layers in a Chinese sphere. Sufficient sunlight poured through the holes to sustain a pallid form of life – or so his intricately calculated diagrams seemed to prove – and even if the air at the core was slightly stale it was nonetheless breathable. If only one could reach the Poles, he explained, an entire inner universe would be within one's grasp.

Symmes presented his theories 'in confused array, and clothed in homely phraseology'[1] and died in 1829 having proved none of them. Yet he was incredibly popular in his time. It was true that some attended his lectures only to laugh, but they came all the same. 'I pledge my life in support of this truth,' Symmes declared in an 1818 circular, 'and am ready to explore the hollow if the world will support and aid me in the undertaking.'[2] In 1822, a Senate vote did, actually, produce twenty-five members in favour of sending an expedition to investigate the existence of such a hole; and three years later Russia offered him a place on a north polar voyage – an invitation he had to refuse through lack of funds.

By the time of his death, Symmes had fallen into disgrace, and 'Symmes's Hole' had become a byword for bogusness, but the appeal of a polar hole lingered, whether it be in the north or south. In 1838, when America sent Lt. Charles Wilkes to explore Antarctica, one of Symmes's acolytes, a man named Jeremiah Reynolds, was asked to join the team. Edgar Allan Poe, at the same time, incorporated Symmes's hole into his famous story, *The Narrative of Arthur Gordon Pym*, wherein a young navigator plunges into the earth's southernmost axis to be greeted by a vast, white figure which could have represented God but which could equally have been one of Symmes's blanched, netherworld inhabitants.

It is easy from a modern viewpoint to scoff at Symmes's fantasies. The truth was that his guess was as good as anybody's. No one knew what was at the North Pole. Legend held that there were undiscovered continents at the world's apexes, Arcadian lands whose benign (and possibly divine) inhabitants waited patiently for humanity to discover them. Another, more rational theory, espoused by many, held that the North Pole was, a temperate sea. In favour of this argument was the fact that ice was known to flow south; it was also known to cling to land masses such as Greenland and other Arctic islands. This suggested that some force was pushing the ice southwards, and that there was no land at the North Pole otherwise the ice would stick to it. Could it be, therefore, that the Pole comprised a tepid lake that pressed down on the surrounding pack to produce the bergs that constantly menaced the North Atlantic whaling fleets? Could it be, even, that this lake was the global cistern that fed the world's oceans? There were gaping holes in this theory (though none to match Symmes's) but in the absence of anything better, it would have to do. The idea that there might yet be land of some kind within the Open Polar Sea was too attractive to abandon entirely – a volcano, an island and even a conical spike of rock were envisaged as the global pivot – but the suggestion, proffered hesitantly by one or two scientists, that there was nothing but ice at the Pole, was dismissed as both defeatist and without foundation.

The allure of the Open Polar Sea was very real. If such a thing did exist, it would allow European navigators speedy access to the lucrative and exotic markets of the Orient. Set against its promise, however, was the seeming impossibility of reaching it. In 1553–4 Sir Hugh Willoughby had led two ships to disaster, eventually perishing with many of his men on the coast of Finland. Not long afterwards, the Dutch explorer William Barents had come to grief above the Russian coast, in the sea that now bears his name. And in the following century, at the other end of Russia, Vitus Bering of Denmark had died in the strait between Alaska and Siberia. These and many other navigators left their names and their bones on the Arctic map, without registering even the possibility that an Open Polar Sea might exist. But the dream continued, and in the early nineteenth century, Sir John Barrow became the latest to perpetuate it.

As Second Secretary to the British Admiralty from 1804 to 1845, and instigator of the world's largest systematic programme of exploration, John Barrow was a passionate believer in the Open Polar Sea. In 1818 he sent two Royal Navy ships to find it, cross it and claim it for Britain. They met the ice pack off Spitsbergen and were driven back in disarray, their timbers smashed and wracked by storms so fierce that their bells rang. Undaunted, in 1827 Barrow sent another expedition under the famous explorer Captain W. E. Parry who had already proved his worth on three journeys into the Arctic. Recognizing that the Open Polar Sea might have to be gained via a tonsure of ice, Barrow equipped Parry with boat-sledges that could be dragged over the floes to a point where they could sail triumphantly to the Pole. Parry and his men hauled their boats manfully across the polar pack and reached a record north of 82°45′ before realizing that, no matter how hard they tried, the ice was drifting south faster than they could walk north. They retreated, having done little to elucidate the matter of an Open Polar Sea.

Symmes, who was then still alive, greeted Parry's failure with contempt. He was ill-disposed towards those who disagreed with him and he still stuck to his theory. 'Had the proposition of concentric spheres, or a hollow globe, been made by an English or French philosopher, instead of a native of the United States,' wrote one of his propagandists, James McBride, 'I very much question, whether so large a share of ridicule would have been attached to its author and adherents.'[3] In his eyes there was an anti-American conspiracy afoot. Barrow's much-publicized ventures encompassed not only the North Pole but the North-West Passage, a seaway that ran through the Canadian Arctic. This was supposed – erroneously as it transpired – to provide a short-cut between the Atlantic and the Pacific and was of as much interest to the United States as it was to Britain. When Parry was despatched to find the North-West Passage, the Symmes faction rose patriotically. 'Parry now is out on his third voyage,' wrote McBride, 'as though there were some hidden mystery there, which the English government is anxious to develop . . . I am induced to believe that they have discovered something in those regions which indicates a state of things different from that heretofore believed to exist.'⁴

Neither Parry the explorer nor Symmes the visionary ever discovered the truth. But John Barrow did, in an odd, posthumous fashion. In 1845, three years before his death, he sent Sir John Franklin to find the North-West Passage. Franklin departed with two of the Royal Navy's finest ice ships, whose screw propellers were powered by locomotive engines of trusted design. He had food for seven years, silver cutlery and 1,000 bound editions of *Punch*. Nothing could possibly go wrong. He entered the Arctic and neither he, his ships nor his 136 officers and crew were ever seen again.

Over the next ten years, scores of ships were sent to find Franklin. They did, eventually, discover relics and skeletons indicating that his ships had become icebound off King William Island to the west of Boothia, a peninsula that juts from Canada's Arctic coast. His crew had then attempted to march south to the Canadian mainland and had perished from a combination of scurvy and starvation. The decade of rescue missions laid bare a mystery that is still being examined today. It also revealed the futility of trying to find a profitable seaway through the ice-choked archipelago of the north. And it put the Arctic firmly on the map. The place was becoming familiar – in the same way perhaps as the moon. But there was one key difference: the moon could be seen, whereas no one knew what was at the Pole – and that, covertly, was what many of Franklin's rescuers wanted to find out.

In one of his last tirades, published in 1846, Sir John Barrow wrote, 'The North Pole is the only thing in the world about which we know nothing; and that want of all knowledge ought to operate as a spur to adopt the means of wiping away that stain of ignorance from this enlightened age.'⁵ His words were still being quoted more than fifty years later.

Between Greenland and the Canadian Arctic lies a body of water known as Baffin Bay. From Baffin Bay three possible sea routes lead on into the Arctic: Smith Sound to the north, Jones Sound to the west and south of Smith Sound, and further still to the south and west,

Lancaster Sound. It was into Lancaster Sound that Franklin had sailed in 1845, travelling west until he reached Cornwallis Island at which point, after a brief reconnaissance to the north, he had turned south down Peel Sound and there, off King William Island, he had met his doom. Naturally, the majority of his would-be rescuers went into Lancaster Sound after him. Their task should have been easy: Franklin's orders had been to sail as far west as possible (Cornwallis Island) and then to strike south in search of the North-West Passage; but if there was no route south he was to head north and see if one could be obtained in that direction. On reaching Cornwallis Island the rescuers saw Peel Sound blocked by ice and, without for one moment considering that it might in other years have been clear, they directed their attentions to the north. By 1852, Franklin had yet to be found and his agents of salvation were becoming puzzled. It seemed as if he had vanished from the map.

That they had not found him was partly due to meteorological mischance: Franklin had gone down Peel Sound in a freakishly warm season. It was also due to misplaced ambition: if the southward route was out of the question that left only the northward, which raised the possibility that Franklin had broken into the Open Polar Sea from which he had been unable subsequently to escape. Changing ice conditions were fully acknowledged here; they would accord nicely with the fact that he had seemingly vanished and, importantly, it would give whoever did find him the chance also to find the North Pole.

Among those who used the Franklin search as an excuse to find the Pole was a British Commander named Edward Inglefield. In 1852 he took the steam yacht *Isabel* into Baffin Bay and made straight for Smith Sound – to which, as he wrote, 'it is well known that Sir John Franklin's attention had been sometimes directed'.[6] Inglefield was guilty of gross fabrication. However confusing Franklin's orders may have seemed, they had never once mentioned Smith Sound. Indeed, since its discovery in 1818, Smith Sound was believed to be a bay, and if not a bay then a channel that was permanently filled with ice. There was no conceivable reason for Franklin to have gone there, and one of the few things that people knew about his expedition was that he had not done so. Nevertheless, Inglefield persisted in his fiction. His was a minor expedition as far as the Franklin search was concerned, but it was a major one in the quest for the Pole. On entering Smith Sound, Inglefield met not ice but open water. It stretched into the distance and he pursued it as far as he was able. His impetus was the declared hope, 'most of all of reaching Franklin and giving him help'[7] – to say otherwise would have cast him as a callous adventurer – but as he sailed further north, 'wild thoughts of getting to the Pole – of finding our way to Bering Strait . . . rushed rapidly through my brain'.[8]

At a latitude of 78°28'N he was forced back by ice and returned to Baffin Bay where he made a fruitless stab at Jones Sound before going up Lancaster Sound like everybody else. He returned to London with no news of Franklin and a clutch of mail from his fellow rescuers. His foray attracted little attention from a public waiting to hear what had happened to their vanished hero. It did, however, cause a stir amongst the secret band of North Polers. Inglefield claimed to have sailed 'one hundred and thirty miles farther north than any navigator',[9] and while this was incorrect – the 80th parallel had been crossed in the Atlantic by at least two previous expeditions – he had certainly travelled further up Smith Sound than anyone else; moreover, he had broached what was possibly a route to the Open Polar Sea. One of the first to respond to his discovery was a young American named Elisha Kent Kane.

Kane was born in 1820, the eldest of seven children in a respectable, upper-class Philadelphia family. His father was a judge, his mother a society beauty and he grew up to become a handsome, well-mannered doctor. He was an unlikely explorer, not only because he was a sprig of the establishment but because, throughout his life, he was constantly ill. He had been a sickly child and had a bad heart; as a student he had suffered so badly from rheumatic fever that his survival was far from certain. Contrarily – or perhaps predictably – he became one of the century's most romantic travellers. 'If you must die, die in the harness,'[10] his father advised him. He therefore explored the Mediterranean, went to Mexico, India, China and West Africa. He trod the catacombs of Thebes, swung on a bamboo rope over a volcanic crater in the Philippines, and commanded a contingent of Mexican guerrillas. He was going to die anyway, he decided, so why waste time being ill at home. (In fact, he was just as ill abroad, catching every regional illness available, and in Mexico was speared in the abdomen.) But none of these setbacks daunted him. He joined the Navy in search of excitement only to find that the sea made him sick and the discipline was too severe for his rebellious nature. His existence was smothered, he wrote, by 'the miserable tediousness of small adventures'.[11] What he wanted was something big, something whereby he could make his name. Accordingly, in 1852, he volunteered as medical officer on one of the missions to find Franklin, sponsored by the New York philanthropist Henry Grinnell.

While Inglefield was sailing up Smith Sound in 1852, Kane sat ice-bound off Cornwallis Island. It was the most uncomfortable, the most terrifying and yet, at the same time, the most rewarding time of his life. He marvelled at the eerie beauty of the scenery; he was exhilarated by the prospect of sudden, unexpected death; he was awed by the cold and by the extent of the sunless winter. Above all, he was delighted to find that, apart from a brief bout of scurvy, which he counteracted with a diet of olive oil, lime juice, potatoes and sauer-kraut, he felt better than he had ever done in his life. On 29 January 1853, he stood alone, a mile from his ship, and gloried as the first sunrise brought to an end eighty-six days of Arctic gloom. 'Never,' he wrote, 'till the grave-sod or the ice cover me, may I forgo this blessing of blessings again!'[12]

The winter of 1852–3 revealed nothing of Franklin's whereabouts – though the graves of three of his crew were discovered on Beechey Island, off Cornwallis Island – and the Grinnell expedition was one of many that closed its books on an empty season. Returning to New York, however, the crew were greeted with applause. Hitherto the North-West Passage had been the exclusive preserve of Britain. Since Elizabethan times, English navigators had sailed messily, and usually disastrously, into its unknown waters. By 1853 there had scarcely been one year in the last thirty-five in which the area had not been visited by one expedition or another. Their exploits had been impressive

and by no means unexciting, but they had been recounted, on the
whole, in the dry manner expected of officers who drew the King's
shilling. The Grinnell expedition was the first American foray into the
Arctic, and it was met with enthusiasm, firstly because it had returned
at all and secondly because its medical officer E. K. Kane was such a
mesmerizing publicist.

Kane lectured to audiences of thousands, thrilling them with
accounts of life in the frozen north. Such was his popularity that he
could ask – and get – payments of up to 1,400 dollars for a single
appearance. When he published his journal in 1854 it became an
instant bestseller. Never before had a tale of Arctic adventure been
told so compellingly. On every page readers shared the author's feelings as he steered them through the vicissitudes of life in the Arctic:
the beards that stuck to tongues when licked, the butter that could
only be carved with an axe, the debilitating effects of scurvy, the
weirdness of Arctic refraction, the ominous rustling of young ice
against the bows, the horrors of being 'glued-up', the terrible sight of
ice floes – a mile wide and weighing more than two million tons –
rearing and splintering as they piled on top of each other. Kane's narrative contained images so sharp that they all but bit his readers'
fingernails for them.

Kane became a hero, his bearded features familiar to citizens across
the country. He acquired a trophy lover – an odd one: Margaret Fox
was a spiritualist, an archetype of the breed, whose double-jointed
toes rapped out in darkened rooms messages from beyond the veil.
Kane also began to harbour delusions of grandeur. 'You are not worthy
of a permanent regard from me,' he told Margaret, in an unorthodox
display of affection. 'You could never lift yourself up to my
thoughts.'[13] She was a mere charlatan, he declared fondly, and her life
was not only tedious but sinful. He, on the other hand, was 'Doctor
Kane of the Arctic Seas'.[14] The Arctic was his calling and he would
return to it as soon as was possible. He visualized a future in which an
improved and educated Margaret Fox would become the wife of a
conquering Kane, the discoverer of the Pole. To his surprise, this
future seemed quite attainable. Despite her objections, Margaret

was packed off to a small village outside Philadelphia, where a miller's wife was employed to give her basic tuition and to safeguard her from the temptations of city life.

Meanwhile, Henry Grinnell was not only happy to sponsor a second mission to rescue Franklin but had no objections to Kane leading it. That Kane was a doctor not a sailor, that he had never commanded a ship, had never led men, had never fitted out an Arctic expedition and was prone to a recurring illness that might prove fatal, was apparently irrelevant, as was the fact that Kane wanted to go up Smith Sound, the spot where Franklin was least likely to be – but the place where Kane might best find an Open Polar Sea.

Throughout the winter and spring of 1853 Kane made his preparations. The 114-ton *Advance*, on which he had previously served, was already fitted out for the ice and needed little further preparation save for the addition of three whaleboats, another smaller boat and a novel, twenty-foot metal dinghy, the gift of its maker, one Mr Francis. All that remained was to find a crew and to order supplies. Here Kane's inexperience and poor health began to show. He fell ill twice with rheumatic fever, suffering the worst bout of his life in April. He feared (unnecessarily) that Inglefield was launching another expedition up Smith Sound – 'Nothing is left ... but a competition with the odds against me', he despaired.[15] When able to work, his urgency to depart led him to skimp on details. 'No one can know so well as an Arctic voyager the value of foresight,'[16] he intoned. But he had no foresight at all. His stores included some 2,000 pounds of pemmican, barrels of salt beef and pork, flour, the standard navy issue of hardtack, and sufficient ingredients to prime a small on board brewery. In addition there was 'a parcel of Borden's meat biscuit, some packages of an exsiccated potato, resembling Edwards's, some pickled cabbage, and a liberal quantity of American dried fruits and vegetables.'[17] On paper it looked fine, representing a good two years' supply of food for what Kane hoped would be a one-year journey. But for all the dried fruit and pickled cabbage, there was not enough Vitamin C in the hold to keep scurvy at bay for that long a period. Blithely, Kane reckoned on being able to procure provisions in Greenland, and to catch enough fish and shoot enough wildlife to keep the expedition healthy – fish and fresh meat were proven anti-scorbutics. But he was honest enough to have doubts. Reviewing his commissariat, he wrote ruefully, 'I can hardly claim to be provident, either by impulse or education.'[18]

If the stores were inadequate, the crew was a mess. Kane signed on two capable people from his previous voyage: Henry Brooks, first mate, and a steward, William Morton. The rest were a mish-mash of seasoned sailors, family friends, green volunteers and the sweepings of New York's docks. There was the medical officer Dr Isaac Hayes, fresh out of medical school; Amos Bonsall, a Philadelphia farmer; August Sonntag, a novice astronomer; Henry Goodfellow, a friend of Kane's brother; John Wilson, a knowledgeable sailing master; Pierre Schubert, a French cook; Jefferson Baker, one of Kane's hunting companions; Christian Ohlsen, a carpenter, the most experienced Polar traveller of the lot; and two wharf rats named William Godfrey and John Blake, who were the last to join what would eventually be a seventeen-strong crew.

The *Advance* sailed from New York on 31 May 1853. Having delivered a warning to Margaret Fox that she should improve herself or else, Kane settled down to his new role as captain. He had worked out a Utopian code of conduct. 'We did not sail under the rules that govern our national ships,' he explained, 'but we had our own regulations, well considered and announced beforehand ... These included – first, absolute subordination to the officer in command or his delegate; second, abstinence from all intoxicating liquors, except when dispensed by special order; third, the habitual disuse of profane language. We had no other laws.'[19] On the understanding that these laws would be obeyed he retired to his cabin and suffered such a prolonged and violent bout of sea-sickness that few of the crew thought he would survive. Within a week he was summoned to imprison Godfrey and Blake for insubordination.

On 20 July the *Advance* reached Upernavik, the northernmost European settlement on the west coast of Greenland, where Kane took aboard two further crew members: Carl Petersen, a Danish dog-driver who had worked previously for British expeditions; and Hans Hendrik, a cheerful Eskimo, aged nineteen. Petersen was dismayed by the supplies and by the crew and formed a poor impression of the captain. He had a premonition that the ship would not survive. Hans was more stoical: 'Still, I thought, if I do not perish I shall return.'[20] Kane also purchased a team of forty-six huskies to augment the six Newfoundlands he already had. With Petersen and Hans to guide him, he hoped to lead these dogs on sledge journeys the following spring. Worryingly, there were no fish to be bought, the cod being late that year. But Kane was not put out. In his opinion everything was going swimmingly.

When Wilson, the sailing master, confessed he had no experience of ice, Kane said not to worry, he knew it like the back of his hand. Take, for example, the old Arctic rule that navigators should steer close to the shore where there was usually open water. In his view this was nonsense. It might be applicable early in the season when everything was choked, but at this time the floes were breaking up and much valuable time could be saved by sailing through them. 'Watch this!' was his unspoken boast as, on leaving Upernavik, he steered the *Advance* into the ice.

Kane had clearly not read his Arctic history. As explorers had recorded, again and again, the floes were a menace. Constantly shifting, they offered no clear passage; and if a wind blew up a ship was liable to be crushed between them. A few days later, having endured a hazardous passage that resulted in the loss of a whaleboat and a spar, the temporary abandonment on nearby floes of several crew members, and being carried tens of miles to the south, Kane was creeping along the coast in traditional manner. Wilson began to have doubts about his captain.

On 31 July they were favoured with 'a gorgeous spectacle, which hardly any excitement of peril could have made us overlook. The midnight sun came out . . . kindling various-colored fires on every part of [the ice's] surface, and making the ice around us one great resplendency of gemwork, blazing carbuncles, and rubies and molten gold.'[21] The *Advance* crunched its way through the jewellery, Kane cheerfully ticking off each headland and promontory that Inglefield had charted. On 7 August, having passed between Capes Isabella and Alexander, the portals to west and east respectively of Smith Sound, he went ashore at Littleton Island, off the western coast of Greenland, and deposited a food cache. In this respect, at least, he was being provident. According to one man, Sir John Ross, who had endured four years in the ice, the only reason Franklin had not yet returned was because he had failed to leave depots of food so that he could walk to safety in the event of his ships being trapped. Kane took note, and therefore, on Littleton Island, he loaded Mr Francis's metal boat with food, blankets and a few yards of waterproof groundsheet. He poured sand and water over the contents, freezing them into a cement-like block that was impervious to marauding wildlife but easily accessible by humans. Returning to the *Advance* he congratulated himself on his foresight. He did not acknowledge, however, that he had further reduced his stock of food. Nor that his well-considered regulations were proving inadequate. On 11 August, Godfrey was again placed under arrest, this time for assaulting Wilson. Then there were the huskies, with which Kane had never come to terms. 'More bother with these wretched dogs!' he wrote on 16 August. 'Worse than a street of Constantinople emptied upon our decks; the unruly, thieving, wild-beast pack!'[22] Starved of food – Kane had never counted on their needs – they ate everything they could find. They devoured two bird's-nests which he had brought aboard and later had a go at his feather mattress. When released, they scampered off 'like a drove of hogs in an Illinois oak-opening'.[23] His men had to row eight miles to retrieve them.

On 23 August, having endured yet another atrocious storm, the *Advance* was at 78°41′, the farthest north any ship had penetrated Smith Sound. Kane gave himself a smug pat on the back. At the same time, however, he began to feel a tinge of worry. Winter was early that year, and the sea had already become a pasty sludge. For his sledge parties to be effective the following spring he needed to sail as far north as possible before being iced in. Yet, as he wrote, 'we are sufficiently surrounded by ice to make our chances of escape next year uncertain'.[24] The crew were equally unhappy. They had no overwhelming desire to find Franklin and, as far as they could tell, neither had Kane. Petersen thought that Kane's sole aim in pushing north was to outdo the British, to overwinter at a higher latitude than anyone else so that, 'the Stars and Stripes ought to wave where no Union Jack had ever fluttered in the polar gale'.[25] On 26 August, a spokesman suggested to Kane that they should turn back. Putting it to a vote he was aghast to find out that of the whole crew only one man, Brooks, saw any point in continuing. It took all his persuasion and the promise that he would look for a winter harbour as soon as they reached the next headland before they agreed to carry on. It was not exactly a mutiny; but neither was it the unquestioning obedience enshrined in the first of Kane's three commandments.

By the 29th they had rounded the headland and the *Advance* was ensconced in a bay that Kane named Rensselaer Harbour. Thereupon, stretching his promise to the limit, he took seven men in a whaleboat to see if a better anchorage lay ahead. The 'Forlorn Hope', as he discouragingly named it, was clad in tin, and the men were each issued with thirty-five pounds of pemmican, a sheath knife and a tin cup. They were also equipped with cummerbunds in which to store their wet socks – body heat would dry them out, Kane reckoned optimistically. The reconnaissance filled Kane with excitement. On 5 September they crossed the mouth of the largest river yet discovered in Greenland. Three-quarters of a mile wide, it was tidal for a full three miles inland. Kane named it Mary Minturn River, after Grinnell's wife's sister. Further on, they saw to the east a dusky, wall-like ridge of ice, the snout of the largest glacier in the Arctic, which Kane later christened Humboldt Glacier. There were deer tracks along the shore, which suggested the promise of fresh meat the following spring. On the 6th he left the boat and walked to a nearby peak to scan the coastline to the north. 'I shall never forget the sight, when, after a hard day's walk, I looked out from an altitude of eleven hundred feet upon an expanse extending beyond the eightieth parallel of latitude,' he wrote. 'Aided by my Fraunhofer telescope, I could see that traversible areas were still attainable.' But, to his frustration, there was no sign of a good anchorage. 'Slowly, and almost with a sigh, I laid the glass down.'[26] Rensselaer Harbour it would have to be. By 10 September he was back with his ship, giving orders to prepare for the coming winter.

Overwintering in the Arctic, a terrifying and unheard-of business less than forty years before, was now, thanks to the pioneers' experience, nothing more than a matter of careful management. Following standard procedures, Kane banked snow against his ship to insulate it against the cold, removed the stores and scientific equipment into separate huts on the shore, dug a fire-hole in the ice against the event of a conflagration, and erected a canopy over the deck to provide extra living space. That done, he and his men settled down for the dark months to come. As Petersen had predicted, the Stars and Stripes flew outside, a triumphant display of Kane's determination to winter further north than any other. Just sixty paces away, however, loomed an iceberg. Like the expedition, it had been trapped before it could escape. It was a dismal neighbour, reminding them constantly that they were now in a region where ice itself fought against ice.

If Kane understood the mechanics of overwintering he was oblivious to its finer points. Of primary importance was the well-being of the crew. Past Arctic commanders had instituted rigorous discipline to keep the men busy while amusing them with plays, masquerades, concerts and even shipboard newspapers. Kane kept everybody busy but he provided few entertainments and the dreary joys of monitoring the observatory instruments at six-minute intervals (for officers) and maintaining a twenty-four-hour watch (for crew) soon began to pall. When not staring out at the motionless ice, his men simply sat there, waiting for spring. The sunless polar winter, which offered at best a semi-twilight, sapped morale. Even Hans, the Eskimo, was fearful: 'Never had I seen a dark season like this, to be sure it was awful, I thought we should have no daylight anymore. I was seized with fright and fell a weeping, I never in my life saw such darkness at noon time.'[27] (At Upernavik the darkest day had at least two hours sunlight.) Fresh food was running short and the main antiscorbutic was grated raw potato – 'It is as much as I can do to persuade the mess to shut their eyes and bolt it,'[28] Kane wrote.

In addition to underprovisioning his ship, Kane had underestimated the amount of fuel required. By the end of February they had used up their oil, burned almost all their candles and were coming to the end of their coal. There was not enough to provide hot water for washing and even less for cooking; the French chef had to close his galley and make do with a saucepan on the main cabin stove. Outside, the temperature hovered between 99° and 82°F below freezing; inside, it reached a melancholy 10°F. It was not painful to breathe, but Kane noted that everybody now did so between compressed lips, as if sipping the air through a straw. Rats, taken aboard in New York, left their nests and ran into the living quarters for warmth. The infestation was so vigorous that Kane had to fumigate the ship with smouldering charcoal. Midway through the process he realized the ship was on fire. Venturing below he was overcome by the fumes and had to be hauled up by his heels. Recovering, he and Ohlsen, the carpenter, went back to douse the flames. The exercise was wasteful and pointless: the rats were soon back, as strong as ever.

Disaster followed disaster. A few days later one of the dogs developed a strange disease akin to rabies and snapped at several people before it was shot. Kane was not disturbed by the loss because it had previously given birth to two pups which looked promising. (There had been other puppies, six of which they had drowned, two of them being made into gloves for the officers, and seven of which had been eaten by their parents.) Shortly afterwards, however, all but six of the fifty-two-strong team died from the same ailment. Any sledge expeditions would therefore have to be man-hauled. And they would have to be hauled by increasingly feeble men for, by midwinter, scurvy had taken hold. Petersen was scathing: 'In the same manner as we most rashly and inconsiderately had gone into winter harbour, all of Mr. Kane's arrangements bore witness to his want of practical skills.'[29] Accustomed to the quiet efficiency and disciplined atmosphere of a Royal Navy expedition, he was appalled at his captain's 'conceited heedlessness and blundering braggartism'.[30]

Kane's lack of leadership became apparent. He criticized his officers while currying favour with the crew. According to Wilson he was, 'peevish, coarse, sometimes insulting . . . the most self-conceited man I ever saw'. He was 'not fit to take charge of men, he does not know how to treat them, and adopts his own ways in spite of all we can say'. The worst crime of all, he was 'actually afraid to offend them'.[31] Godfrey and Blake were persistent offenders but Kane refused to be hard on them. 'Bad fellows both but daring, energetic and strong,'[32] was how he described them. On one occasion Kane offered his own cabin as a prison for Blake. Reviewing his journal he wrote of that period that its pages gave 'evidence of a weakened body and harassed mind'.[33] Perhaps, though, his leniency was not misplaced. Godfrey may have been a troublemaker but in the months to come he was to prove himself time and again as the toughest and most capable man on board.

The sun reappeared on 21 February and Kane rushed to a headland to be the first to greet it. 'It was like bathing in perfumed water,'[34] he recorded. The sight so enlivened him that he ordered his sledge parties to make ready. Throughout the winter, when the daguerreotyping equipment he had purchased in New York would not function due to lack of sunlight, an image of free waters leading to the Open Polar Sea had been developing in his mind. The navigable channel he had glimpsed in September was now fixed as a silvery passage to the Pole. 'The great object of the expedition challenged us to a more northward exploration,'[35] he explained in his journal. Petersen and Ohlsen tried to dissuade him. It was too early in the season; the snow had not yet settled; the temperature was -40°F; and the terrain was difficult. Kane listened with half an ear. He relented to the extent that the men were not to go up the coast but were to aim for a body of land which was visible to the north-west. On 16 March, Brooks, Petersen, Ohlsen and Sonntag, along with three others, were given the six remaining dogs plus a sledge-load of provisions and instructed to build a depot for future operations. Their instructions were to cross the sea and make for the coast of Ellesmere Island – or as Kane called it, Grinnell Land.

While they were away Kane made preparations for another sledge party. On 31 March he wrote that 'Everything looked promising, and we were only waiting for intelligence that our advance party had deposited its provisions in safety . . . Except a few sledge-lashings and some trifling accoutrements to finish, all was ready.'[36] In the light of an oil lamp he was sewing some spare moccasins when Petersen,

Ohlsen and Sonntag stumbled aboard. Their faces were black, their speech was incoherent and their limbs were frozen. Only Ohlsen made any kind of sense, and what he had to report was certainly not the intelligence Kane wanted to hear. Conditions, as predicted, had made travel impossible: on average they had moved only two and a half miles per day; frequently, storms had prevented them moving at all; by the 29th Brooks and three others were crippled by frostbite; crawling into their tent they had sent the remaining members to fetch help. Ohlsen, Petersen and Sonntag had covered the thirty miles back in less than thirteen hours – an astonishing time, if true, given the conditions and their overall weakness. But they had lost their bearings along the way and had no idea where the tent might be. Somewhere to the north-east, Ohlsen guessed. When he had finished his story, he submitted to the attentions of Dr Hayes, who amputated all ten of his toes.

Kane's second group of sledgers – among them Godfrey and Blake – was commandeered as a rescue party. Strapping a comatose Ohlsen to the sledge, in the hope that he might be able to recognize some landmarks, Kane and nine men trudged into the snow. They might as well have left Ohlsen behind. When he came round he exhibited 'unequivocal signs of mental disturbance',[37] and was unable to distinguish one lump of ice from another. Kane now realized his folly in sending Brooks out so early. The terrain was so rough that he abandoned his sledge after twenty miles, and continued on foot. The main bulk of provisions were left by the sledge and each man carried a token amount to see them through what would undoubtedly be a brief dash to Brooks's tent and back. (Ohlsen by this time had regained shaky use of his legs.) But it was not a brief dash. They spent days looking for traces of Brooks's sledge and their food was soon exhausted. In addition, Kane had neglected to bring a stove to melt drinking water. They tried to eat snow but found, after a few attempts, that it took the skin off their faces. 'Any resort to snow for the purpose of allaying thirst was followed by bloody lips and tongue,' Kane recorded. 'It burnt like caustic.'[38]

They struggled for eighteen hours without food or water. They weakened and were seized by trembling fits. Kane himself fainted twice. Then, by chance, Hans the Eskimo spotted some indistinct tracks. Following them, they saw an American flag flying from a hummock. At the bottom of the hummock fluttered another little flag. The staff to which it was attached, barely protruding from a drift of snow, was Brooks's tent pole. The first men to reach it dared not enter. Instead they stood to one side – 'with more kindness and delicacy of feeling than is often supposed to belong to sailors'[39] – and gave Kane the opportunity to crawl into what he fully expected to be a mausoleum. Worming his way through the tent flaps, he saw four bodies. From the darkness within came four feeble cheers. Kane was overcome with self-congratulation. 'They had expected me: they were sure I would come!'[40]

Kane's coming was not a deliverance. True, the rescuers had access to Brooks's provisions, but night was falling, they were exhausted and they needed sleep. The party, now numbering fifteen, had for their shelter a tent that slept eight and which already had four casualties in place. In a rare moment of leadership, Kane allotted each man two hours' sleep in the tent. The rest were instructed to stamp around as best they could in temperatures that reached 75°F below freezing. When everybody had had their two hours the four frostbitten men were sewn into reindeer skins, shoe-horned into two sleeping bags made of buffalo hide and placed on Brooks's sledge. A meagre amount of brandy was slipped into their furs, and the tent plus fifty hours of food were placed on top of them. Then, with the exception of Ohlsen who limped ahead, probing the terrain, the others got into harness and began the troublesome haul back to the *Advance*.

Brooks and his companions, lashed in furs, with only a small hole for breathing, could not see where they were going nor what was happening to them. But the bumping and jolting told them that it was a nightmarish odyssey. Continually, the sledge stuck and its stores, along with its injured, had to be unloaded while it was dragged over ridge after ridge of ice. After each obstacle the fur-bagged casualties were carried back to the sledge where they would stay until they had to be dumped on the ground, groaning, as a new hurdle was overcome.

The cold affected the haulers, who began to complain of sleepiness. They did not feel the chill, they assured Kane; all they wanted was to have a few winks. Kane recognized their sleepiness as a symptom of hypothermia and resisted their demands until Hans dropped unconscious into a drift. Blake, too, fell down and refused to rise. Another man stood 'bolt upright, had his eyes closed and could hardly articulate'.[41] Of the whole party, only Kane and Godfrey were still functioning. With difficulty they erected the tent, placed the worst injured inside it – rummaging in Brooks's bag they were awed to find the brandy frozen – and then they walked in search of the sledge they had abandoned on the way out. The rest were ordered to follow as soon as they recovered.

Kane could remember little of the subsequent trek. 'We were in a strange sort of stupor, and had little apprehension of time,' he wrote. 'I recall these hours as the most wretched I have ever gone through.'[42] He became delirious and had to be pushed along by Godfrey. When his beard froze to his clothes it was Godfrey who sawed him free with a knife. Polar bears wandered across their route, tearing at scraps of cloth abandoned during the outward march. They walked past them as if in a dream. Kane wondered if it was some kind of mirage. (Godfrey, who later published his own self-aggrandizing journal, said that it *was* a mirage.) On reaching the sledge, with its stores of food, they prepared a meal for those to come. Then, when the others had caught up, they moved off again for the *Advance*.

This was the worst stage of the journey. Everybody seemed half-demented, laughing, shrieking and crying as they stumbled along at a rate of one and a half miles per hour. 'I know all my companions were frantic,' Godfrey recorded, 'for they laughed immoderately, gibbered, uttered the most frightful imprecations, mimicked the screams and groans of the invalids, howled like wild beasts, and, in short, exhibited a scene of insane fury which I have never seen equalled in a lunatic asylum. After the lapse of a few minutes the frightful hubbub would suddenly cease; the raving maniacs were changed to sullen and moping idiots, weeping and blubbering like children; and in this condition all would move on mechanically for perhaps half a mile, when, as if all were actuated by one disorderly spirit, another outburst would take place, and the former scene of maniacal fury was re-enacted.'[43] The only moments of quiet came when they paused for a halt and immediately fell asleep; or when, in the face of all wisdom, they ate snow and became speechless with pain. Godfrey, who alone seemed to have a hold on his senses, wrote that he had never felt such a strong urge to commit suicide. 'We were quite delirious,' Kane wrote, 'and had ceased to entertain a sane apprehension of the circumstances about us. We moved like men in a dream. Our footmarks seen after-wards showed that we had steered a bee-line for the brig. It must have been by a sort of instinct, for it left no impress on the memory.'[44] They eventually regained the safety of the *Advance* at 1.00 p.m. on 3 April, having been on the ice for seventy-two hours at a mean tem-perature of minus 41°F.

Hayes, who had been left in charge of the ship, was shocked. His medical school lecturers had taught him many things but never how to deal with a band of raving, ice-clumped lunatics. As his patients thrashed against the pain of thawing flesh, the *Advance* 'presented all the appearances of a mad house'.[45] With remarkable certainty, how-ever, Hayes went to work. He sliced off the frost-bitten toes of four men and pumped morphine into the rest. But Schubert, the French cook, died after losing an entire foot, and Baker, Kane's old hunting companion, went on 7 April, a victim of tetanus. Kane himself recov-ered with a swiftness that amazed Hayes and was up to supervise the burial of the two men – or rather their storage in the observatory until the ground became soft enough for burial. Yet his ordeal had appar-ently taught him nothing.

While he was in the observatory a group of Eskimos approached the ship. They had come from Etah, a uniquely verdant bay on the west coast of Greenland, situated just below Cape Alexander. It was the northernmost human habitation in the world, its people the most isolated of all Eskimos and the most canny when it came to dealing with ice. Using Petersen as an interpreter, Kane bought four of their dogs. These, combined with the remainder of his original pack, would form a full sledge team. Dismissing the Eskimos – one of whom,

Kane was worried to see, was a full head taller than himself – he made plans for further expeditions.

The first party, which included Kane and Godfrey, left on 26 April 1854 to investigate the coast of Greenland. On 14 May they came back, all but dead, having discovered little. 'I may truly say,' recorded Hayes, as he saw Kane tumble aboard, 'that I lost all expectation of seeing him recover, or even rally, from his severe prostration.'[46] According to Hayes's diagnosis, Kane was suffering from frostbite, snow-blindness, scurvy, typhoid and 'dropsical effusions'. The others were little better. 'Both officers and men were all, more or less broken,' Hayes recorded. 'The ship was a hospital.'[47] Only six people were fit for service.

On 18 May it was Hayes's turn. Kane sent him and Godfrey with dogs to explore Grinnell Land. In his journal, Hayes made it seem the simplest thing. They set off with ten days' provisions, crossed the wicked ridges of sea ice, sledged up the coast and at latitude 79°42′N discovered a harbour that they named Cape Frazer. Then they came home. A footnote to Hayes's journal, however, revealed their true suffering. They reached Cape Frazer on the eighth day. At this stage they had forty-eight hours of food for the journey home. Unless they lightened their load they would never make it. On the ninth day they discarded their sleeping bags, huddling for shelter in the lee of snowdrifts. On the tenth day their supplies ran out. They cut off the bottoms of their trousers, smeared them with lamp oil, and fed them to the dogs, throwing in a pair of shoes for good measure. During days eleven and twelve they ate nothing, but their dogs pulled them 120 miles on the strength of their impromptu meal. Hayes had been suffering from snow-blindness since the second day, and his eyes were so bad that when they reached the *Advance* on 1 June he was unable to see it and had to be guided on board.

It was six weeks before Hayes was able to make his report. When he did so, he added an important detail: Godfrey, the expedition's strongest man, had cramped so badly that he had to be put on the sledge during the journey home. What he omitted was equally telling: driven to despair, Godfrey had tried to force Hayes to turn back at gunpoint and had continued only because Hayes wrestled the weapon from him. The casual manner in which Hayes officially addressed Kane in the report was also significant: 'Dr. E. K. Kane, U.S.N., *Commanding Arctic Expedition in search of, &c. &c.*' Taken together, these details reveal that the expedition's physical strength was at breaking point, that Hayes sympathized with Godfrey's position to the extent of not reporting his mutiny,* and that he was so dismissive of Kane's supposed goal that he could not be bothered even to mention Franklin's name. In later years Hayes would proclaim himself one of Kane's staunchest supporters. In May 1855, however, he wanted nothing more than for the ordeal to end.

* The accusation of mutiny did not appear until the second edition of Hayes's journal and may have been a reaction to Godfrey's own exculpatory account, in which it was he who wanted to press on and Hayes who insisted they go back.

2

THE BOAT JOURNEY

Kane took no notice of the warning signals. Spring was now upon them. The ice was melting and Greenland was coming to life. They could catch seals and walruses; they could shoot gulls, ptarmigan and reindeer. Fresh meat was so abundant that they made caches of it beneath the snow. Later on, sorrel sprouted in the damp soil and dwarf willows grew tiny catkins. Their scurvy began to ameliorate. Kane was jubilant. 'This flood of animal life burst upon us like fountains of water and pastures and date-trees in a southern desert,'[1] he wrote. In his excitement he envisaged an age when Europeans and Americans would be as comfortable in the Arctic as they were in New York and London. 'God forbid . . . that civilised man should be exposed for successive years to this blighting darkness,' he said in qualification. But, he added, look at 'the miracle of this bountiful fair season. I could hardly have been much more surprised if these black rocks, instead of sending out . . . the late inroad of shouting Esquimaux, had sent us naturalised Saxons.'[2] Kane's view was that if white people could adapt to the frozen zones they would soon find their way to the balmier realm of the Open Polar Sea. And that sea could not be too far off, as his sighting of clear water the summer before had indicated.

The *Advance* was beset in a small cove on the eastern side of a body of water that would later be named Kane Basin. Hayes had already explored the western side of this basin – Grinnell Land – but the eastern side, the west coast of Greenland, required further investigation. Apart from Kane's brief sortie it was virgin territory. So, another sledge team was despatched to explore further. Its members were Hans Hendrik and William Morton, Kane's steward. They departed on 3 June with orders to 'search to the greatest possible advantage'.[3] Simultaneously, four other men were sent to investigate the Humboldt Glacier.

Of the two parties, the Humboldt group had the richest expectancy. At this stage scientists were still debating the mechanics of glacial movement and the opportunity to study the world's largest known glacier was a godsend to anyone interested in ice. Unfortunately, none of Kane's men *were* interested – they had enough ice to cope with, and the prospect of becoming involved with more held no appeal. They battled the Humboldt's lower chunks for three days before turning back. They were not scientists and had no wish to risk their lives on a crevasse-filled entity that led only to further wastelands. The relatively mundane task allotted to Morton and Hendrik, on the other hand, produced results that exceeded all Kane's hopes. As instructed, they went north until they were stopped by a headland at latitude 81°22′N. Climbing its 500-foot cliffs, Morton saw a channel thirty miles wide that led into an unbroken stretch of clear water. Grey waves rolled unhindered for as far as the eye could see. Here, at last, was the Open Polar Sea.

When Morton and Hendrik had departed Kane had written: 'I am intensely anxious that this party should succeed: it is my last throw.'[4] The joys of spring aside, Kane's theories regarding the habitability of the Arctic were so much wishful thinking without evidence to prove the existence of the Open Polar Sea. Worse still, if Morton and Hendrik returned empty-handed, his travails would be proved pointless and the injuries – not to mention the deaths – incurred during those ghastly sledge journeys of the previous winter would have been in vain. He feared for his enterprise. When the two men handed in their report, Kane blossomed. He had found an approach to the Pole and his venture was justified. In his journal he wrote immodestly: 'I can say that I have led an expedition whose results will be remembered for all time.'[5]

However, Kane congratulated himself too soon. Morton and Hendrik may have reached a higher latitude than any other overland expedition but they had done so at some cost. They had shot three polar bears on the way out and, against Petersen's prior warnings, had eaten the livers. The liver of a polar bear is the only known toxic source of Vitamin A. An overdose of Vitamin A causes headache and fever; the face flushes and the skin peels. Morton and Hendrik suffered all these symptoms and were violently ill. It was to their credit that they continued. Their findings, however, were misleading. The Arctic is a wayward place, whose floes open and close to no discernible rhythm. It is also a place of mirages, where refracted light distorts reality. The channel they had seen – Kennedy Channel, Kane named it, after a friend – happened to be open that year. The Open Polar Sea was an illusion caused by haze, and wind blowing across a body of loose ice. It did not, could not, and never would, exist.

But Kane was certain that it did. 'I do not believe there was a man among us who did not long for the means of embarking upon its bright and lonely waters,'[6] he wrote in his journal. Twelve months before, his opinion might have been valid. Now, Kane alone hankered after the Pole. The crew were still weak from scurvy; some of them were toeless cripples; and had the prospect of advance been mentioned they would have laughed in Kane's face. What they wanted was to escape or, failing that, simply survive the coming winter. But neither option seemed at all likely as they were beginning, uncomfortably, to realize. Throughout July the ice had started to melt, but Rensselaer Harbour was too sheltered to be touched by its retreat. A few narrow leads had opened, allowing Kane to inch the *Advance* southwards. When the leads closed he used gunpowder charges to open them again; and when gunpowder failed his crew limped out to hack a channel with iron spikes. Their efforts gained them a paltry half-mile before they were again beset. On 10 July, Kane sledged south to explore his prospects. After a distance of thirty-five miles he discovered open water: it was freezing rapidly. The *Advance* would not escape that season.

Yet it was impossible for them to remain where they were. The anti-scorbutic promise of spring had been followed by a brief summer and an early winter. The little bits of sorrel they had picked, plus the stores of fresh meat they had laid down, were already gone and although the *Advance* had food to last another year it consisted solely of salted meat. Were they to live on these provisions alone they would be dead from scurvy before next spring. 'There never was, and I trust never will be, a party worse armed for the encounter of a second Arctic winter,'[7] Kane recorded. He toyed with the idea of abandoning ship but balked after lengthy discussions with Hayes. 'Even were it possible, [it] would, I feel, be dishonouring,' he wrote, 'my mind is made up; I will not do it.'[8] Instead he decided to drag the whaleboat over the ice and sail for Beechey Island where, 1,000 miles to the south, deep in the intestines of the North-West Passage, a British fleet was engaged in the quest that had long since been forgotten by himself – the search for Franklin. He hoped to acquire from the British sufficient fresh food to see his crew through the winter, or at least alert them to his predicament.

It was a brave but senseless attempt. The whaleboat measured twenty feet by five and could not have held more than a few months' supplies at best. 'After all, she was a mere cockle-shell,'[9] Kane admitted. Nevertheless, he dragged the boat to open water and set sail. He returned a month later, having been thwarted by a sheet of ice which stretched across the neck of Smith Sound. Petersen jeered at his failure. 'I am confident that this was a great mistake of Dr. Kane. How could he believe it possible to reach Beechey Island and to return again to the ship? But as one could not expect that Mr. Kane, on my word, would desist from his enterprise, I let him depart without expressing my opinion on the subject, and the more so, because he did not at all consult me about it.'[10] And yet, what was Kane to have done? Sat on the ship and waited? At the very least he had improved the health of the six men who accompanied him. Having had access to the more abundant wildlife in the south they were in better condition than those who had remained on the *Advance*, where a diet of cold salt pork, enlivened by twice-daily cups of coffee, and a single helping of soup, had allowed scurvy to take hold again.

On 8 August Kane tried again to blast the ship free with gunpowder. 'Not that there is the slightest possibility of getting through,' he wrote, 'but . . . it looks as if we are doing something.'[11] His assessment was perfectly correct: they made a miserable 300 yards. Ten days later he gave up all hope: 'I inspected the ice again to-day. Bad! bad! – I must look another winter in the face.'[12] They now had 750 pounds of fuel remaining – an insufficient amount to last until summer – and their stores of salt pork, although adequate, offered the prospect of death by scurvy. 'It is *horrible* – yes, that is the word – to look forward to another year of disease and darkness,'[13] Kane wrote in his journal. By his own reasoning he was in an even worse position than Franklin, who was now basking in the (non-existent) Open Polar Sea while his rescuers were glued in the all-too real ice which surrounded it. It was possibly the thought of flying to the north with a reduced body of men that persuaded him to do what he did next. Calling all hands on deck, he acquainted them with the situation and said that if any wanted to take the whaleboat and make for Upernavik they could do so with his blessing. He himself was going to stay, but whatever they decided he would accede to. 'With half a dozen confiding, resolute men I have no fears of ultimate safety,'[14] he wrote.

Half a dozen was what he got, including two men who were too crippled to move and Hans Hendrik whom he had ordered to stay. The rest, eleven in number, voted to leave. Kane was appalled. He had counted on Sonntag, Hayes and Bonsall to take his side; and he had hoped for Ohlsen who, apart from Petersen, was the most capable iceman aboard. Very suddenly, Kane turned vindictive. His published journal spoke only of reasoned discussions, and the necessity of maintaining 'a wholesome, elastic tone of feeling among the men'.[15] His unpublished diary, however, read differently. 'Sonntag's course seemed to me indefensible, adding deceit to treachery, but I say noth-ing to him. Bonsall, whose family are mixed in with my name associations, I truly pity . . . He heard me with tears but adhered to his selfish inclinations.' Ohlsen was 'scheming and non-reliable . . . double-faced, fawning and insincere.' Wilson 'has been reared a gen-tleman but is very weak.' Petersen was 'a cold-blooded sneak'.[16] Not one man was left unspattered by Kane's bile.

He told them he had changed his mind. They no longer went with his approval; instead, those who left would be considered to have quit the expedition and would not be his responsibility; if they came to grief they could expect no help from the *Advance*. And they would have to sign a document to that effect. Wilson came back to the fold, weeping. Ohlsen claimed that, as a Dane, he had not fully understood Kane's initial offer, and asked for pardon. But still he tried to persuade his captain to abandon ship. He 'argued, urged, entreated, almost threatened, behaved like a madman',[17] until Kane lost patience and told him that if he left he would shoot him. None of the others changed their minds, however. Sonntag approached him for an inter-view but any hopes Kane may have entertained of making a convert were soon dashed; all Sonntag wanted was his pay. Hayes, mean-while, calmly packed up the scientific specimens he had collected over the last two summers and delivered them into Kane's hands. Then, on 28 August, the break-away party left the ship with two sledges for the spot where Kane had left the whaleboat. They had been given free access to the supplies and carried food and fuel to last them five weeks – 'the time in which we were expected to reach Upernavik, if at all',[18] Hayes wrote. Behind them Kane nursed 2,000 plants wrapped in brown paper, 200 bird skins packed in a rat-proof chest, several barrels of bones, rocks and fish, a cigar box containing Hayes's minuscule array of entomological specimens, and an over-whelming sense of betrayal.

'Sad as I feel at the dismal prospect ahead,' Kane scribbled angrily, 'anxious as I may be for the fate of those thus severing our connection, I feel that it is a relief, a purgation, ridding me of condemned mater-ial, worthy heretofore, but rotten now.'[19] A few days later, Blake and another man, George Riley, returned with complaints of poor discipline. Riley remained but Blake subsequently rejoined the sledgers on 5 September. Kane's diary, which had lain dormant since 28 August, erupted once more. He started with a quiet justification of his position: 'They are deserters in act and in spirit – in all but the title.' Then he became outraged: 'They leave their ship, abandon sick comrades, fail to adhere by their commander, and are false to the implied trust which tells every true man to abide by the Expedition into which he had entered.' Outrage subsided into martyrdom: 'One satisfaction I have – no slight one – that this misguided party have wanted for nothing. They have had the best of everything, even at self-sacrifice. Their ingratitude is nothing. They would have had the same treatment had they spit in my face. I cannot but feel that some of them will return broken down and suffering to seek a refuge on board. They shall find it in the halving of our last Chip.' Kane's emotions, however, could not be salved by martyrdom alone. Eventually, the boil burst. 'But – but – but - if I ever live to get home – *home!* and should meet Dr. *Hayes* or Mr. *Bonsall* or *Mister* Sonntag,' he wrote, 'let them look out for their skins. If I don't live to thrash them, which I'll try very hard to do (to live, I mean) why then dear brother John seek a solitary orchard and maull [sic] them for me. Don't honour them with a bullet and let the mauling be solitary – save to the principals. It would hurt your Character to be wrestling with such low-minded sneaks.'[20]

The break-aways had elected as their leader Petersen, the most experienced iceman among them. But it was Hayes who acted as their intellectual mentor. He argued that they were doing the others a favour by leaving: the *Advance* was well-stocked with food and with fewer men to bother about Kane could devote his medical attentions more effectively to those who remained. 'If the travelling party should fall by the way,' Hayes wrote in his journal, 'the deaths would probably not be more numerous than if all should continue together; and whatever the fate of that party, the persons at the brig would be in improved condition in the spring.'[21] Coming from a medical man, even one fresh out of college, this was nonsense. Hayes knew perfectly well that the crew would need a miracle if they were not to die of scurvy during the winter. His excuses were a poor justification for what was – as Kane so petulantly but accurately wrote – an act of desertion. He was correct, however, in his assessment of the overall death toll should the party perish. As Kane himself had whispered to one of his loyal companions on 26 August, 'If I get through the winter with half the Ship's company alive, I shall do very well.'[22] In the circumstances it is hard to blame Hayes for his desertion.

The question of the best course of action was one that troubled Hayes repeatedly during the journey south and, indeed, became the leitmotif of his journal. 'What shall we do?' was a sentence he repeated again and again – with good cause. On setting out, conditions were 'incomparably worse'[23] than they had expected. They reached the whaleboat and saw 'ice, ice and nothing but ice'.[24] A brief break-up allowed them to reach open water, where they made for Littleton Island and dug out the metal boat. This, plus a few of the supplies stored within it – but not all; some they left for Kane – gave them extra space as well as extra food. Again, however, Littleton Island was surrounded by ice and they had to wait for a second break-up. Start–stop became the pattern of their escape: at one moment they would be faced with iceless seas; at another they would be locked immobile on the shore. Sometimes they dragged the boats overland, working sixteen-hour shifts across a landscape of ice precipices. Sometimes they hitched a lift on drifting floes. Now it was sunny, with temperatures of 73°F, now they shivered in freezing fog. Rounding Cape Alexander, the storm-blasted gateway to Smith Sound, the metal boat broached to and its contents were lost over-board. Yet, a few miles further on, they were able to relax on a sunny oasis of green hillside where, were it not for the presence of a glacier two miles away, they would have thought themselves in a summer meadow. At each pause in their progress, Hayes's query rose like a smoke signal of distress: 'what shall we do?'

Their moods swung jerkily. 'We congratulated ourselves that the hardest part of the journey was over,' read one of Hayes's journal entries, 'and we seemed to have some ground for anticipating that henceforth all would be plain sailing.'[25] A few days later he wrote: 'This state of inactivity greatly affects our spirits. Every hour is precious, and it is hard to be kept thus closely imprisoned.'[26] Another few days and they were singing their way home. 'Godfrey, who had a penchant for negro melodies, broke out from time to time with scraps from "Uncle Ned", in all its variations, "Susannah", and "I'm off to Charleston, a little while to stay."'[27] Only Petersen seemed unaffected, as he steered them grimly to salvation.

On it went, until at Northumberland Island, some fifty miles south of Cape Alexander and almost within reach of the Eskimo settlement at Etah, they reached an unprecedented low. Their boats were battered and leaking; food was short and a gale was blowing. Blake, who had been appointed cook, struggled to prepare a warm meal. It took half an hour to light the stove and no sooner had the water boiled than a gust of wind blew the stove out. By the time he relit it, the water was covered with a layer of ice. This happened, typically, four or five times with the result that it would be six hours before he emerged, blackened and weeping from the smoke, to announce that dinner was ready. It looked as if Northumberland Island was to be their last resting place. Then, on 12 September, their hopes surged as they were visited by Eskimos from Etah. The leader, a man named Kalutunah, brought them fresh meat – 'walrus-beef' they called it – and seemed very happy to swap more meat for the small quantity of needles they had brought from the *Advance* in anticipation of just such an eventuality. Reinvigorated, they got back into their boats and continued south.

After less than fifty miles they juddered to a halt. They were at a point where normally the sea was free and a few days' sailing would have seen them at Upernavik. But the season was hard that year, and the same necklace of ice that had stopped Kane reaching Lancaster Sound was still in place. Their boats were done – the *Forlorn Hope*, which they had rechristened the *Good Hope* during one of their high points, had been badly damaged and Mr Francis's metal boat, *Ironsides*, had been squeezed twelve inches thinner by floes, its flotation chambers ruined beyond repair. They had two choices: to wait the winter out, hoping that the Eskimos would bring them supplies; or to return immediately to the *Advance*. They chose the former. Dragging the *Hope* ashore, they dismembered it to build a winter hut.

Day after day, a period of 'unmitigated misery',[28] according to Hayes, they hauled stones to create an enclosure fourteen feet long, eight feet wide and four feet high. The *Hope*'s strakes were used as roof timbers, its sails were draped as a roof, and Petersen manufactured a rudimentary chimney out of the *Hope*'s tin sheathing. Its door was two feet wide and three high. They completed the task on 9 October, amidst a shrieking snowstorm, and that evening Hayes was the first man to enter their winter quarters.

The snow was already so deep that he was unable to reach the door and had to tear open a section of the roof. He dropped into their winter home and one by one the others followed him. They found themselves in what Hayes described as a 'cold, fireless, damp, vault-like den'.[29] While they made up a fire - bedding it on pages torn from Hayes's medical manuals, which he had brought for that very purpose – Blake took stock of their provisions. 'There's three-quarters of a barrel of bread,' he said, 'a capful of meat biscuit, half as much rice and flour, a double handful of lard – and that's all.'[30] He was wrong by just one measure: they still had a pint of oil as fuel.

They waited for Kalutunah's Eskimos to arrive but, save for one visit which produced no food and in which Hayes narrowly escaped being eaten by the visiting dog teams, they were left to their own devices. After a week their food supply was exhausted and they were reduced to scavenging for rock lichen, or *tripes de roche*. Ironically, it was Franklin himself who had introduced the world to this unedifying substance during a horrendous trek through the Canadian tundra in 1822. Following the example set by the man they had supposedly come to save, they scraped the thin, black wafers from the rocks, broke them open to reveal the white flesh inside, and tipped them into their stew-pot with some handfuls of bread flour. 'It is disgusting at best, and is scarcely more nutritious than paper,'[31] was how Hayes described the subsequent gruel. It gave them diarrhoea and stomach cramps, and they broke their teeth on the crumbs of rock that came

with it. Given, too, that they had to dig through the snow with their
tin plates to find a single boulder, let alone one growing lichen, many
preferred to go hungry than have anything to do with *tripes de roche*.
Starving, and without any means of transport, their condition was, as
Hayes wrote with understatement, 'fast approaching the horrible'.[32]
What were they to do?

Two weeks after they had settled into the hut, two shapeless lumps
of whiteness fell through the door. It was Kalutunah and another
Eskimo who had travelled thirty-six hours non-stop to bring them a
consignment of meat and blubber. Behind this act of apparent altru-
ism, Hayes and Petersen detected sinister motives. They feared the
Eskimos had come to gauge their strength, to calculate how long it
would be before the strangers died, how long before they could seize
the coveted metal implements and lengths of wood which were unob-
tainable in the Arctic. Hospitable as Eskimos could be in times of
plenty, their code permitted no mercy when times were hard. If food
was scarce the weak were fair prey – earlier explorers had written of
widows and grandmothers being stripped of their possessions and
walled up in an igloo. Food was now scarce and what Kalutunah
wanted to know was how weak the white men were. Petersen, 'a
very Talleyrand in diplomacy',[33] negotiated an agreement whereby
for a few odds and ends Kalutunah and his people would keep them
supplied with food. They were powerful, he said, pointing to the row
of guns stacked outside – weapons could not be brought into the hut
lest condensation dampen their powder – and it was a measure of
their power that they preferred not to go hunting but have others do
the work for them. Kalutunah nodded understandingly. He would
honour the arrangement. But Hayes could tell that although he was
frightened of the guns, he was not fully convinced by Petersen's tale:
'It was clear that he had something running in his head, for I could see
his bright little eyes twinkling with mischief beneath their blubbery
lids.'[34]

For the next few weeks both sides played a careful game. The
Eskimos would visit and would be treated to a display of conspicuous
consumption in which they feasted on the very supplies they had

brought. The guns were displayed. As they ate, Godfrey burlesqued plantation melodies – which impressed the visitors mightily. But, when the Eskimos had gone, the hut-dwellers were left on average with one day's food to see them to the next visit. Until then, they had only *tripes de roche*. It quickly became apparent who had the upper hand. The Eskimos came less and less frequently, and when they did they looked at each other laughingly and sucked in their cheeks in imitation of their hosts' gaunt faces. Once, Kalutunah arrived with his wife. She had walked forty miles in temperatures of 40°F below zero, with a six-month-old baby strapped to her back. Her purpose? Solely to see what the white men looked like. Faced with such blatant mastery of the environment, the white men huddled closer in their hut.

The wood from the *Hope* diminished steadily. Slighter lengths were used as fuel, more impressive bulks were bartered. Petersen carved handles from spare shards, hammering them into strips of hoop iron to create shabby knives which were likewise bartered until, one day, an Eskimo bent the weak blade into a U and flung it contemptuously at their feet. Eventually, they decided to break out. Petersen and Godfrey walked north to seek help from Kalutunah but, having spent three days at his camp, they returned gasping for water and with the news that it was only a matter of time before the Eskimos came to kill them. There was a leader named Sip-Su who took pride in despatching helpless people; he had personally harpooned several lacklustre hunters and wanted the strangers next.

As winter drew in, a flood of Eskimos came to weigh them up. Hayes was astonished: 'Esquimaux are coming from every quarter, and are flying about in every direction.'[35] Among them was a widow who carried dead birds under her arm. She stopped at the hut for a snack and for the chance to make the men weep for her husband who had been lost on an ice floe and thence – she was certain – had been transformed into a walrus. Fox and hare being difficult to obtain, and walrus forbidden, she ate only birds – without pause – slitting their skins with a thumbnail, peeling them back, and dropping their breasts into her mouth. 'This widow greatly interested me,' Hayes wrote. 'She ate birds for conscience' sake.'[36]

When the widow departed, however, Hayes focused on less surreal matters. Parapets of snow were built, behind which the watch stood on twenty-four-hour alert, guns cocked. They called it Fort Desolation. Sip-Su and Kalutunah would pay dearly if they mounted an attack. But as Hayes acknowledged, the Eskimos did not need to attack; they only had to wait until the foreigners starved. 'We were destitute – helpless,' he wrote. 'The only human beings within three hundred miles were seeking our lives. Of what value, now, was the question, *What shall we do?*'[37]

Back on the *Advance*, the crew were asking themselves the same question, though from a different standpoint. It was not the Eskimos that bothered them; it was their captain. Kane's unprofessional notions of command had become unbearable. He boasted and quarrelled with his remaining officers. He developed an irritating habit of dropping French and Latin quotes into the conversation. He flew into unreasonable rages. And, nauseatingly as far as the others were concerned, he began to catch and eat the ship's rats. Wilson described the cabin as 'the most perfect hell hole', from which they escaped whenever possible. 'He has not one friend in the ship left,' he wrote, 'save the lying scamp Morton, whom he bribes, & who tells Mr. K. all he can hear us say.'[38] Kane's habit of going to bed in the early hours and not rising until midday was something else that annoyed Wilson. 'He turns day into night, but makes us all get up at seven bells.'[39] Penned up with such a leader, the men on the *Advance* became increasingly ill at ease.

Kane saw things differently, needless to say. 'Every energy of my nature – a vile foul nature too – is bent to bear myself and those who lean on me out of this great trial,' he wrote in his diary. 'If I let weakness come over me now – we, I mean all of us – are gone.'[40] His rat diet he considered an excellent idea, as the fresh meat kept him free of scurvy. As for his unusual sleeping patterns, these were caused by having to stand two night watches, those of himself and Henry Goodfellow. Kane had hoped that Goodfellow, the man he had enlisted as a favour to his brother, would be a fellow soul with whom he could converse in common. But Goodfellow had become as disenchanted with Kane and the voyage as everybody else. He neglected his duties – which, as a sinecural observer of natural history were virtually nil – and was so openly rude to Kane that the latter dismissed him and, to save argument, stood in for him on his watches. Meanwhile, Goodfellow lolled about, reading books and sipping lime juice. He was 'lazy, dirty, ragged and impudent to everyone', Kane wrote at the end of one night shift. 'He asks me for a glass of lime juice and water. "Yes Henry." So off I go to get it and he now just awake and prepared for a new guzzle and a new nap. He has more cool impudence than any man I ever knew.'[41]

Neither accusation nor explanation could alleviate their physical condition. By December the raw potatoes, which had provided their main source of Vitamin C, were reduced to twelve lonely specimens. Kane grated them into his men's meals but even so, five of the crew were bedridden with scurvy. Morton was so appallingly afflicted that the flesh dropped from his ankle, exposing the bones and tendons. Kane dared not amputate lest tetanus take hold. As for their fuel, it was running out fast. Shelves, beds and bulkheads had already been burned. Now it was the turn of the ship's oak ribbing, a move which did not reduce the *Advance*'s ability to sail, while providing enough firewood to see them through January. On the other side of January, however, awaited the two most violent months of the Arctic winter. For February and March, Kane counted on the three inches of oak sheathing nailed to the ship's hull. Having consulted with Ohlsen, he decided they could sacrifice the wood provided they scavenged no lower than the waterline. This would give them two and a half tons of fuel. And then, he hoped, 'I may get through this awful winter and *save the brig besides!*'[42]

His calculations were posited on a skeleton crew of eight. They made no allowance for extra bodies. At 3.00 a.m. on 7 December 1854, however, Kane was woken by a sudden ruckus. Bonsall and Petersen were back.

3

THE BLOWING PLACE

Confined in their squalid hut, dependent for their survival on a group of increasingly avaricious Eskimos, the boat party had realized that it was impossible to stay where they were. Their options were bleak. They could either continue south by sledge to Upernavik or return to the *Advance*. The former was out of the question: the Eskimos they had encountered thus far were the so-called Arctic Highlanders, the northernmost people on the globe; they knew nothing of the territory which separated them from their southerly cousins in Greenland and could not have guided the strangers through it even if they had wanted to. The latter option involved running the gauntlet of Sip-Su and Kalutunah but there was really no choice: the Americans made plans for an evacuation to the north. Bonsall and Petersen were to lead the way, using their rifles to persuade Kalutunah's men to sledge them to the *Advance*. Once there they would send food to relieve the rest. Hayes and the others were to follow as best they could. 'That all of us would reach Rensselaer Harbour seemed highly improbable,' Hayes wrote, 'yet there was some comfort in looking forward to a struggle which would relieve us of our present uncertainty, and speedily decide our fortunes.'[1]

Bonsall and Petersen departed on 29 November. By means of bluster, persuasion and firepower they were soon being carried on relays of sledges from settlement to settlement towards the *Advance*. Hayes's group, however, was not so thrusting. The effect of Bonsall's and Petersen's departure was palpable. The hut had never been warm at the best of times, but the mercury now quavered below freezing and the muck on the floor began to solidify. At any other time it would have been interesting to discuss the contribution two humans could make to the heat of a shelter, but they were too far gone. An attempt to break free was aborted when one man collapsed with heart problems. Returning to the hut they found they had left the roof open (the door was several feet under snow by this time) with the result that the interior was filled with ice. Neither their body warmth nor the two hours' warmth they permitted themselves each day by lighting the stove could melt it. For three days they sat around the frozen clods, chewing strips of walrus hide. Fort Desolation was renamed Fort Starvation.

When Kalutunah appeared with a small amount of meat they devoured it. They did so against all his protestations that he had no more and they were eating his last supplies. And they were right to do so, for when one of them sneaked out to inspect Kalutunah's sledge he saw whole sides of meat poorly concealed under a snowdrift. Outraged at this blatant evidence of Kalutunah's tactics, Hayes resorted to a desperate ploy: he would drug the Eskimos and steal their sledges. He poured laudanum into the visitors' soup and told the others to make ready. When Kalutunah and his men were snoring they climbed into the Eskimos' travelling furs, which had been removed on entering the hut as was customary, harnessed their dogs and sledges, grabbed the meat and stole off to the north.

It was an embarrassing failure. The dogs ran wild under unfamiliar masters, one team crashing its sledge before running back to the hut. In the time it took for Hayes to redistribute the load between the two remaining sledges, Kalutunah was already coming after them. Before they had gone a few more miles they were overtaken. Standing before them in a motley of discarded blankets, clutching armfuls of tin cups and other Arctic valuables, the Eskimos blocked their path in mute reproach.

In his haste Hayes had not forgotten his rifle. Pointing it at Kalutunah, he told him that unless he and his men guided them to the *Advance* they would all die. If they did as he asked, avoiding Sip-Su, they could have their clothes, dogs and sledges back. The bargain was struck and Kalutunah led them through settlement after tiny settlement on a winding course towards Cape Alexander – 'the blowing place', as Eskimos called it. In the *Ironsides*, Hayes had experienced rough conditions off Cape Alexander; he had no idea, however, how unpleasant it could be when approached on foot. 'The Eskimaux,' he wrote, 'whenever alluding to Cape Alexander, did it with a shrug and a shiver.'[2] He found out why, as the dogs skeltered north through the Arctic twilight.

Cape Alexander was rightly named the blowing place. Beneath its thousand-foot cliffs the ice was constantly shifted by turbulent winds, narrow leads of water opening and closing with treacherous suddenness. Crossing these leads was an impossible task as Hayes discovered when a projecting tongue of ice gave way beneath his weight and dropped him into the sea. Fortunately his furs were almost completely waterproof; but at one place, where his boots joined his leggings, a small amount of water seeped in. As it ran down his leg and pooled at his toes, Hayes knew that they would have to move very fast indeed if he were to avoid frostbite.

Forsaking the disintegrating floes, they took to dry land – or at least the nearest equivalent Cape Alexander had to offer: the ice-foot. Raised some twenty feet above sea level, the ice-foot was created by tides and storm waves freezing repeatedly against the rock face until they formed a platform some ten to fifteen feet wide. Along this platform they now slithered, hoping that it would continue unbroken to the other side of the Cape. Initially their hopes seemed well-founded; the ice-foot was at times wide, at times narrow, but there was always room for the dogs to pick their way. At the Cape's outermost promontory, however, they came to a halt. Here, where the winds were fiercest and the currents strongest, the ice-foot dwindled to a tiny ledge fifteen inches wide. It sloped terrifyingly and below it lay black sea. The Eskimos were all for turning back and circumventing Cape Alexander by the longer, inland route. Hayes refused. Already he had lost sensation in his toes and his calf was burning where the water had trickled down. To turn back would be to lose valuable time – to lose, too, any chance of saving his foot. He therefore scrabbled across the ledge, which luckily extended no further than a few yards, and beckoned the others to follow. How the dogs and sledges made it defied all laws of probability. One minute they were poised at the gap, the next they had careered over, finding purchase in the force of their own momentum and dragging the sledges at an angle behind them. Not one dog slipped and not one item spilled from the sledges. It was unbelievable even to their Eskimo drivers.

From this point the ice-foot widened comfortably and the party was soon able to regroup on the sea where less than two days of fast, frozen travelling separated them from the *Advance*. They reached the ship on 12 December 1854. Hayes could never remember the details of their home-coming, which was perhaps a relief as several of his toes had to be amputated immediately. Kane, however, made up for Hayes's lack of recall. 'We come here destitute and exhausted to claim your hospitality,' ran his version of Hayes's opening speech. 'We know that we have no rights to your indulgence but we feel that with you we will have a welcome and a home.'[3] Hayes may never have said such a thing but it was what he *should* have said, in his captain's opinion, for Kane was feeling sorely tried.

On Petersen's urging he had sent a sledge-load of food to relieve Hayes's party; it had never reached them and had obviously been eaten by the Eskimos to whom it was entrusted. His supplies were smaller, the mouths he had to feed were more numerous, the traitors whom he had cut off were back at his door. On top of this, the depot at Littleton Island had been depleted. This was particularly bad news in that it affected the possibility of their safe return. As Goodfellow wrote, 'The quantity and value of the articles taken . . . are inconsiderable and would scarcely have raised the offence above petit larceny, but the incalculable value of the goods under the circumstances elevates the crime above such an humble place in the Statutebook to the rank of robbery or even piracy.'[4] What was more, when Hayes recovered he had the gall to point out that with the exception of three men – including Kane, who was thriving on his rats – everyone on the *Advance* was helpless with scurvy. The mutineers, however, were scurvy-free thanks to their intake of raw meat. Good thing we went when we did, Hayes said to Kane's fury, or we'd all be like that.

'God of heavens, it makes my blood boil,' Kane wrote in his diary, 'to think that men who have so leaned on me, trusted to me, and like little children been taught by me their very walk, should at last in the midst of a coming winter, set up their juvenile opinions against my own drearily earned judgement of Arctic Ice.'[5] He had nothing pleasant to say about any of them. Bonsall and Sonntag, his erstwhile friends, were described respectively as 'a country boy of low bred training and selfish instincts', and 'a weak, sycophantic *specialité* student, a German Jew employed of a second-rate observatory'.[6] Petersen, as he had previously remarked, was a double-faced mischief-maker. When it came to Hayes, Kane was almost apoplectic. He was 'a vast extenuator of every abomination'.[7] None of them were fit to associate with the loyal members, he announced. Henceforth they would eat separately, sleep separately, and apart from a few necessary duties – such as keeping night watch – would be treated as unwelcome guests. This extraordinary ménage was further complicated by Godfrey and Blake, who made themselves so unpopular that they were told to mess on their own, thus forming a sub-section of pariahdom. Even Kane was losing patience with the pair. After one act of insubordination he attacked them with a belaying pin, very nearly killing Blake with a blow to the skull; when Blake came round Kane told him that next time he *would* kill him.

The company squabbled and fought their way through the winter of 1854–5. Godfrey and Blake continued to be a nuisance, Brooks and Goodfellow came to blows and their captain quarrelled with everybody. Kane's sense of martyrdom evolved into a stubborn isolation where no man was to be fully trusted. 'My task is a hard and thankless one,' he wrote, 'totally unappreciated by my clients and made, thank Heaven, without care or regard for their appreciation or non-appreciation.'[8] The task to which Kane referred was twofold: to keep his crew in good spirits and to preserve their health until they were able to escape. Regarding the former he had failed miserably; as to the latter, it was not really a task at all, for no amount of application could disguise the fact that there was hardly any fresh meat to be had. An arrangement made with nearby Eskimos earlier in the season had produced nothing – the Eskimos themselves were starving – and Hans's hunting forays brought in the tiniest amount of sustenance. By March there were fourteen men down with scurvy and those 'clients' who remained healthy could have been forgiven for their non-appreciation of Kane's regime.

On 20 March Godfrey and Blake tried to escape. Alerted to their plan, Kane lay in wait with a lead bar and once more cracked their skulls. To Kane's dismay Godfrey managed later to slip off unobserved. By now he could not care if Godfrey stayed or went, beyond the effect it would have on his reputation as a commander. 'This wretched man has been the very bane of the cruise,' he wrote. 'My conscience tells me that almost any measure against him would be justified.'[9] He worried for Hans, however, who had been sent on 18 March to coax supplies from Etah, seventy miles away. If Godfrey caught up with him and commandeered his sledge the *Advance* would be stranded; not only would they have lost their most knowledgeable guide and hunter, but also the means to communicate with the Eskimos. As the days passed without any sign of Hans, everybody feared the worst. Petersen managed to shoot a few ptarmigan but they were a poor comfort to men who were now desperate for slabs of raw flesh.

On 2 April, Bonsall spotted Hans lurking on the ice a mile from the ship. He and Kane went out to greet him and were taken aback to find that it was not Hans but Godfrey, riding Hans's dog-sledge on which was piled a trove of walrus meat. Kane was accusatory: Godfrey had only returned to collect his friend Blake. Godfrey was indignant: he had travelled 140 miles in temperatures of –50°F to bring Kane food. Where was Hans, Kane asked? Sick and recovering at Etah, Godfrey replied, and once Kane had taken the food he was going back to join him; he would spend the rest of his life as an Eskimo. Godfrey could consider himself under arrest, Kane retorted, and was to stay where he was while he, Kane, fetched leg irons from the ship. Godfrey said that he couldn't give a fig and ran off across the ice. Bonsall and Kane struggled impotently with their firearms. By the time they sent a shot over his head he had disappeared, laughing, into the hummocks.

Godfrey eventually reached the safety of Etah where, after a solid sleep of fifteen hours he awoke refreshed and without any sign of frostbite. He considered himself safe from Kane's vengeance – after all, it was not everybody who could cover such a distance, even if they were healthy. But Kane was not everybody. Godfrey's defiance was an insupportable blow to his pride. Bent on retribution, he hunted down the deserters like a Wild West marshal. First he launched a raid to bring back Hans, whom he discovered hunting happily on the ice; the Eskimo had not been ill at all, Kane learned, he had fallen in love with a local woman. Enraged, he then went after Godfrey, clutching a pistol and a set of irons. He dragged him from a hut in Etah and marched him at gunpoint all the seventy miles back to the *Advance*. It was a masterly show of strength but one that did little good. Godfrey remained as truculent as ever and Hans slipped away shortly after-wards to rejoin his beloved, never to return.

April was normally a month of release for Arctic dwellers, a period in which a gradual thaw tempted walruses and seals back to the region, announcing the reappearance in succeeding months of a sparse layer of vegetation and the wildfowl, reindeer and musk-ox which came to forage on it. This year, though, the thaw was slow and the game emerged reluctantly. In Etah the Eskimos began to eat their dogs, a sign of utmost desperation. Kane could not crow, as he had done in 1854, about the lush Eden of an Arctic spring. Nor, if the late season was any guide, could he expect the *Advance* to be free that summer. They would have to go home in their three remaining boats, hauling them on sledges overland until they reached open water,

some eighty miles to the south. Taking advantage of the small amount
of fresh meat the season brought him, he ordered his men to eat well
and prepare for the retreat.

Throughout April his scorbutic crew ate, recovered, and rose one
by one to the tasks allotted them. The healthiest were instructed to
take the ship apart, which they did with vigour, dismantling the last
beams to make the sledges which were to carry the boats. The next
strongest flattened curtain rails and hammered them onto the runners.
And the feeblest made bags, boots and clothes from whatever was left
over. Their home for the past two years was plundered to its last ser-
viceable item. Carpeting was made into boot uppers; the gutta percha
speaking tube was cut up for soles and goggles; curtains were transformed into padded quilts; fur clothing was stitched and buttoned to
make sleeping bags; sails were sewn into provision bags which were
waterproofed with a mixture of tar, pitch, flour and plaster of Paris; the
remainder of the canvas was used to make moccasins; the tin chimney
was converted into stoves; and cake tins were bashed into pots. 'We
cut plates out of every imaginable and rejected piece of tinware,'
Kane recorded. 'Borden's meat-biscuit canister furnished us with a
splendid dinner service; and some rightly-feared tin jars, with ominous labels of Corrosive Sublimate and Arsenic, which once belonged
to our department of Natural History, were emptied, scoured, and
cut down into tea-cups.'[10] He set their departure date for 17 May
1855.

The crew complained that it was too early. They would not be
ready by that time. Some could not face the prospect of leaving the
ship. Others feared that Kane was taking the healthy south and abandoning the sick to their own devices. 'I was displeased, indeed, with
[their] moody indifference,' Kane wrote. 'But I showed myself inex-
orable.'[11] Nonetheless, several men threw down their work in disgust.
Kane had to exercise every atom of his authority to restore order.
'The number is unfortunately small of those human beings whom
calamity elevates,'[12] he noted. On 17 May, true to his word, Kane
ordered his crew off the ship – having first forced the 'croakers', as he
called them, to sign a document approving his action. As a final

romantic gesture Kane added the *Advance*'s figurehead to their load. This carved beauty, called Augusta, had led them into the Arctic three years ago with bright blue clothes and pink cheeks. She had since lost a breast to an iceberg, her nose had snagged off and her paint had been stripped by the weather. Even Kane wondered if she was a fitting emblem of hope. But, he consoled himself, she was made of wood; she could always be burned. And so, with Augusta's scarred face pointing the way, they marched south.

It took them a month to reach open water. Working in stages, the rapidly weakening crew man-hauled three boats, 1,500 pounds of food and four invalids across the ice. Kane had optimistically allotted one team to each sledge but it soon became obvious that the entire sixteen-strong contingent was needed to drag just one of them. And so every distance had to be covered again and again. To cross the eighty miles each man walked approximately 316. Kane, meanwhile, on his dog-sledge travelled 1,100 miles to and fro. Scurvy resumed its attack, causing legs to swell, tendons to contract and gums to bleed. At Etah, where they received food from the Eskimos, the disease retreated to its lair. The late spring had at last arrived, and their hosts were so invigorated as to put on a display of ice-hockey, using whale bones as sticks and a walrus flipper joint as a puck. 'How strange this joyous merriment under the monitory shadow of those ice-cliffs!' Kane wondered. 'They were playing as unconcerned as the birds that circled above our heads.'[13] But the scurvy was soon to return. Other problems, too, detracted from their reception at Etah. The smallest of the three boats sank when they put it in the water. And Ohlsen, one of the most valuable members of the party, ruptured his bladder trying to rescue a sledge that had fallen through the ice. Kane tried to keep Ohlsen's condition secret, a futile gesture that did nothing to alleviate the crew's shock when he died a few days later.

On 16 June they were camped within three-quarters of a mile of the sea. 'We see its deep indigo horizon,' Kane exulted, 'and hear its roar against the icy beach. Its scent is in our nostrils and our hearts.'[14] A dark, distant headland marked Cape Alexander, the 'blowing place' which every man of the Petersen–Hayes boat party looked upon with dread. It was surrounded by ridges of squeezed ice and its edges were rimmed with floating sludge. 'How magnificently the surf beats against its sides!' Kane wrote. 'But we have mastered worse obstacles, and by God's help we shall master these.'[15] So, at 4.00 p.m. on 19 June, they pushed their boats into an open stretch of water and headed for Cape Alexander.

'It was an ugly crossing,'[16] Kane wrote, making light of the waves that swamped them faster than they could bail. But by steering into the lee of the ice that lay to the west, rather than hugging the coast, they were able to continue their journey through calmer water. Cape Alexander was the major nautical obstacle in their path, and its successful navigation raised everyone's spirits. Before them, however, lay more than a thousand miles of sea and ice. Their food supplies were low, their fuel meagre and their health disintegrating. For the next forty-nine days they sailed, rowed and hauled their way through Smith Sound and into Baffin Bay. Monstrous scenery greeted them: a 1,100-foot glacier poured into the sea as if tipped from a cauldron; a pyramid of granite, topped by an improbable obelisk, came and went in the fog; red sandstone promontories loomed at dawn, then leered brassily as the flotilla travelled south into the dusk. By the end of June their rations had dwindled to a six-ounce mush of bread dust plus a knuckle of tallow per man per day, and their fuel had run out. When the wind fell and they had to row, Kane could measure his men's weakness by the plash of their oars. They were hit by gales, forced to shelter on floes and at times driven onto land. Somehow they managed to find comfort in disaster. At one unscheduled stop, for example, they met a cliff of nesting seabirds. They ransacked the cliff for three days to the tune of 1,200 eggs per day.

Down they crept along the coast, their supplies gradually running out. By 1 August they were burning oars and sledges to melt water. Their food was exhausted and only the chance capture of a seal saved them from starvation. 'I had not realised how much we were reduced by absolute famine,' Kane wrote. 'They ran over the floe, crying and laughing and brandishing their knives. It was not five minutes before every man was sucking his bloody fingers or mouthing long strips of raw blubber . . . we enjoyed a rare and savage feast.'[17] They were still chewing the intestines as they passed the Devil's Thumb. This distinctive rock on the west coast of Greenland announced their arrival in the whaling grounds. Here they could surely expect help. On 3 August, Petersen spotted an Eskimo paddling his kayak in search of eiderduck. As the boat came closer, Petersen recognized him as an old friend from Upernavik. 'I'm Carl Petersen!' he shouted, waving for attention. 'No you're not,' the Eskimo replied, ploughing away as fast as he could. 'His wife says he's dead.'[18]

For another two days they drifted south, hoping to meet a whaler. Fog rose and they were beginning to despair, when they heard a long, slow, 'Halloo!' 'Dannemarkers!'[19] Petersen whispered. From out of the mist came the *Fraülein Flairscher*, an Upernavik oil-boat plying the coast in search of blubber. Its commander, Carlie Mossyn, was a friend of Petersen. Wringing his hands with excitement, Petersen directed them alongside. As he swapped notes with Mossyn, Kane realized how long he had been away. 'Here we first got our cloudy vague idea of what had passed in the big world during our absence,' he wrote. 'How gently all the lore of this man oozed out of him! he seemed an oracle, as, with hot-tingling fingers pressed against the gunwale of the boat, we listened to his words. "Sebastopol ain't taken." Where and what was Sebastapol?'[20] Mossyn's news of the Crimean War may have been meaningless but it was not long before he spoke of a matter with which they were acquainted – 'our own delusive little speciality',[21] as Kane called it – the fate of Sir John Franklin.

In 1854, travelling overland through the Canadian tundra, an employee of the Hudson Bay Company named John Rae had found the first traces of the lost men. According to local Eskimos the whole expedition was dead. Its ships had sunk and the survivors had starved to death during the gruelling walk to freedom. It would be some years before fuller details came to light but from the relics which Rae obtained it was certain that Franklin and his men had perished. And they had done so more than a thousand miles to the south of Rensselaer Harbour. Kane had wasted three years looking in the wrong place.

On 6 August 1855 they reached Upernavik. After eighty-four days living in the open they found it strange to be back in recognizable civilization. 'Our habits were hard and weather-worn,' wrote Kane. 'We could not remain within the four walls of a house without a distressing sense of suffocation.'[22] Instead they wandered from door to door, drinking coffee and repeating their tale to the eager inhabitants of the settlement. During their recitations it is unlikely that Kane ever once expressed a sense of futility, or regretted that they had lost men, money and their ship, searching for Franklin in entirely the wrong place. Or if he did, he did not mention it in his journal. On the contrary, what Kane felt was triumph. He had taken a ship further north up Smith Sound than anyone else; he had discovered the Humboldt Glacier and had charted great stretches of new coastline; he had overcome mutiny and saved his men from disaster (well, most of them) in a dramatic and well-planned escape; above all, he had, in his own mind, found the Open Polar Sea. He really was 'Doctor Kane of the Arctic Seas'.

4

'AMERICANS CAN DO IT'

Back home, US citizens thought highly of Kane. Already a hero before his departure, he had achieved the status of national icon following the publication in 1854 of his journal describing the first Grinnell expedition. His continued absence on the second prompted comparisons with Franklin, the man whom he was ostensibly meant to be saving. Had Kane disappeared into the same polar ocean? Was he, too, in need of rescue? Congress thought so, and after some debate (for the Franklin business had been running long enough to engender a degree of ennui in official circles), it voted $150,000 to send two ships after the errant polar knight. It was this contingent, under a Captain Hartstene, that caught up with Kane in the autumn of 1855 and brought him back to New York.

Kane's homecoming was one of the most sensational events of the year. Cannon fired salutes, crowds cheered in the streets, and he was so mobbed by reporters and admirers that he had difficulty making his way to Grinnell's home to deliver his report. 'I have no *Advance* with me,' he told his sponsor. 'Never mind,' Grinnell replied. 'You are safe; that is all we care about. Come into the parlour and tell us the whole story.'[1] As Kane did so, the celebrations continued outside.

The next day the *New York Times* filled its whole front page with the news of his return. In succeeding months, Kane's star rose higher and higher. When his journal came out in 1856, under the title *Arctic Explorations*, it sold 65,000 copies and made a mint. Britain's Royal Geographical Society awarded him its Gold Medal, the highest honour it could bestow.* His relationship with Margaret Fox, which he had renewed in his strange hot-and-cold fashion, hit the papers and at once added to his lustre. An exotic explorer with a controversial lover was good copy.

Yet there was a tragic element to Kane's fame. When he docked at New York in October 1855 he looked fit and healthy, tanned and with a trim beard. The ordeal, however, had taken more out of him than he liked to admit. That winter his health worsened under the strain of preparing at breakneck speed his journal, a two-volume affair complete with hefty appendices, that eventually ran to 900 pages, 300 of which were finished by Christmas. He was also stressed by the prospect of rival journals. When his own book was published it said nothing of internal discord; it contained nothing of the boat party's extraordinary journey under Hayes and Petersen – saying merely that it would be covered later, which it wasn't; and it failed outstandingly to address the casualty rate. On every previous Arctic expedition (save Franklin's) the main cause of death had been scurvy; captains were on the whole careful enough to save their crew from frostbite. Kane's men, on the other hand, had died as a result of exposure occasioned by his direct orders. There was hardly a man who had not had some part of himself amputated. Such carelessness was culpable and Kane knew it. When Wilson tried to publish his account of the expedition, Kane paid him $350 to keep it under wraps. It was a waste of money, for Wilson published anyway – albeit a bland nothingness compared to the contents of his notebooks – and almost every other member of the expedition had something to say. Mercifully their contributions were harmless. Morton produced a book which was treated as a hoax.

* There was a political element to the award: Britain's relationship with the US had been frosty; Kane's (and Grinnell's) selfless attempt to rescue Franklin did much to thaw the situation.

Godfrey's ghostwritten journal was ignored. Sonntag refuted an account published under his name. Bonsall wrote a memoir in 1902, too late to have any effect. And Petersen's highly critical *Erindringer fra Polarlandene optegnede af Carl Petersen, Told ved Pennys og Kanes Nordexpeditioner 1850–1855. Udgivne af Lauritz B. Deichmann, Lieutenant. Med Traesnit og Kort over en Deel af Baffinsbay og Smiths-Sund* did not reach a wide audience.

In 1860, when Hayes produced his journal of those missing months, an inkling of the truth emerged. But by then Kane was dead. The completion of his journal took a frightful toll. 'This book, poor as it is, has been my coffin,'[2] he told his publisher on handing over the manuscript. Deteriorating rapidly, he left for Europe in the summer of 1856, accompanied by the steward Morton who had now become his personal valet. His aim was to make a tour of Britain followed by a period of recuperation in Switzerland. Thereafter, who knew where fate might lead him. Wherever it did, it would certainly not be the Arctic. '*This dream is over*,'[3] he emphasized in a letter to his father. Nor would it be anywhere more exotic than a sanatorium if his health failed to improve. He was, according to Grinnell, 'but a skeleton or a shadow of one'.[4] His engagements in Britain took longer than expected thanks to an inescapable series of presentations – which included not only the usual ceremonies but a breakfast with Queen Victoria – and to a relapse which kept him in bed for weeks. When he arose the Swiss season was over. So on 17 November he and Morton left for Cuba, whose warm climate his doctor recommended as the perfect cure. He died there on 16 February 1857, thirteen days after his thirty-seventh birthday, from a series of debilitating strokes.

Kane had always wanted to be somebody and his funeral procession demonstrated just how completely his wish had been granted. For a month his body travelled by ship, river-boat and locomotive from Havana to New Orleans, from New Orleans to Ohio, from Ohio to Cincinnati and from Cincinnati to Philadelphia. Bands played at every major town and the coffin was laid in state at even the smallest stop. Respectful throngs emerged in such numbers that sometimes the cortège could not break through. There were military, civic and masonic processions. Poems, editorials and sermons were published in his honour. When he was finally laid to rest in Laurel Hill Cemetery it took three days for the mourners to file past. His journal 'lay for a decade with the Bible on almost every parlor table in America'.[5] Not until Abraham Lincoln's death would there be such a massive display of grief.

Nevertheless, the 'somebody' Kane had become was an illusion, the product of his own self-publicity. Underneath the adulation and the eulogies lay the fact that Kane was not a great explorer. He had sailed further up Smith Sound than anyone else but not far enough to rate comparison with British pioneers such as William Edward Parry, who had opened the Arctic with such panache in previous decades. He had discovered the Humboldt Glacier but had not investigated it fully. He had undergone fearful privations and had rescued his expedition from disaster – but he had partly been the author of its misfortune. And yet, he had achieved something miraculous: he had discovered – or believed he had discovered – the Open Polar Sea. This, the greatest illusion of all, was Kane's most enduring monument. He became a Colossus whose shadow stretched over the Arctic – as Rhodes's would soon do in Africa – beckoning the world northwards. The Pole was a place whose commercial benefits outweighed potentially all of the Old World's colonies put together. Whoever discovered it would control the swiftest sea route across the globe from west to east. If men of sufficient ingenuity and fortitude could smash through the ice of Smith Sound the world would, literally, be theirs.

Valiant attempts were made to reveal the illusion for what it was. One Dr Henry Rink, who had spent nine years as Inspector in Greenland for the Danish Government, wrote a damning critique of Kane's journal. Dissecting the portion which covered the sighting of the Open Polar Sea, he pointed out that it was impossible for Morton to have covered the terrain described in the time which he claimed it had taken him; it was impossible for him to have taken accurate observations during that period; he did not know how to use a sextant anyway; the horizon to which he said the open sea stretched could not have been very far when viewed from a height of 500 feet; and as to the 500 feet, it was written in various places as 250 feet, 300 feet, 450 feet and 540 feet. Morton had said the coast was full of sea birds and that the temperature was higher than at Rensselaer Harbour – two other details which might have supported the Open Polar Sea theory. Rink said that these could be explained by the bubbles of warm water whose cause he did not know but which frequently disrupted the Arctic ice. Such a bubble would account for the higher temperature and also for the presence of sea birds. In Kane's experience, sea birds might have been common only on large expanses of ocean; in Rink's they flocked to whatever bit of sea was open.

Then Rink turned to Kane's discovery of the Humboldt Glacier. If it did stretch across Greenland's interior, as Kane suggested in one of his appendices, then he had not discovered it at all. If Arctic explorers ever bothered to investigate Greenland's coast in their mad rush north they would find offshoots of the ice cap at the head of every fjord – and Rink knew, because he had spent almost a decade investigating them. In his view, Kane had discovered nothing and the idea of an Open Polar Sea was nonsensical. 'These Polar expeditions,' he wrote, 'do not promise any advantages that can in any way answer to the means and efforts they demand.'[6]

Britain, which had sent two generations of officers into the Arctic, agreed with Rink's findings. At a meeting of the Royal Geographical Society in 1857, veteran after veteran praised Kane's exploits but wasted no time in pointing out his faults. Sir Richard Collinson said that his readings were imprecise and should be adjusted so that they lay at least forty-five miles further south. 'I believe we are quite justified,' he said, 'in rejecting his reckonings altogether.'[7] Sir George Back agreed with him and said the whole business was an underhand attempt to snatch the farthest point north from British hands. Dr Alexander Armstrong, a man of less crustiness and more sense, provided a pertinent summary. 'It appears to me that nothing new has been advanced by Dr. Kane with regard to the existence of water where he is supposed to have seen it,' he announced. 'I must therefore state my conviction that this much talked of Polar Sea or

Basin . . . has no existence except in the vivid imagination of those who feel disposed to portray it.' And then, having spent several very unpleasant years locked in the ice himself, he delivered a broadside against those who had sent him there: 'I have almost universally remarked that the advocates for its existence are those who are least capable of forming an opinion on the subject, from never having been in the Polar Sea.'[8]

Armstrong was wasting his breath. So were Back, Collingwood and Rink. In 1858 the *Proceedings of the Royal Geographical Society* contained a message from Hayes. Morton was well able to use a sextant, Hayes wrote, and if the Royal Geographical Society thought his readings erred on the northward, 'then the only consequence will be that the open sea, if it exists, will be so much nearer to us, and of course proportionately easier of access'.[9] All that talk of warm water bubbles and holes in the ice and opportunistic seagulls was irrelevant. They had to judge Kane's discovery not on their own prejudices but on 'precisely the kind of evidence that was needed, viz. *positive testimony*'.[10] He did not go so far as to accuse them of libel, but he said that it was a bit rich to accuse Morton of inaccuracy without any definite proof that his readings were wrong. Nor did he dwell on Armstrong's crabbiness about who could or could not pronounce on the Polar Sea – a skilful omission that drew every reader's attention to the fact that Armstrong had never been up Smith Sound and was therefore disqualified by his own logic from forming an opinion. Imperial romantics sided with Hayes. In the next volume of the *Proceedings* there appeared a vision of how the Pole might suit the world order. There were too many convicts in Britain now the colonies had stopped taking them, wrote one man. There were coal deposits in the Arctic. Could not the convicts be sent north to mine Arctic coal? The coal would power steamships on their passage over the Pole, would provide heating for the hotels in which travellers would stay, and would rid the nation of its underclass. Exploration, he maintained, was more than the sum of heroes lost and charts filled. It was a commercial, cultural and social imperative which benefited the known and unknown world alike. Very few Americans read the *Proceedings of the Royal Geographical Society* but they, like their

British counterparts, were gripped by the certainty of progress. On either side of the Atlantic, ordinary men and women agreed that the Pole should be taken.

Their respective governments were more realistic. Wrestling with problems larger and more complicated than polar ice, they had no interest in pursuing Kane's dream. Water supplies, gas pipes, safety inspectors, railways, cholera, sewage systems, town halls and workhouses were what concerned them. Hundreds of thousands of government pounds and dollars had been spent on the Franklin search, and now that his fate had been ascertained no more money was forthcoming. People were welcome to chase the Pole but they would have to fund their folly themselves.

Isaac Israel Hayes took up the challenge. Learning from Kane's example he lectured widely on the value of polar exploration. Like Kane, too, he put his words to paper. 'There is nothing in any conceivable state of the facts to deter a prudent man from an enterprise of the kind in question,' he wrote. 'Will the reader endeavour to find a reason to prove that enterprise impracticable or rash? Is it the NATURE OF THE COUNTRY?'[11] This was fighting talk, calculated to raise the hackles of patriotism. Everywhere Hayes went he gathered money and support for another polar expedition. The American Geographical Society was won over by Hayes's arguments, 'deeming it due alike to the cause of science and our national character'.[12] So was the American Philosophical Society, the Academy of Natural Sciences of Philadelphia, the Boston Society of Natural History, the New York Lyceum of Natural History, the Smithsonian Institution and, unexpectedly, the Royal Geographical Society.

By 1859, he had secured the funds for his next trip north. A large part of it came from the pocket of that indefatigable Arctic sponsor, Henry Grinnell. But an equally large part had been raised by Hayes's lectures and by the numerous provincial committees and sub-committees which had been formed to aid the cause. The money was to be spent on a small schooner which, with a crew of fourteen officers and men, would sail for Smith Sound in July 1860. The expedition's aim was to sail through Smith Sound as Kane had done but then, instead of sticking to the Greenland coast, go north up the cliffs of Grinnell Land. During his reconnaissance there, Hayes had noted that the sea was free of ice. There could be no doubt that this was caused by winds coming from the north and in his view Kane's misfortune had stemmed from anchoring to the south, where the *Advance* had been trapped by the body of the ice blown against it. He even had his future harbour planned: Cape Frazer, the sheltered cove which he had reached by sledge with Godfrey. 'Is it too sanguine a disposition which leads me to believe that I shall see again the little flag which I planted upon the coast of Grinnell Land?'he wrote.[13]

There was a certain amount of dissembling as to the actual purpose of Hayes's trip. According to one learned body, 'his return will be fraught with fruits most valuable to science'.[14] Scientific discovery, however, was a fig-leaf so tattered from the number of times it had been snatched aside that it was now a mere convention, a politeness to save the blushes of potential sponsors. As everyone really knew, and as the press had no hesitation in saying, Arctic exploration was a matter of naked ambition. Who would open the ice? Who would reach the Pole first? Even the tiny *Cincinnati News* had the answer. In a brimming editorial it spoke for the nation: 'Americans can do it – and *will.*'[15]

The voice of the *News* was significant. Other newspapers may have had a wider circulation but none had an editor like Charles Francis Hall. Short, thickset and blue-eyed, with broad shoulders and a curly beard, Hall looked like a typical Mid-west settler. His education matched the image: having dropped out of school he had worked as a blacksmith and engraver before becoming editor of the no-account *News*. He was a loner, quick to anger, intolerant, and prone to sudden enthusiasms. He was God-fearing, had a wife, two children and a job. There was nothing to suggest that this scion of America's heartland would become one of its most famous Arctic explorers.

It was Kane's journals that hooked him. Having read them he then read everything available on the subject, and came to two conclusions:

Franklin was in need of assistance; and Eskimos were the key to polar success. Here, Hall was ahead of his time. Anybody who studied Arctic journals from the last half century would have realized that the key to Arctic survival lay in the adoption of Eskimo clothes and an Eskimo diet. Yet the notion of European supremacy still informed every mission that went out. Hall, in his straightforward fashion, saw only what was obvious. If Eskimos could survive so effortlessly in the Arctic then it was surely sensible that future expeditions should not only follow Eskimo customs but be manned by Eskimos. Of course, a white man should lead them – Hall may have lived in Ohio but he was not *that* much out of touch – and he considered himself to be that man.

It was Hayes's lectures that reeled him in. Two weeks after writing his editorial Hall sold his paper, left his family and caught a train to New York. His mission: to sail into the Arctic after Franklin. He had no experience of navigation, of ice, of commanding a ship – in fact, he lacked every skill required for the task. He did not even know what an Eskimo looked like: on seeing a Chinese man he stopped him in the street and asked if *he* was from the Arctic. For none of his deficiencies did Hall care a jot. 'Courage and resolution were all that I needed; and though some persons might not concur in the wisdom or prudence of my effort, still, as my mind was set upon it, try it I would, and try it I did.'[16] As with many things in his life, he felt as if God was backing him – 'it seemed to me as if I had been *called*'.[17] It was his divine duty to go north.

Even as Hall spoke, British teams were man-hauling sledges through the ice in search of further clues as to Franklin's disappearance. Their leader, Francis McClintock, had previously led his men on heroic trudges covering thousands of miles which resulted in little save the death of one man in harness and the hospitalization of his entire team for a year. Now he was back for a second attempt in the area of King William Island. His findings echoed those of Rae. They said, unequivocally, that Franklin and his crew were dead. When the news broke, Hall was unconcerned. He would go to the Arctic whatever. There were questions yet to be answered and he intended to answer them by means of the Eskimos. All he asked was a ship to take him through Hudson Bay from where he would launch the most far-reaching investigation yet into the Franklin tragedy. 'This voyage is one I am about to make for the cause of humanity and science,' he told the American Geographical Society, 'for geographical discovery, and *with the sole view of accomplishing good for mankind.*'[18] His evangelical zeal was attractive. Thomas Hickey, who had served under Kane, wrote in offering his services. And a shipping firm gave him first refusal on De Haven's old ship, the *Rescue*, for the very reasonable price of $2,000.

When Hall arrived in New York he contrived a meeting with Henry Grinnell. The great philanthropist awed him. 'Can it be possible that so poor a creature as I can be worth the consideration of *so worthy a man as he*?'[19] Hall wrote. The interview between semi-educated printer and East Coast sophisticate was improbably fruitful. Grinnell gave him his blessing and $343. Horace Greeley, editor of the New York *Tribune*, donated more money on condition that Hall would write articles for the paper. Waving his wad of dollars Hall traipsed through the docks in search of a crew. He found one man, a whaling captain named Quayle, who might have served his purpose. But Quayle was quickly taken by Hayes, who was currently fitting out his own expedition. Hall was furious. 'I dare not put on paper,' he put on paper, 'the rank inhumanity of Dr. I. I. Hayes – & of Captain P. T. Quayle – here I am, life devoted to rescuing some lone survivor of Sir John Franklin's men and yet within their hearts *must lurk deep damnation.*'[20] In his impetuous manner he decided that Hayes, who had once been his idol, was an agent of Satan. He attacked him viciously: 'I pity him, I pity his *cowardice & weakness*. I spurn his TRICKERY – his DEVILTRY!'[21]

As it happened, the matter of crew members was academic for, with less than $1,000 in his pocket, Hall could not afford a ship to put them in. But such impediments were nothing to a man who had God on his side. In place of a ship he purchased a sturdy boat, and on 29 May 1860 he cadged a lift to the Arctic aboard a whaler named the *George Henry*. The agreed plan was that he would be dropped off on

Baffin Island, to the west of Baffin Bay, and there spend the summer getting to know the Eskimos and learning their language. (He trusted by this time that he would be able to recognize them.) Then, with a bit of luck, the man who had never been to sea in his life would take his boat in search of Franklin on a 2,000-mile return journey through water so hazardous that it made even British navigators quail. The *George Henry* would then pick him up at the end of the season.

5

THE OPEN POLAR SEA

W hile Hall prayed his way northwards, to almost certain doom, Isaac Israel Hayes prepared himself for the Pole. Unlike Hall, he did have a ship, the 133-ton schooner *United States*. It had an undistinguished pedigree, having spent its life hauling freight between the West Indies and Boston. (When Hayes first saw it, it was still laden with sugar cane.) But it was a ship nonetheless – 'a strong, smug, jaunty-looking craft'[1] – and after a complete refit, which involved the usual double- and triple-planking, the reinforcement of the bows with sheet iron, the interior cross-bracing of oak beams and the switch from long-haul to short-tack rigging, Hayes pronounced himself satisfied. Remembering Kane's shortsightedness, he took aboard a vast amount of food and equipment. The latter came in dribs and drabs from well-wishers but the former was personally ordered by Hayes. Eschewing standard pemmican, he favoured dried provisions prepared by the American Desiccating Company of New York. Beef, vegetables, soup and every other staple were ground to a lightweight dust – easy to carry, nutritious to eat. 'Our outfit was altogether of the very best description,' Hayes wrote, 'and our larder contained everything that could reasonably be desired.'[2]

It was the officers, though, that vexed Hayes. Anticipating the readings which trained scientists might undertake in the Arctic, he had hoped to hire a 'corps of well-instructed observers'.[3] Only one man came forward, however, and that was Sonntag, his old companion from the *Advance*, who was currently studying the heavens in Mexico. Otherwise there was a noticeable silence. 'The response,' wrote Hayes, 'was more tardy in its coming than had been at first anticipated.'[4] In contrast, there was no shortage of people willing to serve as crew. According to Hayes he could have fitted out a respectable squadron so great were the numbers. Unfortunately, none of them had any experience of the ice. They declared themselves willing to serve in any capacity but as Hayes commented, this was 'a declaration which too often on this, as on other occasions, I have found to signify the absence of any capacity at all'.[5] For some reason he did not clinch the deal with Captain Quayle – had Hall heard of it he would have exploded – and when he finally completed his muster there was only one man apart from himself and Sonntag who had ever been near the Arctic. His name was Gibson Carruthers, a carpenter who had served under De Haven on the first Grinnell expedition and 'had brought home an excellent record for fortitude and daring'.[6] Unfortunately he died before the ship even reached Smith Sound.

The *United States* left Boston on 6 July 1860, so heavily laden that it was only one and a half feet above the water at the waist. The deck was crammed with boxes, barrels, boards and boats, leaving an area slightly over six feet square for the men to exercise in. The living quarters were cramped and dark; Hayes himself occupied a niche measuring only ten feet by six – 'a dingy, musty cell, fit only for a convict'[7] – and the ceiling was so low in the officers' mess that it was impossible to stand upright. When they hit bad weather the sea flowed the length and breadth of the ship. 'The sailors are sometimes literally drowned out of the forecastle,' Hayes wrote. 'The cabin is flooded at least a dozen times a day.'[8] His precious library of Arctic reference works spent more time sloshing along the deck than they did on their shelves. Yet the crew bore up remarkably well under the circumstances, a fact that Hayes put down to an egalitarian regime of his own devising. Unlike Kane, who had stipulated absolute obedience to his commands, Hayes operated on the rule that every individual was responsible for the well-being of the expedition. Surprisingly, it seemed to work. 'From the beginning to the end of the cruise,' he later wrote, 'I had no occasion to record a breach of discipline.'[9]

The weather that year was good, and as they sailed up Baffin Bay the novice crew were treated to all the wonders of Arctic summer. The sky glowed crimson, gold and purple. The sea was so calm and so clear that at times the ship seemed to be floating in mid-air and those who peered over the rail experienced a sense of vertigo. Icebergs too numerous to count floated past. Hayes amused himself by picking out architectural variations. Here was an Egyptian pyramid, there a Byzantine tower, there a Grecian temple. One berg looked like St Peter's, another like the Colosseum. At night the sun did not set but rolled in a red ball along the horizon illuminating each edifice in turn. Occasionally the seas rose, and now and again the icebergs were threateningly titanic – Hayes saw one monster which he estimated at 2,000 million tons – but in general everything went well. 'We led a strange, weird sort of life,' Hayes wrote, 'A spice of danger, with much of beauty and a world of magnificence.'[10]

They reached Upernavik, where Carruthers died and Hayes took the opportunity to replace him with a Danish seaman, three Eskimo hunters and an interpreter-cum-dog-handler named Peter Jensen. Also, despite a disease (the same strange distemper that had struck Kane's dogs) which had severely reduced Greenland's canine population, thereby jeopardizing whole Eskimo communities, he managed to scrounge several teams of huskies. Conditions, which had been tight before, now became almost insupportable as the new men and animals were squeezed aboard. Somehow a space was cleared on the deck for the huskies, a feat which amazed Hayes. 'Thirty wild beasts on the deck of a little schooner!' he wrote. 'Think of it, ye who love a quiet life and a tidy ship . . . all of them badly frightened and most of them fighting. They made day and night hideous with their incessant howling.'[11]

From Upernavik they made excellent time, sailing through Melville Bay, a much-feared ice-trap which had claimed hundreds of whalers, without so much as a hint of danger. Emboldened by his good fortune, Hayes headed for the promontory of Cape York in the hope of finding Hans Hendrik, the Eskimo hunter who had proved so helpful on Kane's voyage and who had since settled in Etah. Once again, his luck was in. For the past six summers Hans had lain on a 200-foot lookout, scanning the seas for northward-bound ships. He was more than happy to join the expedition – so happy that he insisted on bringing his family to enjoy the experience. Hayes drew the line at Hans's ancient and garrulous mother-in-law and her twelve-year-old son, but was unable to refuse his wife Merkut and the infant she carried in a hood on her back. And so another three souls were packed into the *United States*.

The long-suffering crew at last took umbrage. When the Hendrik ménage was allotted a damp, lightless space in the bow, one man said it was the perfect place for them: if nothing else they would add a bit of padding if the ship hit an iceberg. Hayes, too, began to have doubts. The Hans he knew had been a Europeanized Eskimo. Now, he appeared as dirty and untutored as the rest of his race. 'Six years experience among the wild men of this barren coast had brought him to their level of filthy living,'[12] he wrote disappointedly. He forced them all to have a bath, a novelty which terrified Hans's wife, and then dressed them in red flannels before banishing them below decks. With something approaching impatience, the crew raised sail for Smith Sound.

At Cape Alexander, the expedition met its first serious obstacle. At its best Cape Alexander was hazardous. But this season the warm weather which had given Hayes such a light journey through Baffin Bay showed Cape Alexander at its most awful. Torrents of snow cascaded down its flanks. Miniature tornadoes whirled clouds of white from its summit. Black waves thrashed against its base, spreading towers of spume that were almost taller than the ship itself. Cape Isabella, which formed the western portal to Smith Sound, was scarcely visible. The sun, previously an illuminator of beauty, was obscured by dark, rolling clouds, And from Hayes's Open Polar Sea, thousands of tons of ice ran past at a terrifying speed.

'The imagination cannot conceive of a scene so wild,' Hayes wrote in his journal. 'I have tried in vain to illustrate it with my pencil. My pen is equally powerless. It is impossible for me to convey to this page a picture of that vast volume of foam which flutters over the sea, and rising and falling with each pulsation of the inconstant wind, stands out against the dark sky, or of the clouds which fly overhead, rushing wild and fearful across the heavens . . . Earth and sea are charged with bellowing sounds. Upon the air are borne shrieks and wailings, loud and dismal as those of the infernal blast which, down in the second circle of the damned, appalled the Italian bard.'[13]

Very cautiously, he steered the *United States* into the maelstrom. For days on end the ship wormed through ice and storm. Several times it passed into Smith Sound, only to be spat out by northerly gales. Then, on 1 September, Hayes lost patience. He would meet the ice head-on and batter his way past the cape. As he explained, 'I was determined to do everything rather than go back.'[14] It was a rough ride. The *United States* hit the ice with such force that its iron cladding peeled like sheets of brown paper. In the ensuing tussle they lost a lifeboat, a jib boom and two masts. But they made it safely to the other side, where they licked their wounds in an inlet eight miles to the north-east that Hayes named Foulkes Harbour after one of his Boston sponsors.

His intention had been to overwinter at the 80th parallel or beyond, from where, with the aid of dogs, he would drag boats and men across the ice to the Open Polar Sea. The ice was too fierce and the weather too bad, however, for him to cross to Grinnell Land where he was convinced the sea would be navigable. It was impossible even to move from where he was. So, like Kane, he found himself trapped on the coast of Greenland. He was in exactly the position he had hoped to avoid, to which was added the humiliation of being scarcely above the 78th parallel and some twenty miles south of Rensselaer Harbour. Moreover, the *United States* had received such a battering as to make it unfit for further exploration the next summer – and was possibly in no condition to sail home either. There was a distinct possibility that the expedition would be as great a débâcle as Kane's.

Shrugging his shoulders, Hayes made the ship ready for winter and sent out a few exploratory sledge parties. The second of these, comprising Sonntag, Hans and Jensen, was despatched to Rensselaer Harbour – to take comparative measurements of their position, according to Hayes, although he must also have been driven by curiosity. The first, commanded by himself, went into Greenland's interior, up an outpouring of ice which Kane had named, in one of his less inspirational moments, 'My Brother John's Glacier'. Before he left, however, Hayes decided he should master the art of dog-sledging.

Hayes was keen on his dogs. He even had a pet Newfoundland in his tiny cabin. 'No proprietor of a stud of horses ever took greater satisfaction in the occupants of his stables than I do in those of my kennels,'[15] he wrote proudly. Yet there was a deal of difference between owning dogs and using them, as he soon found out. He had already experienced the wildness of the Greenland husky on the Kane expedition when, during his mutinous boat escape, he had nearly been eaten by a pack of Kalutunah's dogs. Even so, he was unprepared for the harsh methods needed to control them. The dogs responded only to the whip, a stubby weapon whose two-foot-long stock was attached to a length of seal hide which reached four feet beyond the leading dog's traces. At the business end was a small piece of hardened sinew. The whip was difficult to master, but Jensen showed him how. On one practice outing Jensen got fed up with a recidivist member of the team. 'You see dat beast?' he said. 'I takes a piece out of his ear.' 'And sure enough,' Hayes wrote, 'crack went the whip, the hard sinew wound round the tip of the ear and snipped it off as nicely as with a knife.'[16] Hayes was greatly impressed. When he thought he had mastered the technique he took the team out on his own. At once the dogs ran away with him and it was only by turning the sledge upside down and thrashing the trapped animals as hard as he could that Hayes regained order. 'I think they shall remember the lesson,' he wrote, when he returned panting to the ship, ' – and so shall I.'[17]

Hayes and five others set off in mid-October. He had no hope of any great achievement because, as he noted, it was the wrong time of year. Spring was the best time for overland travel, autumn weather being too uncertain. Still, he travelled further than anyone else into Greenland's glacial interior, erecting stakes as he went in order to measure the speed at which the glacier flowed. He went seventy miles inland and reached a height of 5,000 feet above sea level where he faced a stupendous expanse of ice, a 'vast frozen Sahara, immeasurable to the human eye'.[18] Confronting this tremendous plateau Hayes realized his limitations. The temperature was 34°F below zero and the winds so fierce that unless they walked backwards their faces became frostbitten within seconds. With two men already seriously ill Hayes did not dare continue. As he explained, 'longer delay would . . . wholly defeat the purposes of our expedition by the destruction of all of us'.[19] The party barely had the strength to wrap the tent onto the sledge. 'We ran to save our lives,'[20] Hayes recorded. And they did just that, crossing forty miles and descending 3,000 feet before they dared take a rest. When they reached the ship their cramped quarters seemed luxurious beyond belief. Hayes spent several days recovering in his cabin and when he emerged the wolf and bear skins with which they had covered the floor felt like richest carpet. The others recuperated swiftly, the only lasting casualty being one man's nose, which for many weeks remained 'as big as his fist and as red as a beet'.[21]

Sonntag's party departed on 30 October and returned shortly afterwards with bad news. The frozen sea on which he had hoped to sledge to Rensselaer Harbour had unexpectedly opened, blocking his path with a bay of clear water. He had not been able to reach his goal and apart from a battle with a polar bear and her cub, in which he had lost three dogs, he had nothing to report. Hayes was baffled: 'The existence of this open water greatly puzzles me.' He and Kane had met nothing like it at this latitude. 'It is probably merely local,' he decided, 'dependent upon currents and winds.'[22] Absent-mindedly, he chose the very explanation which his opponents had put forward for the non-existence of the Open Polar Sea.

November was a difficult month. The temperature jumped up and down, now freezing now thawing. Sometimes there was heavy rain, yet on one day they had nineteen inches of snow, which was five inches more than had fallen in the entire winter of 1853–4. Hayes found it most disconcerting. He had thirty-four tons of coal aboard which he measured out at four bucketfuls per day to heat the ship. So efficient were their two fireplaces that the main cabin reached a sweltering 75°F – which was fine so long as it was zero outside and the condensation could freeze on the ship's outer walls and housing; but whenever the weather warmed, the accumulated mass dropped onto the floor in two-inch-thick chunks and melted insidiously across the ship.

Problems also arose with the Eskimos. Of the three he had taken on at Upernavik, two had grown so fat and unfit that they were unable to go hunting. One of them became so gross that he could not clamber over a beam which crossed the crew's quarters two and a half feet above the floor; instead he had to squirm under it like a maggot. Only the third, a man called Peter, met with Hayes's approval. 'Peter is a very clever little fellow and withal honest,' he wrote, 'and he has quite taken my fancy.'[23] Hans and his wife, meanwhile, caused endless difficulty. Merkut refused to sew winter clothing for the crew and eventually grew so tired of the expedition that she walked out – only to return after a single night. As for Hans, he was jealous of the small favours Hayes showed Peter and began to persecute him. "He is a type of the worst phase of the Esquimau character,'[24] Hayes wrote. 'Had I crowded upon Hans the best of everything in the vessel, without respect to quantity or usefulness, it would not be more than he covets.'[25] Soon, he came to loathe him: 'his face expresses the same traits as formerly – the same smooth, oily voice, the same cunning little eye, the same ugly disposition. I have very little faith in him.'[26] He had even less faith when, on 19 November, Peter jumped ship and fled south, wearing only a suit of red flannels. A search party recovered a bundle of his belongings not far from

Port Foulkes but he was never seen alive again. Hayes was certain that Hans had persuaded Peter – who could not speak English – that the Americans intended to kill him. Hans denied it absolutely. To which Hayes replied that he would hang him when he uncovered the truth.

The atmosphere worsened when Jensen raided a group of Eskimo graves and brought back several bodies for Hayes's Natural History collection. Unfortunately they happened to be the frozen remains of Merkut's relations. Jensen's lie that the white man would take them home and restore them to life did not satisfy her. So, instead of pickling them for the Smithsonian, as he had intended, Hayes ordered them to be reinterred – more from a desire to shut Merkut up, than from any moral qualms.

The one good aspect of the erratic month was that game could still be hunted and Hayes was able to collect a stock of fresh meat to see them through the winter. Scurvy, he was determined, would not be a feature of this trip and he filled the hold as fast as he could. When the weather finally closed in he had a stock of seventy-four deer carcases, twenty-one foxes, twelve hares, one seal, fourteen eider ducks, eight dovekies, six auks and a ptarmigan. Cached in the snow outside were another thirty deer. The food was needed not just for health but for happiness. Hayes realized that spirits needed to be kept up in the winter months. 'I know by experience what the dark cloud is under which we are drifting,' he wrote, 'and I know that my ingenuity will be fully taxed to pass through it with a cheerful household.'[27] In his opinion, the best way of keeping men happy was to keep them well-fed. He therefore proclaimed an open and unlimited feast on the occasion of each crew member's birthday. The first one soon came around and it was, indeed, a spirit-lifting affair. There was soup, salmon, duck, a huge plum pudding from Boston, blancmange, mince pies, nuts, raisins, olives, cheese and coffee. From his private locker Hayes produced cigars, white wine, madeira and sherry. At the heart of the banquet was a massive thirty-pound venison roast which their Swedish cook had somehow stuffed into the galley stove. The festivities ran into the night, continuing long after Hayes had gone to bed.

Unfortunately – and Hayes should surely have anticipated this – most of the crew had summer birthdays. There were no more feasts that winter. His other ideas for entertainment fell equally short of the mark. A newspaper, *The Port Foulkes Weekly News*, came out on 10 November to great excitement, the men reporting on city news, weather bulletins, 'foreign intelligence' and society clips. To announce its publication one of the youngest officers, the eighteen-year-old George Knorr, gave a rousing speech before the entire ship's company. 'We must carry [the American boundary] to the very Pole itself!' he said. 'And there, sir, we will nail the Stars and Stripes, and our flag-staff will become the spindle of the world, and the Universal Yankee Nation will go whirling round it like a top.'[28]

The thrill soon wore off and *The Port Foulkes Weekly News*, which had never contained any news, never became weekly either. Hayes had also planned a series of theatrical events but these did not materialize. The crew could not be bothered and neither could he. Without saying why, he declared it 'impossible'. They settled down to a monotony of tasks whose meaninglessness was aggravated by the twenty-four-hour Arctic night. 'We live by "bells",' Hayes wrote. '"Bells" make the day and mark the progress of time. But for these "bells", these endless "bells", I believe we should all lie down and sleep on through the eternal night, and wake not until the day dawned upon us in the long hereafter . . . "One bell" calls us to breakfast, two to lunch, and "four bells" is the dinner summons. "Six bells" is the signal for putting out the lights and at "seven bells" we open our eyes again to the same continuous pale glimmer of the kerosene lamp, and we awake again to the same endless routine of occupations, idleness, and *ennui*.'[29]

As if infected by the malaise, the huskies began to die. They frothed at the mouth, wobbled and snapped, then ran barking to the end of the bay where they wheeled and ran barking back. On return they fainted, came to at intervals, then collapsed and died twenty-four hours later. The ailment swept through the ship, reducing the pack from thirty to nine within the space of a week. The prospect of being unable to pursue his spring trip to the Open Polar Sea roused Hayes from his torpor. On 21 December he sent Hans and Sonntag to buy replacements from the nearest village community, 150 miles south. He *had* to get more dogs. But what if the Eskimos would not sell? Then, he decided, tough action would be needed. He would, if necessary, kidnap the whole community at gunpoint and force them to camp at Port Foulkes while he took their dogs north. No sooner had the two men left, however, than Hayes's grim determination lapsed into melancholy. He had a nightmare in which he saw himself walking with Sonntag across the frozen sea; suddenly a floe opened between them and while Hayes gesticulated impotently, Sonntag floated into the distance on a little ice raft. Was it a premonition, he wondered?

The days passed silently and gloomily. 'Each hour of the darkness grows a little longer, and soaks a little more colour from the blood, and takes a little more from the elasticity of the step,'[30] Hayes wrote. He hated the lack of sunlight, he was terrified by the endless silence, and although there was not a single case of scurvy, thanks to his foresight in stocking up with fresh meat, the depression they all suffered was nearly as debilitating. When his pet dog died in January he became increasingly morose and spent more and more time alone in his cabin trying to train a blue fox called Birdie. 'Say what you will, talk as you will of pluck, and manly resolution, and all that sort of thing, this Arctic night is a severe ordeal,'[31] he wrote.

The power of the lassitude that preyed on Hayes was evident in his lack of concern over Sonntag and Hans. Their journey should have taken them three days, maybe a week at the most. They should have been back by Christmas and certainly by the New Year. Hayes, however, did not seem too worried. They would be back soon, he told himself, as he attended to his fox. More than a month after the two men had left the *United States* Hayes came abruptly to his senses. An immediate search party was called for. On 29 January 1861 he was clothing himself for the journey when there came a knock at his door and the ominous words, 'Two Esquimaux alongside.' Instinctively, he knew that Sonntag was dead.

The Eskimos were strangers to him but two days later Hans arrived, accompanied by Merkut's twelve-year-old brother from Cape

York. He was in bad shape and informed Hayes that his dogs had
broken down and he had been forced to abandon them. It was vital
that they be recovered. His mother- and father-in-law had also broken
down, he added unexpectedly. He had left them with the dogs and
they too should be rescued. Hayes could not fathom why Hans
should be returning with his wife's family, when he had been sent to
fetch dogs, but he obediently retrieved them. Once this had been
accomplished Hans told the story of Sonntag's death. It was the most
banal of tragedies. Not having been able to locate the village they had
continued south. Sonntag, who was ahead of Hans, had fallen through
the ice. Hans hauled him out but it was a hard task. 'I cried from
despair for want of help,'[32] he admitted. Once Sonntag was back on
solid ground he ran alongside the sledge while he and Hans raced for
the shelter of an abandoned snow hut. If he had run all the way the
movement might have saved him, but he became exhausted and
climbed on the sledge instead. On reaching the hut he was speechless
and frozen. That night he 'drew his breath at long intervals, and
towards morning only very rarely'.[33] The next day he was dead.
Blocking up the hut, Hans went south. He distributed gifts to the
people of Cape York, picked up his relations and then turned back for
Port Foulkes. Along the way he had been hit by a storm so violent
that 'I tumbled down and could only proceed by creeping.'[34] And
here he was. Dogs, he promised Hayes, would be with them soon
from Cape York.

Hayes grilled him for an hour without eliciting any change in his
story. He could see no reason why Hans should have tried deliberately
to harm Sonntag, especially as Sonntag had treated Hans as his
favourite. All the same, he was suspicious. Surely Sonntag would have
had the sense to keep moving rather than sit on the sledge. Surely he
would have given Hans orders, or instructed him to bring a message
back to the ship. No, Hans swore. It happened just as he said and
Sonntag had not uttered a word from the moment he fell into the
water. Hayes did not believe him, suspecting that his ulterior motive
all along was to make Merkut happy by bringing her family back to
the ship. But twist the circumstances as he might, he could not prove

Hans guilty of murder. Nor could he afford to, for in the absence of Peter, Hans was the best hunter they had. The later revelation that Eskimos had found Peter frozen to death in a snow hut twenty miles south of Port Foulkes, still wearing the skimpy red flannels Hayes had given him, filled him with wrath. More than ever, he regretted taking Hans aboard. 'Had I known him as well then, as with good reason, I knew him afterwards,' he wrote in his journal, 'I would not have gone out of my way to disturb his barbarous existence.'[35]

Of the nine dogs that had survived the epidemic there were now only five, the other four having perished on Hans's journey south. Hayes consigned himself to a future of man-hauling when two things occurred to lift his gloom. The first was the reappearance of the sun, on 18 February – 'Heaven be praised!' he wrote – and the second was the arrival of the dogs Hans had promised. And with the dogs came Kalutunah, the Eskimo on whom Kane's expedition had relied. Kalutunah was now the chief of his people, he told Hayes proudly. There was nothing to fear from Sip-Su, the man having made so many enemies that one night he had been knifed and buried alive. All Kalutunah now wanted to do was to help the white men. Metaphorically if not physically – 'for under the ample furs of this renowned chief there were roaming great droves of creeping things'[36] – Hayes clasped him to his bosom. With the dogs, and with the help of Kalutunah, his exploration could begin in earnest.

The first sledge party of the spring went to Rensselaer Harbour to see if it was possible to reach the Open Polar Sea via Greenland's coast. It was not. Everything had changed since Hayes had last been there. There was no sign of the *Advance* and although the sandstone cliffs were as familiar to Hayes as the shops and warehouses on Broadway the sea was more violently ridged than he had ever seen it. It was a jumble of fragments rising to enormous heights: 'The whole scene was the Rocky Mountains on a small scale.'[37] The cold was killing, at one point sinking to 100°F below freezing. Kalutunah, who had been taken along as a guide, proved hopeless and the white men felt by now they were as good in the ice as any Eskimo. Besides, he 'snored all through the night in the most awful manner'.[38] Hayes felt quite justified in turning back for the *United States* where he put in motion his long anticipated thrust towards Grinnell Land.

On 3 April he left the ship with twelve men divided into three teams, two of them equipped with dogs and the third man-hauling a surprise cargo: a twenty-foot metal boat. Ever since his experience off Cape Alexander in 1853, Hayes had been impressed by metal boats. Now he intended to win the Open Polar Sea with the most technologically advanced dinghy in the world. Kalutunah was not invited to join them. They left in a storm of 'huzzahs' that cheered Hayes hugely. After five or so miles, however, their bravado evaporated. 'Some of them looked as if they were going to their own funerals and wore that "My God! what shall I do?" look.'[39] Two people 'were possessed with a heroic desire to die on the spot',[40] and lay on the snow muttering, 'I am freezing!' – which in fact they were, until Hayes restored them to life. Conditions were worse than on the Greenland Coast. The ice rose in endless hummocks and at times their way was blocked by icebergs, one of which Hayes estimated at 6,000 million tons. 'If a thousand Lisbons were crowded together and tumbled to pieces by the shock of an earthquake, the scene could hardly be more rugged, nor to cross the ruins a severer task,'[41] he wrote. On 6 April they abandoned the boat. It would have taken a hundred men, by Hayes's estimation, to drag it across Smith Sound.

By 24 April, they were thirty miles into Smith Sound. But with the detours around hummocks and icebergs they had travelled five times that distance. One of the sledges had broken, four men were seriously ill and the others were exhausted. 'The chances of ever reaching the west coast with this party looked almost hopeless,'[42] Hayes admitted. Two days later he was even more pessimistic: 'The men are completely used up, broken down, dejected, to the last degree. Human nature cannot stand it. There is no let up to it.'[43] The men agreed in no uncertain terms. As one of them told him, he might as well try to cross New York by the rooftops as tackle this tangle of ice. On 27 April, Hayes gave up. 'There does not appear to be the ghost of a chance for me,' he began his journal for that day. 'Must I own myself a defeated man? I fear I must.'[44] Drearily, he recounted all his misfortunes: the ship driven into early harbour; his trusted lieutenant lost; the dogs dead; his metal boat abandoned; the crew collapsing – the recitation went on and on. Yet the more Hayes listed his misfortunes the more determined he became to overcome them. By the end of the day he had decided to continue. He would take one sledge forward – carrying himself, Jensen, a seaman named MacDonald, plus a young officer, George Knorr – and send everybody else back on the other. And they weren't to waste their time when they got home, he warned. They were to make the ship ready for a frontal assault in the summer. Perhaps he had forgotten that the *United States* was afloat on borrowed time and was barely in condition for the sea, let alone the ice. But the decision stiffened his resolve. 'I renew the struggle tomorrow with hope and determination,' he finished. 'Away with despondency!'[45]

Hayes needed every scrap of optimism he could muster. On the 28 April they advanced one and a half miles – and in doing so travelled an actual distance of twelve miles. The terrain comprised an appalling network of ridges riven by rubbled canyons. Not one inch of the way was over smooth ground and the strain began to tell on all of them. On 3 May they spotted the mountainous coast of Grinnell Land, a sight which sent Hayes into ecstasies of anticipation. 'Oh!' he wrote, 'That I was across the barrier that separates me from that land of my desires . . . the mystic seas which I am seeking through these days of weariness and toil.'[46] But the odds were lengthening against his ever reaching his goal. The dogs were ravenous, Hayes having misjudged the amount of food they would consume, and soon they were eating everything they could get their teeth into. The leather harnesses went first, and then the traces, both of which had to be replaced by lengths of hemp which snapped repeatedly. Next they attacked the sledge, devouring their masters' spare boots, socks and the bindings which kept the whole load in place. When MacDonald dropped his tobacco pouch it was swallowed whole. In a careless moment, Knorr left his meerschaum pipe unattended; down it went. The dogs even ate the expedition's only bar of soap. The men, meanwhile, were physically crumbling. When they reached the other side of Smith Sound, it had taken them thirty-one days to cross eighty miles. The way was now smoother – young, recently formed ice, Hayes noted cheerfully – but on 15 May, Jensen, one of the toughest, collapsed with a bad back and a possibly broken leg. Hayes left him in the care of MacDonald and continued up the coast alone with Knorr. The sun was hot, the ice was getting slushier and in places was smoking. No glaciers were in evidence and gulls were flying northwards. The Open Polar Sea *had* to be nearby.

Three days later, on 18 May, Hayes was stabbing the ice to check for weak spots when his pole suddenly sank into open water. He tried again and again, but everywhere it was the same. The ice seemed to be running out. Climbing a nearby hill, which he estimated to be at least 800 feet high, he gazed northwards. 'The sea beneath me,' he recorded, 'was a mottled sheet of white and dark patches, these latter . . . multiplied in size as they receded, until the belt of the water-sky blended them all together into one uniform colour of dark blue . . . All the evidences showed that I stood upon the shores of the Polar Basin.'[47] He took note of his position: 81°35′, further north by land than anyone yet.

Grinnell Land continued to the north, veering westwards; but of the opposite coast Hayes could see nothing, from which he deduced that Kennedy Channel was either wider than had been reported or that Greenland was finite, and that, at any rate, he had got further than Morton. He built a cairn, and left a message in a bottle announcing his arrival and giving notice that he would be back the next summer with his ship. Then came the raising of the flags. Lacking a staff, he ran a rope between two pinnacles of rock and on this he pinned his emblems. There was the ship's polar ensign, a crimson star on a field of white; there were two masonic pennants; there was a small Stars and Stripes donated by the ladies of Albany Academy; and in pride of place was another Stars and Stripes which had become an icon of polar exploration. It had accompanied an American expedition to the Antarctic in the 1830s under Lieutenant Charles Wilkes; it had followed De Haven into the North-West Passage; it had flown on Kane's *Advance*; and now, on the borders of the Open Polar Sea, Hayes unfurled it once more. He would later pack it up and take it home again, but for the moment he revelled in the sight. He might not have extended America's boundaries to the Pole, but he had put its foot in the door. The flag was flying over an ocean of possibilities, an ocean that, in Hayes's words, 'might lash the shores of distant islands where dwell human beings of an unknown race'.[48]

Back he went, picking up Jensen and MacDonald before he traversed again the horrible mess of Smith Sound. In his euphoria he made light of the journey home – four of his nine dogs just fell over and died in their traces – and when he reached the *United States* on 3 June, having covered a roundabout course of perhaps 1,300 miles in two months, he was raring to go back north. He painted his future in brilliant colours. Steam power could push ships into the Open Polar Sea, he was certain. He would establish a permanent base at Port Foulkes – 'a hunting station or colony',[49] he called it – from which Eskimo hunters could provision steamships for the Pole. The colony could pay its way with sales of walrus ivory, oils, furs and eider down. Jensen thought it a good idea and accepted the post of Superintendent at once. Kalutunah, too, supported the plan. What with the harshness of conditions on the North Greenland coast, and the disease which was killing their dogs, his people were facing extinction. There were now no more than 100 of them left alive, surviving in depleted villages of three families at most. If, however, they could all be brought together, and with the help of the white man's supplies, there was a chance they could ride out the evil period. In an irony that eluded Hayes, the Eskimos on whom his colony would depend were themselves relying on the white men for their own survival.

Before he resorted to steam, Hayes wanted to have one more try by sail. For a month he waited fretfully, checking the posts he had placed on 'Brother John's Glacier' – they had moved ninety-six feet – and generally keeping his men on their toes. With the summer thaw, however, Hayes realized he would be going nowhere north. The *United States* had been so badly squeezed by the ice that it was almost unserviceable. Every board had sprung and handfuls of oakum had to be stuffed into the cracks to make the vessel half-seaworthy. His sailing master advised him that if the ship hit one slab of ice it would fall apart. Very carefully then, Hayes waited for the floes to disintegrate. When they did so, he paid a last visit to Kalutunah to thank him for his help. 'Come back and save us,' the Eskimo begged. Hayes assured him he would, then rejoined the *United States* as it floated to freedom. Heaps of winter ordure, shoals of empty cans, islands of ashes and a flotilla of dead dogs pursued the ship.

But Hayes was never to come back to save Kalutunah's people. Skirting to the west to avoid Cape Alexander, he made a cautious examination of Cape Isabella then slid into Baffin Bay and by 12 August was at Upernavik, where a Danish pedlar came aboard selling little luxuries that the men had not seen for a year. Hayes pounced on him for news of the outside world.

'Oh! dere's plenty news,' he said.

'Out with it man! What is it?' Hayes urged.

'Oh! de Sout' States dey go agin de Nort' States and dere's plenty fight.'[50]

Obviously, this was some garbled report from Denmark, telling of yet another conflict in that war-torn continent. It was not until mail came in from Copenhagen that Hayes realized the awful truth: his country was at war with itself. That America should be at war was bad enough – after all, the underlying premise of its existence was to escape the endless battles which plagued Europe – but that it should be involved in a civil war was inconceivably bad. The prosperous, forward-looking New World which he had left in 1860 was, apparently, as fractured as the Old. Wasting little time over repairs or provisions, the stunned crew prepared the ship as best they could, then raised sail and, 'dove into a villainous fog-bank, out of which came a rush of wind that sent us homeward a little faster than we cared to go'.[51]

When they reached Boston, after a stop-over at Halifax, they felt like trespassers at a funeral. It was dark, it was silent, it was foggy, and the lamps that hung from the ships' masts seemed like brands in a charnel house. There was no sign of life whatsoever, and Hayes was the only man who dared go ashore. He set off for a friend's house to announce his home-coming, but as he wandered through the empty, mist-filled streets he was overcome by dread. It was worse than the darkest Arctic night. Hurrying back to the *United States* he huddled alongside his shipmates and awaited dawn.

Day broke, and Hayes's plan for the conquest of the Arctic faltered. He offered his services to the Union army and was accepted, eventually rising to the rank of Colonel. He still planned to go north again, as he explained in the last pages of his published journal, but he never did so. When the war ended he was too exhausted to carry the baton any further. In a speech to the American Geographical Society in 1868, he apologized, sadly, for his lack of enterprise: 'I have not since been able to gather up what was then lost and scattered, and complete what I had begun.'[52] Apart from a brief voyage up Baffin Bay with an artist friend he never visited the Arctic again. He settled in New York, became a politician and died in 1886, maintaining to the end that the Open Polar Sea was within reach. Later investigations revealed that he had put his farthest north one degree too far. He had probably reached a point that is now called Cape Joseph Goode and which lies at 80°14′. For all his efforts he had not even beaten Kane's steward, Morton.

6

POLAR CRUSADER

'Iceberg was silent; I too was silent. I stood in the presence of God's work! Its fashioning was that of the Great Architect! He who hath builded *such* monuments, and cast them forth upon the waters of the sea *is God* and there can be no other.'[1] The date was Thursday, 21 June 1860. Charles Francis Hall had reached the Arctic.

Travelling north on the *George Henry* under the command of an agreeable captain named Sidney Budington, Hall was enraptured. The pious innocent from Cincinnati could not hide his excitement as he entered the world of his dreams. Everything was new and unexpected (even the sea voyage was a first) and he recorded it all in his journal not just with awe but with an enthusiasm that outstrips any Arctic chronicler before or since. When he witnessed the tricks of refraction, for example, in which distant objects were distorted in size and place so that a tiny hill beyond the horizon hung in the air like a looming mountain, he could not contain himself. 'This *refraction?*' he wrote, disbelievingly. 'It was *Nature turned inside out! Nature turned topsy turvy!!* NATURE ON A SPREE!!! Yes, Nature on a spree!'[2] The Northern Lights which were, like refraction, a perfectly commonplace experience for whalers, excited him to biblical ebullition: 'It seemeth to me as if the very doors of heaven have been opened tonight, so *mighty* and *beauteous* and *marvellous* were the waves of golden light that a few moments ago swept across the "azure deep", breaking forth into floods of wondrous glory. God made his wonderful works tonight to be remembered . . . We *looked*, we SAW, and TREM-BLED.'[3]

At the Greenland port of Holsteinborg, where Budington stopped off to collect stores, Hall fell to his knees in rapture, scrabbling up stones from the beach. 'Thank God, I am at last on arctic land where I have so long wished to be!' he cried. 'Greenland's mountains I greet you.'[4] Childlike, he ran about the place, collecting information and equipment with haphazard carelessness. He bought six dogs for five American dollars apiece; he hobnobbed with the Danish governor and tried out a threadbare Arctic joke concerning the previous governor's wife; he recorded that the Eskimo language had words of more than fifty letters, but he could only remember one of thirty-one – *Piniagagssakardluarungnaerangat* – and then he forgot what it meant. When the crew gathered for an impromptu knees-up, Hall joined in with glee. It was the first time he had ever danced in his life.

On arrival at Baffin Island the *George Henry* was joined by the *Rescue*, the same ship Hall had hoped to command. Both vessels were then hit by a storm that left the *Rescue* in ruins and also crushed Hall's specially ordered boat beyond repair. Hall barely flinched. What were such trivial matters when there was exploration to be done? Bounding inland he immediately encountered a glacier, whose waters he quaffed before praising the Lord. 'On my still bended knees, I thanked God that I lived to behold how manifold and wonderful was the world's creation.'[5] Yet more miraculous things were to occur. '*November 2d*, 1860,' Hall's journal read. 'While intently occupied in my cabin, writing, I heard a soft, sweet voice say, "Good morning, sir." The *tone* in which it was spoken – musical, lively and varied – instantly told me that a lady of refinement was there greeting me. I was astonished. Could I be dreaming? Was it a mistake? No! I was wide awake and writing. But, had a thunder-clap sounded on my ear . . . I could not have been more surprised than I was at the sound of that voice.'[6] No woman had accompanied the *George Henry* and there were certainly no ladies of refinement that he knew of on Baffin Island. But what was another surprise? By then, Hall's life was full of them. He turned to greet his visitor.

Illuminated in the rays shed by the cabin's skylight was a woman dressed in crinoline, flounces, a fringed cape of caribou hide and 'an immensely exaggerated "kiss-me-quick" bonnet'.[7] Before his eyes this virgin apparition peeled off one of her gloves and extended a hand. He rose automatically to shake it. It was a sturdy hand, and as Hall accustomed himself to the glare he realized that the woman to whom the hand was attached was a lot shorter than he had thought. She was not the usual European type. In fact, as he squinted closer, he realized she was an Eskimo.

In 1853 a British whaling captain had persuaded an Eskimo couple, Tookolito and Ebierbing, to accompany him back to London. Over two years they had learned English, had adopted the mannerisms, dress and religion of their host nation and had become minor celebrities. They had been presented to Queen Victoria (like Kane) and had won the hearts of a society that revelled, as no other, in converting others to its own ways. When the novelty wore off they were sent to New York, where they created no less of a sensation. Then they were dropped back on Baffin Island complete with new names ('Joe' and 'Hannah') and a new wardrobe, to be forgotten save by passing whalers who sold them the articles of western civilization to which they had become accustomed. It was Tookolito, or Hannah, who now stood at the door of Hall's cabin. She asked him to visit her home for a cup of tea. Dazedly, Hall accepted.

When he crawled into Tookolito's igloo he saw that she had put aside her European clothes in favour of more practical furs. But she had not forgotten her ladylike manners. Putting down her needles and wool (she had been knitting a pair of socks for her husband) she opened a caddy of black leaves. Did Hall like his tea strong or weak? A delicate cup and saucer was produced, in which Hall was served 'capital tea, and capitally made'.[8] The interview became more and more surreal. Whenever Tookolito coughed she would raise her hand to her mouth and turn her head aside in perfect imitation of London manners. A friend who had also visited the States strolled in to say what he thought of New York – 'G—D—! too much horse – too much house! – too much white people'[9] – thereby earning an oblique rebuke from Tookolito who leaned forward to give Hall a lecture on American morals. What she could not stand was the seamen's swearing. 'I wish they would not do so,' she said. '*Americans swear a great deal – more and worse than the English. I wish no one would swear. It is a very bad practice, I believe.*'[10] She was sure it was a bad influence on her people. Shamefaced, Hall agreed that it was a dreadful state of affairs. He returned shortly afterwards to his ship, favourably bemused.

Nobody but Hall could have had such a bizarre initiation to the Arctic. God-fearing to an almost preposterous degree, he was immune to all setbacks. He was touchingly naïve, spending his first few weeks on Baffin Island clad in a broken hat (he had smashed the crown when he raised it on a boarding pike to celebrate his first ascent of an iceberg) and peering at the scenery through a pair of opera glasses. His supplies were inadequate by normal standards: beyond a few guns, a chronometer, a sextant, a small hoard of tinned pemmican and various other bits and pieces, he carried none of the usual survival kit – no lemon juice or vinegar to prevent scurvy, no winter amusements, no coal to keep him warm – relying instead on his faith and the generosity of Eskimos to keep him alive. Now and then he would lose his temper and rail against adverse situations and obstructive guides; but whenever he did so he quickly regained his sense of purpose. He was a compleat explorer in every sense of the word, prepared to discard all prejudices – save those of religion – and throw himself wholeheartedly into the land and life of the Arctic. So fresh was his attitude that he called the Eskimos what they called themselves – Inuit, 'the people' – rejecting the appellation 'Esquimaux' as deriving from a Cree Indian word which had been further bastardized by French Canadian traders.

Hall declared the Inuit to be 'a kind-hearted, hospitable and well-disposed race of beings'. He fell into their ways with the same lack of inhibition that categorized everything he did. He slept in their igloos and warmed his frozen feet against a pair of bosoms – a suppressed thrill becomes evident in his journal – he adopted their clothes and, above all, he ate their food. '*Eating meat raw or cooked is entirely a matter of education*,'[11] he emhasized in his journal. He re-educated himself with vim. Polar-bear meat was 'passable, with a taste akin to lamp oil, but yet, on the whole good'.[12] Whale-gum could be sliced like mature cheese: 'Its taste was like unripe chestnuts and its appearance like cocoa-nut meat.'[13] Raw venison was 'better than the best of beefsteaks',[14] so tender that it fell to pieces when he lifted it to his mouth; its fat was sweeter than the goldenest butter; and the paunch 'was delightful; its flavour . . . a kind of sorrel acid; it had an *ambrosial* taste.'[15] Of raw seal: '*It is ambrosia and nectar!*'[16] Seal spine was excellent, and slices of whale vertebrae looked just like turkey breast. Whale skin was very palatable with a bit of vinegar and nice enough without. On second tasting he even came round to polar bear. 'Incomparable is the relish with which I have partaken . . . of polar bear meat,'[17] he recorded. A smoking bowl of hot seal blood was delicious. He drank mother's milk from the stomach of a baby seal – a 'great delicacy'. And when he ate a stew of seal brains and entrails, he knew he had arrived: 'I was one of them – one of the honoured few!'[18]

So completely did Hall subsume himself that he became accepted as part of the Eskimo family. His journals stand today as a store of anthropological detail. But Hall was not an anthropologist. He was an explorer, with work to do. Commandeering one of Budington's boats, he spent 1860 and 1861 investigating the neighbourhood with a crew of Eskimos, half of them men and half of them women. (The women, he noted, worked twice as hard as the men.) He did not reach his intended destination of King William Island, but instead sawed up and down the coast of Baffin Island, spending whole months without seeing another white man.

As he did so, the charm of Eskimo life began to wear thin. He found his hosts spoiled by contact with Western traders and much preferred the raw, simple state in which the Danes kept the Eskimos of Greenland. (Contrarily, however, he was quite happy to offer the Eskimos guns if they would act as guides.) He bemoaned the absence of Christianity and advocated the immediate despatch of missionaries to spread the Word. He became emaciated and undernourished. Boils broke out all over his body, even on the bridge of his nose. In a moment of weakness he admitted that he didn't *really* like whale skin. His companions were obstinately independent and refused to do as he said: when Hall insisted that one man, Koojesse, stay awhile while he explored a new bit of land, he received the answer, 'You stop; I go!' Hall was outraged: 'he acts the *devil* with me'.[19] Later, he suspected that Koojesse wanted to murder him. 'I must say that I believe my life is in danger,' he wrote feverishly. 'If I die at the hands of this treacherous people, I die in faith that I am in the performance of my duty. God deliver me from such scenes as I have witnessed among the men Innuits I have with me.'[20] When he tried to sleep the Eskimos kept him awake with a noisy, 'uncouth sort of dance'. 'A hard, weak, weary time did I have of it,'[21] he wrote. If he wanted to do any real exploration it would have to be, 'with a company of *civilised* men'.[22]

Hall charted 1,000 miles of new coastline, ascertained that Frobisher strait was in fact a bay, and discovered heaps of coal and other relics left there in the 1570s by Martin Frobisher, the English navigator after whom the strait was named. Packing them into his old stockings, he preserved them with pride, for as he wrote, 'It may be the English will dispute my discoveries but I covet the opportunity to show the facts.'[23] He also discovered that the Eskimos' oral tradition was flawlessly accurate: centuries after the event, they recounted *exactly* how many ships Frobisher had had on each of his three visits to the area, what he had done and what he had left behind. His towering achievement, however, was to prove that white men could survive in the Arctic without recourse to Western methods. It was a qualified achievement: Hall was content to be a guest of the Eskimos rather than learn the finer points of their lifestyle – how to work a dog-team, how to catch a seal, how to build a sledge, how to make a blubber lamp – and he declared that although the Arctic was tolerable he thought of it, 'not as a place to spend all my life . . . but for *work* to be continued three or five years'.[24] But it was an achievement all the same, and one that would have important repercussions, not least for Hall himself.

When Budington took the *George Henry* home in 1862, Hall went with him and so did Tookolito and Ebierbing, whom Hall hoped to display in New York to raise a few dollars for his next expedition, in which they would act as guides and interpreters. And there would be another expedition, of that Hall was sure. On reaching Newfoundland he took advantage of the new-fangled telegraph to tell Grinnell that, 'I am bound for the States to *renew voyage*.'[25] If the Eskimos of Baffin Island could remember Frobisher, he was certain that the Eskimos around King William Island could remember Franklin.

Hall's homecoming was disrupted, as Hayes's had been, by the American Civil War. So was Grinnell's largesse: as the conflict dragged on his fortune deteriorated by an estimated $500,000. The $20,000 which Hall needed for his next expedition – to King William Island – was not immediately to hand and so, having offered his services half-heartedly to the government, Hall forgot all about the war and embarked on a series of fund-raising lectures. He was not a Kane nor a Hayes, and he hated the auditoriums. 'Lecturing is a curse to my soul,' he wrote to Grinnell. 'Just as soon as I can get out of the uncongenial business I shall do so.'[26] His journal, another potential source of income, which he was preparing to publish with the help of an old Arctic hand, an Englishman named Charles Parker Snow, caused him almost as much distress as the lecture podium. 'I had rather make a dozen voyages to the regions of ice and snow than prepare one book for publication,'[27] he wrote. He made money by leasing out Tookolito, Ebierbing and their new-born son, Tukerliktu, for a two-week stint at Barnum's museum. (They were extremely uncomfortable in the heat and a planned second engagement had to be cancelled.) To curry favour in Britain he decided to present his Frobisher finds in person to Queen Victoria but then, on reviewing the cost of a transatlantic passage and having been advised tactfully that a few sockfuls of coal might not go down well in Buckingham Palace, he sent them to the Royal Geographical Society instead.

Hall employed all the fund-raising tricks he could think of. The Wilkes flag, which having been used by De Haven, Kane and Hayes, had now fallen to himself, was raised at the back of each lecture hall.

Tookolito, Ebierbing and Tukerliktu were displayed at every opportunity. He even went down to the Bowery and sold his damaged hat
for thirty-seven cents. But try as he might, things did not look good.
Thanks to his lecture expenses, 'he was even worse off than when he
started out'.[28] He fell out with Budington, who wanted to take
Tookolito and her family back to the Arctic with him. He became
involved in a lawsuit with Snow, who claimed (exaggeratedly) that
Hall's journal was all his own work.* And on 28 February 1863, little
Tukerliktu died in New York, an event which caused his parents deep
distress. The US government had better things to do with its money
than throw it at the Arctic. The British government had declared a
moratorium on all further expenditure to find Franklin. And Lady
Franklin, usually a staunch promoter of any attempt to find her husband, was not immediately forthcoming. It made Hall very depressed.
In a blue moment he damned the politicking, the tiresome lectures,
the wretched journal and the financial details which were above his
head. He yearned for the uncluttered north. 'The Arctic Region is my
home,' he said, 'when I am there . . . it seems as if I were in an earthly
heaven or a heavenly earth.'[30]

At last, however, the money materalized. It came in sporadically –
a bit from Grinnell, a bit from Grinnell's friends, some from Hall's own
friends, some from scientific organizations (who also lent him a few
items of equipment, but not many because, as they said, he didn't
know how to use them) and a little from public subscription. On 1
July 1864 he left for the Arctic aboard the whaler *Monticello*. So disgusted was he by life at home that he decided he would be away for
a good ten years. Later, he reduced that to three. Ultimately, he would
spend five years looking for Franklin's remains.

Hall's new voyage took him into the region of Repulse Bay, north
of Hudson Bay. It had been first explored by Parry in 1821, and Hall
hoped it would be a good setting-off point for King William Island. He
did eventually reach his goal, from which he returned with fascinating

* The case was thrown out of court. Years later, in retirement, Snow found an
English edition of Hall's book. He scribbled splenetic comments in the margin:
'What a lie!', 'I wrote this!', 'Liar!', 'The whole by W.P.S.'[29]

oral testimony, interpreted by Tookolito, regarding the fate of Franklin's men. In every other respect, however, his second mission was just a protracted version of his first. He started with an encomium on the joys of the Arctic in general and Eskimo life in particular, then he fell ill and was revisited by boils – some of which appeared on his eyelids. Seal blood constipated him, whale skin gave him diarrhoea. An abscess developed on his right eyeball and a second threatened to erupt on his left. The abscesses disappeared, along with the boils, only to be replaced by new troubles. The longer Hall lived in igloos the more he experienced a pain in the left side of his chest, which he put down to the cramped posture he had to adopt when writing his journal in temperatures of minus 42°F, breathing on his pen to keep the ink flowing. His Inuit companions were as obstructive and threatening as before. Of one man he wrote that, 'I had good reason to shoot the savage down on the spot, and know not how long it may be before I have to do so terrible an act to save my own dear life.'[31] On one leg of his journey he was accompanied by a sailor from the *Monticello*, but he proved good for nothing, and despite eating up to eight pounds of meat at a single sitting he managed to contract scurvy and had to be sent back.

Throughout these vicissitudes Hall's diary shimmered in an auroral display of indignant capitals and underlinings. He even began to grow a bit tired of his quest. 'Let no one who has had the like experience as mine, with no other people but savages to deal with, say whether my task has been an enviable one,' he wrote. 'The labor of the writing I have done, without speaking of anything else, has been enough to kill many a man, and has nearly killed me.'[32] He was not going to give up – 'by the aid of High Heaven I will yet succeed'[33] – but he was already thinking of his next mission. To what else could he turn his skills once Franklin was out of the way? A return to normal life was out of the question: by now he was wedded to Arctic exploration; it was, as he described it, his '*work*', a word which he imbued with a sense of grim, crusading urgency. There was only one answer. 'Give me the means,' he declared in March 1865, 'and I will not only discover the North Pole, but survey all the land I might find between Kane's farthest and it, and have my whole soul in the *work*.'[34]

When he returned to America in the autumn of 1869, he said exactly the same thing to Grinnell, albeit in more dramatic fashion. The undiscovered Pole was 'a great, sad blot upon the present age which ought to be wiped out'. And to think that God had given man the world – '*the whole of it*' – Hall hung his head in shame that 'that part of it that must be most interesting and glorious – at least to me – remains as unknown as though it had never been created'.[35] The Civil War was now over and he saw no reason why money should not be available for polar exploration. If it did not come from Grinnell (who had already poured hundreds of thousands of dollars into the Arctic) then it should certainly come from the government. Travelling to Washington, he all but ordered Congress to allocate the resources.

Nobody but he was going to see how it was spent. 'Let it be said that no one should ask of me to accept a subordinate position in an Arctic expedition,'[36] he warned. The message was delivered to Lady Franklin, in response to a projected third Franklin search. But it applied to all his competitors, in particular Hayes who had risen from retirement with the news that he was 'no less earnest than formerly for the opportunity to . . . once more try conclusions with my old foe the Smith Sound ice'.[37] Hall was having no truck with Hayes or anybody else. The Pole would be his alone.

Hayes certainly had no intention of relegating Hall to a subordinate position; he had no intention of letting Hall get anywhere near the Pole at all. Congress was still debating Hall's proposal when Hayes suddenly appeared in Washington with a rival plan. In a speech to the Committee on Foreign Relations he argued that it was he, if anyone, who deserved government funding. A scientist was needed to lead such an important expedition and Hall was not a scientist. Hall retaliated with heavy sarcasm: 'I confess I am not a "*scientific*" man,' he told the Committee. 'Who will dispute the presumption that Dr. Hayes is? Let us all bow to his presumption that he *is* the *savan* of the world.'[38] Hall need not have worried. Hayes's attack was too half-hearted to have much effect. If he was so keen to return to the Arctic he should have done something about it earlier. He came across as a spoiler. And if Hall was not a scientist then neither was Hayes – he was just a doctor with an education.

While waiting for Congress to make up its mind, Hall summoned his wife and their ten-year-old son, Charley, to join him in Washington. Hall's wife was almost destitute and Charley had seen his father for only three months of his life. But if Hall, who had barely mentioned his family in his journals, felt any twinge of remorse he suppressed it quickly. God and ice were calling. When his family returned to Cincinnati, Hall wrote to Grinnell that 'on canvassing the whole matter in relation to my proposed North Pole Expedition with Mrs. H., she concluded that it is best for me to fulfill the mission to which my whole soul is so warmly attached, if I cannot settle down here in the States'.[39] From between the lines emerges a depressing picture: an obsessive man who cared for his wife only to the extent that she supported his project; and a put-upon woman who had finally abandoned hope. When Lady Franklin sent Mrs Hall a cheque for fifteen pounds, it was returned uncashed. She did not want charity. Perhaps, too, she did not want any further connection with her husband's madness.

On 12 July 1870, Congress approved Hall's mission. It was too late to start that year – Hall blamed Hayes's interruption for this – but he knew at least that he would be going, and with $50,000 of government money at his service he would be going in style. Elated, he pranced into friends' houses, pointing upwards with a yell of 'NORTH STAR!' According to an acquaintance, '[the Pole] formed his conversation by day, and, I doubt not, was the substance of his dreams by night'.[40] What would he find when he got there? Would there be land? Yes, there probably would. It would be a continent, a new Australia, and he would colonize it and the Stars and Stripes would fly at the top of the world.

Hall was allocated the USS *Periwinkle*, a steam tug which displaced 347 tons and was reinforced for the Arctic at a cost of $50,000. Thirteen tons of wooden beams were hammered across the interior. It was re-caulked, re-rigged and re-planked. It was coppered. Its propeller shaft, its propeller well and the propeller itself were strengthened against the ice. It was fitted with central heating ducts. It didn't look pretty but that did not matter. Hall was impressed. 'There is no desire in *Uncle Sam* to give bad material or poor work to his Arctic devoted Sons,'[41] he wrote. As to these devoted sons, Hall took the rank of absolute commander. Budington, with whom he had made up, was to be the ship's sailing master and an experienced whaler named George Tyson was to be its assistant navigator. The first mate was Hubbard Chester, from the *Monticello*, and second mate was William Morton, Kane's old steward. Tookolito and Ebierbing came too. A twenty-four-year-old German physician, Dr Emil Bessels, led the three-man scientific team (another of whom was also German) and eight more Germans were enrolled as crew. In all, the twenty-man contingent comprised half Germans and half Americans. Hall was oblivious to the potential friction. 'I have chosen my own men,' he told the American Geographical Society, 'men that will stand by me through thick and thin. Though we may be surrounded by innumerable icebergs, and though our vessel may be crushed like an egg-shell, I believe they will stand by me to the last.'[42] On 29 July 1871, the *Periwinkle* – rechristened the *Polaris* – departed for the Pole.

7

THE SAGE OF GOTHA

To many it must have seemed as if the North Pole was US property. If one discounted Canada and Greenland, the United States was closer to Smith Sound than any other country. Britain and Denmark, the two colonial Arctic nations, were outwardly uninterested in the Pole. The former, which might have used Canada as a springboard, was exhausted by half a century of exploration. And Denmark had only commercial ambitions: Greenland produced a net profit of $250,000 per annum for its tiny European mother and, apart from the occasional coastal foray, the Danes were quite happy to leave things as they stood. There were some in Europe, however, who saw the Pole as very much their own territory, among them August Petermann, an opinionated, disputatious man nicknamed the Sage of Gotha. Born in 1822, Petermann was Germany's most respected geographer. Like Kane, Hayes, Hall and others he had first been attracted to the Arctic by the Franklin disaster. But unlike most Americans, who saw Smith Sound as the only possible approach to the Pole, Petermann had different ideas. He was not so radical as to dismiss the concept of an Open Polar Sea, but for once in the history of polar so-called scientific exploration, he did actually use science to advance a theory supporting its existence. And a very attractive theory it was too. The Gulf Stream, Petermann pointed out, was warm; it flowed north, skirting the western coasts of Britain before hitting Norway, and from Norway it undoubtedly continued on its way. So warm was the Gulf Stream that it enabled humans to survive in comfort where otherwise they would be frozen; the thriving Scottish city of Glasgow, for example, was at the same longitude as the wastes of Labrador. It was silly to think that such a potent force should peter out in Scandinavia. No, Petermann said, it went on, past the east coast of the island of Spitsbergen, to melt a 'thermometric gateway' to the Pole.

Petermann had first voiced his opinion in the aftermath of Kane's voyage up Smith Sound. In 1855 he wrote, 'I feel duty bound to state that Kane's report is apt to cause endless confusion, and to open the door to erroneous ideas if the public really believed him.'[1] But the public did believe Kane. And if they didn't they still read his narrative, a book so popular that Congress voted to buy 15,000 copies for its library – something which could not be said of the Sage's own periodical, *Petermanns Geographische Mitteilungen*. Petermann was put out and for a decade he turned his attentions to Africa, reappearing only in the early 1860s to damn Hayes's expedition as a repetition of Kane's idiocy. In 1865, however, he resurfaced to contradict a preposterous notion laid before the Royal Geographical Society by Rear-Admiral Sherard Osborn.

Osborn was one of the old British school. As a Lieutenant he had taken part in the many Franklin searches sent out by Britain in the 1850s and he was dismayed by the lack of enterprise his country was now showing with regard to the Pole. Britain was the acknowledged master of ice travel: in the effort to find Franklin its naval teams had man-hauled sledges over tremendous distances – more than 1,000 miles at a stretch. But time was passing and the experienced men were dying. Unless something was done, Britain's hard-won Arctic experience would be lost to future generations. What Osborn wanted was a try for the Pole via Smith Sound while there were still people – i.e. himself – who knew how to do it. At his farthest point north Hayes had calculated the Pole to be 510 miles off. The vanishing breed of thousand-milers could cover this easily. Their journey would be across clean, solid ice. Petermann's route, on the other hand, involved ships, unpredictable seas, and the possibility of being frozen in.

Obsorn's purpose had been to goad the British government into action rather than denigrate Petermann's theories. Petermann, however, took it as a challenge. A bitter and increasingly public dispute arose between the two men and their supporters. The British press accused Petermann of trying to gain 'cheap honours for his politically disrupt country'.[2] Petermann replied with jeers at 'greedy British money bags' who wanted the world to 'dance to the pipe of John Bull'.[3] The squabble spread to the US, where one Silas Brent, a hydrographical officer who had sailed with Commodore Perry to Japan in 1854, decided that a second 'thermometric gateway' existed above Bering Strait, caused by the Kuro Siwo (or Kuroshio), the warm ocean current which flowed northwards from Japan. It was in this direction that explorers should head. Hayes took up cudgels for Smith Sound: 'The truth is,' he said of Brent's suggestion, 'this is precisely what ought not to be done.'[4] Brent replied that Hayes had 'failed to see the point and gist of the theory, being wedded to his own dogmas . . . in the face of the thousands of lives, the millions of money, and the three hundred years of time that have been wasted in attempts to reach the Pole.'[5] The American Geographical Society declared in favour of Smith Sound, announcing that Brent 'has not furnished one particle of evidence' in support of his route. Then a fellow officer called Maury came to Brent's defence. And on it went.

The controversy was simmering nicely when Petermann lost patience. Instead of telling the British and Americans how to get to the Pole he would send a German expedition to do the job for them. His first stab, in 1868, involved the *Grönland*, a small schooner carrying eleven men under the command of a thirty-two-year-old Hanoverian named Karl Koldewey. It was not a success. The *Grönland* reached an unspectacular 80°30′N off the west coast of Spitsbergen before being driven back by impassable ice. But Petermann did not mind. This was a preliminary survey. He had better things in mind for 1869. At his own expense he constructed a 140-ton steamship, a big, black, purposeful vessel called the *Germania*, covered with so much iron and braced with such thick beams that he thought it could smash through any amount of ice. In support came the *Hansa*, a 77-ton sailing ship. The total crew on both ships came to thirty-one – fourteen aboard the *Hansa*, seventeen aboard the *Germania* – and the expedition was once again under the command of Captain Koldewey.

Although it was Petermann's private project rather than a government one, it became a symbol of patriotism. 'It rests for German inquiry to open up new domains,' Koldewey wrote, 'in order to show that German sailors are as qualified, as bold, and as persevering as those of other nations.'[6] German firms competed to provide the best supplies for their Arctic heroes. Everything was to be of the finest quality. 'Parsimony could not for a moment be considered at such a time,' the captain noted sternly. 'It would have been misplaced, inhuman, and destructive of the very aim of the expedition had any niggardliness been shown.'[7] When a subscription was opened to recoup some of the costs, the response was avid. Who could resist such a call to national pride? Everybody stumped up – even expatriates as far afield as Honolulu, Tahiti, South America, the East Indies and China.

On 15 June 1869, the two ships left Bremerhaven. King Wilhelm (not quite yet a Kaiser) came down to see them off, cannon were fired, a brass band played uplifting tunes and a crowd of brightly dressed well-wishers lined the banks of the Weser. As the *Hansa* was towed out its cable snapped, an event which was usually seen as a bad omen by sailors but, as Koldewey explained, he and his crew were immune to superstition. The excitement was intense, particularly among the expedition's scientists, none of whom had been aboard a ship before and half of whom had never even seen the sea. Soon they were all feeling seasick, their queasiness aggravated by the smell of fresh varnish, new canvas and the dampness which pervaded every new ship as its timbers adjusted to a marine environment. There were little disputes as the men settled in – such as when and where they should be permitted to smoke – but the great endeavour soon reached an orderly equilibrium.

Petermann had every reason to be proud of the expedition he had set afoot. The *Germania* was just the ship to break through the thermometric gateway. But the *Germania* was not heading up the main body of the Gulf Stream. With the responsibility for Germany's Arctic debut on his shoulders, Petermann's nerve had failed him. Just this once, he would go along with his opponents' theories and accept that the best way north was via coastal waters. The *Germania* and the *Hansa* were therefore to sail for the east coast of Greenland and there determine whether it was possible to create a base for a push to the Pole. Lest anyone accuse him of backsliding, however, he declared that a branch of the Gulf Stream *might* sweep past Greenland.

Petermann's theories allowed for this. In his writings he split the Arctic into two zones. One, into which the Gulf Stream flowed, spread from Greenland in the west to an undetermined point beyond Spitsbergen in the east. It was enclosed by a semi-circle of land which hooped over the Pole from Greenland to finish somewhere north of Siberia. Within this zone the ice was young and free-flowing. In the other zone, to the west of Greenland, it was old and obstinate. The main force of the Gulf Stream clearly flowed to a place above Spitsbergen. But in the 1810s and 1820s whalers had found the east coast of Greenland to be ice-free, thereby suggesting that the Gulf Stream swept around Petermann's enclosure to create an alternative thermometric opening off Greenland. Petermann was unsure whether the Greenland gateway existed, but, as he consoled himself, the Germans were only conducting a mission of reconnaissance; the world should not expect too much.

A touching nervousness overcame the Arctic new boys as they made their way north. Reading and re-reading all the Arctic literature aboard, they wondered what conditions would be like. Would they really be as appalling as the chroniclers told? At the first sign of cold weather they began to fear that they might: 'We thought of the troublous gloominess with which the northern legends enveloped the unknown region; and indeed, began to believe in the influence which a long sojourn in such a climate would have upon mind and body.'[8] The ice drew nearer. They saw their first polar bear and ate their first, hesitant mouthfuls of seal meat. By the middle of July they were off the coast of Greenland and their anxiety was replaced by excitement. 'We stood and felt that we were at the entrance to a new world, whose whole enchantment had thus burst upon us,'[9] Koldewey wrote. There was no clear route through the floes ahead, but he was unperturbed: 'A way for the *Germania* must and should be found.'[10]

It was on this brave premise that the German polar expedition foundered. The *Germania* was quite capable of breaking through ice. The *Hansa*, however, was not. Paul Hegemann, commanding the *Hansa*, had already experienced difficulties keeping up with his more powerful consort, and even as Koldewey spoke those fateful words, on 19 July, the *Hansa* was several miles behind. When it finally came within signalling distance Koldewey raised the flags for Hegemann to come alongside. Before he went anywhere he wanted to discuss the situation with him. Hegemann, however, misread the signal as an instruction to sail west to avoid bad weather. Disbelievingly, Koldewey watched as the *Hansa* steered straight for the thick, coastal ice of Greenland. A bank of fog descended, and that was the last either ship ever saw of each other.

By what inconceivable stroke of mischance or incompetence Hegemann managed to misinterpret Koldewey's message has never been explained. He could surely have seen whether the weather was good or bad, and he knew for a certainty that his ship was ill-equipped to extricate itself once caught in the ice. The only possible reason for his behaviour is that he had been given an order and, unthinkingly, he had obeyed it. The consequences of Hegemann's error were not immediately apparent. The two captains had agreed that in the event of their becoming separated they would rendezvous at Sabine Island, not far from where they had parted. And for a few days Koldewey duly waited there, not overly worried. Then, when the *Hansa* failed to arrive, he began to wonder if his sister ship was in distress. After a week he concluded that it probably was. He therefore continued the journey without it.

Koldewey's action, as inexplicable as Hegemann's, was without parallel in Arctic history. Single ships had, of course, entered the ice in the past – but usually with unfortunate results, and the practice had long been banned by Britain's Royal Navy. Never before, however, had one part of a two-vessel team abandoned the other particularly, as in this case, when the lost ship was the weaker of the two. But Koldewey had been instructed to reach the east coast of Greenland. He had not been told to rescue his companion. Anyway, the *Hansa* might have made its way to the outskirts of the pack and then, having been unable to break in, gone home. Or maybe it was just taking a long time to reach Sabine Island. Ultimately, orders were orders and Koldewey, like Hegemann, obeyed them.

On 5 August, after a brief exchange with the ice, the *Germania* reached the east coast of Greenland at a latitude of 74°18′N. The crew cheered, the German flag was raised and everyone congratulated themselves. 'We found ourselves in a field (which, scientifically, was almost unknown), on a coast respecting which the most unreliable and contradictory reports obtained,' Koldewey wrote. 'And nearly all our discoveries and observations seemed new, thus affording important contributions to the knowledge of the Arctic regions.'[11] Koldewey established a camp on Sabine Island – Hegemann might yet turn up, he hoped – and for the next nine months he sent small excursions into Greenland.

While the men were out, Koldewey's scientists performed their usual observatory rituals with pendulums, magnets and -ometers of every description. All they discovered was that polar bears became very hungry in winter. One man was chased for hundreds of yards, throwing aside his jacket, his waistcoat and his scarf to distract his pursuer and, as the bear caught up, was undoing his belt with which to strangle it when his shipmates came to his aid with rifles. Less lucky was Dr Borgen, whose diary for 7 March 1870 started as follows: 'About a quarter before nine p.m. I had gone out to observe the occultation of a star . . .' He had not gone far when a polar bear cuffed him from behind. 'The next thing I felt was the tearing of my scalp, which was only protected by a skull-cap. This is their mode of attacking seals, but, owing to the slipperiness of their skull, the teeth glide off.' Koldewey heard a cry: 'A bear is carrying me off!' Dashing out with his rifle, he saw a polar bear dragging Borgen away, its teeth fixed in his skull. He fired at the bear which dropped Borgen's head and fastened on his hand. 'After being dragged in this way for about 300 paces,' Borgen wrote, 'almost strangled by my shawl, which the bear had seized at the same time, he dropped me, and immediately afterwards Koldewey was bending over me with the words, "Thank God, he is still alive." The bear stood a few paces on one side, evidently undecided what course to pursue, until a bullet gave him a hint that it was high time to take himself off.'[12] Borgen's injuries were horrible. Two six-inch strips of scalp hung over his ears, his skull was lacerated and at least twenty other wounds had been caused by his passage across the ice. Yet he felt nothing. 'It is worth while mentioning,' he wrote, 'that neither during the act of receiving the wounds nor during the process of healing, which proceeded admirably, did I experience the slightest pain.'[13]*

Further out, Koldewey's man-hauled sledge parties found wonderful things: at 75° there were herds of reindeer and musk-ox (which they mistook for a species of gnu); at the same latitude they saw a 2,000-feet-high cliff, made up of black and white stripes which proved, on closer inspection, to be mixed strata of coal and limestone; at 76° they stumbled on the distinctive stone circles of Eskimo summer camps; and on 15 April they reached 77°1', their farthest north, where Lt. Julius Payer, a young officer on secondment from Vienna, raised both the German and Austrian flags. The expeditions were not very professional: their tents kept falling down, they had no dogs, their travelling clothes were of wool, the furs with which they had been issued were all wrong (in despair Payer actually boned a pair of polar bear legs, complete with pads, and used them as boots) and they suffered from constant dysentery which they dosed with opium.

---

* The African explorer David Livingstone said much the same of a lion attack: 'There was no sense of pain nor feeling of terror. It was like what patients partially under the influence of chloroform describe, who see all the operation, but feel not the knife.'[14]

Their sleeping bags were too small, their fuel arrangements were primitive (twice they set fire to themselves) and the man-hauling was something they had never done, nor, if Payer was to be believed, ever wanted to do again.

Returning from their farthest north, the sun rose briefly at midnight and Payer painted a vivid picture of the scene: 'Radiant lay the endless snowfields in a yellowish, rosy glimmer, over which the wind rolls thick veils of snow, resembling in effect of colour . . . an undulating flow of molten steel, driving away over the diamond-sparkling road, and the long, bluish shadows of the men breaking through the snowy masses as they knocked against each other in their violent and unequal motion, a spectacle and a work for the cursed, which Dante might have held up to the coryphees of his infernal regions.'[15]

Their discomfort was not without compensation: fresh meat, Eskimos and coal – all the requirements for a strike by steam to the Pole. What better discoveries could they have made? Unfortunately, as a British commentator noted, all these things had been found elsewhere. The expeditions 'were, in the main, resultless for all practical purposes. The principal fact on which Koldewey congratulates himself was not that he had achieved anything but that he had reached a point from which to achieve something during the coming summer.'[16] Koldewey never did pursue a summer expedition. He sailed for Germany on 22 July, very glad to be out of the Arctic. When he reached Bremerhaven he heard two pieces of news: Germany was at war with France; and the crew of the *Hansa* was safe.

Hegemann had done his best to keep the appointment on Sabine Island, but no sooner had the *Hansa* sailed west than it was surrounded by floes from which it was impossible to escape. Not yet nipped, but almost as firmly trapped as if it had been, the *Hansa* drifted to the south. By 13 August the crew were beating the ice from the rigging and the two scientists aboard, Drs Laube and Buchholz, were becoming worried. 'It seems bewitched!' Laube wrote, as he watched the rapidity with which ice re-formed on the ropes. 'I did not go to bed that night with the best and quietest of thoughts. We were in the ice, but whether or how we should ever come out again, God only knew.'[17] Hegemann was more sanguine. He had not yet abandoned hope and indeed, after twelve days of valiant tacking, he managed to work the *Hansa* north until it was within thirty-five miles of Sabine Island. But on 25 August he had to admit defeat. The floes were now so tight that not even a boat could have wormed through them. It was his birthday, and they celebrated the occasion with large, gloomy slices of cake.

The ice solidified, imprisoning the *Hansa* on the eastern side of a circular floe two miles in diameter, which was drifting south at a rate of up to six miles per day. Hegemann hoped that, with a bit of luck, the ice would float far enough south for them to be able to escape to open water. But there was no telling if the ship would last that long in the moving ice, so on 27 September he ordered a house to be built 450 yards from the edge of the floe, to which they could retreat with their boats should anything adverse befall the *Hansa*. It was a cosy shack, constructed of the coal bricks they had been carrying for the *Germania*, and when complete it measured twenty feet long by fourteen wide. Hegemann was delighted with the ease at which it went up. 'We only needed to strew finely-powdered snow between the grooves and cracks, pour water upon it, and in ten minutes all was frozen to a strong compact mass, from which one single stone would with difficulty have been extracted!'[18] The roof was covered with sailcloths plus, in a surreal twist, some reed mats which had been left over from the *Hansa*'s last voyage to the West Indies. A stove was installed, alongside which they hung a large, gilt-framed mirror from Hegemann's cabin and an equally ornate and expensive barometer. With these homely touches, plus two months' provisions, the house was as comfortable as could be expected. Later, finding time on their hands, they added a couple of traditional dormer windows.

On 18 October the *Hansa* trembled violently, its masts swaying as if they were being climbed. At the same time an unearthly din came from below. 'The ice,' wrote Hegemann, 'groaned and cracked, squashed and puffed; now sounding like the banging of doors, now like many human voices raised one against another; and lastly like the drag on the wheel of a railway engine.'[19] The floe had started to

swivel, jamming the ship firmly against the coastal ice. Early the following morning a storm hit them from the north-west, squeezing the
floes still closer together. At 10.00 a.m. the *Hansa* began to groan
under the pressure; in the early afternoon its deck seams sprang amidships; by the end of the day its bow had surged a full seventeen feet
into the sky. The stern, however, remained in the ice, being slowly
twisted as if by a gigantic finger and thumb. 'The rising of the ship
was an extraordinary and awful, yet splendid spectacle, of which the
whole crew were witnesses from the ice,' Hegemann wrote, 'and the
conviction that the ship must soon break up forced itself upon our
minds.'[20] Creeping inside, he saw seventeen inches of water in the
hold. He listened but could hear nothing; the leak must be somewhere beyond their reach, probably under the coal. Putting half his
men on the pumps he ordered the others to empty the ship of its
remaining contents. Out came the iron galley range, two stoves, chests
of clothing, piles of bedding, barrels of food, Hegemann's journal and
nautical instruments. 'Round about the ship lay a chaotic mass of het-
erogeneous articles,' Hegemann recorded, 'and groups of feeble rats
struggling with death, and trembling with the cold!'[21] Meanwhile the
storm raged, the temperature sank to 41°F below freezing and down
below the water rose steadily. The men toiled at the pumps, standing
in barrels lest they lose their footing in the semi-frozen sludge which
spewed onto the deck. But nothing could be done. When Hegemann
heard that loose firewood was floating in the fore-peak, he ordered the
pumping to halt. 'Enough! the fate of the Hansa was sealed; our good
ship must go to the bottom!'[22]

The crew sawed down the masts and split them into blocks of firewood which were stacked neatly by the hut. Then, as the *Hansa* sank,
they retreated to their winter quarters. The coal-walled house swiftly
lost its charm. '[Our] new asylum, which was lit by the cabin-lamp . . .
looked like a dreary tomb,'[23] Hegemann wrote, echoing the Arctic
journals he had so eagerly pondered on the way out. It was not yet a
tomb, but as the floe drifted south, past threatening icebergs and
cliffs that reminded Dr Laube of the Alps near Munich, it soon
became an asylum. Dr Buchholz was terrified by their predicament.

1. Henry Grinnell

2. Elisha Kent Kane

3. The Advance *nipped in Smith Sound, 1853*

4. Life in the Advance. *l. to r. Bonsall, Brooks, Kane, Hayes, Morton*

5. One of Kane's sledge parties

6. *Isaac Israel Hayes*

7. *Charles Francis Hall*

8. *Hall's funeral, 1872*

9. The separation of the Polaris, *1872*

10. New Year festivities. The Germania, *1870*

11. Sledgers from the Germania, *1870*

12. The wreck of the Hansa, *1869*

13. The Tegetthoff *drifting north, noon, 21 December, 1873*

14. Searching for a lost dog on Franz Josef Land, 1874

15. Payer's exploration of Franz Josef Land, 1874

16. Divine service aboard the Tegetthoff

17. An Austro-Hungarian carnival on the ice

18. The Tegetthoff *against a lunar halo, 1873*

'As to sleep,' he confided to his diary that first night, 'that was not to be thought of, as the idea of our dreadful position was whistling through my head in the wildest manner... What would become of us when winter really set in, if it already announced its approach with such bitter cold? In vain did I try to think of any means of preservation.'[24] After a number of weeks Buchholz went mad and was confined to his bed.

The weather worsened throughout the winter and they had to put up wooden headboards to stop their pillows freezing to the wall. Hegemann maintained Teutonic discipline to save the others from going the same way as Buchholz. 'We were all actively employed, and daily order and regularity were rigidly kept up,'[25] he wrote. Once a week, on Sunday, they were permitted a single glass of port. All the time they wondered what would become of them. Hegemann's books, which were all they had to go by, offered no solace. 'The experience of former Greenland captains, who had got on the ice on the Greenland coast, told us that their vessels had gone to the bottom,' Hegemann recited, 'and the men had been sometimes lost, and sometimes saved in the boats, after frightful difficulties and dangers, by reaching an Esquimaux settlement on the south-west coast.'[26] It had even happened to Germans. The *Wilhelmine* from Pexel had gone down in 1777: there it was, on page 37 of Lindemann's *Arctic Fishery* in black and white.

In November they shot their first walrus. It took ten men with a pulley to heave it onto the floe, and then they could not skin it easily because it had frozen into a hard stony mass. On Christmas Day they had a small festival. From somewhere or other they cobbled together a tree and unearthed two leadlined caskets which had been presented to them on their departure by learned societies. Out fell a collection of miniature musical instruments: whistles, Jew's harps, and small trumpets. Later came puppets, games of roulette, cracker bonbons and in the evening, chocolate and gingerbread. They were still playing with their children's toys on the morning of 2 January when they heard a rasping noise, as if somebody was shuffling around the hut in enormous shoes. It died away and was soon forgotten. In the

afternoon it came back, this time stronger and more menacing. 'It
was a scraping, blustering, crackling, sawing, grating and jarring
sound,' Hegemann wrote, 'as if a ghost was wandering under our
floe.'[27] They rushed outside with their lamps: the ice was the same as
ever; their three boats were undisturbed; nothing seemed to have
changed. So where was the noise coming from? It was coming from
below: the floe was breaking up.

For forty-eight hours thereafter they were kept inside by a storm.
When they emerged their island had shrunk horribly. The storm had
blown apart the ice, leaving them on a rectangle 1200 yards long and
400 yards wide. Open water was all around them but, tantalizingly, the
leads were not wide enough for a boat. The floe was still their only
means of deliverance.

At 6.00 a.m. on 11 January 1870, while asleep in the hut, they heard
the cry, 'All hands turn out!' Not bothering with the door, they burst
through the roof and emerged into a ferocious storm. 'The tumult of
the elements which met us there was beyond anything we had already
experienced,' Hegemann wrote. 'Scarcely able to leave the spot, we
stood huddled together for protection from the bad weather.
Suddenly we heard, "Water on the floe close by!"[28] A jagged fissure
opened between the hut and the stack of firewood, twenty-five yards
distant. The floe was now only 150 feet in diameter. Watching the
wood drift into the waves they became aware, for the first time, that
the floe was rising and falling with the waves. Hegemann ordered
them to emergency stations: 'We bade each other goodbye with a
farewell shake of the hands, for the next moment we might go down.
Deep despondency had taken hold of our scientific friends; the crew
were still and quiet. Thus we stood or cowered by our boats the whole
day, the fine, pricking snow penetrating the clothes to the skin. It was
a miracle that just that part of the floe on which we stood should from
its soundness keep together.'[29]

On the night of 12 January, having retreated to the hut, they were
again called out. This time it was for an iceberg that threatened to
crush them. It passed by, but not without leaving an impression in
Hegemann's journal: 'What a sight! Close upon us, as if hanging over

our heads, towered a huge mass of ice, of gigantic proportions . . .
Was it really an iceberg, or the mirage of one, or the high coast? We
could not decide the question. Owing to the swiftness of the drift, the
ghastly object had disappeared the next moment.'[30]

The night of 14 January, however, was the worst. Without any
warning, a fissure sliced through the middle of their hut. 'With a
thundering noise an event took place, the consequences of which, in
the first moments deranged all calculations. God only knows how it
happened that in our flight into the open, none came to harm.'[31] For
the next two days they huddled in the boats, half in water, half in
snow, half asleep, half waking, 'and our limbs quivered convulsively as
we lay packed like herrings in our furs'.[32] When the storm passed, on
the 16th, they clawed back what remained of their hut and built a
new shelter, half the size of the original, in the middle of their ever-
shrinking floe. Drifting south, their orderly routine went out of the
window. Who cared how they rationed their resources or how they
spent their days? They had plenty of supplies – the *Hansa* had, after
all, been a supply ship – so why not use them while they still could?
Hegemann's mirror was thrown aside and its gilt frame fed to the
stove. Their Arctic library was stuffed in after it. If the fire sank low
they encouraged it with streams of petrol and brandy. Packets of
tobacco were added to the blaze. To pass the time they made their
gunpowder into fireworks which exploded dully on the ice. All the
while Buchholz lay on his bed, speaking to nobody. For him it did not
matter how they spent their days. They were all doomed.

Hegemann alone still had hope. When the other half of their hut
had floated away he had been able, for the first time, to gauge the
strength of their floe. It was between thirty and thirty-five feet deep,
solid enough to carry them to the southern tip of Greenland, provided
no further splits occurred. Luckily, none did. But when was their drift
going to end? On 18 March he took their position at 64°2′; since their
separation from the *Germania* they had travelled 600 miles down the
coast of Greenland.

The floe moved steadily on (apart from a hiatus when it revolved in
the mouth of a bight for twenty-one days), and on 6 May, at 61°4′, land

birds flocked over them – linnets and snow buntings so tame that they all but sat on the men's noses. In the space of five minutes Hegemann's second officer managed to catch the same bird three times. The snow melted and items they had thought lost – among them the carpenter's chest – came to light. But still there was no navigable water. On 7 May, however, a lead opened to the south-west and Hegemann ordered the boats to be dragged in its direction. When Dr Laube objected, Hegemann explained the situation to him with cold logic: yesterday's position had been 61°4′; today's was 61°12′; the southward current had ended, and if they stayed on the floe they would spend the rest of their lives – a short period – in a circular eddy at the bottom of Greenland. They bade farewell to the ice as if it had been a ship: 'We took one last thankful look at our faithful floe; through numerous dangers and calamities, from the region of terror and death, it had borne us here in 200 days, into a more hospitable latitude; and now, filled with fresh courage, we might hope for a speedy release.'[33]

It was a release, certainly, but it was far from speedy. They started at 4.00 p.m. on 7 May and by the end of the month were still dragging the boats across the ice. At one point Hegemann fainted from the exertion. On 6 June, however, they were in clear water and could raise sail. Not since July the previous year had they been in command of their destiny. The change was magical. Off they sped, stopping at bays to gather sorrel, dandelion and cinquefoil from which, with some pickle, they made their first fresh salad in eleven months. On 13 June they rounded a cape and saw, below a wide semi-circle of mountains, grassy fields in which nestled two red-painted houses. They had reached the Moravian missionary outpost of Friedrichsthal.

Hegemann hoisted the flag and adjusted his telescope. Into the lens swam scenes of homely activity the like of which he had not seen for more than a year. 'At the door of the mission house a blue dress was visible for a moment, and then disappeared; now came a whole company down to the strand; they had seen us . . . A European strode up and down, like an official guardian of order. Was it possible that in Greenland were already to be found harbour-masters and other government officers? What I had first conjectured to be a heap of stones now stood upright. It was a group of oddly-dressed human beings – natives . . . Still it was uncertain whether the missionaries were Danish, but we heard, "That is the German flag! They are our people! Welcome, welcome to Greenland!" Germans, Germans in Greenland! The first word, after so long a time, heard from strange lips was German; the first sound our dear German mother-tongue; and their people the first to offer us help and refreshment – who can describe our wonder and delight?'[34] Before Hegemann's boat touched shore he was wading through the shallows to greet his compatriots.

Herr Gericke, who ran the station, welcomed them solemnly. He listened to their garbled tales for a moment or two then cut them short. 'Wives,' he commanded, 'go and get ready some good coffee; in the meantime we men shall drink a bottle of wine.'[35] Later there were plates of buttered rusks, flagons of home-brewed Greenland beer, cigars and endless rounds of story-telling. Hegemann expressed his joy in three short words: 'This was Germany.'[36]

Delighted as they were with their reception, Hegemann and his crew were disappointed to learn that Friedrichstahl had no steamer link with the outside world. Like almost every settlement on Greenland the missionaries received their supplies on small Eskimo ships – 'women's boats' they were called, for they were indeed operated by women – which made an annual trip to the port of Julianehaab, eighty miles distant. So, having distributed their unwanted possessions – guns, musical boxes, one of the boats – Hegemann's men set sail again. On reaching Julianehaab their reception was distinctly cold. The Danish Governor remembered very clearly that Prussia had annexed his home country's province of Schleswig in 1864 and bore an understandable grudge. When Hegemann recounted his journey on the floe the Governor interrupted it continually with 'That I do not think.'[37] And when he asked for somewhere to stay, the Dane told him that he was willing to house the officers but the men could either sleep in tents or their boats. Hegemann replied that they had no tents and that 'in rainy weather a stay in the boats was not exactly the thing'. At this the Dane sneered, 'If you really have borne so much, a little rain will not kill you.'[38] Hegemann organized a billet for his men in Julianehaab's schoolhouse, arranged for his passage home aboard the *Constanz* under one Captain Bang, and returned to the governor's home where he was delighted to catch his persecutor counting small change. The Governor, he learned, was more commonly known as the manager of Julianehaab's general store.

Hegemann may not have discovered much about Greenland when floating past its eastern coast, but he was deeply interested by what he saw in Julianehaab and its environs. Denmark's Arctic economy was far busier than he had imagined. Apart from the usual oils and furs, Danish ships were taking aboard vast quantities of minerals whose names he had never heard of and whose purpose he could only guess at – something to do with aluminium, he hazarded. He was fascinated, too, by Greenland's history. While waiting for Captain Bang to fill his hold he went on boat trips to find traces of the Vikings who had first settled the island. He saw the remains of houses, outlines of deserted fields and, on the shores of fjords, huddled piles of stones which were described, reverentially, as cathedrals. He visited the area's only cattle farm, tended by a Danish family who had gone native, and was shocked at how swiftly the Nordic bloodline was transformed. The family looked European – they had blond hair and blue eyes – but they lived as Eskimos, sleeping in a communal bed with no regard for conventional decencies. He was appalled when his host's wives wandered about naked, and was disgusted by the sleeping quarters he was offered. A hole was knocked in the cattle byre to make a window, and out of it flew cow heads, entrails and all manner of muck. Given the choice, Hegemann would have preferred to sleep outdoors. 'We were soon convinced that the Greenlander, left to himself, would never appreciate the comfort and advantage of German cleanliness.'[39]

As for the Eskimos, they horrified him. Many were of mixed blood – the Danish workers could not afford a European wife and family – and he was distressed at the way they had adopted local customs. 'I cannot affirm that the Greenland ladies are bashful,' Hegemann wrote, 'for during our stay [in Julianehaab] the cook Luise came in, and quite coolly in our presence made the most critical alterations in her dress.'[40] They were, 'according to our aesthetic opinions, far below the level of the agreeable, and the bodily mien is more repulsive than attractive'.[41] Later he said that they had 'somewhat the appearance of apes'.[42] Without expressing it in so many words, he felt that Denmark was letting the side down. He was very pleased when Captain Bang had loaded the *Constanz* and was ready to sail.

'31 July. No more ice!' Dr Laube wrote in his journal. 'Set south-wards, and – O heavenly music of the word – homewards!'[43] The *Constanz* set them down in Copenhagen, where Hegemann paid a quick visit to a clothing warehouse lest they be arrested as vagabonds, and then they caught a train home, arriving late at night to a country geared for war. The welcome was not as fulsome as he had hoped for – in fact it was non-existent – but at least they were home.

In Britain, Sherard Osborn chortled at the Germans' misfortune. 'It was a very creditable thing to find a young sailor-nation doing its work so well,' he remarked patronizingly, '[but] their efforts had been entirely misdirected by Dr. Petermann, and the result was, as he had anticipated, no addition to our geographical knowledge of the Polar Basin.'[44] Osborn, however, was so desperate to attack the Arctic him-self that he overlooked the real significance of the German expedition. The conclusions of Hegemann and Koldewey were inter-esting. Koldewey's journal exuded patriotic bombast: 'For the first time a German expedition, under the auspices of the black, white and red flag, had visited ... the least known region of the globe.'[45] Hegemann's was more subdued, but slyly telling: 'We cannot flatter ourselves that we have greatly increased the knowledge of Greenland; but we have shown what man's strength and perseverance can accom-plish.'[46] Within a few decades these two attitudes would exemplify all attempts at the Pole. The first viewpoint Osborn could understand – one of his dearest hopes was for Britain to raise its flag on the Pole before anyone else – but the second, that polar exploration was a matter of individuals pitting themselves against the elements, was beyond his comprehension There was no logic to it. Why do such a thing? Where was the justification, scientific or otherwise? He did not live to find the answer, but he did live to see an abominable infringement of what he perceived to be Britain's polar rights. While Britain dithered and prevaricated, yet another nation was about to steal its glory. And it was approaching the matter in a fashion guaranteed to infuriate Osborn. Not content with stirring up the Germans, Petermann had now infected Austria with his theories.

8

A LAND UNKNOWN BEFORE

'Gentlemen!' Carl Weyprecht said, 'this year we have for the first time hoisted the flag in the Arctic region, and we have arrived at results which will bring to life again the faint hopes of finally reaching the Pole. We Austrians have . . . successfully entered the contest.'[1] His audience at the Imperial Academy of Science of Vienna cheered their approval.

Weyprecht, an officer in the Austrian Navy, had recently returned from a voyage to the twin islands of Novaya Zemlya, off the Siberian coast. Accompanied by Julius Payer and an influential patron named Count Johann von Wilczek, he had found at 79°N warm, ice-free waters leading to a fringe of weak floes through which, had he had a steamer, he would have been able to push with ease. Now, on 7 December 1871, he was delivering his findings. 'This sea is the key to the mystic Polynia,'[2] he said, using a Russian term for the Open Polar Sea. 'We are convinced that in this part of the Arctic Ocean greater results may, with equal efforts, be expected than in any other part . . . The Gulfstream theory of Dr. Petermann, which has lately been attacked from different sides, has been fully confirmed . . . we are convinced that a well-equipped and energetically-managed expedition

must succeed in reaching far higher latitudes in this sea than on any
other point of the earth.'[3] One or two cynics wondered what interest
a Middle-European empire could have in the Pole, but Weyprecht
swept them aside. Scientific and national principles were at stake.
Austria was going to 'solve the great problem'.[4]

A thirty-three-year-old Lieutenant, who had been awarded the Iron
Crown and numerous other decorations, Weyprecht had long wanted
to get into the ice, but his services had always been turned down:
Austria had better things on which to waste its cumbersome energies,
and anyway, the Arctic was hardly within its sphere of influence. But
when Payer returned from the German expedition to Greenland,
Vienna felt a challenge to its *amour-propre*. As Weyprecht adroitly
remarked, the Polar battle had 'been carried on for centuries among
civilised nations'.[5] Was not Austria a civilized nation? Its Habsburg
rulers had been on the throne since 1282. It had once controlled most
of Europe, using Latin as its *lingua franca*. It had only stopped calling
itself the Holy Roman Empire in 1806. If a country like Germany,
which was barely five years old, could outfit a polar expedition then
Austria could do it too. So Franz Josef I, Emperor of Austria, King of
Hungary, monarch of all lands from Prague to Venice, decreed that it
should.

The Austro-Hungarian Navy, not one of the world's most celebrated forces, did its utmost. It ordered from Germany a new ship,
the *Admiral Tegetthoff* which, with its 220-ton burden and its 100-
horsepower steam engine, was one of the largest vessels yet to be
sent north. The expedition's command, like that of the Dual Monarchy
whose red-white-red flag it flew, was twofold. Weyprecht was to be in
charge of sea operations while Payer was given authority over any
sorties across land or ice. The two men were very different:
Weyprecht was a career sailor who had been born in Germany, while
Payer hailed from Bohemia and was at heart a poet, whose happiest
times had been when Vienna sent him to explore the Austrian
Alps. (He was also, it was said, the best dog-sledger below the
Arctic Circle.) But differences counted for little in the Austro-
Hungarian Empire, as was shown by the composition of the *Tegetthoff*'s

twenty-two-man crew. They conversed in a Babel of German, Italian,
Magyar and Serbo-Croat – all save two Alpine guides whose Tyrolean
dialect was understood only by Payer – and yet they coexisted peace-
ably and worked together perfectly efficiently. They were a cultural
anachronism united by the ghost of a forgotten Roman tongue. Payer
liked the mix. The Austrians would provide the discipline, the Slavs
and Hungarians would provide the muscle, and the Italians – in whose
language all orders were given – would provide the seafaring skills.
The Tyroleans, meanwhile, would exert their Alpine expertise on the
discovery of land. When the *Tegethoff* left Bremerhaven on 14 July
1872, Adriatic songs wafted from the rigging and the strains of Payer's
zither tinkled over the waves.

The waters through which the *Tegetthoff* sailed were not unexplored.
Swedes and Norwegians had for more than a decade launched
expeditions towards Spitsbergen and eastwards over the top of
Scandinavia. The Russians, too, had done a fair bit of exploring since
the 1820s – but more to find where Siberia stopped than where the
Pole began. Weyprecht, however, dismissed the efforts of his predecessors. The Russians were inscrutably spasmodic, now producing great
feats of exploration, such as those of Baron Wrangel who had sailed
through the Arctic Ocean to the North-East of Siberia in the 1820s, and
now lapsing into periods of secretive indifference. The Scandinavians
were brave but, in Weyprecht's mind, indolent: instead of seeking the
easiest way through the ice they just barged at it until their ships sank or
were iced in; whereupon they sailed home in their boats. Their casualty
rate was disproportionate to the number of vessels lost and this, to
Weyprecht, was a sign of slovenliness rather than efficiency.

On 29 July, at just beyond 74°N, the *Tegetthoff* was faced with a
barrier of ice. Forgetting his earlier remarks about Scandinavian
methods, Weyprecht ran straight at it, emerging in a hole of clear
water. On 2 August he charged another barrier – again successfully.
This was to be his tactic for the rest of his command. At each strike
he noticed with puzzlement that the sea was a lot icier than it had
been in 1871 when he and Payer had sailed to 79° without meeting
a single floe.

In mid-August they reached Novaya Zemlya. For much of the time they had been surrounded by mist, which gave an extra air of mystery to their voyage. But when the weather cleared, usually during the sunlit night, they were smitten by the beauty of the Arctic. 'Where the rays of the sun do not directly fall on it, the ice is suffused with a faint, rosy haze, which deepens more and more as the source of light nears the horizon,' Payer wrote. 'Then the sunbeams fall drowsily and softly, as through a veil of orange gauze, all forms lose at a little distance their definition, the shadows become fainter and fainter, and all nature assumes a dreamy aspect. In calm nights the air is so mild that we forget we are in the home of ice and snow. A deep ultramarine sky stretches over all, and the outlines of the ice . . . tremble on the glassy surface of the water. If we pull in a boat over the unmoved mirror of the "ice-holes", close beside us a whale may emerge from its depths, like a black, shining mountain; if a ship penetrates into the waste, it looks as weird as the "Flying Dutchman", and the dense columns of smoke, which rise in eddies from her funnel, remain fixed for hours until they gradually melt away.'[6] Sometimes, even the mist was magical, clothing the *Tegetthoff* in a low, golden cloud. Had the ship's crows-nest been a bit higher its occupant would have sat in clear sunshine, a solitary being in a world of sky and vapour, travelling silently towards the unknown.

On such occasions it was hard to disbelieve the legends, to doubt that a new and mystical land lay beyond the ice, a realm of wonderment which had been waiting patiently until humankind had found the means to reach it. The steady rhythm of the *Tegetthoff*'s pistons reassured them that they had the means; and with each of Weyprecht's successful charges, the end seemed increasingly attainable.

In their wake came Count Wilczek and friends, who had taken the sail-ship *Isbjorn* to deposit a reserve cache of supplies on the Barents Islands, a string of black, slaty rocks off the north-east coast of Novaya Zemlya. On 20 August, Weyprecht and Payer rowed over to bid Wilczek goodbye. His job was done, they said, and it was time to go home while he still could. Then they sailed north. That afternoon, at 76°32′, they hit solid ice. Preparatory to giving the ice a charge,

Weyprecht moored alongside a floe. The ice, however, made a pre-emptive strike. Without any warning it closed around the *Tegetthoff*, imprisoning it in a solid block. Unable to maneouvre, Weyprecht watched helplessly as his ship was carried off by the Arctic drift. The music stopped.

The *Tegetthoff* was in a singular position, unique in the history of polar exploration to that date. Every previous expedition had been beaten back by southward-flowing currents. It had happened to Parry, whose dash by sledge from Spitsbergen in 1827 had foundered on the southward trend of the ice, and it had happened in recent years, very memorably, to Hegemann. South was the only known direction in which Arctic waters went. Yet here were Weyprecht and Payer being carried *north*. Petermann's theory, or part of it, was therefore correct. The Gulf Stream did continue towards the Pole; but, as the Austro-Hungarians soon became aware, it did not melt the ice before it.

The *Tegetthoff* contained 1,000 days of supplies, and its crew would need every ounce of them because that was very nearly the time it would take before they reached home. 'We must have been filled with despair,' Payer wrote, 'had we known that evening we were henceforward doomed to obey the caprices of the ice, that the ship would never again float on the waters of the sea, that all the expectations with which our friends, but a few hours before, saw the 'Tegetthoff' steam away to the north, were now crushed: *that we were no longer discoverers, but passengers against our will on the ice.* From day to day we hoped for the hour of our deliverance! At first we expected it hourly, then from week to week; then at seasons of the year and changes of the weather, then in the chances of new year! *But that hour never came.*'[7]

For more than a month, Novaya Zemlya slid slowly past on the starboard side. On 2 October the *Tegetthoff* crossed the 77th degree of latitude. The rate of drift increased and by 12 October Novaya Zemlya had become a few shadowy peaks on the horizon. The *Tegetthoff* carried a number of dogs – six Newfoundlands, purchased in Vienna, plus one trained and one wild husky which they had picked up in Norway – who displayed almost human feelings as Novaya

Zemlya disappeared. The Newfoundlands, previously raucous, sat in a dejected heap. The trained husky jumped onto Payer's lap, licking his face, and the wild one (which was so unpleasant they suspected it might have wolf, or even fox ancestry) held its paw out to every passer-by as if it wanted it to be shaken. On the morning of 13 October Novaya Zemlya vanished, and the *Tegetthoff* was alone, drifting north in a bank of cold fog.

Thirteen was a portentous number for the Austro-Hungarian expedition. Its committee had been constituted on the 13th; the *Tegetthoff*'s keel had been laid on the 13th; it had left Bremerhaven on the 13th; it had left Tromsø (where it had called in to collect a Norwegian ice master, an ancient fellow who came aboard wearing a powdered wig) on the 13th; it had reached the ice thirteen days later; and now, on the 13th, with the thermometer at 13°F below zero, they had lost sight of Novaya Zemlya. There was more to come. 'A dreadful day was the 13th October – a Sunday,'[8] Payer wrote. This was the day on which a pressure ridge of ice all but sank the *Tegetthoff*.

'Rushing on deck,' Payer wrote, 'we discovered that we were surrounded and squeezed . . . the after-part of the ship was already nipped and pressed . . . Mountains threateningly reared themselves from out of the level fields of ice, and the low groan which issued from its depths grew into a deep rumbling sound, and at last rose into a furious howl as of myriads of voices. Noise and confusion reigned supreme, and step by step destruction drew nigh.'[9] Here, in a latitude they could not calculate owing to the mist, the current was beating them against an anvil of ice. They had reached Petermann's thermometric gateway and found it closed.

'In all haste we began to make ready to abandon the ship, in case it should be crushed, a fate which seemed inevitable,'[10] Payer wrote. Weyprecht supervised the boats, Payer organized the sledges and the dogs, and other officers took charge of the supplies. What they were going to do with either the boats or the sledges was to Payer a mystery. The sea was a jigsaw of tiny, violent blocks, but nowhere was there a floe the size of the one that had saved the crew of the *Hansa*. A boat, let alone a sledge, would have been swallowed instantly. 'In this very circumstance lay the horror of our situation' Payer wrote. 'For, if the ship should sink, whither should we go, even with the smallest stock of provisions? – amid this confusion, how reach the land thirty miles distant?'[11]

Luckily, they had to do nothing. The nip subsided later in the afternoon and they returned to their quarters. But a second nip came on 14 October, and once again they were all on deck, every man clutching his bundle of necessaries. The boats were loaded with food, ten rifles – Lefaucheur and Werndl – 2,000 cartridges, four sledges, two tents and three enormous, fur-lined sleeping bags capable together of holding the entire crew. The preparations were pointless, for the men had nowhere to go. But, as Payer said, 'we must, for our mutual encouragement, keep up the appearance of believing in them'.[12] Just how pointless he considered them was evident from the random collection of articles he had selected for his own pack: one pair of fur gloves, one pair of woollen gloves, a pair of spectacles against snow-blindness, three notebooks, the journal of his Greenland expedition, a book of drawings, ten ball cartridges, two pairs of stock-ings, a knife, a case of needles and thread, two maps of Novaya Zemlya, six pencils, and a rubber.

The ice calmed on the 17th, and they felt able, for the first time in several days, to remove their clothes before going to bed. While Weyprecht saw that all was shipshape, Payer slipped outside for a last look at the scenery. Even now, in their dangerous situation, he was entranced. The *Tegetthoff* was circumferenced by plains of rumpled, silver ice. And above, in a dark blue sky spotted with clouds, the moon sailed like a freshly minted copper coin.

Their respite was short-lived. Soon afterwards the ice came at them again, and so the alarms continued week after week, month after month. 'Daily – for *one hundred and thirty days* – we went through the same experiences in greater or lesser measure, almost always in sun-less darkness,'[13] Payer wrote. But the *Tegetthoff* held firm. They drifted north-east, their packs at the ready, through Christmas and New Year, through the spring and summer of 1873, the ship accumulating ice until it was sitting in a sizable floe. In July 1873 they tried to measure the floe's thickness with a drill. From the experience of previous expeditions they should have met water after ten feet or so. They bored to the limit of their drill and still encountered ice at twenty-seven feet. In August, as they cast around for seals, or any other kind of fresh meat, the dream of a golden Pole reverted to nightmare. A number of the crew fell ill, and to make life more difficult their floe was threatened by icebergs. The end product of glaciers, icebergs should have alerted Payer to the possibility of land being in the vicinity. But he had become apathetic. Maybe the bergs, like the crew, had drifted north from Novaya Zemlya. 'Not a man among us,' he wrote, 'believed in the possibility of discoveries.'[14] Far more pressing was how to extricate themselves from an apparently hopeless situation. Yet the penultimate day of the month brought a discovery beyond their wildest hopes.

At about midday on 30 August 1873, in latitude 79°43′N, longitude 59°33′E, they were leaning against the bulwarks, staring bleakly into a bank of mist, when suddenly it lifted to the north-east, revealing a range of mountains. By sheer chance, they had drifted towards a new and wholly unknown stretch of land. Was it an island? Was it a peninsula? Was it – *could* it – be part of the Pole itself? Running to the edge of their floe they focused their telescopes. 'We beheld from a ridge of ice the mountains and glaciers of the mysterious land,' Payer wrote. 'Its valleys seemed to our fond imagination clothed with green pastures, over which herds of reindeer roamed in undisturbed enjoyment of their liberty, and far from all foes. For thousands of years this land had lain buried from the knowledge of men, and now its discovery had fallen into the lap of a small band, themselves almost lost to the world.'[15] The *Tegetthoff* was dressed in bunting, grog was made up in an iron coffee pot and to loud hurrahs they christened their find Franz Josef Land. 'All cares, for the present at least, disappeared, and with them the passive monotony of our lives. There was not a day, there was hardly an hour, in which this mysterious land did not henceforth occupy our thoughts and attentions.'[16] Was this or that elevation a headland, or an island, or a glacier? How far did it extend? It seemed to be about sixty miles wide but Payer thought it was probably a lot bigger than that. At last he understood the meaning of the bergs. Their size and number 'were now amply explained – they were indisputable witnesses of [Franz Josef Land's] great extent and its vast glaciation'.[17]

Payer had festered for two years on the *Tegetthoff*, chafing to such an extent that on one occasion Weyprecht had had to threaten him with his revolver. Now he had the chance to do the job for which he had been employed. To his frustration, however, the ice was so broken that neither boats nor sledges had a chance of reaching Franz Josef Land. And then, after so many months drifting north, a wind came up and blew the ship *south*. When the wind turned at the end of September, the *Tegetthoff* resumed its progress north, eventually reaching 79°58', at which point Payer led an expedition to Hochstetter Island – the closest fragment of Franz Josef Land – only to get lost in the mist and return empty-handed. The window for exploration was closing. As winter settled in, the land which had seemed so tantalizingly close became threateningly so. The *Tegetthoff*'s floe broke up as it was beaten repeatedly against the ice besetting Franz Josef Land. On 1 October the distance from the ship to the edge of the floe was 1,300 yards; on 2 October it was 875 yards; and on 6 October it was 200 yards. The *Tegetthoff* splintered under the pressure, sending all men on deck with their bundles. It was like 1872 but worse. 'As we watched the advancing wall of ice, and heard the too well-known howl it sent forth, and saw how fissures were formed at the edge of the floe, the days of the ice-pressures were painfully recalled,' Payer wrote. 'And the thought constantly returned – what will be the end of all this?'[18]

The land he had so longed to visit was visible before him, but the very sight of it had become a torment. It was as unapproachable as ever and if they did reach it, the ship was likely to be broken on the rocks. 'Many were the plans we formed and debated, but all were alike unpracticable, and all owed their existence to the wish to escape from the destruction that stared us in the face.'[19] On 1 November, however, Payer saw a small hope. The *Tegetthoff*'s position had stabilized and the young ice which had formed between ship and shore looked firm enough to support a sledge. Payer left at once. Taking a small team of men and dogs, he climbed a fifty-foot ridge of ice, sledged across the freshly frozen sea and at last stepped onto Franz Josef Land. It was a grim terrain of snow, rocks and broken ice, but as Payer wrote 'to us it was a paradise'.[20] He looked into every rent in the rocks, he touched every block, he was ravished by each crevasse. 'The vegetation was indescribably meagre and miserable [and] the land appeared to be without a single living creature.'[21] No reindeer, no lush pastures. The only perceptible life form was lichen. Yet 'there was something sublime to the imagination in the utter loneliness of a land never before visited; felt all the more from the extraordinary character of our position. We had become exceedingly sensitive to new impressions, and a golden mist, which rose on the southern horizon of an invisible ice-hole, and which spread itself like an undulating curtain before the glow of the noontide heavens, had to us the charms of a landscape in Ceylon.'[22]

An investigative foray was all Payer had time for. Further exploration would have to wait until the spring. They fretted away the months, breaking the monotony with bear hunts, and then on 10 March 1874 (by which time they had killed an impressive total of sixty-seven polar bears) Payer began his overland voyages in earnest. He did so, however, with a sense of fatalism. Throughout the winter their health had deteriorated. Barely eight of the crew were in sound condition. The others suffered from chest complaints, rheumatism and, terrifyingly, scurvy. The worst afflicted was the engineer Otto Krisch, whose diary entries throughout December and January read like a medical casebook: gums swollen and streaked with blood, red spots on hands and feet, pain in the knees and wrists; and day after day, fever, sometimes stabilizing, never improving. But if it was a casebook, it was one like no other, dotted with the rumbling of ice, the shimmering of the Arctic sky and notations of temperature (sub-freezing), wind speed (high) and the hour at which the moon rose (10.00 a.m. for example, on 28 December 1873). On 12 January 1874 Krisch wrote, 'clear, bright weather, severe cold, northern lights above the zenith . . . I can feel nothing but severe pain in my feet and a nameless weakness'.[23] Three days later his entries stopped. In February he rallied to paste a slip of paper into his diary: it was Weyprecht's allocation of men to boats in the event of evacuation; Krisch was to go in the third and last one. From that point his diary remained a blank.

Krisch may have comforted himself that the list was 'in the event of' an evacuation. But the event, unbeknownst to him, had already been decided upon. The ship's store of lemon juice was almost finished and their stock of polar-bear meat – which had done nothing for Krisch – could not last through the summer; nor could their other provisions. There was sufficient to keep them alive until May but in that month the *Tegetthoff* would have to leave Franz Josef Land; and if it could not leave – which was almost a certainty – the men would have to drag their boats south towards open seas. Weyprecht told Payer he could make three expeditions in the months of March and April. He was to survive on what he could carry on his sledge; he could expect no help from the *Tegetthoff*; and if, on returning from his third expedition, he found the ship gone, then he was to head for Europe on his own. Supplies would be left for him.

In Greenland – an expedition so mild that he almost laughed at it now – Payer had been overjoyed at the prospect of virgin territory. 'No more exciting situation can be imagined than that of an explorer in unknown lands,' he had written, 'especially when nature seems to have surrounded [him] with an impenetrable wall, and the earth is as yet untrodden by man.'[24] During the months ahead his enthusiasm sagged. His first journey, with six men, was a preliminary, depot-laying expedition, which lasted only six days. It was time enough, however, for Franz Josef Land to give them a harsh initiation into Arctic travel. In cold that dropped to −59°F their canvas boots turned to stone; their eyelids froze open and shut; fingers and noses became frostbitten. The ever-observant Payer noticed that when a group of men were walking together their breath enveloped them in a cloud of fine ice-needles which rendered them almost invisible. Their progress was accompanied by a curious tinkling noise that he could not explain until he realized it was caused by their frozen exhalations falling to the ground. When, on one odd day, the temperature rose, the effect was magnified by the evaporation of the snow: clear sunlight became a sludgy, yellow-grey dusk and the tinkling turned into a continual hiss. He also noted the clinical effects of intense cold on the human body: he stopped sweating; his nose and eyes ran; he felt an increased urge to urinate and when he did so the urine was bright red; he suffered initially from constipation and then, after a few days, from diarrhoea; his beard became bleached. Josef Pospischill, a stoker from Moravia, was sent back to the ship on the fourth day. He was snow-blind, his hands were frost-bitten, and blood was seeping out of his pores. On the fifth day Payer and the others followed him.

When Pospischill climbed back onto the *Tegetthoff* he was near death. Imagining him to be the sole survivor of some inconceivable disaster, Weyprecht asked him where the others were. Pospischill could not speak, so Weyprecht held his arm out and swivelled him like a weather cock until he pointed in the direction he had come from. Without bothering to put on his furs, Weyprecht ran into the snow. Three and a half hours later he met Payer's team and shep-herded it back to the *Tegetthoff*. The following day, 16 March 1874, one of Payer's two Tyrolean guides, Johann Haller, wrote in his diary: 'This afternoon our machinist Otto Krisch died! God grant him peace rest!'[25] Haller, who with Krisch was one of the few men to keep a regular diary, employed only four exclamation marks in the course of three years. He used two of them on that day.

On 26 March, Payer set out again. With six men and 1,565 pounds of food and equipment, he embarked on a thirty-day grand tour of Franz Josef Land. Disaster hit them on the second day. Having left three men to explore an island, he was leading the other three – among them Alexander Klotz, the Tyrolean guide – across what he christened the Middendorf Glacier. Klotz became frostbitten and so Payer sent him back to the island. His team was thus reduced to two: Midshipman Eduard Orel and Able Seaman Antonio Zaninovich. Halfway across the glacier, Zaninovich fell into a crevasse; with him went all the dogs and their sledge of provisions. Payer's Alpine expe-rience had taught him the necessity of roping a party together. It had not, unfortunately, taught him the dangers of having too heavy a load on one line. 'From an unknown depth,' he wrote, 'I heard a man's voice mingled with the howling of dogs. All this was the impression of a moment, while I felt myself dragged backwards by the rope. Staggering back, and seeing the dark abyss beneath me, I could not doubt that I should be precipitated into it the next instant.'[26] He was at the edge of the crevasse when Zaninovich and the sledge jammed on a ledge thirty feet down. 'I lay on my stomach close to the awful brink, the rope which attached me to the sledge tightly strained, and cutting deep into the snow. The present situation was all the more dreadful as I, the only person present accustomed to the dangers of glaciers, lay there unable to stir ... By and by it flashed into my memory, how I and my guide had once fallen down a wall of ice in the Irtler Mountains, eight hundred feet high, and had escaped. This inspired me with confidence to venture on a rescue, desperate as it seemed under the circumstances.'[27] He called to Orel for a knife and then, hoping that the sledge would remain where it was, he cut the rope. The sledge teetered, did a half turn, and then stuck.

Payer's subsequent acts were of the purest heroism. Throwing off his canvas boots he leaped the crevasse – ten feet wide at that point – told Zaninovich to stay where he was, and then ran to fetch a length of rope from his main party, who were six miles distant. '*Fate Signore*,' Zaninovich called after him. '*Fate pure.*' ('Do it, sir! Do it!') The faster Payer ran, the hotter he became. One by one he dropped his cumbersome protective garments. First to go was a pair of leggings.* Then he tossed aside, in order, his boots, his gloves and his scarf. Soon he was dashing over the ice in his stockings. 'All around me it was fearfully lonely,' he wrote. 'Encompassed by glaciers, I was absolutely alone.'[28] Everything depended on speed, for if a fall of snow should cover his footprints, he would never be able to find his way back in time.

After an hour or so Payer met Klotz. Never the most resourceful of men, Klotz had floundered along in a desultory manner since being

---

* Purchased on his last voyage to Greenland, they were sewn from the skins of birds, the feathers being left on the inside for maximum insulation.

ordered back. He broke down and cried when he heard what had happened, blaming himself for not having been there to help. He was so distressed that he looked as if he might commit suicide. Impatiently, Payer ordered him not to do so, and ran on. When he reached deep snow his run slowed to a wallow. 'It seemed as if I would never reach [my destination]'; he cursed 'with head bent down I trudged on, counting my steps through the deep snow; when I raised it again, after a little time, it was always the same black spot that I saw on the distant horizon.'[29] The black spot, which represented his camp, stayed at the same distance for what felt like hours and then, in a rush, Payer was upon it. Pausing only to drink some water, he grabbed a rope and a pole, and harried the men after him as he sprang off again. 'We ran back for three hours and a half,' he recorded. 'Fears for Zaninovich gave such wings to my steps, that my companions were scarcely able to keep up with me. Ever and anon, I had to stop to drink some rum.'[30] They passed Klotz, and told him to go home. They passed Orel, who had tried to follow his officer only to become mired in snow, and told him to follow them. They passed fragments of Payer's discarded clothing, which he donned piece by piece. And then they reached the crevasse.

'A dark abyss yawned before us; not a sound issued from its depths, not even when I lay on the ground and shouted,'[31] Payer wrote. Then, faintly, he heard a dog whine and Zaninovich's voice telling it to be quiet. Haller, the remaining Tyrolean, was sent down on a rope to bring him up. That done, he went back to retrieve the dogs, who had freed themselves from their traces and were perched on a small ice shelf just above the sledge. Finally, he was lowered to retrieve the contents of the sledge, among them Payer's precious journals which he had kept since the expedition left Bremerhaven. When the operation ended, Zaninovich, the dogs, the sledge and its contents stood unharmed on the glacier. It was a miracle, and Payer celebrated it by broaching the rum from the sledge. As he passed around the mugs he couldn't help noticing that the bottle was a lot emptier than it had been when packed. Zaninovich approached him nervously. Did the Lieutenant mind, he asked, but he'd already had a few tots while dying in the crevasse. Not a bit, Payer told him. Dutch courage was what they all needed. Because they were carrying on.

Payer and his men slogged across glaciers, scrambled through fields of rock and climbed mountains that were now 1,000-feet and then 3,000-feet high. They charted glacier after peak after bay and on 12 April they reached their farthest north. At 82°5′, they stood on a 1,000-foot promontory from which they spotted a far-off cape – Cape Sherard Osborn – and further off still, a blue shadow of mountains which they called Petermann Land. From their position Payer could see open water. Seabirds flocked about him; seals slopped in and out of the sea. Unlike Kane or Hayes, however, he refused to countenance an Open Polar Sea. 'Notwithstanding these signs of animal life, we should not be justified in inferring, from what we saw in a single locality, that life increases as we move northwards. It was a venial exaggeration, if amid such impressions, we pronounced for the nearness of an open Polar sea . . . In enumerating these observations, I am conscious of what attractions they must have for every one who still leans to the opinion that an open ocean will be found at the Pole: subsequent experience, however, will show how little is their value in support of this antiquated hypothesis.'[32]

They built a cairn and left a message in a bottle to tell future explorers that the Austro-Hungarian Empire had got there first. The message, signed by Payer, Orel and Zaninovich, also carried a warning. 'After their return to the ship, it is the intention of the whole crew to leave this land and return home. The hopeless condition of the ship and the numerous cases of sickness constrain them to this step.'[33] Payer led his men 180 miles across slushy snow and creaky ice to the *Tegetthoff* and then, after a short rest, took them out again on his third and final journey. He surveyed an island which he named McClintock, after the most tenacious sledger in the Franklin search, and only then did he submit to Weyprecht's command. The *Tegetthoff* was marooned but it was still, in naval terms, afloat.

On 20 May Weyprecht put his men in harness. There, he said, pointing across the ice, lay Novaya Zemlya. They were going to drag their three boats – massive Norwegian whaling boats, complete with masts and sails – laden with 4,000 pounds of supplies towards it. The distance was approximately 400 miles. It was time to leave.

Probably – almost certainly, in fact – the crew cannot have understood the magnitude of the task ahead of them. If they had it is equally probable that they would have chosen to stay behind and die on the *Tegetthoff*. The boats were so heavy that it took their combined efforts to drag just one at a time. The ice was slushy and sometimes they sank up to their waists before finding a solid foothold. On occasion they had to hack their way through ridges with pickaxes and shovels, only to find after a week's work that the ice had shifted, destroying the path they had so painstakingly made. Gaps opened, forcing them to launch the boats and then, after a few strokes of the oars, haul them onto the next floe. And every obstacle had to be overcome not once but thrice, every distance covered five times. After two months of misery they were no more than nine miles from where they had started.

Weyprecht was an inspiring commander. Whenever the men grumbled he drove them on with blasts of optimism. They *would* succeed, he repeated. They *would* find open seas. They *would* reach Novaya Zemlya and there, he was certain, they *would* find ships of some nationality or other. If there were no ships then they would sail for Spitsbergen, even if it meant spending a third winter in the ice. The depot Wilczek had left on the Barents Islands contained enough food to see them the 1,000-odd miles to Norway if necessary. They *would* get home alive.

Privately, however, Weyprecht believed that they wouldn't. He did not tell the men, but the ice was travelling north almost as fast as they struggled south. In his top pocket he kept a small notebook. It was titled '*Ruckzugstagebuch*', 'Journal of Retreat', and in it he wrote in pencil: 'Every lost day is not a nail but a whole plank in our coffin . . . Dragging the sledges across the ice is only a bluff, for the few miles we gain are of no importance to our purpose. The slightest breeze moves us about in random directions far more than the most exhausting day of labour . . . I put on an unconcerned face to all this, but I am very much aware that we are probably lost if conditions do not change radically . . . I am often amazed at myself, at my own calm when viewing the future. I sometimes feel as if I were not involved at all. I have resolved what I shall do if worse comes to worst, which is why I am so calm. But the fate of the sailors lies heavy on my heart.'[34] The resolution of which Weyprecht spoke had been reached by all the officers before leaving the *Tegetthoff*: if their position became hopeless they would shoot themselves, having first advised the crew to commit suicide too. Not for men of the Imperial Austrian Navy a lingering collapse into scurvy and cannibalism, as had happened to Franklin's expedition. But, bearing Franklin in mind, Weyprecht thought it important that someone find his record of their final days; he did not want to leave a mess for posterity. 'All my thoughts and plans are now directed at depositing my journals in such a fashion that they will be found in future years.'[35]

Such fine thoughts deserved a plaque, but there was nowhere to place such a plaque, just as there was nowhere to deposit Weyprecht's journals. They were surrounded by millions of acres of blank ice. The summer of 1874 was unusually warm, and as they hauled their boats across ever-deeper sludge and ever-wider leads, the physical and mental pressures destroyed Weyprecht's plans for an honourable end. The crew started to fight among themselves. Then they fought with the officers. Finally, the officers fought with each other. 'Payer, is once again so charged with rage that I am prepared for some serious collision at any moment', Weyprecht scribbled. 'In front of the men he made offensive remarks to me about some trivial matter . . . which I could not let pass without reprimand. I told him that in future he should be careful not to use such expressions . . . He then went into one of his rages, said that he still remembered clearly how I had threatened him with a revolver a year ago, assuring me he would steal the march on me next time and declaring outright that he would try to kill me the moment he saw he might not make it home.'[36] Weyprecht's notebook could have been Franklin's or Crozier's, and its tale of disintegration might have continued to the last, empty page were it not for the warm summer. The same weather which had given them poor dragging conditions had also opened the ice. In mid-August, without warning, they hit open water.

'There lay the Open Ocean before us,' ran Payer's journal. 'Never were its sparkling waves beheld with more sincere joy . . . the 15th of August was the day of our liberation – the festival of the Assumption of the Virgin – and our boats were dressed with flags in its commemoration.'[37] They had to row, because there was no wind. That did not bother them – or it did not bother Payer, who sat at the helm: 'With boundless satisfaction,' he wrote, 'we saw the white edge of the ice gradually become a line and at last disappear.'[38] Weyprecht allowed them no pause. From the 15th to the 16th they worked at the oars non-stop. On the 16th they sighted Novaya Zemlya, and were given a few seconds' rest for a cheer. Then it was back to the oars. On 17 August, in mist, they rowed past Wilczek's depot unawares. On 18 August – Kaiser Franz Josef's birthday – they pulled into a bay. It was a comforting place, grassy, mossy and with even a few forget-me-nots poking out. But the ships Weyprecht had promised were nowhere in sight. On they went again. 'The inaccessibility of most places on the coast . . . obliged us to continue our course without going onshore to rest,' wrote Payer, 'although our arms were stiff and swollen with our exertions in rowing.'[39] They searched in vain for a ship but saw only icebergs. 'Stormy weather came up, exhausting our strength and separating our boats, which were taking on so much water the crews had constantly to bail . . . We rowed on mechanically through the endless flood, towards the secret of how this would all end.'[40]

On 24 August the secret became apparent. After ten days of almost constant rowing the *Tegetthoff*'s crew came into view of two Russian whalers, the *Vasily* and the *Nicolai*. Weyprecht went aboard the *Nicolai* and presented its captain, Feodor Valentin, with a letter of safe-conduct with which he had been issued three years previously. Tsar Alexander II, it read, expects all Russian subjects to give aid to the Austro-Hungarian North Polar Expedition. The sailors stood to attention, as Weyprecht's emaciated band climbed the ladder. The journey was over.

The *Nicolai* took the survivors to Norway (at a cost of 1,200 silver roubles) from where they caught a mail ship to Germany, arriving at dusk in the busy, industrial port of Hamburg. The last time Payer had returned from a major Arctic expedition he had been greeted by sombre gloom. This time, however, he and his companions were received as heroes. Clusters of rockets burst into the sky, the piers were decked with lights, crowds yelled and cheered their welcome. Ships sounded their foghorns in a thunderous blast of triumph. There were flags and banners and speeches, all the way from the dock to the railway station, where a special train awaited, garlanded with branches, flowers and yet more flags and banners, to carry them to Vienna.

In Vienna itself, the welcome was even more tumultuous. 'Again and again,' wrote the *Neue Freie Presse*, 'new waves of cheers and hurrahs washed over the carriage in which the two leaders sat. It had been hung with several large laurel wreaths presented to the North Pole travellers during the journey to Vienna. Flowers were tossed into the carriages by the ladies, and both leaders and crew seemed equally amazed at this spontaneous eruption of joy and sympathy from the Viennese. The carriage could make its way only step by step from North Station onto Jagerzeile. The crowd threw itself into the path of the horses and would not allow the carriage to advance. An ever-growing sea of hundreds of thousands stood waiting for them all the way to the heart of the city and parted only very slowly. The streets were black with the throngs, every window in every building was occupied, cheers and waving handkerchiefs greeted them on all sides. At several points the moving crowds were indeed a danger to life and limb. It would be no exaggeration to estimate those taking part in the reception at a quarter-million.'[41]

Down Praterstrasse, across Aspern Bridge to Stuben Gate, through Wollzile, Rothenthurmstrasse, Stephansplatz, the Graben, Bognergrasse and the Hoff, rode Weyprecht and Payer, away from the broad outer rings and into the narrow heart of the old city where the crowds were packed even tighter and balconies swayed under the weight of spectators. At the Roman Kaiser Hotel, where rooms awaited the officers, there were speeches, banquets, presentations of medals, and a visit from Franz Josef himself. At the Dreher Beer Hall on Hauptstrasse, whose proprietor Herr Ott had offered free bed and board to the crew, celebrations were raucous.

Weyprecht and Payer were gratified by the honours but slightly puzzled. What had they done to deserve them? They had discovered a new land, put the Emperor's name on the atlas (it is still there, in Russian, as Zemlya Frantsa-Iosifa) and had made a contribution to science in their analysis of polar currents. They had also alerted Britain and the US to the fact that the Arctic was not their exclusive suzerainty. But they had lost their ship and failed to find the Pole. Franz Josef Land was, by Payer's estimate, a group of islands no bigger than Spitsbergen, containing neither human nor animal life. It did not lead to the North Pole, and neither did the Gulf Stream. There was no thermometric gateway and Petermann's theories were wrong.

So damning were their findings that Petermann withdrew the opinions he had held so vehemently for more than twenty years and proffered an olive branch to his foe, Sherard Osborn. 'It is fortunate for science that the North Pole has not yet been reached,' he wrote to Britain's Royal Society in 1874. 'So, why insist on one way if there are so many ways? They all lead in the end to the one goal that really matters: better knowledge of the Arctic regions.'[42]

There are few instances in Arctic history where a successful voyage ended so dismally. Petermann went into clinical depression and committed suicide on 25 September 1878. Weyprecht caught tuberculosis, and spent the rest of his life railing against the futility of finding the Pole. 'I have never been seasick,' he reportedly told one audience, 'but it might easily happen if I have to listen to any more balderdash about my achievements, about my immortality. Immortal! With this cough?' He was buried in König, Germany, on 31 March 1881. Payer handed in his commission and fled to Paris, where he remarried, became an artist, and painted larger and larger pictures of Arctic tragedy until his death in 1915.

What had disaffected the two commanders? What had disappointed them to the extent that despite a Viennese craze for Payer coats and Weyprecht cravats, they never considered another expedition to the

Pole? The answer lay partly in Weyprecht's *Journal of Retreat*, and partly in the fact that, apart from the Arctic fraternity, few people outside Austria and Germany gave them credit for what they had done. The English-language press noted their achievement but treated it as a side-show: something to be lauded, something to be built upon – as it would be – but not *really* worth attention when set against expeditions such as Hall's through Smith Sound. Predominantly, however, both men were dismayed by the nature of the quest they had undertaken: so much remained to be done; so dubious was the value of the goal. During the voyage, Payer had attempted to lecture the crew in Arctic geography. All went well until he came to the subject of the Pole itself. There, with his blackboard and pointer, barely visible through the condensation of his pupils' breath, he faltered. 'After many painful disillusions,' he wrote, 'the Pole was ascertained to be the intersection of lines in a point, of which nothing was to be seen in reality.'[43]

Weyprecht put it more poetically. 'Here below stand we poor men, and speak of knowledge and progress, and pride ourselves on the understanding with which we extort from Nature her mysteries. We stand and gaze on the mystery which Nature has written for us in flaming letters on the dark vault of night, and ultimately, we can only wonder and confess that, in truth, we know nothing of it.'[44]

9

THE VOYAGE OF THE *POLARIS*

'Glorious is the prospect of the future!'[1] With these words, on 3 July 1871, Charles Francis Hall signed off his last letter to shore before the *Polaris* left America. It was a characteristically ebullient statement. It was also a typically hasty one. Seven days later, his Assistant Navigator, George Tyson, wrote a more sober and, as it turned out, more accurate assessment. 'I see there is not perfect harmony between Captain Hall and the Scientific Corps, nor with some others either. I am afraid things will not work well.'[2]

The friction began with Hall and Emil Bessels, his chief scientific officer. A highly regarded graduate from Heidelberg University, Bessels was a zoologist, entomologist and surgeon – also a friend and protégé of August Petermann. He was slight, with thick, dark hair, a heavy beard and a romantically haunted expression. One female contemporary, obviously impressed, wrote of his 'bright, dark eye, which was susceptible of very varied expression'. He would, she decided, 'pass for a handsome man, built on rather too small a scale'.[3] Hall was less smitten. He hadn't really wanted Bessels to come aboard, fearing that he would spend too much time on scientific observation and not enough on geographical discovery. He had accepted him reluctantly on the urging of Joseph Henry, President of the National Academy of Science, who described him as 'a sensitive man',[4] and had advised Hall to be gentle with him. Bessels, meanwhile, thought Hall an ill-educated, unprofessional amateur. His aims were purely scientific – as Hall rightly deduced – and he had been ordered in no uncertain terms to bring back accurate measurements of everything he encountered.

Already bedevilled by charges of inaccuracy, Hall was jumpy about having scientists on his ship. Before leaving he had tried to anticipate criticisms that he would not know when he got to the Pole, even if he should reach it, with spur-of-the-moment theories. 'On reaching the point called the North Pole, the north star will be directly overhead,' he wrote. 'Without an instrument, with merely the eye, a man can define his position when there. Some astronomers tell me I will find a difficulty in determining my position. It will be the easiest thing in the world.'[5]

It may have been easy – nobody knew for sure – but the United States Government was not risking it. Bearing in mind the disputed findings of Kane and Hayes, it wanted Hall's progress to be logged as thoroughly as was practicable. Bessels's orders instructed him to make four astronomical observations a day, repeated three times against mistakes. He was told to watch the aurora borealis, to make pendulum experiments to determine the forces of gravity in different latitudes, and to record the variation and dip of needles. He was to measure the tides, currents, soundings, bottom-dredging and density of sea water. He was to register temperature, air pressure, humidity, wind velocity, rainfall, the form and weight of hailstones, the character of snow, the speed of glaciers, the frequency of meteors, the presence of ozone, and 'electricity in all its multiform developments'.[6] When putting his observations on paper, he was to do so with complete transparency. 'The evidence of the genuineness of the observations brought back should be of the most irrefragable character,' his orders stated. 'No erasures whatsoever with rubber or knife should be made. When an entry requires correction, the figures or words should be merely crossed by a line, and the correct figures written above.'[7]

Naturally, Bessels could not do all this work himself. Hall, however, had commandeered the meteorologist, Frederick Meyer, to keep the ship's official journal. When Meyer protested (presumably on Bessels's instigation), an angry exchange ensued. Meyer said he had his orders, Hall said he had his. Meyer threatened to resign. Hall said he would not accept it. Then Bessels joined the argument and said that Meyer could go if he wanted to and that if he left the ship so would he and he would take all the German crew with him. A compromise was eventually reached, whereby Meyer continued with the journal for a short time before being replaced by one of the crew. The price, however, was recorded in Hall's orders where, on page six, was the following sentence: 'All persons attached to the expedition are under your command, and shall, under every circumstance and condition, be subject to the rules, regulations, and laws concerning the discipline of the Navy.'[8] (The underlining is Hall's.) Next to it, in Hall's handwriting but signed by Frederick Meyer, was an agreement to abide by this order. It was a bad compromise, one that did not resolve the problem but merely defined and deferred it. For the rest of the voyage the *Polaris* would be split between scientists and explorers, between Germans and Americans.

One can sympathize with Hall. A man who had done all his best work on his own, he was now in command of nineteen men, a role for which he had neither training nor experience. The orders which gave him absolute control as an explorer also demanded specific results from Bessels as a scientist. Without a clear priority of objectives, there was bound to be discord. But one can equally sympathize with the institutions that issued those orders. They had assumed Hall and his scientists would work towards the same goal. Reacting to his fervour, his proven expertise, and a deluge of influential pressures, they had imposed conditions which would have been delightful – well, acceptable – to his competitor Hayes. They hoped that Hall would be like previous commanders, not recognizing that his success stemmed from the fact that he was a loner. Most importantly, they had not made allowance for Hall's choice of officers.

Hall knew his limits and in compensation he had hired what amounted to three captains to serve beneath him. Budington, Chester and Tyson had all led ships into the Arctic and were all expert ice men. Budington was Hall's favourite; not only was he in charge of the ship's day-to-day navigation but in the event of Hall's death or incapacity he was to be his successor. Budington was a capable commander, even if he and Hall had had their differences, and as such should have been able to win the respect of his two subordinate captains. But Budington was a whaler, not an explorer. He did not care about the North Pole, and had no incentive to find it. Nor was he happy with the concept of naval discipline. He stole food from the lockers and filched wine from Hall's private store. Tyson and Chester, already in a dangerous limbo, began to feel that they could do the job much better. By the time the *Polaris* reached Disco Island, on the west coast of Greenland, the ship's executive officers were as divided as the rest of the crew. Hall then hired Hans, the Cape York Eskimo who had worked with Kane and Hayes. Hans came aboard with his wife and three children, thus creating a substratum of distrust between the 'tame' Eskimos, Tookolito and Ebierbing, and the 'wild' ones.

In terms of personnel, Hall's selection was disastrous. Although he would never have admitted it openly, he was out of his depth. He had a premonition that he might not return alive. With him he had brought the journals of his last expedition which he hoped to knock into shape during the current voyage. When Tyson inquired how things were going, Hall said he had left the papers at Disco Island. 'A sort of gloom seemed to spread over his face,' Tyson recorded, 'as if the recollection of something with which they were associated made him uncomfortable, and presently, without raising his head, he added, "I left them there for safety." I saw the subject was not pleasant, and I made no further remark; but I could not help thinking it over.'9

The Arctic, Hall's old and fickle friend, came to his rescue. Conditions were extraordinarily mild that year. In record time, the *Polaris* swept through Smith Sound, passed Cape Alexander without a bother, and by 27 August was at Kane's old quarters. On the 28th they were sailing up a one- to four-mile-wide channel in the ice off the coast of Grinnell Land. At 80°N Budington wanted to stop. With open water ahead, Hall saw no reason for doing so. Neither did Tyson:

'Out on such cowards, I say!'[10] Later that day they passed 81°35'. *'Can't make any thing out of the charts,'*[11] Tyson wrote excitedly. By the evening they had passed Kane's (or Morton's) farthest point north and were in unexplored territory. To the west was a strait which seemed to separate Grinnell Land from another block of land to the north, while to the east a massive fjord (or was it, too, a strait?) appeared to do the same for Greenland. These new territories entered the charts respectively as Grant Land (part of modern Ellesmere Island) and Hall Land; the body of water between them was christened Robeson Channel. Sailing up the coast of Hall Land, Budington urged his commander even more strongly to halt. Tyson dismissed 'these puerile fears'[12] mockingly. 'I see some rueful countenances. I believe some of them think we are going to sail off the edge of the world, or into "Symmes's Hole". But so far we see no worse [ice] than I have seen scores of times in Melville Bay.'[13] Apparently Hall agreed, for on 2 September they reached their northernmost point, 82°16'. Tyson and Chester were all for pressing on; they thought another two or three degrees were entirely feasible. Budington refused and this time he was not going to be gainsaid. Hall did not know what to do. 'He appears to be afraid of offending some one,' Tyson wrote. 'I don't speak my mind; it might be misapprehended and mistaken for self-interest. God knows I care more for the success of the expedition than I do for myself. But I see it's all up, and here we stop.'[14] The 'here' to which he referred was some fifty miles south of their northernmost point, the current having carried them down Hall Land while they argued. There was talk of sailing west to find a winter harbour on Grant Land, 'but the sailing master declared [the ship] should not move from there, and so Captain Hall gave up'.[15] Thus, at 81°38'N, they settled down for the winter in a Hall Land bay measuring twelve miles long by nine wide.

It had been a phenomenally successful season. They had come farther than any previous expedition through Smith Sound. They had charted the area with absolute precision, discovering, thanks to Bessels's observations, that both Hayes and Morton had exaggerated their farthest norths. They had found two new lands which might

well form part of an archipelago reaching to the Pole. They had sub-
stantiated Hayes's claims that a navigable channel existed, if not that
it led to an Open Polar Sea. They had done it all with little sign of bad
weather, and with no physical discomfort or illness. Even the personality clashes seemed to have been forgotten: Bessels, who had shown
exemplary devotion to his duties and to the endeavour as a whole, was
considered an excellent sort; Budington, now that they were safely
anchored, stopped fretting; and when Hall made a speech to say how
well they had all borne up, the crew composed a letter in which they
avowed their confidence and support. Hall replied paternally: 'I need
not assure you that your commander has, and ever will have, a lively
interest in your welfare. 'You have left your homes, friends, and country;
indeed, you have bid a long farewell for a time to the whole civilized
world, for the purpose of aiding me in discovering the mysterious,
hidden parts of the earth. I therefore must and shall care for you as
a prudent father cares for his faithful children. Your Commander,
C. F. Hall.'[16]

What Commander C. F. Hall was feeling when he wrote those
words is lost. Neither he nor his diary survived the voyage. The documentary evidence of the *Polaris* is confined to a few of Hall's letters,
Tyson's journal (written from memory, to his advantage) and statements made by Budington, Chester, Tyson and others on their return.
But an indication of Hall's emotions can be gauged from contemporary
maps. They show Grant Land and Hall Land, separated (wrongly)
from their southern land masses by Lady Franklin Strait and Southern
Fjord. Just above Southern Fjord, on Greenland's west coast, is Polaris
Bay where the expedition wintered. Here, plainly marked at 81°38'N,
61°44'W, is Hall's fear at being so far north, his nervousness at being
in command and his relief at having hopefully settled the disputes
between his three captains. The name reads, 'Thank God Harbour'.

Before leaving Greenland for Smith Sound, Hall had warned his
crew that he would not tolerate any further disobedience and that he
would, 'if necessary die in the performance of his duty as a commander rather than yield a letter'.[17] Perhaps, looking back on it, he felt his
language had been too strong: apart from Budington's continuing

surliness everything else seemed to be proceeding amicably. Perhaps, however, there were others who took his statement at face value and who did not believe, as Hall did, that 'we behold the glory of thy power in this place so long secluded from the gaze of civilized man.'[18] For such as these the coming winter must have been a trial.

Hall sent out a sledge party to explore the surrounding terrain – with woeful results. Three men almost died on a nine-hour journey during which they scaled high hummocks, waded through deep snow and fell, repeatedly, through the ice before lurching back to the *Polaris* with one of the party missing. The lost man was rescued, reeling like a drunkard, and brought back to the ship. He arrived about the same time as his companions were themselves emerging from near coma. 'Captain,' one of them mumbled, 'travelling – in – this – country – is – very – discouraging.'[19] It *was* discouraging, as Hall well knew, so he led the next sledge party himself, taking Hans and Chester with him. He would have taken Tyson (according to Tyson) but was reluctant to leave Budington on his own. 'I do not trust that man,' he told Tyson. 'I want you to go with me, but I don't know how to leave him on the ship.'[20]

Whether Hall did say those exact words is uncertain. Tyson's journal was written from memory and in circumstances stranger than most. They may have been just a dramatic flourish, invented to enliven an already lively story. Even a novice commander like Hall would have known not to risk the expedition's stability by taking sides. And if he did not trust Budington all he had to do was replace him with Tyson or Chester – for was he not, as he had underlined in his orders, in absolute authority? But if Hall *did* say those words, or (allowing for Tyson's recall) something similarly paranoid and disruptive, it reveals more about his state of mind than about divisions within the ship's company. He was not a healthy man. The pains down one side of the body, for example, which he had ascribed on his earlier voyages to writing a journal huddled up in an igloo, may have been caused by a minor stroke. The physical results of a stroke can be so minimal that a sufferer puts them down to other causes. The same sufferer can be oblivious of any mental aberrations –

hallucinations, paranoia, absent-mindedness are common – and will carry on as if in command of all faculties. Possibly another small clot had lodged in the arteries leading to Hall's brain.

Hall and his sledgers departed on 10 October. On 11 October he sent Hans back for a few things he had left behind. The few things ran to a list of seventeen articles, amongst which were their sealskin outfits, fur gloves, the stove for melting water, his chronometer and the dogs' spare traces. He had forgotten virtually everything they needed to survive the trip, including the chronometer, the one instrument with which he could accurately determine his position. It was a staggering display of mismanagement, explicable only by confusion as to who had packed what – or by Hall's failing mind.

Hall came back two weeks later, on 24 October, having climbed a hill from whose summit he was able to confirm what he already knew – that Grant Land and Robeson Channel existed – and with the news that yet more daring exploits were to be ventured in the spring. He was weak. He told Chester that he had been unable to keep up with the dogs – something which surprised him – and had felt so bad the last three days that he had had to sit on the sledge. The first thing he asked for was a mug of coffee, which he was given and which he drank. 'I can go to the Pole, I think, on this shore,'[21] he said. Almost immediately he was violently sick.

Nobody was particularly worried. Hall was tired, he was under stress, and he had just experienced an 80° change in temperature coming into the hot cabin after a fortnight of freezing weather. It was enough to make anyone feel ill. Anyway, Hall had a notoriously bad stomach; he was constantly reaching for a bottle of peppermint oil to soothe his attacks of dyspepsia. There was nothing wrong with the coffee – several people had drunk from the same pot with no ill effects. What they did not consider was that Hall may have had a heart attack. One symptom of a mild heart attack is weakness and sudden, inexplicable vomiting. But such a diagnosis would have seemed alarmist, even if it had been put forward, which it wasn't. No, Hall was fine and a night's sleep would get him back to normal.

Unfortunately Hall was no better the following morning – if

anything he felt worse. As the days passed he began to rave deliriously. He claimed that the coffee had been poisoned – it had tasted unpleasantly sweet and had burned his stomach, he said. He refused to eat or drink anything unless it had first been sampled in his presence. Dr Bessels gave him doses for his stomach and administered daily injections of quinine to reduce his fever. They had no effect. 'The little German dancing master,'[22] as Hall called Bessels, was trying to kill him. He could see poisonous blue vapours whirling around his body. Budington offered to sample the medicine first, but Hall refused. They all wanted to murder him, every single one of them, he raved. No one was exempt from his accusations. Even Tyson, his erstwhile confidant, was damned. Hall became thirsty and asked continually for water. For two days he forbade anyone to come near him save Tookolito, the only person he now trusted. It seemed to work, for on 1 November he was back at his desk trying to complete his journal. 'But he don't act like himself,' Tyson wrote. 'He begins a thing, and don't finish it. He begins to talk about one thing, then goes off on to something else. His disease has been pronounced paralysis and also apoplexy.'[23] In Arctic history, Tyson could recall only one case of apoplexy (the nineteenth-century word for a stroke) and it had occurred decades ago. 'I always thought that might have been heart disease,'[24] he added.

On 3 November Hall was ranting in his bunk again. In moments of lucidity he urged Tyson to continue the struggle. 'If I die, you must still go on to the Pole.'[25] Two days later he was partially paralysed. 'This is dreadful,'[26] Tyson wrote. They took it in turns to watch over him. On the night of 8 November 1871 Chester told Budington that Hall was dying. Budington found Hall sitting on the edge of his bunk, feet dangling and eyes glassy, trying to spell the word 'murder'. He called Tyson to Hall's bedside. 'I got up immediately and went to the cabin and looked at him. He was quite unconscious – knew nothing. He lay on his face, and was breathing very heavily; his face was hid in the pillow. It was about half-past three o'clock in the morning that he died.'[27]

Tyson led a burial detail that night to a spot half-a-mile inland where with pickaxes they hacked a shallow hole. At 11.00 the next morning, by the light of Tyson's lamp, Hall's flag-shrouded coffin was dragged to the grave, the whole crew following in cortège through the Arctic night. 'Thus end poor Hall's ambitious projects; thus is stilled the effervescing enthusiasm of as ardent a nature as I ever knew,' Tyson wrote. 'Wise, he might not always have been, but his soul was in this work, and had he lived till spring, I think he would have gone as far as mortal man could go to accomplish his mission. But with his death I fear that all hopes of further progress will have to be abandoned.'[28]

There was little grief amongst the other officers. 'There's a stone off my heart,'[29] Budington announced. 'We are all right now . . . you shan't be starved to death now.'[30] Frederick Meyer also thought they would be better off with Hall out of the way. According to Midshipman Noah Hayes (no relation of the other Hayes), Bessels laughed, saying Hall's death 'was the best thing that could have happened to the expedition'.[31] Below decks, where Hans and his family were sequestered, somebody crept down and told them not to be fearful: a new father would take charge and lead them home safely.

The strange circumstances surrounding Hall's death became the subject of an inquiry by the Secretary of the US Navy. The board decided that Hall had died of a stroke. Paralysis, slurred speech, delirium – all the evidence pointed that way. One puzzling symptom, fever, did not fit. But without an autopsy there was no telling what else Hall might have suffered from. Maybe he had pneumonia, bronchitis or another infection. Apoplexy was the verdict of history books for almost one hundred years.

In 1968, however, an author named Chauncey Loomis was working on a biography of Hall. He asked permission to exhume the body and test it for poison. Taking a plane to Greenland he dug up the grave. Hall's body was eerily well preserved; the hair was there, as was the beard, the skin was more or less intact and so were the fingernails. When Loomis returned from his mission he sent several slivers of fingernail to be analysed by Toronto's Centre for Forensic Medicine. The findings were startling: Hall may have died from a stroke but he had also been poisoned. In the last two weeks of his life he had ingested toxic quantities of arsenic.

The symptoms of arsenic poisoning are very like those of a stroke – weakness, paralysis, vomiting and sometimes mania. Arsenic tastes sweet and causes a burning sensation in the stomach. The victim has an erratic pulse, vomits and becomes dehydrated – leading to intense thirst. Hall had exhibited every one of these symptoms. But if Hall had been poisoned, the question remained, who had done it?

Was it Budington? The two men had fallen out in the past, and by Tyson's evidence there were signs that they had fallen out again – or, at least, not seen eye to eye. Budington seemed fearful at being so far north and had balked at suggestions that they go further. He had no heart for the trip and had disgraced himself with his pilfering. With Hall out of the way he was in command and could take the *Polaris* home without any shame being attached – indeed, the orders had all but instructed him to do so. Was it Meyer? He had already quarrelled with Hall, and had a low opinion of his egalitarian treatment of the crew – Hall had ordered him, an officer, to be served the same food as the men. Was it Bessels? Like Meyer he had quarrelled with Hall; he looked down on him as an inferior being, unfit to lead a scientific expedition. As the ship's doctor, he had been in constant attendance upon Hall during his illness; it would have been easy enough to poison him by subterfuge – those 'quinine' injections, for example – and the one time Hall rallied was when he refused to let Bessels treat him.

Murder by poisoning was a Victorian speciality and poisoning by arsenic was the most common variant. There are scores of case histories, each of which devolve without exception into a minute study of what the deceased ate or drank and who gave it to him, before probing the motives of the suspect wife or girlfriend – for it was believed to be predominantly a female crime. In Hall's case, however, it is hard to say precisely what he ingested and even more difficult to clarify the movements and motives of the three main suspects, Bessels, Budington and Meyer.

Meyer had no opportunity to keep feeding Hall the arsenic, so was probably innocent. Budington did have the opportunity, being one of

Hall's main carers. But he had offered to taste Hall's food to show it wasn't poisoned and if he wanted to go home that badly his subsequent actions were out of character because he did at one point state his intention to take a sledge party north – though that might have been a bluff. Bessels could have done it – but why? Out of the three suspects he was the one who most wanted to reach the Pole and by all accounts he and Hall had settled their differences. Bessels had more to lose than anybody from Hall's death.

Had a trial been held in court, the prosecution might have pointed to Hall's orders, which said that Budington was to assume command in the event of his death, but that he was to share leadership with Bessels. If he and Bessels disagreed as to the possibility of continuing north Budington was to take absolute charge and bring the *Polaris* home. Budington's later actions could be attributed to self-interest. He may have given the impression of wanting to go north but he never did so and took the ship south as soon as he could. The prosecution would also have noted that during the period in which Hall recovered, he refused to see Budington as well as Bessels. Budington's offer to taste Hall's food might have been a ploy to conceal a later sprinkling of arsenic. Who was to tell if Budington and Bessels had not collaborated? Bessels wanted to reach the Pole. Had he wanted it so badly that he was willing to persuade Budington that with Hall dead they could take joint credit for the Pole? This would explain why Budington did not go home immediately – but then caution had prevailed and he had taken the *Polaris* south.

The defence would then have raised the possibility of Hall having taken the arsenic himself. Arsenic poisoning was commonplace because arsenic was so freely available. It was used for killing rats but it was also a medicine, whose many uses included the settling of unruly stomachs. Some people took it so often that they became habituated. There would have been arsenic crystals aboard the *Polaris* – it contained rats, like any other ship – and there would have been distillations of arsenic in Bessels's cabinet. But Hall had his own medicine chest, which would also have contained arsenic. Could he have dosed himself?

There is no clear answer. If Hall had been murdered, the prime suspect, according to Loomis, was Bessels. He had the means, the opportunity and the expertise to administer fatal quantities of arsenic to a man he disliked. For normal people in normal circumstances, personal antipathy might not be a compelling motive to murder. But Bessells was highly-strung – contemporary pictures and descriptions suggest a more-than-Romantic wildness. Moreover, the conditions in which he operated were as extreme as it is possible to imagine. Bessels's journal, published in Germany, reveals nothing. It is a dry, factual account which makes only passing reference to Hall's death and is concerned mostly with its author's scientific findings. But its respectability does not guarantee innocence. After so many years it is hard to draw any conclusion from the evidence available, and yet a hint of something dubious is evident in the subsequent evasions and contradictions of all parties concerned. If there is a finger to be pointed, it probably points at Bessels.

In America, a suspicious Board of Inquiry took evidence from all parties. Nobody emerged guilty, but nobody emerged spotless either. In the absence of a coroner's court, apoplexy was accepted as the cause of Hall's death. By the time Loomis performed his necessarily limited autopsy all the participants were dead, and so the death of Charles Francis Hall became one more of those weird tragedies which dot Arctic history. Had there been similar crimes in the past – if crime had been committed – and had they been passed off as death by natural causes or accident? British and European Arctic journals are phlegmatic, business-like affairs from which personal details have to be winkled with a pin. American journals – to generalize – contain more popular tales which dwell on the dangers and the heroism of those involved. All were written in the shadow of watchful superiors or an expectant public and were therefore, to an extent, whitewashed. The fragmented accounts of the *Polaris* expedition reveal how thin the whitewash was. They reveal a world of dispute and dislocation. If Hall *had* been murdered there was no reason for it – by rational standards. But as historians have pointed out, rationality had no place in the Arctic. 'I am utterly disgusted with writing and with what I have written,' Noah Hayes said on his return. 'I believe that no man can retain the use of his faculties through one long [Arctic] night . . . for all that he may say and do.'[32]

Hall died at the start of that long night. His successors had to live through the rest of it – and they fared badly.

'No cap'n; nobody cap'n. Cap'n Budington, he cap'n. Captain Tyson, he cap'n. Doctor, he cap'n too. Mr. Chester cap'n. Mr Meyer, cap'n; me cap'n; everybody cap'n – no good.'[33] Ebierbing had the measure of things.

After Hall's death discipline fell apart. Budington's captaincy was confused and erratic. He discontinued Sunday prayers, which in Hall's time had clocked the weeks like a metronome. He issued revolvers and other firearms to every man on board. He raided Bessels's locked cupboard of pickling spirits, and when Bessels objected (the two men came to blows) he had the engineer make spare keys so that the other officers could get in. Then the crew discovered they could break into the store by crawling through the engine shaft. The resulting bouts of drunkenness were dreadful; but as the astronomer Richard Bryan noted, it would have been dangerous to intervene: 'all that could be done was to accept the fact, and keep them quiet and get them to bed as soon as possible'.[34] The bacchanalia only stopped when Bessels spiked the alcohol with emetics. When Bessels asked permission to take out sledge parties Budington refused: he was going to lead them himself. But he never did. He never even left the ship. According to Chester, his 'idea was, that the enterprise was all d—d nonsense; thought the scientific work was all nonsense too; he regarded the whole thing as foolishness'.[35] On Christmas Eve 1871 Tyson wrote: 'Nothing occurring that is pleasant or profitable to record. I wish I could blot out of my memory some things which I see and hear. Captain Hall did not always act with the clearest judgement, but *it was heaven to this*. I have not had a sound night's sleep since the 11th of November . . . If I can get through this winter I think I shall be able to live through anything.'[36] There was no service on Christmas Day.

They did get through the winter and by summer the officers were keen to go exploring. This time Budington did not stop them: 'Whoever wants to go North, let them go, but I won't.'[37] Bessels, Chester, Meyer and Tyson all led expeditions which achieved little – thanks no doubt to Budington's declaration that if the ice broke he would set sail whether they were back aboard or not. On their return, fresh animosities arose. Chester and Tyson began to quarrel. Bessels, previously well thought of, became a 'd—d impostor' who falsified observations he could not be bothered to make. The ship's carpenter, a sensitive soul called Coffin, was so affected by the bitterness that he went mad: enemies wanted to spray him with acid while he slept, he said; he could hear them drilling through the wall behind his bunk. Budington moved him into Hall's old berth from which he quickly decamped, moving from cabin to cabin, from corner to corner, frightened of everyone and everything. He slept in alleyways and by the galley stove, rising pale and terrified when disturbed, a resident ghost around whom the crew learned to tread lightly.

On 12 August 1872, Hans's wife gave birth to a baby boy, an event that surprised everyone, her condition having been disguised by her bulky furs. The crew saw his arrival as a good omen for that same day the ice broke and the *Polaris* escaped into Robeson Channel. Cheerfully, they christened him Charlie Polaris. Three days later, however, Budington drove them into the ice pack and they were beset again. For two months they drifted south, in winds that reached fifty-nine miles per hour and amidst blizzards that reduced visibility to twenty yards. On 12 October they passed Kane's Rensselaer Harbour. The winds were rising and the daylight hours were shortening. They could not tell where they were heading and the ship was leaking badly. Budington's tenuous authority slipped away entirely. With the steam pumps operating full-throttle, consuming tons of coal, he ordered the men to pump by hand. The crew refused and the engineers came out in sympathy, opening the cocks to show him how useless it was to battle such a flood. When he remonstrated they slammed the door in his face.

If they could not tell exactly where they were going they knew that the drift was carrying them south. They knew, therefore, that at some point they would have to enter the perilous strait guarded by Capes Isabella and Alexander. So far they had been protected by the floe in which the *Polaris* sat. But if the floe broke they would stand little chance in the berg-filled bottleneck that lay ahead. At 6.00 p.m. on 15 October their fears were realized: while in the strait a mighty berg crashed into them, squeezing the ship with the pressure of millions of tons of ice. The engineer Schumann ran on deck, shouting that the staves were broken, the pumps couldn't keep up, the ship was sinking. Budington reacted with panic. 'Throw everything on the ice!'[38] he yelled. Everything was confusion, the men heaving food, clothing, coal, beds, bedding and boats over the side in indiscriminate haste. Individuals performed gigantic feats of strength, tossing out barrels and boxes that would normally have required a gang to shift. The Eskimos and their families were among the first to be evacuated, followed by Tyson and a working party whose job was to prevent the massive pile of objects being crushed by the shifting hull.

They toiled for four hours in a black storm, shuttling items to and fro until, at about 10.00 p.m., Tyson became suspicious. The ice seemed to have stabilized and the *Polaris* was no lower in the water than when they had started. Climbing aboard he discovered that it had been a false alarm: all that had happened was that the water in the hold had shifted, there was no hole, and the pumps were coping perfectly well. Disgruntled, he returned to the floe and ordered his team to carry everything back again – and to hurry because he feared the ice might crack. Budington then told them to stop: instead they were to move the boats and material yet farther from the *Polaris*. While Tyson and his men pondered this inexplicable command the floe exploded under their feet. The ship's cables snapped, it heeled over and drifted off. Some of the men ran after it, but they were too slow. 'Goodbye, *Polaris*!'[39] yelled the steward, John Herron. His words were lost in the storm. Blown by a south-easterly gale the *Polaris* vanished swiftly into the darkness.

During the night that followed, Tyson struggled to rescue his party from the constantly splintering floe. Spotting a bundle of furs about to be swallowed by a crack he hauled it to safety and found he had inadvertently saved Hans's three children. In a waterlogged boat he shuttled from fragment to fragment, picking up survivors and rowing them back to the main floe where their main stock of provisions was piled. When day broke he counted eighteen men, women and children huddled around the three boats. He was confident that the *Polaris* would come looking for them. And on 16 October he saw the ship anchored ten miles away. He raised a flag, sure that Budington or one of his lookouts would spot it. They didn't. Tyson tried to launch a couple of boats but was driven back by a sudden storm. When the wind subsided the *Polaris* was nowhere to be seen and the floe was drifting south into Baffin Bay.

Tyson's team now comprised nine white men – predominantly Germans, led by Meyer – one black cook, four adult Eskimos and their five children. The floe on which they sat was a little country in itself, measuring four miles in circumference complete with hillocks and lakes of fresh water. In the terror of flight the men had saved only their clothes, guns and ammunition. (Even the Eskimos were armed.) Tyson had nothing but what he wore – a pair of ragged sealskin breeches, two shirts, a jumper and a cap – and a spare bag of clothes for emergencies. They had three boats, fourteen cans of pemmican, eleven and a half bags of ship's biscuit, one can of dried apples and fourteen hams. On 16 October a chunk of floe broke off, reducing their stores by one boat, six bags of biscuit and their only compass. Then on 23 October it miraculously floated within reach so that they were able to snatch back their lost goods. Apart from what they took from the sea, these supplies were to last them for nine months and 2,000 miles.

Tyson's authority evaporated faster even than Budington's. The Eskimos built igloos for the foreigners and showed them how to hunt, but the trigger-happy crew frightened the seals away. When a seal *was* caught the men ate it on the spot. Meyer made a show of weighing the rations in a home-made set of scales – eleven ounces per person per day – but once they had eaten their portions the men tucked into the rest of the stores. One orgiastic night they broached the cans of pemmican and gorged themselves until they vomited. Tyson could not stop them: he did not speak German and the Germans refused to speak English; also, they were armed and he was not. Meyer was no help, siding with his compatriots. Later, the men burned one of the boats to keep warm. 'We are now living on as little as the human frame can endure without succumbing,' Tyson wrote on 21 November. 'Some tremble with weakness when they try to walk.'[40] On the 27th he moved into Tookolito and Ebierbing's igloo, as the one place he could be sure of hearing English. Thanksgiving was a sad affair and Christmas even sadder. 'The last of our hams, the last of our apples, and the last of our present supply of seal's blood!' he wrote. 'So ends our Christmas feast!'[41] New Year's Day was worse. 'A happy New-year for all the world but us poor, cold, half-starved wretches . . . I have dined today on about *two feet of frozen entrails* and a little blubber.'[42]

They were in the middle of the Arctic winter. On 12 January 1873, with the temperature at minus 40°F, Tyson decided to open his bag of spare clothes. It had been stolen. 'I do not suppose we can hold out,' he wrote. 'As things are going we shall perish here if we stay. *It will be a struggle for life.*'[43] By February the Eskimo children were wailing with cold and hunger; the smallest had nothing to wear and lived in their mother's hoods like Arctic marsupials. The crew, meanwhile, gobbled whatever they could lay their hands on, spurred by Meyer's estimate that the Greenland coast was just a few miles east. He placed them roughly in the latitude of Disco Bay. They *were* in that latitude but they were on the wrong side of Baffin Bay. Without a chronometer to calculate their longitude, Meyer had assumed they were drifting down the Greenland coast when in fact they were floating past Baffin Island to the west. One faction suggested they leave the floe at once and row east to safety – a disastrous course from which they were dissuaded only by their fear of the cold. 'They little know the labor before them,' Tyson sneered. 'They would get to their deaths – that's where they get.'[44] Worryingly, however, he too trusted Meyer's observations. It was the timing, rather than the plan itself, at which he scoffed. April was the month in which they should head east.

Alone, bored, cold, starved of company, confined to an igloo three feet square with nowhere to sit, nothing to read, nothing to eat, his command in tatters, Tyson lapsed into self-pity. 'Notwithstanding all my discomforts, my dark and dirty shelter, my bed of wet and musty musk-ox skins, fireless and cheerless and hungry, without one companion who appreciates the situation, I shall be well content, and even happy, if I can keep this party – worthy and worthless – all together without loss of life until April, when I hope for deliverance.'[45] A rumour reached him that the men actually wanted to *prolong* the trip: having learned that the *Hansa* survivors had been given a 1,000 thaler bonus for their ordeal, they thought they too would receive double pay – and the longer they were adrift the more money they would get. At that Tyson gave up. He lay on the ice and watched the northern sky wheel overhead. 'Ursus Major and Minor,' he wrote. 'Orion, Andromeda, Cassiopeia, the Plaeiades, and Jupiter, so bright – part of Draco too. What a splendid night it would be for telescopic observation! The air is so clear and pure, there is neither cloud nor fog, nor any visible exhalations from this icy land, or frozen sea, to mar the crystal clearness of the atmosphere.'[46]

Throughout February they continued slowly south and Meyer's faulty navigation became apparent. 'They find drifting on an ice-floe not so pleasant,' Tyson remarked approvingly. 'The provisions not holding out as they supposed, they are now *thoroughly frightened*.'[47] Ebierbing and Hans hunted, bringing back small birds and the occasional seal, but it was never enough. The spectre of cannibalism stalked the floe. The Eskimos feared for their children. They had seen the white men eyeing them up, they told Tyson. Idly, Tyson wondered if he ought to commit suicide.

Maybe cannibalism would have broken out, as it had done in Franklin's expedition, destroying the party in a final bloodbath before the floe sank, taking all survivors and all evidence with it. But the floe got there first. On 11 March, it began to crack. A gale whisked off great chunks piece by piece, and sixty hours later the island which they had once counted in miles was reduced to a fragment measuring 75 by 100 yards. Well, at least the Eskimos wouldn't have far to go on their hunting trips, Tyson thought. All they had to do was lie in their igloos and wait: the sea was just twenty yards from where they were camped.

For the rest of March the weather was mild and the game plentiful. Seals and polar bears were shot in such quantities that the fear of cannibalism receded. The men resumed their reckless eating patterns and Tyson discovered that he was interested in life after all. By 22 March he was complaining again. 'These Germans are tremendous eaters and outrageous grumblers,' he grumbled. The reason for his discontent was that the men, in their boredom, had taken to stripping and reassembling their firearms with the consequence that few of them worked anymore – as Tyson found when he picked up a rifle and had three misfires ten feet from a polar bear. 'They seemed possessed with the idea that they can improve every thing . . . nearly every rifle we had upon the ice but [Ebierbing's], which they could not get hold of, has been ruined by their tinkering. They must work away at every thing, and never stop till it is rendered useless.'[48]

Tyson could have worked himself into a rare frenzy if the ice and the weather had held. But on 1 April bergs loomed over the floe, threatening to smash it into crystals. Now was the time, he decided, to escape. On the western horizon lay pack ice across which they might be able to find a route to land; and if there was no such route there would at least be a safer floe than the one they were sitting on. The embarkation was as chaotic as might be expected. They loaded their one remaining boat with every scrap of food and equipment they possessed and then climbed in themselves. The boat nearly sank. One hundred pounds of fresh meat were thrown into the sea along with most of their spare clothes, leaving them with a tent, a few skins and the minimum of food. Some of the men suggested throwing the Eskimo children out too. A small tussle ensued when they saw that Tyson was determined to take Hall's portable writing desk as a memento – a tussle which Tyson, for once, won.

When the boat left it was still dangerously low in the water. Designed for a maximum of eight men it now carried nineteen souls. Space was so cramped that every time Tyson pulled the tiller ropes he risked knocking the Eskimo children overboard. Hans had to scrabble through knees and legs with an empty meat tin to bail the water which poured in with each wave. Day after day, they sailed towards the coast through seas that made them cry out in terror. They rested on floes which split beneath them and on floes so small that there was standing room only. On 8 April, while packed on a small but seemingly stable piece of ice, a fissure zig-zagged between the boat and the tent (between which there was not enough room for a man to walk), tipping Meyer into the water. He scrabbled back onto the floe but chose the wrong chunk. He and the boat would have been lost had not Hans and Ebierbing gone to their rescue, dancing across wobbly stepping stones of ice to bring them back. The immersion in sub-zero waters almost killed Meyer: for a while he stopped breathing until pummelled back to consciousness by the Eskimos; when he came to he was a broken man, frostbitten in both feet and feverish. Tyson had never much liked Meyer, but 'the Count', as the men called him, had been seen as a figure of authority. Without him, Tyson could not see how order was to be maintained.

The night watch now changed every hour instead of every four because the men claimed they were too weak, and each shift made demands on their diminishing reserves. What use was discipline in these conditions? They were bound to die. 'It is getting too dark to see the end,' Tyson wrote. 'It is colder, the ice is closing around us. We can do nothing more.'[49]

On 9 April the weather worsened. A wave washed over the floe, inundating their tent with water and contaminating the small pools of fresh water from which they had been drinking. Thereafter they suffered from thirst as well as hunger. 'Meyer looks very bad,' Tyson wrote on the 15th. 'Hunger and cold show their worst effects on him. Some of the men have dangerous looks; this hunger is disturbing their brains. I can not but fear that they contemplate crime. After what we have gone through, I hope this company may be preserved from any fatal wrong. We can and we must bear what God sends without crime. This party must not disgrace humanity by cannibalism.'[50] On 16 April: 'One more day got over without catastrophe. The ice is still the same. Some of the men's heads and faces are much swollen, but from what cause I can not discover. I know scurvy when I see it, and it is not that . . . Someone has been at the pemmican.'[51] On 18 April Ebierbing shot a seal, which they sucked dry to alleviate their thirst. Meyer, the invalid, came last to the banquet. 'Poor Meyer,' Tyson wrote, 'he is very tall and thin. He has on his hands a monstrous pair of deer-skin gloves, ever so much too large for him. It looked quite pitiable, though almost grotesquely amusing (if the case had not been so serious), to see him striving to gather up some bones, once abandoned, to pick at again for a scrap of meat. The gloves were so large, and his hands so cold, he could not feel when he had got hold of any thing; and as he would raise himself up, almost toppling over with weakness, he found time and again that he had grasped *nothing*. If Doré had wanted a model to stand for Famine, he might have drawn Meyer at that moment and made a success. He was the most wretched-looking object I ever saw.'[52]

Since 9 April the weather had been mild, allowing them to float southwards undisturbed on their floe. They travelled two whole degrees south and were at 53°57′ when a storm hit them on the evening of the 19th. At 9.00 p.m. the sea broke over the floe with such force that it carried off everything that wasn't pinned down. They put the women and children in the boat and held on while waves smashed into them at five-minute intervals. The tent went, so did the piles of skins and clothing. Towards midnight the waves settled into a 15–20-minute rhythm that battered the boat from one side of the floe to the other. In the intervals of calm they hauled it back to the centre, pestered by ice-rocks which flew at them from the darkness. At 7.00 a.m. on the 20th, with water sloshing around their ankles, Tyson ordered yet another evacuation. 'That was the greatest fight for life we had yet had,' he wrote. 'How we held out I know not. God must have given us strength for the occasion. For twelve hours there was scarcely a sound uttered, save and excepting the crying of the children and my orders to "hold on," "bear down", "put on all your weight", and the responsive "ay, ay, sir," which for once came readily enough.'[53]

They reached a floe, rested a while, then moved to another amidst squalls of sleet and rain. '*April 22*. Now, as I recall the details, it seems as if we were through the whole of that night the sport and jest of the elements,' Tyson wrote. 'They played with us and our boat as if we were shuttlecocks. Man can never believe, nor pen describe, the scene we passed through, nor can I myself believe that any other party have weathered such a night and lived. Surely we are saved by the will of God alone, and I suppose for some good purpose of his own. The more I think of it, the more I wonder that we were all not washed into the sea together, and ground up in the raging and crushing ice. Yet here we are, children and all, even the baby, sound and well – except the bruises. Half-drowned we are, and cold enough in our wet clothes, without shelter, and not sun enough to dry us even on the outside. We have nothing to eat; everything is finished and gone. The prospect looks bad.'[54]

Rowing from floe to floe they finally saw, at 4.30 p.m. on 28 April, a steamer flying the Stars and Stripes. They went after it but it did not see them. That night they made a beacon of their remaining seal blubber. The fire went unnoticed. At dawn on the 29th another ship materialized eight miles away. Again they rowed for it but became stuck in the ice. Climbing onto the nearest floe they raised a flag and shouted till they were hoarse, while simultaneously firing volleys into the air. At the third volley the ship responded. It let off three shots and steamed towards them. Then, bewilderingly, it turned south, north and west, before steaming off to the south-west. The three shots had been a fluke, Tyson realized. In an insouciant game of cat-and-mouse the same ship popped out from behind a berg that evening but again slipped away without making contact. At last, at 5.00 a.m. on 30 April 1873 they spotted another ship and this time it saw them too. It lowered boats to pick them up but the castaways could not wait. Throwing everything out of their own boat they pulled towards their saviour and clambered aboard.

It was the *Tigress*, a sealer from Newfoundland, whose crew had little knowledge of the *Polaris* expedition and were initially disbelieving when Tyson told them they had been adrift on the ice since 15

October the previous year. '*And was you on it night and day?*' asked one sailor suspiciously. The question was too much for Tyson. He doubled over and began to make involuntary hacking noises which at first puzzled him. On recognizing the dormant reflex he hacked all the harder. 'My long unexercised risibles thrilled with an unwonted sensation,'[56] he wrote, as for the first time in six months he heard the sound of his own laughter.

By 9 May Tyson and his group were in Newfoundland where they telegraphed to Washington the news of Hall's death, their escape from the ice and the uncertain fate of the *Polaris*. When they returned at last to the US operations were already under way to recover Budington's party. The *Tigress* was commandeered as a rescue vessel, reinforced hastily and sent straight back to the Arctic, with a smaller ship, the *Juniata*, and a tiny steam yacht. It was a Scottish whaler, the *Ravenscraig* from Kirkcaldy, however, which found the survivors and brought them back to safety. They had had almost as bad a time as Tyson's men on the floe. The *Polaris* had sprung a new and nastier leak, forcing Budington, Bessels, Chester and their men to land on the west coast of Smith Sound. They had then dismantled the ship and taken to their boats on which they travelled down the coast for hundreds of miles until they reached the whaling grounds and were rescued by the *Ravenscraig*.

The sensation was immense. As the first reports filtered in, Arctic experts refused to believe what had happened. That the expedition should have unravelled so disastrously – and apparently so incompetently – was just not possible. As for the dramatic escape on the ice floe, it could only be a fiction, some kind of attention-grabbing stunt. But no, it was all true. Hall had died, the mission had collapsed and nineteen men, women and children had, indeed, floated all the way from Smith Sound, down the coast of Baffin Island, past the mouth of Hudson's Bay, to Labrador, a distance of almost 2,000 miles.

It was a remarkable story, on a par with Franklin's in every respect – the voyage into the unknown, the dead commander, the wreck and the retreat – with the fortunate exception that this time the members of the expedition had survived. It had, in addition, the highly news-worthy involvement of women and children: photographers invited the Eskimos to pose for group portraits, tender-hearted mothers sent bundles of clothes to the children and those with a bent for statistics calculated, not without a moist eye, that little Charlie Polaris had been born farther north than anyone in the history of humankind. Tears scalded when Hans and his family were taken back to Greenland: the children were so pleased with their new clothes that they had put them all on at once; you could hardly see their faces. But if one studies the pictures taken of them during that brief flush, a less romantic image emerges. There is one in particular, a group of the floe survivors, in which the Eskimos are sitting in the midst of their white companions. While the white men sprawl, puff their chests, clutch their pipes and look heroic, the Eskimos sit stony-faced, bored, uncer-tain and depressed. They do not partake of the glory, for to them it has no significance. They have stories to tell but in the absence of lan-guage or credibility they offer blank, unsmiling stares. Even allowing for early photographic techniques, and cultural differences, they give the impression that the whole business stinks.

Everything came out in the inquiry: the drunkenness, the poor leadership, the accusations and counter-allegations. It was as if a haemorrhage had burst over a hitherto white sheet. Every member of the expedition was cross-examined, and each had a different interpretation of events, the common strand being a belief that if Hall had lived they would have reached the Pole. But why did Hall not live? How had he died? Hall's own journals had been lost, and those others which had been recovered by the rescue ships at the site of Budington's last beaching made no reference, the relevant pages having been cut out. Where was the evidence? Here the answers jostled awkwardly. A sealed trunk had been tossed into the sea; it had been abandoned on the ice; it had been preserved but later mislaid; various papers had been burned, maybe. The surviving diaries offered hints at best. The Board struggled through the conflicting testimony before deciding that Hall had died of apoplexy.

On 16 February 1874, the American Geographical Society held a reception at the Cooper Institute, over which its President, Judge Daly, presided. All the *Polaris* survivors were on stage and were invited to speak, Tyson getting the biggest cheers of all. Daly produced the old Wilkes flag, which had accompanied every US polar expedition to either the Antarctic or the Arctic. 'It is among the few relics that have been brought back, and Mr. Grinnell requests us to say that he is ready to send it again if there is any other American expedition fitted out for the Pole, but not for any other purpose.'[57] There was applause. They all agreed to lobby Government for extra pay for the survivors. Then Isaac Hayes got up and showed everyone his slides of Greenland, taken on a Stereopticon. It was a cold day, but the *Polaris* men sweated.

10

OSBORN'S LEGACY

'The invisible Sphinx of the uttermost North still protects with jealous vigilance the arcana of her ice-bound mystery. Her fingers still clutch with tenacious grasp the clue which leads to her coveted secret; ages have come and gone; generations of heroic souls have striven and failed, wrestling with Hope on the one side and Death on the other . . . she still clasps, in solemn silence, the riddle in her icy palm – remaining a fascination and a hope, while persistently baffling the reason, the skill, the courage of man.'[1] Thus wrote the editor of Tyson's journal on 1 January 1874. It annoyed Sherard Osborn and his friend Clements Markham intensely.

The full chaos of Hall's last voyage failed to register in Britain. What was noticed, on the other hand, was that he had reached farther north by ship than any other explorer. It was an ominous trend that could not be allowed to continue. Osborn and Markham had been junior officers together in the last British Franklin expedition, and for ten years had been pushing for a new strike at the Pole. They had pestered the Government and the Royal Geographical Society without cease, mustering every inducement available. In 1865 Osborn bemoaned the new school of 'rest and be thankful men',[2] as he called them. Since 1855 the Naval Budget had exceeded £150 million, of which £650,000 had been allocated to scientific research and of that sum a still tinier proportion had been spent on exploration. The Royal Navy was dying from inactivity. 'A wise ruler and a wise people will, I hold, be careful to satisfy a craving which is the lifeblood of the profession,'[3] he told the Royal Geographical Society. 'Would it be too much to ask for a fraction of the vast sum yearly sunk in naval expenditure, for two small screw-vessels and 120 officers and men, out of the 50,000 men annually placed at the disposal of the Admiralty?'[4] He invited members to look at the map. 'You,' he said, 'as a scientific body, have before you an unknown area of 1,131,000 square miles of the globe's surface a sheer blank.'[5]

He read a letter from Edward Sabine, one of Britain's exploring giants who had been to the Arctic as early as 1818: 'To reach the Pole is the greatest geographical achievement which can be attempted, and I own I should grieve if it should be first accomplished by any other than an Englishman.'[6] He cited the support of Grand Duke Constantine, President of Russia's Imperial Geographical Society. He quoted Lady Franklin: 'For the credit and honour of England, the exploration of the Pole should not be left to any other country . . . can there be a moment so fitting as the present?'[7] Then he called on Markham, who delivered an extraordinary broadside of lies. 'The exhilarating and delightful work of charging the ice in Melville Bay, cutting docks, chasing bears and shooting loons and dovekeys, while in the most lovely and striking scenery that can be met with on this earth,' he said of Baffin Bay's ghastliest ice-trap, 'will be exchanged for an Arctic winter, with its gorgeous skies, its genial fellowship, and its rounds of gaiety . . . Suffice it to say that the climate is the healthiest in the world, and that a retreat from Smith Sound to the Danish settlements in summer, is perfectly easy and devoid of danger.'[8] The Admiralty replied that nobody was going to the Pole if they could help it. Besides – as was true – the various bodies could not agree which route was best. They sent Osborn to India to shut him up.

Osborn returned in 1868 and again took the offensive. He chastened the Admiralty for pursuing 'a dead level of mediocrity',[9] and for chuckling at 'the differences of opinion which enabled the dear old navy to hobble on its macadamised highway of crossing royal yards and adhering to routine'.[10] Everybody knew that Smith Sound was the best route. He brought weighty opinions to bear. The Royal Swedish Academy stated of Petermann's Open Polar Sea that, 'This view is in itself so contrary to all experience that it scarcely merits refutation.'[11] And Admiral Lüthe, circumnavigator and President of the Imperial Academy of Sciences at St Petersburg, pooh-poohed the whole argument. 'No matter which line be taken, *provided something be done*. Science will be sure to gain by it, and I see with sincere pleasure that you are beginning to rekindle the question.'[12]

Osborn incandesced. The French were contemplating a naval expedition through Bering Strait but they had also sent in plans of a submarine by which they intend to surge under the ice-cap and emerge at the Pole. The French submarine comprised a tube two metres in diameter, coned at either end for ice-breaking, and equipped with an ornamental balustrade around what passed for a conning tower, from which the commander could, Jules Verne-like, survey his conquest. The submarine was never built and the naval expedition went no further than San Francisco. But, Osborn said, why did Britain not seize the moment while it was within its grasp? He fretted and frothed and all but shook the Admiralty by its epaulettes. They said it was too dangerous and sent him to China.

In 1874 Osborn was back again, fit, tanned and with the Pole still on his mind. The Pole was not too dangerous, he said. Clements Markham had sent his cousin Albert on a whaling trip to the Arctic. Albert's journal, which recorded amongst other events the rescue of Budington's party, announced that the Arctic was perfectly safe. Admittedly, he had only gone into Lancaster Sound, far to the south of Smith Sound, but it was all the same, wasn't it? Clements Markham abetted his cousin's opinions in a book of his own, *The Threshold of the Unknown Region*, in which he deplored Britain's abandonment of the Arctic. 'We, in England,' he wrote, 'have hitherto been condemned by our rulers to the disgrace of looking on while others complete the work so gloriously begun by our ancestors.'[13] And why? Because nobody knew which route was best and they were afraid of disease. What pusillanimous tosh! Hall's expedition had proved Smith Sound to be without question the easiest route; and regarding disease, statistics proved that fewer people died on Arctic expeditions than on any other of the voyages the Royal Navy sent around the globe; in fact, thanks to the purity of conditions and the isolation, you were less likely to catch a cold in the Arctic than at home. As for scurvy, Markham treated it with contempt. 'The scourge of the navy in days gone by, [it] is but little known now,'[14] he said. His book became a bestseller.

Both Markham and Osborn urged the public to consider the scientific benefits to be obtained from polar exploration. 'The mere *coup de théâtre* of hoisting a flag on the spot called our Pole and singing "Rule Britannia" . . . is not the object of my efforts,'[15] Osborn said. Markham wrote much the same: 'It is not by poking about in pack-ice at a distance from land, but by carefully examining hundreds of miles of coast-line that the most useful work is to be done in the unknown region.'[16] Neither man knew quite what the benefits were and when pushed to explain them waffled imprecisely about maps, tides and magnets. To give them credit, however, it was hard to be precise about the unknown – and this was their strongest card. Precision, certainty and an absolute knowledge of the planet's workings were what concerned post-Darwinian Britain. The Arctic was imprecise. It should therefore be brought within the scheme of things.

The public warmed to the prospect. 'A nation's strength is gained by such herculean labours and obstinate struggles,' wrote the *Gentleman's Magazine*, in a display of admirable if confused patriotism. 'Push on for the great secret, and God helping, we shall solve it yet, map out the whole northern seas, and then buckle ourselves to further toils that may still further help humanity.'[17] Support burgeoned, and in August 1874, the British Government granted the possibility of a new Arctic expedition. Then, on 17 November, Prime Minister Benjamin Disraeli gave it his official approval.

Two ships were allocated: HMS *Alert*, captained by George Nares, an old Franklin search hand, and HMS *Discovery*, under one Henry Stephenson. Lieutenant Albert Markham was appointed second-in-command to Nares. Once there had been a time when Britain dithered over the merits of small ships as opposed to large. But that argument belonged to a different age and applied to the shallow waters of the North-West Passage. These steamers were gigantic by previous standards. The *Alert* displaced 751 tons and boasted a 100-horsepower engine. The *Discovery* was 556 tons with 96-horsepower and, like its larger companion, was rigged for sailing as well as steaming. Each ship carried sixty officers and crew and was provisioned for three years. The number of officers alone was larger than the entire company of Hayes's last expedition and included so many lieutenants that they could have formed a collective noun. They were to be accompanied as far as Greenland by a supply ship, HMS *Valorous*, carrying fuel and food to make up for what was expended on the outward journey. Thereafter, the *Alert* would push on through Smith Sound to Robeson Channel and beyond, while the *Discovery* would anchor no farther north than 82° to act as a rescue ship in case the *Alert* became trapped. The total cost of the expedition was £150,000 – several millions today. When Britain did something, the message ran, it did it properly. With this huge display of might it would show the US what the mother country was made of, it would solve lots of scientific conundrums – whatever they might be – and, imperatively, it would get to the North Pole first. Nares's instructions were lengthy, containing pages of scientific this and that,* but the gist was stated in the first paragraph: he was to reach the Pole, and failing that was to go farther north than anybody yet.

Nares's ships left Portsmouth Harbour on 29 May 1875 to

---

* To give an idea of the matters which concerned contemporary scientists, Nares was asked to investigate subjects under the following headings: Ethnology, Mammalia, Ornithology, Ichthyology, Mollusca, Insecta and Arachnida, Crustacea, Annelida, Echinodermata, Polyzoa, Hydrozoa, Spongida, Rhizopoda reticularia, Botany and Geology; he was also to report on the Petermann Glacier, draw up a Meteorological Abstract, record Tidal Observations and keep a full game-book of everything the expedition shot.

resounding applause. 'No one on board our two ships can ever forget the farewell given to the discovery vessels on that occasion,' he wrote. 'Closely packed multitudes occupied each pier and jetty on both sides of the harbour; Southsea beach as far as the castle was thronged to the water's edge; the troops in garrison paraded on the common, the men-of-war in port manned their rigging and as we passed greeted us with deafening cheers, whilst the air rang with the shouts of spectators on shore and on board the steamers, yachts and small craft which crowded the water.'[18] The excitement had even infected Buckingham Palace. In his hand Nares clutched a telegram from Queen Victoria, whose contents read, 'I earnestly wish you and your gallant companions every success, and trust that you may safely accomplish the important duty you have so bravely undertaken.'[19] It was a magnificent send-off, especially by Nares's standards – he was a serious, unflappable man, who wrote according to his character – but it was overshadowed by the absence of Sherard Osborn. The man who had done so much for so long to get these two ships on the water had died suddenly of a stroke, three weeks before. Clements Markham was there of course, enthusiastic and optimistic as ever. (He followed aboard the *Valorous*, taking such a detailed interest in his prodigies that he recorded every personal detail, down to a scar on one of Nares's seamen's big toes.) But it felt strange not to have Osborn with them – and portentous.

By 6 July 1875 the *Alert* and *Discovery* were off Disco Island, where they took on dogs, clothes – too few of the latter – plus an Eskimo dog-handler named Frederick. Later they picked up the indefatigable Hans Hendrik who this time left his wife, Merkut, and children behind. (This was a relief to Nares, Merkut having acquired a reputation for difficulty. Women worried him. He did not want them muddying the cool efficiency of male proceedings. For Nares, one of Frederick's outstanding qualifications was that he was single.) They refilled their water tanks with chunks of ice from a berg, occasioning a near disaster. Wielding his pick, a sailor accidentally knocked off the entire cap, thereby upsetting the berg's equilibrium and forcing him to dance like an acrobat while it revolved in the sea. He was eventually rescued, to the crew's amusement, but Nares wrote dourly that

'The performance . . . involved a certain element of danger, which I should have preferred to avoid.'[20]

On 17 July they left Disco, waved off by Clements Markham. The *Valorous*, on which he was travelling, hoisted a signal on all three mast-heads: 'Farewell. Speedy Return.' The *Discovery* replied, 'Thank you'. So, at length, did the *Alert*. They disappeared into the Arctic fog and Markham sailed back to London with glowing reports of how the expedition was faring.

Throughout the summer of 1875 Britain relished its comeback. 'England again takes her place in the van of discovery,'[21] applauded *Blackwood's Magazine*. 'She has fitted out an expedition with a completeness and an efficiency such as never before characterised any of her previous undertakings.' The Royal Geographical Society, which had supported Osborn and Markham to the hilt, was cock-a-hoop. 'There can be no question but that we do stand in very high public favour,'[22] the President, Sir Henry Rawlinson, told members. The mood was akin to that of a group of schoolboys given permission to go out of bounds. When, on 28 October, the Sultan of Zanzibar attended one of their meetings (members had been warned to be on best behaviour: he was their only foreign Honorary Fellow) he expressed his complete wonderment at the things his British colleagues were getting up to. He would have to read the old Arab chronicles, he said, to remind himself of similar achievements. It was a solemn and graceful speech, which was greeted with applause. Beneath their beards and dark suits, however, the audience were rummaging metaphorically in their shorts for a catapult. The North Pole lay in their sights and they wanted to ping it down as if it were an apple on a tree.

Nares was the wrong man for an orchard raid. A forty-five-year-old Aberdonian, who came from a long line of sea-going forebears, he had been in the Navy since the age of fourteen and was used to orders. He was commonsensical, efficient and had Arctic experience. He was acquainted with sledge travel, having taken part in McClintock's monumental man-hauled sorties in search of Franklin (he was almost one of the fabled thousand-milers) and he knew the ice as well as anybody. He looked upstanding – a painting in London's National

Portrait Gallery shows him as a tall, determined man, bearded, bald and serious – and there could be no doubt as to either his bravery or his competence. 'Whatever man can dare he will dare,' commented *Blackwood's*, 'and no effort of skill or courage will be wanting to bring the expedition which he commands to a successful termination.'[23] But Nares lacked humour, imagination and charisma. He was not a Kane, a Hayes or a Hall. It was bad luck that he had been chosen for this task. He would have been happier where he was, which in 1874 was in command of the *Challenger* Antarctic research voyage. But he had been ordered north, so north he went. His men called him 'Daddy'.

Perhaps, though, the Admiralty had not been so wrong in choosing Nares. Where vim and vision had failed, the stolid, machine-like discipline of the Royal Navy might succeed. There would be no squabbles as to whether or not they should go home. There would be no haphazard abandonment of ships, no embarrassment on ice floes, no question as to who was in command. Nares would see things through to their logical conclusion; if it could not be done he would say so; and he would not let his men die.

Nares and his steamships pushed past Cape Alexander and into Kane Basin, following the same route as Hall. They sprinkled caches of provisions left and right – at no fewer than sixty-mile intervals, as Admiralty orders dictated – and sneered at how badly their predecessors had charted the coast. Kane, Hayes and Hall were hopeless navigators, Nares decided. On the way north he charted a pair of islands, for example, which Inglefield had first described as being two islands but which Kane had later merged into one. Later he discovered that Hayes's charts were miles out (typical) and that Hall had made several tiny mistakes (most irritating). He ignored the fact that his expedition was bigger, better funded and better equipped than any which had entered Smith Sound before. Instead, he chided the Americans like a nanny clearing up after an unruly party.

In late August, the *Discovery* set up permanent winter quarters on Grant Land, to the north of Kennedy Channel. The *Alert*, meanwhile, pressed on up the western coast of Robeson Channel. Aided by a southerly gale which cleared the ice in front of him, on 1 September Nares reached a farthest north by ship of 82°24′. Fifteen days later he achieved 82°27′ where, just before the freeze began, he darted into a bay safe enough for wintering. Within hours the vast blocks of ice through which he had steered, some weighing 30,000 tons or more, coalesced into a solid pack that enclosed the bay completely. The *Alert* was not an ice-breaker; its engines could carry it through loose floes, but any prolonged stretch of ice – even a few feet thick – brought it to a halt. In front of it there rose a barrier fifty feet high through which they had no hope of breaking until the next thaw. Still, it was a good spot in which to spend the winter, shallow enough to keep bergs at a distance while at the same time protected by the barrier to seaward. They named their anchorage Floeberg Beach.

Nares had never been much of a man for the Open Polar Sea hypothesis and the situation supported all his suspicions. Not a speck of water could he see. Hall's expedition had sighted land at a distance, but as Nares peered north through his telescope he saw only frosted hummocks of ice clambering towards the horizon. He dashed to his journal, in which he added more derogatory comments on US practices, leaving Albert Markham to capture the moment. 'Nothing but ice, tight and impassable, was to be seen – a solid, impenetrable mass that no amount of imagination or theoretical belief could ever twist into an "Open Polar Sea"! We were reluctantly compelled to come to the conclusion that we had in reality arrived on the shore of the Polar Ocean; a frozen sea of such a character as utterly to preclude the possibility of its being navigated by a ship; a wide expanse of ice and snow, whose impenetrable fastnesses seem to defy the puny efforts of mortal men to invade and expose their hitherto sealed and hidden mysteries.'[24]

So, the Pole was blocked to ships. The Admiralty, however, had expected this to be the case and had provided Nares with sledges to continue where the ships left off. Dutifully, Nares despatched depot-laying parties to prepare for the spring expeditions. They went west into Grant Land, and north towards the Pole. The dogs were suffering unaccountable fits and, as Nares was a man-hauler at heart, the men floundered on foot to do his bidding. Before they left Nares gave them a warning. One of his many Lieutenants, Wyatt Rawson, recorded it thus: 'the hardest days work we had ever *imagined*, let alone *had*, would not hold a patch on the work we should have sledging'.[25]

The work was more than hard: it very nearly killed them. Lieutenant Pelham Aldrich returned from a trip to the west that left him exhausted. Lieutenant William May, who accompanied him, came back battered and frostbitten. It took five months for his wounds to heal. Albert Markham limped home from the north with one third of his twenty-four-man team frostbitten, three of them so badly that they lost fingers and toes. 'Captain Nares was quite right,' wrote Lt. Rawson, 'he was perfectly right.'[26]

That winter the crew amused themselves in traditional fashion. British captains had always emphasized the importance of keeping their men occupied during the sunless months. Kane's, Hayes's and Hall's journals had all described the monotony of an Arctic winter – a monotony which had possibly been their undoing – and Nares was not going to let his men drift the same way. A skating rink was cleared,* firework displays were held, boxing matches were staged and evening classes were arranged. A newspaper was organized by Pelham Aldrich and every week there were 'Thursday Pops', semi-educational entertainments which comprised songs, readings and tableaux. The first, held on 11 November, featured a talk on 'The Jumping Frog', by Dr Edward Moss. On 18 November, Nares reinstituted 'The Royal Arctic Theatre' which had been founded by Parry on his first wintering in 1819–20 and which had last seen service on the Franklin rescue expeditions more than twenty years previously. The officers dressed up and cavorted on deck in front of the crew, to the hilarity of all. But it was a cold job. As Nares wrote, 'A representation held on the upper deck,

* Sea ice, they discovered, possessed the peculiar property of not being slippery. The rink, therefore, had to be created by pouring fresh water onto a levelled surface and allowing it to freeze.

with a temperature of about twenty degrees below zero, leads everyone to long for the finale at an early hour.'[27] So they went below for the next show, which took place in a balmy 50°F – 'an advantage appreciated by both actors and audience' – against a painted backdrop of Austria, the United States and Britain struggling for the Pole. They had been given so many musical instruments by friends at home that there was a suggestion of forming a band. But as Aldrich was good at the keyboards, and there was a harmonium aboard, they dispensed with the rest. 'He very kindly plays dance music on Thursday evenings,' wrote Nares, 'much to the delight of the numerous dancers.'[29] When not dancing or attending the theatre or enjoying the 'Pops', they set themselves conundrums.* According to Rawson, they were in such high spirits that they had to limit themselves to one joke per day.

One day Nares released a homing pigeon as an experiment. Originally he had had four of them but they had grown sluggish in the cold and had been brought indoors, whereupon two of them had been eaten by the dogs and another by the men. The fourth flew off, flapping south above the ice. The same experiment had been tried by Sir John Ross in the 1830s while he was trapped in the North-West Passage. It had not worked then and it did not work now. The pigeon was never seen again. But the sight of that bird sweeping into the gloom towards a far-off home was a reminder of how they stood. Civilization was thousands of miles away; it was hundreds of miles to the nearest Eskimo settlement in Greenland; and to the north, closer now to them than Edinburgh was to London, lay the Pole. What was it, this Pole? Was it open sea? An island? A hole? Ice? If sea, would it be a maelstrom? If land, would it contain a new race of humans? If a hole, would they fall into it? It must have been hard for anybody with a shred of imagination not to have turned his mind to these questions as the pigeon flew south. Nares struggled to express his feelings. 'Pigeons,' he finally wrote, 'are practically useless for explorers advancing over new territory.'[31]

* An example from Rawson's journal, as devised by the chaplain: 'Why are the two cats we have on board, likely to smell more than any other cats? Because if they only get a little higher they will become Pole cats!'[30]

The *Alert*'s surgeon, Dr Edward Moss, made up for Nares's bland-
ness in a journal that sang with images of the odd and unusual. A
capable artist and a keen observer, he painted (in words and water-
colours) evocative pictures of their daily life: the main saloon, with its
overstuffed chairs, green baize tablecloth, panelled walls and framed
prints, where they emulated at 82°N all the comforts of a Victorian
club; the morning service in which a muffled chaplain preached to his
bearded congregation amidst the yellow glow of an oil lantern, while
ice hung in feathers from the canopy above the deck; the slabby igloos
in which they housed their scientific instruments, and the way in
which these igloos became snowed under so that when he and others
went to take the hourly observations they walked with lamps through
an underground village connected by tunnels. Fresh to the Arctic as
he was, every detail filled him with wonder. Candles less than an
inch thick burned down the centre but melted intermittently on the
outside so that the flames shone through a lattice of frozen wax. Stars
on the horizon did not remain still but swung about, 'in long curves
like the sweep of a goshawk',[32] under the influence of refraction.
Even the air smelled different: 'On first going out into the open,'
Moss wrote, 'there is a faint odour of green walnuts.'[33]

He described his surroundings half in delight, half in fear. 'In this
icy wilderness there is an overpowering sense of solitude, which adds
greatly to the weird effect of moonlight on the floebergs, fantastically
shaped and vague. There is complete silence, but it is broken every
now and then by sudden unearthly yells and shrieks from the still
moving pack, harsh and loud as a steam siren, but unlike anything else
in art or nature.'[34]

The *Alert*'s naturalist, an army officer named Henry Feilden, was
equally thrilled. Of an outing that winter, he wrote, 'The air was so
exhilarating that we hurried over the crisp snow singing, shouting
and laughing . . . And what a moon! Like a great mirror or shield of
burnished steel, not as you see her in the tropics or the
Mediterranean, pale, warm and soft, dimpling land and sea with
shadows, but cold, bright and stern; not a cloud or fleck in the
zenith, but toward the south a pale, delicate green shade with heavy

lines of dark cloud brooding over it told us where the sun many degrees below our horizon was giving light and heat to all we love . . . And then we looked at the great frozen waste in front of us, smooth ice, crooked ice, hummocks, floes and packs all jumbled together in mystic confusion. If a man who looks out upon such a scene, cannot realise his insignificance and the greatness of God, I pity him . . . We trotted back to the ship and as we gathered round our own bright lighted social table, with many luxuries on it, we laughed and talked and were as fully a party as could be found in Christendom.'[35]

Feilden loved the quiet of the Arctic night and took every opportunity to stroll out with his gun on the pretence of adding to his collection of stuffed birds. He killed few specimens but jubilated in the scenery. Once he saw the brightest light in his life: a moonbeam that had been caught in a far-off prism of ice, and which nearly blinded him with its gleam. On another evening he was numbed by the stillness: 'All nature seems to be in a state of repose. It is the same feeling as comes over one when walking home from a London ball at 4 a.m. on a June morning.'[36]

The sun, which had set in October, returned on 1 March 1876 after 142 days – 'the longest period that we know of that any mortal has spent without the sun,'[37] according to Markham – to find the Alerts (as they called themselves) fit and happy. They had hardly noticed the darkness and only one man was ill. Snow had fallen heavily but the wind had been so soft that on only two days had they been prevented from exercising outside. The cold, however, had been intense. For most of February the mercury froze in their thermometers. In early March the temperature dropped to 101°F below freezing, the lowest any man had lived to record. 'One can *see* the body, and the clothes too, losing their heat,'[38] the chaplain recorded in awe. He noted also that the boxing matches had to be cancelled because the combatants were unable to see each other through their breath. One dog's tail froze to the ground, another's tongue stuck to the inside of a meat can, and ice formed in clumps on their coats so that when they moved they rattled like chandeliers.

Under these circumstances it was difficult to argue for the existence of an Open Polar Sea. Contrarily, though, there were signs that there might be land ahead, and not just frozen land, such as Weyprecht and Payer had encountered, but a sunny land where plants grew. Game had been scarce the previous summer – five ducks, three hares, six musk-oxen – and non-existent during the winter. But in March, Nares saw two dozen ptarmigan flying north; flights of geese and ducks followed them a few days later. The ducks and geese returned – there was no water, then – but the ptarmigan did not. Had they found a source of food at the Pole?

The spring sledging started on 12 March with a trek to contact the *Discovery*. A Danish dog-handler named Petersen, whom Nares had hired in Greenland, took Lieutenants Rawson and Egerton south. They returned after four days having covered sixteen miles in a snowstorm. They were all frostbitten. Petersen lost both his feet and died three months later – from exhaustion, according to Nares – but Egerton and Rawson recovered, their frostbite having been mild and occasioned only by trying to rub Petersen's feet back to life. Egerton and Rawson went south again on 20 March with two seamen and, after six days' severe travelling, reached the *Discovery*. All was fine, Stephenson reassured them. So they trudged back to the *Alert*.

At 11.00 a.m. on 2 April the great journeys commenced. Seven massive sledges, manned by fifty-three officers and men, fanned out for the haul. Commander Albert Markham and Lieutenant Alfred Parr went north with two boats (on sledges) plus three support sledges. Another two sledges under Pelham Aldrich and Lieutenant George Giffard went west to Grant Land. Lieutenant Wyatt Rawson, Lieutenant Lewis Beaumont and Dr Richard Coppinger – who had come from the *Discovery* – were later sent east with three sledges to explore Greenland before sledging back down the coast to the *Discovery*. It was a rousing departure, the sledges' silk pennants fluttering in the breeze, bearing heraldic emblems and imposing names such as Marco Polo, Victoria, Bulldog and Bloodhound. The entire crew joined in a hymn before the sledgers picked up their ropes and moved off to three loud cheers. 'A most impressive scene,' recorded

Nares, 'each heart being inspired with enthusiasm, and with a feeling of confidence that the labours, privations, and hardships that the travellers were about to undergo would be manfully battled with.'[39]

For a month the two groups under Markham and Aldrich travelled together across Ellesmere Island, a period in which they discovered to their dismay just how manfully they would have to battle. They floundered through snow that was waist-deep, they used pick-axes and shovels to cut through hummocks that were up to thirty feet high and a quarter of a mile wide, and they shivered in temperatures of more than 45°F below zero. So rugged was the ice that some days they travelled fourteen miles to gain four miles north – hauling, all the while, loads that weighed more than 240 pounds per man. 'We could not but confess that the labour was harder than we had expected, but if others had gone through it we could,'[40] wrote Dr Edward Moss, who accompanied them part of the way with a support sledge. Moss's determination slackened two pages later in his journal: 'Nothing can exceed the monotony of sledge-travelling,' he wrote. 'Day after day the same routine is gone through, day after day the same endless ice is the only thing in sight.'[41] During a whole week the only object they saw that was not white was a distant slab of coastal rock. The terrain, meanwhile, was uncompromising. Moss came to loathe their battle cry: 'One – two – three – Heave!'

The sledgers were individually unidentifiable thanks to their 'Eugenies' – a form of balaclava donated by Empress Eugenie of France, which covered most of the face – and so they daubed their clothes with symbols by which they could be recognized. It fascinated Moss: 'The back view of our sledge-crews was an extraordinary spectacle. One man's back bore a large black anchor with the motto "Hold Fast", another displayed a complicated hieroglyphic savouring of Freemasonry. Here was a locomotive careering over a beautiful green sod and on the next back a striking likeness of the Tichbourne claimant.' Combined with their heraldic sledge-pennants, they must have looked like a crusade gone terribly astray. Moss's journal is a model of decorum and at no time does it state that its author thought that he was part of a mad-house. But the impression comes through nevertheless. 'There again,' he continued, 'was an artistic effort which had cost its author many a week of painstaking execution, but neither he nor anyone else could tell what it was.'[42] When Markham and Aldrich split up on 10 March 1876, the one to go north and the other west, each with two sledges, Moss returned to the *Alert* with the support teams. From miles away, such was the carrying power of the flat, Arctic air, he could still hear the chant, 'One – two – three – Heave!'

As Markham's men clambered over the coastal ice they settled into a regime of haul and sleep, and as they did so they realized that they were not as well-equipped as they had assumed. Their woollen clothes were unsuitable for Arctic travel, absorbing perspiration and freezing until they were hard as boards and it was nigh impossible to do up the buttons. In the mornings they had to beat their trousers with axe heads to make them bend at the knees. Storms kept them in their tents for days, confining them to communal sleeping bags in conditions of hideous discomfort. To save weight the tents had been made of too thin a material, and for similar reasons of economy, the sleeping bags had been built to the tightest possible specifications. Markham found it difficult to sleep in them at all. 'Comfort, with our sleeping-bags and tent-robes frozen so hard as to resemble sheet-iron more than woollen substances, was quite out of the question. The very appearance of our coverlet, when passed into the tent, was sufficient to banish all ideas of comfort or sleep.'[43]

Nares, who had experienced something similar earlier in his career, spoke of it with feeling: 'Very few can possibly realize the utter wretchedness endured by young men in the utmost health & strength & full of life when imprisoned in a heavy gale of wind within a small light tent made of no thicker material than an ordinary cricketing tent . . . compelled to remain lying down at full length cramped up in a compacted space between 28 to 32 inches across for *yourself and companion* for one or two and even three consecutive days – packed in order to economize space, head & tails alternating like preserved sardines . . . where, if your blanket bag allows you to kick it must necessarily be at the risk of striking your next neighbour's nose. Inside the tightly closed blanket bag it is too dark to read and woe betide

anyone who leaves the mouth open. For the whole interior of the
tent is filled with snow drift . . . so fine and light . . . as to be likened
to the motes of a sunbeam . . . forever shifting gradually downwards
and forming a thick & ever increasing deposit on the upper canvas
covering stretched over the cramped men.'[44] In these squalid conditions their clothes thawed, saturating the sleeping bags which then
froze when packed back on the sledges, thereby increasing the weight
of the load and making their next night more uncomfortable still.

Having set off across the Arctic Sea to achieve the expedition's
grand object, Markham became uncertain how long his fifteen-strong
team could last. On 6 March two men had complained of feeling
'seedy'. (Coincidentally, on the same date, two of Aldrich's western
party also complained of weariness, one of them being so weak he had
to be sent back to the *Alert*.) It was exhaustion, Markham assumed.
On 14 April, however, another man collapsed with pains in his legs. 'I
almost think it is rheumatism,'[45] Markham wrote. Three days later
another two broke down. On 19 April so many were ill that Markham
abandoned one of his boats. 'We shall now be able to make a much
more rapid advance,' he wrote, 'if such snail-like progress as ours can
be so termed. It was positively painful & heartrending to see the
tremendous exertions of our small force attempting to drag our heavy
sledge up some high hummocks and probably occupying about ½ an
hour to get her along a few feet.'[46] Without the boat it was still a
monumental task. On rare occasions, they were able to raise sail on
the sledges and let the wind carry them along level stretches. But
mostly it was a matter of smashing the hummocks flat with pick
and shovel. Significantly, Markham now referred to his crew not as
haulers but as road-makers. They smashed and chopped through the
tortuous icescape, falling into snow-covered fissures, struggling over
ridges and taking detours through valleys. Every day they made a
real northing of less than a quarter of the distance they had actually
travelled.

Markham recorded it all in his journal: 'Distance marched thirteen
miles; made good four . . . Distance marched seven miles; made good
one and a quarter . . . Distance marched six miles; made good one

mile . . . Distance made good three-quarters of a mile . . . more small floes and more hummocks and so it goes on.'[47] Nowhere could they see evidence of an Open Polar Sea. 'Is it never going to get warmer?'[48] Markham wondered. In this manner, on 24 April they passed 83°N. More men were now giving way. Their legs hurt terribly, they said, and their joints were swollen. A suspicion formed in Markham's mind; might they be afflicted by something other than exhaustion or rheumatism? On 26 April they encountered a mass of hummocks that spread north, east and west as far as the eye could see. 'We really seem to have arrived at the end of all things,' Markham pencilled in his notebook. 'It is indeed a dismal prospect.'[49] They hauled on.

On the 27th Markham wrote: 'I may mention that today I had of necessity to cross the same floe, on which the snow was knee-deep, no less than thirteen times.'[50] On 3 May: 'The snow drifts are *very, very* deep . . . Once the drift was so deep that the boat sledge was completely buried. We *must* get on.'[51] On 5 May: 'It is a dreary scene we are surrounded by, a desolate, cold and inhospitable looking scene . . . nothing but an uneven and irregular scene of snow and ice.'[52] He was proud of the crippled haulers, who made so light of their illness that they threatened to introduce it to polite society. They were sure that the Marco Polo gait – so-called after the lead sledge – would become an overnight hit in London society. On 7 May it took them a day to cross one hundred yards.

When they reached 83°20′N on 12 May, only two-thirds of the team were functioning, and Markham was forced to admit the truth: they had scurvy. He was bewildered as to how this could be. True, they had only packed four bottles of lemon juice in their provisions, but they had had plenty aboard ship. Normally it took three years or so for the first symptoms of scurvy to become apparent; yet his 'seedy' haulers had fallen ill barely four weeks away from the *Alert* and a year from home. Had he not been assured by everyone – not least his cousin Clements – that scurvy was a thing of the past? It was an impossibility, they had said. Clearly, it was not.

Markham planted the Union Jack where he stood. It was the farthest north any human being had ever stood – indeed, in Markham's estimation it was 'a higher latitude I predict, than will ever be attained . . . With this the country must be satisfied.'[53] In celebration be broached a magnum of whisky – a gift from the Dean of Dundee – and handed cigars to everyone. They sang the 'Union Jack of Old England', the 'Grand Palaeocrystic Sledging Chorus' and 'God Save the Queen', but any triumph Markham may have felt was muted. The Pole was still 400 miles away, and his men were dying. His only choice was to turn back. He comforted himself that, 'as far as the Pole itself is concerned we have most certainly set the matter completely at rest now and for ever, namely that . . . it is *totally and utterly impracticable*. The question also of an Open Polar Sea is unmistakeably settled, its existence can only be in the brain of a few insane theorists.'[54] Nevertheless, it was 'a bitter end to all our aspirations'.[55]

They started south on 13 May, with less than thirty days' food to carry them over a distance it had taken them the last forty-one to cover. The road at least was flat – which was good; their two shovels had broken so many times that the handles were beyond further repair – and they raced down it with their sledge boat that had never seen water. But the scurvy raced faster. On 7 May, only Markham, his second-in-command Lieutenant Parr and two others were at full strength. Everyone else was either on a sledge or just about to be put on one. 'Every day, every hour is of importance to us,' Markham wrote, 'as we know not when we may, one and all, be attacked and rendered useless.'[56] That day he abandoned the boat and its sledge and continued with one sledge alone. On 5 June they reached Grant Land and were forty miles from the *Alert*. But Markham knew it would take them at least three weeks to cover the distance and he was uncertain if his men could live that long. Three days later, there were still twenty-seven miles to go and a marine named George Porter was fading fast.

Lt. Parr, the strongest of them all, volunteered to fetch help. He ran on foot through the snow, carrying only an alpenstock and the makings of a small cup of tea. Twenty-four hours and thirty-five miles later, he climbed aboard the *Alert* on the evening of 8 June, so gaunt and filthy that he was recognizable only by his voice. 'As he crossed the quarter-deck, silently nodding to the one or two who chanced to meet him,' Nares recorded, 'his grave and weary expression was unmistakeable, and in a very few moments the certainty that some sore calamity had occurred had spread through the ship. So travel-stained was he on entering my cabin that I mistook him for his more swarthy friend Beaumont.'[57] On that same day George Porter died.

Royal Navy discipline cranked into action. 'It was a most pleasing sight to me,' Feilden wrote, 'to see the quiet, expeditious manner in which British naval officers meet an emergency. Everybody sat down to tea as quietly as usual. By the time we had finished Capt. Nares came in with a slip of paper detailing the sledges, parties, and supplies to go, and without the slightest noise or bustle in four hours, tents, sledges and tackle were ready, and all hands sitting down to a cup of tea and a snack before starting on this beastly night, as if it was the usual evening's programme.'[58]

By midnight, three sledge parties were on their way to Markham's rescue, the first of which reached him within fifty hours of Parr's departure. When they brought Markham's team back on 14 June, only three men had the use of their feet. Dr Moss was appalled. 'Hardly one of them was recognisable. The thin, feeble voices, the swollen and frost-peeled faces and crippled limbs, made an awful contrast to the picked body of determined men we had seen march north only two months before.'[59] Feilden was so horrified by the account of their sufferings that he refused to record them in his journal, retreating instead to his natural history studies for that day. Subconsciously, however, he gave his own interpretation of Markham's journey. Unbidden, there sprang to mind an incident he had heard from Parr the previous April. 'At 40° [he] watched a little lemming struggling along the floe, it came towards him getting weaker and weaker, it then fell, and when he picked it up it was dead.'[60]

It was much the same for Aldrich as for Markham. He reached 82°16'N, 85°33'W, on 17 May, having named one of the northernmost points on Ellesmere Island after Edward Moss, before scurvy drove him back. Like Markham, he had assumed his men's weariness was caused by physical exertion. When they also complained of sore gums, he realized that they were sick. 'Is scurvy ever got while sledging, sir?'[61] one of them asked him. 'No,' Aldrich lied, the soreness was attributable to the hard tack being too hard. They became weaker and weaker until, by the time Nares's search parties found them on 20 June, four men were strapped to the sledges and another two were limping blindly in their wake. Meanwhile, Aldrich and one other, the fittest remaining of the eight-man contingent, were hauling *both* sledges in a heroically futile attempt to reach safety before they were overtaken by the summer thaw. They would never have made it, travelling at the pace that they did. Even with the help of their rescuers they raced against time. The snow was already turning to slush and more than once during the slog home they fell into the sea as a crust of ice broke beneath them.

If Aldrich and Markham thought they were returning to a safe haven they were mistaken. For scurvy had hit the *Alert* too. In late April, Captain Stephenson had sledged in to see how things stood. Nares assured him that all was well. On 3 May, however, he had a different story. On that day five men reported to Moss with signs of scurvy. Five days later that number had doubled. By 8 June fourteen were down and there was scarcely an able-bodied man on the ship. Following the sledgers' return the number of invalids swelled to insupportable levels. Belatedly, Nares realized how badly they were provisioned. They had subsisted from the beginning on stock Navy fare of salt beef. Anti-scorbutics had been limited in the expectation of their obtaining fresh meat – Hall had reported plentiful supplies of musk-oxen in 'Thank God Harbour'. But they were farther north than 'Thank God Harbour', on a different stretch of land. They had seen little game and had killed less. When the sledge parties left they had already used up most of the Vitamin C stored within their bodies and instead of starting from a point of saturation they were already deep into the twenty-five weeks of grace which scurvy allowed. Ironically, the sledgers had been glad of the salt beef they carried – it made up for the salt they had forgotten to pack – but Nares saw it as the cause of their illness. 'Salt meat should never be supplied for Arctic service,'[62] he said. He also noted that the officers were least affected by scurvy.

Why? Because they had brought their own, privately purchased supplies from home. The hampers into which they tucked each evening at mess had provided just enough Vitamin C to keep them healthy. What Nares could not understand, however, was why the lime juice which every member of the crew had taken daily, had not been sufficient to counteract the deficiencies in their diet. He had no answer to the puzzle, nor any time in which to investigate it. By the end of June the *Alert* had fifty-three crew aboard, only nine of whom were capable of service. Nares had, unquestionably, to return home.

The Revd William Pullen, the *Alert*'s chaplain, agreed with him. Petersen and Porter were dead. The latter had been buried where he fell, a rough cross overlooking the Arctic marking a new northernmost grave. Pullen had read the funeral service over Petersen and unless they left soon he would have to read it over others. On the return of Aldrich and Markham he wrote a poem (a hymn, almost), whose four verses were full of Victorian sentiment but whose last two lines said what everyone felt:

> 'And the breath of His wind shall set us free,
> Through the opening ice to the soft green sea.[63]

The summer of 1876 should have given Nares an opening. It was not there. As Moss said, 'Summer at Floeberg Beach was an affair of weeks, almost days.'[64] Nor was the breath for which Pullen had prayed in evidence. Outside Floeberg Beach the ice was beginning to melt, but the barrier stood as firm as the first day it had formed. Nares could not wait. He blew the ice apart with gunpowder, had his fittest men clear away the chunks, and steamed through the breach into open water, steering down Robeson Channel with the aid of his reduced crew towards the *Discovery*. The soft green sea was thousands of miles away, but the *Discovery* was at a latitude where fresh meat was obtainable. The relief from their scurvy lay there.

*

Of the three sledging expeditions, the eastern, under Beaumont, had been expected to do best. It was heading for land where Hall had reported – and shot – quantities of musk-oxen so there should have been plenty of food. But Hall had shot those beasts in the summer. Beaumont was going there in early spring when nothing was to be had, and he was heading for some of the most daunting mountains and glaciers in the northern hemisphere. Scurvy hit him about the same time as it did the others, and its consequences were as dreadful. Beaumont was quicker than Markham and Aldrich: when substantial numbers fell ill he sent them back on 10 May under Dr Coppinger and Lieutenant Rawson (himself so snow-blind that he hauled blindfold). While recognizing that the sick men had scurvy, he obstinately refused to believe that it might be developing in the others and so, with a reduced team of six he stamped on optimistically.

Draped in harness, Beaumont and his companions ploughed over the north-west coast of Greenland. They slithered across glaciers, so smooth and steep that they had to carve roads in them; in places they took to bare scree. The sledge-runners distorted and buckled under the constant sideways pressure. It was little better on the flat, where the snow was up to four feet deep and no longer crisp and dry but the consistency of wet sugar. 'Walking was most exhausting,' Beaumont recorded. 'One literally had to climb out of the holes made by each foot in succession, the hard crust on top, which would only just *not* bear you, as well as the depth of the snow preventing you from pushing forward through it; each leg sank to about three inches above the knee, and the effort to lift them so high to extricate them from their tight-fitting holes, soon began to tell upon the men.'[65] By 19 May, two men could hardly bend their legs and were reduced to crawling. 'No one will ever believe what hard work this becomes,' Beaumont wrote in his diary. 'Since twelve o'clock it has been my birthday; but I can safely say I never spent one so before, and I don't want to be wished any happy returns of it.'[66]

Their progress was devastatingly slow – two miles a day at best – and they were getting sicker every moment. Beaumont knew by now that the rest of his men had scurvy. They themselves, were not yet aware of it, and he was not going to let them into the secret. 'I did not encourage inspection of the legs,' he wrote, 'and tried to make them think as little of the stiffness as possible, for I knew the unpleasant truth would soon enough be forced upon us.'[67] From where they sat, bedraggled, on 20 May, Beaumont spied a peak beyond the next glacier. He had already set the 23rd as a deadline for turning back – they had barely enough supplies for the return journey – but he hoped that they might yet be able to reach the peak. The view would be valuable in geographical terms; psychologically, too, it would be a fitting point at which to end the journey. Throughout the next two days, however, they were confined to their tent by a blizzard and on the evening of the 22nd, 'a mournful and disappointed party'[68] turned out in the still falling snow for the long haul home.

On the 24th the weather cleared and Beaumont took the chance to climb a 3,700-foot hill in recompense for his disappointment. 'The view was so immense that to sketch it would have been the work of a day,'[69] he wrote, after a six-hour scramble. But it was not the view he would have liked. Inland the glaciers stretched without a break as far as the horizon. To the north, however, his sightline was blocked by haze and mountains. He could not tell how the coast ran nor where it ended – if it did end – nor whether it was lapped by open sea. 'I did not see what I wanted,'[70] he recorded sadly, as he climbed down to the sledge where another snowstorm was blowing up.

Out of a total of seven, only Beaumont and a seaman named Gray were still fit. The rest were 'rather desponding',[71] as Beaumont put it, a masterpiece of understatement which encompassed every stage of scorbutic debilitation. Two men were just capable of hauling; the other three crawled behind on hands and knees. Unlike Markham and Aldrich, who had been able to escape over a ready-cleared road, Beaumont was hampered by poor terrain and evil weather. For days they huddled in their thin tent, while the wind screamed outside. On emerging, they saw that their tracks had been covered by a foot of snow. Before they might have struggled; now they wrestled for their lives.

The new snow had obscured weak patches in the crust of the old, and at every step they and the sledge sank from sight. On 28 May,

Beaumont jettisoned 200 pounds of food and equipment – he could do without the food he decided, as they all had such poor appetites. Thereafter they travelled more swiftly. But on 3 June one man keeled over. They put him on the sledge and continued. On 7 June, another man collapsed and was placed alongside the first. On 10 June, Beaumont decided to make a dash across Robeson Channel for the *Alert*. Accordingly, he threw out every inessential item. The tent went, so did their only gun and the last two items Beaumont carried – his sextant and his knife. Food was all they retained. But when they reached the coast their way was blocked by water and disintegrating ice. They had no option but to head for Polaris Bay, where there was a cache of provisions laid down by Hall's crew years before. 'This was our darkest day,' Beaumont wrote. 'We were forty miles from Polaris Bay at the very least, and only Gray and myself to drag the sick – it did not seem possible.'[72]

Very, very slowly, they hauled southwards. On the 21st they were ten miles from Polaris Bay when they were caught by a gale. They sheltered under a strip of canvas which let in every swirling eddy of snow. 'We were all huddled up in a heap,' Beaumont wrote, 'wet through, and nobody could sleep.'[73] The men with scurvy thrashed constantly to relieve the pain in their joints. When the storm died they were all sodden and to add to the misery of scurvy, the invalids now had pneumonia. On the 23rd another two men were added to the sledge. On the evening of the 24th an occasional hauler, Jones, dropped his rope. A little later, so did Grey. The sledge could go no further. In despair, Beaumont left his men where they were and walked through the snow on his own. If somebody was at Polaris Bay – a forlorn hope – then he might be able to bring help. If nobody was there he was prepared to go back and care for the invalids, giving those who could still walk the choice of making their own way forwards or staying with the sledge – in effect, the choice of dying alone or in company.

Halfway into his journey he met Rawson, Coppinger and Hans Hendrik, driving to his rescue with a dog team. Smoothly they picked him up and carried him back to his abandoned sledge where, with the aid of the dogs, it and its crew continued the journey. Hans brought in a few seals, whose raw flesh was devoured avidly, and so they continued to Polaris Bay where a group of 'Discoverers' was waiting for them.

The last few miles they dragged the sledge over open shingle. It was too late for some: within sight of the Bay, two of Beaumont's men died. On the last day of June, a Sunday, the survivors and their saviours gathered to hear Beaumont read the morning service, 'all of us joining most heartily and fervently in rendering thanks to Almighty God for His gracious mercy and protection towards us'.[74]

Of all the three parties, Beaumont's had suffered the worst. Forty-five years later, the explorer Knud Rasmussen visited the same area of Greenland by dog-sledge. Looking at the glaciers, the rubble and the snowfields over which Beaumont had driven his men, he was struck by what they had done. 'How they managed to pull the sledges up Gap Valley . . . is a perfect riddle to all of us who have looked at the stony pass . . . We others can only bow our heads to those who did it.'[75] Another explorer, Robert Edwin Peary, agreed. A man who rarely praised the efforts of any but himself, even he was forced to admit that it was '[an example] of the most splendid courage, fortitude and endurance, under dire stress of circumstances, that is to be found in the history of Arctic exploration'.[76]

Beaumont's survivors were brought back to the *Discovery* on 15 August, just a few days after the *Alert* made contact with its sister ship. Scurvy had hit Stephenson's crew too. No sooner was everyone aboard than Nares ordered the expedition home. About time, in Hans's opinion. The Americans may have treated him surlily on occasion – perhaps with good reason – but at least the intimacy of their small ships and the exposure of their situation had forced them to treat him as a human being. The British vessels were so large that, isolated within the *Discovery*'s bowels, Hans became an object of gossip and derision. 'I began to perceive that some of the crew were talking about me,' he wrote, 'and had wicked designs towards me.'[77] While the sledge parties were out, he fretted with inactivity. He yearned to be in his element, to escape from this palace of preconception:

'If I should freeze to death it would be preferable to hearing this vile talk about me,'[78] he said. He trusted only Stephenson: 'It was lucky the Commander treated me as a comrade; I did not feel shy in speaking with him, as with other gentlemen.'[79] And he admired only Nares: 'The Captain of our other ship was beyond all praise, one might think he neither slept nor ate.'[80]

It was true, Nares hardly slept a wink or took a bite as he led the two ships down Smith Sound. He personally manned the crows-nest, having occasional meals sent up to him as he directed the *Alert* through the floes. The Arctic sunshine was coming to an end and young ice was forming – frighteningly early – for the next winter. His coal was nearly finished, as was his oil, and below decks his crew were lighting candles in place of lamps.

On 5 September Nares reached a point where his flock of lieutenants wanted to go exploring again – up so-called Hayes Sound, which led westwards off Smith Sound and which may have provided another entry to the Open Polar Sea. (It was, in fact, only a bay.) Nares demurred. They had only a few tons of coal left and he was not willing to risk another year in the ice. Egerton agreed: 'I shall be glad to be clear out of this.'[81] Markham, too, was against such a venture. All he wanted was to be free of the Arctic. 'It was with no small amount of thankfulness,' he wrote, 'that on the 9th of September we emerged from the cold, grim clutches that seemed only too ready to detain us for another winter in the realms of the Ice King, and that we felt our ship rise and fall once more on the bosom of an undoubted ocean swell.'[82]

On 2 November they returned to Portsmouth Harbour. 'I will not dwell on the warm and hearty reception which the officers and men received from all classes of their countrymen,'[83] Nares wrote. But underlying the warmth was a sense of disappointment, for which Nares had only himself to blame. Stopping off in Ireland he had sent a telegram, alerting the Admiralty to his return. Its text clanged through the corridors of power like a funeral bell: 'NORTH POLE IMPRACTICABLE.'

*

Britain was very happy to see Nares home. From Balmoral, on 4 November 1876, Queen Victoria sent a telegram thanking 'these gallant men for what they have accomplished'.[84] Backs were slapped, medals were struck, speeches were given and promotions were issued to every officer save one. Nares was awarded the Royal Geographical Society's Gold Medal, and was presented with a gold watch for his achievement. And it was an achievement, even if the Pole hadn't been reached. The expedition had broken the record for farthest north; it had produced charts which would not be bettered for fifty years; it had brought back scientific findings which would later give rise to some forty published articles and reports; it had taken more than 100 photographs which, if lacking artistry – the main subject was often obscured by blocks of ice – still represented the largest and earliest corpus of Arctic camera-work; and above all it had returned intact. An officer less prudent than Nares might have pressed on in the same spirit as Franklin – and, without doubt, to the same conclusion. There had been fatalities, but no more than on previous expeditions. In the balance of things, the stolid, orderly Nares had done well.

Nares had also provided Britain with a sterling example of its own grit. Not until Scott's death in Antarctica in 1912 would Britons fight so valiantly against the polar odds. Of Parr's life-saving trek to get help for Markham's sledge-team, the President of the Royal Geographical Society, Sir Alcock Rutherford, said, 'I know of nothing more heroic in the annals of war or travel than that solitary walk of thirty miles.'[85] A pundit for the *Quarterly Review* agreed with him. 'There are some defeats which are more glorious than victories; some failures which are grander than the most magnificent success.'[86] It was irrelevant that Britain had failed to reach the Pole. 'We read with such unmixed satisfaction,' the *Quarterly*'s man wrote, 'of the truly heroic endurance exhibited by the sledge parties under Markham and Beaumont that we hardly care to inquire whether any minor objects of scientific interest have been left unattained.'[87]

But in doing so well Nares had also done so badly. 'NORTH POLE IMPRACTICABLE'. These seven syllables tolled resoundingly. They shattered Britain's presumption of Arctic competence, the supremacy of the Royal Navy, the Royal Geographical Society's dreams of conquest and, paramountly, public confidence. They shattered the whole crystal edifice which Sherard Osborn and Clements Markham had taken so long to construct.

It started in the press. 'The Polar Failure', is how one headline announced Nares's return. 'Verily the expedition of 1875–6 has but little of which to boast. It went out like a rocket and has come back like the stick,'[88] wrote *The Navy* magazine. Previously Nares's supporter, it was now his vehement critic. Puce with patriotic frustration, it insisted he be court-martialled for his lack of zeal and for the sin of declaring the Pole impracticable without sufficient cause. He had made the Admiralty a laughing-stock in the eyes of foreign nations. The *Saturday Review* (popular on both sides of the Atlantic) declared that 'the principal officers in command had no heart in the work; that they went because they were appointed and returned as speedily as they could'[89]. Even medical journals joined the chorus. The sufferings of Markham, Aldrich, Beaumont and their men were irrelevant. So were their views (unanimously unfavourable) as to the prospect of attaining the Pole. As for Rutherford and the *Quarterly*, their opinions carried as much weight as a spun farthing. Nares had been sent to plant the Union Jack at the Pole. Instead he had returned with some story about impossibility.

Nares's failure attracted vitriol partly because it had occurred in a slack period of imperialism. The Ashanti War had ended in 1874 and not until the Zulu War of 1877–9 would newspapers be able to drum their shields so noisily. In the interim, Nares was a handy scapegoat. He was not court-martialled but he had to sit through a long and detailed inquiry into why scurvy had been allowed to take hold. From 10 January to 3 March 1877, seven admirals – one of them Inglefield – sat from 11.00 a.m. to 5.00 p.m. every day of the week except Sunday, listening to statements from fifty expert witnesses, twenty-one of whom had been on the expedition. More than 9,000 questions were asked and reams of answers were recorded, creating the largest body of paperwork on the Arctic since the Franklin search.

The findings were published by HM Stationery Office in a 500-page tome whose leather-bound spine carried the words 'Scurvy Report'. It is an unbelievable document, delving into minutiae such as the tannin content of the expedition's tea, the quantity of potash in its lime juice, the fat content of its tinned carrots, the amount of carbon monoxide present in different quarters of the *Alert* and the heights above floor level at which the air was sampled. It shows that Nares's men liked salt beef and disliked salt pork, that they ate regulation amounts of tinned vegetables, that they were fond of chillies and curry powder but wary of cloves or nutmeg, and that an official taster had judged the foods to be of top quality – ruefully, he said he'd never eaten better salt beef in his whole naval service. It records that the men on the *Alert* drank almost 1,000 gallons of rum, twenty-two gallons of port, twenty of sherry, seven of gin, three of brandy, and two of whisky, plus eighteen bottles of champagne and only three bottles of a concoction called Tent. Apparently, some people thought scurvy was caused by 'insufficient exercise and personal filth',[90] and others thought that it was brought about by a lack of eggs. The document contains the medical orders with which each sledge captain was issued, telling him how to restore a man from coma, how to diagnose a broken knee-cap, how to set a fractured leg, how to treat snow-blindness and frostbite, and at painful (and puzzling) length how a catheter should be introduced into the penis to alleviate obstructions of the bladder. The medical orders make no mention of scurvy. The report ends with more than 100 pages of accusatory cross-questioning in small print.

Nares did not come out of it well. Why hadn't he trained his sledge crews better? the panel asked. But he had trained them, he said. Then why hadn't he given them more anti-scorbutics? The two ounces of dried potato per man per day which they had been allocated wasn't much. The Navy's leading medical expert, Dr Armstrong, had advised him to issue lime juice as well. Why hadn't he? Few sledge expeditions in the past had taken lime juice, he replied, and they had not caught scurvy despite being out far longer than his men. Anyway, as Markham's and Aldrich's journals revealed, they had taken bottles of lime juice and little good it had done them. Then why hadn't he given them extra lime juice before they left? But he had, he'd doubled their rations in the preceding weeks. Why then, since the disease had obviously taken hold before the sledgers left, hadn't he followed a healthier dietary regime? Because that was the regime he had been instructed to follow – a standard regime which he had been promised would keep scurvy at bay for at least two years and probably three. So why had his men got scurvy and other expeditions hadn't? All Nares could suggest was that previous expeditions had misreported the disease; they had said they were suffering from exhaustion when really it was scurvy in disguise – the sledge captains had made the same mistake.

The inquiry battered away at Nares, revealing every flaw in his character (and chasms of its own ignorance – one doctor linked scurvy to elephantiasis in India, and another to the direction of the wind in Borneo), before declaring that they didn't know what had caused the outbreak but it was probably lack of lime juice and it was Nares's fault.

The inquiry delivered its verdict in strangled Admiraltese: 'We find that the orders of the Commander of the Expedition for provisioning the three extended and principal spring parties did not include lime juice, thereby deviating from the 11th Article of the Memorandum of Recommendations and Suggestions of the Medical Director-General, furnished by their Lordships for his information, and that the reasons assigned for such deviation being insufficient, the said orders were not proper.'[91]

In fact, the Royal Navy's vaunted efficiency was to blame. As previous expeditions had found that ordinary lime juice froze in its bottles and burst them, the Navy had supplied Nares with a concentrated version. The concentrating process involved boiling the juice in a copper kettle. Copper leaches Vitamin C and heat destroys it. Thus the lime juice with which Nares dosed his men had been stripped of most of its anti-scorbutic properties. The sledgers' body store of Vitamin C would have been depleted long before they started. What lime juice they carried did them little good as, in the conditions they encountered, even the concentrate froze. Having neither the time nor the fuel to thaw it properly, they slept with the bottles clasped to their chests. The meagre essence settled at the bottom and the sips they took from the top had as much benefit as tap water. Ironically, they were victims of a technology designed to save them. None of this would be known, however, until the discovery of Vitamin C in the twentieth century. In the meantime, Nares was considered to be the culprit.

Nares's allies spoke their minds. Clements Markham published an immediate rebuttal of the Scurvy Report, citing sympathetic sources such as the legendary sledger, Sir Leopold McClintock. In a letter to *The Times* on 21 May 1877, Rutherford, as President of the Royal Geographical Society, regretted 'the ungenerous, not to say vindictive, criticism with which the leader of the late Expedition has been persecuted by a certain portion of the Press, more especially that portion representing the medical profession . . . it might almost be inferred that he is a fit subject for the Chamber of Horrors in Baker-Street.'[92] Their support prevented Nares from becoming a complete pariah. He was later knighted and eventually became an Admiral, but he never went to the Arctic again and he never forgot that of all the officers on that expedition, he was the only one not to be immediately promoted. Captain Albert Markham – as he already was by the time of the inquiry – was given a gold watch by the Royal Geographical Society to commemorate his Farthest North. It ticked superbly, and when the British Government introduced daylight saving in 1916, he refused to alter it because it still kept Nares's hours.

Nares, nevertheless, had the last blast. 'I would request our many friends who suggest plans for assisting us over the ice to first mature their propositions in a more temperate region,' he said in a speech to the Royal Geographical Society. 'Without in any way detracting from the suggestions, I may state that no one can realise what Arctic sledge-travelling really means until he has travelled across country, totally on his own resources, say, from London to Edinburgh and back again. If the advocates of ballooning [a sport that was gathering speed] will start from the north of Scotland, carrying their own provisions, visit Iceland, 450 miles distant, and return exactly to their starting point – for a mistake of 20 miles would be fatal – without receiving any outside aid, then only can we entertain the idea of using a balloon.'[93] He was right to attack his critics and visionary in his appreciation of the problems involved in ballooning – which would be used in a subsequent attempt to reach the Pole. Importantly, though, he was hinting that there might be more efficient ways of travelling in polar climes than by the British tradition of heavily manned expeditions sent from big ships.

Britain ignored him. Having led the way, or having wanted to lead it, the nation ran out of puff. With imperial commitments elsewhere it could no longer be bothered with the frozen north. On the streets of London, cockneys thought so mockingly of the North Pole that they adopted it as rhyming slang for 'arsehole'. One officer at the Royal Geographical Society agreed that it was a waste of effort. Possibly a ship might break through the pack off Spitsbergen. What would it discover? Nothing beyond a stretch of ice. 'Let the nation decide,' he wrote sadly. 'Geography has little to gain by it, science perhaps less.'[94]

11

HIS WORD IS LAW

On 18 September 1875, the day on which the *Alert* dropped anchor at Floeberg Beach, Carl Weyprecht rose to address the Forty-Eighth Meeting of German Naturalists and Physicians at Graz in Austria. He wanted to have a word about some 'Fundamental Principles of Scientific Arctic Exploration'. Outwardly there was nothing exciting about the title of his speech. Those present would have expected a précis of recent events, concentrating on German or Austrian achievements. One would clap politely at its conclusion and then proceed to meatier fare.

Weyprecht's speech, however, was revolutionary. After a brief introduction he launched into a tirade against what he called 'the greed for discovery'. 'The mania for this has reached such a pitch, that to-day, Arctic exploration has become a sort of international steeple-chase with the North Pole as its goal,' he said. 'The mere conquest of physical difficulties has usurped the place of real scientific labour. Everywhere the Arctic question is discussed, everywhere the best way to the Pole is a matter of dispute; but few enquire concerning the treasures of science which lie scattered along the way.'[1] His audience must have shifted uneasily. Was this the same Weyprecht who had

brought Austria into the race – his own words – and who had striven
so valiantly to win it for the German peoples? Was their polar hero
dismissing his own achievements – and by extension the ambitions of
a whole *Volk* – as a frivolous pastime? They listened in consternation as
he forged on. 'The investigation of these vast unknown regions about
the Pole will and must be pursued, regardless of cost of money and
human life, so long as man makes any pretension to progress.'[2] This
was more like it. But . . . 'Its great object,' he continued, 'must be a
nobler one than mapping and naming icebound islands, bays and
promontories in this or that language, or reaching a higher latitude
than any predecessor.'[3] Weyprecht's message to the assembly was that
the North Pole, on its own, was not worth the seeking.

In the past there had been arguments over the value of Arctic
exploration. The rationale that it would bring scientific benefits had
always won. But it had always been an excuse, hiding this or that
country's desire to be the first through the North-West Passage or the
first to the Pole. Sponsors, governments or otherwise, had played
along. They cared little about currents, weather patterns or the globe's
magnetic fields. They wanted to plant a flag. Weyprecht was calling
their bluff. If the world – by which he meant Europe and North
America – truly wanted to pursue science then it should forget
competition and unite in an international programme of Arctic observation and analysis. Such a programme would produce something
worthwhile, something which would not involve rash acts of derring-do
and which would be of use to humankind. He was absolutely right, and
by the early 1880s people would be acting on his advice. For the
moment, however, he was unpopular. He had stripped the Pole of its
mystique.

To James Gordon Bennett, proprietor of the *New York Herald*, none
of this mattered. Weyprecht may have been correct in his assessment
of the Pole's worth. Bennett, on the other hand, was not fettered by
the need for scientific justification. His only concern was to sell newspapers, and to do this he had to give his readers news. The discovery
of the North Pole would be very big news indeed.

*

James Gordon Bennett was the nineteenth century's newspaperman par excellence. The only son of a wealthy father – also called James Gordon Bennett, founder of the *Herald* – he was one of the richest men alive. On a personal level, he was slightly revolting. He was an alcoholic playboy of unstable temperament, who had been known to leap naked into the driving seat of a coach-and-four and disappear for weeks on end. He was fond of excitement: apart from his coaching activities he was an accomplished sailor, participating in 1870 in the first transatlantic yacht race; he introduced the sport of polo to the United States; he enjoyed a fight and he was a gambler of distinction. If people objected to his behaviour he responded with wads of cash. When blackballed by all reputable casinos, for example, he simply built his own. Others might have been glamourized by this reputation, Bennett merely garnered a name for shabbiness. He was finally ostracized by New York society for urinating into his fiancée's fireplace at a New Year's Eve party. Thereupon he met his would-be brother-in-law in the last formal duel fought on US soil and fled to Paris from where (clad in chain mail lest the brother-in-law, whom he had failed to kill, rematerialize) he ran the *Herald* with an iron fist.

Bennett's wealth enabled him to do as he pleased. When the trans-atlantic cable proved too expensive he laid down his own. When he tired of Paris he took to the sea aboard an architect-designed yacht, on which a sea-going cow provided him with fresh milk daily. The yacht was called the *Namounia* – but to his terrified New York employees, who never knew when Bennett might suddenly spring ashore and sack them all (he liked to do that) it was known as the *Pneumonia*. Bennett kept live owls in his office as a symbol of wisdom. Bennett had foot-long blue pencils (renewed daily) with which, when not at sea, he edited every word that appeared in the *Herald*. Bennett was the man who, on being reproved for rebuilding his headquarters on a short-lease site – and crowning it with electric owls whose eyes illuminated the surrounding square – retorted, 'Thirty years from now the *Herald* will be in Harlem and I'll be in Hell; so what do we care?'[4] Bennett was likened by one employee to the Caliph of Baghdad. According to the *Herald*'s editor, Ralph Blumenfeld (later the editor of

London's *Daily Express*), 'His word is law.'[5] More than anything, however, Bennett was a man who knew how to make news.

Until now, news had simply been reported. Bennett, however,
created news. Take the British missionary David Livingstone. He
had been lost in Africa for years and by 1869 was given up for dead.
Bennett took his best correspondent to one side and said, 'I will tell
you what you will do. Draw a thousand pounds now and when you
have gone through that, draw another thousand, and when that is
spent, draw another, and when you have finished that, draw another
thousand and so on – BUT FIND LIVINGSTONE.'[6] The correspondent, Henry Morton Stanley, did find Livingstone in 1871 and
gave the world his immortal line, 'Dr. Livingstone, I presume.'
Bennett's blue pencil sliced through Livingstone's reply. 'The
Herald! Who hasn't heard of that despicable newspaper?'[7]

Livingstone's rescue sold copies and Bennett was delighted. He used
the Livingstone–Stanley formula repeatedly, sending correspondents
on hair-raising expeditions around the globe in search of this or that
person or place. The beauty of it all was that should one of his
'Stanleys' disappear in their search for a 'Livingstone' – either human
or geographical – then they too became a 'Livingstone' after whom
another 'Stanley' could be sent. When Stanley himself disappeared on
an expedition for the relief of Emin Pasha, Bennett instructed Edward
Vizetelly to go to Zanzibar. 'It's an awful place, you know. You get the
fever there and die in a week.' To which Vizetelly replied: 'I'll go to
Timbuctoo if you like.'[8] The deal made, they retired to Bennett's
yacht in Beirut harbour, where Vizetelly's last recollection of that
evening was Bennett's invitation to see who could swim around the
vessel without being eaten by sharks. In due course, the Vizetelly
'Stanley' rescued the real Stanley and in due course Gordon Bennett
made money from the tale. The formula worked marvellously until
1879. In that year, Bennett decided to go for the Pole.

The Arctic was not new ground as far as Bennett was concerned. In
1875 he had sponsored a British captain, Sir Allen Young, to take a
small ship, the *Pandora*, in search of the most newsworthy 'Livingstone'
after Livingstone himself – Sir John Franklin. The expedition achieved

little. Nor did a second *Herald*–sponsored expedition to Greenland do much for sales. A land expedition under Lieutenant Frederick Schwatka in 1878–9 was more successful, covering 2,800 miles and returning with the body of one of Franklin's officers – not to mention naming a mountain after Bennett himself. A keen Anglophobe, Bennett had previously been snubbed by the British over the matter of place names. When Prime Minister William Gladstone was shown one of Stanley's maps, on which two African mountains and a river were daubed with the name 'Bennett', he had struck them off. Why had Stanley given them such absurd names, he wanted to know? Now the absurd name stood alongside those of Britain's finest.

These were trifles compared to the Pole. Nares may have reached the highest north to date but in Bennett's view America had paved the way for him. It would be a national shame if the United States did not recapture its Arctic prestige. And it would be an even greater shame if the *Herald* did not play some part in it. In 1877, following a three-hour consultation with Petermann, Bennett was convinced he knew how to reach the Pole. Nares had made it clear that Smith Sound was out of the question. Payer and Weyprecht had proved the futility of following the Gulf Stream off Spitsbergen. There remained the second and as yet untested thermometric gateway via Bering Strait. Bennett would strike there.

Petermann was only too pleased to lend his support. He was still smarting from the criticisms of Sherard Osborn and Clements Markham. He had continually said that Smith Sound was the wrong route and his greatest detractors had proved him right. Withdrawing his overtures of peace, he belaboured the Royal Geographical Society vigorously. Smith Sound was 'an incubus on Arctic research'. It had been 'artificially puffed up', and it was now 'finished'.[9] If the Gulf Stream theory had been refuted it was only because it was so right: the Gulf Stream was obviously so powerful that it had beaten back the ice flowing south from the polar cap, crumpling it into a mass in which Weyprecht and Payer had had the ill luck to become entangled. All one had to do, therefore, was attack the Pole where it was weakest, and one could judge where it was weakest by two criteria: the

amount of ice flowing south – which must thereby create an
expanse of open water behind it – and the prevalence of open water
in other areas. The east coast of Greenland matched the first criterion,
as his own expedition had proved – look at the *Hansa*; simply carried
away by floes – and Wrangel's 'Polynia' off the Siberian coast fitted
the second. 'It is not a waterhole, as has often been asserted,'
Petermann wrote huffily, 'but an extensive open sea, of which we
know as yet very little, but this little with sufficient certainty, that
this open sea is always, summer and winter, every year, found in the
same place.'[10]

When the Royal Geographical Society paid him no attention, he
looked to the US and Bennett. In a *Herald* interview, he stated that
the Nares expedition had resulted only in 'wasted money and lives'.[11]
As could be expected of the British, he concluded, with some justification and to Clements Markham's annoyance. Bennett's proposed
expedition should head for the Polynia through Bering Strait and the
man to lead such a voyage (here, perhaps, one of Bennett's mighty
pencils came into play) should be 'a navigator who goes to work with
the commonsense and determination Stanley showed in Africa'.[12]
Commander George Washington De Long was the chosen one.

A sheltered man of Huguenot descent, De Long looked somewhat
like a disgruntled, provincial doctor. He was balding, wore a large
moustache, and stared at the world through small eyes and *pince-nez*
spectacles with a little ribbon attached. His pictures suggest diligence,
obedience and a slight irritation – a wish to be doing something
else. He had served as commanding officer aboard one of the ships
sent to rescue Hall's expedition and had formed a low opinion of
the Arctic – 'I never in my life saw such a dreary land of desolation,
and I hope I may never find myself cast away in such a perfectly
God-forsaken place.'[13] During this trip, however, he had been
lionized by one of Bennett's special correspondents and on return to
New York he found that the *Herald* had built him up into a conquering
hero of the Kane stamp. Bemused, but not wishing to miss an
opportunity for advancement, he changed tack and became an ardent
Arctophile.

De Long was a complicated person. He was not a particularly good sailor and had once been court-martialled for running his ship aground – a charge against which he defended himself by blaming another. He had also been accused of wanton brutality when running a schoolship for young boys – which may or may not have been true. His journals, however, reveal a man of sensitivity and dry humour who had the gumption to resurrect a flagging career. He threw himself into the Arctic with all the zeal of a convert. 'The Polar virus was in his blood and would not let him rest,'[14] his wife Emma later wrote. He lobbied Grinnell, unsuccessfully, for funds before turning to James Gordon Bennett who was more than willing to sponsor another stab at the Arctic, particularly as the man in charge would be a hero that his own paper had created. De Long was elated. Bennett's fortune and influence were worth more than all the Grinnells in the world – as was shown in 1878 when Bennett pushed Congress into declaring the project a national undertaking.

Bennett did not require the US Navy to provide a ship. He already had that in hand, having purchased the *Pandora* from Allen Young and renamed it the *Jeannette*, after his sister. What he did require was that the *Jeannette* be further strengthened for Arctic service and be accompanied by a naval vessel until the moment it reached the polar pack. This, he insisted, should be done at government expense. That the government's involvement would add extra authority to the venture, as well as saving him money, went unspoken.

Bennett's wealth and influence made things happen quickly, but they did not happen quite as they should have. When the yards got hold of the *Jeannette* they decided the ship was unequal to the task and proposed a refitting that, for boilers alone, cost almost ten times the amount Bennett had been expecting. De Long did his best, cajoling, browbeating and bargaining to reduce this expense. He performed admirably. But then came more alterations and further expenses and, ultimately, the best De Long could do was to fix a time limit after which all costs would be borne not by the Navy but by Bennett. He hoped that he had arranged things to his employer's advantage.

When the hammering ceased, the *Jeannette* had a bow packed ten-feet deep with solid pine; its hull was of oak timbers held in place by wrought-iron straps; below the waterline it was sheathed with 3½ inches of elm; inside, it was braced by a combination of iron beams and wooden trusses that added to the considerable number of bulk-heads and iron trusses already installed by Allen Young. New boilers were fitted; the deck was replaced; additional gunmetal propellers were installed alongside the original copper ones; felt was fitted around every length of exposed ironwork; and a similarly felted porch was erected outside the officers' quarters. For all De Long's efforts, the final bill, as presented to Bennett, was some $50,000. The yards still considered the ship unsuitable for Arctic conditions.

At this, Bennett's support evaporated. He could easily afford the expense but caprice and instability were his hallmarks. It had been understood that he would appear in person to promote De Long's voyage. He did not do so. Absorbed in his eccentric pursuits on the other side of the Atlantic, and seized by a sudden fear of being recognized – and maybe attacked by his ex-fiancée's brother – he could not bring himself to make the journey to the States. 'The country was full of rumours about your coming over,' De Long wrote. 'Everybody in the Department asked me when you might be expected. Of course, I had no answer . . . The uncertainty of your movements seemed to weaken the ardor.'[15]

The promise of a Navy ship to tow the *Jeannette* north disappeared. So did the offer of a support vessel carrying spare food and fuel. If the sponsor could not appear in person then the Navy was not going to support his demands, however influential he was. It would consider the *Jeannette* to be under US naval jurisdiction – but only just.

De Long pleaded constantly with Bennett to exercise his influence, and to show more interest in the project. His pleas were met with vague assurances and, sometimes, silence. The truth was, Bennett had grown cool on the idea. Perhaps he realized that the Pole could not be captured on a journalistic whim. Perhaps, too, he had doubts about Petermann's theories. Certainly, though, he knew it was safer to be a Stanley than a Livingstone, and that the exploits of a rescuer were just as newsworthy as those of a discoverer. It would be much more satisfactory if De Long could capitalize on a disaster rather than become one. As it happened there was a man waiting to be rescued in the very area that De Long was to explore. His name was Baron Nils Adolf Erik Nordenskiöld.

Nordenskiöld was a Swedish explorer of considerable experience who had set himself the task of discovering a North-East Passage. Compared to the tortuous North-West Passage, that had seduced hundreds into its depths, the North-East Passage was a relatively straightforward proposition. It ran to the north of Russia's Siberian coast and its completion required not so much navigational skills as one ice-free summer and the willingness to overwinter until the next year's thaw. Unlike the North-West Passage, the North-East Passage did have a modicum of commercial value, linking the two sides of Russia's Empire as well as providing a conduit for the produce of Siberia.

Nordenskiöld had sailed from Gothenburg on 4 July 1878 aboard the *Vega* and that winter had sent a message overland to Yakutsk, announcing that he was frozen in near the mouth of the Lena River but was optimistic that come the summer he would break free and 'in a few months hail Japan'.[16] As it would eventually transpire, Nordenskiöld's assessment was accurate. But in the meantime the authorities had every reason to doubt it. The annals of Arctic exploration were littered with cheery prospects that had turned sour; and the brink of success was a nasty place with teeth. Word spread that Nordenskiöld was in need of assistance and Alexander Siberiakoff, a Russian merchant who had partly financed the *Vega*, put in motion a rescue mission.

De Long dismissed fears for Nordenskiöld's well-being. 'There seems to be unnecessary alarm,' he told Bennett. 'He is simply frozen in, from what I hear.'[17] To a San Francisco journalist he stated, 'I am as satisfied of Nordenskiöld's safety as I am that tomorrow's sun will shine.'[18] None of this touched the proprietor of the *Herald*. Bennett was much more interested in a good story. Without consulting De Long he wrote to the US Naval Secretary that: 'I am sure you will agree with me that motives of humanity suggest as the very first object the rescue and aid of Professor Nordenskiöld.'[19] The secretary agreed that this aim should 'be kept constantly prominent'.[20] At the same time Bennett wrote to Siberiakoff advising him to delay his plans: what was the point of going to all that expense when the *Jeannette* might be there before him? Siberiakoff, like the US Naval Secretary, agreed that this made sense. When De Long heard that his polar thrust was to be delayed by a search for Nordenskiöld – in his opinion unnecessary – he was angry. Such a task could only hinder his object of getting as far north as possible before the ice closed.

Adding to De Long's distress was the matter of his crew. He had managed to secure several leading men with Arctic experience: Lt. Charles Chipp and Engineer George Melville, both of whom had served on the *Polaris* rescue mission; William Dunbar, an ice master with long experience on New England whalers; and William Nindemann, a carpenter who had served on the *Polaris* itself and who had survived the epic ice-floe escape. Thereafter he was at a loss. His surgeon James Ambler came aboard unwillingly and did so only because he was at the top of the Navy's list for duty. Few crewmen volunteered, so De Long had to scour docksides for men whom he eventually paid slightly more than the going rate. And his Master in charge of navigation, the suave Lt. John Danenhower, was foisted on him by Bennett because he came from a 'good' family. To De Long's dismay he learned that Danenhower had poor eyesight, had suffered a nervous breakdown and had been committed to a lunatic asylum from which only his family connections had released him. Danenhower also suffered from syphilis – though, naturally, he did not advertise the fact. 'I cannot yet bring myself to have that *implicit* confidence in him that I would like to feel,'[21] De Long wrote.

There was also Raymond Newcomb, an enthusiastic but inexperienced naturalist who came equipped with 'an elaborate outfit replete with cups, seins, dredges, taxidermist tools, and countless boxes and bottles of every shape and size'.[22] And there was Jerome Collins, the *Herald* meteorologist, whose main talent lay in making dreadful puns but who was given charge of two inventions that Bennett thought newsworthy novelties in the Arctic: the telephone and the electric lamp. Bell and Edison were both consulted in this regard.

De Long was slightly nervous about his position as head of what he called 'our little family'. As he told his wife, 'I try to be pleasant and agreeable without being familiar, gentle but firm in correcting anything I see wrong, and always calm and possessed. I feel my responsibility and care and I hope I appreciate the delicate position I am placed in of leading and directing so many people of my own age.'[23] He worried about Danenhower, but when Bennett and the Navy both gave orders that he was on no account to dismiss him, De Long conceded. Besides, he had grown to like the man, and Danenhower did seem to know his business.

The *Jeannette* left San Francisco on 8 July 1879, a vessel of 240 tons, carrying an engine of 200 horsepower and laden, so deeply that it wallowed, with provisions to last three years. There was still no sign of Bennett, but De Long carried a telegram from the elusive potentate which went a little way to make amends. 'If icebound,' Bennett had cabled the *Herald*'s New York office regarding De Long, 'I shall spare neither money nor influence to follow him up and send assistance next year, so neither he nor his men will be in danger. I wish this to be an American success. Tell him in case he returns next year, unsuccessful, which I don't believe possible, I shall most certainly send another expedition the following year, and continue doing so until successful, but had rather the victory be his than another's. Should De Long not return next year, or in fact never, the widows of the men belonging to the expedition will be protected by me. Should like him to tell this to his men on departure.'[24] De Long did tell his men (most of whom were unmarried). 'Thank God I have a man at my back to see me through when countries fail,'[25] he wrote happily.

Had he studied the telegram more closely, or had a better insight into his employer's machinations, De Long would have realized what was going on. Not content with casting him as a Stanley in search of the Pole, Bennett was also lining him up as a Livingstone in need of rescue. But De Long was too relieved to be at last on the voyage of his dreams for such subtleties to sink in. The crowds cheered in their thousands along San Francisco's wharves and from Telegraph Hill. A ten-gun salute boomed from Fort Point as the *Jeannette*, escorted by a white-sailed convoy from the San Francisco Yacht Club, headed bravely into the Pacific. 'The ship is now beginning her voyage to that unknown part of the world lying north of Bering Strait,' De Long wrote. 'May God's blessing attend us all.'[26]

A few weeks later, De Long was refuelling in Alaska, where he took on not only coal – a local, low-grade variety that burned more quickly than he liked – but teams of dogs and two indigenous hunters, Alexey and Aniguin, to assist in exploring the land masses he would encounter. He relished his forthcoming adventure in the Open Polar Sea. 'I shall go to the extreme limit of possible navigation that I am able to attain,' he wrote home. 'If the current takes me to the west, you will hear of me through St. Petersburg; but if it takes me eastward and northward, there is no saying what points I may reach; but I hope to come out through Smith's or Jones's Sound.'[27]A group of whaling captains who were in the area came forward to give their opinions as to the *Jeannette*'s chances. Most of them looked positively on the venture. But the last to speak, Captain Nye, had a ruthlessly honest appreciation of its chances. 'Gentlemen, there isn't much to be said about this matter. You, Lieutenant De Long, have a very strong vessel, have you not? Magnificently equipped for the service, with unexceptionable crew and aids? And you will take plenty of provisions, and all the coal you can carry?' To each of these questions De Long replied in the affirmative. 'Then,' said Nye, 'put her into the ice and let her drift, and you may get through or you may go to the devil, and the chances are about equal.'[28] If anything, Nye was giving De Long favourable odds. The region into which the *Jeannette* was heading was famously awful. In the last eight years, thirty-three whalers carrying more than 600 men had drifted north-east from Alaska. None of them had ever returned.

De Long's immediate objectives, however, lay not to the north-east but to the north-west: the tiny Herald Island and the larger Wrangel

Land, which lay off the Siberian coast. In this manner he hoped to show willing over Nordenskiöld's rescue, while continuing to attack the Pole. He was particularly excited about Wrangel Land which, although landed upon, had never been properly surveyed. Some geographers thought it might be a second Greenland; others thought it might even be joined to Greenland itself, creating a land mass that curved voluptuously across the top of the world. Both these ideas had emanated from Petermann. It might have been thought that the Nares expedition had all but spelled out the non-existence of a Polar Sea, let alone the impossibility of a trans-Polar land mass, but facts travelled slowly in those days and their interpretation became muddled, even in academic circles. In the absence of a global network, people could pick and choose from whichever theory caught their fancy. The farther one was from the centre – which was still Europe – the more one could accommodate theories without reference to the facts. De Long, with Bennett's support, was particularly accommodating. His last, touching letter to his wife was dated 27 August 1879. 'Goodbye, my precious darling, with a thousand kisses. With God's help I shall yet do something to make you proud of bearing your husband's name. Do not give me up for I shall one day or another come back.'[29]

Touching the Russian side of Bering Strait, De Long learned that Nordenskiöld and the *Vega* had already passed that way, having successfully completed the first navigation of the North-East Passage. His rescue, therefore, was one less thing to worry about. But the detour had cost valuable time and summer was coming to an end. Infuriated by the delay, De Long nevertheless determined to reach Wrangel Land before the ice closed in. At the beginning of September, with 100 miles separating him from his goal, he raised steam and charged the pack. On the 4th, US whalers spotted a plume of black smoke on the horizon. A bank of fog obscured their view for a few hours and when it lifted the plume was gone. The last sighting of the *Jeannette* boded well. The braced, bulk-headed, elm-clad little ship, with its pine-packed bow, was obviously up to the task.

De Long battered at the ice, seeking every lead that took him towards Wrangel Land. He personally sat in the crow's-nest, directing the helmsman towards any opening that appeared. There were plenty of openings, each of which heightened his expectations, but the open water he spied, which sometimes stretched into lakes hundreds of yards across, was deceptive. Winter was approaching and by the time the ship reached one lake it had sludged over. When De Long directed it to another lake, the same thing would happen. By the end of the month he had abandoned the idea of reaching Wrangel Land. Instead he turned his attentions to Herald Island, a barren pimple some fifty miles to the east. He never reached it.

The ice closed in, heeling the *Jeannette* at an uncomfortable angle and squeezing her so gently that it was some time before De Long noticed the deck sticking underfoot as its boards separated and oozed a mastic of tar and oakum. They were comprehensively nipped. Thereafter began a series of alarms and near-sinkings of the kind Weyprecht and Payer had encountered. 'Living over a powder mill waiting for an explosion would be a similar mode of existence,'[30] De Long wrote wearily. He could have borne the strain better had they discovered something new, but they had not discovered anything and in present circumstances it did not look as if they ever would. 'When we added to our wintering in the pack, with all its uncertainties and terrors, the knowledge that we attained no high latitude our first season, made no discoveries, so far as we know have made no useful additions to scientific knowledge, we cannot help feeling that we are doing nothing towards the object of the expedition.'[31] Most of all, he was disappointed that Petermann's eternal Polynia was nowhere in evidence and that the Kuro Siwo seemed not to have the smallest effect on the Arctic pack.

The US Coast and Geodetic Survey knew why this was so. That winter, having completed a study of currents off the coast of Alaska, it announced that 'The [Bering] Strait is *incapable* of carrying a current of warm water of sufficient magnitude to have any marked effect on the condition of the Polar basin just north of it . . . Nothing in our knowledge offers any hope of an easier passage to the Pole. Nothing in the least tends to support the widely spread but unphilosophical notion that in any part of the Polar Sea we may look for large areas free from ice.'[32] As Dr Thomas Antisell told the American Geographical Society, 'Bering Sea is no real gateway into the Arctic Ocean. It is instead a cul-de-sac.'[33] In the normal course of events this would have elicited a vigorous rebuttal from Petermann. But on this occasion there was no dyspeptic bulletin. The Sage of Gotha had killed himself the previous year, leaving De Long to pursue his legacy alone.

Throughout the winter, as life turned slantwise, and plates slid off the table, small disagreements flared into resentment aboard the *Jeannette*. Newcomb, the naturalist new-boy, was ribbed so mercilessly that he retired into silence. Collins, the *Herald* correspondent who had been touted by Bennett, not only as the expedition's meteorologist but its main scientist, was treated with derision. The electric lights, which De Long had counted on to see them through the gloom, did not work – Edison had not yet perfected his generators – and neither did the telephonic apparatus, whose copper cables lost conductivity when laid across the ice. Collins had also been entrusted with the latest photographic equipment, but while remembering to bring the camera and glass plates, he had neglected to pack the correct developing chemicals. He became an object of fun, and by Christmas was so dejected that he refused to join in the celebrations – such as they were. 'Christmas Day!' De Long wrote in his journal. 'This is the dreariest day I have ever experienced in my life, and it is certainly the dreariest part of the world.'[34]

More worrying, however, than either Collins or Newcomb, was Danenhower. After some deliberation, he reported that his eyes were giving him trouble. Surgeon Ambler inspected him and discovered that he had syphilis. The disease had reached one eye, producing a stringy, mucous-like discharge which, if untreated, could blind him. Having informed De Long, Ambler operated. By candlelight, and with the aid of a magnifying glass, he sliced into Danenhower's eye, releasing a flood of turbid fluid. De Long was sympathetic but could not hide his disgust. Danenhower had come aboard knowing he had a disease and had not told him. He would have to report the matter on his return.

De Long took some comfort in the company of George Melville. The bald, bearded engineer, who had sailed with De Long on the *Juanita*, was a godsend. He was big and bluff, with a laugh that carried everything before it. He could mend and improve anything. He forged new engine rods when they broke and improvised machinery when it was needed. He was an indefatigable source of ingenuity and optimism. When they found that sea ice was salty – Petermann had assured them that it would not be – Melville rigged up a desalination plant using Edison's redundant generator. Again and again Melville proved his worth, twisting the few scraps of metal they possessed into Heath-Robinson-style gadgets that actually worked. 'I believe he could make an engine out of a few barrel hoops if he tried hard,'[35] De Long commented admiringly.

That winter, as the ice solidified under the ship, De Long's crew drifted north, caught in currents similar to those that had seized Weyprecht and Payer. They came within a few miles of Wrangel Land but were unable to reach it. Yet they did see enough to tell them that it was an island. They saw other things too, on their drift. One October night Raymond Newcomb reported an unbelievable sight. A few hundreds yards away a shimmering ball of light hung in the air. Everyone came up to watch it. It pulsated, came near, moved back and then swooped down into the ice before vanishing completely. Collins thought it was to do with the aurora borealis; the more superstitious thought it was a portent; and the term UFO was not used only because it had not been invented.

As the winds changed, pushing them now north-west, now south, now east, in a triangle centred off Wrangel Island, the pack became dispiritingly capricious. At times it sat there, a calm, motionless expanse over which De Long walked at night, marvelling at the beauty of his ship, every spar and rope reamed with ice, outlined against a horizon 'clearly defined as a knife edge, the delicate new moon a little above it'.[36] At other times, however, it rippled and surged around the *Jeannette*, as if circling a prey. On more than one occasion it moved in for the kill. Awoken by Newcomb in the early hours of 12 November, De Long saw the sea alive with floes. They moved apparently at random, in different directions and at different speeds, overtaking, jostling and climbing on top of each other as if in an insane race. Amidst the maelstrom, a flotilla of thirty-foot slabs was heading straight for the ship. As De Long called all hands on deck, the ice moved towards them with a frightful noise, a mixture of screams, rumbles and sudden booms like artillery salvoes. It struck with such force that the men flapped to and fro like puppets as they clung to the rigging. Cakes of ice flew through the ropes and skittered across the boards, knocking people off their feet. Floe after floe piled up, seeming to leapfrog each other in an attempt to get aboard. Meanwhile, the deck bulged so visibly under the impact that De Long expected it to explode beneath their feet. Then, quite abruptly, the onslaught ceased. It was to be just the first of many similar attacks. By Christmas, they were racked by the strain of constant alarms. 'Truly this is no pleasant predicament,' De Long wrote: 'Wintering in the pack may be a thrilling experience to read about alongside a warm fire in a comfortable home, but the actual thing is sufficient to make any man prematurely old.'[37]

The ice now changed tactics. Unable to take the ship by storm it used stealth, squeezing it gently but remorselessly while at the same time rising up its hull. On monitoring its progress De Long recorded that it was crawling upwards at an inch per day. 'We live in a weary suspense,'[38] he wrote. The suspense did not last long.

The *Jeannette* had been built well. Had it not been for all the reinforcements it would already have snapped in two. In January 1880, however, it finally broke under the pressure. A leak in the bow sent water pouring into the forward compartments. The steam pumps were iced up and the hand pumps sputtered uselessly. Designed for level sailing conditions, their intakes were on one side of the ship, but the *Jeannette* was heeled over so sharply that they barely sipped at the water. What little they did obtain froze in the outflow pipes in temperatures that sank to minus 30°F.

De Long sent two seamen, Nindemann and Sweetman, to battle the flood. Waist-deep in a semi-frozen sludge, they stuffed handfuls of oakum into every available gap. But still the sea came in at a rate of sixty gallons per minute. The ten feet of solid pine which they had counted on to break through the ice gave 'no more hindrance [to the water] than that offered by the meshes of a sieve'.[39] Sloshing through the water they built a bulkhead to contain what they could not staunch. The water then made its way vertically through the wall cavities. Nindemann and Sweetman responded with a mixture of plaster of Paris, oakum and old rags. The 'Arctic cement', as De Long called it, encased the flooded compartments; Melville fixed the main pumps; and before long, 'the steam giant was casting out water'.[40] But their measures worked too well. The water which the pumps sloshed overboard froze to the side of the ship, pressing it down into the ice. At the same time, the Arctic cement contained the inflow all too efficiently. Blocked on all sides, yet forced up by the downward pressure of the ship, the water burst through the floor of the crew's sleeping quarters. Once again Nindemann and Sweetman were sent to the barricades. Crawling beneath the boards, they hammered planks into place, plugged holes and applied liberal quantities of Arctic cement. When they finished, the ship was as watertight as it would ever be. De Long had nothing with which to reward their heroism, but in his journal he recommended them both for the Congressional Medal of Honor.

The water which had rushed in at a peak of 4,000 gallons per hour, requiring an expenditure of 1,500 pounds weight of coal a day for the pumps, subsided to 1,650 gallons which was expelled at a cost of 400 pounds. It was still too much for the *Jeannette*'s shrinking supply of fuel. After a few sleepless nights, Melville came up with the solution. He battered together a few strips of wood to support a wind pump whose vanes he made out of empty meat cans. It whirled away and within days the *Jeannette* was operating on just a few pounds of coal per day.

The crew, nevertheless, were not happy. Remembering perhaps the casual manner in which Hall and others had managed their operations, De Long had chosen an authoritarian British approach. Every Sunday he summoned the men on deck and read them the Articles of War. Some did not appreciate his regime. A proposed mutiny was uncovered but it came to nothing, De Long preferring to

believe the would-be mutineers' claim that the man who had reported
them was mad. The informant, a Danish stoker called Iverson, was
put under medical supervision and relieved of all responsible tasks.
Meanwhile, the ship drifted in its triangle, moving slightly to the
south-west with each month. Belatedly, De Long arrived at the same
conclusion as the US Coast and Geodetic Survey. 'As to there being
any warm current reaching to a high latitude, I very much doubt it,'[41]
he wrote in his journal. 'I pronounce a thermometric gateway to the
North Pole a delusion and a snare.'[42]

By the beginning of July they were still fast in the ice, despite
observations which showed a steady progress to the south. Their
bunkers held fifty-six tons of coal which, discounting the thirty
needed for everyday purposes, left sufficient for five days' steaming.
'And with this I have to make the Pole, accomplish the Northwest
Passage, or go back empty-handed,' De Long wrote. 'It makes my
heart sick to think about it.'[43] He became irritated at the lack of
headway: 'The knowledge that we have done nothing [is] almost
enough to make me tear my hair in impotent rage.'[44] From his observations he noticed that they were moving faster towards the South
Pole than to the North. In the end, he supposed, they would drift
along the Russian coast and be deposited ignominiously in the
Atlantic. Was this then, to be the culmination of his ambitions?
Instead of returning in glory he would become a laughing-stock: 'We
and our narratives [will be] thrown into this world's dreary wastebas-
ket and recalled . . . only to be vilified and ridiculed.'[45]

His indignation also concealed a sense of fear – a suspicion that he
might never bring the *Jeannette* home, that he might have to abandon
ship and lead his men over the ice towards Siberia. He estimated the
distance at 250 miles and, what with the condition of the ice, the
weight of boats and supplies to be hauled, not to mention the bedridden invalid Danenhower, he was unsure if they could make it. He
did not like to dwell on the thought. Nevertheless, he ordered boat
sledges to be built and supplies to be stacked against an emergency
evacuation.

The ice seemed to bear them a personal grudge. Following its overt assaults in the winter of 1879, it had managed to sneak aboard by cunning. Throughout the spring and summer the crew found every crevice packed with ice. It materialized in keyholes, cracks and forgotten corners. In De Long's quarters, the driest part of the ship, it glued his bureau to the wall. On opening a bottom drawer for a change of clothes he found it occupied by a 100-pound block of ice which he attacked with a hammer and saw. The ice had scarcely been banished from within when, in November, it resumed its attack from without. De Long greeted its 'horrible yelling and screeching'[46] with resignation. For a while the din was augmented by an eerie humming, which swelled from the bowels of the ship. Lt. Chipp traced it to the tangle of telephone wires which still festooned the *Jeannette*, and which were playing like an Aeolian harp. Collins, who was responsible for the wires and who had previously ascribed the noise to the aurora borealis, was considered even more foolish than before. In this disturbed fashion they entered another long night in Petermann's Open Sea. On 14 November 1880, Dunbar, the ice pilot, told De Long the ship was being squeezed. 'Heard it some time ago,' the captain replied gloomily.

12

In the Lena Delta

Back home, in all spheres of life, technological progress was vaulting forward. Edison had perfected his generators and electric light was beginning to be seen for the first time in public places. Bell's telephones were spreading across the world. A high-altitude treatment for tuberculosis had been discovered. Submarine cables allowed distant continents to speak to each other via telegraph. There were a thousand innovations, large and small, to remind people of the lucky times in which they lived.

Amidst the excitement, however, one or two people remembered the *Jeannette*. The *New York Times* thought something should be done. The *Herald*, its rival, said there was no cause for worry. Bennett himself wrote to Emma De Long on 2 August 1880, saying, 'I hope the silly prophecies of outside irresponsible papers about the *Jeannette* have not frightened you. I am perfectly confident of the absolute safety of the ship and its crew. The very fact of her not having being heard from yet is to me the best evidence of her success.'[1] In Britain, Nares and Clements Markham stated that it was America's duty to send a relief mission if there had been no news from De Long by the end of October. When the end of October came, Isaac Hayes, the Old

Man of the Open Polar Sea, said there was no need for alarm. As he
told the American Geographical Society, 'I do not anticipate that the
Jeannette has been either crushed by the ice or hopelessly beset . . . I
see the face of Mrs. De Long among us . . . And I want to express my
belief that her husband is just as safe tonight, if not as happy, as if he
sat by her side.'[2] The Navy Department agreed with his view that
something should be done in the future but talk of rescue was pre-
mature. Its annual report published in November 1880 repeated (in
strangely similar language) the utterances of Bennett and Hayes: 'The
fact that they have not been heard from seems to indicate that the
vessel is safe and that they may consider themselves able to remain
[in the Arctic] another year at least.'[3] Throughout the debate, the
ghost of Sir John Franklin waved wildly but in vain for attention.

A striking feature of nineteenth-century Arctic exploration was the
refusal by its instigators and participants to learn from the past. Fresh
meat and vegetables, for example, had been known since the 1830s to
keep scurvy at bay – yet off went Nares's expedition with its holds
packed with salted provisions. All indications suggested that the Open
Polar Sea was non-existent – yet people sailed again and again to discover it. Dog-sleds were far and away the most efficient means of
transport – so off went so many with their man-hauled behemoths.
Where small vessels were shown to be most efficient they used large,
where large was appropriate they used small. Where a goal was manifestly best achieved by land they sent ships instead. And when an
early start was recommended, they habitually left too late. De Long's
expedition was no different from any other. The ice into which he
sailed had already killed hundreds – during 1880 it would envelop
another five whaling ships, among them that of the hard-boiled
Captain Nye who had so depressingly assessed their chances of success – and De Long had entered it too late in the season, on too small
a ship, in search of a body of water that did not exist.

It is easy, of course, to criticize from hindsight. Politics, differences
of opinion, the passage of years and the fatally slow transmission
of Arctic knowledge were more to blame for these failures than
stupidity or bloody-mindedness. In the matter of De Long's rescue,

however, the authorities were culpably complacent. John Franklin's tragic expedition of 1845, which had indirectly started the race for the Pole, should have been a warning. Franklin had been considered one of Britain's best Arctic captains. De Long was 'one of the most efficient officers of the Navy'.[4] Franklin had been provided with every novel gadget. So, too, had De Long. Franklin had left with enough food to last at least five years, De Long for three – and his supplies were not only adequate but contained enough Vitamin C to see off scurvy; one small concession to previous experience. When doubts were raised as to Franklin's safety, people had said not to worry: the absence of news was a good omen. They were now saying the same, illogical thing of the *Jeannette*. Franklin and every single man aboard his two ships had died because a rescue had been mounted too late. Would the same happen to De Long?

The similarities between Franklin and De Long were uncanny. When Franklin's fate became uncertain, it had been his wife, Jane, who had spurred people into action – and who, before her death in July 1875, had lent her support to both Sherard Osborn and James Gordon Bennett. Emma De Long now assumed Lady Jane's role, hoping that, unlike her, she would be able to find some trace of her spouse. She badgered officials, twisted influential arms and appealed to the public's sense of duty. At the same time she wrote letters to her absent husband, letters that he would never receive but which she sent all the same. One man who proposed a trip to Greenland was given a few envelopes to deliver. So was a Swede who had the far-fetched idea of flying to the Pole by balloon. In her epistles Emma De Long chided her husband fondly. Why was he keeping her waiting? What was he doing out there? When he got back from the Pole she would give him a telling-off.

Impelled in part by Emma De Long, in part by the spectre of Franklin, but mostly by the *Herald*, whose owner had reviewed the situation and was agitating for a rescue in which one or other of his 'Stanleys' could play a part, the Navy Department announced in the spring of 1881 that two ships were being prepared specifically for a rescue mission: the *Alliance*, which was to investigate the seas off

Spitsbergen, and the *Rodgers*, which was to follow the Pacific route, carrying with it William Henry Gilder, one of Bennett's top correspondents. Gilder, an enterprising man who had accompanied Schwatka on his 1878–79 Arctic expedition, would with a bit of luck be able to find De Long and thus snatch one of the most tremendous scoops since Livingstone. In addition, the *Corwin*, a revenue cutter operating off Alaska, was also told to keep an eye out for the *Jeannette*. The ships left harbour in mid-June but by the end of the year they had discovered nothing. The *Corwin* had been unable to make headway through the ice above Bering Strait; the *Alliance* turned back, having found no sign of the *Jeannette* off Spitsbergen; and the *Rodgers* caught fire and sank, leaving its entire crew stranded on Russia's Chukchi Peninsula.

Those who had been so smug about De Long's safety fell silent. As 1881 turned into 1882, with not a word from the Arctic, the certainty that he was still alive was modified to the probability that he was and then, reluctantly, to the possibility that he was not. And because nobody yet knew what had happened to the *Rodgers*, there was the worrying prospect that it too might be in the same state as the *Jeannette*. Forlornly, Emma De Long carried on writing her letters.

Throughout the winter of 1880–81, the *Jeannette* continued its passive, triangular drift, moving all the time to the west and the south but never fast enough or far enough to give its crew hope of escaping into the Atlantic. Hardened as they were by the first winter, their second passed relatively peacefully. They were able to shoot plenty of bears, so food was not a problem. They enlivened Christmas and New Year with songs, dances and 'a side splitting farce'[5] in which one of the erstwhile mutineers redeemed himself by dressing up in drag. As the new year dawned, De Long treated his men to a rousing speech, a condensed version of which he gave in his journal: 'We had suffered mishap, and danger had confronted as often; we had been squeezed and jammed, tossed and tumbled about, nipped and pressed . . . we had pumped a leaking ship for a year and kept her habitable; we were not yet daunted but were as ready to dare as ever. We were all here, in good health etc. We faced the future with a firm hope of doing something worthy of ourselves, worthy of the enterprise of the gentleman whose name was so closely connected with the expedition . . . and then we could go back to our homes, and with pardonable pride exclaim . . . I, too, was a member of the American Arctic Expedition of 1879.'[6] Four days later, however, he recorded that for all their southward movement they were still 220 miles north-west of the spot in which they had first been beset, and in their travels had covered an actual distance of 1,300 miles – enough to take them to the Pole and back if only they had been moving in a straight line. 'We are drifting about like a modern *Flying Dutchman*,' he complained, 'never getting anywhere but always restless and on the move. Coals are burning up, food is being consumed, the pumps are still going and thirty-three people are wearing out their lives and souls like men doomed to imprisonment for life. If the next summer comes and goes like the last without any result, what reasonable mind can be patient in contemplation of the future?'[7]

Meanwhile, the resentments which had arisen the previous winter hardened into outright rebellion. Collins, still smarting from his perceived belittlement, had a show-down with De Long. He was a civilian, employed by Bennett, and did not have to endure De Long's regime. 'You think you can do with me as you please now, and laugh at the future,' he shouted. 'You are making a mistake common to men of your disposition.'[8] De Long relieved him of his duties. Newcomb, like Collins a civilian, refused to take orders from Danenhower. He, too, was put under arrest, as was a seaman called Starr for disobeying an order given by Melville. And Danenhower, who had endured numerous operations to his eye – sometimes fighting wildly as he saw Ambler approach with his scalpel, magnifying glass and candle – stated that he was getting better and wanted to go back to work. De Long pointed out that he was now blind in one eye and had an infection in the other; if he moved from his darkened quarters he would lose his sight completely. He reasoned at first gently and then forcefully, but Danenhower was obdurate. Eventually, Danenhower joined Collins, Newcomb and Starr in official disgrace. The dogs fell out in sympathy. Long since sent to sleep on the ice, because of their noise and filth, they quarrelled viciously. One dog would fight another, the victim's trace partner would come to its aid, and then the pack would fall on the two of them until one or other was dead. With his officers falling apart and his dogs killing each other, De Long's only comfort was that the men had made no further mention of mutiny.

There was one hope left for the *Jeannette*. In one of his bolder attempts to justify his theory of the Open Polar Sea, Petermann had brought Siberia's rivers into play. These massive bodies of water, such as the Lena and the Kolyma, had their origins in the steppes of central Asia. The heat they absorbed on their way north would, by Petermann's logic, be capable of melting all ice in their path. He was right: the rivers kept the sea free of coastal ice for slightly longer than in those areas where no rivers discharged. Like the Gulf Stream, however, their impact on the larger polar pack was minimal. De Long had yet to prove or disprove this theory, but he distrusted it as he now distrusted all Petermann's theories. 'Let us then hope for something from the much lauded velocity of the spring freshets of Siberian rivers,' he wrote in April 1881, 'for that is about the only Arctic theory that we have not exploded.'⁹

The ice showed no signs of weakening as they inched their way towards the Siberian coast. But on 16 May they spotted an island. De Long was overjoyed. Whether it fitted or not into Petermann's grand Arctic scheme was irrelevant. It was the first land he had seen in fourteen months. He named it, from a distance, Henrietta Island after Bennett's sister. Not long afterwards they saw another, smaller blob which he christened Jeannette Island. Very slowly, the ice swirled them towards these outcrops. They were roughly midway between the two when De Long sent Melville on a dog sledge to explore Henrietta Island. He returned with bad news: it was a barren block of rock inhabited by cliffs of dovekies; and the dogs were an ungovernable disaster. Not having been used for more than a year, they had become slovenly and wild. 'There is no greater violence done the eternal cause of truth,' Melville wrote,' than in those pictures where the Esquimaux are represented as calmly sitting in shoe-shaped sleds with the lashes of their long whips trailing gracefully behind, while the dogs dash in full cry and perfect unison across the smooth expanses of snow. If depicted "true to nature", the scene changes its aspects considerably; it is quite as full of action, but not of progress. A pandemonium of horrors! Dogs yelling, barking, snapping, and fighting; the leaders in the rear, and the wheelers in the middle, all tied up in a knot, and as hopelessly tangled up as a basketful of eels.'[10]

When De Long had seen Melville's flag flying from Henrietta Island he had run immediately to record the occasion in his log. On the way he had neglected to duck the windmill, still pumping valiantly, and was sliced a nasty cut on the forehead. Several stitches and one day later, he remained jubilant: 'Thank God we have at last landed upon a newly discovered part of this earth . . . It was a great risk, but has resulted in some advantage . . . And now where next?'[11]

They had left both islands far behind when, in early June, the ice came at them again. After its previous failure to engulf them it attacked violently and suddenly, tearing the floe on which they sat, tilting the ship onto its side and then squeezing it to death. It became impossible to stand upright. As the deck buckled, De Long ordered everyone onto the ice. Collins, Newcomb and the semi-blind Danenhower helped unload boats and supplies. When they had taken out as much as they could, they set up their tents and watched the ice do its work. On Sunday, 12 June 1881 – the same day the *Alliance* and *Rodgers* set out to rescue them – the *Jeannette* began to vibrate. A humming sound filled the vessel, interspersed by the cracking of the deck seams. The masts swayed as the ice chewed down on the ship and the gang ladders leading to the bridge jumped out of their chucks and drummed on the boards. Finally, at about 6.00 p.m., a spear of ice burst into the coal bunkers. Abruptly, all noise ceased. 'This silence, after the unearthly humming, was the saddest part of all,' wrote Newcomb. 'She had been stabbed in her vitals and was settling fast.'[12] The next day, at 4.00 a.m., the ship sank. 'Turn out if you want to see the last of the *Jeannette*!' shouted the man on watch. 'There she goes! There she goes!'[13]

'Most of us,' wrote Melville, 'had barely time to arise and look out, when, amid the rattling and banging of her timbers and iron work, the ship righted and stood almost upright; the floes that had come in and crushed her slowly backed off; and as she sank with slightly accelerated velocity, the yardarms were stripped and broken upward parallel to the masts; and so, like a great gaunt skeleton, its hands clasped above its head, she plunged out of sight.'[14] De Long and his men crept up to the hole and saluted their ship. A few bits and pieces floated on the surface – a cabin chair among them – but they soon sank, leaving only a solitary signal chest which bobbed, bottom-up, before it too was dragged down.

De Long had done a good job of evacuating the ship. They had adequate amounts of food and fuel, more tea than they would ever need, a good stock of rifles and ammunition and a pile of sealskin clothes which they had sewn from the hides of animals shot during the previous spring and summer. As well as these communal stores, each man had a knapsack containing survival basics: a change of underclothes, a pack of matches, a plug of tobacco, one spare pair of snow-goggles and one spare pair of moccasins. They had five sledges to carry their supplies, which, when they were loaded, weighed between 1,200 and 1,500 pounds. There were also two light dog-sledges for anything left over. In addition, there were three boats mounted on sledges for when they met open water. The whole lot came to a grand total of 15,400 pounds, which was to be dragged by a working force of twenty-two fit men about 200 miles across uncertain summer ice to the coast of Siberia. They set out on 16 June.

The sun was now shining almost around the clock, and to avoid snow-blindness De Long ordered his men to march by night when the glare would be marginally less. Danenhower recorded the routine in his diary: 'At half past five P.M., call all hands, have breakfast, and break camp at half past six; at twelve, midnight, stop one-half hour for dinner; at six A.M., stop for supper and sleep. Ration table during the march to be as follows:-

Breakfast (per man) – Four ounces pemmican, two biscuits, two ounces coffee, two-thirds ounce sugar.

Dinner – Eight ounces pemmican, one ounce Liebig [extract], one-half ounce tea, two-thirds ounce sugar.

Supper – Four ounces pemmican, one-half ounce tea, two-thirds ounce sugar, two biscuits, one ounce of lime-juice.'[15]

Danenhower was slightly disgusted by these rations, which came to less than two pounds of food per man per diem. With the sledges carrying 3,500 pounds of pemmican alone, and with fresh meat undoubtedly to be killed on the march, he felt De Long could have increased the allocation. He was also disturbed by their lack of navigational aids. Surrounded as they were by the biggest ice sea in the world, unmapped and featureless save for mountainous pressure ridges which changed every season, he instinctively felt the need of his instruments. 'I may here state,' he later wrote, 'that the boat compasses were intentionally left behind, because the captain said he preferred the pocket prismatic compasses. We had six splendid Ritchie boat compasses, always kept in the *Jeannette* ready for instant use, but they were, as I said, left behind, much to our detriment at a later period.'[16]

Danenhower complained too much. De Long was doing magnificently for a man who had never before had to face such a task. He kept the men on low rations because, from Weyprecht's journal – part of the library with which Bennett had supplied him – he knew how long it might take to cover the shortest distance. And he did not take the better compasses because they would have added unnecessary weight to the already heavy load (including, incidentally, the semi-blind Danenhower) which his men had to haul. In his immediate position, a pocket compass was as good as any other. All he needed was to know where South lay. That Danenhower had the materials, the leisure and the ability to write his acerbic comments was in itself a measure of how comfortably De Long had arranged their exodus.

The refugees slogged towards Siberia. Their journey was as back-breaking as Weyprecht's – open leads and ridges of ice forced them into long, tiring detours. They had to shove floes into position to bridge gaps in the ice, had to drag their sledges over hillocks and then had to repeat the process several times because the sledges and boats were too heavy to be dragged in unison. Their shoes rotted, so did the moccasins with which they replaced them, forcing some men to walk barefoot over ice that stuck into their feet like needles. There were no landmarks to comfort them, nothing to tell them how far they had come, merely a monotonous jumble of pressure ridges which they overcame with difficulty and in the disheartening knowledge that by next year these obstacles would have vanished completely. For every two miles progress they covered an actual twenty-six – on a good day. Still, they were heading south and that was what mattered. Sooner or later they would come to open water. But De Long had forgotten the drift. That midnight he recorded their latitude as 77°46′N. He did not understand it. He dismantled and reassembled his sextant, checked his charts, and then took a second reading. His observations all told the same story – they were twenty-eight miles north of the point from which they had started.

Revealing his dismal finding to a few chosen officers, De Long changed course from south to south-west, reasoning that if the ice was moving north-west, this tack would at least take partial advantage of the drift and bring them sooner to open water. It worked. For weeks thereafter, they covered real distances of up to thirteen miles per day despite eight men out of thirty-five not working their passage due to illness or arrest. They shot a few seals – 'the meat was not pleasant to the taste,' according to Danenhower, 'and it required the strongest philosophy to enable one to eat it at all.'[17] Walrus sausages, prepared by their two Chinese cooks, were welcomed whole-heartedly, as was the occasional bear steak. On 25 July they sighted land, which gave them a huge fillip. Three days later they landed on it. It was not Siberia, merely an uninhabitable mass of rock like Henrietta and Jeannette Islands, but they greeted it as their salvation. De Long called it Bennett Island, claimed it for the United States and instructed Chipp to give the crew, 'all the liberty you can on American soil'.[18] He named a western cape Emma, after his wife, and freed Collins, Danenhower, Newcomb and Starr. Although not clapped in irons they had been effectively imprisoned by De Long's refusal to let them participate in any worthwhile activity; a punishment that damaged their pride all the more for its apparent pointlessness. 'I come on duty as bugs again,' Newcomb, the naturalist, wrote. 'What a checkered career!'[19]

From Bennett Island they hauled south over the pack. As the leads became wider and the floes smaller, the weighty boats which they had been dragging came into their own. Soon they were spending more time afloat than on the ice and De Long decided the time had come to leave the sledges behind. (They had by now shot and eaten all the dogs save one, which they retained as a mascot.) He detailed his men into three crews: one boat was commanded by himself, another by Melville and the third by Lt. Chipp. With instructions to keep together if possible but if separated to make contact once they had landed, De Long shepherded his crew into the last stage of their journey. Their objective was the Lena Delta, of which he had a map from one of Petermann's many atlases. It charted the river for 200 miles inland and showed a number of important-looking settlements spread along the coast. At one or other of these townships they would surely find help.

Through late August and early September they battled with high seas and rotten floes from whose honeycombed centres the sea jetted in waterspouts twenty feet high. On 11 September they were approximately ninety miles from land and had seven days' full rations remaining. If the weather became no worse, there was a slender chance that De Long might actually bring his crew back alive from one of the most terrifying experiences in Arctic history. Nobody had ever returned from a pinching above the Bering Strait. Nobody had ever walked so far across the vast, lonely fields of the eastern icepack. Even if he had been at times a martinet, De Long could congratulate himself on a triumphant display of leadership.

It was the final approach to Siberia that did for them. As they struggled towards the Lena Delta they were hit by a ferocious storm, that scattered the boats, driving them in different directions. 'The night,' wrote Melville, '[was] an incubus of horrors.'[20] Chipp's boat vanished in the fury. He was never seen again, neither was the ice master

Dunbar nor the carpenter Sweetman – he whom De Long had recommended for a medal – nor the other five men aboard. De Long hit
the Lena delta fair and square, a tribute to his navigation, and waded
ashore with his men through the freezing surf. But Melville was
driven to the east and touched land scores of miles away. Now began
the hardest part of their journey.

The Lena is a vast river. It flows 3,000 miles from start to finish,
drains one million square miles of Siberian plain and has a coastal outflow which measures 260 miles from side to side. Many hundreds of
miles before it reaches the coast it splits into a labyrinth of sluggish
channels separated by low-lying islands of bog which forms a delta
approximately the size of Ireland. With limited supplies, De Long and
Melville headed into this maze and before long were utterly lost.
Petermann's map, which De Long had copied carefully for each boat,
bore no resemblance to reality. The settlements did not exist, or if
they did, were somewhere else. The silty channels of the delta simply
did not accord with what Petermann had published. Separately, De
Long and Melville puzzled over the document, neither of them
knowing where they were nor where the other was. De Long eventually headed south, his old standby, working his way inland by boat
and on foot. Melville, meanwhile, followed the largest part of the
Lena he could find, swearing violently as it meandered in unpredictable directions. 'Bitterly we cursed Petermann and all his works
which had led us astray.'[21]

Towards the end of September, after much hardship and by sheer
good fortune, Melville guided his men to a village where they fed,
rested and came in contact with one of the Cossack messengers who
plied at rare intervals the Tsar's distant wastes. They were lucky
enough, too, to meet up with a convict, a literate thief who promised
to carry their SOS south with the Cossack. The ultimate destination
of these two men was Yakutsk, the largest town in the region. From
Yakutsk special couriers ran to the telegraph at Irkutsk, Siberia's
capital. To reach Yakutsk, however, they first had to get to the
town of Bulun, some 100 miles upriver of the delta. Melville also
wanted to leave for Bulun, to organize a search party for De Long, but

was warned against it by his hosts: such a large, weak group would certainly die along the way, especially as the season was turning. If he waited fifteen days or so for the ice to harden, they would happily sledge him to Bulun. Confident that he had done all he could, and unwilling to risk the lives of his men, Melville agreed to postpone his departure.

Meanwhile, De Long was stitching his way, mile by mile, through the endless filigree of the Lena Delta. Melville had been exceptionally lucky: he had landed on the delta's south-eastern corner, where the river was widest and its path less intricate. De Long, however, had struck the delta at its northern, most tortuous point. His crew was the best of the bunch: he had the stalwart Nindemann, the surgeon Ambler and the Eskimo hunter Alexey, apart from Collins and nine others. If anyone should have succeeded it was De Long. But he did not know where he was going. For weeks he wandered through the maze, finding each village on Petermann's map to be a chimera. Blindly he followed his compass, now shooting a few deer, now detouring along tracks that promised much but delivered nothing. River after river was crossed, equipment was dropped and forgotten, while Petermann's map led them nowhere. Game was migrating fast before the oncoming winter and despite Alexey's efforts their food began to run out. On 3 October they cooked Snoozer, their last dog and their lucky mascot. Their bodies were using stored Vitamin C fast, but thanks to De Long's provisioning on board the *Jeannette* they were a long way from contracting scurvy. Starvation was their greatest worry – and frostbite. In the intense Siberian cold – a long, dry, wind-chilled cold, the fiercest of any land mass in the world, apart from Antartica – frostbite hit them hard.

The mechanics of frostbite are depressingly simple. In extreme cold, the blood vessels constrict to conserve heat. The lack of circulation allows ice crystals to form inside and around the watery cells of the human body. The ice expands, rupturing the cells. When blood starts circulating again, whether from warmth or exercise, it clots on the damaged cells and blocks the flow. Slight frostbite, signalled by a tell-tale whiteness accompanied by blisters, is reversible. Severe frostbite, when the white turns to black, indicates gangrene. Modern antibiotics can deal with gangrene, allowing the infected parts to atrophy without infecting the rest of the body. In De Long's time, however, antibiotics were not known. He and his men watched impotently as their legs and feet blistered and wept. The traditional remedy was a cold massage with snow – a trick which let the blood come back gradually, without impeding circulation – but often this did not work. Toes blackened, cracked and had to be amputated. The worst affected was a seaman named Erikson, whose heels were literally falling apart, chunks of flesh dropping off to expose bone and tendon. He died on 6 October.

The next day they ate the last of Snoozer, and from that point they survived on three ounces of alcohol per day. De Long's eyes, never very good, began to give out. Yet still he believed that they had a chance. On 8 October, he calculated that they were on the island of Tit Ary. According to Petermann's map, the village of Kumakh-Surt was approximately twenty-five miles away and Bulun another fifty. The map, as he knew to his cost, was not reliable – the last major settlement they had made for turned out to be a couple of deserted huts – but it was all he had to go by. He doubted, however, if the weakest members could make even that distance, so he ordered the two healthiest men, Nindemann and Noros, to go ahead in search of help. He gave them a rifle, two ounces of alcohol, and a small, hand-copied version of Petermann's map, plus instructions that if they shot a deer within the next two or three days they were to bring it back. They left on 9 October, with the others moving slowly after them. 'We are now about to undertake our journey of 25 miles,' De Long wrote, 'with some old tea-leaves and two quarts of alcohol . . . I trust in God.'[22]

De Long would have to travel much farther than twenty-five miles to reach safety. For once the map was reasonably accurate; it was De Long's own estimate of his position that was wrong. Bewildered by lookalike islands, by countless identical riverlets, and by constant detours, not to mention Petermann's hazy charting of the northern delta, he was much farther north than he believed. Tit Ary was thirty-five miles away, Kumakh-Surt in the order of eighty. Ignorant of the truth, De Long and his men hobbled south. Nindemann and Noros did not return, which could have meant either that they had met with an accident or simply that they hadn't shot anything or that, best of all, they were returning with assistance. Hoping it was the last option, De Long's team struggled on. Their shoes were now a mess and they bound their feet with strips of canvas cut from their single tent. These makeshift moccasins wore out rapidly and more material was sliced from the tent. Soon there was only a small cover which they dragged over themselves at night. Their alcohol came to an end and still there was no news from Nindemann and Noros.

Everything that could be abandoned was abandoned. But they could not persuade De Long to give up his maps and journals, which were preserved in a heavy, watertight chest. On this point he was adamant. His expedition might be ridiculed but he would not lower it to Franklin's standard; he would never have rescuers wandering Siberia in search of remains, relics and records and then quibbling over what he had or had not achieved. Everything was to be kept on paper, so that future explorers could benefit and his wife could be proud of him. Lugging De Long's box of books, and a roll of maps that was five feet long, they pushed deeper into the Siberian tundra.

On 17 October Alexey died of starvation and exhaustion. They buried him in the ice, conscious that they had lost the one man who had the skills necessary for their survival. On 20 October they had advanced twelve miles and Ambler wrote a message to his brother in Virginia: 'I have myself very little hope of surviving . . . We are growing weaker and for more than a week have had no food. We can barely manage to get wood enough now to keep warm, and in a day or two that will be passed . . . God in His infinite mercy grant that these lines may reach you. I write them in full faith and confidence in help of our Lord Jesus Christ. Your loving brother, J. M. Ambler.'[23] Then he tucked his notebook under his scarf, stuffed the scarf into his trousers to fill out a slack belt, and wrote no more.

De Long continued the tale in his diary. His entries were short, and contained nothing that was good:

Friday October 21st. 131st day. Kaack [sic] was found dead about midnight between the Doctor and myself – Lee died about noon – Read prayers for sick when he found he was going.

Saturday October 22nd. 132nd day. Too weak to carry the bodies of Lee and Kaack out on the ice. The Doctor, Collins and I carried them around the corner out of sight. Then my eye closed up.

Sunday October 23d. 133rd day. Everybody pretty weak. Slept or rested all day and then managed to get enough wood in before dark. Read part of Divine Service – Suffering in our feet – No foot gear.

Monday October 24th. 134th day. A hard night.

Tuesday October 25th. 135th day.

Wednesday October 26th. 136th day.

Thursday ,October 27th. 137th day. Iveson broken down.

Friday, October 28th. 138th day. Iveson died during early morning.

Saturday, Oct. 29. 139th day. Dressler died during night.

Sunday, Oct. 30. 140th day. Boyd and Gorts died during the night – Mr. Collins dying.[24]

On 2 November Melville, accompanied by two dog-drivers, sledged into Bulun. Nindemann and Noros had got there first, barely alive. The two ounces of alcohol with which they had been issued had disappeared quickly. Finding no deer they had scavenged scraps of left-over fish from nomadic huts. When there were no huts they ate Nindemann's breeches and then the soles of their shoes. For ten days they existed on this diet, following Petermann's map through snowstorms and frozen terrain until they were rescued by two nomadic hunters and carried to Bulun, having passed Kumakh-Surt which was, once again, a collection of empty huts. They sent to Yakutsk a scrap of paper on which was writ-ten: 'Arctic steamer *Jeannette* lost on the 11th June; landed on Siberia the

25th September, or thereabouts; want assistance to go for the captain and the doctor and nine other men. Wm. C. F. Nindemann. Louis P. Noros. Reply in haste; want food and clothing.'[25] To this message Melville now added a full account in triplicate of the sinking of the *Jeannette* and his present situation, for despatch to the US minister at St Petersburg, the London office of the *Herald* and the secretary of the US Navy in Washington. However, 3,000 miles lay between Bulun and the telegraph station at Irkutsk; it was not until mid-December that news of the tragedy was tapped out to the world.

Melville had no time to wait for a reply. Taking two sledges, and a rough map prepared by Nindemann and Noros, both of whom were too weak to accompany him, he drove in search of De Long's party – or, as he assumed was the case, their bodies. As he drew near the site of De Long's camp, local hunters brought him notes which they had found under cairns. Plotting De Long's progress through the delta they revealed, among other things, the whereabouts of his logbooks (as opposed to his journals) which he had buried on the shore where he had landed. Melville at once detoured north to retrieve the precious logs. Only then did he resume his search, 'confident that if I could rightly strike De Long's trail I would find him and his party, doubtless dead.'[26] But his drivers rebelled: snow was falling hard and supplies were low. After twenty-three days in the wilderness Melville returned to Bulun with the *Jeannette*'s logs. 'I was now satisfied that I had done all that was possible for me to do at that season of the year,' he wrote. 'Corpses . . . I could find with safety in the early spring.'[27]

That winter saw an unprecedented flurry of activity in the tundra. Cossack couriers galloped between Bulun and Irkutsk, transmitting orders from the Tsar, messages from Washington and 6,000 roubles from Bennett. Melville travelled back and forth, arranging transport for Danenhower and the rest of his boat crew. And one of the *Herald*'s special correspondents, a 'Stanley' named John Jackson, sped east by train and sledge from St Petersburg to Irkutsk with instructions to find De Long (if alive), but more importantly, to find his papers. Already, in America, rumours were circulating that the *Jeannette* had been unsuited to its task. Melville's wife had published a letter from her husband stating that the *Jeannette* was too weak for Arctic travel and, by inference, that the expedition had been mismanaged from the start. The letter attracted widespread criticism of the *Jeannette*'s sponsors and Bennett, as the main sponsor, became uneasy.

Instructing Jackson to forward all material to himself, Bennett gave explicit orders that although he could read what he found he was 'not to air soiled linen'.[28] If De Long's journal contained anything either derogatory or newsworthy, he wanted to handle it himself. By coincidence, Bennett's other 'Stanley', William Gilder, was also heading for Irkutsk to report the loss of the *Rodgers*. En route he intercepted a courier carrying news of the *Jeannette* disaster and, realizing he was in for a scoop, stole the message and substituted one of his own to the effect that he was going north to rescue De Long and retrieve his papers. Simultaneously, Melville was mustering forces for a second march into the Lena Delta. Never before, and certainly never since, have so many US personnel marched through Siberia.

Bennett assured Emma De Long that her husband was alive. In December he wrote that 'Commander De Long has reached the mouth of the Lena safely and is now well and looking after the sick members of the expedition.'[29] Emma – a lock of whose hair was amongst her husband's effects – continued to send loving letters. One of them concerned the balloon-man who was planning to fly to the Pole. 'He told me he would look out for you on the way. No more undertakings like this for my husband or I will get a divorce,' she chided. 'It is evening, I am writing this in the library. Little Sylvie is in bed fast asleep, having said her prayers for her father's health and safety. There is a blazing fire in the grate, the two dogs are stretched out on the fur rug in front of it. How would you like to spend an evening with me? Or is it pleasanter where you are? I suppose I must not tease you.'[30] But despite Bennett's assurances, Emma De Long could not ignore Melville's assessment of her husband's fate. 'I cannot show you my love, my sympathy, my sorrow for your great sufferings. I pray God constantly . . . my own darling husband, struggle, fight, live! Come back to me!'[31]

Melville was the man who eventually found De Long. After delays and many arguments he led a troop of local hunters in search of his captain, taking Nindemann to show him the way. Snow had fallen over the campsite and they found it only because the remains of a tent – four poles lashed together – projected above the surface. Clearing the snow from the site, they were able to reconstruct what had happened. De Long had built a beacon whose smoke would have been visible for miles around and had then waited, starving, for Nindemann and Noros to return. Boyd had clawed his way to the fire and had died there, so close to the warmth he craved that his clothes had singed. In his hands he held Iveson's psalm book, with its inscription: 'Presented by the California Evangelical Society for Foreigners'. Gortz had either crawled or been placed next to the body of Iveson, a few yards away from Boyd. Ah Sam, the Chinese cook, had probably been the next to go. He lay pharaonically on his back, hands crossed over his chest. Ambler had a pistol by his side and blood running from his mouth – into which his fingers were stuffed. De Long? Who could tell how or when he died. His arm was raised (Melville almost tripped over it) and his notebook lay a few feet beyond, as if he had hurled it over his shoulder in his death throes. On inspection, the last entry was 30 October. The final page had been torn out.

Before his death, De Long had stacked the maps and journals on a nearby rise. Melville took charge of them and then buried the bodies. He chose as a grave-site the crest of a 400-foot-high hill fifteen miles away, to which his men dragged the bodies. A communal coffin was constructed from the remains of a native punt – obviously De Long's last means of transport – and then, in a massive box measuring twenty-two feet by seven, Melville lowered the remains into Siberian soil. He erected a wooden cross, carved on it the names and dates of the dead, and then, carrying De Long's maps and every object he found on the bodies – leaving only a bronze crucifix around Collins's neck – he headed for civilization. Behind him, the cross was visible for twenty miles in every direction.

13

FRAM

The United States had never suffered an Arctic disaster on this scale. Of the thirty-three men who had sailed from San Francisco, twenty had died, including the Captain. It was the biggest tragedy since Franklin and it created an equal brouhaha. The first and most urgent question was why the bodies had not been brought home. Bennett had the answer to that. *Herald* men swarmed into Siberia and in January 1884 the bodies were loaded onto a cortège of black railway carriages provided by the Tsar, each man resting in an airtight steel casket donated by the Metallic Burial Case Company of New York. Russian soldiers fired salutes, copies of an epic poem were distributed by the East Siberia Geographical Society and at every stop citizens piled on so many wreaths that special crates had to be built to hold them all. When the bodies reached New York on 20 February, thousands lined the streets to mourn their passing. De Long's burial in Woodlawn Cemetery, the Bronx, would have attracted equal numbers were it not for a snowfall which swept, appropriately, across the city. The *Herald* profited accordingly, reporting the scenes in eye-catching black borders.

By this time, Bennett was beginning to squirm. Since his return

1. Captain George Nares

2. Admiral Sherard Osborn

3. Sir Clements Markham

4. The Duke of Abruzzi

5. The Alert *at Floeberg Beach, spring 1876*

6. Sledgers from the Alert, *1876*

7. *Extricating the* Alert, *1876*

8. *In harness, 1876*

9. The grave of De Long and his companions in the Lena Delta

10. Abruzzi's polar pavilion, 1899

11. The Stella Polare *hit by the ice, 1899*

12. *The officers of the* Jeannette

DANENHOWER.

AMBLER.

CHIPP.

DE LONG.

DUNBAR.

MELVILLE.

NEWCOMB.

COLLINS.

13. The Stella Polare *in Teplitz Bay, 1900*

14. Fridtjof Nansen

15. Otto Sverdrup

16. Hjalmar Johanssen

17. Nansen (r.) meets Jackson at Cape Flora, 1895

18, 19. Nansen (l.) and Johanssen at Cape Flora after their rescue

Danenhower (who had been with Melville's party) had been spreading stories about misconduct and inefficiency among his fellow officers, the stories swelling with each repetition until it appeared that Danenhower had been the only sensible or capable man aboard. Then there was Melville's letter to his wife, which had supposedly said the *Jeannette* was unfit for Arctic service. Why, too, hadn't Melville moved faster to rescue De Long while there was still a chance that he might be alive? There was a feeling that the expedition had been nothing more than a mismanaged, opportunistic publicity stunt, in which a bad crew had been put on a bad ship to satisfy a press magnate's selfish whim. Britain's *Saturday Review* spoke for many when it said: 'These private adventure explorations in circumstances so dangerous . . . are mistakes unless the adventurer goes himself. When a private person, presumably interested only in the chance of having a great discovery somehow tacked on to his name, equips explorers for an adventure of such risk . . . the position of the commander is a very unpleasant one. He feels himself bound to give his owner a run for his money; he is reluctant to quit the quest without something solid and sounding.'[1] It was a reasonable attack on Bennett's style of journalism but it didn't quite fit the facts of the expedition. It had been De Long as much as Bennett who had wanted to reach the Pole. Besides, once in the ice De Long had been unable to give Bennett a run for his money whether he wanted to or not. Nevertheless, a naval court of inquiry was convened to 'investigate the facts connected with the expedition and the alleged unofficerlike and inhuman conduct therein'.[2]

Bennett, Melville and Emma De Long came together in an unlikely alliance, the one wanting to avoid blame, the other to protect his reputation and the third to preserve her husband's honour. They made a formidable team. Bennett promised to use his influence in securing the extra money the Navy needed so badly for modernizing its fleet; Melville sent his wife to a lunatic asylum on a trumped-up charge of alcoholism (she was released as soon as the inquiry was over); and Emma De Long raged impressively against anything said against her husband. The inquiry concluded in January 1884. Nothing concrete had been found, nobody was to blame and everyone had performed outstandingly. They were all free to go home.

Home was a meaningless word to Bennett. He had hardly been 'home' since the duel with his fiancée's brother. He had not visited New York once during the inquiry, conducting all negotiations by telegraph from whatever spot his yacht chanced to touch upon, and he rarely visited the city again. His special reporters continued to roam the globe, but never again did they attain the status of either a Livingstone or a Stanley. Bennett had learned his lesson. He disappeared over the horizon with his yacht, his society mistresses, his cigars, his deckchairs, his cow and a pack of Pekinese dogs.

While investigating the *Jeannette*, the US Navy received news of an even greater disaster. Following Carl Weyprecht's urging, the international community had agreed on a programme of north polar observation for the year 1882. As part of this programme, Adolphus Greely, a Lieutenant in the US Army, had been installed on the west coast of Robeson Channel to take measurements, make observations and perform the usual rituals with thermometers and pendulums. On the shores of Lady Franklin Bay, not far south of the *Discovery*'s anchorage, Greely built the largest encampment the Arctic had seen to date: a wooden blockhouse that he called Fort Conger. Here, in every comfort, he and his team settled down to their duties. But Greely, like so many of his predecessors, harboured dreams of exploration and discovery. He hoped, if not to reach the pole, then at least to travel farther north than Markham had in 1876. And three members of his 'research' party did actually do such a thing: Lt. James Booth Lockwood, Sergeant David Brainard and an Eskimo named Fred Christiansen travelled to the north of Greenland and there, on an island which still bears Lockwood's name, pipped Markham with a reading of 83°24′. However, Lockwood never returned to America to receive his accolade. In a logistical foul-up supplies failed to arrive; forced to evacuate Fort Conger, Greely marched his men south where the expedition withered and died. At one point Greely had to shoot a would-be mutineer. When rescued in June 1884 by Melville (amongst others), eighteen out of Greely's twenty-five men, including Lockwood, had perished of starvation and some of the survivors had turned cannibal, cutting slices from the frozen corpses stored outside their camp. When Greely was helped out of his tent he did not speak of his observations or his men but of the Pole. 'Here we are – dying – like men,' he croaked. 'Did what I came to do – beat the record.'[3]

What with the *Jeannette* and now Greely, the US was sick of the Pole. The Philadelphia *Inquirer* bemoaned, 'the monstrous and murderous folly of so-called Arctic expeditions'.[4] The President himself decided, with massive understatement, that 'The scientific information secured could not compensate for the loss of human life.'[5] The scientific information was actually quite something. Greely's report ran to 1,300 pages and delivered a stream of observations on everything from meteorology to oceanography, from biology to astronomy. It failed to satisfy the public. As the *New York Times* said: 'Let there be an end to this folly.'[6] Greely and Melville, both of whom later attained senior positions in the Navy, agreed. Thus, for almost five years, the States gave up the chase, joining Britain on the sidelines as a wounded and embittered commentator.

If the US was tired of the Pole, other nations were just getting into their stride. The Open Polar Sea had been so thoroughly debunked (if not actually disproved) that nobody believed a ship could either sail or steam to the Pole. But what was the Pole, if not open sea? Some people, clinging to John Cleve Symmes's proposition of the 1820s, still thought it was a hole. In 1878, Symmes's son Americus had resurrected support for his father's theories with a book, *Demonstrating that the Earth is Hollow, Habitable Within, and Widely Open About the Poles*. And in 1885 the Revd William F. Warren published a work called *Paradise Found*, in whose 500 pages he stated that the hole at the Pole led to the Garden of Eden – the aurora borealis being an exhalation of inner global purity – and that people were naturally drawn there because 'mankind would ever have looked back on it as an abode of unearthly and preternatural effulgence, a home fit for the occupancy of gods and holy immortals'.[7] William F. Warren was President of Boston University.

An intriguing, and more plausible, theory ran that the Pole might be a land mass containing clues as to the origins of humankind. It was an attractive idea, first postulated in America, and on 30 March 1886 Major Henry Feilden of the Royal Artillery did his best to explain it to the members of the Norfolk and Norwich Naturalists Society. As a prominent geographer and one of the scientists on Nares's expedition, Feilden had clout. And everything he said seemed to make perfect sense. Life on earth, he said, balanced delicately between extremes of hot and cold, the hottest place being the Equator and the coldest the Poles. In its infancy, the earth had been hot all over – too hot to sustain life. But as the planet cooled the first area to achieve a temperate climate would have been the Poles. Logically, therefore, these would have been breeding grounds for life. Then, as the earth proceeded to cool, and the Poles iced over, animals (of whatever primitive kind) moved south into warmer zones. For some unaccountable reason the earth continued to cool, driving life ever towards the equator; and then the process had reversed, the glaciers had retreated, allowing plants and animals to recolonize the regions they had deserted. At present the globe was in equilibrium.

Feilden's argument was intelligent and tantalizing. It was built on ideas which had been formulated as recently as the 1840s, when scientists had abandoned the Bible and finally admitted the influence that successive Ice Ages had had on the landscape. It envisaged a primordial period and used (tangentially) Darwin's recent theory of natural selection. It drew on the findings of Nares and others, whose fossil specimens demonstrated that Greenland had once been covered in tropical vegetation. And vitally, it drew on research which showed that land masses were rising out of the Arctic Ocean. The ice, once formed, had pressed the earth down with its weight. As it retreated, however, the earth was springing back. The phenomenon had been observed on Spitsbergen, where scientists had found the remains of ancient whaling stations several feet above their original sea level positions. The *Tegetthoff* expedition had discovered similar evidence on Novaya Zemlya. (Even today, Scandinavia inches upwards by the year.) Was it impossible that the North Pole might now be rising to the surface, carrying tokens of humankind's origins? What effect Feilden's speech had on his provincial audience is unknown. The theory does not seem to have carried weight in political and scientific circles. It did, however, give fresh impetus to those who insisted on the importance of reaching the North Pole.

In the absence of governmental intervention, a spirit of free enterprise had seized Europe and America. Financially unsupported by their nations, but with wholehearted popular backing, individuals had begun to kit out expeditions for places like Spitsbergen, Greenland and Novaya Zemlya. Their ambitions were modest, limited as they were by funds, the distance a small steam-yacht could travel, and the endurance of the – often dilettante – men involved. Yet they perpetuated the polar dream and, importantly, sidestepped the bureaucratic floundering which had hindered so many attempts in the past. They were free to experiment, could organize matters to their own liking, and were answerable only to themselves. They preserved a vision of discovery last seen in the time of Sir Joseph Banks, that autocrat of eighteenth-century amateur exploration, and imbued it with all the wealth, vim and technological prowess of the Victorian era. Of course, nationalism was omnipresent. Each man hoped to place his flag farther than that of his foreign competitor. But to this was added a sense of personal competition against the elements – and sometimes against each other – of the kind that Hegemann had first described, following the destruction of the *Hansa*. A new era was unfolding, one that historians would subsequently dub the 'Age of Heroes'.

Scandinavia (specifically, Norway and Sweden) had poked at the Pole on and off for thirty years, its ships probing the areas around Spitsbergen and Novaya Zemlya. Largely forgotten today and unsung at the time – despised even, if one is to believe Weyprecht – these expeditions had produced valuable scientific and geographical results, delivering reports on matters such as the movement of the polar pack, the rise of Arctic land masses and, at a surprisingly basic level, charting the coasts of Spitsbergen and Novaya Zemlya. Their efforts were received politely in Britain and scarcely at all in America, lacking as they did any apparent northward impetus. No Swede or Norwegian had ever launched an all-out serious expedition to the Pole. In the 1890s, however, Scandinavia showed what it could do.

Occupying Europe's northernmost inhabited territory, the Scandinavians lived in, rather than visited, the Arctic zones. They knew how to ski – they (or rather the Lapps) had invented the art in prehistoric times – they were used to prolonged spells of winter darkness and they knew better than any other European or American how to deal with ice and snow. Their entire mythology revolved around coldness, an ice-bound hell replacing the fiery inferno of more southerly climes. As a result, they approached the problem of the Pole with pragmatic confidence. Nordenskiöld had already won acclaim with his competent, almost casual conquest of the North-East Passage. Now it was the turn of a young Norwegian named Fridtjof Nansen to show the world what could be done with a bit of common sense and the right training.

Scandinavia as a whole was in a state of optimistic decline. Its decline stemmed from the fact that it was both backward and politically fragmented. Russia ruled Finland, Norway was linked uneasily to Sweden as part of a Dual Monarchy, and none of the three countries had climbed far up the industrial ladder. Finland was a feudal backwater, Norway was one of the poorest regions in Europe, and Sweden, once a major power, was slipping into obscurity. Its optimism, however, was driven by the endless promise of industrialization, the prospect of agricultural 'improvement' (to use an eighteenth-century term) and, in Norway's case, the romantic ideal of becoming a separate state. Norway wanted to prove itself worthy of international acclaim. Fridtjof Nansen became an icon both of Norwegian independence and Scandinavian worth.

Born in 1861, Nansen was almost an archetypal Scandinavian: he was an expert skier who was tall, blond-haired, blue-eyed and intense. He was also a respected neuro-scientist – certain nerves in the spine are still called after him – who had earned his degree at the University of Christiana (now Oslo) and before whom lay a prosperous career studying nervous anatomy. In 1888, however, he abandoned his studies in favour of exploration, and led a small party on skis to investigate the interior of Greenland. Nordenskiöld, a man whom he admired, thought that Greenland might not be completely covered by glaciers but might contain an inner core of habitable land. Nordenskiöld had tried to ascertain this in 1883 by a sledge-crossing from the west but had been forced to retreat after a few hundred miles, having discovered only a plain of ice. Nansen disagreed with Nordenskiöld's theory: the interior could not possibly be inhabited, he said. He also took issue with Nordenskiöld's methods: a crossing from the west would necessarily be hazardous since its destination was the uninhabited east coast, where an expedition would have little chance of survival unless picked up by ship at a precise rendezvous; a team departing from the east, however, would be heading for relatively well-travelled and well-populated territory and could arrive safely, more or less wherever it wanted. Nansen's plan was flawed in that if he had to turn back he would be stranded on the east coast in just the same situation as a party arriving from the west. But he chose to ignore this. He landed on the east coast of Greenland on 10 August and with four Norwegians and two Lapps, skied, sledged and on occasion was blown across the cap, with the cry: 'Death or the west coast of Greenland.'[8]

They reached the other side on 3 October where by sheer luck they met at Godthaab a Danish inspector doing his rounds. Some antipathy existed between Denmark and Norway regarding Greenland. Vikings from Norway had discovered Greenland in the tenth century. Vikings from Denmark had later occupied Norway. When Denmark had ceded Norway to Sweden in 1814, the Norwegians had resented the fact that Greenland remained in Danish hands. The Danes were aware of this. When Nansen announced himself, the Danish governor struggled for a diplomatic reply. According to Nansen the exchange went, '"Are you Englishmen?" To which I could safely reply in good Norse, "No, we are Norwegians." "May I ask your name?" "My name is Nansen and we have just come from the interior." "Oh, allow me to congratulate you on taking your Doctor's degree."'[9]

Sour Danes aside, Nansen's crossing of Greenland was a display of bravado. When he returned to Scandinavia he was idolized. In Christiana (modern Oslo), where two thirds of the not-very-large population came out to welcome him, Nansen-fever took root and spread throughout the country. 'Nansen here and Nansen there,' wrote a friend. 'Nansen, Nansen, nothing else but Nansen. Nansen caps, Nansen cakes, Nansen cigars, Nansen pens, a Nansen March, and so on *ad infinitum*: the only things I haven't seen are Nansen handkerchiefs.'[10] Shortly afterwards, a Nansen fly button appeared on the market.

In terms of ground covered, Nansen's expedition was irrelevant to the North Pole – indeed, many saw his trip as a triumph for the sport of skiing rather than for discovery. He had, however, introduced a new means of arctic exploration. It was 'the sportsman's method', in the words of one Norwegian, who explained that 'the principle of the new method consists in limiting the number of participants and selecting... a small, trained group, in which all keep pace with each other'.[11] In its rejection of the hefty apparatus of ships, supplies and back-up in favour of small-scale skill and perseverance, the new method was ideally suited to the heroic age. Also, its simplicity and its success made a refreshing change from the orchestrated calamities of recent years. 'Unlike some other expeditions, that of Dr Nansen left behind it nothing but pleasant memories,'[12] said *The Times*. 'We are spared the... painful interest that attaches to many Arctic narratives,' echoed the *Spectator*, 'the horrible details of a timely or just-too-late relief.'[13]

In London, Sir Erasmus Ommaney of the Royal Geographical Society suggested that Nansen should take his new method south and tackle Antarctica – a prescient statement, since it would be by that very method that Roald Amundsen would snatch the South Pole from Scott in 1911. He was even invited by Australia to lead an expedition into Antarctica. Nansen declined. While he had no doubts as to his ability to capture the South Pole, he felt the North Pole was a more profitable goal for Norway. 'It would be best if I went there first,'[14] he said.

On the strength of his Greenland expedition, Nansen the neuro-scientist had become Nansen the explorer. 'It is rather more accidental circumstances which have forced me into that line,' he wrote in 1892, in response to a journalist's inquiry. 'Since than a great many plans and ideas how to explore the unknown Arctic regions have forced themselves upon my mind almost without my help and will, and now I think it to be my duty to try whether they are not right (as I feel convinced that they are) though it is almost with pain that I think of my microscope and my histological work.'[15]

In 1889, the year after his return from Greenland, he came up with a radical idea for reaching the Pole, an idea whose origins lay ironically in De Long's disastrous expedition. In 1884, debris from the *Jeannette* had washed up at Julianehaab, on the south-west coast of Greenland. The debris wasn't much – a few articles of clothing and scraps of paper – but it proved that a current ran east to west across the frozen ocean and if the current could carry clothes then it could also carry a ship – if a ship capable of staying afloat could be built. 'It immediately struck me,' Nansen wrote, 'that this was the way ahead.'[16] He put his plan to the Norwegian Geographical Society in February 1890 in the hope of obtaining a grant. 'Many people believe . . . that the investigation of such inaccessible places as the polar regions ought to be postponed until the development of new means of transport,' he said. 'I have even heard it said that one fine day we will reach the Pole in a balloon and until [then] it would therefore be so much wasted effort to try and reach the goal. [But] among the nations, at this time, there is a noble contest for that goal . . . May Norwegians show the way! May it be the Norwegian flag that first flies over our Pole!'[17] Such an appeal to the national spirit could not fail. In due course the grant was awarded and Nansen went in search of a man who could build him his impossible ship.

That man was Colin Archer, a naval architect of Scottish descent who specialized in vessels for the sealing trade. It was, as he admitted, a daunting task, involving as it did the rejection of every established rule and regulation. But he felt up to it and by October 1892 had produced an extraordinary-looking ship named the *Fram* – Norwegian for 'forward'. With a capacity of 400 tons, the *Fram* was double-ended, with stem and stern of equal sharpness; its body was rounded; and the whole thing was curved like a cockleshell. Unconventional it may have seemed, but Archer assured Nansen it would be perfectly sea-worthy and, most importantly, would serve his purpose in the polar cap. With all its curves there was nothing on which the ice could get a grip, and when squeezed the *Fram* would simply rise upwards – or, as Nansen put it, the ship would 'slip like an eel out of the embraces of the ice'.[18] In effect, he would be drifting not in the pack but on it.

Its shape was not the only unusual thing about the *Fram*. The hull was sheathed in South American greenheart, and braced internally with crossbeams, designed both for strength and elasticity. The gap between the inner and outer planking was filled with a mixture of tar, pitch and sawdust to prevent decay. And the walls of the living quarters were triple insulated with cork, reindeer hair and felt. The doors were also insulated and their sills were raised fifteen inches above the deck to stop cold air flowing in. In all, it was designed not only to be unsinkable (in theory) but to keep Nansen and his crew in comfort for a voyage which he estimated might last as long as five years. Clements Markham was vastly impressed when he visited the *Fram* during construction. He was impressed, too, by Nansen and his daring project, which turned accepted wisdom so thoroughly on its head. On his return to London he persuaded the Royal Geographical Society to donate £300 to the cause.

One reason for Markham's support was to shame Britain into resuming its own polar efforts. Here he met with opposition. The old guard were suspicious of new heroes, as Nansen recorded when he came to lecture at the Royal Geographical Society in November 1892. 'Those old veterans came, one after the other and did their best to . . . pour cold water over me,'[19] he wrote to his wife. Nares, whose horrible experience in the Arctic was still fresh in his mind, was sceptical and 'in a friendly spirit' (which annoyed Nansen greatly) intimated that the project was futile. Another veteran thought he would fail because his way would be blocked by dry land. A third said that he had 'never been an advocate of amateur nautical expeditions'.[20] And a fourth, while admiring the idea in general, advised Nansen to 'dispose of his admirable courage, skill and resources in the prosecution of some less perilous attempt to solve the mystery of the Arctic area'.[21] Nor were

Nansen's ideas much appreciated on the other side of the Atlantic. 'It is doubtful,' said Greely (another man with cause to regret the ice), 'if any hydrographer would treat seriously his theory of polar currents, or if any Arctic travellers would endorse the whole scheme ... Arctic exploration is sufficiently credited with rashness and danger in its legitimate and sanctioned methods, without bearing the burden of Dr. Nansen's illogical scheme of self-destruction.'[22]

Yet Nansen was not dismayed. He had the support of an ageing Sir Leopold McClintock, who declared the expedition 'the most adventurous programme brought under the notice of the Royal Geographical Society'.[23] He also had the support of the populace. Lots of people wanted to sign on for his voyage. A young Roald Amundsen, future conqueror of the South Pole, was among them (his mother forbade him to go). So was a French woman from Algeria, whose qualifications were exceptional spirit and a refusal to admit fear. A British freelance explorer named Frederick Jackson was rejected only because he wasn't Norwegian. When Nansen visited London in 1893, he swished through it like the Lord of Darkness. 'He was dressed,' wrote Jackson, 'in dark clothes, a black cloak, and a soft black hat, suggesting somewhat the regulation stage villain.'[24] Nansen's 'friendly rebuff' gave Jackson ideas of his own. Approaching Alfred Harmsworth, proprietor of the *Daily Mail* and later one of Britain's major press magnates, he obtained funds for an expedition to Franz Josef Land and entered the catalogue of heroes in his own right.

Nansen dismissed both his new rival and his critics. He had an absolute certainty that he would succeed – a certainty that extended to inviting his wife along for the ride, an invitation which she refused only because she was pregnant. Conversely, he relished the prospect of danger, recognizing that the forthcoming battle with the ice would be neither quick nor easy. This fitted his character. He was a man of sharply divided moods, at one moment unstoppably chatty, filling the air with optimistic plans for the future, at others retreating into silence as he pondered the gloom and misery which awaited him. He was aware of this conflict and explained it by his desire to *act*. 'I am young,' he wrote to a friend, 'and as you once said there is possibly some of the aspiring Viking blood in me: a too quiet life attracts me not at all.'[25] His glory was in the doing. If the doing did not succeed, then he would accept the outcome fatalistically.

The *Fram* left Christiana on a dull, grey day - 24 June 1893. It carried a hand-picked crew of twelve and a quantity of tinned provisions so fresh and so varied as to guarantee them immunity from scurvy during the five years they expected to be out. Nansen arrived at his anti-scorbutic diet quite by accident. Scientists had yet to pinpoint the causes of scurvy: they knew it was a deficiency disease; they knew that fresh vegetables and fresh meat cured it; they knew that it had been banished from British ships since the late eighteenth-century by the introduction of lime juice, and they knew that Viking explorers had kept it at bay by loading their longships with Arctic cloudberries. But they did not understand the role Vitamin C played, and would not do so until the second decade of the twentieth century. Nansen's anti-scorbutic success was due to a current dietary fad that variety was important to peak health. So, unwittingly, he took aboard the necessary ingredients to keep his men fit. Not that he cared. 'If, after all, we are on the wrong track, what then?' he wrote during a downswing. 'Only disappointed human hopes, nothing more. And even if we perish, what will it matter in the endless cycles of eternity?'[26]

They also took aboard several pocket aluminium barometers, as recommended by Edward Whymper, conqueror of the Matterhorn and himself an old Greenland hand, plus the latest in dried foods from Germany and Switzerland. In addition, they shipped a new brand of portable cooker – the Primus Stove. Developed in Stockholm, the Primus turned paraffin into gas, thereby utilizing the smallest amount of fuel to produce the greatest heat. It required pumping and gave off a disturbing roar, but was so safe that Scandinavian market women kept one under their skirts to keep off the chill. '*Burns without a wick!*'[27] the advertisements claimed, in mildly astonished terms. More important than the wick was the compactness, lightness and economy of the device. The Primus was approximately 600 per cent more efficient than standard oil or coal burners. It was perfect for the new 'sporting method' of polar travel, and seemed purpose-made for the blubber-free, Eskimo-free, polar wastes into which Nansen's expedition was heading.

Originally, Nansen had planned to follow De Long's route through the Bering Strait and pick up the transpolar current there. In the end, however, he sailed over the top of Norway and followed Nordenskiöld's North-East Passage to Siberia. From there, having collected a team of thirty-four dogs, he headed into the ice off the New Siberian Islands on 25 September.

He was very disappointed at the result. Instead of being carried directly north, the *Fram* followed the same irritating circuit as had the *Jeannette* and the *Tegetthoff*. Now north, now south, it crept triangularly towards its goal. The men were well and healthy and reasonably happy – if a bit disturbed by the moods of their commander to whom they referred, with fear and resentment, as Himself. They suffered none of the usual winter depression, thanks to the provision of electric light. The problems De Long had experienced had long since been ironed out and the *Fram* boasted a generator that could be driven by steam, wind or manual power. Its rigging strung with a line of bulbs, the *Fram* glowed like a seaside pier. Nansen tried to organize a shipboard newspaper but it fizzled out after eight issues. The men were just not interested. They were happy to lie back and – apart from the odd fight – to enjoy the peace. After all, it wasn't often that they had the chance to be well-fed, well-lit (by electricity!) and well-paid for doing nothing. If they needed intellectual stimulus there was the *Fram*'s 600-volume library which contained works by all the latest Scandinavian writers, as well as Jules Verne's novel *Captain Hatteras*, in which a bold captain and his crew sailed, as they were doing, towards the mysteries of the Pole. And if they wanted physical work there were any number of little tasks which required attention. The *Fram*'s stock of skis, for example, many of which were unfinished and experimental, needed to be sorted, graded for different snow conditions, and then waxed – a time-consuming process which involved repeated applications of Stockholm pitch.

Nansen, on the other hand, was frustrated. 'Oh! at times this inactivity crushes one's very soul,' he wrote, 'one's life seems as dark as
the winter night outside: there is sunlight upon no other part of it
except the past and the far, far distant future. I feel I *must* break
through this deadness, this inertia and find some outlet for my energies.'[28] But there was nothing to do except wait. The *Fram* was
working just as it was meant to, rising with every squeeze of the ice
and then settling down once the pressure ceased.

The same lack of drama was felt by citizens at home. In Christiana,
children played The North Pole Game, a board game which reduced
Nansen's well-planned expedition to a few throws of a dice. In
London, *Punch* added its own jolly commentary: 'So Dr Fridtjof
Nansen's off! Cynics will chuckle and pessimists scoff.'[29] Nansen the
'noodle', a 'Norroway chap', was off to the Pole to complete the map.

'Can't something happen?'[30] Nansen raged, as the *Fram* circled
monotonously on. 'Could not a hurricane come and tear up this ice,
and set it rolling in high waves like the open sea?' Nothing did
happen. As a measure of their tedium, Dr Henrik Blessing experimented with morphine and gradually became an addict. The crew,
who had no need of his services, sat around and put on weight. The
months passed and by October 1894, as their second winter began,
Nansen was shimmering through the spectrum of his moods. At times
he was driven to depths of introspection: 'Here I sit among the drifting ice floes in the great silence and stare up at the eternal courses of
the stars, and in the distance I see the thread of life becoming entangled in the complex web which stretches unbroken from the gentle
dawn of life to the everlasting silence of the ice. I see the febrile race,
soap bubbles form and burst. Thought follows thought, everything is
picked to pieces, and becomes miserably small and worthless.'[31]
Poetic analysis was succeeded by self-exhortation: 'I laugh at scurvy,'
he wrote, 'I laugh at the ice . . . I laugh at the cold; it is nothing.'[32]
Then he fell back into self-pity: 'I have never lacked great thoughts
about my intellectual worth. Why was I given a Titan's longings and
then formed like an ordinary worker ant?'[33] The crew became wary of
him and soon started actively to dislike him.

The one surprise came from their soundings. Every authority agreed that the Polar Basin was probably shallow but the further north the *Fram* went, the deeper the water became. Their sounding line ran out and had to be augmented by lengths of iron cable spliced together. On 21 December, they let down 1,000 fathoms and still there was no bottom. That depth would increase to 1,500 and then 2,000 fathoms, still without touching the sea bed. Unnerved, Nansen began to wonder if the earth had a bottomless axis. Were they heading for Symmes's Hole?

On 3 January 1894, as Nansen wished, something happened. A slice of ice, driven by the mysterious pressures of the pack, lurched up and advanced on the *Fram*. They saw it coming but dismissed it until the moment when it climbed over the *Fram*'s deck and threatened to smother the hatch, imprisoning everyone on board. Nansen ordered an evacuation of men and stores. This time it looked as if the *Fram* had met its match. But once again the ship survived Everyone was incredulous, particularly a seaman named Hendrikson who had attacked the ice with a shovel. 'He was a hell of a chap,' wrote one shipmate. 'Afterwards he said, "bugger me, [the ice] heaved both me and the spade, ha ha" . . . in the same tone of voice he tells about how many Russians the Norwegians killed on such and such an occasion on Spitsbergen.'[34]

Nansen saw it as a sign. He had already equipped himself with dogs and skis for an overland trek. The near crushing of the *Fram*, coupled with its obvious lack of progress, decided him. He would wait a year to see if the ship's placid drift brought it any nearer the Pole – by now he was almost certain it would never cross it – and then in spring 1895 he would make a dash for the top of the world. With him he would take one man, whatever teams of dogs were necessary to haul their supplies, several sets of skis, two sledges, and a couple of kayaks. His plan was to ski north with the dogs hauling the supply sledges, then, having travelled as far north as he could, to turn south, feeding the dogs on each other until he reached Franz Josef Land whereupon he would either catch a ride on any ship that might be there or travel the last leg to Spitsbergen by kayak. His confidence

that this daring plan would work came from his experience in
Greenland, where he had learned what could be achieved by ski
travel and where he had been impressed by the seeming invincibility
of Eskimo kayaks. He was certain, too, that the ice would present no
problem. Wandering over it on 15 January 1894, he saw the smoothest
icescape possible, stretching to the limits of sight. Sliding past the
horizon in his imagination, he decided that the Pole was well within
his grasp. 'It might almost be called an easy expedition for two men.'[35]

Nansen's assessment was one of the most foolhardy in the history
of polar exploration. His experience of ice travel had been in
Greenland, whose flattish ice cap was incomparably easier than the
polar pack where hummocks, pressure ridges and stretches of open
water – sometimes covered in snow – formed a maze that led to an
ever-shifting conclusion. His admiration of kayaks came from seeing
them at work in coastal waters where, admittedly, these watertight
slices of skin and bone performed brilliantly. But even Eskimos did
not take kayaks into the open ocean, and most of those who had tried
had perished. As for getting a lift from Franz Josef Land, Nansen
ignored the reality that only a few, hardy men had ever visited the
place since its discovery and that the chance of meeting a ship was
negligible. Nor did Nansen take into account the polar drift which
had baffled so many explorers in the past and which was hampering
the *Fram* just as it would hamper him. His confidence was so great,
however, that he feared more for those he left behind than he did for
himself. 'Imagine if I came home and they did not!' he wrote. 'Yet it
was to explore the unknown Polar regions that I came; it was for that
the Norwegian people gave their money; and surely my first duty is to
do that if I can.'[36]

Preparations went ahead during 1894 and the first months of 1895.
Skis were tested and selected. Sledges were built to Nansen's
own specifications: they were a novel and elastic kind, their broad
runners sheathed in metal to allow fast travel, their leather bindings
flexible enough to cope with rough terrain. Kayaks were constructed
from bamboo and waterproof material, differing from the Eskimo
model only in the provision of holds which were accessible through

hatches in the bow. Casting around the crew, Nansen chose a stoker named Hjalmar Johanssen to accompany him. A drifter, who had been many things, including a prison warder, Johanssen was an all-round athlete who knew how to ski and who had represented Norway at the 1889 Paris gymnastic championships.

Finally, on 14 March 1895, after two false starts, and with the *Fram* sitting just north of the 84th parallel – a record for a ship – Nansen and Johanssen left on their daredevil attempt, carrying provisions to last 100 days. Almost as soon as they had gone an atmosphere of calm descended on the *Fram*. Otto Sverdrup, the Captain, who had suffered an unpleasant two years as Nansen's second-in-command, took control of the ship and began to organize things in a seamanlike fashion. A threatening pressure ridge was hacked down and the *Fram* was made ready to sail as soon as a lead showed itself. Glad to be rid of Nansen and his moods, they settled down for the duration of their drift.

Nansen and Johanssen, meanwhile, were sweeping north at an unprecedented rate. The ice *was* good. In the first week they and their dogs made twenty miles a day and by 29 March they had reached 85°09′N – a new record. Only 300 miles, approximately, remained. Their journey was not without difficulty, though. They, their dogs and their sledges fell through cracks in the ice, to emerge sodden and windblasted. Their tent was an efficient model designed by Nansen – a pyramid, instead of the traditional, horizontal affair with all its awkward guy ropes – but it offered little warmth for defrosting frozen limbs, despite the Primus stove. On 1 April, Johanssen's chronometer stopped, not a disaster in itself but a hindrance, for although Nansen's chronometer was still ticking they now had no means of checking its accuracy.

On 3 April their luck changed. The ice became rougher and rougher, interspersed with ever wider lanes of water. 'These ridges are enough to make one despair,' Nansen wrote, 'and there seems no prospect of things bettering.'[37] This was the day, too, on which they killed their first dog as food for the others. It was a task that saddened both of them for, disreputable and ferocious as the dogs were, they were their only allies in a hostile environment. Most depressing, however, was the realization (if Nansen's chronometer was keeping correct time) that they were now fighting the southern drift. At midday they were at 85°59′, only fifty miles further north than they had been five days earlier. 'It is astonishing that we have not got further,' Nansen wrote in his journal, 'we seem to toil all we can, but without much progress. Beginning to doubt seriously of the advisability of continuing northwards much longer.'[38]

They had covered 115 miles since leaving the ship. The Pole was 240 miles distant and the northernmost part of Franz Josef Land was 370 miles to the south-west – though, as the archipelago had yet to be fully explored, this was guesswork. Even travelling at their best speed it was extremely doubtful whether they could reach the Pole *and* return to Franz Josef Land before their food ran out. At their present rate, struggling both with rough ice and the southern drift, they would never do it. Their one chance was if the ice smoothed out and the drift stopped – then, possibly, they might be able to claim the Pole.

'No, the ice grew worse and worse, and we got no way,' Nansen wrote on 8 April. 'I went on a good way ahead on snow-shoes, but saw no reasonable prospect of advance . . . It was a veritable chaos of ice-blocks, stretching as far as the horizon.'[39] There was no point continuing. If the ice was as bad as this on the way back to Franz Josef Land they would need every day they could get. He therefore decided to change course for the south. 'On this northernmost camping ground we indulged in a banquet, consisting of lobscouse, bread-and-butter, dry chocolate, stewed '"tytlebaer", or red whortle-berries, and our hot whey drink, and then, with a delightful and unfamiliar feeling of repletion, crept into the dear bag.'[40] They had reached 86°13′06″N – a new record by almost three degrees.

To the surprise of both men, their return journey started with days of perfect travelling conditions. 'We sweep over plain after plain,' Nansen wrote in his diary. 'If it continues like this, the journey home will be shorter than I thought.'[41] On 13 April, however, Johanssen's chronometer, which he had reset to match Nansen's, stopped for the second time. When they came to reset it, they discovered that

Nansen's chronometer had stopped too. Anywhere else, a stopped watch would have occasioned nothing more than a brief sense of irritation. Here, on the polar pack, the implications were terrifying. To reach Franz Josef Land, they needed to know their longitude precisely. To measure longitude they needed to know the time, and they no longer had it.

On the way to the Pole longitude had been forgotten. The all-important north–south latitude measurements, which could be taken from the skies, had told them how far they had advanced each day. Now it was the east–west longitude calculations on which their lives depended, for if they got them wrong they would miss Franz Josef Land. Nansen guessed their chronometers had stopped for half an hour but without being certain he reset them for 86°E, a slight eastward exaggeration which he hoped would ensure that if they did not immediately hit land they only had to walk west along a calculable latitude until they did. It was a nerve-wracking decision. If they were much farther west than he thought then they would pass Franz Josef Land on the wrong side and instead of walking towards it would be heading for the Atlantic. And who could tell where the ice had taken them in the interval between the stopping and starting of the chronometers? For the pack had begun its maddening circular drift again, this time carrying them *north*. Nansen's sightings for the 13th showed they were at 86°5′. After days of swift, unimpeded travel they had made just five miles south. How rapidly had the ice carried them east or west?

To cap a terrible day, Nansen had left his compass behind at their last stop. He sloped off to fetch it, leaving Johanssen behind with the dogs. 'Never have I felt anything so still,' Johanssen wrote, once Nansen had gone. 'Not the slightest sound of any kind disturbed the silence near or far; the dogs lay as if lifeless with their heads on their paws in the white snow, glistening in the gleaming sun. It was so frighteningly still, I had to remain where I sat, I dared not move a limb; I hardly dared to breathe.'[42] He was hugely relieved when, after several hours, he heard the grit of skis on the snow and looked up to see Nansen returning with the compass.

The solitude Johanssen experienced was exacerbated in coming weeks by the regular slaughter of their dogs. On 26 April, by which time they had reached 84°46′N, he almost wept when they killed a dog that had been born aboard the *Fram*. It had been born in the ice and now it was dying in the ice without having once seen dry land. He found no comfort in Nansen either. 'He is too self-centred to be anyone's friend, and one's patience is sorely tried. It is silent in the tent; no fun, never a joke. The fellow is unsociable and clumsy in the smallest things; egoistic in the highest degree.'[43]

On 4 June they reached 82°17′N and by Nansen's calculations Franz Josef Land was twenty-five miles away. But they couldn't be certain. 'This is getting worse and worse,' Nansen wrote on 12 June. 'Yesterday we did nothing, hardly advanced more than a mile. Wretched snow, uneven ice, lanes, and villainous weather stopped us.'[44] The snow had become so slushy that even their skis sank into it and leads were opening everywhere. The virtue of their situation was that they could now shoot seals and polar bears – but they were sparing of their magazine, which numbered 350 rounds and which they realized might have to last them a second winter. 'Here we are then,' Nansen wrote from inside their tent, 'hardly knowing what to do next. What the going is like outside I do not know yet, but probably not much better than yesterday, and whether we ought to push on the little we can, or go out and try to capture a seal, I cannot decide.'[45]

They went for the seals, stocking up a good larder for the future. Thus, with a bit of skiing here, a bit of shooting there, and more than a little of kayaking (the kayaks had been damaged during the trek and had to be made watertight with candlewax) they reached on 24 July a point from which they saw land. It was the 132nd day since they had left the *Fram* and Nansen was overjoyed: 'At last we have seen land! Land! Oh wonderful world! After nearly two years we can see something raise itself once more over that everlasting white line out there on the horizon. And this white line, which has spread over this sea for thousands upon thousands of years, and which for thousands of years will continue to spread in the same way – now we will leave it, and all that has happened is the trifle that the narrow track of a little caravan has been drawn in the snow over the white surface; a track which has long since vanished. Now a new life begins for us, because the ice is and always will be the same.'[46]

Disappointingly, however, a new life did not begin immediately. With the exception that Johanssen changed his underwear for the first time in four months, their existence was much the same as before. Instead of forming a neat edge, the pack was a treacherous jumble of frozen surf that shifted and wallowed underfoot. For a fortnight they stumbled and waded across the disintegrating ice, jumping from block to block, dragging their sledges behind them. And all the time the ice continued to move northwards and westwards, threatening to snatch them away from Franz Josef Land at the last moment. On 6 August, however, they finally reached an inlet of open water. They shot their last two dogs, ate a piece of chocolate in celebration, then lashed their sledges across the kayaks to form a catamaran, and left the pack for good. Before them, through a light mist, they saw a collection of floes bobbing on sluggish grey waves, and beyond that a shining glacier pouring from the mountains of Franz Josef Land. 'It was a flood of happiness that filled one's soul at this sight, and which it was impossible to express in words,' Nansen wrote. 'Behind us lay all our troubles, and ahead the waterway lay open all the way home and light and happiness.'[47]

But was it Franz Josef Land? They possessed only a sketchy map by Payer and a slightly improved one by a British explorer, Benjamin Leigh-Smith, who had made two expeditions to the area in the early 1880s. On neither of these did the northernmost headland, Cape Fligely, resemble the outline they saw on the horizon. Without being able to calculate their longitude they could not tell whether they had reached their goal or had struck an entirely new island. If the latter, then where did the new land stand in relation to Franz Josef Land? If to the east, all was well. If to the west, however, they were lost. For the moment, however, that was irrelevant. Having spent 146 days travelling 600 miles across the ice, they paddled thankfully towards shore.

14

MIRACLE AT
CAPE FLORA

In the absence of his expedition leader, Captain Sverdrup was doing very well on the *Fram*. On 15 November 1895 they hit a northernmost of 85°55′5″, nineteen miles south of Nansen's farthest – how he would have raged if he had known – and from there they were on their way home, propelled by a southward drift. The crew had grown stale with inactivity and had taken to drink. Petty squabbles broke out as they prepared for a third winter in the highest latitude known to humankind. 'You cannot conceive how fed up we are,' wrote one man. 'It has got to the point where we can hardly stand each other.'[1] But they were united in the joy of no longer being subjected to Nansen's whims. 'There was a time when I hated Nansen to such an extent that I almost dare not think of it,' the same man wrote, 'but now that feeling has faded to a memory, vague as a fog, of a dark period, and has given way to an ordinary, polite sympathy which makes me concentrate on the good aspects.'[2]

By mid-March 1895 the *Fram* had reached 84°N, 25′E and a fear was growing that 'we will have to celebrate a fourth winter up here'.[3] Sverdrup calmed his men with Viking bravado: if the worst happened they could count on sharing a horn of mead in Valhalla. But Valhalla did not beckon. On 12 August the ice became weak and brittle. At 3.00 a.m. on 13 August they sighted an expanse of dark water to the south-east. And at 3.45 the *Fram* steered through the last floes into open sea. 'WE WERE FREE!' Sverdrup wrote in his journal. 'We paid the final honours to our vanquished antagonist by firing a thunderous salute as a farewell. One more gaze at the last faint outlines of the hummocks and floes, and the mist concealed them from our view.'[4]

That afternoon they sighted a Norwegian ship, the *Sostrene*, and greeted it with further salvoes. The *Sostrene*'s captain came aboard for a night of celebration and to fill them in on all that had happened while they had been away. Sverdrup was interested in only one item of news: had Nansen come home? The answer was no. But, as the captain made himself at home on the *Fram* with a camp bed, fifty bottles of beer and a bottle of whisky, he told Sverdrup and his men something he thought might be of interest: a Swede named Andrée was going to fly to the Pole by balloon.

Salomon August Andrée was tall, fat, broad-shouldered and walrus-moustached. He has been described as a character from a Jules Verne novel and perhaps he did have something of Verne's approach to the earth's mysteries. Born in 1854, he was a lugubrious man who was fascinated by the possibilities of science. As a ten-year-old he had constructed a model balloon, powered by a percussion cap, which had worked perfectly until it came down on – and set fire to – a neighbour's house. Later he experimented with light and darkness, with a view to discovering why polar explorers went so pallid. Were their sallow visages caused by the long Arctic night or were they deceived by the sudden reappearance of the sun? He shut himself in a dark room for a month, to test the matter, and emerged with a satisfactory yellow complexion. He also addressed the problem of how many hard-boiled eggs a man could eat at a sitting. Booking a table at a restaurant, he went in and ordered forty of them, with bread and butter and milk. The waitress asked with a straight face whether he wanted anything else.

Unlike Nansen, who was a true scientist, Andrée was a talented tinkerer, a man who abhorred mystery and who sought by experiment to reduce the world to its rational components. He was passionate, but single-mindedly so. Whenever he felt he might be in danger of falling in love, he squashed the emotion – 'I know that if I once let such a feeling live it would become so strong that I dare not give in to it,'[5] he said. Everything he did was in the service of technology, in which he believed with a devotion approaching zealotry, and by 1885 he was ensconced in Sweden's Patent Office where he was able to admire and adjudicate upon technology in all its forms. He possessed energy and application but lacked charisma and on-the-spot ingenuity. He was the dullest, most unlikely candidate to lead a polar exploration.

The traditional approach had failed so manifestly that maybe it was time for the soulless hand of technology to take over. That, in so many words, was what Andrée said before a meeting of the Swedish Academy in 1895, when he aired his plans to travel to the Pole in a hydrogen-filled balloon, containing himself and two other aeronauts. His speech had patriotic appeal: 'Who, I ask, are better qualified to make such an attempt than us Swedes? . . . [We] must maintain the goodliest traditions in the field of natural science in general, and, not least, in that of polar research in particular.'[6] Patriotism was as attractive to the Swedes as it had been to the Norwegians when Nansen had made a similar appeal, and brought comparable dividends. Andrée received financial backing from King Oscar II of Sweden and Alfred Nobel, the millionaire inventor of dynamite. Nordenskiöld also gave his public support.

On 29 July 1895, Andrée spread his project before the Sixth International Geographical Congress at the Great Hall of the Royal Colonial Institute in London. This time his audience contained heavyweight sceptics. Albert Markham asked how Andrée would know when he had reached the Pole. (By the same methods as anyone else.) And what would happen if he crashed on the ice? (Then he would be in the same position as surface explorers.) Yes, a French scientist said, but what would happen if he crashed in the sea without having prepared the boat he was carrying against such an event?

('Drown,' Andrée replied.) Adolphus Greely, whose survival from his disastrous expedition had made him the voice of America in matters Arctic, then got up and told him to forget the idea, pointing out that his balloon would lose most of its hydrogen through natural seepage before he got halfway there and yet more dead bodies would garland the Pole. Anyway, it was all hypothetical, for Andrée didn't have the funds and would find it impossible to raise them for such a harebrained scheme – much as he, Greely, wished his 'ballooning Arctic friend'[7] luck in doing so. Someone else then said that he regarded 'Herr Andrée's project as foolhardy, and not one to be seriously discussed at a meeting of this character.'[8]

To all these people, some of whom had tried to wrestle the Pole off its pedestal by sheer manly enterprise, Andrée had a very direct response. 'Every minute of latitude covered by the same means [as before] will, no doubt, cost hundreds of thousands in money, and involve great sacrifice of human lives.'[9] *His* expedition was cheaper than any other, it involved only three lives, and it did not depend upon 'sledges drawn by dogs, or a vessel that travels like a boulder frozen into ice'. Besides, he continued, 'can anybody deny that it will be possible, by a single successful balloon journey, to acquire in a few days greater knowledge of the geographical aspect of the Arctic regions than would otherwise be obtainable in centuries?'[10] There was no answer. Then he turned to Greely, who had very noticeably lost more lives than anyone else in recent history and who had scoffed publicly at Andrée's chances of finding money to support his silly project. 'I have the money,' Andrée said, 'and the attempt will be made.'[11]

Ballooning was not a new skill, neither was its application to the polar question particularly novel. For more than a decade, people had wondered if this could be the way forward – De Long, Nares and Bennett among them. But for all the wonder of balloons, they had their drawbacks. They allowed humankind to fly but only at the whim of the wind. Without a steering mechanism they were unreliable, a diversion for rich men who liked to go aloft with bottles of champagne and toast the view. In London's Vauxhall Gardens a captive balloon had long been an entertainment for the middle classes. However, Andrée thought he had solved the problem of steering: drag ropes. By draping a length of rope from the basket to the ground one could influence the way the balloon moved. Drop a rope to the left, and the balloon would be dragged in that direction. Drop a rope to the right and it would move to the other. He knew it worked because he had tried it in Eastern Europe and Scandinavia. In an experiment which took him hundreds of miles across the Baltic Sea and Sweden, he successfully steered his balloon in more or less whatever direction he wanted it to go. (How people beneath felt as his ropes slithered over them is unrecorded.) Between 1893 and 1896 he made nine ascents in which he flew at a height of three miles and covered 240 miles at a stretch. He had been able to steer the balloon at 27° and at times 40° against the wind. On all these voyages he took multiple observations and met nothing which could hinder his ambition to reach the top of the world. He calculated that, with a favourable wind, he could cross from Spitsbergen to Alaska, a distance of 2,200 miles, in less than six days. The Pole itself could be reached in as little as ten hours and a maximum of forty-three.

In a statement to the *New York Times*, Andrée said: 'I don't see that there will be any dangers at all. I have every confidence in the success of my enterprise, and am sure that before long I will find any amount of imitators. I do not care a snap of the fingers what my critics say . . . nothing can prevent me from starting.' His bullish approach won him friends in London society. 'With his engaging manners and design, at once plucky and novel, [he] is the lion of the season's fag end, and has far more invitations that he knows what to do with,'[12] wrote the *Westminster Gazette*.

Clements Markham was fearfully excited. He sent orders to all circumpolar outposts – Weyprecht's experiment was still continuing – to the effect that 'The commanders of these stations will be asked to warn the natives that the balloon is not a devilish or dangerous thing, but that it contains scientific people.'[13] An Austrian newspaper, on the other hand, said that if Andrée hoped to reach the Pole by balloon he was 'simply a fool or a swindler'.[14]

In June 1896, on Dane's Island, one of the northernmost land masses of the Spitsbergen archipelago, Andrée inflated the *Eagle*. It took four days to fill the balloon which, when fully erect, rose almost 200 feet above the men below – the largest balloon the world had ever seen. Unfortunately the wind was wrong and for weeks the *Eagle* bobbled on its mooring while Andrée and his two companions waited impatiently. There was still no change in the weather when, on 14 August, the *Fram* hove into view. Nils Strindberg, one of Andrée's fellow aeronauts, recorded its arrival: 'It was like a dream to see these men, who have spent 3 long years on this ship . . . It is strange, moving, magnificent. [The ship] seems almost sacred . . .'[15] He took them to see the balloon, but Sverdrup's crew had no interest in it. All they could do was play with the stones on the beach in a childlike joy at being on land again.

A French scientist, Henri Lachambre, who had accompanied Andrée, went to visit the *Fram*. He entered the main saloon and stared. It was hexagonal, with brightly-painted red, white and green wainscoting reaching halfway to the ceiling. Above that, the walls were covered with pictures of mythical Norse heroes, a roughly drawn portrait of Nansen and his wife dominating all. It was lit, dimly, by a skylight and a single oil lamp. Off the hexagon, doors led to the sleeping quarters. They were dark and windowless, one lamp in each, the only natural light filtering through from the saloon. Lachambre felt as if he was walking into a shrine.

In the middle of the saloon was a table, on which the men had eaten their meals. In one corner was a sofa. In another was a harmonium. When invited to play, Otto Sverdrup improvised beautifully. Lachambre would have liked to dance but it seemed to him a profane act. Instead, he listened for a while then closed the door silently and went back on deck.

The arrival of the *Fram* disheartened Andrée. On Dane's Island he had prepared a wonderful demonstration of ballooning skill. He had built a shed for the balloon, had dragged ashore the gas-making apparatus, a generator, and the timber to build a house for his men. He had mixed gallons of sulphuric acid and pounds of iron filings to create the hydrogen which would pump the *Eagle* to its desired firmness. The sea was stained so red with the effluent that for miles around visitors thought they were seeing the real colour of the sea bed. And there were visitors: shiploads of tourists came to see what the daring Swede was up to. The northerly wind which had brought the *Fram* home, however, was no use to Andrée. He wanted a strong southerly breeze. It was not forthcoming and so, on 17 August 1896, the *Eagle* was deflated and Andrée returned to the Patent Department. Next year would be the one.

Nansen and Johanssen had landed on what they hoped was part of Franz Josef Land in early August, 1895. It was an uncharted, barren island which was definitely not Cape Fligely. But there were other islands to the south and they headed for them, their spirits rising all the time. 'The sky was overcast,' Nansen wrote at midnight on 17 August, 'but along the whole horizon to the north lay the most wonderful crimson, with gold tinted clouds, like a sunset . . . A wonderful night . . . the water smooth as a mirror, not a piece of ice to be seen . . . It was all like a trip in a gondola.'[16] They camped on floes as a storm blew up and heavy seas began to run past them. On 26 August they battled their kayaks onto a desolate spit of land which bore no resemblance to anything on their maps and resigned themselves to another winter in the ice.

They dug a three-foot-deep hole, built a parapet of stones around it and formed a ridge pole out of a length of driftwood which they then covered with walrus hides to make a roof. In this rudimentary shelter – they called it 'The Hole' – they prepared to sit out 'the third and worst polar night'.[17] Their situation was not life-threatening. They shot enough bears, seals and walruses to see them through until spring so there was no danger of starvation or scurvy. It was the boredom that hit them; that and the uncertainty of their position. If they guessed aright, the southernmost point of Franz Josef Land, where they were most likely to meet help, was 100 miles away. But it was only a guess and they had to live in doubt for at least the next six months. During that time how were they to spend their days?

They did a number of mindless things. They read Nansen's navigation tables and almanac until they were sick of them – and then read them again for 'the sight of the printed letters gave one the feeling that there was, after all, a little bit of the civilised man left'.[18] They made an Eskimo-style lamp fuelled by blubber and thawed their underwear over it, scraping off the grease and adding it to the pool of fat in the lamp. They reminisced about life at home and drew up plans of what they would do next winter in Christiana. At one point, Johanssen noted with awe that Nansen used the familiar form of address for the first time in their entire journey. Sometimes Nansen went outside and marvelled at the aurora, invoking the heroes of Scandinavian mythology. 'Here is the kingdom of giants,' he wrote, 'here Surt [the fire-Titan] ruled the heavens, and the frost giants rule the earth. But some day they will sweep southwards, when Surt's hordes, circled by the flames of the aurora will sough through the air and in roaring winter storms the frost giants will ravage all countries – that will be the twilight of the Gods, the end of all things.'[19] Then he returned to the 'Hole' and introspected: 'Christmas is on the way, the season of joy. The meat cauldron is bubbling cheerfully on the stove. I sit here and stare into the flickering flames . . . What is the strange power that fire and light have that all creation seeks them?'[20] Most of the time, however, they just slept.

On 19 May 1896, the ice opened and they were able to resume their journey. But, in their relief at being afloat, they became careless. On 12 June, while climbing a berg in order to obtain their bearings, they moored the kayaks too loosely. When they turned around the vessels had drifted out to sea. This was the worst conceivable disaster for, apart from being their only means of transport, the kayaks contained all their food, clothing and ammunition. Without them, they were dead. Pausing only to hand Johanssen his watch and strip off his coat, Nansen dived into the sea. People had fallen into the Arctic Ocean before but this was the first time anyone had swum in it voluntarily. Johanssen slithered impotently at the edge of the berg. He knew that it could only be a few minutes before Nansen's limbs cramped in the cold. Nansen knew it too – but, as he later recorded, 'there drifted all our hope, and whether I stiffened and sank here, or returned without the kayaks, the result seemed much the same'.[21] Hampered by his clothes and by the icy coldness he floundered through the sea, the kayaks seeming to drift farther away by the minute. After a while, he thought he was gaining on them. 'My courage rose, and I carried on with renewed strength. Little by little, however, I felt my limbs becoming stiffer and unfeeling. I understood that I could not manage much more, but now it was not all that far, and if only I could hold out we were saved. So I forced myself on. My limbs became weaker and weaker the shorter the distance.'[22] His arms froze, so he turned on his back and kicked with his feet. From this point, as he knew, he had only a short time before his legs also froze. He beat the clock by the smallest margin. His arm hit one of the kayaks and he flung it woodenly onto the canvas. Then came the boarding. 'I tried to pull myself up, but the whole of my body was so stiff with the cold that this was an impossibility.'[23] Finally with a supreme effort, he hooked one of his legs onto the frail catamaran and swung himself up.

Paddling the kayaks back was almost as bad as swimming to rescue them. Bitten by the wind, his clothes freezing, Nansen forced his arms into motion. Blood began to flow and before he reached shore he was able to shoot two guillemots with a single discharge (retrieved them, too). But when he landed he was in a poor state: he was pale, his long hair and beard were frozen, he frothed at the mouth, shivered incessantly and had difficulty speaking. Johanssen stripped him, put him to bed and when he woke up a few hours later, fed him the two guillemots he had shot. Nansen then consumed a bowl of soup and declared himself fit for anything. And, amazingly, he was.

Three days later, however, they met a pack of walruses. On shore, walruses are somnolent and vulnerable – the two Norwegians had shot scores of them, some from a distance of six feet. But in the sea, they can become fierce and aggressive. On 13 June the walruses came after the catamaran and, before Nansen and Johanssen could shoot them, they had sunk their tusks into the kayaks, crippling them fatally. Luckily they were close to shore – yet another bit of unrecognizable coast – and were able to drag the kayaks up for repair. It took them four days to patch the craft, using all their meagre resources. On the morning of 17 June they were cooking a last meal when Nansen thought he heard dogs barking. Johanssen could hear nothing save birds on a nearby cliff. But Nansen insisted, and skied to investigate. A few hours later, he heard voices. They seemed to be English. Rounding a hummock he saw first a dog and then a human being. It was Frederick Jackson.

The Jackson–Harmsworth expedition had left the Thames in 1894 and had set up camp near the south-western tip of Franz Josef Land at a point called Cape Flora. Since then, in an efficient – but today largely forgotten – manner it had begun a thorough survey of the archipelago, supplied at regular intervals by the *Windward*, a small steamer that carried provisions, equipment and letters from civilization. The expedition numbered eight men in all, who lived and worked in a settlement of seven wooden huts on the shore of Cape Flora. One of Jackson's men had spotted Nansen from a distance and had alerted his commander to the presence of another human in the wilderness. 'Oh, nonsense,' Jackson had replied, 'it is a walrus surely?'[24]

'A tall man, wearing a soft felt hat, loosely made, voluminous clothes, and long shaggy hair and beard, all of which were reeking with black grease, presented himself,' Jackson recorded. 'His complexion was that of native Central Africa, excepting for one or two white spots in the neighbourhood of his eyes and mouth ... This much suggested the physiognomy of a Music Hall celebrity of long ago, "the One-Eyed Kaffir".'[25] He thought initially that it might be a stranded British sailor, then noticing the skis decided it was more likely a Scandinavian walrus hunter who had lost his ship. As they spoke, however, Jackson realized who the man was. It was hard to connect this ragamuffin with the Faustian figure who had spurned him at the Royal Geographical Society. But there could be no mistake. 'Aren't you Nansen?'[26] he asked.

In Jackson's own words, 'A more remarkable meeting than ours was never heard of.'[27] It was, indeed, an extraordinary stroke of luck that these two explorers should chance upon each other in the hundreds of thousands of square miles of empty polar ice. If not for the walrus attack, neither man would have known of the existence of the other: Jackson would have carried on exploring. and Johanssen would have paddled off to certain doom. The unlikelihood of their meeting was reinforced by Jackson's later revelation that he had charted the island on which they had spent the winter without even noticing 'The Hole'. It was as dramatic as the encounter between Livingstone and Stanley and, unconsciously or not, Jackson greeted Nansen with the same clumsy words that Stanley had used: 'I congratulate you most heartily, you have made a deuced good trip of it, and I am awfully glad to be the first person to congratulate you.'[28]

Nansen was brought back to Cape Flora while a team went out to rescue Johanssen and the kayaks. Jackson insisted on both men posing in their filthy clothes while he took some photographs and his team gave three cheers – 'This appeared to please Nansen very much and he frequently exclaimed, "This is splendid!",'[29] Jackson recorded – then he let them have a bath, a shave and a haircut. The sight of Nansen naked shocked him. Expecting a skeleton, he noted that he was 'pale, fat and very anaemic.'[30] When put on the scales Nansen weighed fourteen stone seven pounds, a stone and a half above his normal weight. Discounting constipation and piles, which were the unavoidable result of a meat-only diet, he was too healthy to be true. Nansen was then clothed, fed and offered a chair to sit upon. The chair unnerved him. After months of either skiing upright or resting horizontally on the snow, the halfway house of a chair seemed unnatural. When he got used to it, however, he gave in: 'A strange feeling came over me . . . At one stroke of changing fate, all responsibility, all troubles were swept away from a mind that had been oppressed by them during three long years . . . My duty was done: my task was ended; now I could rest, only rest and wait.'[31]

The *Windward* not being due for several weeks, Jackson gave his guests the run of the island. He escorted Nansen to a secret cliff where he could shoot loons on the wing. But Nansen was afraid of heights and had to be helped down, ruining in the process a pair of trousers Jackson had lent him. They talked of Franz Josef Land –

once, for forty-eight hours at a stretch – and came to an agreement about who should name which features. Jackson said Nansen could name everything within sight of 'The Hole', even though Jackson had already charted it himself: 'he has discovered very little to name, and I think it hard lines on the chap,'[32] he reasoned. Nansen asked if he could use Jackson's maps in his journal and Jackson agreed. 'It is very decent of him to think of it,' he wrote, 'some would have published that portion of the map without consulting me.'[33]

This was a subdued and polite Nansen, a far cry from the over-bearing 'Himself' on the *Fram*. The long trek had shaken him badly. 'Nansen repeatedly remarks that nothing will ever induce him to undertake such a journey again,'[34] Jackson noted in his journal. He also jotted down a slightly schoolmasterly warning for future explorers: 'I only trust that Dr. Nansen's extraordinary immunity from penalty will not lead the inexperienced to suppose that one may go larking about within the Polar Circle with merely a dog and a gun and that all things will be well with them.'[35]

Jackson was unstinting in his praise for Nansen. '[He] has made an extraordinary journey, which for daring I consider is without parallel.'[36] He felt an affinity for him because, in his own way, he too was an innovator. Breaking free from British tradition, he had equipped himself with skis, sledges and dogs which – in a very un-British fashion – he knew how to use, having undergone a period of training in Russia. He was toying, too, with the idea of ponies or reindeer as draught animals and had devised a collapsible aluminium boat for crossing channels of water. The reason for his keenness on new means of transport was a belief that he would be able to reach the Pole from Franz Josef Land, which he hoped might be the southernmost tip of a land mass reaching to the top of the globe. When Nansen reported that Franz Josef Land was in fact an archipelago, Jackson's enthusiasm was undimmed. If Nansen could travel south across the pack then he, Jackson, could travel north across it. At once he began to build copies of Nansen's sledges and kayaks in preparation for an attempt to break the Norwegian record. For all his tuttings about inexperienced amateurs, he had not taken in a word that Nansen had said.

Nansen for his part felt affronted that Jackson should prepare so openly to steal a lead using the methods his guests had shown him. But the ramifications of explorers' etiquette are endless; Jackson probably took the view that having salvaged Nansen's expedition he was entitled to the proceeds of the wreck. The Norwegians were not worried. 'Skiers, the Englishmen are not,' Johanssen wrote. 'I do not believe they will reach as far as us; in fact, I am certain, from what I have seen of them.'[37] Nansen agreed. Their assessment was eventually proved correct: Jackson's expedition went no further than the northern tip of Franz Josef Land. Meanwhile, the Britons bustled blithely away, and Nansen began to exert his forceful presence. 'I have never met anyone who had such a magnetic personality, and such a profound confidence in himself,'[38] recorded one of Jackson's cohorts. Jackson himself, while noting that Nansen had a tendency to disparage all other explorers, wrote that, 'I like him very much, and we get on A.1. together.'[39]

In the early hours of 25 July, the *Windward* arrived at Cape Flora with Jackson's supplies. The unloading took a week and was followed by several days of bad weather, but on 7 August the two Norwegians were lifted off Franz Josef Land and six days later delivered to Norway where, at the port of Vardo, Nansen monopolized the telegraph lines for several hours before continuing down the Norwegian coast. He was hailed at Hammerfest and cheered at Tromsø, where he had an emotional reunion with the men of the *Fram*, followed by a tersely polite encounter with Andrée, and on 9 September he finally steamed into Christiana. Every vessel in the harbour came out to welcome him. 'There were flags high and low,' he wrote, 'salutes, hurrahs, waving of handkerchiefs and hats, radiant faces everywhere, the whole fjord one multitudinous welcome. There lay home, and the well-known strand before it, glittering and smiling in the sunshine. Then steamers on steamers again, shouts after shouts; and we all stood hat in hand, bowing as they cheered.'[40] He was escorted into town by the King and Queen of Sweden, passing under an arch of 200 white-clad gymnasts before he arrived at the Royal Palace, which was to be his abode for the next days and where his wife and daughter were waiting for him.

Amidst the acclaim there were only two voices of complaint. One came from the playwright Henrik Ibsen who, on being asked why he wasn't attending the fête, replied, 'It's a Red Indian deed, and it's being celebrated by Indian war dances, and I don't belong there.'[41] The other came from Johanssen, Nansen's forgotten shadow, who skulked unhappily in the background. 'Now when I think of how wonderful I thought it would be to say goodbye to all the ice and to all suffering, and compare that feeling with my reality now,' he wrote, 'I find that reality, after all, is not so wonderful as it appeared to me in the midst of our hard life.'[42]

From Britain to Hungary, plaudits flooded in. The steward of the *Windward* had to fight off people wanting to buy Nansen's old clothes. And when Nansen published his journal, *Farthest North*, a two-volume tome of 300,000 words which he wrote in an unbelievable two months, his fame multiplied. He sold the book for stupendous sums to publishers in Norway and elsewhere in Europe, where it received glowing reviews. Edward Whymper, conqueror of the Matterhorn, and explorer of Greenland, wrote that Nansen had made 'almost as great an advance as has been accomplished by all other voyages in the nineteenth century put together . . . He is a Man in a Million.'[43] The Russian anarchist, Prince Peter Kropotkin, said that he and Johanssen were 'true heroes of our century'.[44]

They *were* true heroes and heroes very much of their age, if not the entire century. Hitherto, the success of Arctic explorers had been judged as much by the manner in which they overcame self-inflicted disaster as by their achievements. The tribulations of Kane, Hayes, Hall, Nares and the like provided excellent newspaper copy and gave naval authorities on both sides of the Atlantic much to think of. But they had not delivered the geographical goods. On a standard atlas, schoolboys could measure the progress of most expeditions by scratching sub-divisions on the smallest unit of their wooden rulers. The *Fram*, however, had meandered over vast distances and Nansen had very nearly reached the Pole in one of the most exciting odysseys to date. Moreover, everyone had survived. As people began to realize, clear, scientific planning was the clue to the Pole; romantic, wishful endeavour was not – even if, as in the Nares expedition, it had been undertaken by the world's most professional navy.

The one hostile note came from Jackson. Since Nansen's arrival in Norway, a surge of expectation had arisen concerning the English explorer's chances. Like Jackson himself, the British public saw no reason why he should not be able to cover Nansen's tracks but in reverse. The expedition's sponsor, Alfred Harmsworth, encouraged such thinking. 'We may rest assured that just as the records of Lockwood and Markham have been lowered by Nansen, so will Nansen's farthest north be beaten,' he wrote in the *Daily Mail* on 15 August 1896. 'The fact that Mr. Jackson and his party are remaining in that strange home of theirs in, what is, in fact, probably the most desolate country in the world, points to the conclusion that he is alive to the splendid possibilities of his position. May we wish him good luck in reaching the Pole.'[45] Three days later, 'I know him well enough to be convinced that he will strain every nerve to push forward . . . The opportunity of reaching the highest known latitude ever attained will obviously not be allowed to pass.'[46]

Neither, obviously, was the opportunity of reaching a higher circulation to be allowed to pass. This was the same Harmsworth who had earlier said that the main purpose of the expedition was scientific, and that even if Jackson reached the Pole he would consider the venture a failure were the scientific work not completed. But now was not the time to emphasize that side of things. In Bennett-like fashion, Harmsworth had a keen understanding of what his readers wanted to read. Circulation of his newspapers did indeed go up, but so high were hopes raised of Jackson's success that when he returned in September 1897, having travelled no further than the top of Franz Josef Land, the disappointment was acute. After making a successful series of observations spanning three years, and having conducted a respectable exploration of a little-known territory, Jackson was spoken of only in terms of failure. On his departure in 1894 *The Times* had hailed him as 'a modern Ulysses, to whom scarcely any region of the earth is unfamiliar'.[47] Now all it could say was that he should have stayed another year and tried again – and this was one of Jackson's more positive clippings.

Jackson found it hard to accept. In his frustration he turned on Nansen, whom he perceived as the leech on his glory. He said that Nansen had used his map in *Farthest North* without proper acknowledgement, and he took exception to a statement that Nansen could have survived the trip without his help. 'This,' he wrote, 'I can only regard as the result of elusive visions arising from the optimism produced by the safety of an armchair and cigar . . . I can positively state that not a million to one chance of Nansen reaching Europe existed, and, but for our finding him on the ice, as we did, the world would never have heard of him again.'[48] Petulantly, he went on to suggest that Nansen had deserted his ship. In a flight of fancy he announced that the world was now riven by the question of the map, and that rival camps of Jacksonites and Nansenites roamed the streets hardly daring to talk to each other. It was a mean-spirited attack, with nothing to commend it – as any reader could see, Nansen had given Jackson full and uncharacteristically grovelling recognition for his help. It was sad to see Jackson so reduced. That, however, was one of the less pleasant characteristics of the age of heroes: there was never room for more than one.

Nansen was untouched. He stood so high in popular opinion that nothing could damage him. Supporters wanted him to be Prime Minister of an independent Norway and cartoonists portrayed him as a future king. He rejected both positions, declaring his preference to lead an expedition to the South Pole. But he never went. His experiences on the ice had drained him and for the rest of his life he explored by proxy. He supported Otto Sverdrup on a voyage through the quadrant west of Greenland, where he supposed a string of islands might connect with those of Franz Josef Land. He also encouraged (and financed) Roald Amundsen's 1903–06 blast through the North-West Passage. Later, he lent Amundsen the *Fram* for his conquest of the South Pole – and, incidentally, secured Johanssen a place on the team. Content with his laurels, he left the North Pole to others.

There were many challengers keen to better Nansen's record. The most persistent of them was an American called Robert Edwin Peary, who had been probing a route via Greenland for some while. The most immediately threatening, though, was Salomon Andrée. The big Swede was still intent on the Pole, and in 1897 he returned to Spitsbergen with his balloon.

15

THE FLIGHT OF THE *EAGLE*

The Arctic had become so familiar to Britons that by now it was part of their social calendar. *The Times* spoke of the Arctic 'season' with the same reverence as it announced Henley Regatta, the Ascot races and the day on which grouse shooting commenced. Travelling to Greenland was beyond most, but Spitsbergen was well within reach of the fashionable. Norwegian steamers ran a regular service to the island, where there was a hotel and a post office which issued its own Arctic stamps. Mountaineers climbed Spitsbergen's crags, fishermen flogged its waters, historians investigated the remains of settlements dating from the seventeenth century, and the less energetic went there simply for the glory of its jagged, perma-frosted landscape. In the Arctic season of 1897, tourists were delighted to learn that Andrée was once again inflating his balloon on Dane's Island. They sailed in their scores and were rewarded handsomely for their trouble by the spectacle that awaited them.

Within its scaffolding, which had survived the last winter remarkably well, Andrée's *Eagle* bulged and strained like a captive toad. It comprised triple envelopes of pongee silk – the lightest yet sturdiest material available – made up of 3,360 squares, each of which had been hand-tested for resilience, glued together and reinforced with 153,110 yards of stitching. The outer layer had been double-varnished on both sides; it was dark, to attract the sun's heat and therefore discourage settling snow; and it was contained within a net of Italian hemp, soaked in vaseline to prevent it absorbing atmospheric moisture. The whole balloon had a capacity of 170,000 cubic feet and when the visitors arrived in July, it was covered with a team of sailors and technicians who bounced over its surface testing the seams of every square of silk for gas-tightness.

Everything about the *Eagle* spoke of professionalism. For extra power it had three sails, comprising 818 square feet of silk, which hung like aprons from its midriff. Its steering was provided by three drag-lines, measuring 3,300 feet in total but of uneven lengths to prevent them tangling. Each line had a weak point, 165 feet from the end, designed to snap if it should snag on an obstruction. In addition, the lines were made up of several lengths, connected by screw fittings so that if they snagged again, the lower sections could be released by twisting the rope from above – 'altogether unnecessary,' wrote Andrée, '[but] it affords a certain sense of security'.[1] Ingeniously, the drag-lines were also to act as ballast, Andrée's theory being that if the balloon lost height a greater length of rope would rest on the ground, thus increasing its buoyancy. If the balloon were to gain height, its ascent would be checked by the greater weight of rope it had to hold in the air. Operating on a similar principle were eight separate ballast lines which would come into play if the balloon dropped to 231 feet above ground. The lines would cause a bumpy ride as they snaked over the ice but this was all part of Andrée's planning, for each jerk would dislodge any snow or ice which had settled on the canopy. With these arrangements in place he expected confidently that the *Eagle* would speed over the Pole at an average altitude of 480 feet. If the balloon needed to stop for any reason, it carried three 66-pound anchors, and three grapnels one of which was fitted to a quick-release vent that could deflate the *Eagle* within two minutes in case of emergency. In the extremely unlikely event of its sinking to the limit of its ballast, there was an extra seven hundredweight of sand to be thrown out. As a last resort they could jettison the basket and live in the rigging.

The basket was well-designed if not capacious. A wicker cylinder of two metres in diameter, covered in tarpaulin, it contained three berths and had a single entry port which led to its roof. The roof itself provided daytime living space, protected from the elements by a skirt of silk in which holes were cut so that Andrée and his men could take readings as they flew north. From the roof, a rope ladder led to the carrying ring which linked the basket to the balloon. Here their provisions were arranged in sacks and baskets – calculated to last three and a half months but extendable to six. Strung around the ring and the basket were three sledges, a tent and a canvas boat (in case of evacuation), a collection of twelve cork buoys to be flung out to mark their progress (an especially large one was reserved for the Pole) and cages containing thirty-six carrier pigeons donated by Stockholm's *Aftonbladet* newspaper. As for the galley, it was a gem. Open flames could not be allowed in the basket, nor could they be permitted on the roof, mere feet from the inflammable hydrogen trapped within all those squares of pongee silk. One of Andrée's friends therefore constructed a cooking apparatus which dangled twenty-six feet below the basket and which, 'by means of special devices',[2] could be ignited and doused by remote control from above. It came with a mirror set at an angle of 45° so that if the chef hung out of the basket he could check the progress of his meal.

Lest anybody have the slightest doubt as to what it was all about, Andrée had stamped his purpose on every piece of equipment. Branded into wooden items, engraved on metal ones, sewn onto flags, painted on the balloon, printed on the car, abbreviated on small surfaces, written in full where space allowed, were the words 'Andree's Polar Expedition 1897'.

It impressed everyone. Even the King and Queen of Sweden-Norway came to Dane's Island to bid Andrée *bon voyage*. Andrée and his fellows scuttled to make impromptu gifts. One man gave them a box of balloon-silk handkerchiefs, another a crown made out of rubber gas-hose, another a small-scale model of the *Eagle*. But the celebrations could not disguise the dauntingly experimental nature of the project. None of Andrée's theories had been proved in the Arctic and none of his contraptions had been tested – which frightened off at least one man. Nils Strindberg stayed with the expedition, but Nils Ekholm, who had volunteered for the first flight, withdrew his services. He feared that the fabric of the balloon would leak. The pongee silk squares had been varnished impeccably but each of the tiny stitch holes which held them together – all eighty-six miles of them – represented a possible outlet for gas. He had noticed on its previous inflation that the balloon had started to wilt and he did not want to participate in its final collapse. His place was taken by Knut Fraenkel, a twenty-five-year-old Stockholm physicist.

In photographs, Andrée, Fraenkel and Strindberg display no sign of fear. There they stand, tall and fleshy – they were vast, these Swedes – in their heavy overcoats and Homburgs (or in Andrée's case a ridiculously small rowing cap), posing incongruously against the mountains of Spitsbergen. They seem unconcerned about their fate. Andrée remained 'calm, cold and impassible', according to an associate, 'not a trace of emotion [was] visible on his countenance; nothing but an expression of firm resolution and an indomitable will'.[3] But Andrée had secret doubts. Like Ekholm, he knew that the balloon leaked, yet he could not retreat, having taken the project so far. He had a premonition that he would die, and said as much in a preamble to the will that he wrote before his departure. But, as he had also said, following one of his experiments, 'Dangerous? Perhaps. But what am I worth?'[4]

On 11 July 1897 the wind swung in the right direction and at 1.43 p.m. Andrée and his companions climbed into the basket. 'Strindberg – Fraenkel – let us go!' Andrée cried. Three minutes later he gave the order, 'Cut away everywhere!'[5] The *Eagle* rose majestically out of its scaffolding and swept across the harbour in a north-easterly direction, its drag-ropes furrowing the sea below. It had barely reached a height of 300 feet, however, when it dipped abruptly, struck by a stream of cold air flowing from the surrounding mountains. The onlookers' cheers turned to exclamations of dismay as the basket sank halfway into the water. It rose, sank again, and then, as the crew jettisoned ballast, struggled into the air. Within a few minutes it was at a height of 1,600 feet and speeding over Vogelsang Island in the distance, where Strindberg threw out a sealed tin containing a last letter to his fiancée. They were moving at twenty-two miles per hour, a rate at which, as one man calculated, would see them to the North Pole within two days. But the relief on Dane's Island was short-lived. At some point during its dip the balloon's guide ropes had become twisted – either that or they had caught on a rock – with the result that the release attachments had unscrewed. Two-thirds of the length of all three guide ropes had dropped off. Turning round, the spectators saw them lying on the shore, still neatly coiled, their ends leading into the water. With the loss of his ropes and with the sand that had been thrown out as the basket hit the water, Andrée had been deprived of approximately 1,500 pounds of ballast. And unless he dropped so low that the remaining stubs hit the ice, he had also lost his ability to steer.

Up above, in the grey sky, the *Eagle* was moving fast. The assistants watched as it dwindled to the size of an egg and then vanished into a cloud. 'Instinctively we drew together without saying a word,' wrote one man. 'There is nothing, nothing whatever in the distance to tell us where our friends are; they are now shrouded in mystery.'[6] The *Eagle* was never seen again.

On 15 July, one of Andrée's carrier pigeons landed on a Norwegian sealer. Its message, written on the 13th, reported that the *Eagle* had reached 82°2′N – 'All well on board.'[7] So, it appeared that he was going to reach the Pole after all, despite his leaky stitching and the loss of his drag-ropes. In two days he had reached a latitude it had taken Nansen six months to accomplish. But Andrée never returned to tell the world of his triumph. In September, a report came in from Siberia that a balloon had been spotted briefly in the province of Jenisseisk, but it was impossible to confirm. The year 1897 passed without further word: Andrée had warned that he might not be heard of until the next summer if he was forced to overwinter in Siberia or Alaska. By autumn of 1898, however, after a number of rescue missions had returned empty-handed, it was certain that Andrée, Fraenkel and Strindberg had perished in the ice.

A few missives arose from the grave, such as a buoy which was discovered in August 1900 by a Norwegian woman scavenging the coast for flotsam. Dropped from the *Eagle* at 10.00 p.m. on 11 July 1897 it read, 'Our journey has hitherto gone well. We are still moving on at a height of [830 ft.] . . . We are now over the ice, which is much broken up in all directions. Weather magnificent. In best of humours . . . Above the clouds since 7.45 GMT.'[8] What had happened between the sending of this optimistic note and the unknown date when disaster struck, nobody could tell. The Arctic had swallowed Andrée's expedition at a gulp, and the odd morsels it spat out offered no solution to the greatest polar mystery since Franklin.

In the summer of 1930 a Norwegian ship, the *Bratvaag*, landed on an insignificant lump of rock and ice to the east of Spitsbergen called White Island. The *Bratvaag* was after seals and normally would not have landed on White Island. But it also carried a number of scientists, and on their insistence the captain stopped so that they could investigate the geology and glaciology of this undocumented island. They found three skeletons, several rolls of undeveloped film and a number of journals. The relics were taken back to Tromsø where forensic specialists developed the films and transcribed the sodden, fragmented journals. When they announced their findings the town was swamped by journalists from every major newspaper in the world. Here was the complete record, in pictures and words, of Andrée's flight.

In October 1930, the Swedish Anthropological and Geographical Society published the story. At the outset, it seemed, Andrée had not been dismayed by the loss of his drag-ropes. He had taken up one of the ballast lines and spliced it onto the broken end of one of the drags so that he would have at least some degree of control. But steering the balloon was to prove of infinitesimal importance compared to the problem of keeping in the air. Andrée had greatly underestimated the way in which the dramatic temperature switches of these regions would affect the *Eagle*. When the sun shone the gas expanded, the balloon rose, and all was well; when it hit a cloud, on the other hand, the gas shrank, and the balloon dropped. And all the time the hydrogen was leaking through the stitches. Water collected on the canopy, adding further downward pressure on the balloon. Later the water froze and in the absence of the guide lines, which were meant to have given such a bumpy ride as to knock it off, the ice continued to accumulate. (Not that the lines would have made any difference, as events proved.) Throughout the 11th, Andrée had full opportunity to observe how the balloon reacted to clouds. From an initial high-point of 600 metres it dropped to 100 metres, leaped up to 500 metres, dropped back to 250 metres, then soared to 700 metres. Sometimes the changes were gradual, sometimes they were alarmingly rapid: on one occasion they fell 500 metres in less than half an hour. The speed at which they descended and the length of time they stayed down depended on the size and thickness of the cloud. Fortunately, none of the clouds they encountered were that thick or that large and they never had to wait longer than forty-five minutes before rising again.

Stops and starts aside, it must have been a glorious experience. For most of that first day they were above cloud level, floating along under a bright sun with not even the sound of the wind to disturb their calm. They released carrier pigeons, threw out buoys, joked, opened packs of sandwiches, took turns in urinating off the top of the basket and were, as Andrée said in his message, in the best of humours. Towards the end of the day, however, they spotted a towering altocumulus to the north-east. It was a vast mass, covering a quarter of the horizon and they were heading straight for it.

At eleven minutes past midnight on the morning of 12 July, the *Eagle* entered the cloud. It fell so swiftly that within four minutes the drag-rope was touching the ice and an hour later so were the ballast ropes. Soon the balloon was at sixty-five feet, a height it would maintain for another twelve hours. Their journey now became a staccato hopscotch of leaps and bounds as the ballast ropes began to work in the way they had been designed. But the jolting failed to dislodge the ice on the canopy and the burden increased remorselessly, forcing the *Eagle* down, both by its weight and its effect on the gas. At 3.00 p.m. the basket hit the ice for the first time. It struck twice, shortly after 4.00 p.m. Between 4.45 and 5.15 there were eight touches. By 6.30 it was hitting the surface every five minutes. Soon it was every one minute. At the same time the wind speed kept altering: one hour they might be galloping along at seventeen feet per second, the next hobbling at twelve inches per second; at one point, in the eye of a cyclone, they remained perfectly motionless.

Worryingly, the wind kept changing direction – north, east, west, north-east, south – until Strindberg's orderly chart of their progress dissolved into an ant's nest of tiny, cramped numerals. Even if all three guide ropes had been working they would have had no effect: designed to exert a gentle influence against a constant breeze they could not have coped with such violent switches. As it was, the *Eagle*'s single, makeshift drag was useless – worse than useless, in fact, because as they bounced on their circular course, stamping the ice every 500 feet or so, the drag caught on a block of ice. At that point the wind changed from north-east to south-west and the rope wrapped itself around the block, bringing the balloon to a dead stop. Slowly, the *Eagle* rose into the air and sat there, thirty-five feet above the surface. The time was 10.00 p.m., it was dark under the cloud and a fine drizzle was falling.

The free-spirited *Eagle* had become, temporarily, a captive balloon, and Andrée's men were very happy that this was so. The day had been exhausting. Much of it had been spent jettisoning ballast – a rope, several bags of sand, the buoys, five rungs of a rope-ladder, then another six rungs and finally the whole ladder, more sand, shovels, anchors, another line, even the heavy knives for cutting the ropes. Everything save their scientific equipment, their sledges, their food and their boat was flung out pell-mell. When Andrée climbed aloft to defecate, Fraenkel and Strindberg watched the altimeter only partially in jest – they themselves had taken to spitting out of the door to lighten the load. 'We . . . have not had any sleep, nor been allowed any rest from the repeated bumpings, and we probably could not have stood it much longer,'[9] Andrée wrote in his journal. At 11.20 p.m. he told the other two to go to bed. 'I mean to let them sleep until 6 or 7 o'clock if I can manage to keep watch until then. Then I shall try to get some rest myself.'[10]

Throughout that night, while Fraenkel and Strindberg slept, Andrée gave vent to his feelings. As the balloon swayed and twisted, rose and sank incessantly, he huddled over a lamp, his notebook on his knee. 'It is not a little strange to be floating here above the Polar Sea,' he began. 'To be the first that have floated here in a balloon. How soon, I wonder, shall we have successors? Shall we be thought mad or will our example be followed? I cannot deny but that all three of us are dominated by a feeling of pride. We think we can well face death, having done what we have done. Is not the whole, perhaps, the expression of an extremely strong sense of individuality which cannot bear the thought of living and dying like a man in the ranks, forgotten by coming generations? Is this ambition?' He paused a while. 'The rattling of the guide-lines in the snow and the flapping of the sails are the only sounds heard, except the whining [of the wind] in the basket.'[11]

How odd, that expression of Andrée's emotions: wistful, wondering, yet detached. He spoke as if he had already reached the Pole – and he probably thought that he would, once this temporary setback had been overcome. Like modern passengers crossing the Arctic in a jet, he could see the unwelcoming environment below, but had implicit faith that technology would bring him to safety – even though, in his case, the ice was just a few yards beneath him and he knew that the balloon leaked. His musings reflected the heroic mindset: a determination to break free of the common mould, to reject mediocrity and to create a lasting memorial. But Andrée was not cut out to be a hero, either in a physical or moral sense. He was not a leader, nor an improvisor, nor a visionary. He was a man who had taken a chance on a new venture, like thousands of other Victorian entrepreneurs. And therein lay the tragedy – and, in a way, the triumph – of his expedition. He was an ordinary person, whose ordinary ambitions had led him into extraordinary circumstances.

At about 9.00 on the morning of 13 July, the sky began to lighten. Small patches of blue could be seen through the clouds and at the same time the wind reverted to its previous direction, allowing the balloon to disentangle itself from the ice. Off they floated again to the east, rising by midday to a height of 200 feet, at which point they lowered the cooking apparatus and prepared a large Châteaubriand steak. 'A good and invigorating meal,'[12] noted Strindberg. By 2.30 p.m., however, they were back in the fog and once again scraping over the pack. Yet still they seemed to have felt no sense of unease. When Strindberg climbed onto the carrying ring to escape the vibrations he found it 'confoundedly pleasant'.[13] At 6.00 p.m. a small fire broke out in the basket – they were unconcerned. Two hours later they threw out another 650 pounds of ballast, including 440 pounds of precious food, and the balloon rose slowly to 130 feet. 'Altogether it is quite splendid!'[14] wrote Andrée.

The splendour did not last. At 5.30 on the morning of 14 July, after four and a half hours of continual bouncing, Andrée decided they would have to come down. The *Eagle* gave an obliging leap into the air, he pulled the release string and at 7.30 a.m. he wrote a final entry in his flight log: 'We jumped out of the balloon.'[15]

They were at 82°56′N, 29°52′E. The pack was a mess of drifting ice, intersected by leads and lined with pressure ridges in between which lay pools of meltwater. The sky was cloudy, a light rain was falling, a faint breeze came from the south-east and the temperature was at freezing. The *Eagle* lay beside them, a semi-tumescent mound of gas, trailing an empty skein of silk to which were attached the ropes, sails and basket. It was at least 192 miles to the northernmost point of Spitsbergen, 210 miles to Franz Josef Land – though anything might lie in between, for nobody had ever visited this part of the Arctic. They had no experience of ice travel and their thin, woollen clothes offered little protection against the climate. They were lost, they were cold and they were hungry.

But *still* they refused to worry. Andrée set up the tent and for the next seven days they removed everything from the *Eagle* that could be used or eaten – 'excellent pumpernickel',[16] Andrée exclaimed – while planning their next move. Prior to their departure, a number of supply depots had been arranged to assist a possible retreat. One of these was on Spitsbergen and another on Cape Flora, where Jackson had left among other things, eight gallons of Dewar's Scotch whisky – 'since inscribed on a memorial tablet in my mind, "Deeply Regretted.

R.I.P.,"'[17] the Englishman had written. They could head for either of these two points or wait, like the *Fram*, until the polar drift shunted them into clear water. A wait was possible but impracticable: their canvas boat was good for crossing leads but too small for the sea travel which would sooner or later be inevitable. Of the landward options, Spitsbergen was nearest. But Spitsbergen was big and empty; it offered no shelter; its over-fished waters were visited infrequently by whalers; and without skis they had no means of reaching an inhabited point before winter. Cape Flora, on the other hand, had a large stock of food; they could winter in Jackson's huts; and there was a greater possibility of meeting a whaler in the summer.

They set out for Cape Flora on 22 July, hauling three sledges loaded with 200 kg of food and equipment apiece. 'Hummocks, walls, and fissures in the sea alternating with melted ice,' Strindberg recorded. 'One day passes like another. Pull and drudge at the sledges, eat and sleep.'[18] All the same, 'I am in excellent health . . . We are sure to come home by and by.'[19] On those first days they ate sandwiches and little pots of caramel as if on a picnic, then lay back and swapped campfire yarns of a unique nature. 'We discuss our mental characteristics and our faults,' Strindberg wrote. '[It is] very educative.'[20] At one point, Andrée told them how he had got his job in the Patent Bureau.

On 26 July they dumped part of their load, finding – as others had before them – that the struggle of dragging one sledge then returning for the others was more than they could manage. Increasingly they ate not sandwiches but joints of fresh meat, the encroachment of hungry polar bears having become a near-daily occurrence. They walked through fog so thick that they could hardly see the leads before they fell into them. On 31 July they had to cross ten leads in six hours. Yet they were still tourists, even if circumstances said that they were not. When Fraenkel, the biggest and gentlest giant among them, developed a blister on his heel it occasioned much tutting and an immediate reprieve from duties.

On 4 August, Andrée realized they were not going to reach Cape Flora. His readings told him that although he and his men were walking south-east, the pack was carrying them west. Therefore he headed for Spitsbergen, which he thought could be attained in six or seven weeks. For a month they trudged, hauled, splashed across pools of water, waded through snowdrifts, climbed ice-hills and crossed countless leads. Unperturbed and sure of reaching safety somehow, they drew up plans for their next polar expedition: the balloon should have metal-lined guide ropes; the living quarters should be in the carrying ring; and 'the gas to be somewhat heated by boiling water in the car'.[21]

Some days it was 'dreadfully heavy going',[22] according to Andrée, but on others, 'We knew that we were moving onwards more quickly than usual and at every turn of the leads we asked ourselves in silence if we might not possibly journey on in this glorious way to the end.'[23] They were in their sixth week of travel when it became apparent they would never make Spitsbergen. The drift had changed course yet again. In the first week of September it had driven them northwest and then it had turned about and by the middle of the month was carrying them south-east at speed – a full degree in three days – towards the gap between Spitsbergen and Franz Josef Land. In mid-September they resigned themselves to spending a winter on the ice.

They built a shelter out of snow blocks on one of the thicker floes and shot a number of seals and polar bears so that for the immediate future at least they would not go hungry. Their sledges were battered but intact, as was the boat, which meant they still had scope for manoeuvre. But if conditions were reasonable, they could still have been a lot better. The Swedes suffered from the cold: their ballooning clothes offering some protection against the wind but no insulation from the chill of the pack. Their new diet gave them alternating bouts of diarrhoea and constipation, the worst affected being Fraenkel who complained 'almost constantly',[24] according to an exasperated Andrée. (In diligent style he recorded, each day, the frequency and fluidity of every motion passed.) They could not count on being able to kill seals and bears indefinitely and Andrée's suggestion that they live off plankton – he had constructed a net in which to catch them – had slight appeal. Nor were they very happy when their stove refused to light. 'Our humour is pretty good,' Andrée wrote, 'although joking and smiling are not of ordinary occurrence.'[25]

The drift carried their floe southwards but, luckily, also a little to the west. On 17 September they spotted a rounded shield of white glacier which was called variously White Island or New Iceland on their maps. They hovered 1,000 yards off its coast until a south-easterly drift pushed them beyond its sight. At 5.30 a.m. on 1 October, their floe splintered. 'We heard a crash and thunder, and water streamed into the hut,' Andrée wrote. 'The floe that remained to us had a diam. of only 80 ft., and the one wall of the hut might be said rather to hang from the roof rather than to support it ... We were frivolous enough to lie in the hut the following night.'[26] Then the drift changed and swirled them around so that they were again within touching distance of White Island.

The last legible sentence in Andrée's diary reads, 'No one had lost courage; with such comrades one should be able to manage under, I may say, any circumstances.'[27]

There were two volumes of Andrée's diary and only the first could be properly deciphered by the experts in Tromsø. The second had been spoiled by water and stained by ice. From its torn, blackened remains only a few portions of a few sentences could be made out. The right-hand section of the last page read:

```
..................................................bad weather and we fear
.........................................we keep in the tent the whole day
.........................................................so that we could
.................................................................on the hut
...........................................................to escape
.....................................................................like
.................................................out on the sea
..............................................crash . . . grating
...............................................................drift-wood
.................................................................[p]ermits.[28]
```

Extrapolating from these fragments and the remains that the investigators found, a tentative guess can be made as to the fate of Andrée and his balloonists. They had somehow made their way onto White Island and, having dragged their boat and sledges beyond the reach of the waves, had erected their tent. After pulling driftwood into a pile and lighting it, both for warmth and as a beacon to passing ships, they had cooked a few meals on the fire and then, after delving into their stock of bear meat, they had fallen ill.

The nature of their illness is unknown but it was probably trichinosis, a parasitic disease caused by eating meat infected with the trichina worm. The symptoms are diarrhoea, nausea and a stiffening and swelling of the muscles. If untreated it can be fatal. The three men would have ignored the diarrhoea, having suffered from it on and off since leaving the balloon (had they already contracted a mild form of the disease from one of their early kills?) but when the vomiting began, and when their limbs began to swell, they would have known they were in trouble.

One can only hazard at the way in which they tried to cure themselves. They had no medicine, their chest having been thrown overboard as they strove to keep the balloon aloft – and even had they retained it, its collection of mild tinctures and powders would have been useless. Whatever they did, it did not work. Strindberg, the strongest and most capable of the trio, was the first to succumb. His body was placed between two jutting boulders and piled over with rocks. Fraenkel went next. He collapsed near the shore, perhaps trying to drag more driftwood to the fire. Andrée, whose bones were found propped against a rock, was the last. He had sat down and then, stiffly, quietly, and probably still wondering how everything had gone so wrong, he had died.

16

'I *MUST* HAVE FAME'

At the end of 1897, the year in which Andrée and his companions died on White Island, the Arctic seemed to belong to Scandinavia. The *Fram* had completed its drift through the pack, Nansen had undertaken his epic ski adventure and Andrée – as far as the world knew – had probably reached the Pole. In addition, Otto Sverdrup was out there aboard the *Fram*. Shortly after his return, Nansen had bounded up to Sverdrup and asked him if he wanted to take the ship north again. The answer was yes, and now Sverdrup, without Nansen, was charting a huge area to the west of Greenland, a project that would take four years and would encompass 100,000 square miles of unexplored Arctic ice.

To the regimes of *fin de siècle* America and Britain, any further investment in north polar exploration was a waste of money – besides, the Antarctic looked a lot more enticing. Clements Markham was already interviewing a young torpedo captain named Robert Falcon Scott to lead an expedition to the South Pole, for although Nansen had lain quiet since his last venture one never knew what he might be planning with his skis and a proper, man-hauled expedition was needed to pre-empt him. But there was one man who refused to

relinquish the dream of conquering the North Pole. His name was
Robert Edwin Peary.

Otto Sverdrup, who had crossed Greenland with Nansen and had
captained the *Fram*, was not a polar fanatic. Despite his fantastical
whiskers which sprang in all directions from his face, giving him the
air of a hastily groomed berserker at a wedding, he was a quiet, dutiful man. When he took the *Fram* back to the Arctic in 1897, he did so
with the intention of letting it drift where it would. He would steer it
to the top of Smith Sound and then let it go, taking dog-sledges to
investigate nearby coastlines. He had no designs on the Pole: he was
a professional, not a risk-taker. He was a little baffled, therefore, to be
greeted in October 1898 by a strange figure who wandered into his
camp on the east coast of Ellesmere Island. Sverdrup had just lit a fire,
and was about to have dinner. Hospitably, he ordered coffee beans to
be ground for their fur-clad guest.

'Are you Sverdrup?' the man asked. 'My ship is frozen in . . . There
is no way of getting through Robeson Channel. It has frozen fast.'[1]

Robeson Channel was where the *Fram* was heading next. Sverdrup
would have liked to have asked him more, but the stranger strode off,
refusing the offer of coffee. The meeting went so quickly that the
man had hardly removed his mittens to shake hands when he put
them back on again and disappeared. Sverdrup thought it very odd.
His abrupt visitor was Peary.

Born in 1856, into a family of New England merchants, Robert
Edwin Peary was undoubtedly the most driven, possibly the most
successful, and probably the most unpleasant man in the annals of
polar exploration. It has been said of many historical figures that they
were made for their destiny, but none were made so forthrightly as
Peary. Having lost his father at the age of two, he was brought up by
his mother alone, a situation which he seems to have resented. He
developed into a solitary youth, self-reliant, fond of long walks and
empty spaces, intelligent but with a cruel sense of humour – he liked
to trip up his grandfather, for example, for the joy of seeing the frail
man fall. This antagonistic approach to life might have led him down

a number of unsavoury paths, had he not as a teenager read Kane's narratives and decided to emulate them. He wanted to be an explorer and he worked hard at it. He was a big child and grew up to be a large man: 'Tall, erect, broad-shouldered, full-chested, tough, wiry-limbed, clear-eyed, full-mustached, clear-browed complexion, a dead shot, a powerful, tireless swimmer, a first-class rider [and] a skilful boxer and fencer.'[2] This was not the hyperbole of hero worship, it was a completely accurate description of a physical superman. And it was written by Peary himself. His only physical weakness was a lisp, a relic from childhood which he had long since overcome but which emerged (unnervingly) when he was angry.

His ambition matched his physique. He trained as a civil engineer and took a job with the US Navy which left him dissatisfied. As he explained to his mother at the age of twenty-four, 'I feel myself overmastered by a resistless desire to do something. I do not wish to live and die without accomplishing anything or without being known beyond a narrow circle of friends.'[3] These sentiments had been expressed by others, but nobody had been so candid in their greed for fame as Peary. 'I wish to acquire a name which shall be an "open sesame" to circles of culture and refinement anywhere,'[4] he wrote in the same letter. In another letter he was even more revealing: 'I must be the peer or superior of those about me to be comfortable.'[5] He accepted a posting to Nicaragua, which he thought might create an opportunity for the fame he desired. He pictured himself emerging from the jungle in his thirties, 'perfectly at home in any company, yet always bearing with me an indefinable atmosphere of the wildness and freedom of the woods and mountains, master of German, Spanish, and French, and as a speciality, (all these things being mere accomplishments) a knowledge of the Isthmus equalled by no man living'.[6]

Nicaragua gave him a taste for the wilds. He described to his mother the 'feverish anxiety' of struggling over mountains or pushing past a turn in a river to capture a glimpse of unknown territory. 'I am glad,' he wrote, 'that my lot is cast upon the world now rather than later when there will be no new places, when every spot will have felt the pressure of man's foot, and earth and air, and fire and water, the grand old primal elements and all that is in them, will be his abject slaves.'[7] But Nicaragua did not fulfil him: it was exciting, but he needed something stronger.

On a trip to Washington in 1885 he visited a bookshop and picked up a 'fugitive paper on the Inland Ice of Greenland'.[8] Immediately, he knew that the Arctic was his destiny. 'A chord, which as a boy had vibrated intensely in me . . . was touched again. I read all I could upon the subject . . . and felt that I must see for myself what the truth was of this great mysterious interior.'[9] The mysterious interior of which he spoke was that of Greenland, but in his mind Greenland was a stepping stone to an even vaster enclosure of uncertainty – the Pole.

Since Nansen's drift, scientists were in agreement as to the nature of the Pole: it comprised a quantity of loose, seaborne ice, and as such did not require further exploration. Peary did not care about science. If he reached the Pole he would have fame and fortune. Nothing could match such an achievement, and nothing else could satisfy him. From the moment he picked up that paper on Greenland, his goal was set. The Pole would be his, and his alone. Anybody who set foot in the same direction was guilty – in his favourite word – of 'forestalling' him.

In 1886, Peary took a summer's leave from the Navy and went to Greenland with the object of crossing it side to side at its widest point by dog sledge. He failed, travelling less than 100 miles into its interior, but returned with the boast that he had penetrated 'a greater distance than any white man previously'.[10] Actually, Nordenskiöld had tried the same thing two years before, and if he personally had not travelled as far as Peary, his two Lapland companions had gone a long way further. Peary ignored this: the Laplanders were not 'white men'. 'I will next winter be one of the foremost in the highest circles in the capital, and make powerful friends with whom I can shape my future,' he wrote home, adding, 'Remember, Mother, I *must* have fame, and I cannot reconcile myself to years of commonplace drudgery and a name late in life when I see an opportunity to gain it now and sip the delicious draught while yet I have youth and strength and capacity to enjoy it to the utmost . . . I want my fame now.'[11]

But fame eluded him, and when Nansen crossed Greenland in 1888, albeit by a shorter route, Peary was horrified. 'This forestalling of my work,' he wrote, 'was a serious blow to me.'[12] He became indignant when Nansen published his journal. His discoveries were 'hardly greater than I had obtained . . . [he has] profited much by my experience,'[13] he told his mother, dismissing the traverse as a pretentious, copy-cat affair. That Nansen had been planning his voyage since 1882, long before Peary had even thought of Greenland, was of no consequence. He was a forestaller.

Peary did not acknowledge it, but he had been forestalled in principle as well as practice. 'The time has arrived now for an entire change in the expeditionary organisation of Arctic research parties,' he had written in 1885. 'The old method of large parties and several ships has been run into the ground . . . The new plan of a small party depending largely on native assistance . . . deserves to be recorded as the American plan, and another successful expedition will make it permanently such and put us far ahead in the race.'[14] But this was old hat. The idea of sledge crews living off the land had been pioneered in the 1850s by a Scot named John Rae and that of 'native assistance' had been perfected in the 1860s by Charles Francis Hall. As for taking a small party instead of a large one, that had been advocated by Nansen back in 1882 and would later be used both on his Greenland crossing and on his journey with Johanssen from the *Fram*. When Peary claimed to have read all he could on the Arctic he must have been exaggerating or, charitably, have had access to a very small library.

However, in his diary of 1885 he did contemplate a novel method of conquering the Pole, one so scheming that even the British had not thought of it. 'If colonisation is to be a success in the polar regions let white men take with them native wives,' Peary wrote, 'then from this union may spring a race combining the hardness of the mothers with the intelligence of the fathers. Such a race would surely reach the Pole if their fathers did not succeed in doing it.'[15] He not only contemplated this method but put it into practice, fathering at least two part-Eskimo children on future expeditions.

But Peary was right in one very important respect. Although his

'American plan' may have been borrowed from others, he said that it should be applied to the 'American route'. Alone amongst explorers since the Nares and Greely débâcles, Peary saw Smith Sound and Greenland as an avenue to the Pole. In June 1891, having been granted leave from his post as civil engineer and having raised the necessary $10,000, he went back there aboard the *Kite*, with the intention of landing as far north as was practicable, and from there taking a sledge diagonally across Greenland to its northernmost point.

The expedition started inauspiciously, with Peary breaking a leg halfway through the voyage, an event which caused some discussion as to whether the ship should turn back. Even though he was bedridden and immobile, Peary refused to contemplate a retreat and so the *Kite* continued until, on 27 July, having been driven back by the ice, it anchored at a point to the south of Cape Alexander. Not since 1818 had a ship made such little headway through Smith Sound. Peary, who had spent the last few weeks in his cabin, peering suspiciously at a compass to ensure his orders were being obeyed, was carried onto the west coast of Greenland strapped to a plank.

A team of six individuals followed Peary ashore. This did not detract from his idea of a small, fast-moving party: he still intended taking only one man with him on the sledge trip. But the enterprise needed to return with some scientific kudos. During that winter – he did not mean to start sledging until the following year – and while he was away, his team would be pecking at the rocks, mapping the immediate neighbourhood and taking all those readings whose fathomless columns filled the appendices of every Arctic journal. Peary also needed the men as a back-up, in case anything should go wrong. For this was to be an entirely land-based expedition. The *Kite* (which had sailed with nine fare-paying tourists) was to go home that year, returning at intervals to deliver supplies and, when necessary, to bring Peary back. In the meantime, the team would live in a wooden hut, specially strengthened and insulated according to Peary's own designs, liaising as required with the Eskimos at nearby Etah.

Peary had chosen his companions carefully. 'They were all young, and in addition to possessing first-class physique and perfect health,

were men of education and attainments. I believe this to be the type
of man best fitted to endure with minimum unfavourable effect the
ordeal of the Arctic winter, and to effectively execute a two or three
months' dash on sledges, where intelligent will-power, youthful elasticity, and enthusiasm rise superior to the stolid endurance of muscles
hardened by years of work.'[16] Men, in fact, similar to himself – but not
equal. Nobody, in Peary's estimation, could match up to himself and
if he commended his team he did so in the manner of his contemporary, the satirical writer Ambrose Bierce. 'Commendation,' Bierce
wrote in his famous *Devil's Dictionary*, 'the tribute that we pay to
achievements that resemble, but do not equal, our own.'[17]

Peary's men included Langdon Gibson, ornithologist and hunter;
Eivind Astrup, a Norwegian ski expert who hero-worshipped his
leader; John Verhoeff, a geologist and meteorologist who had contributed $2,000 to the expedition; Frederick Cook, a genial but
inexperienced young doctor from Manhattan, who had just gradu-
ated and who had treated three patients in the first six months of his
practice; and Matthew Henson, Peary's 'body servant', whom he had
met while buying a pith-helmet for Nicaragua and whom he had
impulsively hired as a valet. Of them all, only Henson had any
experience of the Arctic, having served a long tutelage on a whaler.
But Henson was no threat in Peary's eyes, because he was a servant
and he was black – or of mixed blood, having a complexion like 'a
well-fingered copper coin'.[18] Speaking of him as if he were a family
pet, Peary said that 'His intelligence and faithfullness, combined with
more than average pluck and endurance, as shown during several
years that he had been with me through varying experiences, part of
the time in Nicaraguan jungles, led me to regard him as a valuable
member of the party.'[19] The sixth, and most surprising member of
Peary's team was not a man. She was Josephine, his wife.

Josephine's inclusion in the expedition raised many eyebrows and
caused not a little disquiet. Was not the Arctic a male domain? Should
a delicate flower of American womanhood be forced to face the icy
tempests? Peary did not care. He had always stated that women were
necessary to keep up a man's spirits, and if Eskimos had taken their

wives with them on other expeditions he saw no reason why he should not take Josephine on this one. Anyway, she was not a delicate flower. In some ways she was as tough as her husband. Peary later wrote: 'She has been where no white woman has ever been, and where many a man has hesitated to go . . . I rarely, if ever, take up the thread of our Arctic experiences without reverting to two pictures: one is the first night that we spent on the Greenland shore after the departure of the *Kite*, when in a little tent on the rocks – a tent which the furious wind threatened every moment to carry away bodily – she watched by my side as I lay a helpless cripple with a broken leg, our small party the only human beings on that shore . . . Long afterward she told me that every unwonted sound of the wind set her heart beating with the thoughts of some hungry bear roaming along the shore . . . Yet she never gave a sign at the time of her fears, lest it should disturb me.

'The other picture is that of a scene perhaps a month or two later, when – myself still a cripple, but not entirely helpless – this same woman sat for an hour beside me in the stern of a boat, calmly reloading our empty firearms while a herd of infuriated walrus about us thrust their savage heads with gleaming tusks and bloodshot eyes out of the water close to the muzzles of our rifles, so that she could have touched them with her hand . . . I may perhaps be pardoned for saying that I never think of these two experiences without a thrill of pride and admiration for her pluck.'[20]

Again, there is a hint of the patronising tone Peary used to describe Henson – Ambrose Bierce would have had something to say about the word 'pluck' – and when he spoke of Josephine's bravery it was in terms of his own. Nevertheless he did love her, and she was indeed a remarkable woman who possessed the same determination and fortitude as her husband. The only lack of wisdom Peary showed in having her aboard was not to do with her gender but her character, for she was almost as domineering as he. One Peary was hard enough to stomach – two were insupportable. The men quailed under their strictures – at one point Peary forbade anyone to travel more than 500 yards from the ship – and Verhoeff, in particular, could not stand it. 'I will never go home in the same ship with that man and that woman,'[21] he confided to Cook. He did not have to. After a foray to nearby Inglefield Gulf he took a short-cut home and vanished. His route led across a glacier and although search parties tracked his footsteps going in, they found none coming out. The verdict was that he had fallen into a crevasse.

Peary sledged for the north of Greenland on 30 April 1892, accompanied by Astrup. On 5 July they reached their goal, a spot which Peary named Independence Bay. Climbing one of its surrounding cliffs he was greeted by a breathtaking vista. 'A few steps more,' he wrote, 'and the rocky plateau on which we stood dropped into a giant iron wall that would grace the Inferno, 3,800 feet to the level of the bay below us. We stood upon the north-east coast of Greenland; and, looking far off over the surface of a mighty glacier on our right and through the broad mouth of the bay, we saw stretching away to the horizon the great ice-fields of the Arctic Ocean . . . Silently Astrup and myself took off our packs and seated ourselves upon them to fix in memory every detail of the never-to-be-forgotten scene before us. All our fatigues of six-weeks' struggle over the ice-cap were forgotten in the grandeur of that view.'[22]

From his vantage point Peary was able to confirm that a stretch of water separated Greenland from a mountainous block of land to the north. He named them respectively Peary Channel and Peary Land. Then he and Astrup set off for home. They were lucky to make it. Peary had pared their supplies so finely that their margin of safety was wafer-thin. The journey took longer than expected and it was only Astrup's chance shooting of some musk-oxen that saved them from starvation. But when they reached base, Peary was jubilant. He had proved that Greenland was finite, thereby banishing for ever the last of Petermann's ghosts. He had also undertaken the fastest, longest, most efficient sledge journey in the Arctic to date, covering some 1,100 miles in eighty-five days. Nansen had travelled 235 miles in 1888 and had taken forty days to do so. Peary and Astrup had travelled four and a half times the distance at twice the speed.

There could be no quibbling with Peary's sledge times, nor his competence in Arctic exploration. When he returned to the United States he received the fame for which he had yearned. The press was full of his exploits and even his erstwhile forestaller, Nansen, wrote to congratulate him on his 'wonderful achievements and grand results'.[23] It was a generous tribute compared to Peary's remarks on Nansen's own achievements. 'Certainly not many will better understand what a piece of work you have performed,'[24] Nansen said, 'and not many have awaited with more impatience to hear what you would find in the unknown North of the inland ice.' He signed himself, 'Your Admirer.'[25]

As the conqueror of Greenland, Peary commanded staggering lecture fees – as much as $2,000 per day – and he pumped the circuit with the same stamina he had shown in the Arctic, giving 165 speeches within a period of 103 days. He hated speaking in public yet, compelled to make money and to augment his reputation, he performed in sterling fashion – 'perform' being the operative word. A typical Peary event involved a stage designed to resemble an Eskimo camp on which he and Henson would appear dressed in their Arctic furs. Henson would chivvy on a team of tame huskies which draped themselves around Peary's feet, staring pale-eyed at the audience while the great man spoke. Then, at the conclusion of the speech, they would raise their heads and howl, bringing a chill of polar solitude to the most cramped and over-heated hall. It was magisterial.

Peary's showmanship concealed a number of awkward truths. In Astrup's journal there was no mention either of a Peary Channel or of Peary Land – for the good reason that they did not exist. Peary had either been deceived by refraction or had made it all up. 'Peary Land' was not an island but the most northerly part of Greenland, separated from the main block by nothing. Peary Channel was also a chimera. 'The outcome,' as one eminent explorer has written, 'was a map that was virtually worthless and misled other explorers into taking risks they should not have taken, with loss of life and unnecessary suffering as the result.'[26] These errors, however, would not be discovered for many years and in the meantime Peary was readying himself for another Arctic expedition, funded in part by the receipts from his lecture appearances and partly by gifts from wealthy admirers. He intended to revisit the same areas as before, but this time he was not bothered with such pallid concerns as the insularity of Greenland – though he was still slightly uncertain about the 'remaining gaps in the northern . . . coast-line',[27] which may have meant Peary Channel – but its potential as a staging post for a route to the Pole.

Before he set out for the Pole, Peary had to leap a mundane but significant hurdle. He was still employed by the US Navy and, having already been granted two long periods of absence (on full pay), it was felt that he should start doing what he had been hired to do. This was where the cleverness of his lectures came in. The wistful howling of the dogs added more than atmosphere; it resurrected a popular desire for Arctic adventure, and it said that here was a man – not a government man but a free-spirited individual – who had the ability to grasp the nettle. The message reached those who wielded power, and when Peary appeared before them his physical presence reassured them that their sponsorship was well placed. One convert was General I. J. Wistar, President of the Philadelphia Academy of Natural Sciences, a body that had long been active in Arctic exploration and which had helped fund Peary's last expedition. Wistar was an influential man, and also a patriot. He had a quiet word with the Secretary of the Navy and all was fixed. So on 8 July 1893, a few weeks after finishing his lecture tour, Peary was steaming north once again.

The manning and mechanics of the expedition were as before: a team of twelve – larger than Peary wanted, but still smaller than many other expeditions – which would then be whittled down to a privileged few who were deemed fit to take part in the quest. They would be dropped off by a ship – not the *Kite* this time, but a similarly sized vessel named the *Falcon* – would overwinter, and then while a chosen few went north, the remainder would gather up what scraps of scientific knowledge remained to be found in the vicinity. Everything was as before with one exception and one addition.

The exception was that hardly anyone from his previous expedition wanted to accompany him. One taste of Peary's leadership was enough for most, and only Astrup, Henson (who had little choice) and

Cook volunteered to join him. But even Cook, the happy-go-lucky chancer, later dropped out. His refusal sprang not from any personal animosity – Peary seemed to have quite liked him – but from an unwillingness to accept the terms of Peary's contract. On the previous trip, Peary had insisted that nobody publish their findings, that everyone was to give him their journals which would then become his property and that they would not write, lecture or disseminate any information about the expedition until a year had passed. When Cook asked if he could publish his modest findings in a medical journal Peary refused – it would detract from his own fame. In Cook's view there was little to be gained from working in these conditions.

The addition was Josephine Peary – or, rather, the child she was carrying inside her. In absolute disregard of public opinion, Peary took his pregnant wife with him on the *Falcon*. On 12 September 1893, in Anniversary Lodge, as Peary called his hut, Josephine Peary gave birth to a baby girl. Her name was Marie Ahnighito and she was the first white child to be born so far north. The Eskimos of Etah were wonderstruck, travelling for miles to see the blue-eyed infant whom they christened the 'Snow baby'. Peary was proud: he had proved that white people could live and breed and survive in the Arctic. In fact he had proved nothing, save that he had hauled his wife north at the end of her term. The only credit was due to Josephine who had been brave enough to believe in her husband. (The primitive conditions in which she gave birth were no worse, and possibly better, than those endured by some mothers of the time.) Nevertheless, Peary congratulated himself on having adapted to an Arctic lifestyle.

Of those who really lived in the Arctic, Peary was condescendingly appreciative: 'I have often been asked, "Of what use are Eskimos to the world?" They are too far removed to be of value in commercial enterprises, and furthermore they lack ambition. They have no literature, nor, properly speaking, any art. They value life only as does a fox, or a bear, purely by instinct. But let us not forget that these people, trustworthy and hard, will yet prove their value to mankind. With *their* help, the world shall discover the Pole.'[28] He valued them;

he called them 'my children', 'my Eskimos', but he did not see them as human beings. Like Henson, they belonged to a subspecies who had been placed on the earth to help further his own quest. He did not bother to learn their language (Henson could speak it fluently) and in the course of his Arctic career he wrote nothing that could be construed as an ethnographical study. His scientific interest was restricted to a collection of photographs, many of which depicted naked women.

Peary did, however, learn from the Eskimos the skills he needed for survival in the Arctic. When he went travelling he carried no tent but built igloos instead; where the English wore cotton and wool, and the Scandinavians dressed in Iceland sweaters and windcheaters, Peary wore Eskimo furs; where others struggled with sleeping bags, Peary slept Eskimo-style in the clothes he wore. In return, Peary trained the Eskimos in what he proudly called the 'Peary System' of exploration, which consisted of three separate parties: the first to prepare the ground and build shelters at designated resting places; the second to haul caches of food in their wake; and the third, the polar group, which would follow behind, carrying a minimum of supplies so that they would be fresh for the big push. Once again, none of this was exactly new. A similar system of tripartite sledge travelling had been employed by the British during the Franklin rescue missions forty years before. But if Peary could claim credit for none of the individual details he was the first to bring them together, combining European and Eskimo techniques to produce the most efficient method yet of travelling long distances in the Arctic. Unlike his suspect eugenics, this was a marriage that worked.

When he sailed on the *Falcon*, Peary had not yet perfected his system. Like Captain Robert Falcon Scott, who would later take a team of horses to Antarctica, Peary decided to experiment with South American burros (donkeys) as beasts of burden. This was an unwise move for, unlike meat-eating dogs, the burros were herbivores and had to be fed bulky bales of hay. Nor was Peary confident enough to employ Eskimo methods on his own. That winter he sent a team to Etah to persuade the Eskimos to help him. If they refused they were to be kidnapped at gunpoint. Luckily, guns were not needed. Lured by gifts of iron and the promise of unlimited knick-knacks, one Eskimo family came to Anniversary Lodge of their own free will. But their assistance offered no protection against the series of natural calamities that befell Peary's expedition.

In September 1893, Astrup went inland to set up a chain of food depots. He was struck first by gastric fever and then by foul weather. When he crawled back to camp, three of the precious sledges had been 'blown away without leaving a vestige'.[29] The following month, Peary too ventured inland. When he left, he was certain that Anniversary Lodge was as stable and as secure as could be: the huts were situated well above the high-tide level; a little steam launch and a whale-boat had been dragged to safety; the burros and their hay, the dogs and their sledges were far from the sea. But on 31 October, while Peary was advancing over Greenland, a nearby glacier calved, dumping such a huge amount of ice into the bay that a tidal wave undid all his preparations. '[It] burst up through the solid ice near the shore in a roaring cataract of water and foam; rolled the steam launch, which had been hauled up for the winter at the head of the harbour, over and over and stove her in; dashed the whale-boat *Faith* . . . a hundred yards up the valley and ruined her; then receding, carried down with it into the vortex of grinding ice-cakes all [the] oil barrels, the dory, several bales of hay from the burro stable, and a number of puppies.'[30]

'The fates and all hell are against me,' Peary said, '*but I'll conquer yet.*'[31] An expedition to the north in March 1894, however, covered only 128 miles before its members succumbed to illness and the elements. During one three-day period, at an altitude of 5,000 feet, the wind speed approached fifty miles per hour and the thermometer hovered between -50° and -60°F – which, with the added factor of wind chill, was an effective temperature of approximately -125°F. Men dropped back, dogs fell sick and sledges broke. They deposited several caches of food before retracing their steps. 'The judgement will be that this storm beats the record as the most severe experienced by any Arctic party,'[32] Peary wrote when he returned to base on 18 April. It was no consolation at all to find that, during his absence,

Astrup had recovered from the gastric complaint which had plagued him throughout the winter and had conducted a small but very successful mission of his own to the south, towards the hinterland of Melville Bay. Such behaviour was beyond the pale. How dare Astrup act on his own initiative – and how dare he succeed where Peary had failed?

Searching for a face-saving feat, Peary remembered the discoveries of Sir John Ross. One of the most ebullient and cantankerous of Arctic explorers – also, in an eccentric way, one of the most successful – Ross had left Britain in 1818, with instructions to find the North-West Passage. He did not find it; instead he found a tribe of Greenland Eskimos who lived so far north that they had lost contact with their relatives to the south. These Eskimos – the Arctic Highlanders, as Ross called them – were unique in many ways but in particular for their use of iron. In the mineral-free Arctic, iron was prized above anything else and the Arctic Highlanders were the only Eskimos who had access to a natural supply of it. They described their mother lode to Ross as a 'Mountain of Iron', but taking their absence of mining skills with their propensity to exaggerate, Ross suspected that their iron might come from a meteorite – a suspicion that was confirmed when he submitted samples to scientists at home. Since that date the Arctic Highlanders had become familiar to every explorer who approached Smith Sound. They were the same Eskimos who had assisted Kane, Hayes and all the others – Peary included. But everybody had been too intent on the quest at hand to bother with irrelevancies such as where the Eskimos obtained their metal. So, while expeditions came and went, the Mountain of Iron remained untouched and unseen save by its owners. Peary decided to change that.

By Peary's time the Arctic Highlanders were in decline. As the globe's northernmost people, they had always survived on the limit. Now, through a combination of harsh winters and a disease which was killing their dogs – the same disease that Kane and Hayes had reported – their numbers had dwindled until they could be counted in the low hundreds. They retained, however, the skills of sledging and hunting that had allowed them to survive so long. And they still had their Mountain of Iron, which gave them that vital edge.

When Peary told his Eskimos to take him to the Mountain of Iron, they were reluctant. They did not believe in a God but they had sacred places and the Mountain of Iron was among them. The journey to the Mountain was difficult, they said, and could only be performed at certain times of the year. They really didn't want him to go there. But Peary insisted and as he and his fellows had been so generous with their gifts they agreed to lead him to the spot. The Mountain of Iron turned out to be three meteorites called 'Dog', 'Woman', and 'Tent'. The Dog weighed 300 pounds, the Woman three tons and the Tent 100 tons. For centuries the Eskimos had hacked at these chunks of ferrous manna, paring slivers to edge their harpoons, to form arrow-heads and to make knives. They were culturally priceless, having made it possible, as Peary wrote, 'for an entire aboriginal tribe, the most northerly one upon the earth, probably the smallest, and perhaps the most interesting, whose habitat is metal-barren, to rise from the stone to the iron age.'[33] Thoughtfully, Peary scratched his initials on the Woman. At a future date he might be able to do something more with these treasures than merely discover them.

When he returned to Anniversary Lodge that summer, the men were in a state of near mutiny. Like Verhoeff on the previous voyage, they'd had enough of the Pearys. Two of them were still bedridden from the spring march, and all of them were hungry, the food supplies having run low. When the *Falcon* returned in August 1894, they clambered aboard with gratitude. Peary, however, opted to stay for another year, with Henson and another volunteer, Hugh Lee, to keep him company. 'The other members of my party had discovered that Arctic work was not entirely the picnic they had imagined,' Peary wrote, 'and wisely regarding discretion as the better part of valour, had decided to return home; Lee and Henson alone possessed the grit and loyalty to remain.'[34] Peary was not being entirely straight here. The *Falcon* had arrived with only a limited amount of food, rendering it impossible for the whole party to stay, even if they had wanted to. According to the second-in-command, Samuel Entrikin, there were some who were willing to endure another winter if they could be certain of being fed. 'His men served him well, the best they could under the conditions,'[35] Entrikin remarked. But Peary was glad to see them go. From the outset he felt his team was too large – or so he later said. In reality he wanted to see the back of them so that he ran no risk of being forestalled, as he almost had been by Astrup's display of independence. He allowed Henson and Lee to stay only because the one was his servant and the other his unquestioning admirer – a young, inexperienced hero-worshipper, just as Astrup had been before he outgrew his boots. When the *Falcon* sailed on 28 August 1894, Peary waved it goodbye with relief: 'So ends with the vanishing ship the ill-omened first half of my expedition and begins the second.'[36]

The second was hardly better than the first. On 8 October he and Henson went with an Eskimo to check the route which the spring party had pioneered. On the second day they were hit by a storm so fierce that the Eskimo went home, leaving Peary and Henson pinned to a glacier. It took the Eskimo four days to reach camp, nearly starving and so weak that he crawled the last few miles. Peary and Henson shivered it out, before retreating too. 'Plans for the future failed me,' Peary wrote. 'Interest in anything refused to be aroused . . . happy scenes and memories, before this devil of Arctic exploration took hold of me, rose and ranged themselves opposite to the precious hours of my life being wasted . . . till it seemed as if with this, and the unceasing hiss of the wind and snow, I should lose my reason.'[37] He was unable to locate any of the depots laid down in the spring.

That winter Peary became depressed. His wife and daughter had sailed back on the *Falcon* and he felt their absence badly. 'Cold and more cheerless yet seems the room tonight,' he wrote to Josephine on 6 January 1895, 'and I stretch yearning across to you from a sad heart. Never have I felt more lonely than tonight, never if God grants me to take you in my arms again will I leave you for so long again. The past runs black, the future blacker. Matt [Henson] is still sick, Lee in a condition that I fear for his sanity, and I feel at times that I am going mad. I have lost my sanguine hope, my elan, I am an old man; I think at times perhaps I have lost you.'[38] By March 1895, however, he had regained his spirits and strength and was ready to face the journey – though not without some trepidation. Almost a ton and a half of food, including all his pemmican and alcohol, had been stored in the 1894 depots which he could no longer locate. This left only a minimum of food for the outward journey and nothing for the return. Once at Independence Bay, and on the way back to Anniversary Lodge, he and his companions would have to live off the land – if there was anything to be killed. It was very nearly a suicide mission, and Peary knew it. 'I shall do all that a man can do,' he wrote in a last letter. 'The rest is in His hands.'[39] He did not ask for rescue: 'It is unnecessary to enumerate possibilities, as once I have put a hundred miles of the Great Ice between me and the Lodge no human help could find or avail us in the event of a catastrophe.'[40]

Peary, Henson and Lee started for Independence Bay on 1 April 1895, accompanied by six Eskimos who dropped back after the first 100 miles, leaving Peary and the others to continue with three sledges and forty-two dogs. Five hundred miles later, only eleven dogs remained, of which three were fit only for eating. Lee, meanwhile, was at breaking point. This was the critical moment. Should they turn back while they had enough food (just) to see them back to the lodge, or should they continue for Independence Bay and gamble on finding game there? Peary chose to drive on. Leaving Lee where he was, to be picked up on their return, he and Henson headed for the coast. 'I felt,' Peary wrote, 'that in that cool, deliberate moment we took the golden bowl of life in our hands, and that the bowl had suddenly grown very fragile.'[41]

They did finally reach Independence Bay, but in the two weeks they spent there they were too concerned with stocking up for the return trip to do any exploring. On 1 June, having bagged a number of musk-oxen and having added practically nothing to Peary's map of the area, they began their retreat. They had nine dogs and food to last fourteen days.

It was an incredible journey. Peary pushed them on at speeds of up to twenty miles per day, all but killing Lee who begged to be left behind to die. 'We will all get home or none of us will,'[42] Peary replied. On they went, Peary taking greater and greater risks to find the shortest route. Lee later said he was so careless in crossing crevasses that it was as if he wanted to kill himself. To this he attributed the motive that Peary would rather die than return home a failure – which was not without foundation as, from its underprovisioned outset to the decision to carry on after 500 miles and then to race back from Independence Bay, every step of the expedition seemed to have been driven by a death wish. They survived, however. In the last week of June 1895 they limped into Anniversary Lodge, starving, half-demented (Peary thought Henson was trying to poison him) and with one dog left out of the forty-two with which they had begun the trip. The journey was a stupendous example of bravery and fortitude, one which perhaps only Peary could have seen to a successful conclusion. But it had achieved absolutely nothing. Greenland was no better explored and the North Pole no nearer than when they had left Anniversary Lodge. Peary had failed – which was worse, much worse, even than being forestalled.

And yet, if he had failed in one respect he had succeeded in another. On his return to the States he took with him two of the Eskimos' meteorites, the Dog and the Woman. In 1897 he came back with reinforcements and took the Tent. The Eskimos believed the Tent had a soul, and Peary, too, wondered if it possessed some supernatural force as he dragged it the eighty yards to his ship. 'The dogged sullen obstinacy and enormous inertia of the giant against being moved; its utter contempt and disregard of all attempts to guide it or control it when once in motion; and the remorseless way in which it destroyed everything opposed to it, seemed demonaic.'[43] If, in the darkness, a sledge chanced to strike it, 'a spouting jet of scintillating sparks lit the gloom, and a deep note, sonorous as a bell, a polar tocsin, or the half-pained, half-enraged bellow of a lost soul answered the blow.'[44] But Peary was a match for any demon.

The triplet of magical stones turned Peary's failure – of which the public were only vaguely aware – into a triumph. He had captured the essence of Eskimo life, the mysterious and potent emblems of Arctic culture which had eluded all other explorers for eighty years. Had he bottled the Northern Lights he could not have been received more warmly. He excused his actions in terms which would have been well understood by an age accustomed to acts of cultural desecration. The Eskimos had no further use for the meteorites because they could buy iron from explorers like himself, he said – which was true, in a way – and they were of far more worth to western scientists than to the Eskimos themselves. The Smithsonian Institution in Washington eventually bought them for $40,000, ascertained that they were like most other meteorites, and placed them in its collection. They remain there today.

Peary also helped the anthropological department of the Smithsonian with a 'gift' – for which the institute paid hard cash - of several Eskimo skeletons which he had exhumed and six live specimens, three grown-ups and three children, whom he had lured south with the promise of 'nice warm houses in the sunshine land, and guns and knives and needles and many other things'.[45] The Eskimos were housed in the museum's basement where they gradually died of pneumonia. Observing decencies, the Smithsonian held a funeral to appease one of the boys whose father was among the early casualties. Inside the coffin was a log: his father's body was dissected by medical students then sent to a macerating plant where the flesh was stripped and the bones reassembled to form a display at the Natural History Museum of New York. By May 1898, four of the Eskimos were dead.

Peary had known most of them personally. One of them had been the son of Kalutunah, Kane's and Hayes's old adversary-cum-friend. He had even known the names of some of the people whose skeletons he had dug up. He had promised them the earth to save his reputation, and they had saved it. As first the adults died, and then a young girl, Peary distanced himself. He had taken responsibility for delivering them and then, if they had wanted, taking them back to the Arctic on his next trip. It was too bad if they perished in the interim. The two surviving children were later shipped home. One died in the Arctic, the other – who had seen his father's mock funeral – drifted back to America where he succumbed to the influenza epidemic of 1918.

Meanwhile Peary was treated as a hero. In 1897 the American

Geographical Society awarded him a Gold Medal and the following year so did the Royal Geographical Society, where Clements Markham described him as 'without exception, the greatest glacial traveller in the world'. Still he had yet to reach his goal, and as he approached forty he began to doubt if he ever would. 'I shall never see the North Pole unless some one brings it here,' he announced. 'In my judgement such work requires a far younger man than I.'[46]

17

'A FEW TOES AREN'T MUCH . . .'

Peary's despondency was short-lived. By 1898 he was already planning his next expedition to the Pole, not via Greenland this time, but up Kane Basin and Ellesmere Island where, having established a colony of Eskimos as his northerly base, he would bide his time until the moment he could 'shoot forward to the Pole like a ball from a cannon'.[1] Again the US Navy raised an objection. They had hired the man as a civil engineer, and were paying him as such, but had seen nothing of him for almost a decade. There was a post waiting for him at Mares Island on the West Coast – far from those schemers in Washington – and, not unreasonably, they wanted him to fill it. Once again Peary was ahead of them. Rallying to his cause were a collection of politicians and plutocrats who wanted the U.S. to win the polar race and also, possibly, to have their names immortalized at the finishing line for the naming of distant points after his sponsors was one of the most persuasive gifts Peary had to offer. As he put it in a fund-raising letter, 'if I win out in this work, the names of those who made the work possible will be kept through the coming centuries floating forever above the forgotten and submerged debris of our time and day'.[2] After all, he added, the only reason people remembered Ferdinand of

Spain was because he sent Columbus to discover America. Thus was born the 'Peary Arctic Club'. The club would not hold its first meeting until 1899, but the concept was there, as was a core group of would-be Ferdinands, headed by Senator Morris Ketcham Jesup, who provided the financial backing to get Peary's new expedition under way and the political influence to ensure that their man would be free to lead it. To the Navy's indignation, it was President Roosevelt himself who signed the order giving Peary all the leave – the *paid* leave, moreover – which he needed in order to accomplish his objective.

Peary sailed on 4 July 1898 aboard the *Windward*, the same ship which had brought Nansen back from Franz Josef Land and which had been donated by Alfred Harmsworth. Perhaps Peary enjoyed this coincidence. The vessel which had rescued his rival Nansen from the ice would be the one in which he, Peary would reach the Pole. But the *Windward* had come to him badly prepared. It was neither as strong as he would have liked nor was it as powerful, an industrial strike in Britain having prevented the installation of the larger engines he had been promised. The *Windward* made a maximum of three and a half knots in the most favourable circumstances – far from the battering ram he needed if he was to break through the ice in Smith Sound. He could have waited until better engines were installed but there was no time as a 'disturbing factor in the appropriation by another of my plan and field of work had now entered the fray'.[3] He had to move fast because, as he wrote in the *Bulletin of the Geographical Society of Philadelphia*, 'I did not wish to be distanced in my own domain.'[4] The 'disturbing factor' was Sverdrup.

While Peary had been plotting his route to the Pole, Otto Sverdrup had been planning a trip to explore the northern Arctic islands. There was no rivalry in Sverdrup's mind. He stated plainly that he had no designs on the Pole and made abundantly clear that he was interested in the more scientifically profitable regions to the west of Greenland. Such excuses had been used by every 'scientific' expedition since the days of Kane, but in this case they were genuine. Why should Sverdrup bother with the Pole, having all but reached it on the *Fram*'s first voyage? Why should he dispute the belief, held almost universally since Nansen's return, that the North Pole was nothing but an ice-covered sea? Besides, to try and better Nansen in the ship which Nansen had built and which Nansen had lent him for the purpose of meaningful discovery, would have been dishonourable.

Peary had no sense of honour other than his own, which was why he resented Sverdrup's intrusion in 'my own domain'. He did not believe that the Norwegians – who had, incidentally, mounted a far stronger and more capable expedition than his own – were going north for altruistic purposes. As he said to Jesup, it was 'an unprincipled attempt . . . to appropriate my route, my plans and my objects'.[5] In Peary's lexicon of the unforgivable, 'appropriation' was giving 'forestallment' a run for its money. According to one source, however, Peary had been fed details of Sverdrup's outfit by the US consul in Bergen. As Sverdrup had been planning his expedition for at least as long as Peary, it may have been Peary who was guilty of appropriation.

Whatever the case, this was to be Peary's most wretched and futile voyage. The *Windward* made its way through Smith Sound under the command of an experienced captain named Robert Bartlett. Peary had learned from his previous expeditions and trimmed his team to include only the finest. The cannonball sledgers whom Bartlett would fire at the Pole comprised Peary, Henson and one Dr Tom Dedrick. There were to be no others, save for the Eskimos they recruited en route. That first winter, the *Windward* found an anchorage at Cape D'Urville on the western shore of Kane Basin, but Peary hoped yet to reach Greely's old station, Fort Conger. This barn-like wooden dwelling had housed Greely's team during the year of international polar co-operation, and was still intact. It also contained fuel and food which Peary hoped to use for his own purposes. Sverdrup's *Fram* was tucked in a score or so miles to the south of Cape D'Urville. The Norwegians presented no threat but Peary felt compelled to warn them off. And that was why, in October 1898, Sverdrup's dinner was interrupted by a stranger in furs warning him that Robeson Channel was closed.

The abrupt meeting between Peary and Sverdrup did not appear in Peary's journal, save for one oblique reference. But Henson recorded his reaction. Pacing the cabin floor Peary cried, 'Sverdrup may at this minute be planning to beat me to Fort Conger! I can't let him do that . . . I'll get to Conger before Sverdrup if it kills me!'[6]

He did reach Conger before Sverdrup and it did nearly kill him. With Dedrick, Henson and two Eskimos he sledged north on 20 December 1898 and attained Conger eighteen days later. By the light of his last oil he located Greely's cooking range and the officer's stove and lit a fire in both of them. Of that day Sverdrup, to the south, wrote, 'I have a suspicion that it was the coldest twenty-four hours I have ever experienced.'[7] The temperature was -69°F and Sverdrup's men had to put Primus stoves under their Iceland jerseys to melt the ice which had accumulated on their bodies. (It was so cold that snow fell *within* Sverdrup's sealed tent.) For Peary, out in the open and exposed to the wind, conditions were unbearable. When the stoves were lit in Fort Conger he admitted to Henson that he no longer had sensation in his feet.

'Matt handed a bucket to Ahndloo and told him to fill it with snow,' wrote Henson's biographer. 'Then he inserted the blade of his knife under the top of Peary's sealskin boots. He ripped the boots from both feet, and gently removed the rabbit-skin undershoes. Both legs were a bloodless white up to the knee and, as Matt ripped off the undershoes, several toes from each foot clung to the hide and snapped off at the first joint.

'"My God, Lieutenant! Why didn't you tell me your feet were frozen?" Matt cried.

'"There's no time to pamper sick men on the trail," Peary replied tersely. Then he added thoughtfully, "Besides, a few toes aren't much to give to achieve the Pole."'[8]

Dedrick amputated six of Peary's toes. For the next month Peary lay in his bed, while storms raged outside. During 'those interminable black days',[9] as he called them, twelve dogs died from eating tainted food and Henson had difficulty persuading the two Eskimos not to take the remaining animals and abandon them. 'I could not at times repress a groan at the thought that my God-given frame was mutilated forever,' Peary wrote in his diary, 'still I never lost faith . . . I *knew* that

I should yet do the work which I had set before myself.'[10] On the walls of Fort Conger he inscribed a quotation from Seneca: '*Inveniam viam aut faciam*,' – 'Find a way or make one'. As soon as possible, when the weather cleared, the group returned to the *Windward*, their leader strapped to a sledge and dictating his journal to Dedrick as they went. They completed the journey of 250 miles in eleven days in temperatures of -60°F. On arrival Dedrick cut off another two of Peary's toes, leaving him with just the little toe on each foot.

Sverdrup was fascinated by the *Windward*. He did not know what had happened at Fort Conger but had seen sledges plying to and fro. Shortly after Peary's return he sent his second-in-command, Victor Baumann, to see how things were. Baumann reported that Peary was confined to his cabin and was initially too bad-tempered to see him. He did, however, have a revealing interview with Bartlett who told him that he was frightened for the expedition and that if the ice broke he would leave at once. But Bartlett feared his 'chances of putting away were anything but favourable',[11] and he thought it unlikely they would be able to walk out. Baumann agreed. 'The worst of it all, as regards the crew,' he wrote, 'was that they were badly equipped with clothes, and quite unfitted for a long journey on the ice. In any case, it was Peary's own intention to push northward in spite of every-thing.'[12] The next morning Baumann was finally granted an audience with Peary and explained the purpose of his visit – to see where Peary was going so that Sverdrup could avoid duplicating his efforts. Peary was tight-lipped. Not only did he refuse to say where he was going, he also refused to say where he had been, making no mention of Fort Conger. When Baumann sympathized with the loss of his toes, Peary responded grandly: 'You must take your chances up here, you know.'[13]

This puzzling encounter left Sverdrup none the wiser as to Peary's intentions, so he shrugged and got on with the job. In 1899, while Sverdrup sledged west across Ellesmere Island, Peary returned to Fort Conger in the hope of finding a route north. It was madness. His toes had not yet healed and the wounds began to open under the strain of travel. Once again he had to be brought back to the ship on a sledge. To compensate for this failure he railed at Greely's inefficiency in allowing his men to perish, back in 1884. Peary and his Eskimos had been able to shoot plenty of game and were it not for his feet they would have survived in perfect comfort at Fort Conger. Greely was clearly not of the same calibre as himself. 'The horrors of Cape Sabine are not inevitable,' Peary later wrote. 'They are a blot upon the record of American Arctic exploration.'[14] What Peary did not dwell upon were the entirely different circumstances of the two expeditions and that, although Greely's men may have starved, they had never been so careless as to become frostbitten – something which Peary could not say of himself.

After these two fruitless forays anyone other than Peary would have abandoned the race. But not he. Shifting the *Windward* to the opposite side of the Kane Basin he attacked the Greenland coast in the spring of 1900, shuffling northwards on his broken feet in search of the Pole. His drive was unquenchable. He furiously wanted to beat his competitors, past and present. He was also impelled by a sense of semi-divine urgency. 'There is something beyond me,' he wrote to Josephine, 'something outside of me, which impels me irresistibly to the work.'[15] *The work.* How reminiscent of Hall were those words, with their undertones of evangelism and Protestant ethic. But Peary was not a religious man. All he shared with Hall was an obsession. Ever since the Franklin era, people had written of explorers that the polar virus was in their blood. Peary had a more virulent strain of the virus than anybody yet. He *had* to press on – at whatever cost.

In 1900 the world was toasting a new century, albeit one in which nothing much had changed: Britain was at war in South Africa, Russia was occupying Manchuria, France was subjugating the Sahara, and Germany was establishing colonies in Tanzania and Namibia. Rubber-hungry Belgium was milking the Congo, Portugal was tightening its grip on Angola and Mozambique, and America was smashing Spanish control of the Philippines. Austria-Hungary was encroaching southwards into the Balkans and the Ottoman Empire was congratulating itself on yet another massacre of the Albanians. In the Far East, the Boxers were laying siege to Peking, and Japan was preparing its navy for the ultimate demolition of the Tsar's fleet in the war of 1905.

Oblivious to it all, Robert Edwin Peary plodded northwards up the west coast of Greenland.

On 8 May he reached 83°24'N, the highest point attained by Lockwood and Brainard on the Greely expedition From there the two men had seen a headland to the north, Cape Washington. Peary could see it too and hoped fervently that it was not the top of Greenland. For anybody even to have seen it before he did would have been a blow. Fortunately, when he reached Cape Washington, there was another headland to the north. 'It would have been a great disappointment to me,' he explained, 'after coming so far to find that another's eyes had forestalled mine in looking first upon the coveted northern point.'[16] Several days later he did eventually reach Greenland's northernmost point, which he named Cape Morris Jesup after his most influential backer. His sense of triumph was diminished, however, when he took his first steps on the Arctic Ocean. Travelling over the rough and broken ice, he realized how difficult was the task he had set himself. On the Greenland ice cap he had been able to cover more than twenty miles per day. Here, he was pressed to make half that speed. Reflectively, he turned back for Fort Conger, completing the 400-mile distance in a space of nineteen days. He would wait until another spring arrived and another avenue presented itself.

Life at Fort Conger was getting better by the year. Game was plentiful, so was fuel. Peary had demolished Greely's single large house to make three smaller, more heat-efficient huts and the left-over debris burned well. In addition there was seal blubber and even some coal, which Henson sledged in from a seam discovered by the Nares expedition. 'Wonderful this cabin,' Peary wrote, 'this mellow life, this warmth.'[17] He had never spent a happier time in the Arctic, 'so free from annoyance, worry, or irritation'.[18] Like a chess player, he focused his mind solely on his next move, brushing all distractions away. A typical Peary day went as follows: rise at 5.30 a.m., drink a quart of coffee, see what Dedrick was up to at 8.00, and then spend the rest of the morning writing or devising more compact ways of packing his supplies; at midday he would have lunch (made by Dedrick), then drag in some more wood for his stove and potter about with his equipment until 6.00 p.m. when supper was ready (again, often made by Dedrick), after which he would write, read and plan, before turning in at 11.00 p.m. His last act of the day would be to chop kindling for his next morning's brew of coffee.

But if Peary was happy with these arrangements, Dedrick was not. As the expedition's doctor he felt he was not getting the consideration to which he was entitled. He received the impression that he was a supernumerary to be called on when toes required amputation but otherwise to be left in the kitchen. He was lonely, too: Peary lived in single-minded solitude and Henson spent most of his time with the Eskimos. On the few occasions Henson spoke to him, he did so without respect. His confidence eroding, Dedrick woke Peary from his polar trance and demanded some action be taken. He wanted it known that he was second-in-command, in title at least, and he wanted Henson and the Eskimos to recognize this. Peary had a word with Henson, but it was a half-hearted affair, as is clear from the notes Peary jotted down before delivering his admonition: 'You have been in my service long enough to show me respect in small things . . . Have a right to expect you to say sir to me always . . . That you will pay attention to me when I am talking to you and show that you hear directions I give you by saying yes sir, or all right sir . . . Have no fault to find when we are alone together, but when doctor or number of Eskimos present or when we are on board ship you are very different . . . Now is there anything which, if different, would make things pleasanter for you?'[19]

Peary resented these irritations. They distracted him from his planning, his packing and repacking of the sledges, his tinkering, his wood-chopping and his morning quart of coffee. Whatever he said to Henson merely papered over a widening breach. That winter, with the doctor still dissatisfied, Peary fired him, ordering him to return to the States at once. But Dedrick refused to go further south than Etah, where he said the Eskimos needed him. Then, when an epidemic broke out at Cape Sabine, he crossed Kane Basin because he was needed there, too. Every so often he would return to Fort Conger because he said they needed him there as well. It was extraordinary and without precedent. Nobody had ever dismissed a man like that in

the Arctic, telling him to pack his bags and walk home. And nobody
had ever reacted as Dedrick did, by going native and hanging around
in the hope of being reinstated. Peary called him that 'crazy doctor'.[20]

No less bizarre were the events being played out to the south.
While Peary was sledging up Greenland, the *Windward* had sailed back
for supplies and on its return journey had brought Josephine and
Marie Peary with it. The ship was then nipped off Cape Sabine and
forced to winter there – which would have been fine had it not been
for a young Eskimo woman who also came aboard. Allakassingwah, or
'Ally' had been Peary's mistress earlier in the expedition and, as she
told Josephine cheerily, was carrying his child. 'You will have been
surprised, perhaps annoyed, when you hear I came up on a ship,'
Josephine wrote to her husband in a letter that would not be delivered
until spring 1901, 'but believe me had I known how things were with
you I should not have come.'[21] It says a lot for Josephine – or perhaps
Peary – that the two women not only survived a winter in the enforced
proximity of a ship but put up with each other reasonably well.

Then there was Cook, who had been sent north in August 1900 to
see if Peary was in need of assistance. Already antagonistic to Peary,
Cook was aghast at what he encountered. Dedrick was 'living in
underground holes as wild men do',[22] and the Eskimos were dying in
handfuls from what Peary described as dysentery but which Cook,
like Dedrick, recognized as an epidemic. He later called it 'one of the
darkest unprinted pages of Arctic history'.[23] Cook went to Fort
Conger, where he diagnosed Peary as anaemic and unfit for service.
'You are through as a traveller on foot,' he said, 'for without toes and
a painful stub you can never wear snowshoes or ski.'[24] He also advised
Peary to eat more raw meat, to which Peary replied that he would
sooner die. When Cook left, Peary carried on as before: packing,
planning and drinking coffee.

Peary did nothing else for the duration of 1901: conditions were
either unfavourable or unconducive. In March 1902, however, he
hobbled north with Henson, travelling up the west coast of Kennedy
and Robeson Channels, and reaching the northernmost point of
Ellesmere Island in early April. The Arctic Ocean sat there, in its

crinkly, fissured vastness, and Peary went over it. He reached 84°17'N before his way was barred by a wide lead of open water. He waited for it to freeze but it did not do so, and on 21 April he admitted defeat. On his retreat he noted that Nares's Palaeocrystic Sea, supposedly formed of immovable, centuries-old ice, was in fact as volatile as the rest of the Arctic pack. During his journey north, he had been pushed twelve degrees to the west by the drift. In these circumstances it would be even more difficult to reach the Pole than he had imagined.

This was the most crushing blow Peary had suffered to date. 'The game is off,' he wrote in his diary. 'My dream of sixteen years is ended . . . I have made the best fight I knew. I believe it has been a good one. But I cannot accomplish the impossible.'[25] Reviewing his life he realized how much his obsession had cost him, how long he had been away from his wife and family, how many things he had missed during those years in the ice. His daughter hardly knew him, another child had been born and had died in his absence, and his mother too had died. And what did he have to show for it? 'Now a maimed old man, unsuccessful after the most arduous work, away from wife and child, mother dead, one baby dead. Has the game been worth the candle?'[26]

Never had Peary sunk so low. 'As I look out on the scenery that a few years ago would have filled me with enthusiasm, as I think of my high hopes then, and contrast them with my present lack of energy, of interest, of elation; as I think of the last four years and what I have been through; as I think of all the little petty details with which I have been and am still occupying myself, it all seems so small, so little worth the while that I could cry out in anguish of spirit.'[27]

The *Windward* picked him up on 5 August 1902 – and Dedrick too, which further soured Peary's mood – bringing with it a devastating piece of news. From the past four miserable years, Peary had emerged with one consolation: without the aid of a ship, he had travelled further north from an Arctic landmass than any other human being. But now he learned that he did not even have that honour. In 1900, an Italian expedition under the Duke of Abruzzi had reached 86°34' from Franz Josef Land, a full 137 miles further north than Peary.

He had failed.

18

THE POLAR DUKE

During his protracted duel with Greenland, Peary had paid scant attention to events elsewhere on the polar map. Confident in his choice of route and in the certainty that nobody would ever better Nansen in the Scandinavian and Siberian ice pack, he had ignored the North-Eastern approach entirely. But others had not, and the activity had been intense. Russian ships had explored new islands off Siberia, the British mountaineer Sir Martin Conway had made the first crossing of Spitsbergen, and Prince Albert of Monaco would later map part of its coastline. Germans and Swedes were out there, as were individuals like Walter Wellman, an American who made several disastrous attempts at the Pole from Spitsbergen and Franz Josef Land, returning from his latest fiasco, in 1899, to the headline: 'WELLMAN BACK, A CRIPPLE'.

Another American was Evelyn Baldwin, whose voyage to Franz Josef Land in 1901 was sponsored lavishly by the chemical magnate William Ziegler. 'The Baldwin–Ziegler Expedition was organised *to reach the Pole*,' Baldwin announced. 'Neither scientific research, nor even a record of "Farthest North," will suffice; only the attainment of that much-sought-for spot where one can point only to the south can satisfy our purpose.'[1] Baldwin's only triumph was in the scale of his failure. Having wasted his coal trying to find a sea route above the archipelago he made a single sledge foray and, in the words of one man, 'succeeded in losing more than 300 dogs and 30,000 pounds of pemmican'.[2] A second Ziegler expedition was sent out under Baldwin's subordinate, Anthony Fiala, but although Fiala was less calamitous than Baldwin his three stabs at the Pole took him no further north than 82°. 'An ill conceived, badly managed, undisciplined venture,' was how Britain's Henry Feilden described the expedition. '[Fiala is] utterly incompetent – he may be a fairly good cook but not a leader of men.'[3] On his return to America, Fiala found work in a New York sports goods shop.

They were a motley crowd, these explorers of the eastern routes. Some capable, some misguided and some downright ridiculous, they have been swept under the carpet of Arctic history. (Though it must be said, in extenuation, that it was harsh to praise Fiala only for his cooking.) However, their antics should not be overlooked for they show that Peary by no means held a monopoly on the Pole and that the 'American route' to which he devoted himself for so long was considered the least practicable by his contemporaries. They also demonstrate, as Baldwin's statement made clear, that people did not care what Clements Markham and his ilk thought. So what if the Pole was, scientifically, a waste of time? They still wanted to reach it. Their ardour survives in crinkly folios of newspaper archives, the odd geographical bulletin, one or two books focusing on the sporting delights of the Arctic – climbing, mainly, and shooting – and the amazing journal of the Duke of Abruzzi.

From his official photographs, Luigi Amadeo Giuseppe Mario Fernando Francesco de Savoia-Aosta, Duke of the Abruzzi, looks like any other European aristocrat of the time – stiff, bemedalled, uniformed and epauletted, with a waxed moustache and a monocle that is absent only, one feels, because he had forgotten to bring it to the studio. He comes across as solitary, reserved and dignified, as befitted a scion of Europe's oldest royal family, the House of Savoy, which since 1861 had occupied the Italian throne. But the photographs do not do him justice. In reality he was vigorous, a man of daring, and an intrepid mountaineer. He had helped conquer the Alps and could count among his list of first ascents that of Mount St Elias in Alaska. Later, he would make his name in the Himalayas. In the 1890s, Abruzzi was the fresh face of Italy, a nation which was scarcely thirty years old. Why should Italy not stamp its mark on the world with a polar expedition, just as Germany had done in the 1860s? Abruzzi was the ideal person to do it. That he was of royal blood would also bolster the never-very-secure status of the Italian throne.

Succeed or fail, Abruzzi felt that the venture would be worthwhile. 'The practical use of Polar expeditions has often been discussed,' he wrote. 'If only the moral advantage to be derived from these expeditions be considered, I believe that it would compensate for the sacrifices they demand. As men who surmount difficulties in their daily struggles feel themselves strengthened for an encounter with still greater difficulties, so should also a nation feel itself still more encouraged and urged by the success won by its sons, to persevere in striving for its greatness and prosperity.'[4]

In 1898, therefore, Abruzzi ordered 120 dogs to be kept for him at the Russian port of Archangel, and on 16 January 1899, he arrived unannounced at Christiana to pump Nansen for information. He was only twenty-six years old, twenty years younger than Peary and twelve years younger than Nansen. He knew about ice-work, was inured to the freezing conditions of high-level mountaineering, and was willing to risk everything for the glory of Italy. Nansen warned him what to expect. Abruzzi listened carefully and six months later was on his way to the Pole.

Outside of war, members of European royalty were not famed for their participation in matters of physical endeavour – a sad state of affairs, because their wealth and influence afforded them limitless opportunity in that direction. Abruzzi, however, was different: untrammelled by the need for governmental approval or public subscription, he simply opened his coffers and went ahead. Having collected the necessary men and materials, he purchased a 570-ton whaling ship, the *Jason*, which he renamed the *Stella Polare*, at a total cost of £38,413, and arrived at Archangel on 30 June 1899. Half his crew were Norwegian, a mix which he feared might prove explosive, given the overtly nationalistic nature of the expedition, but to his pleasure, 'Italians and Norwegians behaved throughout this voyage as though the crew were composed of one nationality. I had comrades with me, rather than subordinates.'[5]

From Archangel, his plan was to sail for Franz Josef Land, where he would set up a depot of eight months' provisions at Jackson's old base, Cape Flora, then find an anchorage as far north as possible. That autumn he would set up a string of depots on the northern islands of the archipelago and the following spring he would use these for an attempt at the Pole. If the *Stella Polare* sank or became iced in, he and his team would retreat to Cape Flora and wait there for a pre-arranged relief ship to pick them up – or, if the relief ship failed, escape by boat to Novaya Zemlya or Spitsbergen.

It was very much like Nansen's trek from the *Fram* but in reverse. Indeed, according to one commentator, it was drawn up 'under the personal advice and superintendence of Dr. Nansen, who aided in every possible way the success of the expedition'.[6] Perhaps Nansen did have a hand in things – the *Stella Polare*, in its previous incarnation as the *Jason*, had been the same ship which had transported him to Greenland; Abruzzi took Nansen sledges and Nansen kayaks – but Nansen's role was probably restricted to describing the obstacles Abruzzi might face on the pack. If he had had any major say in the expedition he would have insisted they take skis. Abruzzi, however, preferred to travel by foot and by sledge. Superficially this was an odd decision for, since Nansen's Greenland trip, skiing had spread from Norway to the Alps and had established itself as a popular pastime for Europe's elite. But Abruzzi had none of Nansen's technical expertise, was ignorant of which skis to use in various conditions, did not know how to prepare or repair them, and was, anyway, more at home with an ice-axe and alpenstock, two items which, to judge by every account of the pack's hummocks and ridges, would be just as useful as skis.

The first thing Abruzzi noticed on reaching Archangel was the wretched condition of the 120 dogs he had bought. 'They were placed in an enclosure of about 20 yards long, and 10 wide, and chained up, each separately to boards fastened to the ground,' he wrote. 'Our arrival was greeted by furious barking which even the whips of [my agent] and his men could not silence. There were coats of all sorts: black, white, yellow, short-haired, long-haired; small and straight ears, large and hanging ones. The biggest were not higher than 24 inches, and their state of emaciation, owing to the journey, the heat, and the flies, inspired me with serious misgivings as to whether these animals would ever be able to accomplish 1,200 miles drawing all that was requisite for the expedition.'[7]

More encouraging was the dribble of dignitaries who came aboard the *Stella Polare* to wish Italy's first Arctic expedition *bon voyage*. There was His Excellency Morra, Ambassador to St Petersburg, Russia's Grand Duke Vladimir, the Counts Oldofredi and Rignon, the Chevalier Silvestri, and Colonel Nasalli. None of them was very notable except Grand Duke Vladimir, and he was only there by chance, but Abruzzi thought it a good show given the difficulty of reaching Archangel. '[It] left a most grateful remembrance behind,' he wrote, 'which accompanied us into the desolate Arctic regions and more than once cheered us during the long winter nights.' At sundown on 12 July, he herded the dogs onto his ship. 'This work lasted two hours and was accompanied by a most infernal noise, which informed the inhabitants of Archangel that our departure was close at hand.'[8] That evening, the *Stella Polare* slipped anchor and after a triple 'Hurrah' sailed down the Dvina into the White Sea for Franz Josef Land.

Four days later they were at Cape Flora and in early August they reached 82°04′N, their highest point for the season. An anchorage was found at 81°47′ in Teplitz Bay on Prince Rudolf Island, the northernmost island of the archipelago, from where Abruzzi began his depot-laying expeditions. On 7 September, however, the *Stella Polare* was hit by a pressure ridge which heeled it over, punched leaks in both sides, and sent water flooding into the engine room. Abruzzi ordered the ship to be evacuated. Personally, he was convinced it would never float again, but his second-in-command, Captain

Umberto Cagni, thought something might be done. Abruzzi therefore left him to his devices while he oversaw the all-important construction of their winter quarters.

Not for Abruzzi the squalor of an igloo or the utility of a wooden hut. Instead, the Italian camp was a marvellously stylish edifice, unlike anything that had been seen in the Arctic before. At its heart were two tents, above which was erected a second layer of canvas, and enclosing the lot was a third, and still larger tent. The central two tents formed the living quarters, complete with wooden floors, stoves, camp beds and feather mattresses; the galley occupied the space between the inner tents and the second layer; and the stores were packed between the second tent and the third. Three doors separated the living quarters from the elements, retaining heat so effectively that when Abruzzi turned off the stoves at night the temperature never sank below zero. He had built himself a triple-insulated, fully-functioning Arctic pavilion.

When Cagni completed the ship's repairs on 15 November, Abruzzi's joy was complete. 'I did not believe it possible,'[9] he wrote admiringly. But on 23 December, while charging north with supplies for his depots, Abruzzi suffered a setback. Hit by a sudden storm, he and Cagni lost their way and in the darkness drove their sledges into the sea – or, as Abruzzi put it, 'passed rapidly from the glacier into the bay in a rather abrupt manner and against our wishes'.[10] They survived the experience – which 'served as a lesson to all of us'[11] – but Abruzzi lost the tops of two fingers to frostbite. He tried to forget his 'little troubles' during the Christmas festivities – champagne, raffles, fireworks, feasts and bonfires – but the wounds healed slowly and brave as he was, he was no Peary. Besides, a Prince of the House of Savoy could not risk any further disfigurement. When the Pole party left in the spring, it was led by Cagni rather than Abruzzi.

Except for rank there was little to choose between the two men: they were mountaineering companions – Cagni had accompanied Abruzzi on the ascent of Mount Elias – and they were equally well-acquainted with snow and ice. If anything, Cagni was the more accomplished of the pair, having a practical bent that his titled comrade lacked: if the sledges broke on the way north Cagni would be the man to fix them. Abruzzi, therefore, appointed him to the command without resentment and in complete confidence of his ability to carry the Italian flag to the Pole. 'I could not have entrusted [the expedition] to a leader more gifted with energy and activity, more prompt at finding expedients or endowed with greater moral and physical endurance,'[12] he wrote.

After a false start in February, Cagni departed the royal camp on 11 March 1900 with ten men, 102 dogs and thirteen sledges, each sledge carrying 510 pounds of supplies – amongst which, apart from the usual pemmican and tinned goods, was a lightweight carbohydrate which foreigners called 'Italian paste' and Cagni knew as pasta. The sledges were constructed according to Nansen's specifications, their runners edged with metal and saturated with a mixture of pitch, stearine and tallow. Cagni also carried Nansen kayaks, modified to include sails, rowlocks and pumps. He refused, however, to accept the sleeping bags which Nansen had specified. Scandinavians slept in a sitting position, spines upright. They had short beds and short covers. Cagni liked to sleep on his back, and had the bags lengthened to suit. He also liked to walk. Instead of using skis or snowshoes, Cagni and his party wore insulated Nordic footwear called *finneskos*, in which they would run alongside the sledges, the latter having been deliberately overloaded so that the men could keep pace with the dogs.

Not all of the party were expected to reach the Pole. Cagni had divided his caravan into three sections, each of which would turn back at different intervals when its supplies were finished. Thus the first group would drag supplies for the second, returning to camp after fifteen days. The second would drag food for the third, splitting off on the thirtieth day. And the last, under Cagni, would continue with three men, five sledges and forty-eight dogs for a further fifteen days, carrying food for a maximum of sixty days' travel, including the return journey. In that it involved stages, Cagni's scheme mimicked the Peary system. Otherwise, the two men could not be compared. Peary's field was Greenland, where he could count on Eskimo help. Cagni was crossing an emptiness before the likes of which Peary had retreated in despair. But Cagni would have done well to imitate Peary's survival techniques. He could be forgiven for not knowing how to build an igloo and for relying on tents instead, but surely he should have been aware of the advantages of fur clothing. Instead he took the usual European woollens (made by Jaeger). In fact, he positively rejected the fur gloves he had been issued because he said they restricted his movements. And so he suffered accordingly.

For the first few weeks they made little more than seven miles a day, hampered by the severest weather Cagni had ever experienced. In temperatures of 80°F below freezing, the metal in the sledges and ice-axes became brittle as glass. Dogs froze and died in the night. Boiling soup solidified before the bowl could be emptied. Their sleeping bags were like wood. 'Sleep?' wrote Cagni. 'I do not know how or when we slept, for every little noise was heard by all of us, and without a tremendous effort of will we should never have come out of that sleeping-bag, where we lay without comfort, but also without that mass of suffering which inevitably awaited us on issuing therefrom. Half an hour after we got up our underclothing had already become a cuirass of ice.'[13] Fumbling in the cold, they lost six hours every day simply setting up and striking camp.

As the weather improved and their loads lightened they gathered speed, at one point covering eighteen miles in a single day. On 22 March the first three-man group, under Lieutenant Chevalier Francesco Querini, turned back for home. Then on 31 March, the second group of three, led by Dr Achille Cavalli, followed suit. Both parties dropped out earlier than planned because Cagni had revised his schedule. If he were to travel north for forty-five days that would mean a total of ninety days in the field, and an estimated return date of early June. It was imperative, however, that he be back before the end of May to avoid being trapped by the thaw. He therefore reduced his outward journey to a maximum of thirty-seven days and brought forward the departures dates of his support teams to match. No sooner had the second team left, however, than Cagni changed his mind. Confined to their tent for two days by a storm, 'tormented by the phantasy of non-success in the desperation of our impotence',[14] Cagni and his companions – three Alpine guides by the names of Simone Canepa, Alessio Fenouillet and Giuseppe Petigax – decided they were being over-cautious. If they went on two-thirds rations they could prolong their march by a couple of weeks; their loads would become lighter with each meal, allowing them to travel faster; and as the sledges were successively emptied they could abandon them and feed the redundant dogs to the others, thereby saving on the pemmican which the dogs usually ate. They were bound to meet better conditions further north and their return would be so light and easy that they would positively fly back and still make the May deadline. They dreamed of 'extending [their march] to the extreme limit of what was reasonable, of pushing on till every hope was exhausted!'[15]

It was a hare-brained scheme that conflated opposing calculations of time, distance and weight and which took no account of reality. Their sledges were so battered that only their bindings held them together. The kayaks were also in tatters – those that had not been dismantled to repair the sledges. And their food-saving plans worked directly against their weight-saving ones. But they had gone Pole-mad. Having made their decision they put it into practice at once, eating only one meal in the next two days, 'and by this little sacrifice we thought we had deserved better weather'.[16]

Propelled by their mania, they covered record distances – up to twenty-eight miles per day, despite stumbling through hummocks so labyrinthine that it took them hours to escape the maze. On 21 April they reached 85°28′N and saw mile after mile of smooth ice stretching before them. By rights they should have stopped two or three days previously, but Cagni's men shouted 'Forward! Forward!',[17] so forward they went. On the 22nd, 'we started, smiling to each other, but all of us were very agitated and nervous'.[18] By midday they were at 85°48′N and conditions were not as perfect as they had seemed. They took greater risks, hopping from old ice to new, dodging pressure ridges and crossing leads on ice islands, driven always by 'the influence of fear',[19] as Cagni put it, but making steady progress. At 3.00 p.m. on 23 April they stood at 86°05′N and Nansen's record was within their grasp. They were tired but, 'The temptation was stronger than our weakness, and after half-an-hour's rest we again started on our journey.'[20]

'The remembrance of that march is like a dream to me,' Cagni later wrote. 'We did not feel the fatigue; it seemed that life on that endless white plain consisted of placing one foot before the other, and we seemed to find in this mechanical movement peace of mind and repose for the body. So we went on for many hours. Seven o'clock passed, eight o'clock, and even nine o'clock, and we were marching still.'[21] It was 10.00 p.m. before they finally stopped. That evening they drank all the brandy in their medicine chest and as Cagni admitted, 'we went to sleep rather late'.[22] Their hangovers lasted until noon the following day.

On the evening of 24 April, at 86°33'N, 64°30'E (later adjusted to 86°34') they gave up. Their euphoria had deserted them, and a sober count of their supplies showed that they only had thirty days' food remaining. They had beaten Nansen by twenty-one miles, the thermometer registered 60°F below freezing, and it was time to go home. Cagni went outside and stared north, towards the Pole, fewer than 250 miles distant. 'The air was limpid, the wind ranged between north-east and north-west, innumerable were the points – dark blue, white, sharp, and blunt, often of the most curious forms – of the great blocks of ice which the pressure had raised; and further away on the clear horizon, in the form of a crown extending from east to west, was a bluish wall, which, seen from afar, appeared insurmountable. It was for us *Terrae ultima thule.*'[23]

Initially, the return journey was easy. Following their old tracks they sliced through the snow, the dogs careering ahead so fast that Cagni and his men had trouble keeping up. Two hundred and fifty miles separated them from Franz Josef Land, and according to Cagni's calculations their provisions would last them at least 360 miles if conditions held fair. He suspected they might need some of these extra miles, for the drift had taken them slightly to the west during their march north, and so he had compensated by altering course to the south-east. If the drift continued at the same rate he expected to arrive ten miles east of Franz Josef Land; if it increased slightly, they

would probably hit it dead on. Their only fear was being caught by
the thaw, for their remaining kayaks had been so badly smashed that
it would take at least a week to mend them. But, at their current
speed, this was unlikely to be a problem.

In the space of four days they covered a whole degree south, and on
28 April Cagni was feeling confident: 'If this progress continued for
three or four more days longer,' he wrote in his journal, 'we should be
almost safe from any surprise on the part of the ice-pack.'[24] By the end
of the month they had travelled ninety miles in six days, which meant
that if they averaged just seven miles per day – their worst ever – they
would be at the *Stella Polare* before the end of May. Cheerfully, they
laid bets on when they would get back. Canepa plumped for 23 May,
Petigax the 26th, Cagni the 27th and Fenouillet, at whose pessimism
they scoffed, chose the 30th. Secretly, Cagni agreed with Fenouillet,
but he was sure he had a period of grace before the thaw started in
earnest. 'It would be enough for me to reach [base] in the first week
in June, and I should still consider that I had made a splendid
march!'[25] he wrote.

In those first halcyon weeks Cagni struggled to keep up. The three
others had made a living from climbing the Italian Alps around Aosta
and were superbly fit. But Cagni, although an amateur mountaineer,
had perforce spent most of his life on the deck of a ship and was
pressed to match his companions. The nervous energy which had
sustained him on the way north evaporated. 'I was frequently obliged
to be dragged along,' he wrote, 'my legs were weak and so heavy that
I could not take five steps continuously.'[26] He stopped eating pemmican because he thought it gave him diarrhoea and thus became
weaker still. He also had a frostbitten finger which, as it turned gan-
grenous, sent shooting pains into his armpit. When it became too
much to bear he travelled on a sledge, doped with opium. As they
pushed south, all of them resorted to drugs, dribbling drops of cocaine
into their eyes to alleviate snow-blindness.

On 2 May, while blockaded in their tent by a two-day storm, Cagni
took the opportunity to attend to his finger, which had swollen almost
to the thickness of his wrist and was black with gangrene. He

described the treatment with chilling calmness. 'I clear away all the black part with a lancet, which I hold in my left hand. As soon as I introduce the point of the blade into the flesh, an incredible quantity of matter issues forth, which gives me great relief. I take away a covering of dead flesh, and there remains sticking out of the wound a piece of bone, which has all the appearance of being dead. When I press the end, I feel a great pain in my whole arm. I consider that, if I leave this useless projection, the smallest blow will cause me intense suffering, and I therefore set about cutting it off; but I only have scissors, and the little bone is very hard, so that I suffer a great deal while taking a piece off. Over this little operation, which a doctor would have performed in three minutes, I passed fully two hours . . .'[27] Canepa was so revolted that he fled the tent, preferring to take his chances in the storm than endure the sickening sights and smells within. Cagni allowed himself no time for recuperation. The following day he covered a distance of eighteen miles, his whole arm aching unbearably – but he did not mention his discomfort to the others for, as he wrote, 'it seems to me that yesterday's operation rather upset them'.[28]

Every day they seemed to be going faster and faster. They could not believe their luck as they sped over plains of flat ice, making twelve, fifteen, twenty miles per day. On 8 May they were practically at 83°. 'What a latitude!'[29] Cagni exclaimed in delight. The *Stella Polare* was less than two degrees – 120 geographical miles – to the south. 'From this moment we feel we can live free of anxiety.'[30] Two days later, however, he crept out while the others were asleep and took his longitude. The ice had drifted further and faster than he had expected, carrying them to 50°E, eight full degrees (fifty-seven miles or so) west of Prince Rudolf Island. 'It is a very serious deviation,'[31] he wrote. But they were well up on their projected distances and if they changed course to the east he calculated it would add only a couple of days to their trip. On 12 May, having travelled at least forty miles east, Cagni again took the longitude. To his mystification, they were approximately twelve miles *west* of his last reading. Another few days would have to be tacked onto their journey. 'We are, however, about eighty miles from the island,' he consoled himself, 'and no matter how slow our progress may be, we shall reach it before the end of two weeks.'[32] On three-quarter rations they had food for twenty-three days.

The thaw which Cagni had hoped might be late had instead started early, and they often sank to their waists in wet snow, while canals of open water blocked their way with greater frequency. Yet they plugged on at a reasonable, if diminished speed, and the warm weather brought compensations. Sometimes it was so hot that they sweated just standing still, and at night they slept half-way out of the sleeping bag. Cagni's finger, too, was on the mend. Since his makeshift amputation, he had feared he would lose the whole finger from the amount of pus he drained daily from the tip. By mid-May, however, he was feeling much better. 'But,' he wrote on the 18th, 'these considerations do not greatly diminish the anxiety which is coming over me more and more every day – a terrible anxiety with regard to our fate. After marching for nine days towards the south-east, we are nearly on the same meridian.'[33] Actually, it was worse than that. From a longitude reading which Cagni snatched amidst increasingly foggy weather, they were almost at 49°E, nearly one degree closer to Greenwich than they had been on the 10th. For the last week and a half they had been on a treadmill which span faster than they could walk.

Cagni pencilled a few calculations in his journal. On two-third rations they could live another fifteen days. If they ate the dogs they could last a bit longer. But the determinant was their fuel. They had one Primus stove and one case of fuel left. Although the thaw was upon them, the melt which collected on the ice was too salty to drink without first being distilled. The fuel would last until 10 June. 'We shall struggle to the last,' he wrote on 20 May, 'and, if we must fall, we shall fall fighting. May God protect us!'[34]

On the morning of 29 May Cagni again took their longitude – 'which I pretend to find comforting'.[35] It showed that in six days they had made less than one degree east; another six degrees lay between them and Franz Josef Land. The ice was getting rougher and the leads broader, widening at times into lakes almost a mile wide, around which they had to detour. On the evening of 30 May, Cagni wrote, 'We have worked for twelve hours continuously and made an advance of 1,000 yards. If we go on at this rate, we shall not get to Teplitz Bay even by next year.'[36] The guides, who had hitherto vied to outpace each other on the ice, were nervous when it came to water. Cagni, the lagger, became Cagni the leader. When they reached a lead, he pranced over it on tiny blocks of ice. If the lead widened to a lake he repeated the trick, dragging his men behind him on the largest available floe. 'One cannot imagine how easy it is to move them,' he wrote. 'A rope of only an inch and a half in circumference can tow a rather thick piece of ice measuring as much as 200 square yards super-ficially, and forming a mass weighing, perhaps, 1,000 tons.'[37] Easy it may have been, but it was not a speedy means of travel and all the time their supplies were diminishing.

They sliced their food thinner, used their fuel less, boiling a pint and a half of water per man every twenty-four hours. If they added a bit of snow to their flasks and shook it hard they could eke out the contents for three days. On 2 June they started eating their dogs. On 3 June their saucepan burst. Not long after that their Primus stove also broke. No bears or seals were in evidence so they used dog fat to cook their meals in a patched and leaking pan. Cagni feared they would never be able to tell the world what they had done. 'Oh!' he wrote, 'we must carry and we shall carry this news to our Prince.'[38] On the 7th, however, he calculated their longitude and found it was practi-cally the same as it had been at the beginning of the month. 'In seven days of severe toil we have not advanced three feet to the east!', he cried. 'What will become of us?'[39]

As it was patently impossible to make any headway to the east, Cagni decided to abandon the struggle for Prince Rudolf Island – which was by now miles to the north-east – and head instead for Cape Flora to the south. But the Arctic was having none of it. 'We cannot go to the south,' Cagni wrote on the morning of the 9th. 'It seems as though it were done on purpose; when we wanted to go to the east the best ice was always to the south; and now that we have decided on going in that direction the state of the ice forces us to go towards the east.'[40] Back they went, therefore, to their battle with the drift. At 2.00 p.m., to their relief, they saw land. Cagni recognized it as Cape Mill, a headland they had passed in the *Stella Polare* on their way north. 'At that moment, it seemed to us as though we rose again suddenly to life,' he wrote, 'and now [we] see that we are sure of being saved!'[41] Racing forward, they battled for an hour with the ice, climbing a hummock shortly after 3.00 p.m. to get their bearings. The Arctic had another little joke in store for them.

Cape Mill had gone. Cagni was uncomprehending. He was certain he had seen it. He remembered its shape perfectly, having sketched it from the deck of the *Stella Polare*. He could not have been mistaken. But there was no land to be seen, just an expanse of broken ice that stretched off to join the sky. 'We are dismayed and terrified,' he wrote. 'Can what we have seen an hour ago have been a hallucination? It cannot be ... as Petigax suggests, a jest of the Fata Morgana. It would be too cruel and improbable a joke; neither do I wish to believe in a strong effect of refraction, which might have shown us the land still hidden below the horizon; it was too high and well defined.'[42] Whatever Cagni liked to believe or disbelieve the fact remained: Cape Mill was not there. That evening they camped amidst a heavy fall of snow and huddled morosely in the tent. Normally the evenings were a time of discussion, in which they bolstered their spirits with talk of friends and family, of the lavish meals they would eat when they returned to Italy. But this night they were silent. 'I think that in our minds the conflict between doubt and hope is so great that it paralyses our power of thinking,' Cagni wrote. 'I am so agitated that I cannot close my eyes all night.'[43]

The next day was a Sunday and their morning prayers were answered when at 10.30 a.m. they again saw Cape Mill. It was nearer than they had supposed, just twenty miles away, and before it, at a distance of fifteen miles, rose the white, tortoise-shaped hump of Harley Island. They had no explanation for the events of the previous day and they did not care. Pleading for it not to be another mirage they began to run for land.

For the next two days they ran, while the Arctic teased them with haze interspersed by flashes of sunlight. 'On the horizon, which is hidden by fog,' Cagni recorded, 'there appear and disappear continually, as in a magic lantern, the very dim outlines, sometimes of Harley Island, sometimes of Cape Mill, and of the other dark rocks which form the coast.'[44] As their goal blinked in and out of sight, the ice changed nature. Here it broke into chunks, shifting randomly from place to place, there it solidified to form a smooth, water-logged marsh through which they waded up to their hips. At last, on 13 June, they reached the solid ice surrounding Harley Island, but they did not stop there. They continued over the pack, heading north-east for nearby Ommaney Island. They could have crossed the remaining miles to Cape Mill but this would have not helped them: however rotten the ice was, they made better speed on it with their sledges than if they took to the rocky mainland. Ommaney Island was reached on 14 June. 'After ninety-five days of life on the pack, our feet touched land!'[45] Cagni wrote. He did not stay long to enjoy it. Prince Rudolf Island was roughly thirty miles away and their food was coming to an end. 'What length of time should we require in order to cover these last thirty miles?' Cagni wondered. 'It was a question of life and death.'[46] They had two sledges and twelve dogs remaining. If they ate everything on the sledges and all their dogs, they could live for two weeks at the outside. Cagni, who was not given to overstatement, wrote: 'We ran frantically.'[47]

Day after day they ran, twenty hours at a stretch, eating when they could and sleeping when it was impossible to advance. The Arctic toyed casually with its victims. It sent hummocks so hard that the Italians snapped their ice-axes trying to cross them. It broke the ice into channels that caused hours of frustrating delays. It lured them onto floes that unexpectedly floated off into open water. It blocked their vision with snowstorms and fog. Then, on 20 June, when they were camped in the middle of a wide lake on a floe measuring sixty yards in diameter, with Prince Rudolf Island just a few miles away, the Arctic played a final trick.

In a great upheaval, the pack began to move. The wind was from the south-west but the current was from the opposite direction and the current was the stronger of the two. Slowly, Cagni's ice island shifted away from Prince Rudolf Island. He tore the sails off his kayaks and planted them on the floe. Now it was the wind which was more powerful, driving them slowly back towards the shore. But then the current changed again, charging the floe landwards with vicious intensity. Cagni had seconds to get his men and dogs together. As the floe hit the shore they leapt off, scurrying for safety while the ice rippled over their tracks in a heaving mass. On 23 June, having hauled themselves and their sledges over the rocks and ice of Prince Rudolf Island, they crossed a pass and saw below them the *Stella Polare*.

Abruzzi, who had been looking to the north, was alerted by a shout from the south: 'Cagni is back!' He could not believe the state they were in. 'The seven dogs which survived . . . were merely skin and bone. The only part of their outfit they had brought back that was still capable of being of any use was their tent, and this had been mended. The framework of the kayaks had been broken and their canvas torn . . . The sledges which remained had been mended with pieces of other sledges. All that was left of their cooking utensils was the outer covering of the stove, a saucepan which had been mended, and their plates. The Primus lamp had been replaced by a pot, in which dog's grease had been burned for the last few weeks. The sleeping bag had been thrown away, and only the thick canvas lining kept. Their clothes were in rags.'[48]

Dr Cavalli was the first man to greet the survivors, running across the snow to shake their hands as they descended the glacier above Teplitz Bay. 'He is there at the head of his men and waving his cap like them, and crying out, "Hurrah! Hurrah! Hurrah!" Cagni wrote. 'A few minutes later we are in each other's arms. I clasp the hands of the men [one of whom] says to me: "Do you know Querini has not come back?" I look at Cavalli as though stupefied; he bows down his head.'[49]

Never, while marching north, or on his retreat south, had Cagni worried about the fate of his support teams. All they had had to do was go home, which should have been a straightforward and risk-free task:

the ice was good, as was the weather, and the track was easy to follow. The second detachment, under Cavalli, had come back with no problems. But the first, under Querini, had vanished. Nobody knew what had happened to him. Maybe he had lost his way with the westward drift and might still be alive somewhere on the ice. Maybe he had reached land and was lingering on an outpost of Franz Josef Land. Or maybe an ice floe had broken beneath him, tipping his party into the sea. Despite repeated searches, the men at Teplitz Bay had found no trace of Querini and his two companions. Their fate, to this day, remains unknown.

Abruzzi decided it was pointless staying on Prince Rudolf Island for a second year. Querini was not going to come back. And to send another sledge expedition to the Pole would have been futile. He was of the firm opinion that Franz Josef Land was finished as far as the Pole was concerned. It was too far away, the drift was too treacherous and the ice was too thick. The proper spot was Greenland, where a ship could penetrate farther north and where, if a sledge team was driven south by the drift, it could be certain of hitting land. He himself would not be going there, but he looked forward with almost vengeful anticipation to another man doing so. 'May the day at least not be far off when the mystery of the Arctic regions shall be revealed, and the names of those who have sacrificed their lives to it shine with still greater glory – the day when a small band of men, subduing these inhospitable and repellent lands, shall avenge all the past sacrifices and the lives so sadly lost in this obstinate struggle, which has lasted for centuries.'[50]

That August he laid seventy mines of gun-cotton and gunpowder in the seventeen-foot-thick ice surrounding his ship – and on the shore, too – and literally blew the *Stella Polare* out of Teplitz Bay. On 6 September 1900 they were back in Tromsø where Abruzzi began the lengthy but enjoyable task of telegraphing the world. His first concern was for his cousin, the King of Italy, to whom he sent two long telegrams couched in courtly terms, describing the expedition's achievements and its sufferings and begging His Majesty to accept their homage etc. To Nansen he sent a shorter and less expensive message: 'STELLA POLARE ARRIVED ... EXPEDITION REACHED EIGHTY SIX THIRTY THREE'.[51]

The hero of the polar pack received the news with philosophical gloom. 'Is it the struggle towards the goals which makes mankind happy?' he wrote in his diary. 'What is the value of having goals for their own sake? ... they all vanish ... It is merely a question of time.'[52]

19

FARTHEST NORTH

14 November 1902. 'My dear, dear Father,' began Marie Ahnighito Peary's letter. 'Of course I know the papers are not always right, but I read that the Peary Arctic Club are trying to get your consent to go north again. I think it is a dogs [sic] shame and wish every member of the Club were dead then you would not have to go in the first place. I know you will do what pleases Mother and me and that is to stay with us at home. I have been looking at your pictures it seems ten years and I am sick of looking at them. I want to see my father. I don't want people to think me an orphan. Please think this over.'[1]

Peary had thought it over. On the date of his daughter's letter he was already limbering up for another polar expedition. After his latest defeat he had been willing to give up the game, certain that nobody could go further on foot than he, but Abruzzi's success now forced him back to the Arctic. It was galling that he should be forestalled and more so that this perceived insult be displayed to the public in Abruzzi's glossy-papered, two-volumed, very exciting journal which contained hardly a mention of Peary.

'We have conquered! We have surpassed the greatest explorer of the century!'[2] Abruzzi's men had cried. They referred to Nansen not

Peary. When Abruzzi wrote a condensed account of his journal for the British market it was entitled *Farther North Than Nansen*, not 'Farther North Than Peary'. Not only had Peary been beaten to a farthest north but in the eyes of many he was not even part of the race. When he had returned to the States after his prolonged and uncomfortable spell in Greenland, he was greeted by the *New York Times* with the laconic headline, 'Peary Failed To Reach The Pole'.[3] Failure on the ice was something Peary could accept, albeit grudgingly. To be ignored, however, was unbearable. If he had thought of giving it all up, he now changed his mind. 'Next time I'll smash all that to bits,' he said to Henson. 'Next time!'[4]

He launched an immediate propaganda campaign, consisting of lectures and articles designed to boost his achievements in Greenland and to raise money for another expedition. 'The gain to the world by the results of my work in the Arctic regions are of far more value than if I had discovered the Pole,' he told *The World* newspaper. 'The full result of my labors cannot be fully ascertained or even imagined until the observations I have taken have been worked out by scientists . . . the work I have done, I am vain enough to think, is great.'[5] This, from a man whose scientific attainments were virtually non-existent, was an exaggeration. He conceded as much a few months later when he wrote to Henry Bryant, President of the Philadelphia Academy of Sciences: 'You and I are no longer chickens, and we both know that no man would give a few facts of so-called scientific information the slightest weight, if balanced against the Pole.'[6] Peary, a supreme publicist, knew that a column of newsprint was worth a thousand facts. The applause began to swell. Peary collected another three gold medals, was promoted from Lieutenant to Commander, was elected President of the American Geographical Society and was lauded by Beaumont – now Admiral Sir Lewis Beaumont – who had served under Nares and who, in a speech to the Royal Geographical Society, said that Peary had achieved more than anybody before him.

But Beaumont's praise cut two ways. The aspect of Peary's journey which he most admired was that he had started 400 miles farther south than his predecessors via Smith Sound, yet had still managed to sledge farther north. In true British fashion, when Beaumont praised Peary's achievement he was referring to physical achievement, just as when Amundsen reached the South Pole the British public would idolize his competitor Scott for his toughness in coming second. Toughness, although admirable, was not all. Scott would lose his life thanks to poor methodology and an obsessive desire to succeed. Peary had lost his toes for similar reasons: starting with a 400-mile disadvantage was not entirely wise; neither was travelling in winter to Fort Conger to beat imaginary competition particularly level-headed.

Trickles of anti-Peary sentiment seeped into the press. In James Gordon Bennett's *Herald*, Dr Dedrick revealed several unsavoury details of the Greenland expedition: Peary had refused to pay him his salary, had threatened to leave him behind and had branded him insane. He wrote of 'Mr Peary's almost inhuman treatment of me without provocation during the last year.'[7] He threatened to write other things too, but that, as he said, 'would entail a long, and to me, shameful story'.[8] Watchful eyes also noticed that when Sverdrup's hugely successful expedition returned from the Arctic, having discovered among other things Axel Heiberg Island, to the west of Ellesmere Island, Peary altered his story to indicate that he might have discovered it too. He said he had seen something which he called Jesup Island and which was probably Sverdrup's Axel Heiberg Island. Peary made no mention either of Peary Channel or Peary Land, two features which he had described very precisely on his first journey to Greenland.

The whiff of misconduct, personal or professional, was disheartening. More so was Beaumont's well-meant implication that Peary had been incompetent. What distressed Peary most, however, was the growing impression that he was attacking the Pole in the wrong manner and from the wrong direction. He had got nowhere, at great cost, with his Smith Sound explorations – nowhere, that was, when compared to Nansen and Abruzzi on the ice above Franz Josef Land. Might he not be better advised to drift in a ship like the *Fram*, and follow the route which had proved so successful for the Norwegians and Italians? The rot spread to the Peary Arctic Club, one of whose members wrote, 'Having lost faith and hope, we are in a mood of masterly inactivity, if not actually moribund. Peary's experience has definitely taught him that . . . Greenland as a route and Etah as a base must be abandoned.'[9] They had misjudged their man, as Peary was quick to tell them. A drift, he wrote, 'is in no way suited to a man of my temperament who can endure almost anything so long as he feels that his own exertions will have some bearing upon the final result; but who would fret himself to death if he were a helpless piece of flotsam'.[10] He was quick, too, to damn Abruzzi's success, 'which missed by a hair's breadth being a complete catastrophe . . . Further I believe Abruzzi's accomplishment marks the limit by that route'.[11] Ironically Abruzzi agreed with him, devoting a whole chapter of his journal to an explanation as to why Greenland was the best way forward. But Abruzzi was read by few, whereas Peary was heard by many.

In his lectures, Peary had emphasized the difficulties he had overcome, hoping thereby to prove his capacity to defeat the Arctic. The plan misfired, and the more he spoke of the terrors, the more his would-be sponsors shrank from sending him back to face them. Henry Bryant, who favoured the drift approach, and whom Peary had approached for funds, was not appeased by his arguments. 'After hearing you lecture and reading your article,' Bryant wrote, 'I am more than ever impressed with the almost insuperable obstacles to be overcome [via Smith Sound] . . . To put the matter briefly in my humble opinion, the chances of success are not promising even under your experienced and resolute leadership.'[12]

Bryant's letter was typical of hundreds. For an uncomfortable few months Peary despaired. The Pole had become his career, his life, his dream. He had travelled further over the ice than anyone else (discounting, possibly, McClintock during the Franklin search), he had developed the so-called 'Peary System', had perfected the use of Eskimo survival techniques and had spent more than a decade in the Arctic. He was an explorer, but the Navy was waiting. If nobody believed in him, he would have to spend the rest of his days in mundane naval service. Luckily, Senator Morris Ketcham Jesup still believed in him and still had the ear of President Roosevelt. On 5

September 1903, Peary received orders from the Secretary of the Navy which not only gave him paid leave but instructed him to seek the Pole. 'The attainment of the North Pole should be your main object,' the Secretary wrote. 'The discovery of the poles is all that remains to complete the map of the world . . . Our national pride is involved in this undertaking, and this department expects that you will accomplish your purpose and bring further distinction to a service of illustrious traditions.'[13]

Before he went anywhere, Peary had to raise money and have his feet fixed. In their present painful condition they would have been a crippling disability on any protracted journey across the ice. Under the scalpel of a prominent New York surgeon, therefore, the remaining two little toes were shortened, and the front of the foot was slit open so that the pad could be brought forward to cushion the stubs of the others. When the operation was finished, Peary possessed two fully functioning feet, but was left with a strange, skating gait which became familiar to the inhabitants of New York and Washington as he slid through the streets, knocking at door after influential door in search of funds. Jesup gave a mighty $50,000, George Crocker, a railway magnate, donated an equal sum and General Thomas Hubbard of the National Geographic Society stumped up $20,000. The remainder came from Peary's own pocket, and from mortgages that, if called in, would have left him bankrupt. With this money, he launched a polar expedition that combined elements both of Nansen's and his own previous expeditions.

One hundred thousand dollars went into the construction of the *Roosevelt*, a ship whose design owed much to that of the *Fram*. In cross section it was egg-shaped, its thirty-inch-thick sides connected by a maze of crossbeams which would keep a nip at bay long enough for the ship to rise out of the ice. As befitted the man who would command it, the *Roosevelt* was built to attack as well as to survive. Its bow was flared like an inverted snow-plough for cutting through floes, and it was driven by hefty 1,000-horsepower engines connected to oversize propellers. Using this prototype ice-breaker, Peary planned to batter his way through Smith Sound to the top of Greenland, collecting Eskimo families as he went. When the *Roosevelt* was snugly iced in, he then intended to sledge and walk north with Henson, deploying his Eskimos according to the Peary System, until he reached the Pole.

The rest of his money was spent on the twelve-strong company who would work the *Roosevelt* and, in the case of Professor Ross Marvin, take whatever scientific observations were required. The ship was commanded by Robert Bartlett from Peary's previous expedition. A mere thirty years old, Bartlett was an experienced ice-master with a physique so powerful and a temper so colourful that when he shouted – as he often did – drops of sweat evaporated visibly on his neck. He had taken the job on Peary's explicit promise that he would be among the team to reach the Pole, but other than Bartlett Peary intended taking no white men with him to the Pole. As he had learned from experience, they had contrary opinions, minds of their own and an uncomfortable access to the press.

The *Roosevelt* left Manhattan's West Side piers on a sizzling Sunday, 16 July 1905. A month later, the ship was at the gates of Smith Sound, taking on Eskimos who were so eager to enlist that all Peary had to do was sound his horn and whole communities flocked to the water's edge. When the *Roosevelt* left Etah on 16 August it was packed to the brim. 'Below decks,' Peary wrote, 'the ship was filled with coal until her plank sheer was nearly to the water; on deck were more than two hundred Eskimo dogs; and on the top gallant forecastle, and the tops of both forward and after deck houses were over half a hundred Eskimos, men, women and children and their belongings.'[14] The Eskimos knew what they were meant to do: the men were to help Piulersuaq (Peary's Eskimo name) on his journey; the women were to prepare clothes for Piulersuaq and his companions. They knew that they were to be paid in valuable currency: guns, axes, knives, mirrors, beads and other items of cheap hardware which Peary had purchased in bulk. And they knew that Piulersuaq was seeking something at the top of the world. But they were not entirely sure what it was that he sought – clearly, though, it was something useful and something metal, otherwise Piulersuaq would not be so desperate to find it. (Had he not been so eager to take their meteorites?) In Europe and America, jokes about the Pole had become commonplace. Was there a pole at the Pole? Was it made of wood? Was it a thick pole or a thin pole like hop-growers used? Was it striped like a barber's pole? Every variety of pole had been played out in the pages of *Punch* and other humorous magazines. Unconsciously, the Eskimos used the same imagery but applied their own values. They called it the 'Great Nail'.

A fire had damaged the *Roosevelt*'s boilers, cutting its power by half, but still the ice-breaker managed to hammer its way through Smith Sound. Bartlett later said that every day seemed likely to be his last, but Peary loved it. 'In all my experience,' he wrote, 'I recall nothing more exciting than the thrill, the shock of hurling the *Roosevelt*, a fifteen-hundred ton battering-ram, at the ice to smash a way through, or the tension of the moment when, caught in the grip of two resistless ice-fields, I have stood on the bridge and seen the deck amidships slowly bulge upward, and the rigging slacken with the compression of the sides.'[15] The ship vibrated like a violin string as the floes squeezed it, but the designers had done their work well and always it rose up safely. 'Ah, the thrill and tension of it,' Peary wrote, 'the lust of battle, which crowded days of ordinary life into one.'[16] He relished the sewing-machine sound of the big engines down aft, the whirr of the twelve-inch steel shafts and the thrashing of the wide-bladed propellers. He described almost in ecstasy the grating snarl of the ice as the ship's steel-shod bow flung it aside in whirling fragments. This was power and he revelled in it. Their progress, he said, 'was no more to be denied than the force of gravity'.[17]

Winter commenced on 1 September, 'with snow driving in horizontal sheets across the deck, the water like ink, the ice ghastly white, and the land invisible except close to us as we almost scrape against it on the port side'.[18] Four days later, spewing plumes of black smoke, the *Roosevelt* arrived at Cape Sheridan, about two miles north of Nares's 1875 anchorage, and here, with its bows facing the Pole, it came to rest. 'I do not believe there is another ship afloat that would have survived the ordeal,'[19] Peary wrote in self-admiration, ignoring the Nares expedition entirely. Unlike Nares, whose journal – along with those of his Lieutenants – was inward-looking and dwelled on difficulties rather than potential, Peary captured the sensation of standing at the outer limits of the globe, of staring into the unknown, Half-fearful, half-excited, he wrote: 'The northern-reaching fingers of all the rest of the great world lay far behind us below the ice-bound southern horizon. We were deep in that gaunt frozen border land which lies between God's countries and inter-stellar space.'[20]

In February 1906, his Eskimos having slaughtered herds of musk-oxen, Peary began his advance towards the Great Nail. Teams of men were sent to Point Moss, one of the northernmost headlands which Nares's men had mapped on Ellesmere Island, from where they were to deposit food depots on the pack at intervals of fifty miles. The Arctic night was still upon them, and they sledged to and fro in a depressing gloom. But when Peary arrived at Point Moss on 5 March, the moon was shining brightly and the landscape was brilliantly monochrome. This was a good omen. Equally good was the fact that the Pole was less than 500 miles away. On his last expedition Peary had covered more than that distance across Greenland. 'If I can do as well this time we shall win,' he wrote. 'God and all good angels grant it, and let me seize this trophy for the Flag.'[21]

At its conception, the 'Peary System' had relied on small numbers. This time Peary took a vast team, every member of which would be needed. Shortly after his start, on 6 March, with Henson leading and Peary agitating from the rear, twenty-eight men and 120 dogs were working back and forth across the ice. Mile by mile the leaders hacked through obstructions while the support groups shuttled supplies over the ice. On 26 March, Henson reached what would be known as the 'Big Lead', a strip of open water, in places two miles wide, which marked the separation of Greenland's continental shelf from deeper waters, and which became their major landmark in an otherwise featureless waste. Here, 124 miles from Point Moss, Peary took his first longitude reading (until now he had had no real idea where he was) and discovered the ice had carried him eighty miles west. To this infuriating realization was added the frustration of being unable to cross the Big Lead. They waited at its edge for a precious

week until the temperature suddenly dropped, a film of ice materialized, and they were on their way again.

Three days later, however, Peary, Henson and six Eskimos ran into
a blizzard that pinned them down for yet another week. In his desperation, Peary paced back and forth across the ice for three hours
every day. When the wind was too strong for him to walk, he crawled.
He knew by now that he would never the reach the Pole – at his current speed of six or seven miles per day it would take him two months
just to get there, let alone get back. The only prize he had a chance of
claiming was that of farthest north. On 13 April, when the weather
cleared, he dropped all unnecessary baggage and ran with his team for
the record. Run they must have, if Peary's journal was to be believed.
In the next two days, despite having to cross eleven leads, he claimed
they made sixty miles. On 21 April, after an average daily northing of
nineteen miles – three times their previous speed, without taking into
account the drift which, in its arbitrary manner had now carried them
five degrees to the east – they stood at 87°06′N, thirty-six miles farther
than Cagni. Peary did not bother to camp, but turned back at once. 'As
I looked at the drawn faces of my comrades,' he wrote, 'at the skeleton
figures of my few remaining dogs, at my nearly empty sledge . . . I felt
I had cut the margin as narrow as could reasonably be expected.'[22]

Everything about this final rally was mysterious. How had they
managed, at one point, on bad ice, to cover what must have been,
including detours, thirty miles a day, a distance that had eluded both
Cagni and Nansen? Had they really passed 87°? Peary offered no calculations, no explanations, just his word that this was the latitude he
had read. He took no longitude with which he might have pinpointed
his position. Nor were there any trained observers to support him, as
Bartlett, contrary to their agreement, had been left behind. Peary's
journal and diaries, which had never been precise, became even
vaguer on his return journey.

He chose not to follow his outward route but to slice straight down
the 50th meridian towards Greenland, along whose game-rich coasts
he could then cut back to Cape Sheridan at his leisure. And this,
apparently, he did. The ice was in constant motion, breaking behind

them as they rushed south. But the winds and currents which broke it seemed to have no effect on Peary's course, which continued to be due south. At the Big Lead they were lucky to find a bridge of fragile ice blocks over which they scrambled speedily. But two days later, they met a *second* Big Lead, half a mile across and stretching east and west as far as the eye could see. They camped beside it, roasting their dogs on fires fed by redundant sledges and waiting, hoping, for the lead to close. Instead of closing, however, it opened wider. At an unrecorded date, fortunately, the temperature sank low enough to cover it with a skin of ice. They were uncertain if it would bear their weight but with summer approaching they had to cross. If they did not, they would drift east until the ice melted and they fell into the sea. Peary was now in a dilemma similar to that faced by Cagni and Nansen. Abruzzi's supposition that Greenland was large enough to catch off-course parties was mistaken.

Where or when Peary made his crossing is unknown. That he did make it, however, is indisputable. According to polar experts, his journal is too explicit to doubt. 'Once started, we could not stop, we could not lift our snowshoes,' he wrote. 'It was a matter of constantly and smoothly gliding one past the other with utmost care and evenness of pressure, and from every man as he slid a snowshoe forward, undulations went out in every direction through the thin film incrusting the black water. The sledge was preceded and followed by a broad swell. It was the first and only time in my Arctic work that I felt doubtful as to the outcome, but when near the middle of the lead the toe of my rear kamik [boot] as I slid forward from it broke through twice in succession I thought to myself, "this is the finish," and when a little while later there was a cry from someone in the line, the words sprang from me of themselves: "God help him, which one is it?" but I dared not take my eyes from the steady, even gliding of my snow-shoes, and the fascination of the glossy swell at the toes of them.'[23] Silently, the lead opened behind them.

Their next leg took them across a jumble of hillocks – 'a hell of shattered ice as I have never seen before and hope never to see again'[24] – which occupied the 113 miles between their current position and the coast of Greenland. 'It did not seem as if anything not possessing wings could negotiate it,' Peary wrote. He did get across it, according to his journal, still heading directly south, and his feet hurting so badly that he ground his teeth until his jaw ached. On 9 July, close to the shores of Greenland, they met one of their support teams headed by Fireman Charles Clark of the *Roosevelt*. Clark and his three men had sledged north from Point Moss but had turned back at the Big Lead and had lost their way in the same storm which had delayed Peary for a week. Since then they had travelled southwards across the ice, hoping to hit land before the drift spilled them into the ocean. They were at the end of their resources, being on the point of burning their last sledge to cook their remaining dogs. If Peary had not stumbled across them and then, with his knowledge of the region, guided them to places where game was to be found on the Greenland coast, they would certainly have died. Peary now had twelve men to look after, which he did with consummate skill, leading them down the coast until they crossed the frozen sea and arrived at the *Roosevelt*, every one of them alive.

For Clark it was an incredibly lucky meeting. Later, however, Peary's critics would claim it was more incredible than lucky. Apart from the coincidence of the two parties crossing tracks, how was it possible for Clark and Peary to have arrived at the same position on the same date? The figures did not add up. Clark had been travelling south from the Big Lead, since 26 March. Within the same period Peary had run ostensibly to 87°06'N and back again, over ice no easier and perhaps worse than that faced by Clark, had then walked over the same ice as Clark, yet had still managed to catch up with him. Either Clark had moved at a snail's pace or Peary had travelled with super-human speed – neither was impossible, though neither was likely. Or maybe Peary had not gone as far north as he claimed.

Polar experts have since come to several conclusions, the most charitable being that Peary might have bested Cagni by a few miles but was compelled to exaggerate the distance so that in placing himself safely above 87°N he would not have to face an inquiry in which Cagni's firm readings were set against his own incomplete and very hazy ones. Less complimentary is the judgement that Peary never went north at all after the Big Lead, but just drifted east and then recrossed it to continue south at the same time as Clark, inventing everything else. Every Peary expedition had involved questions. Did Peary Land or Peary Channel exist? Was Jesup Land real, and was it Axel Heiberg Island or not? Now there was another uncertainty.

Had Peary truly reached a farthest north he should have been happy to go home. But on 2 June, a week after his return to the *Roosevelt*, he was back on the ice, wearing a pair of tin-soled shoes, to conduct an exploration of Ellesmere Island's northern coast, accompanied by two Eskimos. By Peary's standards this valuable work was irrelevant and unproductive. But he needed to bring his sponsors a tangible prize, a piece of land which bore their name, so he scrabbled for the crumbs which Aldrich and Sverdrup had left on the table. He reached Aldrich's farthest west on 16 June and managed to discover enough inlets and capes before he hit Cape Colgate, just above Axel Heiberg Island, to satisfy his requirements. The way in which he did it carried his usual stamp. On 16 June he wrote, 'What I saw before me in all its splendid, sunlit savageness was *mine*, mine by the right of discovery, to be credited to me, and associated with my name, generations after I ceased to be.'[25] And when he named features of the terrain after his sponsors he couldn't help throwing in a bit of mystery. On 26 June, from Cape Colgate, he reported seeing, 'snow clad summits of [a] distant land in the northwest, above the ice horizon. My heart leaped the intervening miles of ice, as I looked longingly at this land, and in fancy I trod its shores and climbed its summits.'[26] He called it Crocker Land, after one of his more influential supporters.

But Crocker Land did not exist, as an expedition discovered in 1914 when it went out for the very purpose of exploring it. Had Peary been misled by a trick of Arctic refraction? Such things were not unknown. In 1818, the British explorer John Ross had seen a range of mountains blocking the entrance to Lancaster Sound which he had called – by strange coincidence – Croker Mountains. They were no more than a play of the light but they appeared so solid that Ross staked his career and reputation on their existence. Had the same thing happened to Peary? Or was there a more sinister explanation, that he had invented Crocker Land to please his sponsor and to add extra lustre to the expedition? The discovery of Crocker Land was made public in his account of the trip, *Nearest the Pole*, which was published in 1907. But in his diary for the 26 June, and in the three messages he placed subsequently in cairns along the coast, there is no mention of such an island. The nearest he came to describing the view north was when he wrote of the 27th and 28th, 'fine clear days giving a good view of the northern horizon'.[27] He said nothing of Crocker Land to Bartlett, Henson or any other person aboard the *Roosevelt*. He did not offer a speck of scientific evidence to locate its position – and none was ever asked for. All one can say for certain of Crocker Land, and all Peary's other geographical ultimates, is that they accorded with his perception of reality and that maybe his quest had become more real to him than the landscape in which he played it out. He had often said that the Arctic was *his* world. And so it was.

The 300-mile journey back to the *Roosevelt* was horrible. The summer was upon them and their trail took them through a 'devil-inspired labyrinth of lakes and rivers set in a morass of knee-deep slush'.[28] Peary's furs were sodden and stinking; his clothes were rotting on his body; his tin soles were worn thin and broken; and his feet 'were hot, aching, and throbbing, till the pain reached to my knees'.[29] He and his companions pick-axed a road along which they shoved, dragged, hoisted and lowered their sledges with such difficulty that Peary sent one of the Eskimos ahead to ask Bartlett for men to help them complete the last miles. The men returned, but they came with unwelcome news: the *Roosevelt* had broken free of the ice and was now twenty miles further south in a bad condition. The rudder was broken, two of the four propeller blades had snapped off and the ice had punched holes in the hull, one of them below the waterline and so large that, according to Bartlett, a boy could almost have crawled through it. When Peary reached the *Roosevelt* and saw the damage, his response was straightforward: 'We have got to get her back, Captain. We are going to come again next year.'[30]

The ship was 'a complete wreck', as Bartlett wrote in his log.

Nevertheless, they rigged up a temporary rudder and repaired the holes with a mixture of oakum, rags and cement, before steaming south with the pumps working around the clock. Bartlett directed affairs with superb seamanship, but even he thought they were doomed. 'I used to go on deck and decide that we would sink in a few minutes and then go down and make a last entry in my diary,' he wrote. 'Then I'd come up again and we'd still be afloat and I'd try to explain how it was possible for a wreck like ours not to sink . . . All the time the jury rudder we had rigged was being punished worse and worse and the bottom was getting more holes punched in it. Most of our men had given up hope long ago. Only Peary was at all optimistic.'[31]

They beached at Etah on 16 September and added more patches to the *Roosevelt*'s disintegrating hull, packing the new gashes and nailing canvas over them. Their coal was running out, their food was low and winter was not far off. All Bartlett's instincts told him that they should run south as soon as the ship was afloat. But Peary had promised his Eskimos that when the expedition was over he would provide them with walrus meat and then land them at whatever place they desired, even though he knew that any delay would worsen the long and stormy journey ahead. Bartlett was humbled: '[He] had given his word and he never broke it, so the thing was done. It is no wonder these people loved and respected Peary. No other man in the past or future can or will get these people to do what he did.'[32]

The *Roosevelt* left Etah on 26 September in the darkness of a snowstorm. Peary, still in his own world, chatted cheerfully about plans for the future, while Bartlett battled to keep the ship going in what has been described as 'one of the classic tales of the sea'. The stokers swept the bunkers for the last shovelfuls of coal dust and then started on the interior bracing, cutting down beams and feeding them into the furnaces. When the beams were finished they went ashore and collected blubber, green timber and coal which they dynamited from frozen caches left by previous expeditions. They were attacked by the ice and hampered by gales. They lost the *Roosevelt*'s main anchor, its rudder and most of its cables. By the time they entered the safety of southern waters, and tried to make their way into St Peter's Canal, on Cape Breton Island, the ship was unworkable. The most powerful vessel to have gone north swung this way and that, then ran headlong into a mudflat, reared over a fence and poked its nose into a field where a girl was milking a cow. The milkmaid fled in terror and the cow galumphed after her. As Bartlett said, 'The poor old *Roosevelt*, as well as ourselves, was ready for the insane asylum or the dump heap.'[33]

20

1909

'I t would be useless to deny that I am disappointed that Commander Peary failed to reach the Pole.'[1] When Morris Ketcham Jesup said those words to the *Washington Post* on 3 November 1906, he spoke for the nation. Peary had promised he would reach the Pole and had returned instead with a farthest north and a sighting of Crocker Land, neither of which were what was wanted. The National Geographic Society awarded him another Gold Medal and was dutiful in its praise. President Roosevelt congratulated him in person and secured him yet another three years' leave in which to finish the job. But this time Peary had to battle to raise money for his next expedition. However he dressed up his story he had not delivered the goods and people had become tired of him, as became evident when Peary's *Nearest the Pole* appeared in the bookstores. He had expected to make $100,000 from it, but he did not even cover his advance of $5,000: it sold only 2,230 copies. Nor did Peary have much luck when he and Bartlett toured the country on a by-now familiar lecture tour. 'I was rebuffed, laughed at, offered jobs, sympathized with and in a hundred ways resisted,'[2] Bartlett wrote.

Peary played every card he could. The Pole must be captured, 'for the honor and credit of this country',[3] he told the National Geographic Society. He repeated the message to the *New York Times*: 'the attainment of the Pole spells national prestige'.[4] He portrayed the Pole (untruthfully) as 'the last great geographical prize which the world has to offer adventurous men'.[5] But still the response remained lukewarm. 'It was a glorious fight but we failed,'[6] Bartlett recorded philosophically. In 1907 he left Peary to struggle on, and departed for Newfoundland to drum up a bit of money from sealing. There he was wrecked, losing his ship and all profits.

So disappointing was the reaction to Peary's proposed expedition that 'Symmes's Hole' made a comeback with the publication in 1906 of William Reed's *The Phantom of the Poles*. According to Reed the interior had a climate similar to that of San Francisco, contained 'vast continents, oceans, mountains and rivers' and was 'peopled by races yet unknown to the dwellers upon the earth's exterior'.[7] The aurora borealis, he said, was caused by forest fires burning in the interior. Reed was almost as anxious as Peary for the Pole to be reached (but for different reasons) and offered all would-be explorers the following advice: 'As soon as you adopt the belief that the earth is hollow, perplexing questions will be easily solved, the mind will be satisfied, and the triumph of sensible reasoning will come as a delight never to be forgotten.'[8]

Peary was not comforted by Reed's words. He had spread the cloth for a banquet but nobody was interested in joining him; and as he sat alone at the table, a ghost rose from behind his chair. Of the six Eskimos he had brought from the Arctic in 1897, the youngest survivor was a boy called Minik. It was Minik's father who had been put through the macerator and whose bones had been bleached for display in New York's Museum of Natural History. Minik had been only six when it happened, and since then he had been adopted by a man named Wallace, one of the museum's employees. All had gone well, and Minik had been accepted and indeed loved by the Wallace family. Jesup contributed to his upkeep, Minik took the additional names of Peary Wallace, forgot his own language and was set to join the American melting-pot – but he had never, by tacit agreement, been told what had happened to his father. In 1901, however, Wallace was caught embezzling money, upon which Jesup forced him to resign and cut off the allowance. Wallace, his life ruined, waited patiently to take revenge on Jesup, Peary and the whole Arctic fraternity. When Peary hit the campaign trail, Wallace struck.

'GIVE ME MY FATHER'S BODY,'[9] read the *World*'s headline on 6 January 1907. Its front page was covered with illustrations of a fur-clad Minik kneeling before the Museum, his arms outstretched beseechingly. Columns of weeping prose told 'The Pathetic Story of Minik, the Esquimau Boy, Who is Growing Up in New York, and Is Going to Find the North Pole Some Day, but Who Now Wants Most the Bones of his Father.'[10] Minik did not want to go to the Pole, but he was understandably upset by the revelation that he had attended the funeral of a log and that his father's remains were now on public display. The *San Francisco Examiner* later ran an article suggesting that Minik wanted to shoot Peary. 'I can never forgive Peary,' he was quoted as saying, 'and I hope to see him, to show the wreck he has caused.'[11] The Peary Arctic Club organized a swift repatriation for Minik, but he railed against them even as he left for the Arctic. 'You're a race of scientific criminals,' he said. 'I know I'll never get my father's bones out of the American Museum of Natural History. I am glad enough to get away before they grab my brains and stuff them into a jar! . . . You Americans will never discover the North Pole.'[12]

Onto this lugubrious scene sauntered Dr Frederick Cook, snuffing Peary's candles with a fresh pall of misery. In recent years Cook had emerged as an ice-man of stature: in the 1890s he had led a couple of expeditions to Greenland; and in 1898–9 he had taken part in a Belgian expedition to the Antarctic aboard the *Belgica*, with Roald Amundsen as first mate, during which he had made a name for himself by his professionalism, his experience and his cheerfulness. Against their will and the captain's orders, he persuaded the crew to eat raw meat, and in doing so ensured that this first wintering in the southern ice did not result in wholesale death from scurvy. When the *Belgica* was trapped for weeks in the ice it was Cook's cheerfulness that maintained morale and his advice that secured their release.

Amundsen wrote that the *Belgica*'s escape was 'due first and foremost to the skill, energy and persistence of Dr. Cook'.[13] Later, he described Cook as 'a man of unfaltering courage, unfailing hope, endless cheerfulness, and unwearied kindness . . . his ingenuity and enterprise were boundless.'[14] The Royal Geographical Society of Belgium awarded Cook a Gold Medal and King Leopold II was so impressed that he took time from counting his Congo profits to confer a knighthood on him. Cook's reputation blossomed. The Peary Arctic Club wrote glowingly of him and showed its appreciation of his abilities by sending him north in 1901 to administer to Peary's stalled Greenland expedition. In 1906, when a team set off to conquer North America's highest mountain, Mount McKinley in Alaska, it was the sleepy-eyed Dr Cook who first set foot on the 20,320-foot summit. His account of the climb was a bestseller, flying off the shelves faster than bookshop assistants could shove Peary's journal aside to make room for it.

In July 1907, Cook left for Etah with a wealthy sponsor named John R. Bradley. Ostensibly it was a game-hunting expedition, for narwhal horns, walrus ivory, seal hide and bear pelts, but Cook took a suspiciously large quantity of supplies. Rumour said that he was trying for the Pole. At the time, Peary rejected this as a slur. 'Cook is an honourable man,'[15] he told a fellow explorer, Vilhjalmur Steffanson. Yet that autumn, just after Peary had announced he would not be able to take the *Roosevelt* north until 1908, due to lack of funds and the huge amount of work needed to repair the ship, Bradley came back with a message from Cook. 'I have hit upon a new route to the north pole and will stay to try it. By way of . . . Ellesmere and northward . . . over the Polar Sea seems to me a very good route. There will be game to the 82d degree, and here are natives and dogs for the task. So here is for the pole.'[16]

Peary's polar construct fell apart. *His* world was being invaded by another man, who was planning to use *his* Eskimos, whom *he* had trained, over a route that *he* had pioneered. That neither the Arctic nor its inhabitants were actually his was irrelevant. Cook was poaching, clear and simple. On investigation, Peary heard that Cook might have falsified his conquest of Mount McKinley, posing for photographs on a similar-looking foothill. There was no evidence, but Cook's companions were adamant that he could not have reached the top. Handily, Cook was not there to rebut the accusation. In his absence, gossip was spread that Cook was now going to fake the North Pole just as he had done McKinley. When a friend warned him of it, Peary said, 'Oh no, I do not believe Cook would do that.'[17] Cook may have been a rival but he was not an impostor. He had performed well on the 1891–2 Greenland expedition with Peary, as Peary himself had admitted, and although the two men had their differences, Cook's polar expertise was unimpeachable.

Nevertheless, something had to be done. Peary sent a letter to the National Geographic Society, lambasting not Cook but Bradley, a man who had a dubious past and was known in New York as 'Gambler Jim'. 'I have been informed,' Peary wrote, 'that he was at one time a card sharp on the Mississippi River until turned out. It is a well-known fact that he is the owner of a gambling hell in Palm Beach, in which I am told women, as well as men gamble.'[18] Cook's expedition, he said, should receive 'the distinct dis-approval of all reputable Geographic and scientific organizations and individuals'.[19] Then he attacked Cook too. 'Dr. Cook's action in going north . . . for the admitted purpose of forestalling me [is] one of which no man possessing a sense of honour would be guilty,'[20] he told the *New York Times*. He insisted to the Explorer's Club that he would not accept the offer of its Presidency unless they promised to investigate Cook's proof that he had reached the Pole – if indeed he did reach it.

The one good thing which Cook did for Peary was to awaken interest in the Pole. Jesup died in January 1908 but his wife gave Peary $5,000, and the wealthier members of the Peary Arctic Club donated larger sums. Peary started a fresh fund-raising spree, targeting businesses this time and emphasizing the commercial benefits of sponsorship. While Peary waited for the money to trickle in – which it did, slowly but surely – he was importuned by a small flood of crank letters, 'simply oozing with inventions and schemes'.[21] Flying machines were popular, as were automobiles guaranteed to run over the roughest ice. One man was sure a submarine would do the trick, although he was less sure how it would emerge through the pack having once gone beneath it. A manufacturer of portable sawmills offered to sell Peary his latest model which, when set up on Greenland, would produce enough planks to build a covered tunnel to the Pole. Another man said the sawmill was nonsense and that in its place Peary should erect a central kitchen from which soup could be pumped through hoses to invigorate parties on the ice. The suggestion Peary liked best, however, came from a man who had perfected a cannon – Peary would understand if, for reasons of commercial secrecy, he did not reveal its precise workings – with which the explorer could be blasted to the Pole. 'This was surely a man of one idea,' Peary wrote. 'He was so intent on getting me to the Pole that he seemed utterly careless of what happened to me in the process of landing there or how I should get back.'[22]

The vision of Peary soaring meteorically to the Pole, helmet on head, clad in furs and with his moustache swept back by the wind, was an appealing one. If it was completely mad it was also a happy indicator of how far opinion had swung in his favour. But favour also brought pressure. Having set himself up as the man who would succeed – and having cried wolf so many times before – Peary now had to show that he could do it. In the months during which the *Roosevelt* was brought back into commission he came under intense strain. His public and his backers willed him on, but he was in his fifties, he had spent the last two decades of his life in the Arctic and this was his final chance. He was not sure he was up to the challenge.

He steeled himself by attacking his perceived competitors, who included not just Cook but every explorer in the world. It did not matter what they were doing: if they were after fame, Peary would beat them to it. He issued a challenge to the British explorer Ernest Shackleton, who had left for Antarctica in 1907, announcing that he would reach the North Pole before Shackleton reached the South. In the words of the *New York Times*, it was 'an international race between the American explorer and Lieut. Ernest Shackleton . . . Despite the fact that Lieut. Shackleton has a year's start, Peary, nevertheless, expects to get further north than the British explorer does south, and to let the world know the results of his expedition before Shackleton reports his results.'[23] Admittedly, there was competition among Western nations, as there always had been, to open up the world's remaining empty spaces, but such cross-fertilization of ambitions was absurd. No North–South race was in progress, or it if was, Peary seemed to be the only contestant aware of it.

The 6th of July 1908 was one of the hottest days New York had known for years: seventy-two people collapsed and thirteen died from the heat. In these conditions the *Roosevelt* left its berth at the foot of East Twenty-Fourth Street for what Peary knew, win or lose, would be his last voyage to the Pole. Its departure was accompanied by all the usual rumpus – crowds cheered, ships fired salutes, factories let off their sirens and a group of convicts on Blackwell Island came out to wave the expedition off. The following afternoon, at the Roosevelts' summer home on Long Island, the President himself came aboard to wish Peary *bon voyage*. 'I believe in you, Peary,'[24] he said as he clambered back over the rail.

Peary's crew was much the same as in 1905–6. Bartlett was there, so was Henson and Professor Marvin. There were only three 'tenderfeet', as Peary called them: George Borup, a twenty-one-year-old college athlete, Dr John Goodsell, the surgeon, and Donald Macmillan, a Massachusetts PT instructor. They were selected for their fitness and for their Americanness – Peary was adamant that everything about his expedition be American with the exception of Newfoundland-born Bartlett, whom he considered near enough the proper thing – but mainly they were chosen because Peary liked the cut of their jibs. 'A season in the Arctic is a great test of character,' he wrote. 'One may know a man better after six months with him beyond the Arctic circle than after a lifetime of acquaintance in cities. There is a something – I know not what to call it – in frozen spaces, that brings a man face to face with himself and with his companions; if he is a man, the man comes out; and, if he is a cur, the cur shows as quickly.'[25]

His plan also differed little from 1906. The main changes were that he planned to leave from Cape Columbia, forty miles west of Point Moss and ten miles farther north; and he intended, if possible, to make his base camp well above the Big Lead, leaving less than 200 miles to be covered by the final party. He also took precautions against the *Roosevelt* having to repeat that rudderless, fuelless journey home, which had almost done for it on the last expedition. It was equipped with a steel-bound spare rudder and as much coal as it could carry, while a support ship, the *Erik*, was enrolled to ferry a further 800 tons of coal to Etah. The *Roosevelt*'s damaged boiler had been fixed and its engines tweaked so that for short periods they could double their already impressive output. There was one alteration which Peary did not make, and that was to supply kayaks for crossing the Big Lead. It was the simplest and most obvious thing to do, after the delays and perils the Big Lead had caused him. But he wasn't skilled in their use; he was, and always had been, a land traveller; and he was getting old. His last trip would be done the only way he knew how.

Peary's published account of this expedition was ghostwritten by a woman named Elsa Barker, whose style, to put it politely, was of the time. 'The divine fire that produces literature cannot be hired by the week,' she told Peary, 'nor does it come at call.'[26] However it arrived, it left a scorching impression on the page. Of Peary's parting with his wife Josephine, for example, Barker wrote: 'Another farewell – and there had been so many! Brave, noble little woman! You have borne with me the brunt of all my Arctic work.'[27] The divine fire came to Elsa frequently, but here and there one can detect the blander hand of Peary, and he is at his most forthright when describing 'his' Eskimos. On reaching Smith Sound in late July, he remarked that, 'I know every man, woman, and child in the tribe, from Cape York to Etah.'[28] It was a statement of fact. He had visited the place off and on for twenty years, and had left such a mark that serving on his expeditions had become as valid a part of Eskimo existence as hunting and fishing. He had brought them articles of unquantifiable value – wood for their sledges, pots for their cooking, iron for their spears and steel knives – and in doing so had almost singlehandedly changed their culture. But he refused absolutely to change it more than necessary. 'My plan,' he wrote, 'has been to give them such aid and instruction as would fit them more effectively to cope with their own austere environment, and to refrain from teaching them anything which would tend to weaken their self-confidence or to make them discontented with their lot.'[29] To Christianize them, he thought, would be a nonsense, for 'the cardinal graces of faith, hope and charity they seem to have already'.[30] As for resettling them in Canada or the States, he scoffed at the idea: the diseases of 'civilization' would wipe them out in three generations or less. Why should anyone want to civilize them anyway? 'They are healthy and pure-blooded; they have no vices, no intoxicants and no bad habits – not even gambling. Altogether, they are a people unique upon the face of the earth. A friend of mine well calls them the philosophical anarchists of the North.'[31] He looked on them still with a patronising sense of superiority, but this was a different Peary from the one who had sent Eskimos south to the Smithsonian and who had stolen their sacred stones. He had mutated with age into a more likeable human being.

But not that much more likeable. At Anoatok, a village to the north of Etah, Peary discovered a twenty-nine-year-old German named Rudolph Franke, a member of Cook's hunting party who had been left behind to guard a cache of goods – skins, ivory, and other valuable trophies worth $30,000 – while Cook went north with two Eskimos, a sledge and a canvas boat, in search of the Pole. Franke, who had accompanied Cook part of the way, had a bad leg, was suffering from scurvy and in Henson's words was 'the most hopelessly dirty, unkempt, filth-littered human being any of us had ever seen'.[32] Quite what happened next is open to conjecture. One man said that Peary refused to feed Franke, or even give him a cup of coffee until Bartlett smuggled him aboard. Another wrote that Franke was a madman, clutching a grubby piece of paper and screaming, 'Look! I can go away. I have permission from Dr. Cook . . .' whereupon Peary turned to the crew and said, 'That, gentlemen, is an example of what can happen to a white man in the Arctic.'[33] An Eskimo later said that

Peary stole Franke's dogs; Franke later said that he had to surrender Cook's furs and ivory, 'just as the enemy has to hand over their arms to the victorious party',[34] (but at the time he remarked only that he had given Peary a narwhal horn worth $1,000). Peary later claimed that Frank was so ill that he had no alternative but to send him home.

The records of this encounter are muddled, but they agree on several facts: that Peary later presented the narwhal horn to President Roosevelt; that Franke was given a berth on the *Erik* – for which Bradley was charged $100 – but was not allowed to take any of Cook's belonging with him and was searched as he came aboard to make sure he had nothing hidden in his clothes; that when Franke left for America on the *Erik* on 18 August 1908, Peary's bosun, one of his cabin boys and a wealthy sportsman, Harry Whitney, took his place as guardians of Cook's hut; that their task while Peary was away was to collect the same goods as Cook had stored in his hut; and that by the time they had made their collection Cook's hut was empty. Neither did the notice which Peary pinned to the door of Cook's hut redound to his credit: 'This house belongs to Dr. F. A. Cook, but Dr. Cook is long ago dead and there is no use to search for him. Therefore, I, Commander Robert E. Peary, install my boatswain in this deserted house.'[35] Cook was not dead, and Peary had no evidence to suggest that he was. But as Peary was demonstrating, this was *his* world.

The *Roosevelt* left Etah not long after the *Erik*, its decks crammed with sixty-nine Eskimos and 246 dogs. 'It is to be doubted if anywhere on the Seven Seas there was ever a more outlandishly picturesque vessel than ours at this time,'[36] Peary wrote, to be followed hastily by Elsa Barker. 'Imagine this man-and-dog-bestrewn ship, on a pleasant, windless day . . . The listless sea and the overarching sky are a vivid blue in the sunlight – more like a view in the Bay of Naples than one in the Arctic. There is a crystalline clearness in the pure atmosphere . . .'[37] Bartlett's description of the journey was more pungent: 'To my dying day I shall never forget the frightful noise, the choking stench and the terrible confusion that reigned aboard.'[38] The dogs fouled every inch of the deck and although the excrement was shovelled regularly overboard, its stink filled the crew's nostrils. He recorded an evening when they opened a can of peaches after dinner. 'The odor about us was so powerful that the peaches simply felt wet and cold on one's tongue, having no fruit flavour whatsoever.'[39]

The *Roosevelt* barged through the ice, using its super-charged engines when Peary gave the word, Bartlett hanging out of the crows-nest to steer it through the floes, until it reached Cape Sheridan on 5 September. Peary at once ordered the Eskimos and their reeking dogs to decamp. He also emptied the holds, allowing the *Roosevelt* to creep further into the shelter of the shore, and at the same time reducing their dependency on the ship. If the *Roosevelt* sank, as it almost had on the last expedition, their stores would still be intact, providing a base depot from which they could sledge to the safety of Etah. It was quite a sight: for a quarter of a mile, Cape Sheridan was strewn with piles of coal and boxes of food, while in three separate places the crates were stacked to create box-houses measuring fifteen by thirty feet, roofed with canvas, the tops of the crates facing inwards so that if the occupants needed anything they just had to reach up, 'the contents taken out, as needed, as from a shelf, the whole house being one large grocery'.[40] The box-houses could hold the whole crew plus Eskimos, if necessary, and Peary was so proud of his Arctic village that he christened it Hubbardville, after the President of the National Geographic Society.

Life in Hubbardville was comfortable enough, but Peary had problems with his dogs. More than a hundred died before he traced the cause to a consignment of tainted whale meat. He also had problems with the Eskimos, some of whom developed an illness called *piblokto*. In some ways it was akin to the mysterious, distemper-like disease (also called *piblokto*) which had been endemic in their dogs ever since the days of Kane and Hayes. 'The manifestations,' Peary wrote, 'are somewhat startling. The patient, usually a woman, begins to scream and tear off and destroy her clothing. If on the ship, she will walk up and down the deck, screaming and gesticulating, and generally in a state of nudity, though the thermometer may be in the minus forties. As the intensity of the attack increases, she will sometimes leap over the rail upon the ice, running perhaps half a mile. The attack may last

1. The crew of the Eagle. *Front, l. to r. Fraenkel, Andrée, Strindberg*

2. Testing the seams of the Eagle. *Dane's Island, Spitsbergen, 1897*

3. The Eagle

4. The Eagle *taking off from Dane's Island, 1897*

5. The Eagle *shortly after its forced landing on the Arctic pack, 1897*

6. Robert Edwin Peary, 1897

7. Dr Frederick Cook, 1892

8. Josephine Peary and an Eskimo family during her husband's 1891–2 expedition to Greenland

9. Matthew Henson, 1892

10. Peary's 1909 dash for the Pole

11. Peary's companions (Henson centre), supposedly at the North Pole

12. Mussolini (far left, front row) hands over the Norge.
Nobile is third from left, followed by Amundsen and Ellsworth

13. The Norge *leaving Spitsbergen, 1926*

14. Peary in his travelling furs

a few minutes, an hour, or even more, and some sufferers become so wild that they would continue running about on the ice perfectly naked until they froze to death, if they were not forcibly brought back. When an Eskimo is attacked with *piblokto* indoors, nobody pays much attention, unless the sufferer should reach for a knife or attempt to injure some one. The attack usually ends in a fit of weeping, and when the patient quiets down, the eyes are bloodshot, the pulse high, and the whole body trembles for an hour or so afterwards.'[41] Children were never afflicted, but *piblokto* would break out among their parents every couple of days, sometimes hitting five people in the space of twenty-four hours. Peary diagnosed it as 'a fear of the future',[42] which maybe it was – many Eskimos were nervous of what lay ahead – but research has since suggested that *piblokto* is caused by lack of calcium. Whether the result of depression or a deficient diet, Peary found that *piblokto* could be alleviated by promises of gifts to come and by freeing the Eskimos to hunt.

Throughout the winter a stream of men and sledges transported food and equipment ninety miles to Cape Columbia, where they created Crane City, a miniature version of Hubbardville. It was from here, on the last day of February 1909, that the first of Peary's teams departed for the Pole. Bartlett led the way, he and his Eskimos blazing a trail with pick-axes, while the support teams commanded by Goodsell, Macmillan, Borup and Marvin followed at regular intervals. Peary was the last to leave Crane City, on the afternoon of 1 March, by which time there were nineteen sledges, twenty-four men and 133 dogs strung out across the ice.

The travelling was bad: Bartlett's party chopped through pressure ridges as high as two-storey houses; leads opened and closed in their wake; and the drift carried them east, west, north and south. They took measurements every five days – but the days on which the sun was clear at noon were rare, so that they had no real idea where they were heading. Fifty miles out they met the Big Lead, and they waited a week for it to close, swearing at the delay. Bartlett described the wait as 'Hell on Earth'.[43] Henson agreed, but in more temperate language. 'It was exasperating,' he wrote. 'Seven precious days of fine weather

lost; and fine weather is the exception, not the rule, in the Arctic . . .
we were ready and anxious to travel . . . but were perforce compelled
to inactivity.'[44] When it did close, Bartlett, accompanied now by Peary,
pushed on. 'It is *vital* you overtake us and give us fuel,'[45] Peary wrote
on 11 March in a note that he left in an igloo for Ross Marvin, the next
commander down the line.

Three days later Marvin came up, 'men and dogs steaming like a
squadron of battleships',[46] and delivered all the fuel the forward parties could need. The other heavy divisions, under Goodsell and
Macmillan, had already turned back, and for a while Marvin was
given the opportunity to break new ground. The lanky professor
continued with them until 25 March – Borup having been dismissed
on the 19th – before being sent back with two Eskimos, a man
named Kudlikto and his younger cousin. By 28 March, Peary had
crossed the 87th parallel and was beyond his previous record for the
farthest north. The ice ahead was flat and fine, and he began to
wonder if this time he might succeed. 'I had believed for years that
this thing could be done and that it was my destiny to do it,' he
cautioned himself, 'but I always reminded myself that many a man
had felt thus about some dearly wished achievement, only to fail in
the end.'[47]

Peary did not heed his own caution. From the notes he jotted in his
diary margins, he was already anticipating triumph. 'March 26: Have
set of ivory mounted sledge implements made . . . Ivory mounted
snowshoes? Think up some ivory articles to be made for the home
folks . . . Present sextant . . . to Navy Museum (Annapolis?). Have
my eye glasses mounted for constant use. Have extra pair ditto as a
present to someone . . . March 28: Suggest sending piece of fringe to
each local or state division D.A.R. . . piece of N.P. bearskin fringe for
souvenirs to women. The N.P. flag with white bar. This as a stamp on
all N.P. articles?'[48]

On 31 March, Bartlett recorded a latitude of 87°47′N. He, like
Peary, was optimistic. The Pole was 133 miles off, and if they continued
at their average speed over the last six days of eleven miles per day, it
could only be twelve days before they were there. Bartlett, in his

enthusiasm, thought it might even be done in eight. But Bartlett would not be going to the Pole: on 1 April Peary revealed that he was taking Henson instead. This was Peary's second breach of promise – the first having occurred in 1906, when he swore that if Bartlett commanded the *Roosevelt* north he could accompany him to the Pole. In justification Peary said that Henson was the better dog-handler and worked more efficiently with the Eskimos – which was true. 'He was part of the travelling machine,'[49] as Peary said. Dubiously, however, he also said that Henson lacked the fibre for the return journey. 'He would not have been so competent as the white members of the expedition in getting himself and his party back to land,' he explained. 'He had not, as a racial inheritance, the daring and initiative of Bartlett, or Marvin, MacMillan, or Borup. I owed it to him not to subject him to dangers and responsibilities which he was temperamentally unfit to face.'[50]

When Bartlett published his memoirs in the 1930s he was philosophical about Peary's decision, accepting that Henson was a better traveller – but notably not endorsing Peary's racial theories. On his return to America, however, he told the *New York Herald* of his distress: 'I really didn't think I would have to go back . . . Then the Commander said I must go back – that he had decided to take Matt Henson . . . It was a bitter disappointment. I got up early the next morning while the rest were asleep and started north alone. I don't know, perhaps I cried a little. I guess perhaps I was just a little crazy then. I thought that perhaps I could walk on the rest of the way alone. It seemed so near.'[51] In his memoirs, of course, he said he had been a little crazy when he talked to the *Herald*. But that was then. The *Herald* interview, with its description of a final, northward gesture, is more convincing. And even in the memoirs, there is a small hint of resentment. 'It's all in the game,' Peary told him. 'And you've been at it long enough to know how hard a game it is.'[52] 'He wasn't heartless,' Bartlett wrote, 'he was just businesslike. He was always that way.'[53]

Peary revealed just how businesslike he was in a less mealy-mouthed explanation of their parting. 'The pole was something to

which I had devoted my life; it was a thing on which I had concentrated everything, on which I had expended some of myself, for which
I had gone through such hell and suffering as I hope no man . . . may
ever experience, and in which I have put money, time, and everything
else, and I did not feel under those circumstances I was called upon to
divide with a man who, no matter how able and deserving he might
be, was a young man and had only put in a few years in that kind of
work, and who had, frankly, as I believed, not the right that I had to
it . . .'[54] Henson and the Eskimos clearly did not count as men. They
also did not know how to take readings with a sextant. On this last
stage of the journey, significantly, Peary would be the only one who
knew where they were, the only one who could say whether they
had reached the Pole or not.

   Peary, Henson and four Eskimos, Egingwah, Seeglo, Ootah and
Ooqueah left for the north on the morning of 2 April carrying fuel and
food for forty days, fifty at a pinch. Immediately – and unaccount-
ably – their speed picked up. 'I had not dared to hope for such
progress as we were making,'[55] Peary later wrote in his journal. His
diary margins began to fill up: 'April 4: Have special pair of "Peary
North Pole" snowshoes made. Raised toe and heel, curved body, lac-
quered bows, ebony crossbars, silver keel & name plate white gut
lacing . . . Have Henson make pattern "Peary North Pole sledges" . . .
for miners, prospectors, lumbermen, explorers, children. April 5:
North Pole coats, suits, tents, cookers at Sportsmen Show with male
& female attendants in Eskimo costume . . . Jewel for Order of the
North Pole. Have Borup take a 5" × 7" . . . portrait of me in deer or
sheep coat with bear roll (face unshaven) & keep on till satisfactory
one obtained. Have Foster colour in a special print of this to bring out
the gray eyes, the red sunburned skin, the bleached eyebrows and
beard, frosted eyebrows, beard. April 6: Have Harper's take entire
matter, book, magazine articles, pictures & stories (100). Kane got 75
from his books, Nansen 50 for his . . . flag with diagonal white bar to
be my personal flag.'[56] Then, suddenly, he stopped.

   At some point on 6 April 1909 – Peary said it was the morning,
Henson the afternoon – Robert Edwin Peary arrived at the North

Pole. It had taken him not twelve days (as expected), nor eight (as Bartlett had hoped), but a mere four, travelling at an average speed of more than thirty miles per day. 'The Pole at last!!! The prize of 3 centuries, my dream and ambition for 23 years. *Mine* at last. I cannot bring myself to realize it. It all seems so simple & commonplace, as Bartlett said [on reaching his farthest north], "just like every day". I wish Jo could be here with me to share my feelings. I have drunk her health & that of the kids from the Benedictine flask she sent me.'[57] That's what Peary wrote in his diary – or at least that is what he inserted in his diary on a loose sheet of paper. The pages for the seventh and eighth of April are blank, leaving his account of those two days to be written up at a later date for his published journal.

According to the journal – and to Henson's memoirs, the only other record of their conquest – they built two igloos and planted the ice with flags: the Stars and Stripes, sewn by Josephine, Peary's old college pennant, the 'World's Ensign Liberty and Peace', the Navy League flag and the Red Cross flag (at this date bearing not a simple white cross but an elaborate Maltese one). They posed for photographs, named the spot Camp Jesup – 'the last and most northerly camp on the earth',[58] Peary told Henson – and left a message in a cairn, saying that Peary had 'formally taken possession of the entire region and adjacent, for and in the name of the President of the United States of America'.[59]

Peary took thirteen readings to ascertain his position, and described minutely the way in which he did so. He built a semi-circular poacher's shelter of ice, facing south, in which he placed an artificial horizon comprising a wooden trough, filled to the brim with mercury and resting on a mat of fur lest it freeze on contact with the ice. The trough pointed lengthways to the south, and on its sides were balanced two glass panes, joined at the top to form an inverted V, which protected the mercury from the wind and from snow or frost crystals in the atmosphere. He then threw down a fur at one end of the trough to insulate him from the cold and to block refraction from the ice, while he lay down and aimed his sextant at the sun's reflection in the mercury. 'The principle on which the latitude of the observer is obtained from the altitude of the sun at noon is very simple,' Peary explained. 'It is this: that the latitude of the observer is equal to the distance of the center of the sun from the zenith, plus the declination of the sun for that day and hour. The declination of the sun for any place at any hour may be obtained from tables prepared for that purpose, which give the declination for noon of every day on the Greenwich meridian, and the hourly change in the declination. Such tables . . . I had with me on pages torn from the "Nautical Almanac and Navigator."'[60] The result was 89°57′N.

Assuming he was wrong by at least ten miles, Peary continued north until he was past the Pole and heading south. Whereupon he marched back to where he guessed the Pole to be. 'Certain reflections intruded themselves which, I think, may be fairly recorded as unique,' he wrote. 'East, west and north had disappeared for us. Only one direction remained and that was south. Every breeze which could possibly blow upon us, no matter from what point of the horizon, must be a south wind.'[61] Stirring stuff, and with Peary's 'how-to' guide on celestial navigation, authoritative into the bargain. But not entirely convincing.

He took no longitude readings, assuming that he was on the same meridian as Cape Columbia. It was almost impossible that he should still be on that line, however. In his defence, longitude was unimportant in a race for the highest latitude. But it was something he could and should have measured and which had a bearing on the daily distances which led him to the Pole, for if he had been carried either east or west, the deviation would have placed him miles to the south. And at no point in his journey did he offer proof that he had checked the variation of his compass, or even consulted it. He simply said that he went north by the sun. Either he or Bartlett must have made adjustments, otherwise they would not have known where they were heading – the magnetic North Pole being to their south-west in the Canadian Arctic — but there is no mention of them. Any set of positional figures can be falsified, but the more there are the more they

can be cross-checked against each other. Peary produced only his latitude readings: two pages of sums which any student possessing the
Nautical Almanac and Navigator could have written as a theoretical
exercise.

How had Peary reached the Pole so swiftly after leaving Bartlett?
Thirty miles per day was an unbelievable rate, even if the ice had
been flat as a pancake. But was the ice that flat, over that distance,
that near the Pole? Peary admitted in his journal that they had to
cross open leads. This indicated that the ice was moving, and if the
ice was moving – as it usually does – then it would have formed
pressure ridges. (Modern aerial photographs show constant pressure
ridges over the area Peary claimed to have covered.) Previously,
Peary had always added an extra 25 per cent onto his distances to
allow for obstructions and detours. In this case he did not. Perhaps,
however, for one season, the ice was free of pressure ridges and no
detours were necessary – it was possible: Cagni had recorded twenty-
eight miles in one day over smooth ice; Nansen had been lured from
the *Fram* by the vision of flat plains ahead. But then there was the
southward drift. When Bartlett tramped over the pack on his last,
despairing gesture, his readings showed that in the time it took him
to walk five miles north he had been pushed one and a half miles
south. In these conditions Peary would have moved south at least
two miles a day and as many as five, therefore covering not 133 miles
in four days but possibly 150. Without pressure ridges this brings
the average daily rate to thirty-seven miles per day With pressure
ridges – and it is hard to believe he met none – Peary would have had
to run for as much as fifty miles per day, every day. If one accepts that
there was no southward drift during those four days, maybe even a
northern drift; if one accepts that there was no longitudinal drift
either – on 7 March, Borup and Marvin had noted that the polar
swirl hauled bergs out of sight within a matter of hours; if one accepts
that he encountered no pressure ridges on his bee-line zip to the
Pole; and if one accepts his latitude readings (written in an authenti-
cally shaky hand), then, and only then, could Peary have done what
he did.

It is impossible, however, to accept what Peary did next. His party left Camp Jesup at 4.00 p.m. on 7 April. According to Henson, Peary was so exhausted that he had to be carried on a sledge, swaddled in furs. Yet they reached the camp where they had split from Bartlett at midnight on 9 April. In fifty-six hours they had traversed 133 miles of fractured polar ice which it had taken them four days to cross on the way north.

There have been endless analyses of Peary's conquest of the Pole, the most thorough being that of Wally Herbert, a British explorer who has not only walked to the Pole but continued to the other side of the polar pack. These analyses present, in minute detail, all the flaws in Peary's account of his discovery. But the most damning proof lies in Peary's own documentation. Under no circumstances could he have completed the return journey in the time he claimed. Modern explorers have been to the Pole on snowmobiles and with dogs and on skis, but nobody has yet equalled Peary's supposed average of thirty miles on his final northward stretch. One can point to discrepancies: nobody has ever gone to the Pole in the same manner as Peary, with a massive support team, a pre-prepared track and fresh dogs for the final stretch; nobody has been there and back along the same route and in the same circumstances; and nobody, conceivably, has been as tough or as driven as Peary. In the same vein, some explorers have met heavy pressure ridges but others have seen open fields of ice of the very kind Peary said he travelled over and have testified that his claimed speeds for the northern march are neither impossible nor improbable. All these points are worth considering. So is Peary's declaration that their passage back was hastened by northerly winds and a southward drift. But the distances of almost sixty miles per day which he claimed for the southern journey are fantastical. Unless Peary was a superman – and Henson, Egingwah, Ootah, Ooqueah and Seeglo were supermen too – he could not, by his own evidence, have done it.

Peary thought he had done it – done it, that is, as far as anybody could tell – and wrote a postcard to his wife, headed '90°N Lat (North Pole) Apr 7th':

My dear Jo,

I have won out at last. Have been here a day of the finest weather. I start for home and you in an hour. Love to the 'kidsies'.

Bert.[62]

Then he started scribbling in his margins again: 'April 9 . . . send photo Pres. & self shaking hands to him . . . send R[oosevelt] a Pole Peary sledge. April 10. U. S. made Melville & Schley Admirals and Greely Brigadier General for their Arctic work. England knighted James and John Ross, Parry, Franklin, Nares, McClintock, Richards (?), Beaumont, etc. etc. Paid Parry $125,000. April 19 . . . have aluminium case Harvard watches repaired by makers & put gold hunting case for presents. One properly engraved to be given to Bridgman [one of his supporters]. This watch carried by me to the North Pole, is given to my friend H. L. Bridgman as a slight token of my appreciation of his invaluable assistance and loyal devotion to the cause for years, R. E. Peary.'[63]

They hurtled south at indescribably fast speeds, following the 84th line with scarcely a digression, and crossing an iced-over Big Lead without hazard, before reaching Cape Columbia on 23 April. For two days, on and off, they slept in the remains of Crane City, during which period Peary wrote a tribute to himself in his diary. Naturally, it was a glowing tribute. But against his marginal jottings, his lack of scientific documentation, and his imprecise catalogue of all that had happened since he had left Bartlett at 87°47', it gives the impression of a man returning to reality. Previously, Peary had claimed tutelage over the whole Canadian Arctic land mass. He now rejected that claim. Whoever wanted Greenland, Ellesmere Island, Axel Heiberg Island and all the rest – they could have it. His world was now the North Pole. He had shifted his boundaries to a safely unattainable distance, the game was over and Ellesmere Island could be New York for all he cared.

'My life work is accomplished,' he wrote. 'The thing which it was intended from the beginning that I should do, the thing which I believed could be done, and that I could do, I have done. I have got the North Pole out of my system after twenty-three years of effort, hard work, disappointments, hardships, privations, more or less suffering, and some risks. I have won the last great geographical prize, the North Pole, for the credit of the United States. This work is the finish, the cap and climax of nearly four hundred years of effort, loss of life, and expenditure of fortunes by the civilized nations of the world, and it has been accomplished in a way that is thoroughly American. I am content.'[64]

21

PRINCE OF IMPOSTORS

Peary arrived at the *Roosevelt* on 27 April, completing the distance from Cape Columbia in two marches of forty-five miles. Bartlett, who had resumed command of the ship on the 24th while his commander was recuperating at Crane City, came forward to greet him. If he wondered how Peary had managed to catch up so quickly, how he had managed to travel at least 300 miles farther but reach the ship only three days behind him, he made no mention of it. 'I congratulate you, sir, on the discovery of the Pole,'[1] he said. Peary laughed cheerfully. Then Bartlett told him that Marvin was dead.

The story, as related by Kudlikto, was that Marvin had risen one morning to reconnoitre the track ahead, as was customary, leaving Kudlikto and his cousin to strike camp and follow him with the sledges. Out of sight and beyond earshot, Marvin had fallen through thin ice into the Big Lead. His death had not been quick. He must have struggled and shouted, buoyed up by his snowtight outfit, for several long minutes before the cold and water took him. Unaware of their leader's dilemma, the Eskimos had packed the sledges, harnessed their dogs, and followed at leisure. At the Big Lead they saw a wide pool of open water in the centre of which the back of Marvin's fur jacket bobbed just below the surface. The broken edges of the ice showed that he had fought desperately to scramble out, but in doing so had only widened the hole. The Eskimos could do nothing to help. They left Marvin's body where it was, and ran over the Big Lead while the ice still held.

Peary was genuinely shocked. He had formed an honest regard for the skinny Cornell scientist. He had also hoped to bring his expedition home intact. Marvin's death was a personal blow and also a blot on Peary's polar accomplishments. He became tight-lipped when the Pole was mentioned, refusing to discuss it with anyone, and kept his distance from Henson, who tried repeatedly to talk about their experiences. When Goodsell questioned him, he replied flatly that 'I have not been altogether unsuccessful'.[2] His avoidance of the subject has been interpreted as an admission of guilt – that he had not reached the Pole – but to give Peary his due he had always been a responsible leader. On the way north he had noted all the graves he had passed, each death reminding him of previous, disastrous forays: Sonntag, Ohlsen, Hall, Petersen, men from the Nares expedition, and men from Greely's. Now Marvin was to be added to the list. That a man under his command had died was, to Peary, a sign of failure.

Having erected several cairns and a vast, four-pronged signpost bearing copper plates on which were punched readings for all of Peary's northernmost records and a list of the people who had accompanied him on his final journey, the men of the *Roosevelt* left Cape Sheridan on 17 July. A month later, after a relatively easy voyage south, they landed at Anoatok to collect the two men they had left in Cook's hut – the bosun, John Murphy, and the cabin boy, Billy Pritchard – plus Harry Whitney, the rifle-toting sportsman who had hitched a ride north in search of trophies new. Here they learned that Cook and his two Eskimos had passed through on their way south, dropping off a few packages before they continued to Upernavik where Cook expected to catch a ship home. The three men were reticent about Cook's visit, but Peary called Pritchard into his cabin and wrung it out of him. 'He said he didn't want Mr. Peary or anyone else to know it,'[3] said Pritchard, squirming under what he described as

Peary's third-degree interrogation. Know about what? Well, Pritchard had overheard Cook tell Whitney, having sworn him to secrecy, that 'I've been to the Pole.'[4] Cook had beaten Peary to the North Geographical Pole on 21 April 1908.

'To us up there at Etah, such a story was so ridiculous and absurd,' Henson wrote. 'We knew Dr. Cook and his abilities ... and aside from his medical ability, we had no faith in him whatsoever. He was not even good for a day's work, and the idea of his making such an astounding claim as having reached the Pole was so ludicrous that, after our laugh, we dropped the matter altogether.'[5] But, as Peary knew, Cook *was* good for a day's work. Maybe for several days. Maybe for weeks and months. Maybe good enough to have forestalled him. He took Murphy, Pritchard and Whitney aboard but insisted they leave behind Cook's packages and the potential evidence they contained.

When the *Roosevelt* reached Indian Harbour, Labrador, news of Cook's conquest was already on the telegraph. Borup reacted excitedly. 'He's handed them a gold brick!'[6] he cried. Peary looked up sternly from his desk. Was there any better way of putting it? Borup shook his head. Peary therefore ordered a telegram to be tapped out. It was for the *New York Times*, and it was printed on 11 September. 'Do not trouble about Dr. Cook's story or attempt to explain any discrepancies in his statements,' it read. 'The affair will settle itself. He has not been to the Pole on April 21st, 1908, or at any other time. He has simply handed the public a gold brick. These statements are made advisedly, and I have proof of them. When he makes a full statement of his journey over his signature to some geographical society or other reputable body, if that statement contains the claim that he has reached the pole, I shall be in a position to furnish material that may prove distinctly interesting material for the Public. Robert E. Peary.'[7]

Peary telegraphed every interested party, reiterating his message. Not since the Duke of Abruzzi had the wires hummed at such expense.

Cook's story was a straightforward one. Leaving Greenland in spring

1908, he had sledged with his Eskimos across Smith Sound, across Ellesmere Island and up the east coast of Axel Heiberg Island, from the tip of which he had driven north with two sledges, twenty-six dogs and half a ton of provisions. By 11 April half the food was gone and the Pole was approximately 200 miles away. But ten days later, on reduced rations, at an average of just under twenty miles per day, he managed to reach the sought-after spot. 'I had culminated with success the efforts of all the brave men who had failed before me,' he later wrote (with the aid of his editor who, like Peary's Elsa Barker, was prone to the divine fire). 'I had finally justified their sacrifices, their very death . . . It seemed that the souls of these dead exulted with me, and that in some substrata of the air, in notes more subtle than the softest notes of music, they sang a paean in the spirit with me.'[8] On the way north he had sighted a new land to the west, which he had named Bradley Land after his main supporter. So, to cap his victory, he decided to return via Bradley Land. But Bradley Land, like Peary's Crocker Land, did not exist. Cook and his Eskimos became lost on the ice and were almost starving when they reached Amund Ringnes Island, far to the west and the south of Axel Heiberg Island. Living off the land, they marched south and east, spending five winter months in an Eskimo grave on Devon Island, before staggering back to Greenland in the spring of 1909, where they found Peary's men in charge of their hut.

Many apparently simple situations conceal complications and Cook's story was no exception. That he had reached the top of Axel Heiberg Island was certain – Franke, a reliable witness, had accompanied him that far. That he had endured an extraordinary winter in virtually Stone-Age conditions can be acknowledged - he had to have been somewhere the last year and he lacked the provisions to support himself and his men in anything approaching comfort. But that he had been to the Pole was far less certain. According to Cook, he had kept winter depression at bay by writing up his journal. Armed with four pencils and one eraser, he scratched away in a self-invented form of shorthand, until he had completed 150,000 words. The material on which he wrote comprised two booklets, a prescription pad, and his larger journals, erased as necessary, on which he had recorded his journey to date.

Four pencils do not last 150,000 words, and no matter how small you write or how short a shorthand you use, you cannot get that number of words onto the few pages Cook claimed to have used. (If you wish to put it to the test, transcribe this book, which contains approximately 150,000 words, onto any size of paper you choose. You may write in the margins and are allowed to use both sides.) Cook swore, however, that his journal, both booklets and his prescription pad – why had he taken it? at which apothecary were the Eskimos to redeem his scrip? – contained his proof and his record of reaching the Pole. He also swore that he had left them with Whitney – for no explicable reason – while he walked south to Upernavik, the port from which he hoped to catch the speediest ship home. Cook did make this journey to Upernavik, a distance as the crow flies of more than 500 miles and on foot maybe half that again, which had never before been crossed by Eskimo or foreigner. From Upernavik he travelled down the coast on a variety of vessels until, on 20 June 1909, he caught a ship to Denmark. The ship sailed via Lerwick, in the Shetland Isles, where he wrote a 2,000-word despatch which he left with the Danish Consul. 'If you want it, send for it,'[9] he cabled the *New York Herald*. All he asked was £3,000. And he had photographs.

Like a spider, James Gordon Bennett rose from his lair. Since the *Jeannette* disaster he had restricted his operations in the Arctic, sending correspondents to report in minor fashion on unimportant missions. A devotee of exploration, he had contributed to all Peary's previous expeditions but he had neglected the last one. According to Bartlett there had been a mix-up. One of Bennett's editors had personally paid the sum of $4,000 for Peary's narrative. (Peary was to repay the money if he did not attain 90°N.) But Bennett had sacked him in one of his fits of madness, and he had gone to the *New York Times* with his scoop. According to other sources Bennett had become bored with Peary's constant failures and had withdrawn his support. Either way, when Bennett received Cook's cable, he realized something big was afoot. He moved fast. On 2 September 1909, the day after the message arrived, the *Herald* devoted five whole pages to Cook's conquest of the Pole. By the 3rd the story was in every major American and European newspaper.

'In the wildest flights of my imagination I never dreamed of any world wide interest in the Pole,' Cook later stated. 'I regarded my entire experience as purely personal. I supposed that the newspapers would announce my return, and that there would be a three days' breadth of attention, and that would be all.'[10] Such a statement seems unbelievable. Cook must surely have known what to expect when the news broke. But all the evidence suggests that he did not. In fact, he comes across as naïve to the point of simple-mindedness. When he reached Copenhagen on Saturday, 4 September, he was engulfed by a 'whirlwind of excitement'.[11] Mobs burst through the police cordon as he came ashore, snatching at his clothing to grab a souvenir. By the time he was hustled, dazed, into his carriage, he had already lost his hat, one of his cuffs and several buttons. In the banquets and presentations that followed, he appeared so bland and innocent that reporters could not bring themselves to disbelieve his story. The London newspaperman, W. T. Stead, spoke for the majority when he said, 'I think that almost all of us who went to Copenhagen would agree . . . that he does not strike us as a man, but rather as a child – a naïve, inexperienced child, who sorely needed someone to look after him . . . his inability to protect his own interests . . . was almost pitiful.'[12] In Stead's opinion, 'Everything a clever rogue would do instinctively, if he wished to hoax the public, Dr. Cook did not do.'[13] This, however, only addressed the question of Cook's cleverness. Hard-boiled, heavyweight that he was, Stead seems not to have considered the possibility of Cook being a stupid rogue.

Some journalists dissented. One man, Philip Gibbs of London's *Daily Chronicle*, asked to see Cook's diary. At that, 'a strange defensive look'[14] came over Cook's face. All his material was at Etah, he said. On being pressed, he became suddenly angry. 'You believed Nansen, and Amundsen, and Sverdrup,' he retorted. 'They had only their story to tell. Why don't you believe me?'[15] Gibbs didn't believe him because he had no proof, whereas all the others had been supported by witnesses. He also noted, from the few figures Cook offered, that his mileage appeared exaggerated, that his measurements were too precise to be credible, and that he had difficulty in deciding whether his thermometer readings were in Celsius or Fahrenheit. So Cook changed his story and hinted that his original papers were in the hands of the University of Copenhagen. (The university denied this.) Then he said that some of them were in America. Then he said that all of them were. Gibbs was at first puzzled and then incredulous. Cook's air of innocence did not fool him – though it did impress him: apart from that one irritable outburst, Cook sustained his role immaculately. 'I must now say that this man Cook is the most remarkable, most amazing man I have ever met,' Gibbs wrote. 'I will say honestly that I am filled with a sense of profound admiration for him. If he is an impostor he is also a very brave man – a man with such iron nerve, such miraculous self-control, and such magnificent courage in playing his game, that he will count for ever among the greatest impostors of the world. That and not the discovery of the North Pole shall be his claim to immortality.'[16]

Also puzzled was a Danish journalist, Peter Freuchen, who had travelled in the Arctic and could make head nor tail of Cook's timetables. But the establishment and the public were on Cook's side. He was a respected explorer, so why should his word be doubted? One man was so incensed by Gibbs's carping that he challenged him to a duel. Freuchen received a more reasoned rebuff from his editor, who spiked a critical article with the words, 'We cannot wine and dine a man one day and call him a fraud the next.'[17]

Ironically, Cook *was* being wined and dined when the controversy broke. At a banquet for journalists, held in Copenhagen's pleasure park Tivoli, their host received a telegram. He handed it to Stead in disbelief. Stead read the message aloud: 'In a wire from Indian Harbour, Labrador, dated September 6, 1909, Peary says: Stars and Stripes nailed to the Pole.'[18] There exists a photograph taken just after the announcement. A flushed Cook stands centre-stage, with a garland around his neck, looking uncertainly at a point off-camera.

Sverdrup is on his right, the guest of honour, glaring as manically as ever. On Sverdrup's side of the room the guests also face the camera. But on the other side (Cook's side, the sceptical side) the journalists are in a state. One man puffs his cheeks in surprise and excitement. Others stare openly at Cook, waiting for his response. 'I am proud that a fellow American has reached the Pole,' Cook said, after the flash had popped. 'There is glory enough for us all. He is a brave man, and I am confident that if the reports are true his observations will confirm mine and set at rest all doubts.'[19] With these placatory words, the assembly dissolved and the argument began.

At the time of Nansen's drift, Jackson had written of the world being divided into two camps over what had happened in Franz Josef Land. His assessment of a little-known dispute had been optimistic. (Most people at the time did not know who Jackson was and cared less.) But now the world really was split, as an increasingly media-driven society wavered between Peary and Cook. The *New York Times* stuck by its man, claiming that Peary was honest and Cook a crook. An influx of cables arrived from Peary, one of which stated that on interviewing Cook's Eskimos they had said that they never been out of sight of land. 'Do not trouble about Cook's story. I have him nailed,'[20] he telegraphed the editor. Nares came out in his favour, and Melville branded Cook a fake. The British explorer Ernest Shackleton, having at first congratulated Cook, also edged onto Peary's side, and Evelyn Baldwin, the American who had made such an expensive mess of his expedition to Franz Josef Land, added his pro-Peary tuppenceworth.

Possession, however, was nine-tenths of the law. Cook had staked his claim to the Pole before Peary and he had the public, most of the press and, above all, Bennett's mighty *Herald* on his side. When Cook arrived in New York on 21 September 1909 he was greeted by screaming hordes. Dr Cook toys were on sale in the shops – one could buy the solo figurine in furs or a smaller one complete with sledge – and a celebratory hat had been available to women since the 5th. Two-feet tall, made of fuzzy brown fur and decorated with a snowlike plume on the left side, the Dr Cook hat was the fashion equivalent of horsemeat.

As the *New York Tribune* said, 'It . . . looks massive and solid enough to supply a good soup stock in case of Arctic exigency.'[21] But it was out there, and it had his name on it. New York gave Cook the freedom of the city; Brooklyn wanted to erect a statue in his honour; Harlem lit up its streets in celebration of his feat; and all the while the *Herald*'s headlines boomed their support.

'If you only can keep still and not discuss this creature until you have had an opportunity to see what he and others have said it would be far better,'[22] Josephine Peary counselled her husband on 12 September. But Peary charged on with disastrous consequences. When he and his supporters tried to stamp Cook a fraud, it rebounded against them. Why should he be a fraud? was the question asked by most. And why should Peary take it upon himself to say that he was? Cook himself put it very nicely: 'Commander Peary has as yet given to the world no proof of his own case. My claim has been fully recognized by Denmark and by the King of Sweden . . . A specific record of my journey is accessible to all, and everyone who reads can decide for himself. When Peary publishes a similar report then our cases are parallel. Why should Peary be allowed to make himself a self-appointed dictator of my affairs?'[23] Cook's argument had flaws. The specific record to which he alluded was the one which had appeared in the *Herald* (Bennett paid an extra $25,000 to serialize it), but Peary's own report had come out in the *New York Times*, so they were equal on that count. Also, Cook's claim had not been fully recognized by anyone; they had merely taken his word that he had done what he said he had done. But people agreed with Cook's last comment. Peary's attacks were mean-spirited and vicious – 'neither sportsmanlike, scientific nor ethical',[24] according to the *New York Tribune*. His own story was hardly more believable than Cook's. The Peary brigade had ridiculed Cook's daily mileage on the grounds that an average of seventeen miles or so was impossible. But here was Peary in the *New York Times* with a mileage of twenty-five miles and more.

Cook's star continued to rise. He embarked on a lecture tour that paid him – purportedly – $10,000 per appearance. When the *Toledo Blade* polled its readers, 550 thought Cook had reached the Pole as opposed to ten who supported Peary. 'I know Peary the explorer,' Cook said adroitly. 'As such he is a hero in Arctic annals and he deserves the credit of a long and hard record. To Peary the explorer I am still willing to tip my hat, but Peary's unfounded accusations have disclosed another side to his character, which will never be forgotten.'[25] A church on Long Island was so impressed by Cook's martyrdom that it sealed a copy of his *Herald* despatch in its cornerstone.

To and fro the arguments went, as the *Times* and *Herald* fought to win readers. Meanwhile, the men in the ring took their own stances. Cook was the calm, well-mannered chap who appealed to mothers and vicars. Peary, still in the north, was the hairy gladiator. 'He looked a good deal like a dramatised miner,' wrote one reporter, 'in his square cut blue flannel shirt, rough black trousers and huge brimmed sombrero. His sandy moustache bristled out on both sides like two rough brushes twisted to a point. There was a two-day growth upon his cheek. But his skin was as clear as a woman's and remarkably smooth for a man of his years. Every inch of him, every ounce of him was hard as Bessemer steel; his muscles danced and squirmed under his shirt as he moved and breathed. Whenever he spoke he heaved out his great chest, gestured slightly with his freckled, well kept hands, and made a peculiar gurgling sound in his throat, his Adam's apple sticking out in the loose flesh as if it had been a lump of coal.'[26] The description was biased, but Peary definitely had the physical edge over Cook. As the days passed, he gained the evidential advantage too.

For a start, the Peary Arctic Club discovered that Cook's photographs of the North Pole, which the *Herald* had published alongside his narrative, were cropped versions of ones he had taken six years previously in Greenland. Also where were Dr Cook's proofs? Dr Cook still had no coherent answer. 'The impression seems to prevail that Mr. Harry Whitney has records of importance with him,' Cook said. 'He may not know that he has them, for they are packed with my instruments which I left in his care.'[27] Whitney did not have them, as a *New York Times* reporter soon found out. (He did not have the instruments either, thanks to Peary.) Cook then declared that he had left *some* original documents with Whitney but most of them were duplicates of material which Cook now had in his possession. It would take him several months to prepare everything for inspection. In all fairness, however, he ought to launch another expedition to recover the packages Peary had forced Whitney to leave behind. When he did find them, the University of Copenhagen should have first refusal.

Digression followed delay. Meanwhile, disturbing news came in of Cook's ascent of Mt. McKinley. A Cornell University professor had visited the area and had reported that, 'the almost unanimous verdict of Alaskans knowing that country [was] that the feat was impossible'.[28] On its own this meant nothing: every ascent of every major peak in the world has been disputed, and never more vehemently than by people who claim to know the region best. But one of Cook's own guides, Edward Barrill, admitted that Cook had climbed no higher than 5,000 feet. He also swore that Cook had made him forge his diary of the climb and that the photographs of the summit which Cook had published were of a similar peak no more than 8,000 feet high. When Cook was asked to produce his own diary a familiar story emerged. 'I do not see that it is material,'[29] he responded. Anyway, the diary was at the bottom of a trunk and rather hard to get at. But he would happily organize another expedition to the top of McKinley to retrieve the brass canister which he'd left there as proof of his conquest.

Even Bennett was bemused by Cook's willingness to climb a mountain rather than rummage through a trunk. Fred Printz, another of Cook's guides, extrapolated the situation for all to understand in *The New York Times*: 'I am just as sure as I'm living that Cook never saw the North Pole. Any man who would make the representations he did as to his alleged ascent of Mount McKinley is capable of making statements credited to him in the press about the North Pole achievement.'[30] The *Herald*'s support thinned visibly and so did that of the public. Peary, who had arrived home in late October 1909, filled the void. He presented the National Geographic Society with his own proofs and, because they were not entirely clear to the layman, talked a three-man sub-committee through their finer points.

It was a sham: the three men were all supporters of Peary and two of them were personal friends; they did nothing more than read his journal aloud to each other; and when they examined his instruments for accuracy they did so in a railway station at twilight. The journal may not even have been the original: Bartlett remembered it as a dirty, greasy booklet; but the one which the sub-committee saw surprised them by its cleanliness. As for its contents, they were no more verifiable than Cook's. But the National Geographic Society accepted them at face value. The verdict was decided before the assessment. 'Every one who knows Peary by reputation knows he would not lie,'[31] wrote one of the adjudicators.

On 4 November the sub-committee's minutes read:

'Whereas, Commander Robert E. Peary has reached the North Pole, the goal sought for centuries; and

Whereas, this is the greatest geographical achievement that this society can have opportunity to honor: Therefore

Resolved, that a special medal be awarded to Commander Peary.'[32]

In Peary's ghostwritten journal – for instalments of which *Hampton's Magazine* paid a record $40,000 – there is a picture of the medal. On the obverse, above an image of an iced-in ship, Peary glowers forth from a wreath of furs and laurels. On the reverse a stylized team sets out with dogs towards a representational Polar Star. It comes with a caption that leaves the reader in no doubt as to Peary's glory: 'THE SPECIAL GREAT GOLD MEDAL OF THE NATIONAL GEOGRAPHIC SOCIETY OF WASHINGTON (This medal is four inches in diameter).'[33]

Cook did not fight Peary's proofs. He resorted instead to a cloak-and-dagger subterfuge. On 24 November 1909 he cut his hair, shaved his moustache, pulled a black hat over his face and caught a train for Toronto. From Toronto he took a ship to Liverpool, and from Liverpool he went to an undisclosed location in France. His secretary, a man named Walter Lonsdale, ferried his documents to Denmark in a sealed strong-box, for the perusal of the University of Copenhagen. For a while, mystery surrounded Cook's whereabouts. One report said he was in a sanatorium. His lawyer, the alliteratively named

H. Wellington Wack, said he was in Naples. H. Wellington Wack also said that Cook was victim to 'one of the most diabolical plots that has been hatched against an explorer or any other man'.[34] Three secret agents were after him, two men and a woman, ready to seduce his secretary, drug his champagne, and ransack his cabin. Wack's statement was not so silly: the Peary Arctic Club had approached Pinkerton's to investigate Cook. But as Wack so grandly said, 'we hired detectives to watch their detectives'.[35] Cook eventually turned up in Marseilles.

The University of Copenhagen was supportive of Cook. It refused an application by the National Geographic Society to attend the sitting, declaring that it had no scientific standing and that its approaches were 'little less than an insult'.[36] When Cook's bolted, iron-bound chest was opened, however, it contained nothing but a bundle of seventy-seven typewritten pages and no diary. The Danes were angry. Cook was declared an impostor and a swindler. Knud Rasmussen, an erstwhile supporter, now said that Cook's papers were 'almost impudent . . . no schoolboy could make such calculations. It is a most childish attempt at cheating.'[37] But wait, said Lonsdale, Cook's handwritten diary was on its way. His wife was bringing it over in secret to avoid the machinations of Peary's myrmidons. After all Cook's evasions about the exact whereabouts of his original papers, one can imagine the apoplexy of the Copenhagen experts. When the diary did arrive, it was no more convincing than the other material. The writing was peculiarly legible for a document that had been written, so Cook said, while wearing two pairs of mittens. In fact, the experts said, it appeared that 'important parts of it are manufactured'.[38] In conclusion, they were 'of the opinion that the material transmitted for examination contains no proof whatsoever that Dr. Cook reached the North Pole'.[39] The *New York Times* reported their findings gleefully on 21 December under the headline, 'COOK'S CLAIM . . . REJECTED; OUTRAGED DENMARK CALLS HIM A DELIBERATE SWINDLER'.

Conciliatory statements were made. *The Sun* said that 'Cook was too hastily acclaimed as the discoverer of the North Pole. Let us not be too hasty in acclaiming him the prince of impostors . . . Insane delusions are caricatures of the time and place where they are developed.'[40] But it was hard not to believe in Cook's guilt, especially if one considered the business of Dunkle and Loose. George Dunkle worked in insurance, Captain August Loose was supposedly in navigation, and Cook had hired them to help with his journal. Dunkle and Loose (if those were their real names) were shady characters and, as the Peary Arctic Club claimed, they had crossed the accepted bounds of assistance. The *New York Times* published Dunkle's affidavit that the pair had accepted $2,500 to forge Cook's observations, with another $1,500 to follow if Copenhagen accepted them. It was untrue, Lonsdale replied. Cook had employed the men 'for the purpose, not of fabricating records, but merely checking observations by the doctor'.[41] On finding they intended to fake his records, Cook had thrown them out of his hotel room. Nobody cared. The very names Dunkle and Loose oozed skulduggery. And now, with further accusations emanating from Denmark, the world knew that Cook was the lowest form of snake.

Pursued by cries of 'shameless swindler' and 'infamous wretch', stripped of his membership of the Explorers' Club of New York, of which he had once been President, Cook ran. He had already left Marseilles for Algeciras, and was living there under an assumed name when his wife caught up with him, carrying the diary which he hoped would prove his case. Their rendezvous was touching. Marie, his wife, did not know her husband's address or the name he was living under. Cook knew only that Marie had arrived. They wandered through the streets looking for each other until they finally met on a bench in a small park. Marie gave him the diary, which Cook sent to Lonsdale in Copenhagen and then the couple left for South America. To the press, 'his flight was a confession'.[42]

Mr and Mrs Cook sailed around South America, stopping at Buenos Aires, daring the Straits of Magellan, touching at Santiago where, Cook having been recognized, they returned overland to Buenos Aires. Mrs Cook left her husband at this point, and went back to New York to look after their children. Cook wandered alone through Paraguay before catching a ship to London where he based himself

incognito at the Hotel Capitol in Pall Mall. In disguise he attended a
lecture at the Royal Geographical Society on May 1910, given by
Peary. 'I stood twenty yards from Peary, and none recognised me,'[43]
he chortled. At some point during the last twelve months Cook had
become seriously unhinged.

Peary's lecture ended with his being awarded a Gold Medal
designed by Katherine Scott, wife of the Antarctic explorer Robert
Falcon Scott, and he added a picture of it to Appendix III of his journal just after the National Geographic's four-inch medal. The medal
was disappointingly small compared to its predecessor, and carried the
caption, 'THE SPECIAL GREAT GOLD MEDAL OF THE
ROYAL GEOGRAPHICAL SOCIETY OF LONDON (Actual
size).'[44] Nor did it carry any acknowledgement that he had reached
the Pole, merely praising him 'For Arctic exploration from 1886 to
1909'.

The Royal Geographical Society was wise to be cautious. When it
voted on Peary's claim, only seventeen members of its thirty-five-
man board were present, and of these seventeen only eight came out
in favour of Peary, seven voted against and two abstained – hardly a
show of confidence. The reason for their hesitation can be found in
the jotted examination of Peary's proofs, preserved today in the Royal
Geographical Society's archives. Their leading navigational expert
studied Peary's material and concluded that it was possible, with the
instruments Peary possessed, to take the readings he had. He also said
that those readings were consistent with his having reached the North
Pole. Therefore, 'He either took them and got close to the Pole or
"faked" them, to defraud the public and is an impostor of the very
worst type. *There is no other possible explanation of the case.*'[45] Then, forsaking logic, he decided that Peary must have reached the Pole
because his reputation for integrity was too well-known for him to
have lied. A compass specialist pointed out the lack of compass readings and said that they only had Peary's word that he had gone north;
and a chronometer expert said that the instrument was so faulty that
the few longitude sightings could not be relied upon and that if Peary
had not travelled in a straight line (which was doubtful) he would be

some distance away from the Pole. To which the navigational expert replied that Peary must have gone north, and must have travelled in a straight line, because otherwise his readings would not show that he had stood at the Pole. To settle the matter, a member of staff was told to give Bartlett lunch at his club and pump him for information. The employee returned (having been asked to leave the club because of Bartlett's language) with the following report: 'He said that Peary had treated him badly in not letting him go on that last leg with him, but he honestly thought he got there, or so close that it made no odds.'[46] On this shaky analysis, and the marginal vote which accompanied it, Peary's conquest of the Pole was confirmed.

Where the Royal Geographical Society led, other scientific bodies followed. On the final pages of his journal, Peary listed an impressive tally of awards. Gold medals were heaped upon him from the Philadelphia Geographical Society, the Chicago Geographical Society, the Imperial German Geographical Society, the Royal Italian Geographical Society, the Imperial Austrian Geographical Society, the Hungarian Geographical Society, the Royal Belgian Geographical Society, and the Royal Geographical Society of Antwerp. The Royal Geographical Society of Scotland gave him a silver model of a sailing ship, Edinburgh University made him a Doctor of Law, the Royal Netherlands Geographical Society made him an Honorary Member and so did the Manchester Geographical Society.

Peary was riding high. His minimum fee for a lecture was $1,000 and one auditorium paid him $7,500. Meanwhile, he had received an advance on his journal for $15,000. President William Howard Taft sent him his personal congratulations and the US Navy approved his retirement in 1911 with the rank and pension of a Rear-Admiral, back-dated to 6 April 1909. His naval colleagues resented his promotion, pointing out the unfairness of rewarding officially a man who had never commanded a ship of the line, who had never served in any capacity other than civil engineer, and who had been on protracted leave for almost twenty years. But their protests fluttered off before the gale of Peary's acclaim. As Peary so popularly said, 'The discovery of the North Pole stands for the inevitable victory of courage, persistence, endurance, over all obstacles. In the discovery of the North Pole is written the final chapters of the last of the great geographical stories of the Western Hemisphere which began with the discovery of the New World by Columbus. Here is the cap and climax, the closing of the book on 400 years of history. The discovery of the North Pole on the 6th April, 1909, by the last expedition of the Peary Arctic Club, means that the splendid frozen jewel of the North, for which through centuries men of every nation have struggled, and suffered and died, is won at last, and is won for ever, by the Stars and Stripes!'[47]

The fame for which he had striven since adolescence was now his. And who could deny him it? He had struggled more fiercely, travelled farther, and single-handedly done more than anybody else to reach the Pole. Maybe he had not stood on the top of the world – Wally Herbert, in his exhaustive study of Peary's journals, estimates that he might have come within sixty miles of the geographical North Pole – but he had near as damn it done so. Had he gone those extra miles, what would he have proved? That he could read his sextant that bit farther north? There is nothing to differentiate the Pole physically from its environs: no stick, no stone, no summit, no land, no hidden treasure, no race of alien beings. There is nothing to find except the limit of one's endurance and a test of one's navigational skills. This we now know and by these criteria Peary deserves his fame.

But they did not know then what we know now, and by the standards of the time, Peary had failed. He had not proved definitively that there was nothing save ice at the Pole nor had he been able to pinpoint with accuracy the spot at which he had turned back. His distances were suspect, his diary was inconclusive and the impartial scientists who awarded him his laurels did so in a manner that was neither impartial nor scientific. What he *had* proved beyond doubt was his ability to beat Cook in the battle for public sympathy, and it was this determination to overcome the man that undermined his achievement in overcoming the Arctic. Instead of a clear-cut victory, or even a clear-cut disaster, of the kind that would soon emerge from the Antarctic, the world had to deal with a prolonged and increasingly tedious controversy.

The battle of proof had been hard for both men. Cook had suffered a nervous breakdown and so, to a lesser extent, had Peary. But although Peary had apparently won, Cook refused to go away. In 1911, *Hampton's Magazine* offered him a chance to present his own side of the story in a four-part serial. His journal, *My Attainment of the North Pole*, was to be published later that year but the article in *Hampton's* gave him the opportunity for a preliminary skirmish before battle recommenced. Unfortunately, Cook had not read the small print. Tucked away in his contract were the words, 'no editorial guarantees whatsoever'. This meant that the magazine could do what it liked with his copy. And that is what it did. What Cook had written as a rebuttal emerged as an admission of guilt which *Hampton's* advertised as 'DR. COOK'S CONFESSION'. Under the editorial pencil he said that he had no idea whether he had reached the Pole or not and that the American public was incapable of understanding the mental condition under which he had been suffering when he made his claims. The defeat was so complete that when his journal was published it was laughed out of the bookshops. 'DR. COOK CONFESSES HE DIDN'T CONFESS,'[48] jeered the *New York Times*. Cook retreated once again, sniping at his enemies from a crumbling redoubt of credibility.

He sued everyone who questioned the truth of his statements, but all his lawsuits failed. For this he blamed Peary, who had smothered him with a 'leprous blanket of infamy'.[49] He wrote that, 'I found myself the object of a campaign to discredit me in which, I believe, I stand the most shamefully abused man in the history of exploration.'[50] His conspiracy theory was without foundation, for there were plenty of people willing either to support him or attack Peary. But their efforts were thwarted by Cook's own mendacity. In 1910, a team recreated his ascent of Mt. McKinley, determined to prove that Cook had climbed it. They found that, after a certain point, his map 'abruptly departs from reasonable accuracy into complete fantasy'.[51] Later, an expedition went to Etah to recover Cook's original diary. His belongings had been scavenged by Eskimos but they were able to retrieve a sextant and a few other items. There was no diary, however, nor any evidence that such a thing had existed. The Eskimos swore that his packages had contained no papers; moreover, they had only opened the packages because Dr Cook had left without paying his debts.

Despite Cook's lies, some people still spoke up for him, only to be silenced by the clamour of patriotism. 'To discredit Robert E. Peary, after all his years of endeavour,' said one man, 'must necessarily discredit American scientists who have put the stamp of their approval upon his labors . . . it would seem that the only thing for Congress to do would be to accept the verdict of the National Geographic Society without further humiliation of the American explorer.'[52] In 1916, however, Congressman Henry Helgesen uncovered the National Geographic Society's sub-committee's adjudication of Peary's proof. He was appalled by the slipshod manner in which it had treated the material and demanded that Rear-Admiral Peary be stripped of his rank and the pension that came with it. In Helgesen's words, Peary's 'claims to the discoveries in the Arctic regions have been proven to rest on fiction and not on geographical facts'.[53] What he said was true, but it was ignored in the debate over America's involvement in the First World War. Helgesen died the following year and his lengthy analysis of Peary's shortcomings was consigned to the archives of the *Congressional Record*, its 120 columns of small print to be picked over by future Cookites seeking to re-establish their hero's reputation. (There still exists a Frederick A. Cook Society devoted to that very task.) But even had Helgesen lived it is doubtful whether his report would have received much popular attention. When the doughboys sailed for Europe in 1917, polar squabbles were the last thing on their mind.

Peary did not participate in the war. He was invited to enter politics but refused: he was too busy fighting his old enemy Greely, the latest man to question his record; and any nomination might involve the troublesome business of the Pole. Besides, he had no training for politics, and he was ill. On one of his early Greenland expeditions, Peary had been diagnosed by Cook as suffering from anaemia. In those days anaemia was used to describe any form of unnatural paleness and included the depression attendant on a sunless winter. But Peary now had real anaemia – pernicious anaemia – for which there was no cure. He tried to ignore it. A fellow sufferer who wrote to him received the following reply: 'Searching physical examination by independent doctors have shown that every organ is sound, healthy, and in smooth running order; my appetite is first class, and I sleep like a man who has worked hard all day. My blood pressure, the doctors tell me, is that of a man of forty . . . Within the past weeks three doctors independently have stated that I was over the top, out of the woods, every chance for a complete recovery. I have not at any time felt any apprehension in regard to my condition because I could not believe that a perfectly sound, smooth-running machine could be put out of commission permanently because the steam pressure had run a bit low.'[54] To his wife he said, 'Jo, we have won many fights. We are going to win this one.'[55]

The man who had wanted his name to live for ever fought against his own mortality. He took his blood-cell counts at regular intervals, noting always the highs. But the diary in which he kept track of his illness – a far more detailed diary than he had kept on his voyage to the Pole – showed his lows. 'Tendency to nausea much of the day . . . Perspiration at breakfast . . . Group photo . . . Distinctly tired feeling . . . Mutton chops and baked beans . . . Uncomfortable feeling disappears, but much annoyed by stinging sensation in left nostril preventing sleep till midnight . . . Near vomiting before breakfast . . . Flush and perspiration after breakfast.'[56] Slowly, the superman broke apart. On Friday, 19 February 1920, at noon, Robert Edwin Peary fell into a coma. He died at 1.20 a.m. The next Monday he was interred in Arlington Cemetery. Planes flew over his grave, troopers fired volleys and a Navy bugler ended the ceremony.

One of Peary's biographers, John Edward Weems, finishes his book with a romantic quote from Peary's journal: 'I can hear the eager yelping of the dogs, the shouting of the drivers, and the forward rush of every man and sledge, as after days of weary travel across the ragged sea ice, every man and dog spurts for the shore of that untrodden land lying a few yards ahead in the brilliant Arctic sunlight.'[57] Was this the memory that Peary took with him to the grave? Or was it a letter from

Josephine, written in 1905: 'I hope you will live to know that you have reached the Pole; then you will be content to die, whether anyone else knows it or not.'[58] More likely it was the latter. He did die, he was content, and nobody knew if he had done it.

22

THE LAST HEROES

B y the time of Peary's death in 1920, his position as conqueror of
the Pole had received widespread popular acceptance, buttressed
as it was by the support of the National Geographic Society, many of
the world's learned bodies and, importantly, the passage of time. In
the immediate aftermath of his conquest, however, the controversy
with Cook left many people in doubt as to whether the polar question
had actually been solved. If it was so difficult, given the nature of the
evidence, to adjudicate between the two claimants, how then was it so
easy to say that either man had actually reached the Pole? A young
explorer named Gregoriy Yakovlevich Sedov decided to settle the
matter by leading his own expedition to the Pole. As he said in a
memo to the Tsar's Central Hydrographic Directorate, dated 22
March 1912, 'we will show the world that Russians are equal to the
ordeal'.[1]

Virtually unknown in the West, but revered in Russia as one of its
greatest Arctic explorers, Sedov was a man of innate talent. Born in
1877, the son of an illiterate Azov fisherman, he did not go to school
until he was fifteen. When he was eighteen he ran away to Rostov,
where he enrolled in navigational classes, on completion of which he

earned his master's ticket then fought his way into St Petersburg's elite Naval College. On graduation he applied himself to the North-East Passage which he saw, presciently, as being of major importance both to Russian trade and the development of Siberia. In 1909, while Peary was attacking the polar pack, Sedov sledged across the Siberian tundra with minimal funds and manpower to complete a thorough survey of the region. The next year, in a ship, he produced a deluge of information about the coastline, which encompassed data on navigable approaches, underwater hazards, characteristics of the sea-bed, the quirks of the tides, the supply of fresh water and the availability of furs for trading. So impressive were his surveying skills and his tenacity in the field that he was rewarded with the rank of Second-Lieutenant in the Imperial Russian Navy – a rare promotion for one who lacked money or title.

Although Sedov had toyed for almost a decade with the idea of travelling to the North Pole, the North-East Passage was his main concern. As he very sensibly said, 'We are far from the Pole when the coasts lying next to the Motherland as yet remain a mystery to us.'[2] But the dispute surrounding Peary's conquest, coupled with a disturbing inquiry in 1911 from Julius Payer's son as to the possibility of hiring a Russian ice-breaker to take him to the Pole, forced Sedov to consolidate his plans. In 1912 he petitioned the government for 50,000 roubles to support an expedition from Archangel that would map the unknown segments of Franz Josef Land before sledging north to take the Pole. The task, he states, was 'of importance not only to the nation, but to all mankind'. And, he added, he was willing to die for it – a theme which he maybe pursued too energetically, stating: 'the noble impulses of men striving to sacrifice their lives for science should not be thwarted by the absence of material means to fulfil those tasks'.[3]

Asked to support an apparent suicide attempt, and noting that the plan showed signs of hastiness, the government was not forthcoming. Sedov had 'their sympathy in principle' but he could not have their money. Like his US contemporaries, Sedov turned therefore to the press and to the public. The *Noyoe Vremya*, a newspaper whose proprietor, a man named Suvorin, was no more a stranger to the value of publicity than James Gordon Bennett or Alfred Harmsworth, took up his case. Suvorin supplied some of the money and his readers – predominantly the educated elite; scientists and artists mostly – donated the rest. The total fell short of the sum Sedov wanted but it was enough to buy a ship, fill its holds with provisions and to hire a crew.

In September 1912, Sedov arrived in Archangel to take command of the *Svatoy muchenik Foka*. It was a shabby, 273-ton sealer, built in 1877 and badly in need of an overhaul. Yet it was still afloat and its 100-horsepower engine could force its iron-sheathed bow through the ice at a rate of six knots. Onto this vessel Sedov loaded twenty-seven men – fourteen of whom were to be explorers, including six scientists of various disciplines – plus a limited selection of low-grade supplies. Smelling a profit, the Archangel merchants had equipped the *Foka* with the shoddiest material they could find: the clothes were thin, and could not last more than one winter; the coal was sufficient for four weeks' steaming at best; and the food was an invitation to scurvy, comprising mostly salted meat and salted fish with no fresh meat or vegetables. Then, no sooner had Sedov taken men and supplies aboard, than the port authorities announced the *Foka*'s waterline was a few inches lower than regulations permitted and it could not leave the harbour. 'Sedov flew into a rage,' one of his companions reported, 'and ordered the deck cargo to be pitched on the quay. Boxes, barrels, whatever came to hand, flew over the rails.'[4] Thirteen days later, having slashed through jungles of red tape, he was permitted to start his voyage. 'Where there is order, there is victory,'[5] he consoled himself caustically, as he sailed out of Archangel.

Already the victim of profiteering, indifference and bureaucracy, Sedov now fell prey to the Arctic. Instead of reaching Franz Josef Land in the first year, he was forced by storms to overwinter on Novaya Zemlya – an event he did not welcome, for he had planned to send the *Foka* home once it had dropped his exploring party, and the stranded crew now put an extra strain on his already insufficient supplies. Resignedly, he put his confinement to good use, embarking on a thorough survey of the north-west coast by dog-sled – on one occasion he covered 620 miles in fifty-seven days – and taking a stream of meteorological readings. When he sent some of the men home with his findings in 1913, the Hydrographic Office was so impressed that it invited Nansen to admire the results. 'Very useful,'[6] was his verdict. Nansen seems to have considered Sedov less of an explorer than a surveyor, which perhaps explains his cool response: compared with his own voyage on the *Fram*, Sedov's was of minor importance. Had he realized that Sedov was merely killing time on Novaya Zemlya before continuing to Franz Josef Land and the Pole he might have been more appreciative. He might also have been able to exert influence on his behalf. For Sedov had sent back not only his findings and several crew members but a request for more supplies. The request was ignored. Later that year, Sedov despatched another group of surplus men, bearing a similar request. This, too, was ignored. While Nansen returned unconcernedly to Norway, Sedov was left to capture the Pole with the smallest amount of fuel and food allocated to any explorer in Arctic history.

The pictorial records of Sedov's expedition are scant, being restricted to a few poor quality photographs in which uniformed silhouettes pose on unknown headlands, their vast, black flags frozen mid-billow against a grainy Arctic sky. It is hard to gauge the characters of these shadow men, but their actions show that they must have been incomprehensibly tough. Stripped of crew, short of fuel and with scurvy already evident amongst his men, Sedov continued on his quest for the North Pole. He had his team shoot bears and seals to alleviate their salt-meat diet; he had them collect driftwood to feed the *Foka*'s furnaces; he even tried to tame bear cubs for use as draught animals in case the dogs fell ill. The scientists made polite noises of disquiet, to which Sedov replied with equally polite orders to be silent. On 11 September 1913, he wrote, 'Today the officers made me a fine gift: through the officer of the watch, they proposed turning back. At first this really amazed me, then it pained me, because I had to refuse them.'[7] The *Foka* left Novaya Zemlya for Franz Josef Land on 16 September and reached Cape Flora ten days later, by which time the remaining coal had been consumed and the stokers were making use of blubber, ropes and old sails. The doubters were now appreciative of their leader. 'Without his unshakeable persistence and talents as an ice-captain, we could scarcely have achieved success,'[8] wrote one man.

At Cape Flora they discovered a small amount of coal left behind by Anthony Fiala, leader of the second Ziegler expedition. Into the furnace it went, followed by the remains of Frederick Jackson's wooden huts, an allowance that enabled them to steam to the next island north. There, however, they were hemmed in by a new season of ice. Their fuel was by now reduced to 660 pounds of coal dust, a number of walrus hides and a few empty barrels and boxes. That winter they fed their stove with blubber and the partitions between the officers' cabins. By Christmas only three men were healthy, all the rest having scurvy. Sedov was among the afflicted. On 2 January 1914 he wrote, 'Legs completely paralysed.' On 8 January: 'Sadness in my heart. My health is deteriorating. I sit, or lie, shut alone in my cabin.' A month later: 'Am writing orders and letters home. May these all be posthumous?'[9] Yet he refused to give up. 'He would not abandon [the Pole] because of that,' wrote an officer, 'and would go north until he was down to his last crust.'[10]

Still suffering from scurvy, Sedov departed on foot, on 15 February, for the Pole. He took with him two volunteer sailors, three sledges, twenty-four dogs and enough food to see them to the top of the world. He hoped to pick up supplies left by Abruzzi and Fiala, but even with these reinforcements he knew he was unlikely to return alive.

Before he left he delivered a valedictory speech to his comrades. 'This order may possibly be my last word,' he began, 'may it serve for you all as a souvenir of our mutual friendship and love.' A few sentences later he faltered. 'He stood for a few moments with his eyes closed, as if gathering his thoughts, in order to say some final words,' wrote one man. 'But instead of words, a scarcely audible groan was torn from him and tears glistened in the corners of his closed eyes . . . With an effort, Gregoriy Yakovlevich got control of himself, looked at us all, and began to speak, at first jerkily, but then more smoothly and calmly as his voice became firmer ". . . I am setting off on this journey not as strong as I might be, or as I would wish to be at this important moment. The time has arrived, and we are beginning the first Russian attempt to reach the North Pole . . . Today is a great day for us and for Russia. But can we really go to the Pole with this equipment? Can I really expect to reach it with these supplies? . . . Our supplies are exhausted . . . and we ourselves are not as strong in health as we should be. But this does not prevent us from carrying out our duty. We will do our duty.'"[11]

Off the three men went to do their duty, in temperatures of –104°F. 'The going is atrocious,' Sedov wrote on the 17th. 'Our dogs are suffering terribly.' Three days later, 'Going is abominable . . . My legs have become bad again and my bronchitis is worse. It is very difficult to walk and even harder to breathe.'[12] By the 22nd Sedov could no longer move his legs and had to be carried on a sledge. The other two urged him to turn back but 'he would just smile and shake his head'.[13] Sedov's last journal entry came on 1 March. Two days later he died. They had not even reached Prince Rudolf Island.

'I took a clean handkerchief and covered our leader's face with it,' one of the seamen wrote. 'For the first time in my life, I did not know what to do, and began to tremble with an inexplicable fear.'[14] The two seamen were, indeed, in an unenviable position. Their food and fuel were almost exhausted, their leader was dead, they were unsure how to find their way home and, to compound matters, a three-day blizzard covered the sledges and froze two of their dogs to death. When the weather cleared they buried Sedov with the flag he had hoped to fly at the Pole and then began their retreat. After a terrible journey in which their fuel ran out, their dogs died of cold and hunger, and in which their navigation was impeded by snowstorms and fog, they reached the *Foka* on 19 March.

For the next four months, as the Russians waited for the ice to open, flocks of seabirds arrived on the island, providing a welcome change of diet which enabled the crew to recover from their scurvy and even gave them the strength to survey the nearby islands. They finally broke free on 25 July and steamed for Cape Flora, feeding the bulwarks and inner decks into the furnace as they went. By the time they reached their destination almost every combustible article save the hull, the masts and the upper deck had been burned, reducing the ship to little more than a shell. They counted, however, on being able to scavenge a few more scraps from Jackson's huts to see them through the ice until they were able to raise sail in clear seas.

Already the scene of one miraculous encounter – that between Jackson and Nansen – Cape Flora was about to witness another. It was only by mischance that the *Foka* stopped there. Were it not for the shortage of fuel it would have steamed straight past the place. And had it done so, another pair of corpses would have been added to the Arctic tally. For as the *Foka* smoked towards Cape Flora, two figures paddled desperately in kayaks towards it. They were from the *Svatoy Anna*.

The *Anna* had left Russia in September 1912 on a journey through the North-East Passage, but had become beset in the southern Kara Sea and from there had been dragged north by the Arctic drift. Unprepared for a winter in the ice, the crew had two options: to stay with the ship and hope the drift pushed them into the Atlantic; or to walk to Franz Josef Land in search of help. In the end they did both, half the crew remaining on board while the other half trekked over the ice. Nothing was ever heard of the *Anna* or its crew again; of the landward party, the two men who reached Cape Flora were the only survivors.

Carrying the human salvage of two disasters, the *Foka* struggled south for the motherland, arriving in Archangel on 6 September. In another country and at another time, its homecoming might have been cause for celebration. But in the late summer of 1914, Russian's attention was directed towards the progress of the First World War. Sedov's expedition received a few short notices in the press, the Navy treated his demise as a welcome end to a parvenu irritant, and his findings were dismissed as irrelevant. The last, and perhaps the most tragic, of the Arctic heroes sank into oblivion. Consigned to the archives, his journals gathered dust under Tsarist and Soviet rule, not to be opened until 1956, forty-five years after their author had perished.

The Age of Heroes, and the society that had produced it, collapsed with the First World War. At the turn of the century, 'bigness' had been a catchphrase associated with heroism – the big goal, the big endeavour, the big result. (Peary had always been talking about doing something big.) Big things and heroic deeds had been seen as an antidote to the charmless routine of industrialism. But the war of 1914–19 cast a shadow so colossal that big deeds became commonplace. The duty which had beckoned Sedov in 1914 called more than thirteen million men to their deaths in the succeeding five years. Against the horror of the trenches, polar exploration was considered a self-indulgent and at times unpatriotic pastime. In 1916, when Shackleton and his crew were released from entrapment in the Antarctic, Winston Churchill wrote from Flanders: 'When all the sick and wounded have been tended . . . when every hospital is gorged with money, and every charity subscription is closed, then and not until then would I concern myself with those penguins. I suppose, however, something will have to be done.'[15] In 1919, when the armistice was signed, heroism was a word used more in anger than in admiration.

By the 1920s there were few Arctic heroes left in service. Nansen had abandoned exploring for a career in politics. Abruzzi, having commanded the Italian Navy during the First World War, was too busy consolidating the shaky position of his royal house. Nares had died in 1915 and most of his lieutenants were in retirement. Of Peary's men, Borup had drowned in a boating accident before the war; Macmillan was still in the field, but that field was the Canadian Arctic, not the Pole – it was he who discovered in 1914 that neither Crocker Land nor Bradley Island existed. And Bartlett's ardour had faded too. In 1913 he had captained a fantastically bad expedition under the American explorer Vilhjalmur Stefansson, which resulted in a near-repetition of the *Jeannette* disaster. Stefansson had jumped ship off Alaska, leaving Bartlett plus crew to fend for themselves. Their ship, the *Karluk*, had drifted with the ice, forcing its crew onto

Wrangel Island from where Bartlett walked over the polar cap to Siberia, trudging hundreds of miles to find an ice-breaker that had not been requisitioned for war purposes. Of the pre-war heroes only Roald Amundsen, a citizen of neutral Norway, still preserved the flame. But where was he to turn his attentions?

Like Peary, Amundsen had always wanted to be an explorer, to do something notable. As a child he had read of Franklin's tribulations and it was this that had set him off. He had trained rigorously – more even than Peary – for polar conditions and although physically slight had expanded his muscles so impressively that when he applied for military service the examining doctor called his colleagues to view the specimen before him. Amundsen's training proved its worth when he became the first to sail through the North-West Passage in 1903–06 and then, in 1911, to beat Scott to the South Pole. The measure of his confidence was that before sailing for Antarctica he had been planning to take the *Fram* – borrowed from Nansen – on a drift to the North Pole. On learning of Peary's success, he changed his mind. 'This was a blow indeed!' he wrote. 'If I was to maintain my prestige as an explorer, I must quickly achieve a sensational success of some sort.'[16] So he went south and did just that. During the war, Norway being neutral, he traversed the North-East Passage – 'I had nothing else to do'[17] – and after the war, untouched by the world's altered perception of size, he went after one more 'big thing'. He would fly from one side of the north polar cap to the other. In this he had the support of a small body of scientific and exploratory experts. A flight such as Amundsen proposed would resolve all remaining questions.

It was a project he had been contemplating for some while, but his every attempt was dogged by misfortune. The planes were not delivered when promised, when they arrived they did not work, or when they did work they weren't capable of making the journey. At one point he had to register himself bankrupt after an unscrupulous agent ran up huge bills on his behalf. Preparing such an enterprise was something for which Amundsen was ill-suited, involving as it did a knowledge of machinery and a sound grasp of business, two qualities which he lacked outstandingly or which, as he preferred to put it, he had not had time to acquire. His greatest asset was his physical fitness – in 1922, at the age of fifty, he ran 800 miles through the snows in Alaska in sixteen days to disprove a heart specialist who had warned him he would die if he took any more strenuous exercise. But physical fitness did not make planes fly.

By the fall of 1924, Amundsen was in despair. A lecture tour of the United States had failed to raise money or to produce a sympathetic backer of the sort Peary had enjoyed throughout his career. In New York, Amundsen desponded: 'As I sat in my room in the Waldorf-Astoria, it seemed to me as if the future had closed solidly against me, and that my career as an explorer had come to an inglorious end. Courage, will-power, indomitable faith – these qualities had carried me through many dangers and to many achievements. Now even their merits seemed of no avail. I was nearer to black despair than ever before in my fifty-four years of life.'[18] His gloom was interrupted by the telephone. He answered it reluctantly, expecting a time-waster or, worse, one of his many creditors. Instead, it was Lincoln Ellsworth, the son of a Chicago millionaire. As Amundsen recorded happily, 'Mr. Ellsworth explained that he had an independent income and a strong thirst for adventure.'[19]

By the following spring the Amundsen–Ellsworth Arctic Expedition was at Spitsbergen. Ellsworth senior had donated $85,000, on the condition that his son stopped smoking, and with this money Lincoln Ellsworth had purchased two Dornier flying boats, four crew to fly them, fuel sufficient to carry them 1,200 miles, and a plentiful supply of tobacco. The Dorniers took off on 21 May 1925, and as an excited Amundsen wrote, '[we] shaped our course to carry us towards the North Pole.'[20]

Previously, Amundsen had announced, 'I had no interest in the Pole itself – Peary's splendid achievement in 1909 had destroyed the value of that prize for all later explorers.'[21] It was a semi-truth. Having been the first explorer to conquer the South Pole and the North-West Passage, and having crossed the North-East Passage, Amundsen now wanted to add the North Pole to the other scalps on his belt. Besides, there was still a belief that a body of land, maybe of continental proportions, was hidden somewhere in the Arctic. Stefansson had been trying to find that land mass above Canada when he abandoned Bartlett and the *Karluk* in 1913. Stefansson had failed – Amundsen thought little of him: in his biography, *My Life as an Explorer*, he dismissed him in a chapter, 'Mr. Stefansson and others'. Still, given the controversy over who had found the Pole, or if it had been found at all, Amundsen half hoped that there might yet be land at the Pole, or if it lay elsewhere, that he might be able to discover it from the altitude at which his Dorniers flew. 'This particular part of the Arctic Ocean was unexplored, and we might possibly make some discovery about land, besides,'[22] he wrote.

The Dorniers – named N-24 and N-25 – reached only 87°14' before N-24 developed engine trouble. Seeing a stretch of open water below them – the first that they had met on their flight over the cap – Amundsen and Ellsworth decided to land. The Dorniers came down and on inspection the engineers declared that N-24's engines were 'utterly out of commission'. Then the open water began to sludge over. Six hours after landing, the crew were chipping at the ice to stop the planes being frozen in. 'Here we were,' wrote Amundsen, 'landed upon the ice with airplanes equipped for landing upon water . . . and with provisions adequate for full nourishment for only about three weeks.'[23] Never, except perhaps for Andrée's balloonists, had a group of men been less prepared for an escape over the polar pack.

For twenty-four days, twenty-four hours a day, they chopped at the ice to create a skiway over which the N-25, the plane on which their survival depended, could take off. During this period they survived on eight ounces of food per day – half the rations which Peary had fed to his dogs, Amundsen noted. By 15 June they had carved a navigable strip. Abandoning all surplus supplies they climbed aboard the N-25. Soon the over-laden plane was on its way.

'The most anxious moments of my life were the last two seconds,' Amundsen wrote. 'As we gained speed, the inequalities on the ice multiplied their effect upon us and the fuselage swayed from side to side with such a careening motion that more than once I feared we should be thrown over on one side and have one of our wings crushed. Nearer and faster we approached the end of our runway, but still the bumping motion indicated we had not left the ice. Still gaining momentum, but still hugging the ice, we approached the brink . . . and then we rose. An enormous sense of relief swept over me, but it lasted only an instant. There, dead ahead of us, and only a few yards away, loomed [a] twenty-foot hummock . . . We were headed straight towards it . . . Thoughts and sensations crowd fast at such a moment. The seconds seemed terrible hours. But we did clear it – we could not have had more than an inch to spare. At last we were on the way.'[24] On 15 June 1925, with thirty minutes of fuel remaining, and with its ailerons refusing to respond, the Norwegian pilot, Hjalmar Riiser-Larsen, crash-landed N-25 in the sea off Spitsbergen. Three weeks later, Amundsen and Ellsworth were in Norway where, undaunted by their near-disaster, 'we immediately proceeded with plans for a more ambitious undertaking'.[25] They would fly to the Pole in an airship.

There were several good reasons for choosing an airship over a plane: they were safer, they could cover greater distances without refuelling and they could hover. As Amundsen observed, the great advantage to hovering was that a closer and more detailed inspection of the terrain could be made. Unspoken, though probably in his mind, was that if an airship could hover it could also let down a man on a rope. If there was a continent at or near the pole, a man lowered on a rope could therefore walk upon it. Such a man could name the continent after himself. And such a man could be Amundsen. Against these advantages was the expense of an airship – for the $200,000 cost of a new model, they could have purchased four Dorniers and still had money left over. But in 1926 an opportunity arose to purchase a second-hand Italian dirigible which could be delivered to Spitsbergen with pilot and crew for just $75,000. Ellsworth dug into his pockets and the deal was made.

It was not the first time airships had been used in the Arctic. Walter Wellman, the American journalist/explorer who had nearly crippled himself on a sledge expedition in 1899, was one of the pioneers of polar aeronautics and in the first decade of the twentieth century he had made several attempts at the Pole not by balloon – the fate of Andrée had seen to that – but by the new-fangled means of a hydrogen-filled dirigible. His expeditions were over-ambitious, unsuccessful and conceived in an overly simplistic fashion. But one has to admire the spirit in which they were carried out. On New Year's Eve 1905, Wellman received a cable from his editor at the *Chicago Record-Herald*: 'Build an airship and with it go find the North Pole.'[26] Without hesitation he did as he was bidden. 'Here,' he explained in the phraseology of the time, 'was an opportunity to attempt a big thing.'[27]

Gathering the necessary men and machinery, he headed in 1906 for Virgo Harbour on Dane's Island, the site from which Andrée's balloon had taken off. The untested engines broke on their bench-trial and he went home without even having inflated the craft. He returned in 1907 with a new and better dirigible – the second largest in the world after the *Hindenburg* – and this time he did take to the air, travelling only fifteen miles, however, before being blown inland where he crashed into a glacier. The entire trip lasted just three hours. A third attempt in 1909 was even worse: his new dirigible came down in the sea, had to be towed home and, as Wellman and his crew were dolefully emptying its fuel tanks, it rose suddenly into the air and, on reaching an altitude where its fabric could no longer contain the expanding gas, it burst, showering the onlookers with debris. ('The most thrilling thing I've ever seen,'[28] one man recorded.) Rejecting the Pole, Wellman attempted a transatlantic flight in 1910. The results were equally unhappy: his dirigible developed engine problems, drifted 1,000 miles to the south and crashed in the sea off Bermuda. He became a laughing-stock, and when rival journalists learned he had taken a cat aboard, they had a field day. 'We can fully understand why Wellman and his companions embarked on a voyage which for foolhardiness exceeds anything in the field of human recklessness,' wrote one paper, 'but what gets us is how a perfectly sane cat ever consented to go.'[29] Wellman never went into the air again.

Wellman's failures did much to discredit the idea of reaching the

Pole by airship. Critics, however, did not take into account the infant state of dirigible technology at the time – Wellman's gondolas, for example, resembled elongated Canadian canoes – nor the character of Wellman himself. One journalist reported his methods in excoriating terms: 'Since August 1 [he] has followed the Spartan regime he set himself without complaint. As usual through the hard and trying period of preparation Mr Wellman left his rough Louis XIV couch ... at 8 o'clock this morning ... At the breakfast table Mr. Wellman ate the frugal but sustaining meal which wide experience in the wildest hotels along Broadway and other channels of travel has taught him is best for adventurers. He rarely has more than steak, eggs, buckwheat cakes, potatoes, fruit, biscuits and coffee for breakfast. A pause in training might be expected here, but Mr. Wellman is made of sterner stuff. He returned to his room, got his strength together, and when a newspaperman called up and asked "when the old gas-bag was going up", Mr Wellman told him to go where a gas-bag would explode ... [he] would go when he was ready for the trip, and did not give a rump-de-dump whoop-de-do for what other folks said about it.'[30] Wellman's imperious manner irritated his workers and on one occasion a French mechanic had to be restrained from doing him a physical injury.

Serious explorers considered his exploits the poorest form of advertising stunt: Nansen visited Virgo Harbour in 1912 and on seeing the skeleton of Wellman's airship hangar scoffed heartily at the 'ruins of that great humbug'.[31] The memory of Wellman's incompetence lasted almost a decade: when an Australian named George Wilkins proposed an Arctic flight in 1919, manufacturers would not sell him an airship at any price for fear of the bad publicity he would attract.

By the mid-1920s, however, dirigible technology had advanced. German engineers led the way, wartime experience having enabled them to produce airships that could roam the globe. Known as Zeppelins, after Count Ferdinand von Zeppelin (who had not only pioneered their design but had investigated in 1910 their application in the Arctic), they were now manufactured in Italy, under strictures laid down by the Treaty of Versailles. But although the factories had changed hands, German-designed zeppelins were still better than anything else on the market. After the First World War Britain and America had produced their own airships, based on captured German models, but they were shoddy things with an unreliable record and a history of explosions. If one wanted the real article one went to Italy.

Moreover, airships were no longer the playthings of journalists but serious transcontinental vessels. An amateur like Wellman would never have been allowed near the controls of the sleek dirigibles which were now visible over every major capital from Berlin to New York and – soon – Tokyo. To control an airship, with all its fiddly controls governing elevation, sideways steering and variations in gas pressure, one needed an experienced pilot, and the best pilots were to be found where the best dirigibles were being made – in Italy. Amundsen and Ellsworth were being perfectly sensible, therefore, in choosing an Italian-built airship that was crewed and piloted by an Italian aviator. Where they might have made a mistake was in choosing Colonel Umberto Nobile as the pilot.

Nobile was a small, proud, excitable man who weighed nine and a half stone and was devoted to his pet dog, a terrier named Titina who accompanied him on all his flights. He was not the best pilot in the world, nor indeed in Italy, but he was a skilled airship designer, whose dirigibles were in international demand. He would later be employed by Stalin to construct the biggest and best airship in existence – an early example of the arms race which came to nothing – and he had designed the N-1, the airship which Amundsen had contracted to buy. Amundsen was happy to have him aboard, on the grounds that the man who had built the ship would be the best one to mend it if it went wrong. When he and Riiser-Larsen travelled to Rome, however, Nobile treated them to a wild display of his driving skills. Fancying a dip in the resort of Ostia, the two Norwegians accepted Nobile's offer to drive them there in person. '[He] proved to be a most eccentric chauffeur,' Amundsen recalled. 'So long as we were proceeding on a straight and level stretch of highway he drove steadily at a rational speed. The moment, however, we approached a curve in the road where an ordinary driver would slow down as a matter of course, Nobile's procedure was directly the opposite. He would press the accelerator down to the floor, and we would take the blind curve at terrific speed. Halfway round, as I was convulsively tightening my grip on the seat with my hands and shuddering with fear of disaster, Nobile would seem to come out of a cloud of abstraction, realize the danger, and frantically seek to avert it. He would jam his brakes on with all his strength, which, of course, with our centrifugal momentum, threatened to topple us over. To prevent this, he would then start zigzagging with his front wheels . . . Riiser-Larsen, who is one of the most sensible men I ever knew, was sitting muttering to himself that we should certainly all be killed.'[32]

After this terrifying ride in a machine whose speed probably did not exceed forty to fifty miles per hour on the straight, the two men conferred in their hotel room. Should Nobile be dropped from the project, a badly shaken Amundsen asked. No, said Riiser-Larsen, it was often the case that madmen on the ground became paragons of steadiness in the air. And the Italian was the ideal man to pilot the airship: 'He had handled her on many flights, and of course would be familiar with every trick and peculiarity about her.'[33] Nobile was therefore accepted. Not accepted, on the other hand, was an offer from Benito Mussolini that Amundsen could have the N-1 for free provided it flew the Italian flag. This was dismissed as a blatant piece of fascist propaganda. Mussolini's suggestion that the flight be called the Amundsen–Ellsworth-Nobile Expedition was similarly rejected. It could only be known as such in Italy, Amundsen said ('to gratify local . . . pride'[34]), but in the wider world it would be strictly him and Ellsworth who were credited. 'I was delighted to share the national honours with my beloved American friend,' he explained, 'I did not want to share them with the Italians. We owed them nothing but the opportunity to buy and pay for a second-hand military dirigible . . . It was our idea. It was financed with our money, and it would be made in the craft we had bought and paid for.'[35]

On 29 March 1926 the N-1, now christened the *Norge*, was officially handed over to Amundsen at Ciampino airport outside Rome.

Mussolini attended the ceremony, wearing his smartest civilian clothes. Amundsen, too, put on his best formal suit – which he hated – and with a bowler hat perched on his disproportionately large head looked 'as if the weight would drive his tapered legs into the earth and anchor him there'.[36] He, Mussolini, Nobile and various Italian dignitaries posed for a publicity shot, Nobile sharing the foreground with Mussolini, everyone grinning hugely. Then Amundsen left for King's Harbour, Spitsbergen, leaving Nobile to follow on the *Norge* when the weather was right.

Nobile's departure was set for 3 April and on that date Mussolini turned up again at Ciampino, more comfortably dressed and wearing a plaster on his nose, the result of a mismanaged assassination attempt the previous day.* The winds, however, were too strong for Nobile's liking and he declined to take off. Mussolini applauded his decision. 'You'll succeed,' he said as he drove off. 'You'll go – and come back victorious.'[38] He did not attend a week later when the *Norge* finally rose into the air – with the Italian flag secretly painted on its hull – and headed for Spitsbergen on a circuitous route that took it over France to Britain, and then via all major Scandinavian cities to Leningrad, where there was not only a voluminous storage hangar but a wealth of professors whose ballooning experiments had given them more knowledge about Arctic flying conditions than anyone on earth. 'All, some more or less, thought it probable that ice or snow would form on the envelope of the dirigible, in such quantities as to bring us down,'[39] Nobile wrote. The Leningrad experts cited the fate of a tethered balloon which had been sent into the clouds, only to sink back under the weight of an inch-thick coating of ice that had formed in a few minutes. Glumly, Nobile resumed his flight to Spitsbergen, serenaded from below by a Soviet band, and arrived at King's Harbour on 7 May, slipping into the hangar which Amundsen had had built for him.

Amundsen had never had expectations of being first to the Pole. Although a loyal friend and supporter of Cook, he recognized Peary's

---

* His assailant was the Hon. Violet Gibson from Ireland, who had fired a pistol but had only managed to graze her target's nose. 'Fancy! A woman!'[37] Il Duce is reported to have said.

claim. 'I know Admiral Peary reached the Pole,' he said flatly. 'The reason I know it is that I knew Peary. [That he had the] ability to fake his observations is perfectly true. The answer to any doubt on that score is simply that Peary was not that kind of man.'[40] It was an argument used by many during the protracted polar squabble: if you knew the man you knew he was honest. But there was another argument which said that even if Peary had reached the Pole it was necessary to revisit it in order to make the scientific observations which were lacking in his journal. As one magazine said when analysing the Cook-Peary dispute, 'Whatever be the truth, the results of these two expeditions are equally meagre and valueless.'[41]

In venerable tradition, Amundsen espoused scientific advance as an excuse for adventure. He was not alone in doing so. Even as the *Norge* was making its way to Spitsbergen, Robert Bartlett was steering a ship towards the same destination. On board, he carried Robert Evelyn Byrd and Floyd Bennett, two of America's pioneering airmen, and the plane in which they hoped to fly to the Pole. Also on board was a team of Pathé cameramen to record the event. Neither Amundsen nor Byrd said they were competing against each other but the press said it for them. The race for the Pole had begun all over again.

Amundsen was angered not by his American competitors – to whose impending arrival he had yet to be alerted – but by Nobile. During the flight from Rome, Nobile had refused to let the Norwegians wear the cold-weather suits which Amundsen had ordered at great expense from a tailor in Berlin. They weighed too much, Nobile said, and on an Arctic flight every ounce of fuel counted. But as Amundsen noted, Nobile and his men came aboard in thick furs. Then in Spitsbergen, Amundsen tried to teach the Italians how to ski in case the *Norge* crashed and they had to make their way home on foot. They fell all over the place. 'If we have to get down on the ice you will not leave us Italians and save yourselves,'[42] Nobile pleaded. Amundsen agreed that he would not, but he seethed at the slur. 'That this man had let the thought even enter his head,' he wrote, 'that men of our past record could be so base that he would need such a reassurance, only reveals his own mind.'[43] Nobile had also asked permission for the *Norge* to fly back to Spitsbergen once it had reached the Pole, a request that Amundsen dismissed as a sign of cowardice.

When Bartlett, Byrd and Bennett reached Spitsbergen on 29 April 1926, Amundsen realized the threat. Releasing himself from Nobile's ski lessons, he radioed Byrd that he could not land. There was a Norwegian gunboat already moored at the single pier and a whaler about to join it. Under no circumstance could he come ashore. Reluctantly, Amundsen allowed Bartlett to moor his ship temporarily against the gunboat, but he would not let Byrd take his plane on to Spitsbergen. It would be four days at least before the pier was free and in the meantime Byrd could either try the space in front of the gunboat – 'We would surely have gone aground,' Byrd wrote in his diary. 'I cannot understand.'[44] – or he could wait a safe distance away.

Anchored 300 yards offshore, Byrd became impatient: 'We cannot wait for days,'[45] he fumed. On the night of 30 April he ordered his men to construct a pontoon from the ships' boats and – 'Great work' – the plane was brought to dry land. The Pathé men were there to film the unloading but one of Amundsen's men announced that it was forbidden on Norwegian soil. Byrd was angry. 'Great sportsmanship,' he wrote in his diary. 'They deny us dock, deny movie, make us move out in stream. The Viking valor.'[46] Once on land, however, Byrd faced new problems. When he took his plane on a trial flight the skis with which it was fitted broke before the machine could take off. One of the less patriotic Norwegian officers, a pilot named Lieutenant Bernt Balchen, came over to help. He fashioned new skis from a couple of oars, rubbed them with grease and advised Byrd to leave at night when the ice would be more slippery. With that he wished him *bon voyage*.

In his published account, Amundsen took pains to explain that he had not intended to hinder Byrd. 'He fully understood the reasons for everything that happened,' he wrote, 'and he and I were then and are now on terms of the most cordial friendship.'[47] Byrd professed similar sentiments: Amundsen and Ellsworth were 'great sports', he said in his own journal. But Byrd's diary revealed his true feelings. 'In spite of everything the Norwegians do I intend to be a sport and be dignified and calm. They have made it very difficult,'[48] he wrote on 1 May. The next day, 'Took lunch with Amundsen who professes great friendship but gave Lt. Balchen (who is a peach and wanted to help us and has helped us) orders not to come near again.'[49]

The principle of sportsmanship was lost on Amundsen. His exploring career had been based on competitiveness and much as he liked to deny it he was now engaged in a competition to be the first man to fly to the Pole. Ironically, it was Nobile, the man Amundsen loved to hate, who was most anxious about Byrd beating them to their goal. He urged them to get the *Norge* aloft as swiftly as possible. Amundsen and Riiser-Larsen laughed at him. They laughed all the more when Byrd came ashore – the American plane could never take off with skis like that. But when Balchen came to Byrd's aid they stopped laughing. And they did not smile on the night of 8 May when they heard the roar of a triple-engined Fokker taking off for the north, with Byrd and Floyd Bennett at its helm. Fifteen and a half hours later, Amundsen and his crew were at dinner. One man remarked that Byrd and Floyd Bennett ought to be back by now, if they were ever coming back. At that moment, in the distance, they heard the drone of the Fokker. Byrd had done it.

Byrd's flight, since hailed as one of the milestones of Arctic and aeronautical exploration, was truly heroic. He and Floyd Bennett had flown to the Pole in an unpressurized aeroplane, the noise of its engines so great that they could only communicate by scribbled notes, and whose heating was almost non-existent – Byrd suffered frost-nips while taking his readings – and which, if it had been forced to land would never have been able to take off again. (They carried pemmican and a collapsible boat with which they hoped to reach Greenland if they crashed; but these precautions would only have prolonged their lives briefly.) Shortly before the Pole one of the engines started to leak oil, a sign of impending failure, but Byrd still continued – and if his journal is to be believed, how could he stop?

'At the end of this unknown area lay our goal, somewhere beyond the shimmering horizon,' Byrd wrote. 'We were opening unexplored regions at the rate of nearly 10,000 square miles per hour, and were experiencing the incomparable satisfaction of searching for new land ... I had a momentary sensation of great triumph. If I could explain the feeling I had at this time, the much-asked question would be answered: "What is this Arctic craze so many men get?"'[50] He circled what he assumed to be the Pole from the readings he took on his sextant and sun-compass – a new development that obviated the need for magnetic positioning – and then, when his compass broke on the return journey, he navigated blind to Spitsbergen where he was met by Amundsen's team with 'nine good Norwegian cheers'.[51]

By any standards Byrd had done well. On his return to New York he was greeted by a ticker-tape reception and awarded the Congressional Medal of Honor. Songs and poems were composed in his honour. Parents named their children after him. Even Amundsen had praise (with faint damns) for his flight: 'If considered only as a feat of navigation, Commander Byrd's exploit is one of the most remarkable on record.'[52]

But had he reached the Pole? Byrd's readings were later studied and approved by the National Geographic Society – the same body which had awarded Peary his victory – but doubts were soon raised by less partial observers. When Byrd went back to America, Bernt Balchen went with him and on closer acquaintance with Byrd's plane – which he flew across the continent – he decided that the Fokker could never have reached the Pole in the time Byrd claimed. Balchen later said that Floyd Bennett had admitted, in private, that they had just flown around for a while before coming home.

In 1960, Professor G. Lilequist of the University of Uppsala studied the prevailing weather conditions at the time of Byrd's flight and, coupling this with the output of the Fokker's engines, declared that Byrd could not have reached the Pole. Thirteen years later another aeronautics authority decided that Byrd could have come within fifty miles of the Pole. Then in 1979 Finn Romme, one of Byrd's later flying companions, revealed that Byrd himself had admitted to having come no closer than 150 miles to the top of the world. Meanwhile, the National Geographic Society continued to support Byrd's claim.

Reading his diaries, and the scraps of paper which he passed to Floyd Bennett, it is hard to believe that he did not come at least within sight of the Pole. His calculations are there in pencil: average speed, 85 miles per hour; time spent in the air, eight and a half hours; distance covered, 722 statute miles; therefore, at the hour at which he did his sums, he was twenty statute miles from the Pole. But these calculations assumed he travelled in a direct line. The written messages which he passed to Floyd Bennett show that they were blown off course. And there are erasures in his diary which hint that his original readings placed him well to the south – but these can be construed as recalculations. The charitable answer is that Byrd believed he had reached the Pole and if he had not done so precisely, he should not be condemned for it. Flying at a height of 2,000 feet, he could see fifty miles in every direction. 'There was no sign of land,' he wrote. 'If there had been any within 100 miles radius we would have seen its mountain peaks, so good was the visibility.'[53] But like Peary, he may not have done what he thought he had done and the Pole might therefore still be open.

Back at King's Harbour, Spitsbergen, Amundsen and Nobile were still squabbling about manning, precedence and weights. Nobile resented having to reduce his air crew to accommodate what he saw as Amundsen's cronies, and although he was willing to accept the services of competent men like Riiser-Larsen he objected to taking the likes of Fredrik Ramm, a Norwegian journalist who, at fourteen and a quarter stone, was a redundant burden. Amundsen, meanwhile, resented Nobile's instructions that to save weight they could take no clothes other than the ones they were wearing. Their flags, too, could be no more than pennants, Nobile said, there was no margin for heavy staves and banners. Nobile was right to be concerned about weight because he had the example of Britain's R.34 airship in his mind. In 1919, the R.34 had made the first east–west crossing of the Atlantic and before leaving, in order to conserve fuel, its captain had ordered a 200-pound crewman to stand down. Midway through the flight, however, the captain had discovered that the man had stowed aboard. His extra weight was so critical that when the R.34 reached New York it had only two hours' flying time left. Nobile did not want to be in that position above the polar pack.

Amundsen retorted slyly by capturing the seats. They were made of velvet-upholstered aluminium and, weight and space being at a premium, there were only two of them. He and Ellsworth would sit in them throughout the expected seventy hours of flying. Nobile could stand, like the rest of the crew, or sit on one of the many crates stamped 'Bovril' which littered the interior.* Trivial as it maybe was, the seating arrangement emphasized Nobile's status as a hired employee on the great Amundsen–Ellsworth expedition.

At 10.00 a.m. on 11 May 1926, the *Norge* took off – having been piloted out of its hangar by Riiser-Larsen, while Nobile, in Amundsen's words, '[stood] fatuously to one side, doing nothing'[54] – and started its voyage towards Alaska.

Clive Holland, a recent chronicler of Arctic exploration, describes Amundsen's narrative of the journey thus: 'The Norwegians heroically man the rudders, write telegrams, plot the course; Ellsworth heroically holds the chronometer; the Italians invisibly keep the thing in the air.'[55] Which is about as good an analysis of Amundsen's journal as you can get. But according to Amundsen's subsequent memoirs, published in 1927, the Italians – Nobile to be precise – were far from invisible. In this later, slightly unbalanced version, Nobile was a menace, veering from hysteria to apathy, grabbing the controls at one moment, then forgetting that he had them as the airship sank towards the ice and Riiser-Larsen came forward to snatch them from disaster. Nobile would publish a refutation long afterwards, in 1961, stating the opposite: that it was he and his crew who did most of the work while the Norwegians – whom he had had to train over a period of just a

---

* Known today for its familiar brown jars of meat-extract, Bovril was then famous as, among other things, a supplier of pemmican to polar explorers. Both Scott and Shackleton took Bovril pemmican on their Antarctic expeditions.

month – conned the airship under his supervision, plotted their course and, in Ramm's case, did nothing save loom burdensomely in the background, scribbling notes. The truth probably lies somewhere between the two. Apart from their leaders' dispute the Norwegian and Italian teams seem to have worked amicably and efficiently together. What all three versions agree on, however, is that the two men after whom the expedition was named played the least part. Ellsworth did hardly anything and Amundsen, in his own words, merely peered out of the porthole. 'He is for the most part occupied in the peaceful occupation of looking out through the window,' he wrote of himself, 'and studying the ice-conditions that are constantly changing. His gaze is often far away and dreamy: "I wonder what I shall see next."'[56]

In the first hours of 12 May, Amundsen saw the Pole. It was Ellsworth's birthday, and to celebrate the occasion Nobile came forward with cups of egg-nog. Then, at about 1.30 a.m., Amundsen called, 'Ready with the flags.' Riiser-Larsen took a reading with his sextant: 'Now we are there.'[57] Nobile lowered the *Norge* to 600 feet, throttled down the engines and, in the ensuing silence, the flags were solemnly dropped. The 'beautiful double-sewn Norwegian flag'[58] was first, then came the Stars and Stripes of America. In keeping with Nobile's instructions, neither of them was 'much larger than a pocket handkerchief'.[59] But then came the Italian flag. 'Imagine our astonishment,' Amundsen wrote, 'to see Nobile dropping overside not one, but armfuls of flags. For a few moments the *Norge* looked like a circus wagon of the skies, with great banners of every shape and hue fluttering down around her.'[60] All these emblems were as nothing, though compared to the vast flag which Nobile's men dragged out of a heavy oak case and proceeded to squeeze out of the window. It was so large that they had difficulty getting it out and once released it threatened to snag the *Norge*'s propellers before it fell onto the ice. 'Ours was the most beautiful,'[61] crowed Renato Alessandri, an Italian rigger. Amundsen, who had been told to reduce weight to a minimum, was infuriated. The flags, let alone the oak case in which the largest one was stored, must have weighed 100 pounds. 'Fortunately,' wrote the grim Norwegian, 'I have a sense of humour, which I count one of my chief qualifications as an explorer.'[62]

From the Pole to Alaska, their flight became more difficult. Ice formed on the dirigible, just as the Russians had said it would, and although Alessandri climbed out of a window and crawled up a ladder to hack it off – as he had successfully done before – he was unable to gain a footing on the slippery shell. The speed of their flight caused fragments of ice to break off and fall into the propellers from where they flew out, puncturing the balloon so frequently that the supply of emaillite, a substance designed to mend tears in the envelope, began to run out. The interior of the main cabin became increasingly shambolic. '[It] was horribly dirty,' Nobile wrote. 'The dozens of thermos flasks heaped on the floor, near the little cupboard where we kept the charts and navigation books, presented a particularly sad spectacle: some of them empty, others overturned, others broken. Coffee and tea had been spilt everywhere, and all over the place were the remains of food. In the midst of all this mess there stuck out picturesquely Amundsen's enormous feet, with his grass-stuffed shoes, his diver's gaiters and red and white gloves.'[63]

They flew through fog and clear air, seeing no land below them – alas for Amundsen's ambitions – and landed on Alaskan soil at 7.30 a.m. (GMT) on 14 May. They had spent 70 hours and 40 minutes in the air, had flown over 3,180 miles of virgin territory, had confirmed the non-existence of an Arctic land mass or an open sea and Amundsen, along with his colleague Oscar Wisting, who had accompanied him to the South Pole and was one of the Norwegian team aboard the *Norge*, had become the first people to visit both ends of the earth's axis. More importantly, although nobody knew it, the expedition had become the first to indisputably reach the North Pole. 'Thanks for the journey!' Wisting said to Nobile, and side by side the Italian and the Norwegian watched as the *Norge* was deflated. 'Our great adventure,' Nobile wrote,' was finished.'[64]

The adventure was finished, but not their journey. They still had to get home, which they did in typically disputatious fashion. A ship carried them to Seattle where Amundsen - dressed in a set of miner's clothes which he had purchased to replace the outfit he had been wearing ever since Spitsbergen – prepared to greet the press. As at the Pole, however, his arrival was upstaged by Nobile. 'Imagine,' he wrote, 'our astonishment when . . . Nobile appeared from below apparelled in the most resplendent dress uniform of a colonel in the Italian army.'[65] After all the admonitions to save weight, Amundsen was disgusted that Nobile should have been keeping a uniform in readiness for the occasion. 'This was nothing less than double-dealing,' he seethed. '[But] it was beneath my dignity to enter a competition for the moment's precedence with this strutting upstart.'[66] Accordingly it was Nobile, not Amundsen, who was presented by a little girl with a bunch of flowers; it was Nobile who was treated as the leader of the expedition; and it was Nobile who was placed at the head of the banquet tables – until Amundsen, finding it within his dignity after all, reminded officials of his position.

The two men parted company at Seattle. Amundsen went home to sort out his bills, write his journal, castigate the Aero Club of Norway for mismanaging his affairs, and to try and sell the film rights of the flight. Nobile, meanwhile, conducted a lecture tour through what Mussolini called the 'Italian colonies' of America, concluding with an interview with President Coolidge. He sailed for Italy at the end of July, arriving in Naples on 2 August. 'It was sunset,' he wrote. 'The gulf was sprinkled with hundreds of white sails coming to meet us; flights of aeroplanes were whirling about the sky; farther off, in the direction of Rome, we saw the well-known silhouettes of two of our airships: a solemn moment which will be for ever engraved on my mind.'[67]

The quest for the North Pole was finally over. It had provoked acts of heroism and folly, had led its protagonists through scenes of beauty and vistas of despair, had tantalized scientists and inflamed the imaginations of artists and adventurers alike. Governments and individuals had been drawn into its dream-like depths, spurred in equal measure by sound theories and myths of wildest fancy. In the history of exploration – perhaps in the history of the world – no point on the earth's surface has aroused such intense curiosity or been the object of such desperate desire. The North Polar explorers had had a cold time of it – as evidenced in the snail tracks of suffering that dotted the Arctic map – but had reached a triumphant conclusion. Yet what did the triumph mean? In imperial and commercial terms the North Pole was valueless. Scientifically its discovery brought no immediate benefits to humankind. Nothing had been found save the same ice which previous explorers had battled for hundreds of years, and little had been proved save the ability of humankind to reach a set of coordinates which it had itself invented. After so many years of delusion and disappointment, of wild hopes and shattered dreams, it was maybe fitting that the struggle for the Pole should end not with a bang, or even a whimper, but the steady hiss of escaping gas.

But maybe it was fitting that the North Pole *should* be a disappointment, that its discovery *should* be marked by petty feuding and a sense of anti-climax, and that it *should* have been reached without any of the participants realizing that they were the first to do so. For the Pole as a geographical entity had long since ceased to be important. In some ways it did not even need to be discovered, for its navigational status was already an accepted fact, its location never in doubt. The British poet Lewis Carroll had suspected this long ago. In 'The Hunting of the Snark', published in 1876, the year in which Nares had returned home, he included the following verse:

> 'What's the good of Mercator's North Pole and Equators,
> Tropics, Zones, and Meridian Lines?'
> So the Bellman would cry: and the crew would reply
> 'They are merely conventional signs!'

Robert Bartlett had said much the same when lecturing about his journey with Peary. 'How did you know you had reached the Pole?' a journalist asked. Bartlett responded with a question: had he ever crossed the equator in a ship? Of course, said the journalist. Well, roared Bartlett, did he feel the keel bump?

During the Franklin search, Britian's poet laureate, Lord Tennyson, had written, 'There is nothing worth living for but to have one's name inscribed on the Arctic chart.'[68] Fifty years later Peary enticed sponsors with the same argument. Many did, in person or by proxy, stamp their name on the map. Almost every polar explorer and most of their backers are immortalized somewhere within the Arctic Circle: a cape or island here, a bay or channel there, some of the features major, others minor, but all recognizable nevertheless as landmarks. At the Pole itself, however, the map remains empty. Not even Peary, who had fought the hardest to reach it, and who had yearned more than any for fame, could devise a means of christening the expanse of ice he had discovered at the top of the world.

In a way, Symmes's theory had been proved correct. If not exactly a hole, the Pole comprised an absence of all those goals towards which explorers traditionally strode. Nothing awaited its conquerors save an empty grail of solar readings. But if it was a conventional sign in one respect, it was unconventional by every other standard. At 90° north, one stands at a point where time and direction are stretched to their conceptual limits: in the course of a year there is only one day and only one night; a short stroll takes in every point on the compass; within minutes one crosses every time zone on earth. There is little wildlife and such as exists is opportunistic: a few seals; a rare, confused bird; the odd fox or bear that has wandered from its southern habitat. It is almost elemental. It is the nearest one can get to leaving the planet without actually doing so. Here, one walks on water.

The North Pole was the greatest goal which humankind set itself in the nineteenth and twentieth centuries and it remains to this day a paradigm of exploration. Since the 1920s it has been visited many times and in various fashions. In 1948, a Russian expedition under Alexander Kuznetsov flew to the Pole and became the first to definitely set foot on it. An American, Ralph Plaisted, went there on motorized sledge in 1968. A Briton, Wally Herbert, sledged to it in 1969 – supported by air drops – and then continued sledging, in one of the most heroic feats of endurance in modern history, until he reached the other side of the Arctic Ocean. In recent decades it has been reached by all manner of conveyance – the most unlikely being a 200cc Yamaha motorcycle driven by Shinji Kazamas of Japan in 1987. There have been one-man attempts, women-only attempts, and Grand Tour attempts in which the North Pole has garlanded a series of extreme conquests that include the South Pole and the summit of Everest. None of these achievements should be dismissed as solipsistic, for they all involve bravery and ingenuity. But they come after the fact.

In a rare flight of fancy Peary once compared geographical discovery to a fairy tale. 'There is a certain intoxication in such work,' he said, 'in the thought, "my eyes are the first that have ever looked upon this scene, mine the touch that has wakened the sleeping princess".'[69] Modern travellers to the Pole can never recreate that sensation. The extraordinary voyages of Kane, Hayes, Hall, Nares and De Long, the Odysseys of Cagni, Nansen and Peary, the pioneering thrill experienced by aeronauts such as Andrée, Byrd and Nobile, are practicably unrepeatable. If there is an image that epitomizes the quest for the North Pole it is not the insulated, orange-clad and eminently practical expeditions which are mounted today but the memory of a fur-clad Ross Marvin and his dogs, steaming into view on the northern side of the Big Lead, as he brought Peary the supplies which would carry him towards the top of the world.

EPILOGUE

L ike those who have been to the moon, North Polar explorers
seem to have been marked permanently by the experience. On
their return they often succumbed to a malaise of indifference and at
times depression; their subsequent careers were frequently blighted
by tragedy and disappointment. Those least obviously affected –
Greely, Melville, and Nares, for example, all of whom rose to high
rank in their professions – were still burdened by their Arctic past. For
the men who dared the Pole nothing, apparently, was ever quite the
same.

Following his drift on the *Fram*, Nansen formed an ambition to go
to the South Pole. So did Peary, who told Bartlett that they had the
men, the dogs and the experience – why not give it a try? But neither
man put his plan into action. They were mentally and physically
unable to repeat their ordeal. Instead Hjalmar Johanssen did it for
them. Having become steadily more depressed following his polar
trek from the *Fram* with Nansen, he was granted, on Nansen's urging,
a place in Amundsen's Antarctic team of 1911. For reasons of intran-
sigence he was not allowed to be part of the group which made it to
the South Pole. He shot himself on 4 January 1913.

Julius Payer, explorer-turned-artist, devoted his later years to painting scenes of Arctic disaster that resembled ever more closely and ever more icily *The Wreck of the Medusa*. He expired on 29 August 1915 at a spa in the Julian Alps. His diary contained doom-laden predictions which foretold a revolution in Russia, the murder of the Tsar, the liberation of Poland, bankrupt nations, millions of dead, the destruction of cities, of navies and commerce, and the spread of plagues. All of these things came about. As for the discovery of Franz Josef Land, he said it meant nothing to him. Nothing at all.

By the end of the First World War, James Gordon Bennett had plundered his funds so thoroughly and disrupted the *Herald* so comprehensively that he was almost penniless. He spent his last years in France where he ranted against the Boche – reportedly it was he who coined the term – and then, following the advice of a clairvoyant who said that he would die on his seventy-seventh birthday, he did just that on 10 May 1918. He was lowered into a grave which, on his orders, was adorned at each corner by a stone owl. His papers were sold to rival concerns and the only legacy today of the man who invented news and who sent De Long to the Pole is the *International Herald-Tribune*.

Nobile went to the North Pole again by airship in 1928. He crashed on the pack, losing his dirigible and many of his men. Roald Amundsen went to his rescue. He took off on a seaplane and was never seen again. Wreckage which later washed up on the shores of Scandinavia suggested that Amundsen and his crew had come down in icy water and had survived for a while – but not long enough. Reviled by Mussolini, Nobile spent several years in the Soviet Union before moving to the United States and then Spain. He published his memoirs in 1961, giving a dignified version of Amundsen's *Norge* narrative. 'I was astonished and distressed to find a very scathing criticism of myself,' he wrote. 'With the personal side of this I do not intend to deal.'[1] He died on 19 July 1978, at the age of ninety-three.

Fridtjof Nansen almost bucked the trend. In 1922 he was awarded the Nobel Prize for his support of Europe's displaced minorities. Shortly after the war, when Amundsen was aiming to fly to the Pole by plane, Scandinavian papers published cartoons of the great explorers, wafting effortlessly towards the top of the world on wings – two Norwegian spectres differentiated by their profiles: Nansen's forceful jowls and Amundsen's beaky nose. Having seen what Amundsen had done in 1926, Nansen planned his own trip by airship to the Pole. Once again, however, he could not bring himself to do it. He died in 1930 to be mourned by hundreds of thousands.

Cook rambled on from disgrace to disgrace. He tried to refute Peary's claims: 'I shall now, having felt the smarting sting of the world's whip, and in order to justify myself, use the knife,'[2] he wrote. But his accusations were mean and petty and no one believed them. He became a property salesman, specializing in oil fields, and when one property yielded no oil he was fined $14,000 and given fourteen years nine months in jail for misrepresentation. Speaking in 1923, his trial judge delivered a searing verdict: 'Now, Cook . . . This is one of those times when your peculiar and persuasive personality fails you, doesn't it? You have at last got to the point where you can't bunco anybody. You have come to the mountain and you can't reach the latitude . . . Oh God, Cook, haven't you any sense of decency at all?'[3] Such was the stigma attached to him that when Roald Amundsen visited him in jail the National Geographic Society promptly cancelled a lecture engagement. He was paroled in 1930 and pardoned by President Roosevelt in 1940. The oil-free land which he was accused of selling later produced millions of gallons of oil. He died in 1940, his last testament being, 'I have been humiliated and seriously hurt. But that doesn't matter any more. I'm getting old, and what does matter to me is that I want you to believe that I told you the truth. I state emphatically that I, Frederick A. Cook, discovered the North Pole.'[4]

In his twenty-year fulmination against the injustice of the world, its geographical societies, its exploring community, its legal system and life in general, Cook could take some solace from news that showed Peary's polar journey to have been flawed, not in its achievement – that still stood – but in its management. In 1926 the truth of Ross Marvin's death came to light. He had not fallen into the Big

Lead as reported, thus dying heroically in the struggle: instead he had been murdered. The two Eskimos who had accompanied him back to Greenland were Kudlikto and Kudlikto's cousin, the latter known as 'Harrigan' from a song he had picked up on the *Roosevelt* and which he sang ceaselessly. Somewhere along the way, Harrigan became exhausted and asked to ride on the sledge. Marvin refused. Harrigan repeated his request a while later. Marvin still refused. Kudlikto interceded on Harrigan's behalf but Marvin's answer remained the same. So Kudlikto shot Marvin and with Harrigan's help pushed his body through the ice. Then the two Eskimos continued to safety, presumably with Harrigan on the sledge and, presumably, making the same speed they would have done had Marvin let him get on in the first place. Kudlikto was not brought to justice: the murder had taken place on no land over which any country held jurisdiction; he could not be prosecuted under international maritime law as he was not a sailor and the deed had not happened at sea; nor could anybody be bothered to snatch him from Greenland and bring him home to be tried under a legal system of which he was entirely ignorant. The matter was laid to rest amidst the dry shuffling of judicial excuses. It did, however, leave a stain on Peary's reputation as a leader.

Robert Bartlett never got over his experience with Peary. He returned to the Arctic again and again. Some of his voyages were successful but others – like the *Karluk* expedition – were harrowing failures. He wrote a few books, the last of which sold so badly that its earnings failed to cover his tobacco allowance. His crews, already accustomed to his temper, were horrified at the prospect of Bartlett abandoning the weed. But Bartlett had mellowed. During the Second World War he, too, succumbed to post-polar apathy. 'I wonder if winning,' he wrote, 'is worth fighting for?'[5] He died on 28 April 1946.

The only one not to give in was Emma De Long. She edited her husband's journal and completed her own memoir which was published in 1938 under the title *Explorer's Wife*. She died in 1940 at the age of ninety, having spent her last years on a farm in New Jersey.

She continued to receive visitors until the end, maintaining the same optimism which had been evident in her letters dated sixty years previously. 'I don't think my husband died in vain, do you?'[6] she asked one journalist sweetly.

Appendix

PAPER ON SCURVY
BY DR DONNET AND
DR FRASER
(1877)

Symptoms, Pathology, and Causes

The evidence given to the Committee has reference to scurvy, not only as it appeared in Arctic Regions, but likewise in Africa, Asia Minor, the Crimea, India, Australia and various parts of the United Kingdom. In every place where observed, the distinctive characters of scurvy were unchanged. Instances also have been given in evidence which prove that the disease is not confined to the White Race, but is met with in the Negro, the Lascar, the Indian, and the Esquimaux, and presents the same essential characters in all races.

Symptoms – The symptoms which are observed in the course of scurvy, and which characterise the disease, are shown in evidence to be as follows:– The colour of the face changes, the skin grows sallow and assumes a leaden hue, and the countenance may afterwards become bloated, and the eye assume a heavy expression. A general debility prevails, and an apathy of manner is noticed; there is feebleness of the knees and ankles, and pains – resembling the flying pains of rheumatism – attack various parts of the body. Swelling of the joints, with rigidity, accompany these symptoms. This rigidity is especially observed in the hams, for which site a predilection seems to exist in the case of men engaged in walking exercise. The gums swell, grow spongy, and bleed from the slightest cause. The breath becomes fetid. The skin is dry and rough; and petechiæ are observed about the legs and thighs, as small reddish brown specks at the points where the roots of the hair perforate the skin. Sleep at this period of the disease is readily obtained; the appetite usually remains good; there is some constipation, but no fever. Sometimes, there is breathlessness with sense of tightness of the chest, for which auscultation generally fails to reveal a cause. Night blindness has sometimes been observed as a symptom of scurvy.

With the advance of the disease the symptoms become aggravated, the petechiæ extend, coalesce, and assume the form of large maculated patches; the skin loses its elasticity, readily pits and frequently breaks, and the ulcer which follows assumes a spongy appearance, and resembles what sailors graphically term 'bullock's liver'. The smell from this ulcer is offensive.

The low spirits become confirmed, and the unfortunate patient indulges in the gloomiest of ideas; the fetor of the breath is now intolerable; the gums protrude as spongy masses from the mouth; the teeth become loose in the socket, and frequently fall out.

In this advanced condition, every slight scratch degenerates into an ulcer, old scars break out afresh, and hæmorrhages are now frequent from different parts of the body in the form of epistaxis, hæmoptysis, hæmatemesis, hæmaturia, and scorbutic dysentery. The urine is high coloured and small in quantity; the pulse is small and indicates a weak state of the circulation.

The mind is anxious and desponding, the intellect is clear, but towards the latter end this anxiety and despondency give way to apathy and indifference.

The breathlessness, which was remarked at the onset of the disease as a troublesome but not a continuous symptom, now increases, is frequently attended with faintings, especially on any exertion, and is sometimes accompanied with sanguineous effusion into the substance of the lung, and into the pleuræ and other cavities. Death occurs suddenly in many instances.

Pathology – The examination which has been made of the bodies of men who have succumbed to scurvy has shown that the morbid appearances chiefly relate to the effusion into the cellular tissues of the body; these are the peculiar characteristics of scurvy. There are solid fibrinous effusions in the substance of the gums, and more especially in the intermuscular spaces, more abundant usually in the lower extremities than in the upper, there are also fibrinous effusions between the periosteum and the bone, constituting what are termed scorbutic nodes. The colouring matter of the blood, also, may ooze through the walls of the vessels without rupture of the vessels. The viscera generally are not affected.

The blood is reduced in density, it contains a greater quantity of water and fibrine, and a smaller quantity of red corpuscles, albumen, and inorganic constitutents than healthy blood, and it exhibits an abnormal tendency to coagulate. These characters cannot, however, be regarded as the essential conditions distinctive of scurvy; they represent only incompletely the deterioration of the blood that exists as a result of depraved nutrition.

Causes – The evidence is all but unanimous that the want of fresh vegetable food, or of some of the constituents which compose fresh vegetables, and probably also fresh animal, food is the cause of scurvy.

What Mr. Busk said with regard to the causation of the disease, seems to embrace the general spirit of the evidence. He considered scurvy to be 'essentially a consequence of defective rather than of deficient nutrition . . . a species of starvation,' due to the want of 'a particular element, of the nature of which we are entirely ignorant,' but which is, 'according to most authorities, afforded solely by fresh vegetable juices; whilst some are of the opinion that fresh animal flesh, in the raw state more especially, and milk, are also possessed of powerful antiscorbutic properties.

SOURCES AND REFERENCES

The following abbreviations have been used for archive material:

OS   – Osterreichisches Staatsarchiv
RGS – Royal Geographical Society
SPRI – Scott Polar Research Institute

The original journal of Elisha Kent Kane (extracts from which are cited as G. Corner and O. Villarejo) is held by the Historical Society of Pennsylvania. The journals of Charles Francis Hall (cited C. Loomis) are courtesy of the Smithsonian Institute, Washington, DC. The papers of Robert Edwin Peary (cited P. Berton, W. Herbert and J. Weems) can be found in the United States National Archives, Washington, DC.

1   The Gateway

1 I. Spufford, *I May Be Some Time*, Faber, London, 1996, p. 64.
2 *Alaska Journal*, Winter 1984, p. 30.
3 Spufford, op. cit., p. 68.
4 Ibid., p. 70.
5 J. Barrow, *Voyages of Discovery and Research in the Arctic Regions*, John Murray, London, 1846, pp. 316–17.

6   E. Inglefield, *A Summer Search for Sir John Franklin with A Peep into the Polar Basin*, Thomas Harrison, London, 1853, pp. xvi–xvii.

7   Ibid., p. 65.

8   Ibid.

9   Ibid., p. 71.

10   W. Elder, *Elisha Kent Kane*, Childs & Peterson, Philadelphia, 1858, p. 37.

11   G. Corner, *Doctor Kane of the Arctic Seas*, Temple University Press, Philadelphia, 1972, p. 68.

12   E. Kane, *The US Grinnell Expedition in Search of Sir John Franklin*, Harper, New York, 1854, p. 293.

13   E. Kane and M. Fox, *The Love-Life of Dr. Kane*, Carleton, New York, 1966, p. 48.

14   Ibid., p. 49.

15   Corner, op. cit., p. 117.

16   E. Kane, *Arctic Explorations*, Vol. I, Childs and Peterson, Philadelphia, 1856, p. 25.

17   Ibid., p. 19.

18   Ibid., p. 25.

19   Ibid., p. 16.

20   H. Hendrik (trans. H. Rink), *The Memoirs of Hans Hendrik*, Trubner & Co., London, 1878, p. 22.

21   Kane, *Arctic Explorations*, op. cit., p. 37.

22   Ibid., p. 64.

23   Ibid., p. 65.

24   Ibid., p. 83.

25   O. Villarejo, *Dr. Kane's Voyage to the Polar Lands*, University of Pennsylvania Press, Philadelphia, 1965, p. 64.

26   Kane, *Arctic Explorations*, op. cit., p. 102.

27   Hendrik, op. cit., p. 24.

28   Kane, *Arctic Explorations*, op. cit., p. 171.

29   Villarejo, op. cit., p. 77.

30   Ibid.

31   P. Berton, *The Arctic Grail*, Viking, London, 1988, p. 254.

32   Kane, *Arctic Explorations*, op. cit.

33   Ibid., p. 172.

34   Ibid., p. 162.

35   Ibid., p. 163.

36   Ibid., p. 187.

37   Ibid., p. 189.

38   Ibid., p. 190–91.

39   Ibid., p. 192.

40   Ibid.

41   Ibid., p. 194.

42   Ibid., p. 195.

43   W. Godfrey, *Godfrey's Narrative of the Last Grinnell Exploring Expedition*, J. T. Lloyd, Philadelphia, 1860, p. 155.

44   Kane, *Arctic Explorations*, op. cit., p. 198.

45   Ibid., Vol. II, p. 355.

46 I. Hayes, *An Arctic Boat Journey*, Richard Bentley, London, 1860, p. 17.
47 Ibid., p. 19.

2 The Boat Journey

1 E. Kane, *Arctic Explorations*, Vol. I, Childs & Peterson, Philadelphia, 1856, p. 245.
2 Ibid.
3 Ibid., p. 257.
4 Ibid., p. 258.
5 P. Berton, *The Arctic Grail*, Viking, London, 1988, p. 258.
6 Kane, op. cit., p. 306.
7 Ibid., p. 312.
8. Ibid.
9 Ibid., p. 315.
10 O. Villarejo, *Dr. Kane's Voyage to the Polar Lands*, University of Pennsylvania Press, Philadelphia, 1965, p. 85.
11 Kane, op. cit., p. 342.
12 Ibid., p. 343.
13 Ibid.
14 Ibid., p. 349.
15 Ibid.
16 G. Corner, *Doctor Kane of the Arctic Seas*, Temple University Press, Philadelphia, 1972, pp. 176–7.
17 Villarejo, op. cit., p. 166.
18 I. Hayes, *An Arctic Boat Journey*, Richard Bentley, London, 1860, p. 37.
19 Corner, op. cit., p. 177.
20 Villarejo, op. cit., pp. 169–70.
21 Hayes, op. cit., p. 31.
22 Villarejo, op. cit., p. 171.
23 Hayes, op. cit., p. 34.
24 Ibid., p. 41.
25 Ibid., p. 75.
26 Ibid., pp. 106–7.
27 Ibid., p. 110.
28 Ibid., p. 152.
29 Ibid., p. 158.
30. Ibid.
31 Ibid., p. 180.
32 Ibid., p. 154.
33 Ibid., p. 170.
34 Ibid., p. 168.
35 Ibid., p. 241.
36 Ibid., p. 199.
37 Ibid., p. 237.
38 Berton, op. cit., p. 274.
39 Ibid., p. 278.
40 Corner, op. cit., p. 186.

41   Berton, op. cit., p. 279.
42   Kane, op. cit., p. 433.

3   The Blowing Place

1   I. Hayes, *An Arctic Boat Journey*, Richard Bentley, London, 1860, p. 269.
2   Ibid., p. 311.
3   G. Corner, *Doctor Kane of the Arctic Seas*, Temple University Press, Philadelphia, 1972, p. 188.
4   O. Villarejo, *Dr. Kane's Voyage to the Polar Lands*, University of Pennsylvania Press, Philadelphia, 1965, p. 172.
5   Ibid., p. 175.
6   P. Berton, *The Arctic Grail*, Viking, London, 1988, p. 287.
7   Ibid.
8   Ibid., pp. 288–9.
9   E. Kane, *Arctic Explorations*, Vol. II, Childs & Peterson, Philadelphia, 1856, p. 84.
10   Ibid., p. 174.
11   Ibid.
12   Ibid., p. 175.
13   Ibid., p. 207.
14   Ibid., p. 245.
15   Ibid., pp. 245–6.
16   Ibid., p. 257.
17   Ibid., p. 288.
18   Ibid., p. 290.
19   Ibid., p. 291.
20   Ibid., p. 292.
21   Ibid., p. 293.
22   Ibid., p. 294.

4   'Americans can do it.'

1   G. Corner, *Doctor Kane of the Arctic Seas*, Temple University Press, Philadelphia, 1972, p. 224.
2   W. Elder, *Elisha Kent Kane*, Childs & Peterson, Philadelphia, 1858, p. 218.
3   Corner, op. cit. p. 243.
4   Ibid., p. 241.
5   D. Malone (ed.), *Dictionary of American Biography*, Charles Scribner, New York, 1995, p. 257.
6   *Journal of the Royal Geographical Society*, Vol. 28, p. 287.
7   *Proceedings of the Royal Geographical Society*, Vol. 2, p. 200.
8   Ibid., p. 200–201.
9   *Proceedings of the Royal Geographical Society*, Vol. 3, p. 148.
10   Ibid.
11   I. Hayes, *An Arctic Boat Journey*, Richard Bentley, London, 1860, p. 344.
12   Ibid., p. 356.
13   Ibid., p. 351.
14   Ibid., p. 371.

15 C. Loomis, *Weird and Tragic Shores*, Macmillan, London, 1972, p. 44.
16 C. Hall, *Life with the Esquimaux*, Vol. I., Sampson, Low, Son and Marston, London, 1864, p. 5.
17 Ibid., p. 4.
18 Ibid., p. 10.
19 Loomis, op. cit., p. 55.
20 Ibid., p. 58.
21 Ibid., p. 59.

5 The Open Polar Sea

1 I. Hayes, *The Open Polar Sea*, Sampson, Low, Son and Marston, London, 1867, p. 7.
2 Ibid., p. 11.
3 Ibid., p. 3.
4 Ibid.
5 Ibid.
6 Ibid., p. 34.
7 Ibid., p. 133.
8 Ibid., p. 21.
9 Ibid., p. 16.
10 Ibid., p. 42.
11 Ibid., p. 49.
12 Ibid., p. 60.
13 Ibid., pp. 69–70.
14 Ibid., p. 76.
15 Ibid., p. 107.
16 Ibid., p. 93.
17 Ibid., p. 95.
18 Ibid., p. 120.
19 Ibid.
20 Ibid., p. 121.
21 Ibid., p. 138.
22 Ibid., p. 155.
23 Ibid., p. 102.
24 Ibid.
25 Ibid., p. 104.
26 Ibid., p. 139.
27 Ibid., p. 111.
28 Ibid., p. 180.
29 Ibid., p. 183.
30 Ibid., p. 184.
31 Ibid., p. 201.
32 H. Hendrik (trans. H. Rink), *The Memoirs of Hans Hendrik*, Trubner & Co., London, 1878, p.39.
33 Ibid.
34 Ibid.
35 Hayes, op. cit., p. 61.

36 Ibid., p. 232.
37 Ibid., p. 257.
38 Ibid., p. 251.
39 Ibid., p. 268.
40 Ibid., p. 269.
41 Ibid., p. 281.
42 Ibid., p. 285.
43 Ibid.
44 Ibid., p. 286.
45 Ibid., p. 289.
46 Ibid., p. 295.
47 Ibid., p. 315.
48 Ibid., p. 318.
49 Ibid., p. 342.
50 Ibid., p. 397.
51 Ibid., p. 399.
52 *Journal of the American Geographical Society*, 1870, p. 24.

6   Polar Crusader

1 C. Hall, *Life with the Esquimaux*, Vol. I, Sampson, Low, Son and Marston, London, 1864, p. 23.
2 Ibid., p. 83.
3 Ibid., p. 156.
4 Ibid., p. 39.
5 Ibid., p. 107.
6 Ibid., p. 163.
7 Ibid.
8 Ibid., p. 168.
9 Ibid., p. 101.
10 Ibid., p. 168.
11 Ibid., p. 134.
12 Ibid., p. 107.
13 Ibid., p. 135.
14 Ibid., p. 182.
15 Ibid., Vol. II, p. 209.
16 Ibid, Vol. I, p. 227.
17 Ibid., Vol. II, p. 80.
18 Ibid., Vol. I, p. 290.
19 Ibid., Vol. II, p. 143.
20 Ibid., p. 144.
21 Ibid., p. 131.
22 Ibid., p. 144.
23 J. Nourse, *Narrative of the Second Arctic Expedition made by Charles F. Hall*, Govt. Printing Office, Washington, 1879, p. 8.
24 Hall, op. cit., Vol. I, p. 318.
25 Nourse, op. cit., p. 4.
26 Ibid., p. xvii.

27 Ibid., p. 39.
28 Ibid., p. 25.
29 C. Loomis, *Weird and Tragic Shores*, Macmillan, London, 1972, p. 177.
30 *Journal of the American Geographical Society*, Vol. III, p. 406.
31 Nourse, op. cit., p. 308.
32 Ibid., p. 238.
33 Ibid, p. 261.
34 Ibid., p. 158.
35 Loomis, op. cit., p. 229.
36 Nourse, op. cit., p. xxi.
37 *Journal of the American Geographical Society*, 1881, p. 120.
38 Loomis, op. cit., p. 239.
39 Ibid., p. 234.
40 Ibid., p. 250.
41 Ibid., p. 249.
42 *Journal of the American Geographical Society*, Vol. III, p. 407.

7 The Sage of Gotha

1 C. Holland (ed.), *Farthest North*, Robinson, London, 1994, p. 54.
2 Ibid., p. 63.
3 Ibid.
4 *Journal of the American Geographical Society*, 1870, p. 26.
5 Ibid., p. ci.
6 K. Koldewey, *The German Arctic Expedition of 1869–70*, Sampson, Low, Marston, Low and Searle, London, 1874, p. 6.
7 Ibid., p. 17.
8 Ibid., p. 57.
9 Ibid., p. 73.
10 Ibid., p. 74.
11 Ibid., p. 309.
12 Ibid., pp. 407–10.
13 Ibid., p. 410.
14 D. Smith, *Arctic Expeditions*, Fullarton, Jack & Co., London, 1880, p. 782.
15 Koldewey, op. cit., p. 440.
16 Smith, op. cit., p. 773.
17 Koldewey, op. cit., pp. 90–91.
18 Ibid., p. 103.
19 Ibid., p. 106.
20 Ibid., p. 108.
21 Ibid., p. 112.
22 Ibid., p. 109.
23 Ibid.
24 Ibid., p. 110.
25 Ibid., p. 117.
26 Ibid., p. 101.
27 Ibid., p. 127.
28 Ibid., p. 131.

29 Ibid., p. 131.
30 Ibid., p. 132.
31 Ibid., p. 133.
32 Ibid., p. 134.
33 Ibid., p. 148.
34 Ibid., pp. 176–8.
35 Ibid., p. 178.
36 Ibid.
37 Ibid., p. 222.
38 Ibid.
39 Ibid., p. 207.
40 Ibid., p. 188.
41 Ibid., p. 208.
42 Ibid.
43 Ibid., p. 261.
44 *Proceedings of the Royal Geographical Society*, Vol. XV, p. 112.
45 Koldewey, op. cit., p. 571.
46 Ibid., p. 264.

8 A Land Unknown Before

1 J. Wiggins (ed.), *The Austro-German Polar Expedition under the command of Lieut. Weyprecht*, William Carr, London, 1875, p. 30.
2 Ibid., p. 10.
3 Ibid., pp. 12–25.
4 Ibid., p. 30.
5 Ibid.
6 J. Payer, *New Lands Within the Arctic Circle*, Vol. I, Macmillan, London, 1876, p. 133.
7 Ibid., p. 150.
8 Ibid., p. 167.
9 Ibid., pp. 163–4.
10 Ibid., p. 165.
11 Ibid., p. 167.
12 Ibid., p. 173.
13 Ibid., p. 168.
14 Ibid., p. 277.
15 Ibid., p. 279.
16 Ibid., pp. 279–80.
17 Ibid., p. 280.
18 Ibid., p. 287.
19 Ibid.
20 Ibid., p. 288.
21 Ibid., p. 289.
22 Ibid.
23 O. Krisch, *Das Tagebuch des Maschinisten Otto Krisch*, Leykam-Verlag, Graz-Wien, 1973, p. 113.

24 K. Koldewey, *The German Arctic Expedition of 1869–70*, Sampson, Low, Marston, Low & Searle, London, 1874, p. 353.
25 J. Haller, *Erinnerungen eines Tiroler Teilnehmers an Julius v. Payer's Nordpol-Expedition*, Universitätsverlag Wagner, Innsbruck, 1959, p. 63.
26 Payer, op. cit., Vol. II, p. 144.
27 Ibid., p. 145.
28 Ibid., p. 147.
29 Ibid., p. 148.
30 Ibid., p. 149.
31 Ibid.
32 Ibid., p. 154.
33 Ibid., p. 166.
34 OA-B/205 – cited C. Ransmayr.
35 Ibid.
36 Ibid.
37 Ibid., p. 265.
38 Ibid., p. 266.
39 Ibid., p. 270.
40 J. Payer, *Die Oesterreichisch-Ungarische Nordpol-Expedition*, Alfred Holder, Wien, 1876, p. 443.
41 *Neue Freie Presse*, 26 September, 1874 – cited C. Ransmayr.
42 C. Holland (ed.), *Farthest North*, Robinson, London, 1994, p. 72.
43 Payer, op. cit., p. 221.
44 Wiggins, op. cit., p. 335.

9   The Voyage of the *Polaris*

1 E. Blake (ed.), *Arctic Experiences*, Sampson, Low, Marston, Low & Searle, London, 1874, p. 133.
2 Ibid., p. 142.
3 Ibid., p. 130.
4 C. Loomis, *Weird and Tragic Shores*, Macmillan, London, 1972, p. 254.
5 *Journal of the American Geographical Society*, Vol. III, pp. 70–71.
6 Blake, op. cit., p. 110.
7 Ibid., p. 109.
8 Loomis, op. cit., p. 267.
9 Blake, op. cit., p. 147.
10 Ibid., p. 148.
11 Ibid.
12 Ibid., p. 149.
13 Ibid., p. 148.
14 Ibid., p. 150.
15 Ibid.
16 Ibid., p. 154.
17 Loomis, op. cit., p. 269.
18 Blake, op. cit., p. 467.
19 C. Davis, *Narrative of the North Polar Expedition*, Government Printing Office, Washington, 1876, p. 130.

20 Blake, op. cit., p. 155.
21 P. Berton, *The Arctic Grail*, Viking, London, 1988, p. 390.
22 Loomis, op. cit., p. 325.
23 Blake, op. cit., p. 162.
24 Ibid.
25 Ibid.
26 Ibid.
27 Ibid.
28 Ibid., p. 165.
29 Loomis, op. cit., p. 330.
30 Blake, op. cit., p. 474.
31 Ibid., p. 476.
32 Berton, op. cit., p. 393.
33 Ibid.
34 Loomis, op. cit., pp. 302–3.
35 Blake, op. cit. p. 471.
36 Ibid., p. 171.
37 Berton, op. cit., p. 394.
38 Blake, op. cit., p. 198.
39 Loomis, op. cit., p. 290.
40 Blake, op. cit., p. 219.
41 Ibid., p. 233.
42 Ibid., p. 237.
43 Ibid., p. 240.
44 Ibid., p. 247.
45 Ibid., p. 243.
46 Ibid., p. 247.
47 Ibid., p. 242.
48 Ibid., p. 306.
49 Ibid., p. 314.
50 Ibid., p. 318.
51 Ibid.
52 Ibid., p. 319.
53 Ibid., p. 321.
54 Ibid., pp. 322–3.
55 Ibid., p. 332.
56 Ibid.
57 J. Wright, *Geography in the Making*, American Geographical Society, New York, 1952, p. 89.

10   Osborn's Legacy

1 E. Blake, *Arctic Experiences*, Sampson, Low, Marston, Low & Searle, London, 1874, p. 19.
2 *Proceedings of the Royal Geographical Society*, Vol. IX, p. 43.
3 Ibid., pp. 52–3.
4 Ibid., p. 53.
5 Ibid., p. 54.

6 Ibid., p. 58.
7 Ibid., p. 148.
8 Ibid., pp. 143–5.
9 *Proceedings of the Royal Geographical Society*, Vol. XII, p. 93.
10 Ibid., p. 94.
11 Ibid., p. 96.
12 Ibid., p. 108.
13 C. Markham, *The Threshold of the Unknown Region*, Sampson, Low, Marston, Low & Searle, London, 1873, p. 117.
14 Ibid., p. 274.
15 *Proceedings of the Royal Geographical Society*, Vol. XII, p. 102.
16 Markham, op. cit., p. 270.
17 *Gentleman's Magazine*, Vol. XV, p. 45.
18 G. Nares, *Narrative of A Voyage To The Polar Sea*, Sampson, Low, Marston, Searle & Rivington, London, 1878, Vol. I, p. 2.
19 Ibid., p. 1.
20 Ibid., p. 26.
21 *Blackwood's Magazine*, Vol. CXVII, p. 778.
22 *Royal Geographical Society President's Addresses*, 1869–75, p. 94.
23 *Blackwood's Magazine*, Vol. CXVII, p. 789.
24 Markham, op. cit., p. 141.
25 SPRI – MS 38. Rawson's diary, Vol. II.
26 SPRI – MS 38. Rawson's diary, Vol. II.
27 Nares, op. cit., p. 195.
28 Ibid.
29 Ibid.
30 SPRI – MS 38. Rawson's diary, Vol. III.
31 Nares, op. cit., p. 200.
32 E. Moss, *Shores of the Polar Sea*, Marcus Ward, London, 1878, p. 42.
33 Ibid., p. 41.
34 Ibid., p. 42.
35 RGS – Feilden Journal.
36 Ibid.
37 RGS – Markham to his mother, 26.10.76.
38 *Fraser's Magazine*, Vol. XIV, p. 789.
39 Nares, op. cit., p. 283.
40 Moss, op. cit., pp. 56–7.
41 Ibid., p. 59.
42 Ibid.
43 *Proceedings of the Royal Geographical Society*, Vol. XXI, p. 113.
44 RGS – Nares papers.
45 SPRI – MS 396/2. Markham's Journal.
46 Ibid.
47 Nares, op. cit., pp. 353 ff.
48 SPRI – MS 396/2. Markham's Journal
49 Ibid.
50 A. Markham, *The Great Frozen Sea*, Daldy, Isbister & Co., London, 1878, p. 232.

51 SPRI – MS 396/2. Markham's Journal.
52 Ibid.
53 RGS – Markham to his mother, 26.10.76.
54 Ibid.
55 Nares, op. cit., p. 375.
56 Ibid., p. 385.
57 Ibid., p. 344.
58 RGS – Feilden Journal.
59 Moss, op. cit., p. 64.
60 RGS – Feilden Journal.
61 Nares, op. cit., Vol. II, p. 34.
62 *Report of the Committee appointed by the Lord Commissioners of the Admiralty to enquire into . . . The recent Arctic Expedition, HM Stationery Office, London, 1877, Minutes of Evidence*, p. 3.
63 Ibid., p. 49.
64 Moss, op. cit., p. 69.
65 Nares, op. cit., Vol. II, p. 100.
66 Ibid., p. 101.
67 Ibid., p. 102.
68 Ibid., p. 103.
69 Ibid., p. 105.
70 Ibid.
71 Ibid.
72 Ibid., p. 108.
73 Ibid., p. 110.
74 Ibid., p. 113.
75 K. Rasmussen, *Greenland by the Polar Sea*, Heinemann, London, 1921, p. 96.
76 R. Peary, *Nearest the Pole*, Hutchinson, London, 1907, p. 332.
77 H. Hendrik, *Memoirs of Hans Hendrik*, Trubner & Co., London, 1878, p. 89.
78 Ibid., p. 90.
79 Ibid., p. 97.
80. Ibid., p. 98.
81 SPRI – MS 174/5 – Egerton's Journal.
82 A. Markham, op. cit., p. 399.
83 Nares, op. cit., Vol. II, p. 186.
84 Nares, op. cit., Vol. II, p. 186.
85 *Proceedings of the Royal Geographical Society*, Vol. XXI, p. 96.
86 *Quarterly Review*, Vol. 143, p. 186.
87 Ibid., p. 152.
88 B. Riffenburgh, *The Myth of the Explorer*, Oxford University Press, Oxford, 1994, p. 83.
89 *North American Review*, March 1877, p. 236.
90 *Report of the Committee* . . . op. cit., p. xxi.
91 Ibid., p. iv.
92 *The Times*, 21 May 1877.
93 *Proceedings of the Royal Geographical Society*, Vol. XXI, p. 105.
94 Nares, op. cit., Vol. I. p. xl.

11 His Word is Law

1 C. Weyprecht, *Fundamental Principles of Scientific Arctic Investigation*. An Address delivered before the 48th meeting of German naturalists and physicians at Graz, on the 18th September 1875, Stein, Vienna.
2 Ibid.
3 Ibid.
4 R. Blumenfeld, *RDB's Diary*, Heinemann, London, 1930, p. 53.
5 Ibid., p. 34.
6 D. Seitz, *The James Gordon Bennetts*, Bobbs-Merrill, Indianapolis, 1928, p. 279.
7 R. O'Connor, *The Scandalous Mr. Bennett*, Doubleday, New York, 1962, p. 112.
8 F. Bullard, *Famous War Correspondents*, Pitman, London, 1914, pp. 281–2.
9 RGS – Petermann to the President of the Royal Geographical Society.
10 Ibid.
11 L. Guttridge, *Icebound*, Paragon, New York, 1988, p. 40.
12 Ibid.
13 Ibid., p. 17.
14 Ibid., p. 21.
15 Ibid., pp. 52–3.
16 Ibid., p. 45.
17 Ibid., p. 47.
18 Ibid., p. 45.
19 Ibid., p. 46.
20 Ibid., p. 47.
21 Ibid., p. 89.
22 Ibid., p. 81.
23 Ibid., p. 78.
24 G. De Long, *The Voyage of the Jeannette*, Kegan Paul, Trench & Co., London, 1883, pp. 72–3.
25 Ibid., p. 72.
26 Guttridge, op. cit., p. 9.
27 R. Newcomb, *Our Lost Explorers*, American Publishing Company, Hartford, 1882, p. 27.
28 Ibid., p. 29.
29 Guttridge, op. cit., pp. 76–7.
30 De Long, op. cit., p. 174.
31 Ibid., p. 199.
32 Guttridge, op. cit., p. 94.
33 Ibid., p. 94.
34 De Long, op. cit., p. 203.
35 Ibid., p. 80.
36 Ibid., p. 213.
37 De Long, op. cit., p. 177.
38 Guttridge, op. cit., p. 120.
39 Ibid., p. 131.
40 G. Melville, *In the Lena Delta*, Longmans, Green & Co., London, 1897, p. 14.

41 De Long, op. cit., p. 373.
42 Ibid.
43 Ibid., p. 391.
44 Ibid., Vol. II, p. 467.
45 Ibid., Vol. I, p. 411.
46 Ibid., Vol. II, p. 484.
47 Ibid., Vol. II, p. 487.

12 In the Lena Delta

1 L. Guttridge, *Icebound*, Paragon, New York, 1988, p. 161.
2 *Journal of the American Geographical Society*, Vol. XII, pp. 272–3.
3 Guttridge, op. cit., p. 165.
4 Ibid., p. 166.
5 G. De Long, *The Voyage of the Jeannette*, Vol. II, Kegan Paul, Trench & Co., London, 1883, p. 498.
6 Ibid., p. 500.
7 Ibid., p. 504.
8 Guttridge, op. cit., p. 157.
9 De Long, op. cit., p. 540.
10 G. Melville, *In the Lena Delta*, Longmans, Green & Co., London 1987, p. 18.
11 De Long, op. cit., pp. 566–9.
12 R. Newcomb, *Our Lost Explorers*, American Publishing Company, Hartford, 1882, p. 306.
13 Melville, op. cit., p. 31.
14 Ibid., pp. 31–2.
15 Newcomb, op. cit., pp. 208–9.
16 Ibid., p. 209.
17 Newcomb, op. cit., p. 184.
18 Ibid., p. 311.
19 Guttridge, op. cit., p. 201.
20 Melville, op. cit., p. 71.
21 Guttridge, op. cit.
22 De Long, op. cit., p. 721.
23 Guttridge, op. cit., pp. 254–5.
24 De Long, op. cit., pp. 798–9.
25 Newcomb, op. cit., pp. 116–17.
26 Melville, op. cit., p. 209.
27 Ibid., p. 221.
28 Guttridge, op. cit., p. 271.
29 Ibid., p. 274.
30 Ibid., p. 275.
31 Ibid., pp. 275–6.

13 *Fram*

1 L. Guttridge, *Icebound*, Paragon, New York, 1988, p. 293.
2 Ibid., p. 313.

3 D. Brainard (ed. B. James), *Six Came Back*, Bobbs-Merrill, Indianapolis, 1940, p. 312.
4 P. Berton, *The Arctic Grail*, Viking, London, 1988, p. 485.
5 Ibid.
6 Ibid.
7 *The Alaska Journal*, Winter 1984.
8 F. Nansen (trans. M. Gepp), *The First Crossing of Greenland*, Vol. I, Longmans, Green & Co., London, 1890, p. 5.
9 Ibid., Vol. II, pp. 171–2.
10 R. Huntford, *Nansen*, Duckworth, London, 1997, p. 126.
11 Ibid., p. 131.
12 Ibid., p. 145.
13 Ibid.
14 Ibid., p. 147.
15 RGS – Nansen to Mrs. Tweedie, 1.5.1892.
16 Huntford, op. cit., p. 148.
17 Ibid., pp. 149–50.
18 F. Nansen, *Farthest North*, Vol. I, Constable, London, 1897, p. 62.
19 Huntford, op. cit., p. 162.
20 *Geographical Journal*, Vol. I, p. 31.
21 Ibid., p. 32.
22 Nansen, op. cit., Vol. I, pp. 50–52.
23 Ibid., p. 41.
24 F. Jackson, *The Lure of Unknown Lands*, G. Bell & Sons, London, 1935, p. 55.
25 Huntford, op. cit., p. 147.
26 Nansen, op. cit., Vol. I, p. 263.
27 Huntford, op. cit., p. 165.
28 Nansen, op. cit., Vol. I, pp. 355–6.
29 Huntford, op. cit., p. 188.
30 Nansen, op. cit., Vol. I, p. 356.
31 Huntford, op. cit., p. 198.
32 Nansen, op. cit., Vol. I, p. 369.
33 Huntford, op. cit., p. 217.
34 Ibid., p. 226.
35 Nansen, op. cit., Vol. I, p. 330.
36 Ibid.
37 Ibid., Vol. II, p. 136.
38 Ibid., p. 137.
39 Ibid., pp. 140–41.
40 Ibid., p. 142.
41 Huntford, op. cit., p. 271.
42 Ibid., p. 272.
43 Ibid., p. 274.
44 Nansen, op. cit., Vol. II, p. 226.
45 Ibid., p. 227.
46 Huntford, op. cit., p. 296.
47 Ibid., p. 301.

14 Miracle at Cape Flora

1 R. Huntford, Duckworth, London, 1997, p. 323.
2 Ibid., p. 324.
3 Ibid., p. 346.
4 F. Nansen, *Farthest North*, Vol. II, Constable, London, 1897, p. 621.
5 S. Andrée, *The Andrée Diaries*, John Lane, London, 1931, p. 10.
6 Ibid., p. 38.
7 *Report of the Sixth International Geographic Congress, held in London, 1895*, p. 225.
8 Ibid.
9 Ibid., p. 223.
10 Ibid., p. 224.
11 Ibid., p. 226.
12 B. Riffenburgh, *The Myth of the Explorer*, Oxford University Press, Oxford, 1994, p. 158.
13 *Geographical Journal*, Vol. VII, p. 325.
14 Andrée, op. cit., p. 40.
15 Huntford, op. cit., p. 350.
16 Ibid., p. 307.
17 Ibid., p. 310.
18 Nansen, op. cit., Vol. II, p. 395.
19 Huntford, op. cit., p. 319.
20 Ibid.
21 Ibid., p. 335.
22 Ibid.
23 Nansen, op. cit., Vol. II, p. 447.
24 F. Jackson, *The Lure of Unknown Lands*, G. Bell & Sons, London, 1935, p. 165.
25 Ibid., p. 166.
26 RGS – Jackson to Bromwich, 10.7.1896.
27 F. Jackson, *A Thousand Days in the Arctic*, Vol. II, Harper, London, 1899, p. 66.
28 Ibid., pp. 62–3.
29 RGS – Jackson to Bromwich, 10.7.1896.
30 Jackson, *The Lure* . . . op. cit., p. 167.
31 Nansen, op. cit., Vol. II, p. 466.
32 Jackson, *A Thousand Days* . . . op. cit., p. 74.
33 Ibid., p. 71.
34 Ibid., p. 91.
35 Ibid., p. 73.
36 RGS – Jackson to Bromwich, 10.7.1896.
37 Huntford, op. cit., p. 345.
38 Ibid., p. 352.
39 RGS – Jackson to Bromwich, 10.7.1896.
40 Nansen, op. cit., Vol. II, p. 516.
41 Huntford, op. cit., p. 358.
42 Ibid., p. 354.
43 Ibid., p. 362.
44 Ibid.

45 Riffenburgh, op. cit., p. 155.
46 Ibid., p. 154.
47 Ibid., p. 153.
48 Jackson, *The Lure* ... op. cit., pp. 168–71.

15 The Flight of the *Eagle*

1 S. Andrée, *The Andrée Diaries*, John Lane, London, 1931, p. 53.
2 Ibid., p. 51.
3 H. Lachambre and A. Machuron, *Andrée and his balloon*, Constable, London, 1898, p. 301.
4 Andrée, op. cit., p. 6.
5 Lachambre, op. cit., pp. 300–301.
6 Ibid., p. 305.
7 Andrée, op. cit., p. 89.
8 Ibid., p. 76.
9 Ibid., p. 85.
10 Ibid.
11 Ibid., p. 86.
12 Ibid., p. 88.
13 Ibid., p. 445.
14 Ibid., p. 92.
15 Ibid., p. 95.
16 Ibid., p. 357.
17 F. Jackson, *The Lure of Unknown Lands*, G. Bell & Sons, London, 1935, p. 212.
18 Andrée, op. cit., p. 451.
19 Ibid., pp. 449–50.
20 Ibid., p. 451.
21 Ibid., p. 443.
22 Ibid., p. 395.
23 Ibid., p. 393.
24 Ibid., p. 398.
25 Ibid., p. 401.
26 Ibid., p. 412.
27 Ibid.
28 Ibid., pp. 415–16.

16 'I *must* have fame.'

1 P. Berton, *The Arctic Grail*, Viking, London, 1988, p. 511.
2 J. Weems, *Peary: The Explorer and the Man*, Eyre & Spottiswoode, London, 1967, p. 53.
3 W. Herbert, *The Noose of Laurels*, Hodder & Stoughton, London, 1989, p. 45.
4 Ibid.
5 Ibid., p. 47.
6 Ibid., p. 48.
7 Ibid., p. 49.
8 R. Peary, *Northward over the Great Ice*, Vol. I, Methuen, London, p. xxxiv.
9 Ibid.

10 Ibid., p. 39.
11 Weems, op. cit., p. 84.
12 Peary, op. cit., p. xxxvii.
13 Weems, op. cit., p. 100.
14 Ibid., pp. 69–70.
15 Ibid., p. 72.
16 Peary, op. cit., p. 45.
17 A. Bierce, *The Enlarged Devil's Dictionary*, Doubleday, New York, 1967, p. 42.
18 Herbert, op. cit., p. 66.
19 Peary, op. cit., p. 47.
20 J. Peary, *My Arctic Journal*, Longmans, Green & Co., London, 1893, pp. 4–5.
21 F. Cook, *My Attainment of the Pole*, The Polar Publishing Co., New York, 1911, p. 63.
22 R. Peary, op. cit., pp. 343–4.
23 Herbert, op. cit., p. 89.
24 Ibid.
25 Ibid.
26 Ibid., p. 88.
27 R. Peary, op. cit., p. 550.
28 R. Peary, *Nearest the Pole*, Hutchinson, London, 1907, p. 390.
29 R. Peary, *Northwards . . .* op. cit., Vol. II, p. 72.
30 Ibid., pp. 75–6.
31 J. Hayes, *Robert Edwin Peary*, Grant Richards & Humphrey Toulmin, London, 1923, pp. 25–6.
32 R. Peary, *Northwards . . .* op. cit., Vol. II, p. 100.
33 Herbert, op. cit., p. 107.
34 R. Peary, *Northwards . . .* op. cit., Vol. II, p. 155.
35 Herbert, op. cit., p. 99.
36 Weems, op. cit., p. 149.
37 R. Peary, *Northwards . . .* op. cit., Vol. II, p. 294.
38 Herbert, op. cit., p. 101.
39 Ibid., p. 104.
40 Ibid.
41 R. Peary, *Northwards . . .* op. cit., Vol. II, pp. 467–8.
42 Weems, op. cit., p. 164.
43 R. Peary, *Northwards . . .* op. cit, Vol. I. pp. 572–3.
44 Ibid., p. 574.
45 K. Harper, *Give Me My Father's Body*, Profile Books, London, 2000, p. 19.
46 Berton, op. cit., p. 520.

17   'A few toes aren't much . . .'

1 W. Herbert, *The Noose of Laurels*, Hodder & Stoughton, London, 1989, p. 110.
2 Ibid., p. 154.
3 R. Peary, *Nearest the Pole*, Hutchinson, London, 1907, p. 296.
4 Herbert, op. cit., p. 111.
5 P. Berton, *The Arctic Grail*, Viking, London, 1988, p. 522.
6 B. Robinson, *Dark Companion*, Hodder & Stoughton, London, 1948, p. 134.

7 O. Sverdrup, *New Lands: Four years in the Arctic Regions*, Vol. I, Longmans, Green & Co., London, 1904, p. 98.
8 Robinson, op. cit., p. 138.
9 Herbert, op. cit., p. 115.
10 Ibid.
11 Sverdrup, op. cit., p. 115.
12 Ibid., pp. 115–16.
13 Ibid., p. 117.
14 R. Peary, *The North Pole*, Dover, New York, 1986, p. 95.
15 Herbert, op. cit., p. 121.
16 Peary, *Nearest . . .* op. cit., pp. 325–6.
17 J. Weems, *Peary: The Explorer and the Man*, Eyre & Spottiswoode, London, 1867, p. 191.
18 Ibid.
19 Ibid., p. 193.
20 Ibid., p. 198.
21 Ibid., p. 190.
22 F. Cook, *My Attainment of the North Pole*, The Polar Publishing Co., New York, 1911, p. 484.
23 Ibid.
24 B. Riffenburgh, *The Myth of the Explorer*, Oxford University Press, Oxford, 1994, p. 171.
25 Peary, *Nearest . . .* op. cit., p. 344.
26 Weems, op. cit., p. 200.
27 Ibid., pp. 200–201.

18   The Polar Duke

1 B. Riffenburgh, *The Myth of the Explorer*, Oxford University Press, 1994, p. 156.
2 Ibid.
3 RGS – Feilden papers.
4 L. Abruzzi (trans. W. Le Queux), *On the Polar Star in the Arctic Seas*, Vol. I, Hutchinson, London, 1903, p. vii.
5 Ibid., p. viii.
6 H. Wright, *The Great White North*, Macmillan, New York, 1910, p. 426.
7 L. Abruzzi, *Farther North than Nansen*, Howard Wilford Bell, London, 1901, p. 4.
8 Ibid., p. 5.
9 Abruzzi, *On the Polar Star . . .* op. cit., Vol. I, p. 143.
10 Abruzzi, *Farther North . . .* op. cit., p. 23.
11 Ibid.
12 Abruzzi, *On the Polar Star . . .* op. cit., p. 189.
13 Abruzzi, *Farther North . . .* op. cit., p. 43.
14 Ibid., p. 49.
15 Ibid.
16 Ibid., p. 50.
17 Ibid., p. 55.
18 Ibid., pp. 55–6.

19 Ibid., p. 57.
20 Ibid., p. 58.
21 Ibid.
22 Ibid., p. 59.
23 Ibid., p. 60.
24 Abruzzi, *On the Polar Star* . . . op. cit., Vol. II, p. 500.
25 Ibid., p. 504.
26 Ibid., p. 500.
27 Ibid., p. 508.
28 Ibid., p. 509.
29 Ibid., p. 515.
30 Ibid., p. 517.
31 Ibid., p. 519.
32 Ibid., p. 526.
33 Ibid., p. 534.
34 Ibid., p. 540.
35 Ibid., p. 559.
36 Ibid., p. 562.
37 Ibid., p. 561.
38 Ibid., p. 569.
39 Ibid., p. 578.
40 Ibid., p. 582.
41 Ibid., p. 583.
42 Ibid., p. 584.
43 Ibid., p. 585.
44 Ibid., p. 588.
45 Abruzzi, *Farther North* . . . op. cit., p. 73.
46 Ibid.
47 Ibid., p. 75.
48 Abruzzi, *On the Polar Star* . . . op. cit., Vol. I, p. 269.
49 Ibid., Vol. II, p. 612.
50 Ibid., Vol. I, p. 322.
51 R. Huntford, *Nansen*, Duckworth, London, 1997, p. 383.
52 Ibid.

19 Farthest North

1 W. Herbert, *The Noose of Laurels*, Hodder & Stoughton, London, 1989, p. 151.
2 L. Abruzzi, *On the Polar Star in the Arctic Seas*, Vol. II, Hutchinson, London, 1903, p. 486.
3 B. Riffenburgh, *The Myth of the Explorer*, Oxford University Press, Oxford, 1994, p. 168.
4 B. Robinson, *Dark Companion*, Hodder & Stoughton, London, 1948, p. 169.
5 Riffenburgh, op. cit., p. 168.
6 Ibid.
7 Herbert, op. cit., p. 149.
8 Ibid., p. 150.
9 Ibid.

10 Ibid., p. 155.
11 Ibid.
12 Ibid., p. 156.
13 Ibid.
14 R. Peary, *Nearest the Pole*, Hutchinson, London, 1907, p. 33.
15 W. Hobbs, *Peary*, Macmillan, New York, 1936.
16 Peary, op. cit., p. 44.
17 Ibid., p. 45.
18 Ibid., p. 47.
19 Ibid., p. 46.
20 Ibid., p. 51.
21 Ibid., p. 101.
22 Ibid., p. 135.
23 Ibid., pp. 145–6.
24 Ibid., p. 146.
25 Ibid., p. 190.
26 Ibid., p. 206.
27 P. Berton, *The Arctic Grail*, Viking, London, 1998, p. 564.
28 Peary, op. cit., p. 225.
29 Ibid., p. 240.
30 R. Bartlett, *The Log of Bob Bartlett*, Putnam's, New York, 1928, p. 166.
31 Ibid., pp. 168–9.
32 Herbert, op. cit., p. 200.
33 Bartlett, op. cit., p. 178.

20   1909

1 B. Riffenburgh, *The Myth of the Explorer*, Oxford University Press, Oxford, 1994, p. 169.
2 R. Bartlett, *The Log of Bob Bartlett*, Putnam's, New York, 1928, p. 182.
3 R. Peary, *Nearest the Pole*, Hutchinson, London, 1907, p. ix.
4 P. Berton, *The Arctic Grail*, Viking, London, 1988, p. 566.
5 Ibid.
6 Bartlett, op. cit., p. 182.
7 *The Alaska Journal*, Winter 1984, p. 31.
8 Ibid., p. 32.
9 K. Harper, *Give Me My Father's Body*, Profile Books, London, 2000, p. 83.
10 Ibid.
11 Ibid., p. 137.
12 Ibid., p. 145.
13 Riffenburgh, op. cit., p. 170.
14 R. Amundsen, *My Life As An Explorer*, Heinemann, London, 1927.
15 J. Weems, *Peary: The Explorer and the Man*, Eyre & Spottiswoode, London, 1967, p. 230.
16 Riffenburgh, op. cit., p. 171.
17 Weems, op. cit., p. 231.
18 Berton, op. cit., p. 567.
19 Ibid., p. 568.

20 *New York Times*, quoted 9 September 1909.
21 R. Peary, *The North Pole*, Dover, New York, 1986, p. 17.
22 Ibid., p. 18.
23 Riffenburgh, op. cit., p. 169.
24 Peary, op. cit., p. 27.
25 Ibid., p. 19.
26 Berton, op. cit., p. 570.
27 Peary, *The North Pole*, op. cit., p. 29.
28 Ibid., p. 44.
29 Ibid., p. 47.
30 Ibid.
31 Ibid.
32 M. Henson, *A Black Explorer at the North Pole*, Bison Books, Lincoln, 1989, p. 26.
33 B. Robinson, *Dark Companion*, Hodder & Stoughton, London, 1948, p. 208.
34 Berton, op. cit., p. 570.
35 Herbert, op. cit., p. 221.
36 Peary, *The North Pole*, op. cit., p. 74.
37 Ibid.
38 Bartlett, op. cit., p. 185.
39 Ibid.
40 Peary, *The North Pole*, op. cit., p. 125.
41 Ibid., p. 167.
42 Ibid., p. 167.
43 Henson, op. cit., p. 89.
44 Ibid., p. 91.
45 Peary, *The North Pole*, op. cit., p. 232.
46 Ibid., p. 235.
47 Ibid., p. 259.
48 Berton, op. cit., p. 583.
49 Peary, *The North Pole*, op. cit., p. 272.
50 Ibid., p. 273.
51 H. Horwood, *Bartlett: The Great Canadian Explorer*, Doubleday, New York, 1977, pp. 87–8.
52 Bartlett, op. cit., p. 195.
53 Ibid.
54 Berton, op. cit., pp. 578–9.
55 Peary, *The North Pole*, op. cit., p. 282.
56 Berton, op. cit., pp. 583–4.
57 Herbert, op. cit., p. 247.
58 Henson, op. cit., p. 132.
59 Peary, *The North Pole*, op. cit., p. 297.
60 Ibid., pp. 288–9.
61 Ibid., p. 290.
62 Herbert, op. cit., p. 253.
63 Berton, op. cit., p. 584.
64 Peary, *The North Pole*, op. cit., p. 316.

21   Prince of Impostors

1 R. Bartlett, *The Log of Bob Bartlett*, Putnam's, New York, 1928, p. 197.
2 W. Herbert, *The Noose of Laurels*, Hodder & Stoughton, London, 1989, p. 256.
3 P. Berton, *The Arctic Grail*, Viking, London, 1988, p. 586.
4 Ibid.
5 M. Henson, *A Black Explorer at the North Pole*, Bison Books, Lincoln, 1989, p. 176.
6   Bartlett, op. cit., p. 204.
7 *New York Times*, 11 September 1909.
8 F. Cook, *My Attainment of the North Pole*, The Polar Publishing Co., New York, 1911, p. 287.
9 Ibid., p. 465.
10 Ibid., p. 455.
11 Ibid., p. 466.
12 Berton, op. cit., p. 600.
13 Ibid.
14 P. Gibbs, *Adventures in Journalism*, Heinemann, London, 1923, p. 42.
15 Ibid., p. 43.
16 *New York Tribune*, 9 September 1909.
17 Berton, op. cit., p. 601.
18 Herbert, op. cit., p. 283.
19 Ibid.
20 Berton, op. cit., p. 602.
21 B. Riffenburgh, *The Myth of the Explorer*, Oxford University Press, Oxford, 1994, p. 177.
22 Ibid.
23 Berton, op. cit., p. 604.
24 Riffenburgh, op. cit., p. 182.
25 Herbert, op. cit., p. 289.
26 Ibid., p. 287.
27 Berton, op. cit., p. 605.
28 Ibid., p. 606.
29 Ibid., p. 608.
30 *New York Times*, 9 September 1909.
31 Ibid., p. 300.
32 R. Peary, *The North Pole*, Dover Publications, New York, 1986, p. 364.
33 Ibid.
34 Berton, op. cit., p. 611.
35 Ibid.
36 Herbert, op. cit., p. 302.
37 *New York Tribune*, 22 December 1909.
38 Berton, op. cit., p. 613.
39 Herbert, op. cit., p. 305.
40 Ibid., p. 306.
41 Ibid., p. 304.
42 Ibid., p. 307.
43 Ibid., p. 310.

44 Peary, op. cit., p. 365.
45 RGS – Peary material.
46 Ibid.
47 Herbert, op. cit., p. 17.
48 Riffenburgh, op. cit., p. 190.
49 Cook, op. cit., pp. 509–10.
50 Ibid., p. 8.
51 Herbert, op. cit., p. 310.
52 Ibid., pp. 325–6.
53 Berton, op. cit., p. 621.
54 J. Weems, *Peary: The Explorer and the Man*, Eyre & Spottiswoode, London, 1967, p. 321.
55 Ibid., p. 319.
56 Ibid., pp. 319–20.
57 Ibid., p. 326.
58 Ibid., p. 324.

22   The Last Heroes

1 Canadian Slavonic Papers, 1973, p. 505.
2 Ibid.
3 Ibid., p.506.
4 Ibid., p. 508.
5 Ibid., p. 511.
6 Ibid., p. 512.
7 Ibid., p. 513.
8 Ibid., p. 514.
9 Ibid., p. 516.
10 Ibid.
11 Ibid., pp. 516–17.
12 Ibid., p. 517.
13 Ibid.
14 Ibid., p. 518.
15 R. Huntford, *Shackleton*, Cardinal, London, 1989, p. 489.
16 R. Amundsen, *My Life as an Explorer*, Heinemann, London, 1927, p. 64.
17 Ibid., p. 77.
18 Ibid., p. 119.
19 Ibid.
20 Ibid., p. 123.
21 Ibid., p. 104.
22 Ibid., p. 123.
23 Ibid., p. 124.
24 Ibid., pp. 127–8.
25 Ibid., p. 132.
26 P. Capelotti, *By Airship to the North Pole*, Rutgers University Press, New Brunswick, 1999, p. 47.
27 Ibid.
28 Ibid., p. 90.

29 Ibid., pp. 93–4.
30 Ibid., p. 49.
31 Ibid., p. 98.
32 Amundsen, op. cit., pp. 138–9.
33 Ibid., p. 133.
34 Ibid., p. 157.
35 Ibid., pp. 136–7.
36 A. McKee, *Ice Crash*, Souvenir Press, London, 1979, p. 44.
37 Ibid., p. 46.
38 Ibid.
39 U. Nobile, *My Polar Flights*, Muller, London, 1961, p. 42.
40 Amundsen, op. cit., p. 225.
41 *Discovery*, April 1921, p. 88.
42 Amundsen, op. cit., p. 166.
43 Ibid.
44 R. Byrd, *To The Pole*, Ohio State University Press, 1998, p. 74.
45 Ibid.
46 Ibid., p. 75.
47 Amundsen, op. cit., p. 167.
48 Byrd, op. cit., p. 75.
49 Ibid., p. 76.
50 R. Byrd, *Skyward*, Putnam's, New York, 1928, p. 196.
51 Amundsen, op. cit., p. 170.
52 Ibid., p. 171.
53 Byrd, *Skyward*, op. cit., p. 193.
54 Amundsen, op. cit., p. 173.
55 C. Holland, *Farthest North*, Robinson, London, 1999, p. 248.
56 R. Amundsen and L. Ellsworth, *The First Flight Across the Polar Sea*, Hutchinson, London, 1927, p. 116.
57 Ibid., p. 120.
58 Ibid.
59 Amundsen, op. cit., p. 183.
60 Ibid., p. 184.
61 Nobile, op. cit., p. 64.
62 Amundsen, op. cit., p. 184.
63 Nobile, op. cit., p. 67.
64 Ibid., p. 82.
65 Amundsen, op. cit., p. 212.
66 Ibid., pp. 212–13.
67 Nobile, op. cit., p. 90.
68 P. Berton, *The Arctic Grail*, Viking, London, 1988, p. 627.
69 *Journal of the American Geographical Society*, Vol. XXIX, p. 117.

Epilogue

1 U. Nobile, *My Polar Flights*, Muller, London, 1961, pp. 92–3.
2 F. Cook, *My Attainment of the Pole*, The Polar Publishing Co., New York, 1911, p. 6.

3 P. Berton, *The Arctic Grail*, Viking, London, 1988, p. 622.
4 W. Herbert, *The Noose of Laurels*, Hodder & Stoughton, London, 1989, p. 321.
5 H. Horwood, *Bartlett: The Great Canadian Explorer*, Doubleday, New York, 1977, p. 169.
6 L. Guttridge, *Icebound*, Paragon, New York, 1988, p. 333.

Picture Sources

Section 1

1 *Henry Grinnell* © Author's collection
2 *Elisha Kent Kane M.D., U.S.N.* © Author's collection
3 *The Pack off Sylvia Headland* © Author's collection
4 *Life in the Brig* © Author's collection
5 *Crossing the Ice Belt at Coffee Gorge* © Author's collection
6 *Dr Isaac Israel Hayes* © Royal Geographical Society, London
7 *Charles Francis Hall* © Author's collection
8 *Burial of Captain Hall* © Author's collection
9 *The ship broke away in the darkness, and we lost sight of her in a moment* © Author's collection
10 *Neujahr 1870 (New Year 1870)* © Royal Geographical Society, London
11 *Scene der Schlittenreise nach Norden (Scene from the sledge journey to the north)* © Royal Geographical Society, London
12 *Die Hansa als Wrack (The Wreck of the Hansa)* © Royal Geographical Society, London
13 *Noon on December 21st, 1873* © Royal Geographical Society, London
14 *Fruitless attempt to rescue Matoschkin* © Royal Geographical Society, London
15 *The Sledge in a snow storm* © Royal Geographical Society, London
16 *Divine service on deck on board the Tegetthoff* © Royal Geographical Society, London
17 *The Carnival on the Ice* © Royal Geographical Society, London
18 *The Moon with its Halo (Tegetthoff)* © Royal Geographical Society, London

Section 2

1 *Sir George Nares by Stephen Pearce (1819–1904)* © National Portrait Gallery, London
2 *Sherard Osborn by Stephen Pearce (1819–1904)* © National Portrait Gallery, London
3 *Sir Clements Markham* © Royal Geographical Society, London
4 *H.R.H. Luigi Amedeo of Savoy. Duke of the Abruzzi* © Author's collection
5 *Floeberg Beach, spring* © Author's collection
6 *Sledgers from the Alert, 1876* © Scott Polar Research Institute, Cambridge
7 *Extricating the Alert, 1876* © Scott Polar Research Institute, Cambridge
8 *One of the Nares sledge crews* © National Maritime Museum, Greenwich
9 *Cairn Tomb, Monument Hill, Lena Delta* © Royal Geographical Society, London
10 *The hut by moonlight* © Author's collection

11 *The Polar Star after the ice pressure* © Author's collection
12 *Officers of the Jeannette* © Author's collection
13 *The Bay of Teplitz, from the east* © Author's collection
14 *Nansen takes a walk* © Royal Geographical Society, London
15 *Captain Sverdrup in his cabin* © Royal Geographical Society, London
16 *Lieutenant Hjalmar Johanssen* © Royal Geographical Society, London
17 *Meeting of Jackson and Nansen* © Royal Geographical Society, London
18 *Dr Nansen* © Royal Geographical Society, London
19 *Johanssen at his house, Cape Flora* © Royal Geographical Society, London

Section 3

1 *On the bridge of the Svensksund: Messrs. Fraenkel, Andrée, Svedenborg, and Strindberg* © Royal Geographical Society, London
2 *On top of the balloon* © Royal Geographical Society, London
3 *Andrées Balloon (1 January 1897)* © Royal Geographical Society, London
4 *The Eagle rising from the Danes Island on July 11th 1897* © Royal Geographical Society, London
5 *The Eagle immediately after landing on the ice floe July 14th 1897* © Royal Geographical Society, London
6 *Admiral Robert E. Peary (1886–1897)* © Royal Geographical Society, London
7 *Dr Frederick Cook, 1892* © Library of Congress
8 *A summer day – Ikwa and family* © Royal Geographical Society, London
9 *Matthew Henson, 1892* © Library of Congress
10 *Typical difficulties of working sledges over pressure ridges* © Royal Geographical Society, London
11 *Peary at the North Pole cheering the 'Stars and Stripes'* © Royal Geographical Society, London
12 *Mussolini delivering airship to Norway (left to right Mussolini, Calant, Nobile, Amunsden, Ellsworth, Thommessen (29 March, 1926)* © Royal Geographical Society, London
13 *The Norge leaving Spitsbergen, 1926* © Scott Polar Research Institute, Cambridge
14 *Peary in his North Pole costume* © Royal Geographical Society, London

BIBLIOGRAPHY

Abruzzi, L. (trans. W. Le Queux), *On the 'Polar Star' in the Arctic Sea* (2 vols), Hutchinson, London, 1903
——*Farther North than Nansen*, Howard Wilford Bell, London, 1901
Amundsen, R., *My Polar Flight*, Hutchinson, London, 1926
——*My Life as an Explorer*, Heinemann, London, 1927
Amundsen, R. and Ellsworth, L., *The First Flight Across the Polar Sea*, Hutchinson, London, 1927
Andrée, S., Strindberg, N. and Fraenkel, K. (trans. E. Adams-Ray), *The Andrée Diaries*, John Lane, London, 1931
Astrup, E. (trans. H. Bull), *With Peary Near the Pole*, Pearson, London, 1898
Barrow, J., *Voyages of Discovery and Research in the Arctic Regions*, John Murray, London, 1846
Bartlett, R ., *The Log of Bob Bartlett*, Putnam's, New York, 1928
Berton, P., *The Arctic Grail*, Viking, London, 1988
Bessels, E., *Die Amerikanische Nordpol-Expedition*, Engelmann, Leipzig, 1879
Blake, E. (ed.), *Arctic Experiences: containing Capt. George E. Tyson's wonderful drift on the ice-floe*, Sampson Low, Marston, Low & Searle, London, 1874
Blumenfeld, R., *R.D.B.'s Diary*, Heinemann, London, 1930
Brainard, D. (ed. B. James), *Six Came Back*, Bobbs-Merrill, Indianapolis, 1940
Bryce, G., *The Siege and Conquest of the North Pole*, Gibbings, London, 1910
Byrd, R., *Skyward*, Putnam's, New York, 1928
Byrd, R. (ed. R. Goerler), *To the Pole*, Ohio State University Press, 1998
Capelotti, P., *By Airship to the North Pole: An Archaeology of Human Exploration*, Rutgers University Press, New Jersey, 1999
Conefrey, M. and Jordan, T., *Icemen*, Boxtree, London, 1998
Cook, F., *My Attainment of the Pole*, The Polar Publishing Co., New York, 1911
——*Return from the Pole*, Burke, London, 1953

Corner, G., *Doctor Kane of the Arctic Seas*, Temple University Press, Philadelphia, 1972

Crockett, A., *When James Gordon Bennett was Caliph of Baghdad*, Funk & Wagnalls, New York, 1926

De Long, G. (ed. E. De Long), *The Voyage of the Jeannette* (2 vols), Kegan Paul, Trench & Co., London, 1883

Elder, W., *Elisha Kent Kane*, Childs & Peterson, Philadelphia, 1858

Fairley, T., *Sverdrup's Arctic Adventures*, Longmans, London, 1959

Feilden, H., *Notes from an Arctic Journal*, West, Newman & Co., London, nd.

Fox, M., *The Love-life of Dr. Kane*, Carleton, New York, 1866

Gibbs, P., *Adventures in Journalism*, Heinemann, London, 1923

Gilder, W., *Ice Pack and Tundra: an account of the search for the Jeannette*, Sampson, Low, Marston, Searle & Rivington, London, 1883

Giudici, D., *The Tragedy of the Italia*, Appleton, New York, 1929

Godfrey, W., *Godfrey's Narrative of the Last Grinnell Arctic Exploring Expedition in search of Sir John Franklin, 1853–4–5*, J. T. Lloyd, Philadelphia, 1860

Greely, A., *Three Years of Arctic Service* (2 vols), Richard Bentley, London, 1886

Guttridge, L., *Icebound*, Paragon, New York, 1988

Hall, C., *Life with the Esquimaux* (2 vols), Sampson Low, Son, and Marston, London, 1864

Hall, T., *Has the North Pole Been Discovered?*, Richard C. Badger, Boston, 1917

Haller, J. (ed. F. Haller), *Erinnerungen eines Tiroler Teilnehmers an Julius v. Payer's Nordpol-Expedition*, Universitätsverlag Wagner, Innsbruck, 1959

Harper, K., *Give Me My Father's Body*, Profile Books, London, 2000

Hayes, I., *An Arctic Boat Journey*, Richard Bentley, London, 1860

——*The Open Polar Sea. A narrative of a voyage towards the North Pole*, Sampson Low, Son, and Marston, London 1867

——*The Land of Desolation*, Sampson Low, Marston,Low & Searle, London, 1871

Hayes, J., *Robert Edwin Peary*, Grant Richards & Humphrey Toulmin, London, 1923

Heilprin, A., *The Arctic Problem and narrative of the Peary Relief Expedition*, Contemporary Publishing, Philadelphia, 1893

Hendrik, H. (trans H. Rink; ed. G. Stephens), *The Memoirs of Hans Hendrik*, Trubner & Co., London 1878

Henson, M., *A Black Explorer at the North Pole*, Bison Books, Lincoln, 1989

Herbert, W., *The Noose of Laurels*, Hodder & Stoughton, London, 1989

Hobbs, W., *Peary*, Macmillan, New York, 1936

Hoare, J., *Arctic Exploration*, Methuen, London, 1906

Holland, C. (ed.), *Farthest North*, Robinson, London, 1994

Horwood, H., *Bartlett: the Great Canadian Explorer*, Doubleday, New York, 1977

Hoyer, L. (trans. M. Michael), *Nansen: a family portrait*, Longmans, Green & Co., London, 1957

Huntford, R., *Nansen*, Duckworth, London, 1997

Inglefield, E., *A Summer Search for Sir John Franklin with A Peep into the Polar Basin*, Thomas Harrison, London, 1853

Jackson, F., *A Thousand Days in the Arctic* (2 vols), Harper & Bros, London, 1899

——*The Lure of Unknown Lands*, Bell, London, 1935

Kane, E., *The US Grinnell Expedition in Search of Sir John Franklin*, Harper, New York, 1854
——*Arctic Explorations in the years 1853, 1854, 1855* (2 vols), Childs & Peterson, Philadelphia, 1856
Keely, R. and Davis, G., *In Arctic Seas*, Gay and Bird, London, 1893
Koldewey, K. (trans. C. Mercier; ed. H. Bates), *The German Arctic Expedition of 1869–70 and narrative of the wreck of the 'Hansa' in the ice*, Sampson Low, Marston, Low & Searle, London, 1874
Krisch, O., *Das Tagebuch des Maschinisten Otto Krisch*, Leykam-Verlag, Graz-Wien, 1973
Lachambre, H., Machuron, A., *Andrée and his balloon*, Constable & Co., London, 1898
Loomis, C., *Weird and Tragic Shores: The story of Charles Francis Hall, Explorer*, Macmillan, London, 1972
Lopez, B., *Arctic Dreams*, Picador, London, 1987
McKee, A., *Ice Crash*, Souvenir Press, London, 1979
McKinlay, W., *Karluk*, Weidenfeld & Nicolson, London, 2000
Macmillan, D., *Four Years in the White North*, Medici Society, London, 1925
Malaurie, J., *Ultima Thule*, Bordas, Paris, 1990
Malone, D. (ed.), *Dictionary of American Biography*, Charles Scribner, New York, 1995
Markham, A., *A Whaling Cruise to Baffin's Bay and the Gulf of Boothia*, Sampson Low, Marston, Low & Searle, London, 1874
——*The Great Frozen Sea: A personal narrative of the voyage of the 'Alert'*, Dalby, Isbister & Co., London, 1878
——*A Polar Reconnaissance: Being the voyage of the 'Isbjorn' to Zemlya in 1879*, C. Kegan, Paul & Co., London, 1881
Markham, C., *The Threshold of the Unknown Region*, Sampson Low, Marston, Low & Searle, London, 1873
——*A Refutation of the Report by the Scurvy Committee*, Griffin, Portsmouth, 1877
Markham, C. (ed.), *Papers Relating to the Arctic Expedition of 1875–6*, Clowes & Son, London, nd.
Markham, M. and F., *The Life of Sir Albert Hastings Markham*, Cambridge University Press, Cambridge, 1927
Melville, G., *In the Lena Delta*, Longmans, Green & Co., London, 1885
Nansen, F. (trans. M. Gepp), *The First Crossing of Greenland* (2 vols), Longmans, Green & Co., London, 1890
——*Farthest North* (2 vols), Constable & Co., London, 1897
Nares, G., *Narrative of A Voyage To the Polar Sea* (2 vols), Sampson Low, Marston, Searle, & Rivington, London, 1878
Newcomb, R., *Our Lost Explorers: the narrative of the Jeannette Arctic Expedition*, American Publishing Company, Hartford, 1882
Nobile, U. (trans. F. Fleetwood), *My Polar Flights*, Frederick Muller, London, 1961
——*With the 'Italia' to the North Pole*, Allen & Unwin, London, 1930
Nordenskiöld, A. (trans. A. Leslie), *The Voyage of the Vega*, Macmillan, London, 1883
Nourse, J. (ed.), *Narrative of the Second Arctic Expedition made by Charles F. Hall*, Government Printing Office, Washington, 1879

O'Connor, R., *The Scandalous Mr. Bennett*, Doubleday, New York, 1962

Payer, J., *New Lands Within the Arctic Circle. Narrative of the discoveries of the Austrian ship Tegetthoff in the years 1872–1874* (2 vols), Macmillan, London, 1876

——*Die Oesterreichisch-Ungarische Nordpol-Expedition*, Alfred Holder, Wien, 1876

Peary, J., *My Arctic Journal*, Longmans, Green & Co., London, 1893

Peary, R., *Northwards over the Great Ice* (2 vols), Methuen, London, 1898

——*Nearest the Pole*, Hutchinson, London, 1907

Petermann, A., *Das Nordlichste Land der Erde*, Justus Perthes, Gotha, 1867

——*Papers on the eastern and northern extension of the Gulf Stream*, United States Hydrographical Office, Washington, 1872

Petermann, A., Freeden, W., Muhry, A. (trans. E. Knorr), *Papers on the . . . Gulf Stream*, Government Printing Office, Washington, 1871

Ransmayr, C. (trans. J. Woods), *The Terrors of Ice and Darkness*, Paladin, London, 1992

Rasmussen, K. (trans. A. and R. Kenney), *Greenland by the Polar Sea*, Heinemann, London, 1921

Report of the Committee appointed by the Lords Commissioners of the Admiralty to enquire into . . . the recent Arctic Expedition, HM Stationery Office, London, 1877

Riffenburgh, B., *The Myth of the Explorer*, Belhaven Press, London; Scott Polar Research Institute, Cambridge, 1993

Robinson, B., *Dark Companion*, Hodder & Stoughton, London, 1948

Seitz, D., *The James Gordon Bennetts*, Bobbs-Merrill, Indianapolis, 1928

Smith, D., *Arctic Expeditions, British and Foreign*, Fullarton, Jack & Co., London, 1880

Spufford, F., *I May Be Some Time*, Faber, London, 1996

Sverdrup, O., *New Lands: four years in the Arctic regions* (2 vols), Longmans, Green & Co., London, 1904

Vaughan, R., *The Arctic: a history*, Alan Sutton, Stroud, 1994

Villarejo, O., *Dr Kane's Voyage to the Polar Lands*, University of Pennsylvania Press, Philadelphia, 1965

Weems, J., *Peary: the explorer and the man*, Eyre & Spottiswoode, London, 1967

Wiggins, J. (ed.), *The Austro-German Polar Expedition under the command of Lieut. Weyprecht*, William Carr, London, 1875

Wrangel, F. (ed. E. Sabine), *Narrative of an Expedition to the Polar Sea in the years 1820, 1821, 1822 & 1823 commanded by Lieutenant, now Admiral, Ferdinand Von Wrangel, of the Russian Imperial Navy*, James Madden, London, 1840

Wright, H., *The Great White North*, Macmillan, New York, 1910

Wright, J., *Geography in the Making: The American Geographical Society, 1851–1951*, American Geographical Society, New York, 1952

Young, A., *The Two Voyages of the 'Pandora' in 1875 and 1876*, Edward Stanford, London, 1879

Journals, Newspapers, Periodicals

Alaska Journal
American Geographical Society Journal
Blackwood's Magazine
Daily Mail

Discovery
Fraser's Magazine
Gentleman's Magazine
London Illustrated News
New York Herald
New York Times
New York Tribune
Polar Record
Proceedings of the Royal Geographical Society
Quarterly Review
Canadian Slavonic Papers
Royal Geographical Society Journal
Royal Geographical Society President's Addresses
The Times

INDEX

Abruzzi, Duke of: character and background, 315–16; Arctic expedition (1899–1900), 316–32; his journal, 333–4, 336; later years, 397

Academy of Natural Sciences of Philadelphia, 56

Admiral Tegetthoff (Weyprecht and Payer's ship), 112, 113, 115, 116, 117, 119

Advance (Kane's ship), 10–14, 19–22, 25–30, 32, 37–9, 44, 73

airships: on Amundsen–Ellsworth expedition (1926), 401, 405, 411–14

Albert of Monaco, Prince, 314

Aldrich, Lieutenant Pelham: on Nares's expedition (1875–76), 167, 168, 171, 172, 173, 177–8

Alert, HMS (Nares's ship), 161–2, 163, 164, 165–6, 171, 173, 183

Alessandri, Renato, 413

Alexey (Eskimo): on De Long's expedition (1879–82), 223, 225

Allakassingwah (Peary's mistress), 312

Alliance (De Long rescue ship), 213–14

Ambler, James: on De Long's expedition (1879–82), 200, 205, 215, 223, 225, 229

American Geographical Society, 56, 79, 91, 94, 157; awards Gold Medal to Peary (1897), 303; Peary elected president of, 334

American Philosophical Society, 56

Amund Ringnes Island, 372

Amundsen, Roald, 238, 241, 267, 350–1; attempts to fly to the Pole (1925), 398–401; airship expedition to the Pole (1926), 401, 405–7, 411–14; his reception, 415; death (1928), 420

Andrée, Salomon August: character and background, 253–4; plans balloon trip to the Pole (1895), 254–6; attempt on the Pole (1896), 257–8; attempt on the Pole (1897), 269–74; remains found on White Island (1930), 274; story of his expedition published (1930), 274–82

Anniversary Lodge (Peary's hut), 294, 296, 301

Anoatok (village), 356, 370

Antisell, Dr Thomas: on Bering Sea as gateway to the Arctic Ocean, 205

Archangel, 317, 318, 392, 396

Archer, Colin: designs *Fram*, 239–40

Arctic expeditions: chronology, xv–xxi; overview, 415–17, 418

ABRUZZI (1899–1900): arrives at Archangel, 317; condition of the dogs, 317–18; visited by dignitaries, 318; arrives at Prince Rudolf Island, 318; ship punctured and repaired, 318–19; hit by a storm, 319; Cagni and team set out for the Pole, 320; Querini and Cavalli turn back, 321; Cagni's progress, 322; Cagni and team reach 86°34′, 323; their return journey, 323; Cagni weakens, 324;

Arctic expeditions: ABRUZZI (1899–1900)
    continued
        Cagni amputates his own finger, 324–5;
        ice drift takes them off course, 325–8;
        they see mirage of Cape Mill, 328; they
        reach Ommaney Island, 329; they reach
        their ship, 330; Querini and his team
        vanish, 331; the return home, 331–2
    AMUNDSEN–ELLSWORTH (1925): flying boats
        take off, 399; they develop engine
        trouble, 401; they take off again and
        nearly crash, 401–2; they crash-land off
        Spitsbergen, 401
    AMUNDSEN–ELLSWORTH (1926): airship takes
        off, 412; the journey, 412–13; Amundsen
        sees the Pole (12 May), 413; flags
        dropped on the Pole, 413; the flight to
        Alaska, 414; their reception, 414–15
    ANDRÉE (1896), 257–8
    ANDRÉE (1897): preparations, 269–72;
        balloon takes off but loses altitude,
        272–3; guide ropes drop off balloon,
        273; balloon goes missing, 273–4; crew's
        skeletons recovered (1930), 274; story
        of expedition published, 274–82
    BALDWIN (1901–2), 314–15
    BYRD–BENNETT (1926): dispute with
        Amundsen, 408; journey to the Pole,
        409–10; return home, 410; doubts about
        Byrd's findings, 410–11
    COOK (1907–9): leaves for Etah, 351; claims
        to have reached the Pole, 371; his story,
        371–2; doubts about his story, 372–3;
        reception at Copenhagen, 374
    DE LONG (1879–82): leaves San Francisco,
        201; winters on the ice pack, 204–6;
        Danenhower treated for syphilis, 205;
        ship struck by ice slabs, 207; ship
        flooded, 207–8; fears for crew's safety,
        211–13; rescue missions, 214; disquiet
        among the crew and the dogs, 215–16;
        reaches Henrietta Island, 216; ship sinks,
        217–18; crew marches to Siberia, 219;
        reaches Bennett Island, 220; crew
        marches to Lena Delta, 221–2; Melville
        and his men become detached from De
        Long, 222; De Long and his men get
        frostbite, 223; Nindemann and Noros
        search for help, 224; De Long's diary,
        226; Nindemann and Noros reach Balun,
        226; Melville searches for De Long, 227;
        further rescue missions, 227–8; Melville
        finds De Long and his men dead, 229
    FIALA (1903–5), 315
    FRANKLIN (1845), 5, 48
    GREELY (1882), 232–3
    HALL (1860–62): reaches Baffin Island, 81;
        Hall's encounter with Tookolito, 82–3;

Hall lives with Eskimos, 83–4; Hall
    charts coastline, 85
HALL (1864–69): explores Repulse Bay, 87;
    Hall falls ill, 88
HALL (1871): departs for Pole, 91;
    disagreements among crew, 133–5;
    progress and discoveries, 135–6;
    reaches 82°16′, 136; Hall falls ill and
    dies, 138–40
HAYES (1860–61): leaves Boston, 62; reaches
    Baffin Bay, 63; reaches Upernavik, 63;
    picks up Hendrik and family, 64; storm
    at Cape Alexander, 64–5; winters in
    Greenland, 66; Hayes has trouble
    controlling the dogs, 66–7; explores
    Greenland, 67; problems with the
    Eskimos, 68–9; birthday parties, 69; *The
    Port Foulkes Weekly News*, 70; huskies
    begin to die, 70; Hendrik and Sonntag
    travel to get replacement dogs, 71;
    Sonntag dies, 71–3; Kalutunah and dogs
    arrive, 73; expedition to Smith Sound,
    74; Grinnell Land sighted, 75; dogs
    become ravenous, 75; they reach 81°35′,
    76; flags raised, 76–7; return to ship, 77;
    return to Upernavik and then Boston, 78
HERBERT (1969), 417–18
INGLEFIELD (1852), 6–7
JACKSON (1894–97), 263–6
KANE (1853–55): preparations, 10–11; leaves
    New York, 11; reaches Upernavik, 11;
    leaves food cache at Littleton Island, 13;
    crew wish to turn back, 14; discoveries,
    14; winters at Rensselaer Harbour,
    15–17; dogs develop disease, 16; Ohlsen
    and others get frostbite, 18; rescue party,
    18–19; their journey back, 19–21; deaths
    of crew members, 21; meeting with
    Eskimos, 21–2; further explorations, 22;
    Godfrey mutinies, 22–3; evidence of
    Open Polar Sea, 25; Morton and
    Hendrik eat polar bear livers, 26; Kane
    attempts to sail to Beechey Island by
    whaleboat, 27; Hayes and others vote to
    leave, 28–9; Kane brands them
    deserters, 30; the breakaway party's
    journey south, 31–2; they build a winter
    hut, 33; they eat *tripes de roche*, 33–4;
    their encounter with Eskimos, 34–6;
    Kane begins to eat rats, 36; Kane's crew
    get scurvy, 37; Bonsall and Petersen
    return to the ship, 37; Hayes drugs
    Eskimos and tries to escape, 39–40;
    Hayes's party make for Cape Alexander,
    40; they reach the ship, 41; Godfrey
    escapes, 43; Kane arrests Godfrey at
    Etah, 44; Kane decides to leave, 45; they
    march south, 46; Ohlsen dies, 46; they

KANE (1853–55) *continued*
head for Cape Alexander, 47; they are
picked up, 48; they reach Upernavik, 49
KUZNETSOV (1948), 417
NANSEN (1888): traverses Greenland, 237–8
NANSEN (1893–96): anti-scorbutic diet, 242;
carries Primus stoves, 242–3; travels to
New Siberian Islands, 243; Nansen
becomes frustrated, 244; ship nearly
crushed by ice, 245; Nansen and
Johanssen sledge north, 247; ice drift
takes them off course, 248; their
chronometers stop, 248–9; Nansen has
to retrieve his compass, 249; they sight
land and reach it, 250–1; they build
'The Hole', 258; uncertain of their
position, 258; they lose their kayaks
and Nansen swims after them, 259–60;
kayaks attacked by walruses, 260–1;
rescued by Jackson, 261–2
NARES (1875–76): leaves Portsmouth, 162–3;
picks up Hendrik and family, 163; leaves
Disco Island, 164; winters in Floeberg
Beach, 166–8; Nares releases homing
pigeon, 168; Moss's journal, 169, 172–3;
Feilden's journal, 169–70; Markham and
Aldrich cross Ellesmere Island, 172;
Nares describes conditions in the tents,
173–4; Markham's men suffer from
exhaustion and scurvy, 174–5, 176;
Markham reaches 83°20′, 175;
Markham's return journey, 176; Parr
returns to ship for help, 176–7; Aldrich's
journey, 177–8; scurvy hits the *Alert*,
178–9; Beaumont's exploration of
Greenland, 179–80; Beaumont's men get
scurvy, 180–1; Beaumont heads for the
Alert, 182; Beaumont's team rescued,
182–3; return to Portsmouth, 183–4
NORDENSKIÖLD (1878–79): expedition to
find North-East Passage, 199; Bennett
proposes rescue mission, 199–200; De
Long's rescue mission, 200; De Long
hears that Nordenskiöld is safe, 203
PEARY (1886): fails to cross Greenland, 286
PEARY (1891–92): Peary breaks a leg, 288;
winters on west coast of Greenland,
288; his team, 289; Verhoeff vanishes,
291; reaches Independence Bay, 291;
'discovers' Peary Channel and Peary
Land, 291
PEARY (1893–95): preparations, 293;
Josephine Peary gives birth, 294; tidal
wave, 296; Peary marches north but is
beaten back, 296; journey to Mountain
of Iron, 298; the *Falcon* returns, 298–9;
Peary's second expedition, 299; journey

to Independence Bay, 300; return
journey, 300–1; Peary takes back
meteorites to USA, 301–2
PEARY (1898–1902): preparations, 304–5;
leaves home, 305; meeting with
Sverdrup, 306–7; reaches Fort Conger,
307; Peary loses eight toes to frostbite,
307–8; returns to Fort Conger, 308;
Peary journeys north, 309; reaches
Cape Morris Jesup, 310; Peary's
relations with Dedrick, 311; Peary's
illegitimate child is born, 312; Peary
visited by Cook, 312; journey to
Ellesmere Island, 312; Peary becomes
depressed, 313
PEARY (1905–6): leaves New York, 338; ship's
progress, 339; reaches Cape Sheridan,
339; begins advance to the Pole, 340;
Henson reaches Big Lead, 340; reaches
87°06′, 341; return journey, 341–4; Peary
explores Ellesmere Island, 344; claims to
have discovered Crocker Land, 344–5;
return journey, 345; ship is damaged,
345; ship reaches Etah, 346
PEARY (1908–9): leaves New York, 354;
meets Franke, 356–7; leaves Etah, 357;
reaches Cape Sheridan, 358; Eskimos
fall ill, 358–9; teams march north,
359–60; Peary and Henson head for the
Pole without Bartlett, 361–2; they arrive
at the Pole (6 April 1909), 362–3; Peary
takes readings, 363–5; return journey,
366; reaches Cape Columbia, 367
PETERMANN (1868), 94
PETERMANN (1869): leaves Bremerhaven,
95; Hegemann misinterprets
Koldewey's signal, 97; Koldewey
proceeds on *Germania*, 98; Dr Borgen
savaged by a polar bear, 98–9; they
reach 77°1′, 99; the *Hansa* is
surrounded by ice floes, 100–2; the
Hansa sinks, 102; Hegemann and men
drift on floe, 102–3; floe breaks up, 104;
nearly crushed by iceberg, 104–5;
fissure slices through hut, 105; they
take to the boats and reach
Friedrichsthal, 106; they reach
Julianehaab, 107; they arrive in
Copenhagen, 109
SEDOV (1913–14): arrives at Archangel, 392;
winters at Novaya Zemlya, 392–3;
arrives at Franz Josef Land, 393–4;
Sedov and his men get scurvy, 394;
Sedov sets out for the Pole, 394–5;
Sedov dies, 395; survivors rescued, 396
SVERDRUP (1898–1902): 305–6; 307, 308,
335
WELLMAN (1906, 1907 & 1908), 401–3

WEYPRECHT–PAYER (1872–74): leaves
 Bremerhaven, 113; reaches Novaya
 Zemlya, 114; Wilczek deposits
 supplies, 114; ship is carried by ice
 drift, 115–16; ship is nearly crushed by
 ice, 116–17; discovery of Franz Josef
 Land, 118–19; illness among the crew,
 120, 122; Payer explores Franz Josef
 Land, 122; Zaninovich, dogs and sledge
 fall into crevasse, 122–3; Payer runs for
 help, 123; Payer rescues Zaninovich,
 124–5; journey to Novaya Zemlya,
 125–8; they reach Novaya Zemlya, 128
Arctic Explorations (Kane), 51
The Arctic Grail (Berton), x, xi
Arctic Highlanders, 38, 297
Armstrong, Dr Alexander: attacks idea of
 Open Polar Sea, 54–5
Astrup, Eivind: on Peary's expedition
 (1891–92), 289, 291; his journal, 292; on
 Peary's expedition (1893–95), 293, 296,
 297
Axel Heiberg Island, 335, 344, 372

Back, Sir George: attacks Kane, 54
Baffin Bay, 5, 6, 47, 63, 78, 81
Baffin Island, 84, 149
Baker, Jefferson: on Kane's expedition
 (1853–55), 11, 21
Balchen, Lieutenant Bernt, 408, 409, 410
Baldwin, Evelyn: Arctic expedition (1901–2),
 314–15; supports Peary against Cook, 376
ballooning, 255–6
Bang, Captain, 108, 109
Barents, William, 3
Barents Islands, 126
Barker, Elsa (Peary's ghostwriter), 355, 357
Barrill, Edward, 379
Barrow, Sir John: belief in Open Polar Sea, 4;
 and North-West Passage expedition
 (1845), 5; on North Pole, 5
Bartlett, Robert: on Peary's expedition
 (1898–1902), 306, 308; on Peary's
 expedition (1905–6), 338, 339, 341, 345–6,
 347; on Peary's lecture tour, 348; on
 Peary's expedition (1908–9), 354, 355,
 357–8, 359, 360, 360–1, 369; sails to
 Spitsbergen with Byrd and Floyd (1926),
 407, 408; later years, 397–8, 422
Baumann, Victor: on Sverdrup's expedition
 (1898–1902), 308
Beaumont, Lieutenant (later Admiral Sir)
 Lewis: on Nares's expedition (1875–76),
 171, 179–84; praises Peary, 334–5
Beechey Island, 8, 27
Belgica (Cook's ship to Antarctica), 350, 351
Bennett, Floyd: Arctic expedition (1926),
 407, 408, 409–10

Bennett, James Gordon: motives for Polar
 exploration, 192; character, 193–4;
 sponsors search for Livingstone, 194;
 sponsors search for Franklin, 194–5;
 collaborates with Petermann, 195–6;
 collaborates with De Long, 197; plans to
 rescue Nordenskiöld, 199–200; organises
 search for De Long, 227–8; attacked in
 Saturday Review, 231; publishes Cook's
 story, 373–4; later life, 232, 420
Bennett Island, 220, 221
Bering, Vitus, 3
Bering Strait, 94, 195, 196, 203
Berton, Pierre, x, xi
Bessels, Dr Emil: on Hall's expedition
 (1871–73), 91, 136, 137, 140, 141, 145, 146,
 155; disagreement with Hall, 132–4;
 possible murderer of Hall, 142–3, 144
Bierce, Ambrose, 289
'Big Lead', 340, 342, 343, 355, 359, 367, 369
Blackwood's Magazine: praises Nares's
 expedition, 164, 165
Blake, John: on Kane's expedition (1853–55),
 11, 17, 18, 20, 29–30, 32, 42, 43
Blessing, Dr Henrik: on Nansen's expedition
 (1893–96), 244
Blumenfeld, Ralph, 193–4
Bonsall, Amos: on Kane's expedition
 (1853–55), 11, 28, 29, 37, 38, 39, 42, 43, 44;
 publishes account of expedition, 52
Borgen, Dr: on Petermann's expedition
 (1869), 98–9
Borup, George: on Peary's expedition
 (1908–9), 354, 359, 360, 365, 371; later
 years, 397
Boston Society of Natural History, 56
Bovril, 412n
Bradley, John R.: on Cook's expedition
 (1907–9), 351; attacked by Peary, 352
Bradley Land, 372, 397
Brainard, Sergeant David: on Greely's
 expedition (1882), 232
Bratvaag (ship), 274
Brent, Silas: thermometric gateway theory,
 94
Brooks, Henry: on Kane's expedition
 (1853–55), 11, 14, 17, 18, 19, 20, 42
Bryan, Richard: on Hall's expedition
 (1871–73), 145
Bryant, Henry, 334, 336
Buchholz, Dr: on Petermann's expedition
 (1869), 100, 101–2
Budington, Sidney: on Hall's expedition
 (1860–62), 80, 81, 86; falls out with Hall,
 87; on Hall's expedition (1871–73), 91,
 134–5, 136, 137, 138, 141, 145, 146, 155;
 possible murderer of Hall, 142–3
Bulun (Siberian town), 222, 226, 227

burros (donkeys): on Peary's expedition (1893–95), 295
Byrd, Evelyn: Arctic expedition (1926), 407, 408–10; receives Congressional Medal of Honour, 410; doubts about his claims, 410–11

Cagni, Captain Umberto: on Abruzzi's expedition (1899–1900), 318–30
Camp Jesup, 363, 366
Canepa, Simone: on Abruzzi's expedition (1899–1900), 322, 324, 325
cannibalism: on Greely's expedition (1882), 233
Cape Alexander, 31, 40–1, 46–7, 64, 78, 135, 147, 165, 288
Cape Breton Island, 347
Cape Colgate, 344
Cape Columbia, 355, 359, 367, 369
Cape D'Urville, 306
Cape Flora, 261, 262, 278, 279, 317, 318, 327, 393–4, 395, 396
Cape Frazer, 22
Cape Isabella, 64–5, 78, 147
Cape Joseph Goode, 79
Cape Mill, 328, 329
Cape Morris Jesup, 310
Cape Sabine, 311, 312
Cape Sherard Osborn, 125
Cape Sheridan, 339, 341, 358, 370
Cape Washington, 310
Cape York, 64, 72
Carroll, Lewis, 416
Carruthers, Gibson: on Hayes's expedition (1860), 62, 63
Cavalli, Dr Achille: on Abruzzi's expedition (1899–1900), 321, 330
Centre for Forensic Medicine (Toronto): investigates Hall's death, 141–2
Chester, Hubbard: on Hall's expedition (1871–73), 91, 134, 135, 136, 138, 145, 146, 155
Chipp, Lieutenant Charles: on De Long's expedition (1879–82), 200, 210, 220, 221
Christiansen, Fred: on Greely's expedition (1882), 232
Churchill, Winston, 397
Cincinnati News: supports Hayes's expedition (1859), 57
Clark, Charles: on Peary's expedition (1905–6), 343, 344
Coffin (carpenter on Polaris), 146
Collins, Jerome: on De Long's expedition (1879–82), 200–1, 205, 215, 217, 220, 223, 229
Collinson, Sir Richard: doubts Kane's findings, 54
Constantine, Grand Duke, 159

Constanz (ship), 108, 109
Conway, Sir Martin, 314
Cook, Frederick: on Peary's expedition (1891–92), 289; drops out of Peary's 1893–95 expedition, 294; joins Peary (1900), 312; expedition to Antarctica (1898–99), 350–1; 'climbs' Mount McKinley (1906), 351, 352, 379, 386; Arctic expedition (1907–9), 351, 370–1; claims to have reached the Pole, 371; his story, 371–2; doubts about his story, 372–3; reception at Copenhagen, 374; dispute with Peary, 376–81, 386–7, 390, 407; University of Copenhagen declares him an impostor, 381; accused of forgery, 382; goes on the run, 382–3; his journal, 386; diary not recovered, 386–7; later years, 421
Coppinger, Dr Richard: on Nares's expedition (1875–76), 171, 180, 182
Cornwallis Island, 6, 8
Corwin (De Long rescue ship), 214
Crane City, 359, 367
Crocker, George, 337
Crocker Land, 344–5, 348, 397

Daily Chronicle, 374
Daly, Judge (President of American Geographical Society), 157
Danenhower, Lieutenant John: on De Long's expedition (1879–82), 200, 201, 205, 215, 217, 218–19, 220, 227; spreads stories of misconduct on expedition, 231
Dane's Island, 257, 269, 402
De Long, Emma (wife of George), 197, 211, 213, 214, 228, 231, 422–3
De Long, Commander George Washington: character and background, 196–7; collaborates with Bennett, 197; Arctic expedition (1879–82), 200–29; death, 229; burial, 230; inquiry into expedition, 231–2
Dedrick, Dr Tom: on Peary's expedition (1898–1902), 306, 307, 308, 310, 311–12, 313; attacks Peary, 335
Devil's Thumb, 48
Devon Island, 372
Disco Island, 135, 149, 163, 164
Discovery, HMS (Stephenson's ship), 162, 163, 164, 165, 171, 183
Disraeli, Benjamin: approves British expedition to the Arctic (1874), 161
dog-sledging, 66–7
Dunbar, William: on De Long's expedition (1879–82), 200, 210, 222
Dunkle, George: accused of forging Cook's observations, 382

Eagle (Andrée's balloon), 257–8, 269–71, 272–3, 274–6, 278

Ebierbing (Eskimo): meeting with Hall, 82; goes to America, 86; at Barnum's museum, 86; on Hall's expedition (1871–73), 91, 135, 145, 149, 150, 153

Egerton, Lieutenant: on Nares's expedition (1875–76), 171, 184

Egingwah (Eskimo): on Peary's expedition (1908–9), 362, 366

Ekholm, Nils: withdraws from Andrée's expedition (1897), 272

Ellesmere Island, 17, 136, 172, 284, 312, 340, 344, 351, 372

Ellsworth, Lincoln: attempts to fly to the Pole with Amundsen (1925), 399–401; airship expedition to the Pole with Amundsen (1926), 401, 405–7, 411–14

Emin Pasha, 194

Entrikin, Samuel, 298–9

Erik (Peary's support ship, 1908–9), 355, 357

Erikson (seaman): on De Long's expedition (1879–82), 224

Eskimos: Kane's expedition (1853–55) and, 32, 34, 35–6, 38, 39; Hall recognises importance of, 58; on Hayes's expedition (1860–61), 63, 68; language, 81; Hall's encounter with, 81–3; Hall's opinion of, 83–5; Hegemann's opinion of, 108–9; Peary's opinion of, 294–5; 'exhibited' at Smithsonian Institution, 302; on Peary's expedition (1905–6), 338–9; on Peary's expedition (1908–9), 355–6, 358

Etah, 32, 43, 44, 64, 288, 295, 346

Explorer's Wife (Emma De Long), 422

Falcon (Peary's ship), 293, 298, 299

Farther North Than Nansen (Abruzzi), 334

Farthest North (Nansen), 265

Feilden, Henry: on Nares's expedition (1875–76), 169–70, 177; theory of the Pole as a land mass, 234–5

Fenouillet, Alessio: on Abruzzi's expedition (1899–1900), 322, 324

Fiala, Anthony: Arctic expedition (1903–5), 315

finneskos (footwear), 320

Floeberg Beach, 166, 179

flying boats: on Amundsen–Ellsworth expedition (1925), 399–401

Foka (Sedov's ship), 392, 393, 395, 396

Forlorn Hope (boat), 14, 32–3, 35

Fort Conger, 232, 306, 307, 308, 310

Foulkes Harbour, 65

Fox, Margaret, 9–10, 51

Fraenkel, Knut: on Andrée's expedition (1897), 272, 276, 279, 280, 282

Fram: as Nansen's ship, 239–40, 243, 244, 245, 252–3, 257, 267, 283, 284; as Sverdrup's ship, 306

France: plans submarine mission to the Arctic, 160

Franke, Rudolph: encounter with Peary at Anoatok, 356–7

Franklin, Sir John: expedition to find North-West Passage (1845), 5; his fate, 48

Franklin, Lady (wife of Sir John), 87, 89, 90, 159

Franz Josef I: supports Austrian mission to the Arctic, 112; welcomes Weyprecht and Payer home, 129

Franz Josef Land: discovered by Weyprecht and Payer (1873), 118–19; explored by Payer and others (1873–74), 120, 121–2, 122–5; Nansen's and Johanssen's journey to, 248–51; Jackson–Harmsworth expedition to (1894), 261; Sedov's expedition to (1913–14), 393–4

Fraülein Flairscher (boat), 48

Frederick (Eskimo): on Nares's expedition (1875–76), 163

Frederick A. Cook Society, 387

Freuchen, Peter: doubts Cook's story, 375

Friedrichsthal, 106, 107

Frobisher, Martin: Arctic expedition (1570s), 85

frostbite: on Kane's expedition (1853–55), 18, 21, 22; on Nares's expedition (1875–76), 167, 171; on De Long's expedition (1879–82), 223–4; on Peary's expedition (1898–1902), 307–8; on Abruzzi's expedition (1899–1900), 319, 324–5

Gentleman's Magazine: advocates British expedition to the Arctic, 161

George Henry (Hall's ship), 59, 60, 80, 81, 86

Gericke, Herr, 107

Germania (Petermann's ship), 95, 96, 97, 98

Gibbs, Philip: doubts Cook's story, 374–5

Gibson, Langdon: on Peary's expedition (1891–92), 289

Giffard, Lieutenant George: on Nares's expedition (1875–76), 171

Gilder, William Henry, 214, 228

Gladstone, William Ewart: snubs Bennett, 195

Godfrey, William: on Kane's expedition (1853–55), 11, 13, 17, 18, 20, 21, 22, 23, 32, 35, 42, 43, 44; publishes account of expedition, 52

Godthaab, 237

Goodfellow, Henry: on Kane's expedition (1853–55), 11, 36–7, 41–2

Goodsell, Dr John: on Peary's expedition (1908–9), 354, 359, 360, 370

Grant Land, 136, 137, 139, 171, 176

Greeley, Horace: makes donation to Hall's expedition, 59

Greely, Adolphus: Arctic expedition (1882),

232–3; sceptical of Nansen's expedition, 241; sceptical of Andrée's expedition, 255

Grinnell, Henry: sponsors search for Franklin (1852), 8–9; sponsors search for Franklin (1853–55), 10; welcomes Kane back to New York, 50; sponsors Hayes's expedition (1859), 56; makes donation to Hall's expedition, 59; decline in fortunes, 86; sponsors Hall again, 87

Grinnell Land, 17, 22, 25, 65, 74, 75, 135, 136

Grönland (Petermann's ship), 94

Gulf Stream: Petermann's theory of, 93, 96, 115; theory supported by Weyprecht, 111–12; disproof of Petermann's theory, 130

Hall, Charles Francis: background, 57; plans Arctic expedition, 58, 59–60; Arctic expedition (1860–62), 80–6; meeting with Tookolito, 82–3; fund-raising attempts, 86; Arctic expedition (1864–69), 87–9; asks Congress for funding, 89; his wife, 90; Congress supports his plan (1870), 90; plans Arctic expedition (1871), 90–1; Arctic expedition, illness and death (1871), 132–40; burial, 140–1; suspicions over his death, 141–5; inquiry into 1871–73 expedition, 156

Hall Land, 136, 137

Haller, Johann: on Weyprecht/Payer expedition (1872–74), 122, 124

Hampton's Magazine, 380

Hansa (Petermann's ship), 95, 97, 98, 100, 101, 102, 105

Harley Island, 328, 329

Harmsworth, Alfred, 241, 261, 266, 305

Harrigan (Eskimo): murder of Marvin and, 422

Hartstene, Captain: brings Kane back to New York, 50

Hayes, Dr Isaac Israel: on Kane's expedition (1853–55), 11, 18, 21, 22, 23, 28, 29, 30–1, 31–2, 33, 34, 35, 36, 38, 39, 40, 41, 42; publishes account of expedition, 52; defends Kane's findings, 55; advocates further Polar exploration, 56; plans Arctic expedition (1859), 56, 61; Arctic expedition (1860–61), 62–78; receives news of American Civil War, 78; joins Union Army, 79; presents plan to Congress, 89; dispute with Brent, 94; addresses American Geographical Society (1874), 157; on De Long's absence, 211–12; death (1886), 79

Hayes, Midshipman Noah: on Hall's expedition (1871–73), 141, 144–5

Hayes Sound, 184

Hegemann, Paul: on Petermann's expedition (1869), 97, 98, 100, 101, 102, 103, 104–5, 106–7, 108

Helgesen, Congressman Henry: casts doubts on Peary's claims, 387

Hendrik, Hans: on Kane's expedition (1853–55), 12, 15, 19, 25, 26, 28, 43, 44; on Hayes's expedition (1860–61), 64, 66, 68–9, 71–3; on Hall's expedition (1871–73), 135, 138, 139, 150, 152, 153; returns home, 156; on Nares's expedition (1875–76), 163, 182–3, 183–4

Henrietta Island, 216

Henry, Joseph, 133

Henson, Matthew: on Peary's expedition (1891–92), 289; on Peary's lecture tour, 292; on Peary's expedition (1893–95), 293, 298, 299, 300; on Peary's expedition (1898–1902), 306, 307, 311, 312; on Peary's expedition (1905–6), 340, 341, 345; on Peary's expedition (1908–9), 354, 356, 359–60, 361, 362, 363, 366, 370, 371

Herald Island, 202, 204

Herbert, Wally, x–xi; analysis of Peary's claims, 366, 385; sledges to Pole and traverses Polar pack (1969), 417–18

Herron, John (steward of *Polaris*), 147

Hochstetter Island, 119

Holland, Clive, 412

Holtsteinborg, 81

Hubbard, General Thomas, 337

Hubbardville, 358

Humboldt Glacier, 14, 25, 49, 53, 54

huskies: on Kane's expedition (1853–55), 16, 39; on Hayes's expedition (1860–61), 66, 70, 73, 75, 77; on Weyprecht's expedition (1872–74), 115–16; on De Long's expedition (1879–82), 216, 217; on Abruzzi's expedition (1899–1900), 318

Ibsen, Henrik, 265

Imperial Academy of Science of Vienna, 111

Imperial Geographical Society (Russia), 159

Independence Bay, 291, 300, 301

Inglefield, Edward: search for Franklin (1852), 6–7

Inglefield Gulf, 291

Inquirer (Philadelphia): attacks Arctic expeditions, 233

Ironsides (metal boat), 32, 40

Isabel (Inglefield's yacht), 6

Isbjorn (Wilczek's ship), 114

Jackson, Frederick: rejected for Nansen expedition, 241; meeting with Nansen on Franz Josef Land (1894), 261–2; plans expedition to the Pole, 263; high hopes of his success, 266; attempt ends in failure, 266; dispute with Nansen, 267

Jackson, John: searches for De Long, 227

Jeannette (De Long's ship), 197–8, 201, 203, 204, 207, 217, 227–8, 231, 239
Jeannette Island, 216
Jenisseisk, 273
Jensen, Peter: on Hayes's expedition (1860–61), 63, 66, 69, 75, 76, 77
Jesup, Senator Morris Ketcham, 305, 306, 336, 337, 348, 349, 350, 352
Jesup Island, 335, 344
Johanssen, Hjalmar: on Nansen's expedition (1893–96), 247–51, 258–62; returns home, 264; misses the ice, 265; on Amundsen's Antarctic expedition (1911), 419
Jones Sound, 5
Journal of Retreat (Weyprecht), 131
Julianehaab, 107, 108, 239
Juniata (yacht), 155

Kalutunah (Eskimo leader): Kane's expedition (1853–55) and, 32, 33, 34, 35, 36, 38, 39, 40; Hayes's expedition (1860–61) and, 73, 74, 77, 78
Kane, Elisha Kent: early expeditions, 7–8; search for Franklin (1852), 8–9; popularity of, 9; Arctic expedition (1853–55), 10–49; returns to New York (1855), 50; receives Royal Geographical Society's Gold Medal, 51; publishes journal (1856), 51; illness and death (1857), 52; funeral procession, 52–3; appraisal, 53
Kane Basin, 165, 306
Karluk (ship), 397, 400, 422
Kazamas, Shinji: reaches the Pole on Yamaha motorcycle (1987), 418
Kennedy Channel, 26, 76, 312
King William Island, 5, 6, 84, 87
King's Harbour, 406, 411
Kite (Peary's ship), 288, 290
Klotz, Alexander: on Weyprecht/Payer expedition (1872–74), 122, 123–4
Knorr, George: on Hayes's expedition (1860–61), 70, 75, 76
Koldewey, Karl: on Petermann's expedition (1868), 94; on Petermann's expedition (1869), 95, 97, 98, 99, 100; his journal, 109
Koojesse (Eskimo): Hall and, 85
Krisch, Otto: on Weyprecht/Payer expedition (1872–74), 120–1, 122
Kropotkin, Prince Peter: praises Nansen, 265
Kudlikto (Eskimo): on Peary's expedition (1908–9), 360, 369; murders Marvin, 422
Kumakh-Surt (Siberian village), 224, 225, 226
Kuro Siwo (ocean current), 94, 204
Kuznetsov, Alexander, x–xi; first to set foot on the Pole (1948), 417

Lachambre, Henri: visits the *Fram* (1896), 257
Lady Franklin Strait, 137

Lancaster Sound, 6, 7, 32
Laube, Dr: on Petermann's expedition (1869), 100–1, 102, 106, 109
Lee, Hugh: on Peary's expedition (1893–95), 298, 299, 300–1
Leigh-Smith, Benjamin, 251
Lena Delta, 221, 222, 223
Leopold II (king of the Belgians): knights Cook, 351
Lilequist, Professor G.: doubts Byrd's claims to have reached the Pole, 410
Littleton Island, 13, 31, 41
Livingstone, David, 99n, 194
Lockwood, Lieutenant James Booth: on Greely's expedition (1882), 232–3
Lonsdale, Walter, 380, 381, 382
Loomis, Chauncey: investigates Hall's death, 141–5
Loose, Captain August: accused of forging Cook's observations, 382
Lüthe, Admiral, 160

McBride, James, 4–5
McClintock, Francis: search for Franklin, 58
McClintock, Sir Leopold, 189, 241
McClintock Island, 125
MacDonald (seaman): on Hayes's expedition (1860–61), 75, 76, 77
Macmillan, Donald: on Peary's expedition (1908–9), 354, 359, 360; later years, 397
Markham, Albert: whaling trip to the Arctic, 160; on Nares's expedition (1875–76), 162, 166, 167, 170, 171, 172, 173, 174–6, 177, 184; receives gold watch from Royal Geographical Society, 189; sceptical of Andrée's expedition, 254
Markham, Clements: advocates British expedition to the Arctic, 159, 160–1; on Nares's expedition (1875–76), 163; defends Nares against Navy inquiry, 189; fears for De Long's safety, 211; supports Nansen, 240; supports Andrée, 256; praises Peary, 303
Marvin, Professor Ross: on Peary's expedition (1905–6), 338; on Peary's expedition (1908–9), 354, 359, 360, 365; death, 369–70, 421–2
Mary Minturn River, 14
May, Lieutenant William: on Nares's expedition (1875–76), 167
Melville, George: on De Long's expedition (1879–82), 200, 206, 208, 215, 216–17, 218, 221, 222–3, 226–7, 228, 229; subject of inquiry, 231; on Greely rescue mission, 233; supports Peary against Cook, 376
Melville Bay, 64, 136, 297
Merkut (Hans Hendrik's wife), 64, 68, 69, 146, 163

Meyer, Frederick: on Hall's expedition (1871–73), 134, 141, 146, 148, 149, 152; possible murderer of Hall, 142–3
Middendorf Glacier (Franz Josef Land), 122
Minik (Eskimo), 349–50
Monticello (Hall's ship), 87, 91
Morton, William: on Kane's expedition (1853–55), 11, 25, 26, 36, 37; publishes account of expedition, 51; on Hall's expedition (1871–73), 91
Moss, Dr Edward: on Nares's expedition (1875–76), 167, 169, 172–3, 177, 179
Mossyn, Carlie, 48
'Mountain of Iron', 297, 298
Murphy, John, 370
Museum of Natural History (New York), 349, 350
Mussolini, Benito, 405, 406
My Attainment of the North Pole (Cook), 386
'My Brother John's Glacier', 66, 77
My Life as an Explorer (Amundsen), 400

Nansen, Fridtjof: background, 236–7; traverses Greenland (1888), 237–8; plan to reach Pole, 239; Arctic expedition (1893–96), 242–51, 258–62; returns home, 264; his journal, 265; dispute with Jackson, 267; praises Peary, 292; advises Abruzzi, 317; reaction to Abruzzi's expedition, 332; praises Sedov, 393; scoffs at Wellman's airship attempt on the Pole, 403; later years, 267, 397, 420–1
Nares, George: Arctic expedition (1875–76), 162–84; character, 164–5; receives Royal Geographical Society's Gold Medal, 185; appraisal of expedition, 185–6; attacked in the press, 186; subject of inquiry, 186–9; fears for De Long's safety, 211; sceptical of Nansen's expedition, 240; supports Peary against Cook, 376; later years, 189–90; death (1915), 397
The Narrative of Arthur Gordon Pym (Poe), 2
National Academy of Science, 133
National Geographic Society: awards Gold Medal to Peary, 348; Peary presents proofs to, 379–80; approves Byrd's findings, 410
The Navy (magazine): attacks Nares's expedition, 186
Navy Department (USA): contemplates De Long rescue mission (1880), 212; search for De Long (1881), 213–14
Nearest the Pole (Peary), 345, 348
Neue Freie Presse: reports Weyprecht/Payer reception, 129
New Siberian Islands, 243
New York Herald, 192, 193, 335, 361, 373, 377, 379
New York Lyceum of Natural History, 56

New York Times: news of Kane's return home, 51; attacks Arctic expeditions, 233; Peary writes in, 349; attacks Cook, 376, 381
New York Tribune, 377
Newcomb, Raymond: on De Long's expedition (1879–82), 200, 205, 206, 215, 217, 220
Nicolai (Russian ship), 128
Nindemann, William: on De Long's expedition (1879–82), 200, 207–8, 223, 224, 225, 226, 229
Nobel, Alfred, 254
Nobile, Colonel Umberto: chosen to pilot Amundsen–Ellsworth airship, 404–5; on Amundsen–Ellsworth expedition (1926), 406, 407, 409, 411–14; upstages Amundsen at reception, 415; further airship expedition to the Pole (1928), 420
Nordenskiöld, Baron Nils Adolf Erik: expedition to find North-East Passage (1878), 199, 203, 236; rescue mission, 199–203; theory of habitability of inner Greenland, 237; supports Andrée's expedition, 254
Norge (Amundsen–Ellsworth airship), 405–6, 412–14
Noros, Louis P.: on De Long's expedition (1879–82), 224, 225, 226
North Pole: location of, 1
North-East Passage: Nordenskiöld's expedition to find (1878), 199, 203
North-West Passage: Franklin's expedition to find (1845), 5
Northern Lights: Hall on, 80–1
Northumberland Island, 32
Norwegian Geographical Society, 239
Novaya Zemlya: Weyprecht's expedition to (1871), 111; Weyprecht reaches (1872), 114; Sedov reaches (1912), 392
Noyoe Vremya: supports Sedov's Arctic expedition, 391–2
Nye, Captain, 202, 212

Ohlsen, Christian: on Kane's expedition (1853–55), 11, 16, 17, 18, 19, 28, 29, 37, 46
Ommaney, Sir Erasmus, 238
Ommaney Island, 329
Ooqueah (Eskimo): on Peary's expedition (1908–9), 362, 366
Ootah (Eskimo): on Peary's expedition (1908–9), 362, 366
Open Polar Sea: theories of, 3; expeditions to find, 4, 7, 10; Kane and, 25–6, 49, 53; Rink and, 53–4; Armstrong and, 54–5; Hayes and, 67–8, 76–7, 79; Petermann and, 92–3; Weyprecht and, 111–12; Payer and, 125; Markham and, 176; US Coast and Geodetic Survey and, 204–5

Orel, Eduard: on Weyprecht/Payer
expedition (1872–74), 122, 123, 125
Osborn, Rear-Admiral Sherard: dispute with
Petermann, 93–4; makes fun of
Petermann's failure, 109; is vindicated,
130; advocates British expedition to the
Arctic, 158–9, 161; death (1875), 163
Oscar II (King of Sweden), 254
overwintering, 15

Parr, Lieutenant Alfred: on Nares's
expedition (1875–76), 171, 176–7; praised
by Royal Geographical Society, 185
Parry, Captain William Edward: expedition
to find Open Polar Sea (1827), 4
Payer, Lieutenant Julius: on Petermann's
expedition (1869), 99, 100; on Weyprecht's
expedition to Novaya Zemlya (1871), 111;
Arctic expedition (1872–74), 113–28;
reception in Austria, 129–30; later life,
130, 420
Peary, Josephine (wife of Robert): on
husband's expedition (1891–92), 289–91;
on husband's expedition (1893–95), 294,
299; winters at Cape Sabine (1900), 312
Peary, Marie Ahnighito (daughter of Robert
and Josephine), 294, 299, 312, 333
Peary, Robert Edwin: praises Beaumont's
exploits, 183; character and background,
284–6; attempts to cross Greenland
(1886), 286; envious of Nansen, 287; on
inter-breeding with Eskimos, 287;
expedition to Greenland (1891–92),
288–91; lecture tour, 292, 293; Arctic
expedition (1893–95), 293–301; sends six
Eskimos to Smithsonian Institution, 302;
receives American Geographical Society
Gold Medal (1897), 303; receives Royal
Geographical Society Gold Medal (1898),
303; plans next expedition, 304–5; Arctic
expedition (1898–1902), 305–13; loses
eight toes to frostbite, 307–8; propaganda
campaign, 334; elected president of
American Geographical Society, 334;
praised by Beaumont, 334–5; criticised,
335–6; granted leave (1903), 337;
undergoes surgery on feet, 337; Arctic
expedition (1905–6), 338–47; readings
open to doubt, 343–4; his journal, 345;
receives National Geographic Society
Gold Medal, 348; incurs enmity of Minik,
349–50; attacks Cook and Bradley, 351–2;
challenges Shackleton, 353–4; Arctic
expedition (1908–9), 354–68; arrives at the
Pole (6 April 1909), 362–3; accuracy of his
readings, 363–5, 383–4; doubts about his
rate of progress, 365; flaws in his account,
366; congratulates himself, 367–8, 384–5;

learns of Marvin's death, 369–70;
dismisses Cook's claim to have reached
the Pole, 371; dispute with Cook, 376–81,
386–7, 390, 407; presents proofs to
National Geographic Society, 379–80;
receives second Royal Geographical
Society Gold Medal, 383; other awards
and distinctions, 384; appraisal of, 385;
denounced by Helgesen, 387; illness and
death (1920), 387–8
Peary Arctic Club, 305, 333, 335–6, 350, 351,
352, 378, 381
Peary Channel, 291, 292, 335, 344
Peary Land, 291, 292, 335, 344
'Peary System' of exploration, 295, 336, 338
Peel Sound, 6
Periwinkle, USS (later Polaris), 90, 91
Perry, Commodore Matthew, 94
Peter (Eskimo): on Hayes's expedition
(1860–61), 68–9, 72
Petermann, August: Gulf Stream theory, 93,
96, 115; attacks Kane's theories, 93;
dispute with Osborn, 93–4; Arctic
expedition (1868), 94; Arctic expedition
(1869), 95–109; appraisal of 1869
expedition, 109–10; Gulf Stream theory
disproved, 130; collaborates with Bennett,
195–6; commits suicide (1878), 130
Petermann Land, 125
Petersen, Carl: on Kane's expedition
(1853–55), 11–12, 13–14, 17, 18, 27, 28–9,
30, 32, 33, 34, 35, 37, 38, 39, 41, 42, 43, 48;
publishes account of expedition, 52
Petigax, Giuseppe: on Abruzzi's expedition
(1899–1900), 322, 324, 328
The Phantom of the Poles (Reed), 349
Philadelphia Academy of Sciences, 334
piblokto (disease): developed by Eskimos
during Peary's expedition (1908–9),
358–9
Plaisted, Ralph: reaches the Pole on
motorized sledge (1968), 417
Poe, Edgar Allan, 2
Point Moss, 340, 343, 355
polar bears: eaten by Kane's men, 26; attack
on Dr Borgen, 98–9
Polaris (Hall's ship), 132, 134, 135, 146, 147,
155
Polaris Bay, 137, 182, 183
'Polynia', 196, 204
Port Foulkes, 68, 72, 77
The Port Foulkes Weekly News, 70
Porter, George: on Nares's expedition
(1875–76), 176, 177
Pospischill, Josef: on Weyprecht/Payer
expedition (1872–74), 122
Primus stoves: on Nansen's expedition
(1893–96), 242–3

Prince Rudolf Island, 318, 327, 329–30
Printz, Fred, 379
Pritchard, Billy, 370–1
Pullen, Revd William: on Nares's expedition (1875–76), 179
Punch: commentary on Nansen's expedition, 244; jokes about the Pole, 339

Quarterly Review: praises Nares's expedition, 185, 186
Quayle, Captain P.T., 59, 62
Querini, Lieutenant Chevalier Francesco: on Abruzzi's expedition (1899–1900), 321, 330–1

Rae, John, 48, 287
Ramm, Fredrik, 411, 413
Rasmussen, Knud: praises Beaumont's exploits, 183
rats: infestation on Kane's ship, 16; eaten by Kane, 36
Ravenscraig (ship), 155
Rawlinson, Sir Henry, 164
Rawson, Lieutenant Wyatt: on Nares's expedition (1875–76), 167, 168, 171, 180, 182
Reed, William: hollow earth theory, 349
refraction: Hall on, 80; Peary possibly misled by, 344–5
Rensselaer Harbour, 14, 26, 38, 48, 66, 67, 73, 146
Repulse Bay, 87
Rescue (Hall's ship), 81
Reynolds, Jeremiah, 2
Riiser-Larsen, Hjalmar, 401, 404, 405, 409, 411
Riley, George: on Kane's expedition (1853–55), 30
Rink, Dr Henry: critique of Kane's journals, 53–4, 55
Robeson Channel, 136, 139, 146, 166, 182, 284, 312
Rodgers (De Long rescue ship), 214
Romme, Finn: doubts Byrd's claim to have reached the Pole, 410–11
Roosevelt: Peary's ship (1905–6), 337–8, 339, 343, 345–7; Peary's ship (1908–9), 354, 355, 357
Roosevelt, President Theodore: grants leave to Peary, 305; congratulates Peary, 348; wishes Peary success (1908), 354
Ross, Sir John, 13, 168; expedition to find North-West Passage (1818), 297; misled by Arctic refraction, 344
Royal Colonial Institute, 254
Royal Geographical Society: awards Gold Medal to Kane, 51; doubts Kane's findings, 54–5; won over by Hayes's arguments, 56;

petitioned by Osborn, 158–9; praises Nares's expedition, 164; awards Gold Medal to Nares, 185; awards gold watch to Markham, 189; donation to Nansen expedition, 240; awards Gold Medal to Peary, 303; awards second Gold Medal to Peary, 383; doubts Peary's claims, 383–4
Royal Geographical Society of Belgium: awards Gold Medal to Cook, 351
Royal Swedish Academy, 160
Rutherford, Sir Alcock: praises Alfred Parr, 185; defends Nares against Navy inquiry, 189

Sabine, Edward, 159
Sabine Island, 97, 98, 100, 101
'The Sage of Gotha' *see* Petermann, August
St Peter's Canal, 347
San Francisco Examiner, 350
Saturday Review: criticises Nares's expedition, 186; criticises De Long's expedition, 231
Schubert, Pierre: on Kane's expedition (1853–55), 11, 21
Schwatka, Lieutenant Frederick: search for Franklin (1878–79), 195
Scott, Katherine, 383
scurvy: on Kane's expedition (1853–55), 10, 16, 31, 37, 46; on Hayes's expedition (1860–61), 69; on Weyprecht/Payer expedition (1872–74), 120; on Nares's expedition (1875–76), 174, 175, 176, 177–9, 180–1, 182, 183; inquiry into incidence of during Nares's expedition (1875–76), 186–9; on Nansen's expedition (1893–96), 242; on Sedov's expedition (1913–14), 393, 394; symptoms, pathology and causes, 424–6
Sedov, Gregoriy Yakovlevich: background, 390–1; plans expedition to Franz Josef Land, 391–2; explores Novaya Zemlya (1912–13), 392–3; expedition to Franz Josef Land (1913–14), 393–4; attempts to reach the Pole, 394–5
Seeglo (Eskimo): on Peary's expedition (1908–9), 362, 366
Shackleton, Ernest: challenged by Peary, 353–4; supports Peary against Cook, 376
Siberiakoff, Alexander, 199, 200
Sip-Su (Eskimo leader), 35, 36, 38, 40, 73
Smith Sound, 5, 6, 7, 13, 27, 31, 47, 49, 64, 65, 74, 76, 77, 135, 155, 284, 288, 306, 355
Smithsonian Institution, 56, 302
Snow, Charles Parker: Hall's journals and, 86, 87
Sonntag, August: on Kane's expedition (1853–55), 11, 17, 18, 28–9, 42; on Hayes's expedition (1860–61), 62, 66, 67, 71, 72

Sostrene (ship), 253
Southern Fjord, 137
Spitsbergen, 126, 245, 400, 406
Stanley, Henry Morton, 194
Stead, W.T., 374, 375
Steffanson, Vilhjalmur, 351, 397, 400
Stella Polare (Abruzzi's ship), 316, 318, 330, 331
Stephenson, Henry: Arctic expedition (1875–76), 162, 178, 184
Strindberg, Nils: with Andrée on Dane's Island (1896), 257; on Andrée's expedition (1897), 272, 276, 278, 279, 282
Svatoy Anna (ship), 396
Sverdrup, Otto: as captain of *Fram*, 247, 252, 257, 267; charts area west of Greenland, 283, 284; Arctic expedition (1898–1902), 305–6, 307, 308, 335
Swedish Anthropological and Geographical Society: publishes story of Andrée's expedition (1930), 274–82
Sweetman (carpenter on *Jeannette*), 222
Symmes, Americus (son of John Cleve Symmes): revives father's theories (1878), 233
Symmes, John Cleve: 'hole' theory of the Poles, 1–2, 233, 349; on Parry's expedition (1827), 4

Taft, President William Howard, 384
Tennyson, Lord, 417
Teplitz Bay, 318, 327, 330, 331
The Threshold of the Unknown Region (Clements Markham), 160
Tigress (ship), 154, 155
Tit Ary (island), 224
Tookolito (Eskimo): meeting with Hall, 82–3; goes to America, 86; at Barnum's museum, 86; on Hall's expedition (1871–73), 91, 135, 140, 149
trichinosis: possible cause of Andrée's death, 282
tripes de roche (rock lichen), 33–4, 35
Tukerliktu (Eskimo), 86, 87
Tyson, George: on Hall's expedition (1871–73), 91, 132, 134, 135, 136, 138, 140, 145–55; speaks to American Geographical Society (1874), 157; his journal, 158

United States (Hayes's ship), 61, 62, 65, 71, 75, 77, 78
Upernavik, 11, 49, 63, 64, 78, 370, 373
US Coast and Geodetic Survey: on Open Polar Sea, 204–5

Valorous, HMS (supply ship), 162, 164
Valentin, Feodor, 128

Vega (Nordenskiöld's ship), 199, 203
Verhoeff, John: on Peary's expedition (1891–92), 289, 290–1
Victoria, Queen: wishes Nares success, 163; congratulates Nares and his men, 185
Virgo Harbour, 402, 403
Vizetelly, Edward, 194
Vogelsang Island, 273

Wack, H. Wellington, 381
walruses: Nansen's expedition (1893–96) and, 260
Warren, Revd William F.: 'Garden of Eden' theory, 233–4
Washington Post, 348
Weems, John Edward, 388
Wellman, Walter, 314; attempts to reach the Pole by airship (1906, 1907 and 1909), 401–3
Weyprecht, Carl: expedition to Novaya Zemlya (1871), 111; Arctic expedition (1872–74), 113–28; reception in Austria, 129–30; later life, 130; his journal, 131; attacks 'greed for discovery', 191–2
White Island: Andrée's remains found on (1930), 274, 282
Whitney, Harry, 357, 360, 370, 373, 378–9
Whymper, Edward: praises Nansen, 265
Wilczek, Count Johann von: on Weyprecht's expedition to Novaya Zemlya (1871), 111; sails to Novaya Zemlya (1872), 114
Wilhelmine (ship), 103
Wilkes, Lieutenant Charles: expedition to Antarctica (1838), 2
Wilkins, George, 403
Willoughby, Sir Hugh, 3
Wilson, John: on Kane's expedition (1853–55), 11, 13, 16–17, 29, 36; publishes account of expedition, 51
Windward: as Jackson's supply ship, 261, 262, 264; as Peary's ship (1898–1902), 305, 306, 308, 309, 312, 313
Wistar, General I.J.: supports Peary's 1893–95 expedition, 293
Wisting, Oscar, 414
Wrangel, Baron, 113
Wrangel Land, 202–3, 204, 206, 398

Young, Sir Allen: search for Franklin (1875), 194–5

Zaninovich, Antonio: on Weyprecht/Payer expedition (1872–74), 122, 123, 124, 125
Zanzibar, Sultan of, 164
Zeppelins, 403–4
Ziegler, William, 314, 315